X-MEN
LONGSHOT

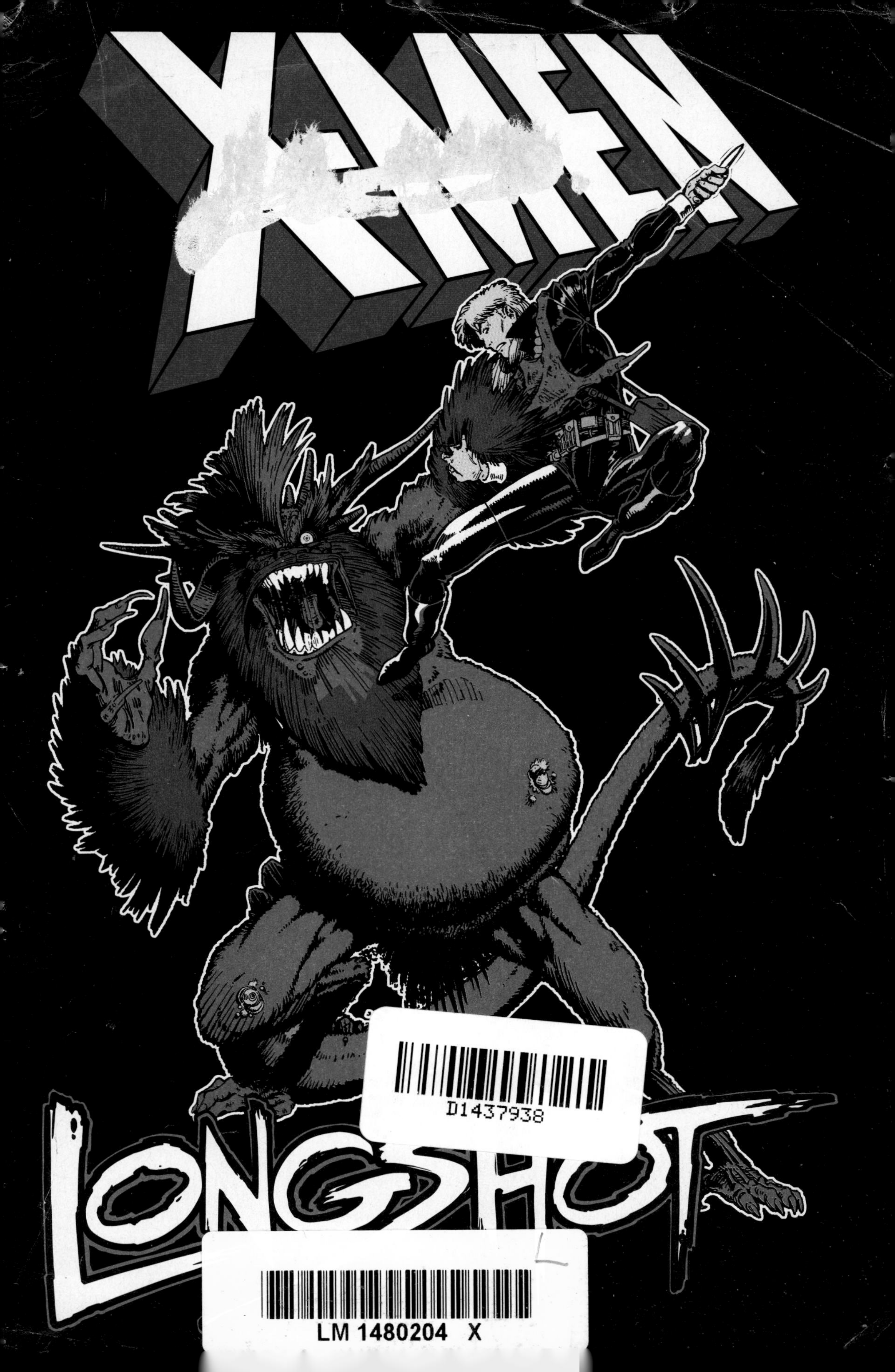

X-MEN

WRITER
ANN NOCENTI

PENCILER
ARTHUR ADAMS

INKERS
WHILCE PORTACIO
WITH BRENT ANDERSON

COLORIST
CHRISTIE SCHEELE

LETTERER
JOE ROSEN

ASSISTANT EDITORS
BOBBIE CHASE, MARC McLAURIN
& MARC SIRY

EDITOR
LOUISE SIMONSON

FRONT COVER ARTISTS
ARTHUR ADAMS & CHRIS SOTOMAYOR

BACK COVER ARTIST
ARTHUR ADAMS

X-MEN: LONGSHOT. Contains material originally published in magazine form as LONGSHOT #1-6. Second edition. First printing 2013. ISBN# 978-0-7851-6711-2. Published by MARVEL WORLDWIDE, INC., a subsidiary of MARVEL ENTERTAINMENT, LLC. OFFICE OF PUBLICATION: 135 West 50th Street, New York, NY 10020. Copyright © 1985, 1986 and 2013 Marvel Characters, Inc. All rights reserved. All characters featured in this issue and the distinctive names and likenesses thereof, and all related indicia are trademarks of Marvel Characters, Inc. No similarity between any of the names, characters, persons, and/or institutions in this magazine with those of any living or dead person or institution is intended, and any such similarity which may exist is purely coincidental. **Printed in the U.S.A.** ALAN FINE, EVP - Office of the President, Marvel Worldwide, Inc. and EVP & CMO Marvel Characters B.V.; DAN BUCKLEY, Publisher & President - Print, Animation & Digital Divisions; JOE QUESADA, Chief Creative Officer; TOM BREVOORT, SVP of Publishing; DAVID BOGART, SVP of Operations & Procurement, Publishing; C.B. CEBULSKI, SVP of Creator & Content Development; DAVID GABRIEL, SVP of Print & Digital Publishing Sales; JIM O'KEEFE, VP of Operations & Logistics; DAN CARR, Executive Director of Publishing Technology; SUSAN CRESPI, Editorial Operations Manager; ALEX MORALES, Publishing Operations Manager; STAN LEE, Chairman Emeritus. For information regarding advertising in Marvel Comics or on Marvel.com, please contact Niza Disla, Director of Marvel Partnerships, at ndisla@marvel.com. For Marvel subscription inquiries, please call 800-217-9158. **Manufactured between 3/6/2013 and 4/8/2013 by R.R. DONNELLEY, INC., SALEM, VA, USA.**

10 9 8 7 6 5 4 3 2 1

COLLECTION EDITOR
MARK D. BEAZLEY

ASSISTANT EDITORS
NELSON RIBEIRO & ALEX STARBUCK

EDITOR, SPECIAL PROJECTS
JENNIFER GRÜNWALD

SENIOR EDITOR, SPECIAL PROJECTS
JEFF YOUNGQUIST

PRODUCTION
JERRON QUALITY COLOR & JOE FRONTIRRE

COLOR RECONSTRUCTION
**JAMISON SERVICES
& USA DESIGN GROUP**

SVP OF PRINT & DIGITAL PUBLISHING SALES
DAVID GABRIEL

EDITOR IN CHIEF
AXEL ALONSO

CHIEF CREATIVE OFFICER
JOE QUESADA

PUBLISHER
DAN BUCKLEY

EXECUTIVE PRODUCER
ALAN FINE

LONGSHOT

INTRODUCTION BY ANN NOCENTI

It's been at least two decades since Arthur Adams and I created Longshot, and it's difficult to access the intent of those youngsters. I was not familiar with the vast genealogical tree of the Marvel Universe when I answered an ad in the Village Voice for an "editorial and writing" job. Greeting me at the office on Madison Avenue were giant Captain America and Spider-Man cutouts, tilted and frayed, gazing at me askance, an obvious pretender to their domain.

Once inside the fortress I was broadsided by a tsunami of history and character. There were multiple universes, alien invasions, every character seemed to have a doppelganger or an evil version, had already died and been resurrected, found out that their sister was really their mother, gone to hell and back, and, ultimately, had a thousand more parallel lives on T-shirts and lunch boxes. It was a knot of mythos and soap opera and beach towel franchises. To keep their fertile minds occupied, the Marvel staff would do things like tie helium "thought" balloons to their heads, come to work dressed in nothing but Saran Wrap, glue their office furniture to the ceiling so they could work upside down, hold paddle ball "whack-offs," decide to run that month's comics out of bathroom stalls converted into offices, or simply show you their gun collection and cackle. There was a wonderful guy who ran the bullpen — he'd tell you to rub his big belly for luck — and an in-house letterer who felt the heat coming off the top of your head and pinched your fingernails to tell you what vitamins you lacked. The place was as full of panache and zing! as the stories that spilled out of it. I loved it. And that's how I want to remember it.

As an overwhelmed newcomer, I craved something simple. I'd read the bios of the characters I was in charge of, and they read like Cliff Notes for a Dostoyevsky novel. I was dying to be part of this wonderment, but needed to start...slow and simple.

I believe choosing the name Longshot had something to do with bending the odds: the whole enterprise was a long shot. There was a T.S. Eliot line: "purification of the motive in the ground of our beseeching," which I liked to recite before going out drinking in college. I'd had luck with that one, so decided motive and luck were tied together. And I thought the cat that slunk around my Manhattan loft looked cool when his one eye glowed in the dark, so I burdened Longshot with that affectation. One glowing eye. The reigning super heroes were candy-colored, but I was into film noir and chose black, or maybe Arthur did. Longshot was a tabula rasa, created out of a curiosity: if we forget who we were, then who are we? I had him drop to Earth an amnesiac...cliché now, to have a character with no memory, but back then it seemed fresh. And super heroes seemed so sexed-up (something I came to appreciate), but at the time I wanted Longshot to be a bit childlike, without a big swinging machismo. Longshot was a grab bag, a monster built of whatever was floating in the ethers of my world at the time. At least, that's the way I recall it.

Just as I was building my monster, some art samples arrived on my desk. Three blue pencil pages of the Beast washing dishes and tossing them to another X-Man to dry. These pages were genius. Full of dizzy charm, antics, fluid energy, humor... and they came with a note from a guy named Art Adams.

I sent Arthur my thousand-page opus about who I thought Longshot was, along with descriptions of Mojo, Ricochet Rita, Gog 'n Magog, Major Domo and other minions. Arthur sent back a deluge of creativity so astounding in its breadth and power that it compelled me to create even deeper and more complex origins. His tossed-off sketches of extra minions, like the six-armed chick and the ram-head guy, were so compelling they became major characters. The next thing we knew we were sucked into the wonder that is the Marvel Universe and, well, the stories weren't so simple anymore.

Not that any of this would have happened without Louise Simonson. She was the brilliant, prescient editor who allowed two dithering babies such as Arthur and I to have our very own comic. The one you hold collected now. Back then, in the times before some lipstick salesman wandered in and bought the company and corporatized it, it was easy to make comics. You had an idea, an editor said "Sounds cool. Why not?" and you did it. Now there are pitches and proposals and committees, and a character like Longshot would be so tangled in red tape from it all he'd end up consigned to the reject bin long before he'd ever be given a chance to jump up and stick to a wall. Sigh.

About the caveats at the end of some of these paragraphs, about the fragility of recollection. I have been perplexed by the overlap of story and memory. For a long time I had a vivid memory of a tiny me riding a giant horse when very young. Later, when my family's Super-8 movies were transferred to video, I saw that I was in my father's lap, and that he was riding the horse. Why had I removed him from the memory? Was that closer to the essence of what was to come in life? Me, riding a horse alone? The idea of deep origins that we are so sure of, and of the stories we tell ourselves about who we are, and the suspicion that perhaps all memories are rewritten stories, all this led to the idea of Longshot having no past but rather a story he had to discover along the way. And maybe that's all it was, and all memory is, a story we tell ourselves. Or try to tell others. The actress Ingrid Bergman once said, "Happiness is good health and a bad memory." Forgetting is part of health. Remembering who you are now, not then.

I'll say one more thing about comics. Writing them for ten or so years kept me infantile. Developmentally challenged. I still live half my life in a fantasy world. Hallelujah.

Ann Nocenti

Ann Nocenti by Arthur Adams

SUPER EDITOR

THE ENERGETIC, EFFERVESCENT...
...SUPER EDITOR!
VS
THE TOTALLY AWESOME MIGHT OF...
...TEDDY-BEAR-MAN!

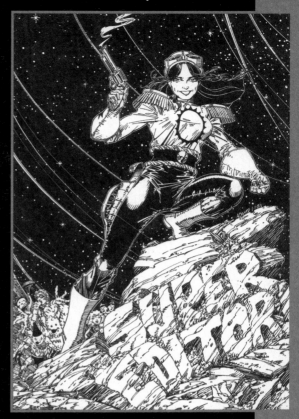

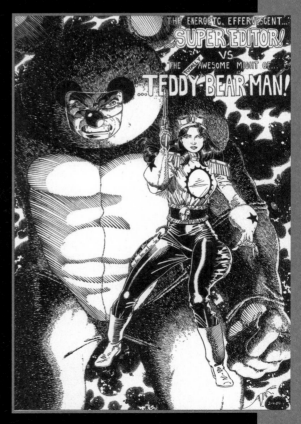

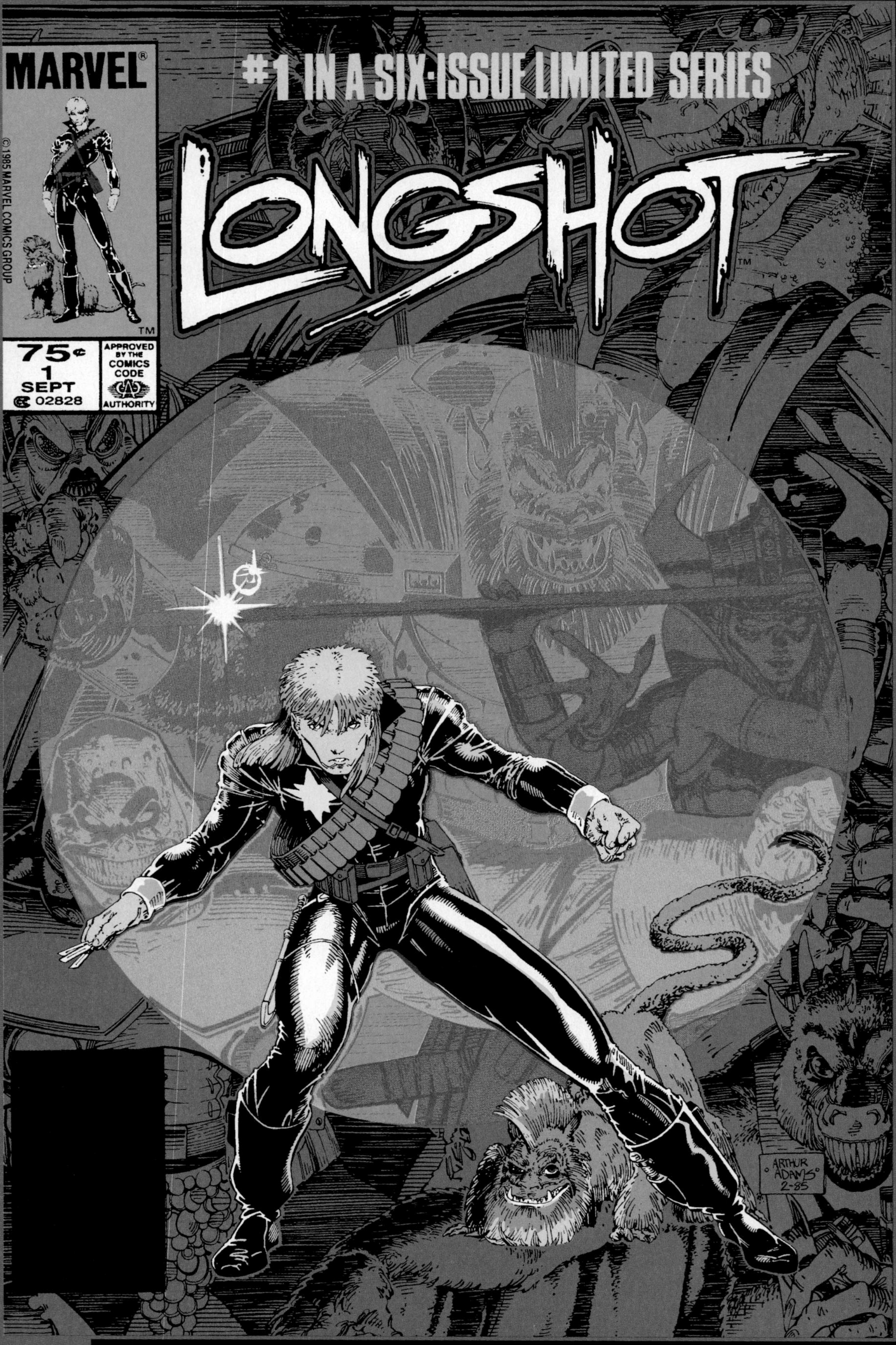
MARVEL®
#1 IN A SIX-ISSUE LIMITED SERIES
LONGSHOT™
© 1985 MARVEL COMICS GROUP
75¢
1
SEPT
02828
APPROVED BY THE COMICS CODE AUTHORITY
ARTHUR ADAMS 2-85

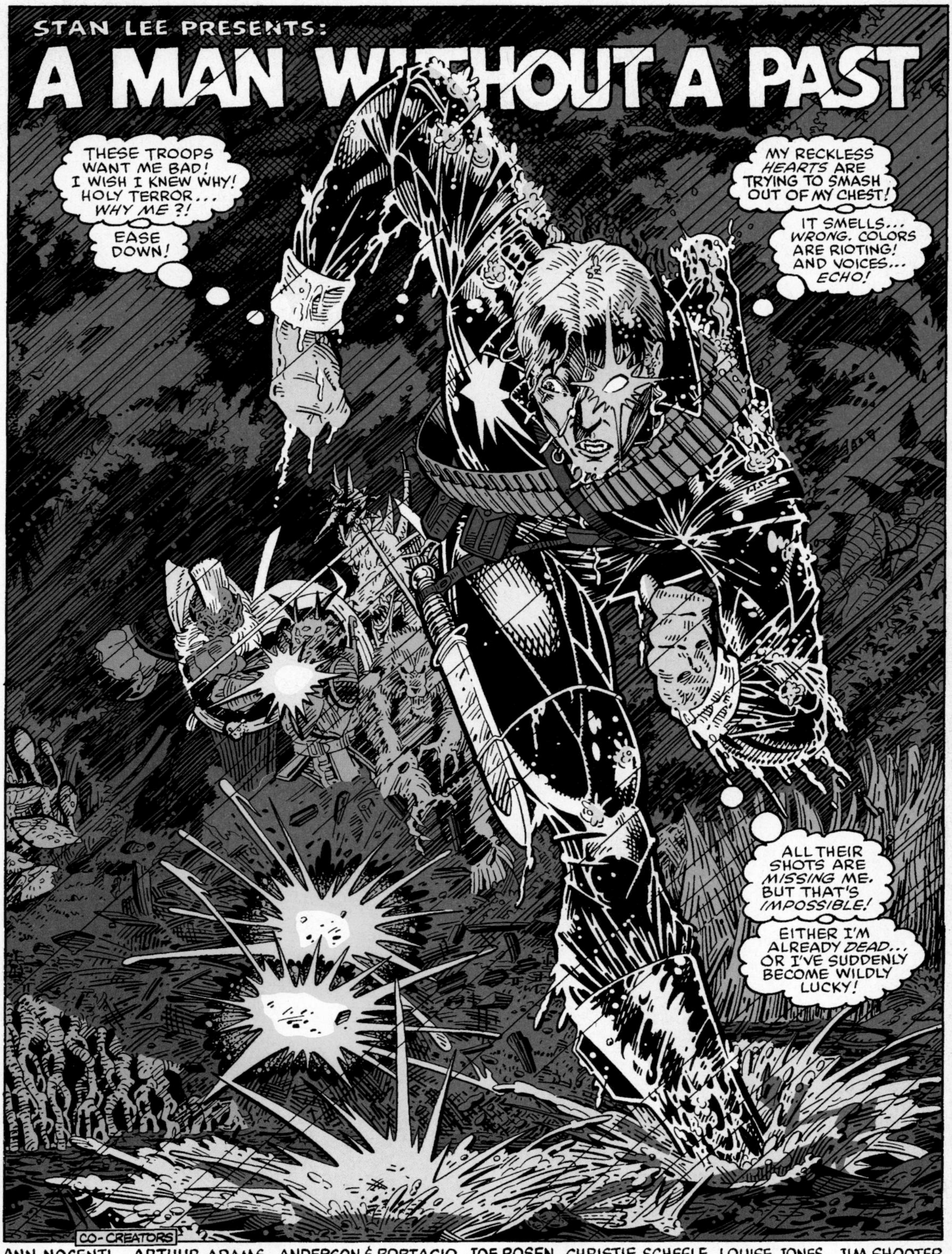
STAN LEE PRESENTS:
A MAN WITHOUT A PAST
THESE TROOPS WANT ME BAD! I WISH I KNEW WHY! HOLY TERROR... WHY ME?!
EASE DOWN!
MY RECKLESS HEARTS ARE TRYING TO SMASH OUT OF MY CHEST!
IT SMELLS... WRONG. COLORS ARE RIOTING! AND VOICES... ECHO!
ALL THEIR SHOTS ARE MISSING ME. BUT THAT'S IMPOSSIBLE!
EITHER I'M ALREADY DEAD... OR I'VE SUDDENLY BECOME WILDLY LUCKY!
CO-CREATORS

ANN NOCENTI WRITER · ARTHUR ADAMS PENCILS · ANDERSON & PORTACIO INKS · JOE ROSEN LETTERS · CHRISTIE SCHEELE COLORS · LOUISE JONES EDITOR · JIM SHOOTER EDITOR IN CHIEF

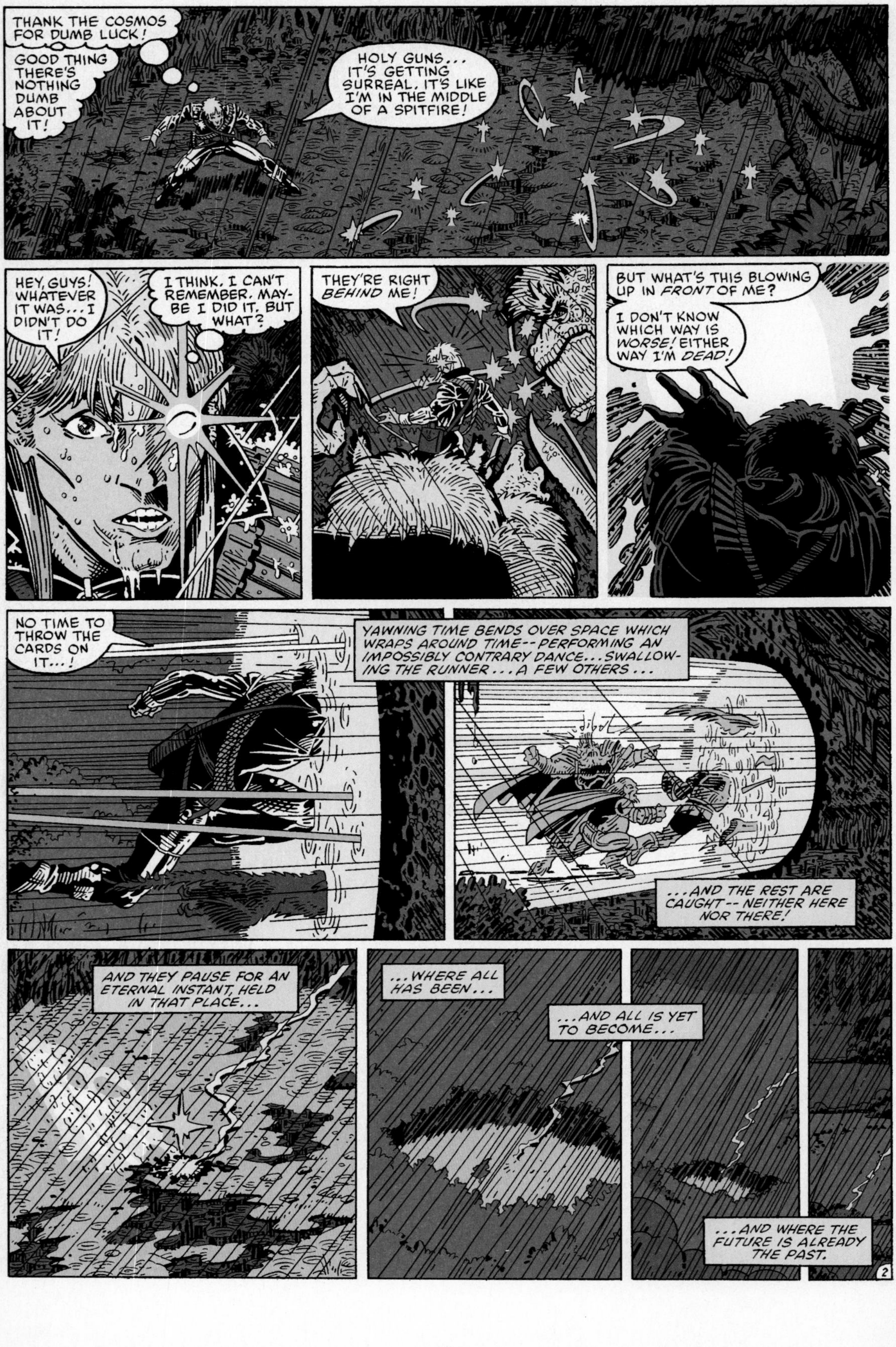
THANK THE COSMOS FOR DUMB LUCK!
GOOD THING THERE'S NOTHING DUMB ABOUT IT!
HOLY GUNS... IT'S GETTING SURREAL. IT'S LIKE I'M IN THE MIDDLE OF A SPITFIRE!
HEY, GUYS! WHATEVER IT WAS... I DIDN'T DO IT!
I THINK. I CAN'T REMEMBER. MAY-BE I DID IT. BUT WHAT?
THEY'RE RIGHT BEHIND ME!
BUT WHAT'S THIS BLOWING UP IN FRONT OF ME?
I DON'T KNOW WHICH WAY IS WORSE! EITHER WAY I'M DEAD!
NO TIME TO THROW THE CARDS ON IT...!
YAWNING TIME BENDS OVER SPACE WHICH WRAPS AROUND TIME--PERFORMING AN IMPOSSIBLY CONTRARY DANCE...SWALLOWING THE RUNNER...A FEW OTHERS...
...AND THE REST ARE CAUGHT--NEITHER HERE NOR THERE!
AND THEY PAUSE FOR AN ETERNAL INSTANT, HELD IN THAT PLACE...
...WHERE ALL HAS BEEN...
...AND ALL IS YET TO BECOME...
...AND WHERE THE FUTURE IS ALREADY THE PAST.
2

UPSTATE NEW YORK.

OH, SAINTS HEAR ME! BLESSED MARY...PETER PAUL, *HELP!*

RALPH THERE'S SOME KINDA ELECTRICAL STORM!

RAALPH THE CAR'S GONE BERSERK!

RAAALPH WE'RE GONNA KILL THAT OLD LADY!

AWRIGHT, I *SEE* IT, ROSE! SHUT UP ALREADY!

I'M DEAD. ARCHANGEL GABRIEL?

OUT OF THE WAY, MA'AM... AND YOU'LL LIVE TO A RIPE OLD AGE OF 300!

K-K-KRAK!

KARASH!

WOW! HE SAVED HER! DON'T THAT BEAT THE ODDS.

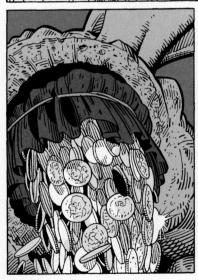

RALPH, LOOK! MONEY! IT WAS HIDDEN BEHIND THAT GARGOYLE!

SOME CROOK'S GONNA BE MAD!

BUT MAN, AIN'T *WE* LUCKY!

OBOY! I CAN BUY COMICS AN' CANDY...AN' COMICS!

3

9

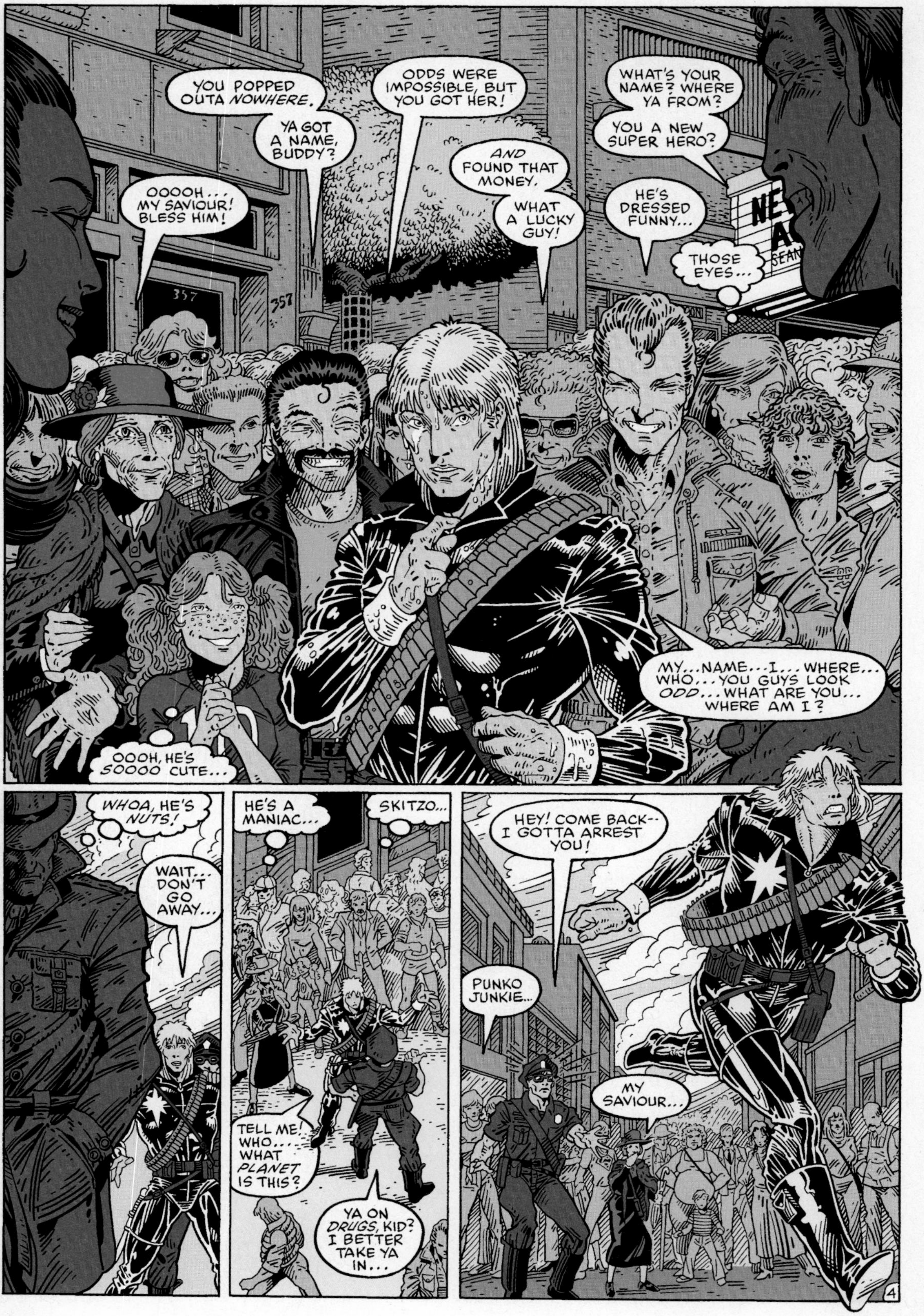
YOU POPPED OUTA *NOWHERE.*
YA GOT A NAME, BUDDY?
ODDS WERE IMPOSSIBLE, BUT YOU GOT HER!
WHAT'S YOUR NAME? WHERE YA FROM?
YOU A NEW SUPER HERO?
OOOOH... MY SAVIOUR! BLESS HIM!
AND FOUND THAT MONEY.
WHAT A LUCKY GUY!
HE'S DRESSED FUNNY...
THOSE EYES...
MY...NAME...I...WHERE... WHO...YOU GUYS LOOK *ODD*...WHAT ARE YOU... WHERE AM I?
OOOH, HE'S *SOOOO* CUTE...
WHOA, HE'S *NUTS!*
WAIT... DON'T GO AWAY...
HE'S A MANIAC...
SKITZO...
TELL ME! WHO... WHAT *PLANET* IS THIS?
YA ON *DRUGS*, KID? I BETTER TAKE YA IN...
HEY! COME BACK-- I GOTTA ARREST YOU!
PUNKO JUNKIE...
MY SAVIOUR...
4

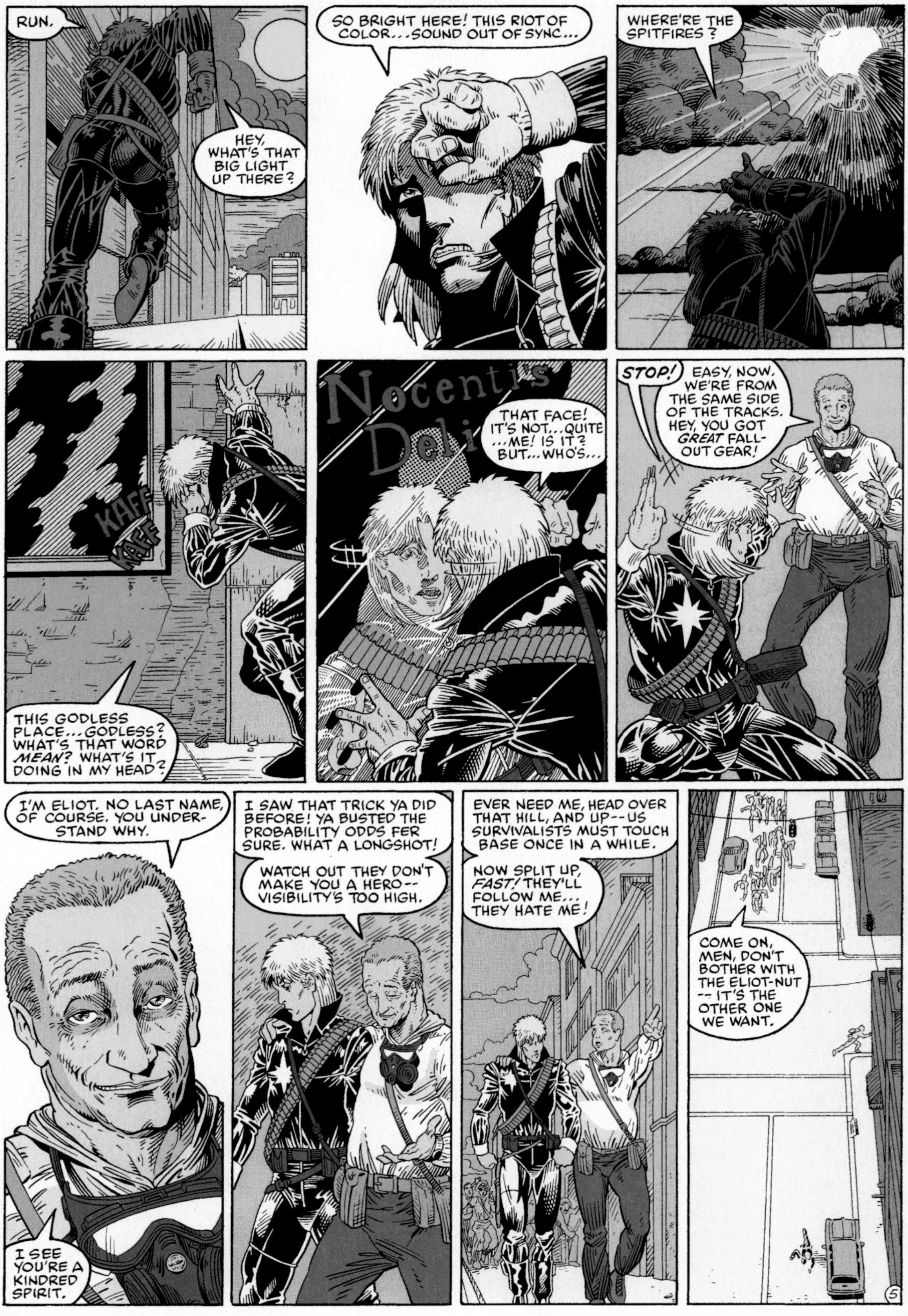
RUN.
HEY, WHAT'S THAT BIG LIGHT UP THERE?
SO BRIGHT HERE! THIS RIOT OF COLOR...SOUND OUT OF SYNC...
WHERE'RE THE SPITFIRES?
KAFF KAFF
THIS GODLESS PLACE...GODLESS? WHAT'S THAT WORD MEAN? WHAT'S IT DOING IN MY HEAD?
Nocenti's Deli
THAT FACE! IT'S NOT...QUITE ...ME! IS IT? BUT...WHO'S...
STOP!
EASY, NOW. WE'RE FROM THE SAME SIDE OF THE TRACKS. HEY, YOU GOT GREAT FALL-OUT GEAR!
I'M ELIOT. NO LAST NAME, OF COURSE. YOU UNDERSTAND WHY.
I SEE YOU'RE A KINDRED SPIRIT.
I SAW THAT TRICK YA DID BEFORE! YA BUSTED THE PROBABILITY ODDS FER SURE. WHAT A LONGSHOT!
WATCH OUT THEY DON'T MAKE YOU A HERO-- VISIBILITY'S TOO HIGH.
EVER NEED ME, HEAD OVER THAT HILL, AND UP--US SURVIVALISTS MUST TOUCH BASE ONCE IN A WHILE.
NOW SPLIT UP, FAST! THEY'LL FOLLOW ME... THEY HATE ME!
COME ON, MEN, DON'T BOTHER WITH THE ELIOT-NUT --IT'S THE OTHER ONE WE WANT.
5

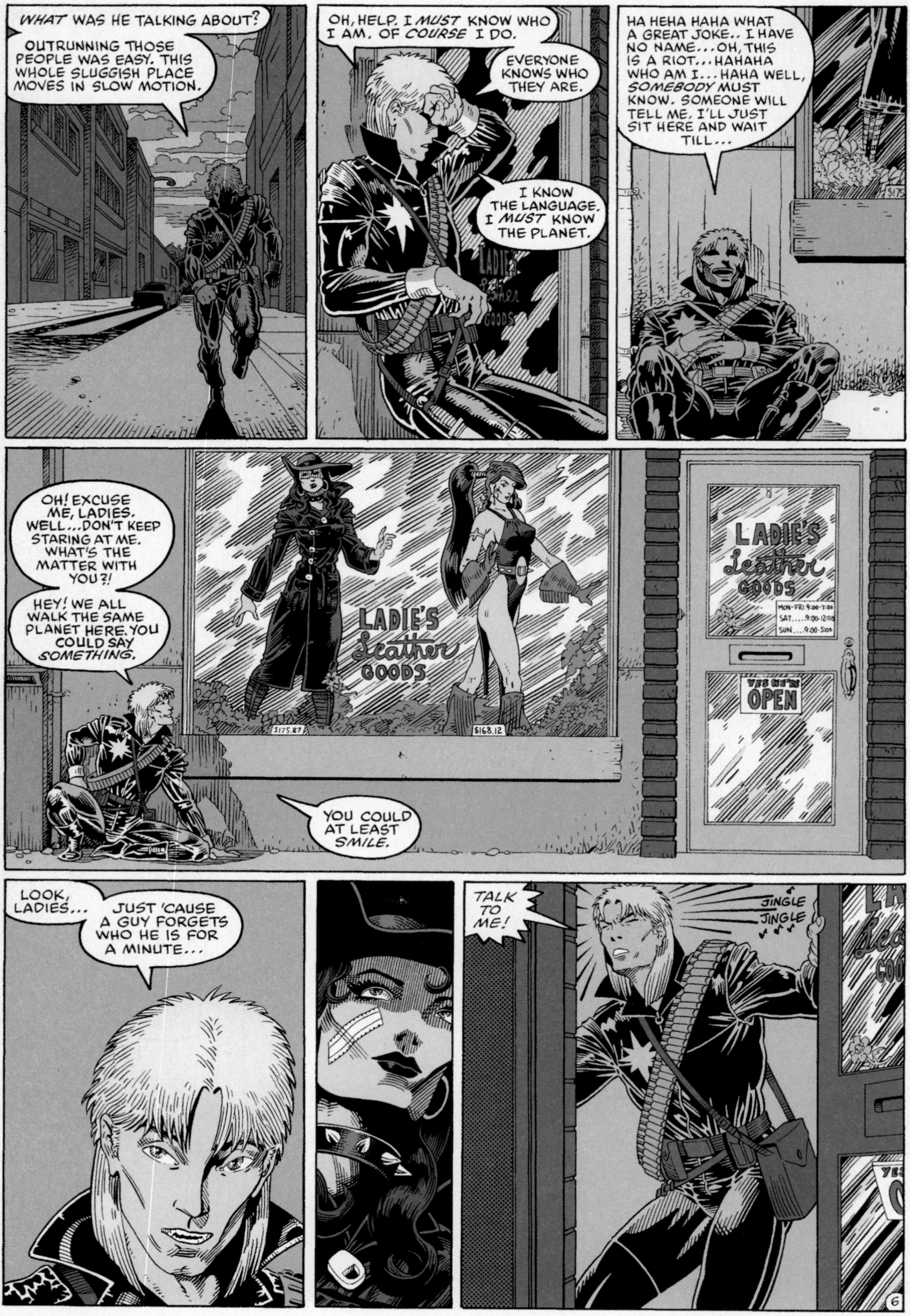

WHAT WAS HE TALKING ABOUT?
OUTRUNNING THOSE PEOPLE WAS EASY. THIS WHOLE SLUGGISH PLACE MOVES IN SLOW MOTION.
OH, HELP. I MUST KNOW WHO I AM. OF COURSE I DO.
EVERYONE KNOWS WHO THEY ARE.
I KNOW THE LANGUAGE. I MUST KNOW THE PLANET.
LADIE'S Leather GOODS
HA HEHA HAHA HAHA WHAT A GREAT JOKE.. I HAVE NO NAME...OH, THIS IS A RIOT...HAHAHA WHO AM I...HAHA WELL, SOMEBODY MUST KNOW. SOMEONE WILL TELL ME. I'LL JUST SIT HERE AND WAIT TILL...
OH! EXCUSE ME, LADIES. WELL...DON'T KEEP STARING AT ME. WHAT'S THE MATTER WITH YOU?!
HEY! WE ALL WALK THE SAME PLANET HERE. YOU COULD SAY SOMETHING.
LADIE'S Leather GOODS
$175.87
$168.12
LADIE'S Leather GOODS
MON-FRI 9:00-7:00
SAT....9:00-12:00
SUN....9:00-5:00
YES WE'RE OPEN
YOU COULD AT LEAST SMILE.
LOOK, LADIES...
JUST 'CAUSE A GUY FORGETS WHO HE IS FOR A MINUTE...
TALK TO ME!
JINGLE JINGLE
6

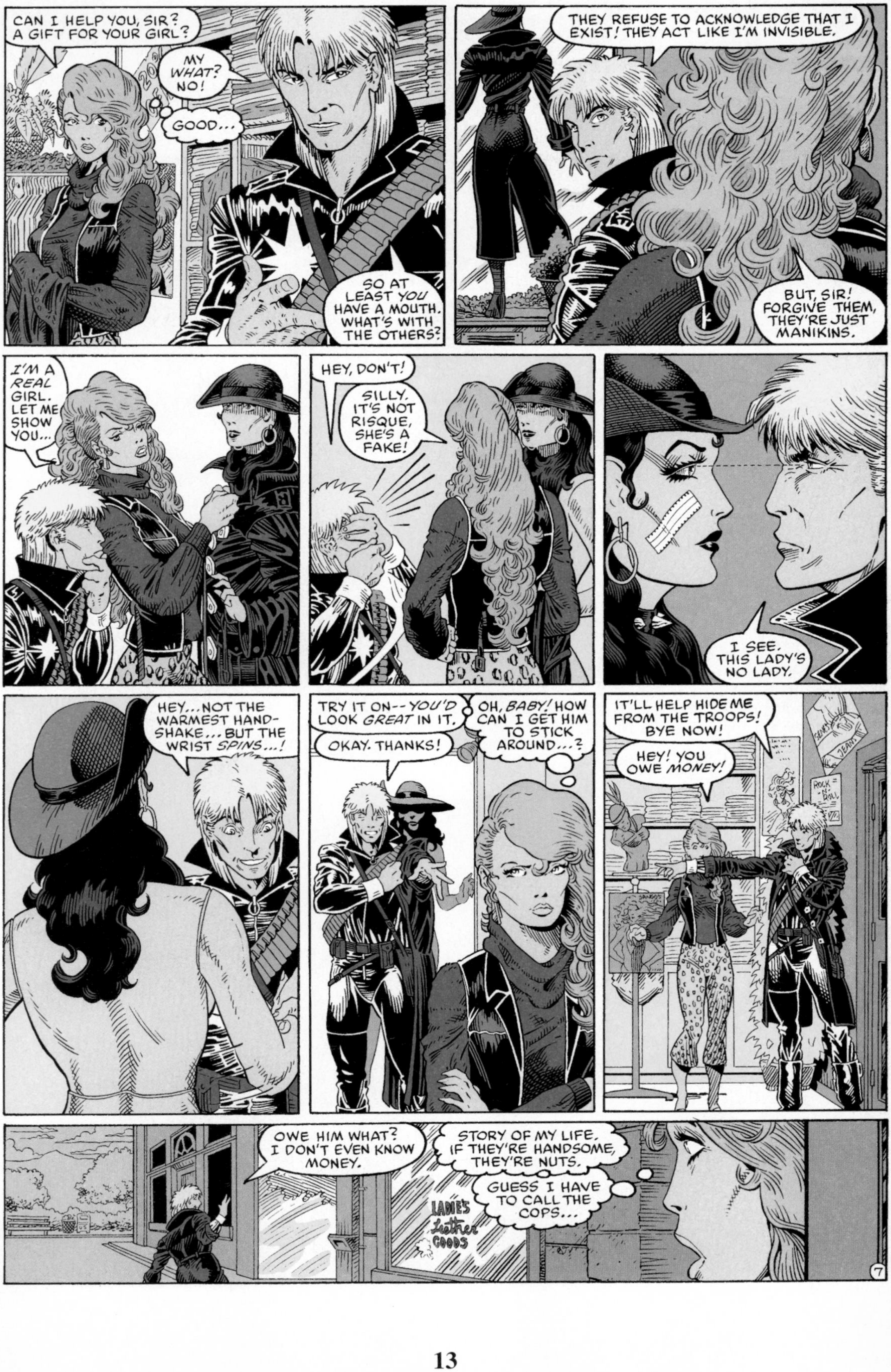
CAN I HELP YOU, SIR? A GIFT FOR YOUR GIRL?
MY WHAT? NO!
GOOD...
SO AT LEAST YOU HAVE A MOUTH. WHAT'S WITH THE OTHERS?
THEY REFUSE TO ACKNOWLEDGE THAT I EXIST! THEY ACT LIKE I'M INVISIBLE.
BUT, SIR! FORGIVE THEM, THEY'RE JUST MANIKINS.
I'M A REAL GIRL. LET ME SHOW YOU...
HEY, DON'T!
SILLY. IT'S NOT RISQUE, SHE'S A FAKE!
I SEE. THIS LADY'S NO LADY.
HEY... NOT THE WARMEST HAND-SHAKE... BUT THE WRIST SPINS...!
TRY IT ON-- YOU'D LOOK GREAT IN IT.
OKAY. THANKS!
OH, BABY! HOW CAN I GET HIM TO STICK AROUND...?
IT'LL HELP HIDE ME FROM THE TROOPS! BYE NOW!
HEY! YOU OWE MONEY!
ROCK-N-ROLL
OWE HIM WHAT? I DON'T EVEN KNOW MONEY.
STORY OF MY LIFE. IF THEY'RE HANDSOME, THEY'RE NUTS.
GUESS I HAVE TO CALL THE COPS...
LADIE'S Leather GOODS
7

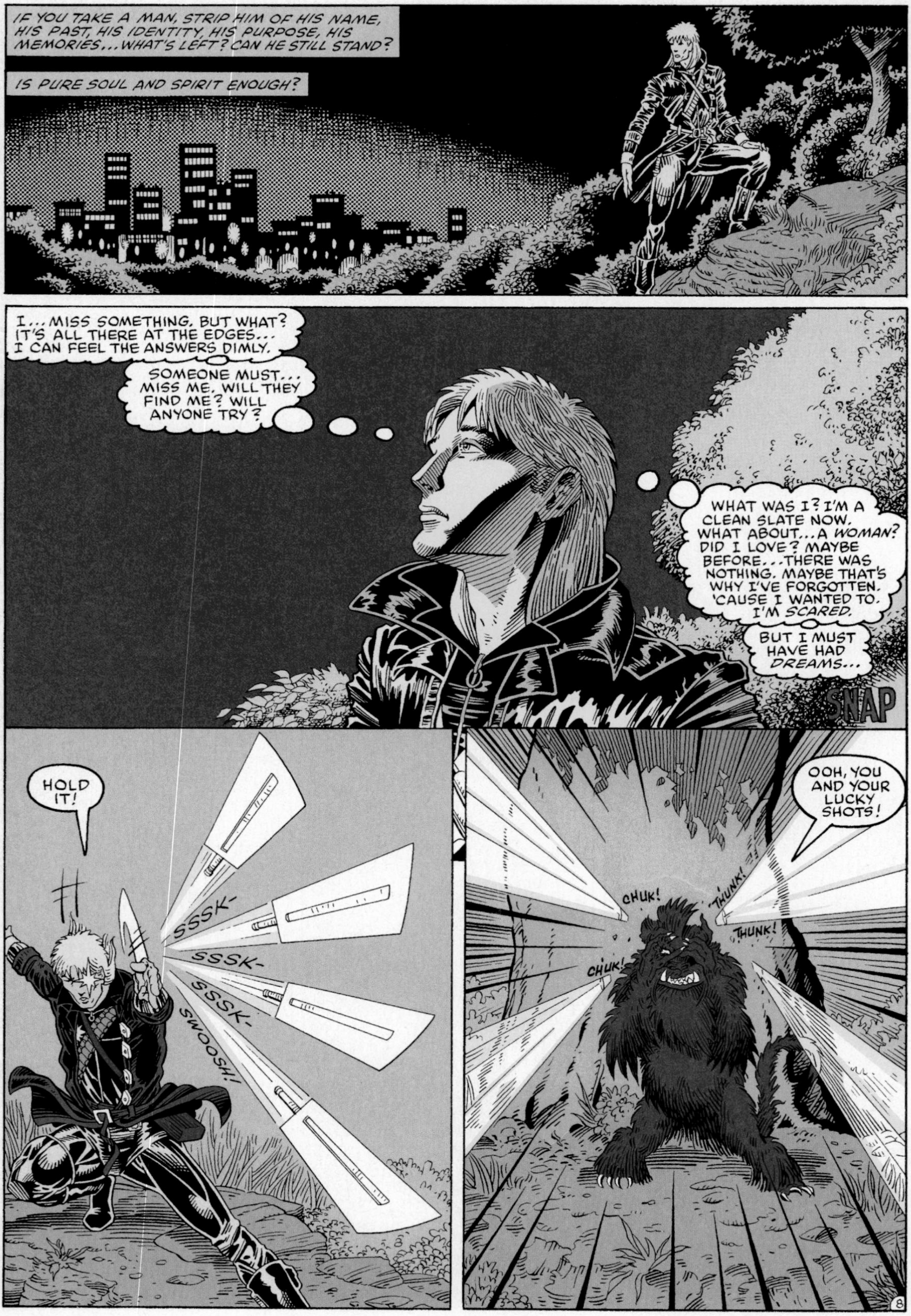

IF YOU TAKE A MAN, STRIP HIM OF HIS NAME, HIS PAST, HIS IDENTITY, HIS PURPOSE, HIS MEMORIES... WHAT'S LEFT? CAN HE STILL STAND?
IS PURE SOUL AND SPIRIT ENOUGH?
I... MISS SOMETHING. BUT WHAT? IT'S ALL THERE AT THE EDGES... I CAN FEEL THE ANSWERS DIMLY.
SOMEONE MUST... MISS ME. WILL THEY FIND ME? WILL ANYONE TRY?
WHAT WAS I? I'M A CLEAN SLATE NOW. WHAT ABOUT... A WOMAN? DID I LOVE? MAYBE BEFORE... THERE WAS NOTHING. MAYBE THAT'S WHY I'VE FORGOTTEN. 'CAUSE I WANTED TO. I'M SCARED.
BUT I MUST HAVE HAD DREAMS...
SNAP
HOLD IT!
SSSK-
SSSK-
SSSK-
SWOOSH!
OOH, YOU AND YOUR LUCKY SHOTS!
CHUK!
THUNK!
THUNK!
CHUK!
8

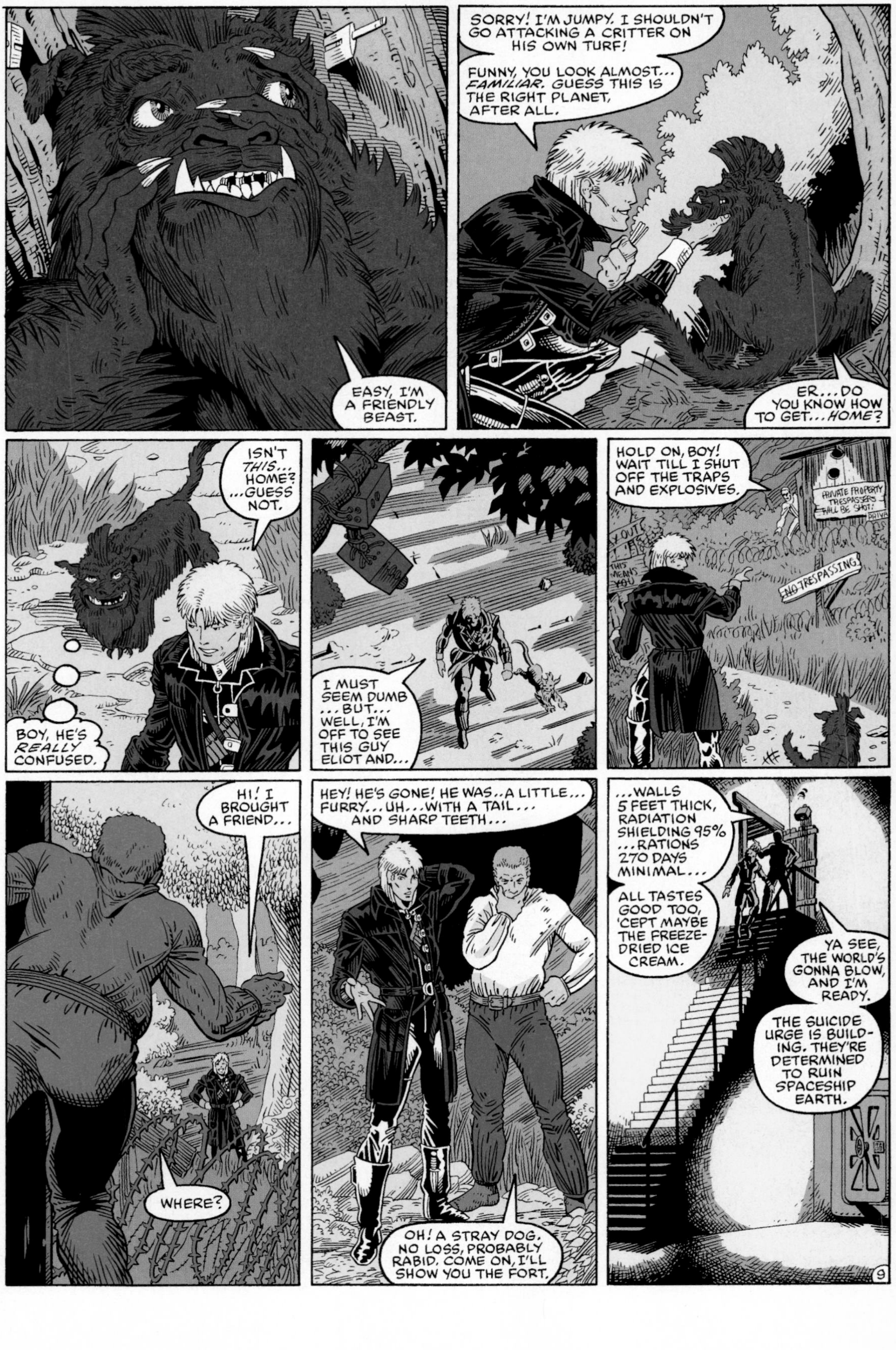
EASY, I'M A FRIENDLY BEAST.
SORRY! I'M JUMPY. I SHOULDN'T GO ATTACKING A CRITTER ON HIS OWN TURF!
FUNNY, YOU LOOK ALMOST... *FAMILIAR.* GUESS THIS IS THE RIGHT PLANET, AFTER ALL.
ER...DO YOU KNOW HOW TO GET...*HOME*?
ISN'T *THIS*... HOME? ...GUESS NOT.
BOY, HE'S *REALLY* CONFUSED.
I MUST SEEM DUMB ...BUT... WELL, I'M OFF TO SEE THIS GUY ELIOT AND...
HOLD ON, BOY! WAIT TILL I SHUT OFF THE TRAPS AND EXPLOSIVES.
PRIVATE PROPERTY TRESPASSERS WILL BE SHOT!
THIS MEANS YOU
NO TRESPASSING
HI! I BROUGHT A FRIEND...
WHERE?
HEY! HE'S GONE! HE WAS..A LITTLE... FURRY...UH...WITH A TAIL... AND SHARP TEETH...
OH! A STRAY DOG. NO LOSS, PROBABLY RABID. COME ON, I'LL SHOW YOU THE FORT.
...WALLS 5 FEET THICK, RADIATION SHIELDING 95% ...RATIONS 270 DAYS MINIMAL...
ALL TASTES GOOD TOO, 'CEPT MAYBE THE FREEZE-DRIED ICE CREAM.
YA SEE, THE WORLD'S GONNA BLOW, AND I'M READY.
THE SUICIDE URGE IS BUILDING. THEY'RE DETERMINED TO RUIN SPACESHIP EARTH.
9

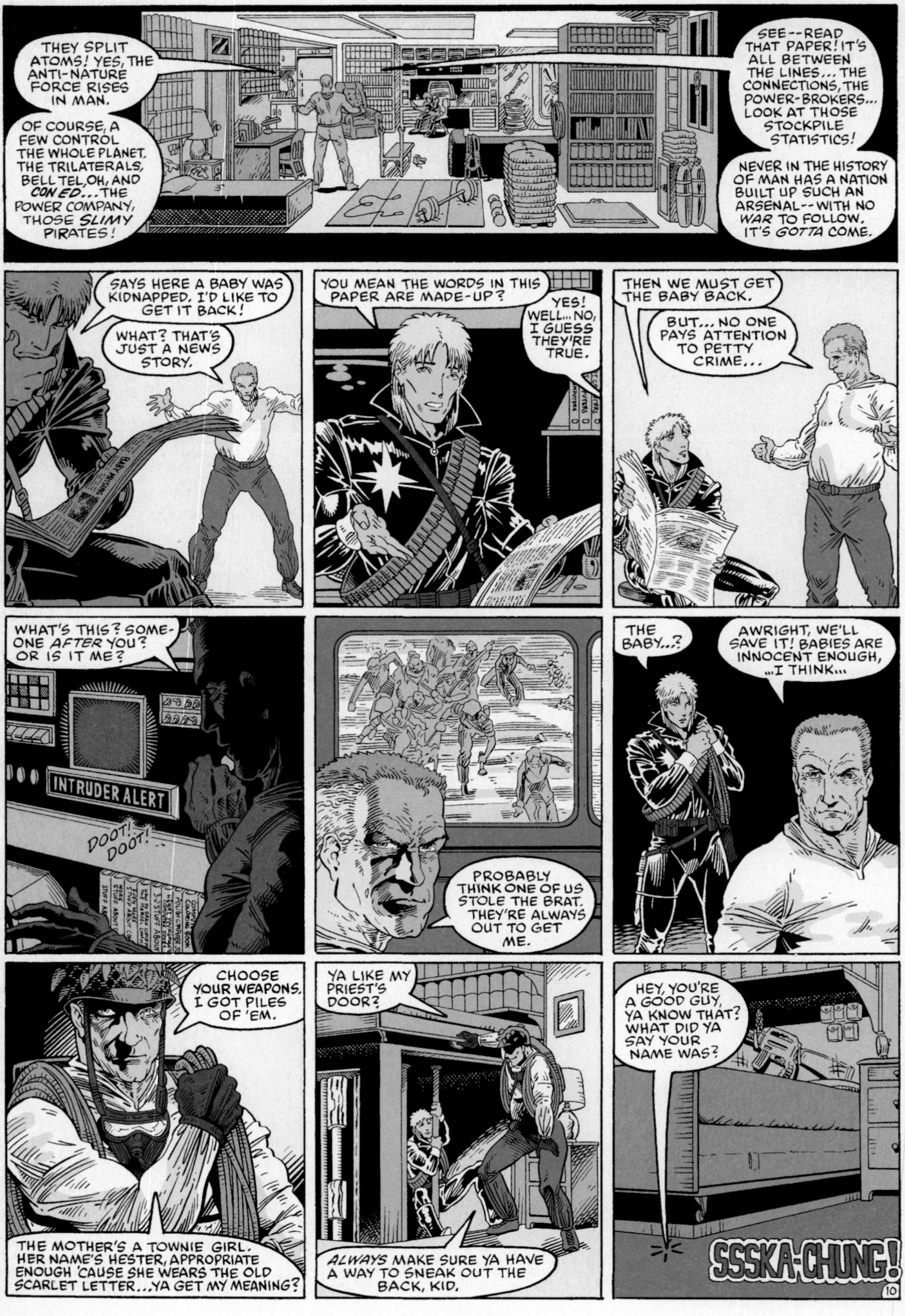

THEY SPLIT ATOMS! YES, THE ANTI-NATURE FORCE RISES IN MAN.
OF COURSE, A FEW CONTROL THE WHOLE PLANET. THE TRILATERALS, BELL TEL, OH, AND CON ED... THE POWER COMPANY, THOSE SLIMY PIRATES!
SEE--READ THAT PAPER! IT'S ALL BETWEEN THE LINES... THE CONNECTIONS, THE POWER-BROKERS... LOOK AT THOSE STOCKPILE STATISTICS!
NEVER IN THE HISTORY OF MAN HAS A NATION BUILT UP SUCH AN ARSENAL--WITH NO WAR TO FOLLOW. IT'S GOTTA COME.
SAYS HERE A BABY WAS KIDNAPPED. I'D LIKE TO GET IT BACK!
WHAT? THAT'S JUST A NEWS STORY.
BABY MISSING
YOU MEAN THE WORDS IN THIS PAPER ARE MADE-UP?
YES! WELL... NO, I GUESS THEY'RE TRUE.
THEN WE MUST GET THE BABY BACK.
BUT... NO ONE PAYS ATTENTION TO PETTY CRIME...
WHAT'S THIS? SOME-ONE AFTER YOU? OR IS IT ME?
INTRUDER ALERT
DOOT! DOOT!
PROBABLY THINK ONE OF US STOLE THE BRAT. THEY'RE ALWAYS OUT TO GET ME.
THE BABY..?
AWRIGHT, WE'LL SAVE IT! BABIES ARE INNOCENT ENOUGH, ...I THINK...
CHOOSE YOUR WEAPONS. I GOT PILES OF 'EM.
THE MOTHER'S A TOWNIE GIRL. HER NAME'S HESTER, APPROPRIATE ENOUGH 'CAUSE SHE WEARS THE OLD SCARLET LETTER...YA GET MY MEANING?
YA LIKE MY PRIEST'S DOOR?
ALWAYS MAKE SURE YA HAVE A WAY TO SNEAK OUT THE BACK, KID.
HEY, YOU'RE A GOOD GUY, YA KNOW THAT? WHAT DID YA SAY YOUR NAME WAS?
SSSKA-CHUNG!
10

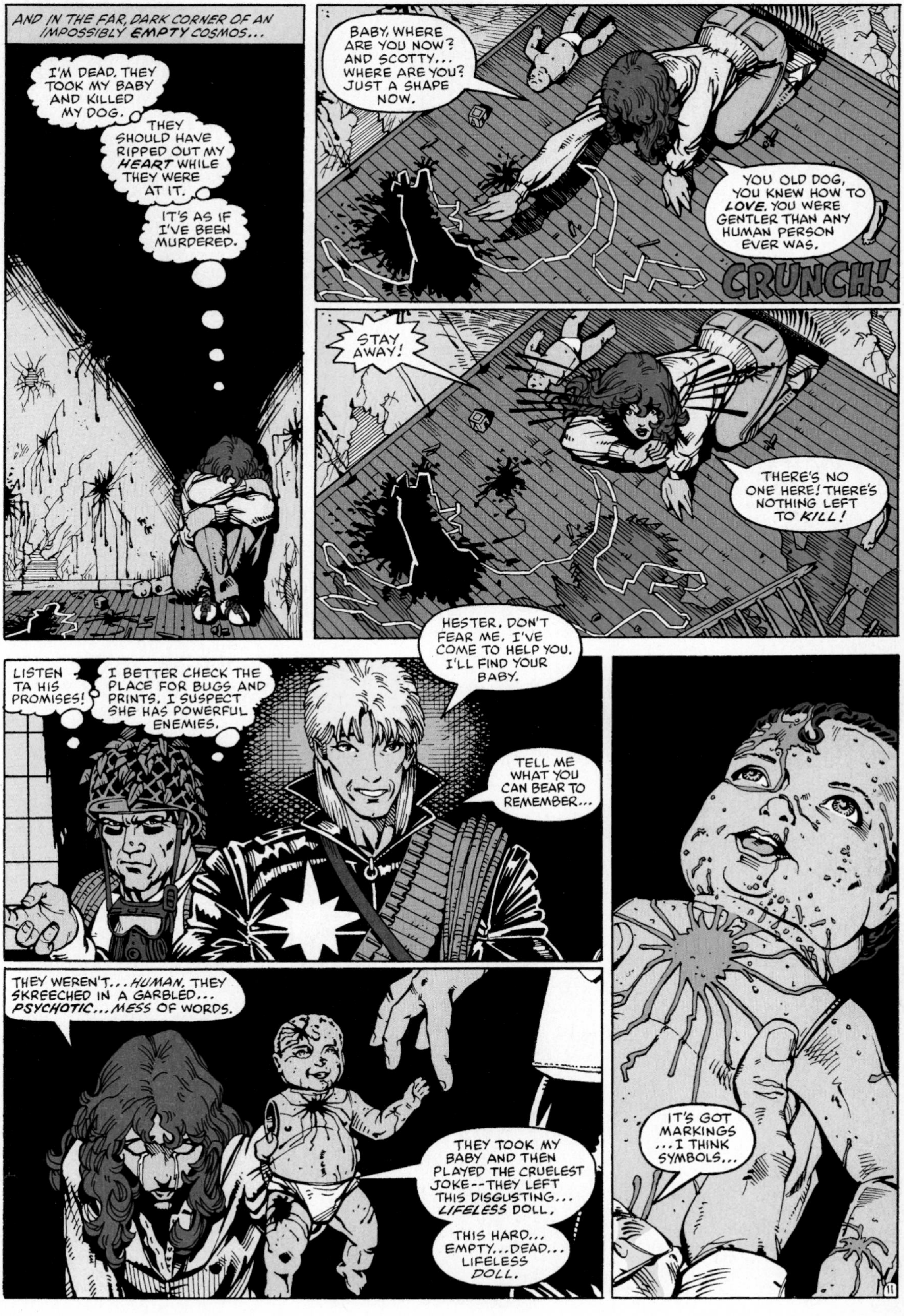
AND IN THE FAR, DARK CORNER OF AN IMPOSSIBLY EMPTY COSMOS...
I'M DEAD. THEY TOOK MY BABY AND KILLED MY DOG.
THEY SHOULD HAVE RIPPED OUT MY HEART WHILE THEY WERE AT IT.
IT'S AS IF I'VE BEEN MURDERED.
BABY, WHERE ARE YOU NOW? AND SCOTTY... WHERE ARE YOU? JUST A SHAPE NOW.
YOU OLD DOG, YOU KNEW HOW TO LOVE. YOU WERE GENTLER THAN ANY HUMAN PERSON EVER WAS.
CRUNCH!
STAY AWAY!
THERE'S NO ONE HERE! THERE'S NOTHING LEFT TO KILL!
LISTEN TA HIS PROMISES!
I BETTER CHECK THE PLACE FOR BUGS AND PRINTS. I SUSPECT SHE HAS POWERFUL ENEMIES.
HESTER. DON'T FEAR ME. I'VE COME TO HELP YOU. I'LL FIND YOUR BABY.
TELL ME WHAT YOU CAN BEAR TO REMEMBER...
THEY WEREN'T... HUMAN. THEY SKREECHED IN A GARBLED... PSYCHOTIC... MESS OF WORDS.
THEY TOOK MY BABY AND THEN PLAYED THE CRUELEST JOKE--THEY LEFT THIS DISGUSTING... LIFELESS DOLL.
THIS HARD... EMPTY... DEAD... LIFELESS DOLL.
IT'S GOT MARKINGS ...I THINK SYMBOLS...

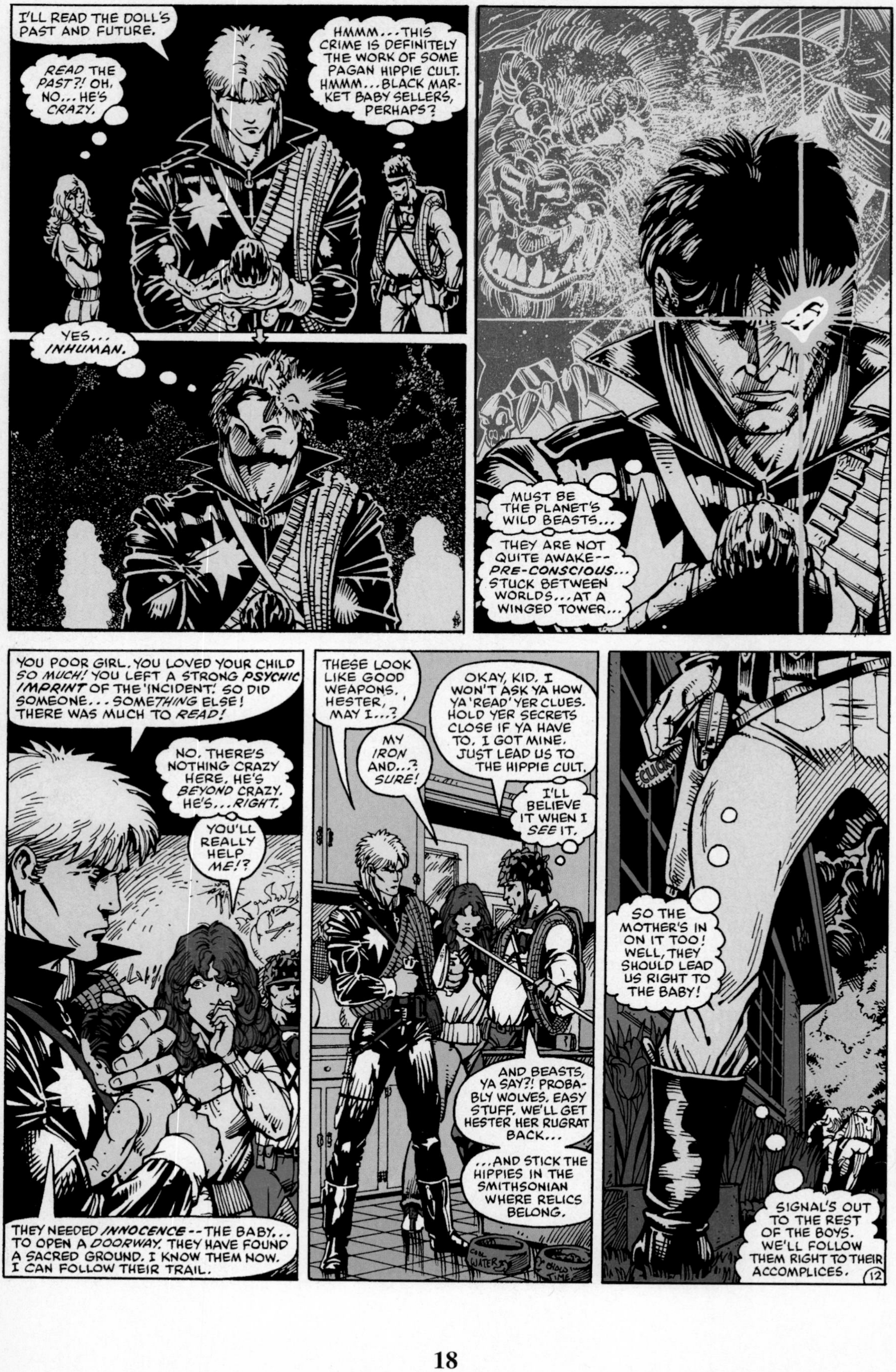
I'LL READ THE DOLL'S PAST AND FUTURE.
READ THE PAST?! OH, NO... HE'S CRAZY.
HMMM...THIS CRIME IS DEFINITELY THE WORK OF SOME PAGAN HIPPIE CULT. HMMM...BLACK MARKET BABY SELLERS, PERHAPS?
YES... INHUMAN.
MUST BE THE PLANET'S WILD BEASTS...
THEY ARE NOT QUITE AWAKE-- PRE-CONSCIOUS... STUCK BETWEEN WORLDS...AT A WINGED TOWER...
YOU POOR GIRL. YOU LOVED YOUR CHILD SO MUCH! YOU LEFT A STRONG PSYCHIC IMPRINT OF THE 'INCIDENT.' SO DID SOMEONE... SOMETHING ELSE! THERE WAS MUCH TO READ!
NO. THERE'S NOTHING CRAZY HERE. HE'S BEYOND CRAZY. HE'S...RIGHT.
YOU'LL REALLY HELP ME!?
THEY NEEDED INNOCENCE--THE BABY... TO OPEN A DOORWAY. THEY HAVE FOUND A SACRED GROUND. I KNOW THEM NOW. I CAN FOLLOW THEIR TRAIL.
THESE LOOK LIKE GOOD WEAPONS, HESTER, MAY I...?
MY IRON AND...? SURE!
OKAY, KID. I WON'T ASK YA HOW YA 'READ' YER CLUES. HOLD YER SECRETS CLOSE IF YA HAVE TO. I GOT MINE. JUST LEAD US TO THE HIPPIE CULT.
I'LL BELIEVE IT WHEN I SEE IT.
AND BEASTS, YA SAY?! PROBABLY WOLVES. EASY STUFF. WE'LL GET HESTER HER RUGRAT BACK...
...AND STICK THE HIPPIES IN THE SMITHSONIAN WHERE RELICS BELONG.
CLICK
SO THE MOTHER'S IN ON IT TOO! WELL, THEY SHOULD LEAD US RIGHT TO THE BABY!
SIGNAL'S OUT TO THE REST OF THE BOYS. WE'LL FOLLOW THEM RIGHT TO THEIR ACCOMPLICES.
12

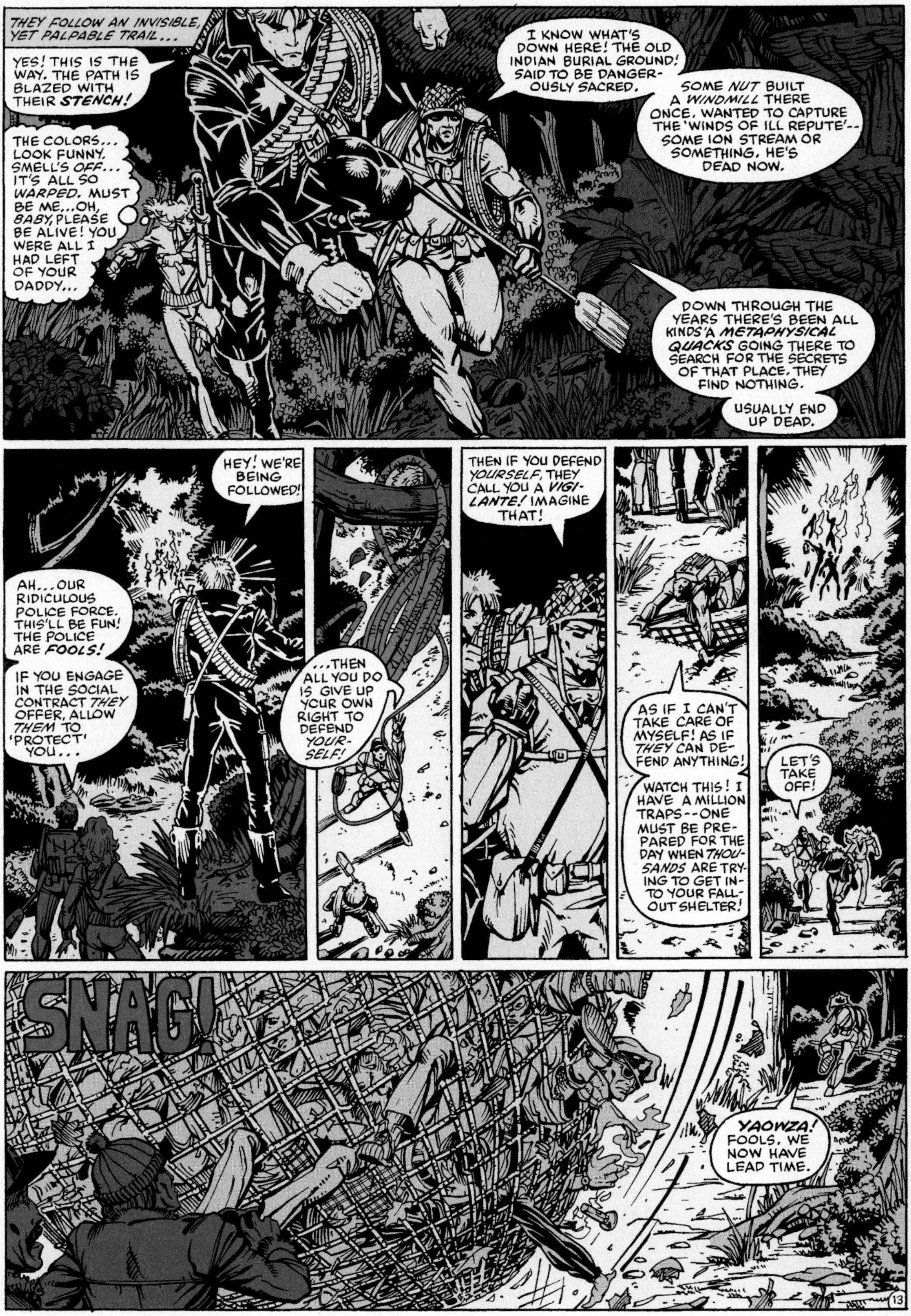
THEY FOLLOW AN INVISIBLE, YET PALPABLE TRAIL...
YES! THIS IS THE WAY. THE PATH IS BLAZED WITH THEIR STENCH!
THE COLORS... LOOK FUNNY. SMELL'S OFF... IT'S ALL SO WARPED. MUST BE ME...OH, BABY, PLEASE BE ALIVE! YOU WERE ALL I HAD LEFT OF YOUR DADDY...
I KNOW WHAT'S DOWN HERE! THE OLD INDIAN BURIAL GROUND! SAID TO BE DANGEROUSLY SACRED.
SOME NUT BUILT A WINDMILL THERE ONCE. WANTED TO CAPTURE THE 'WINDS OF ILL REPUTE'-- SOME ION STREAM OR SOMETHING. HE'S DEAD NOW.
DOWN THROUGH THE YEARS THERE'S BEEN ALL KINDS'A METAPHYSICAL QUACKS GOING THERE TO SEARCH FOR THE SECRETS OF THAT PLACE. THEY FIND NOTHING.
USUALLY END UP DEAD.
HEY! WE'RE BEING FOLLOWED!
AH...OUR RIDICULOUS POLICE FORCE. THIS'LL BE FUN! THE POLICE ARE FOOLS!
IF YOU ENGAGE IN THE SOCIAL CONTRACT THEY OFFER, ALLOW THEM TO 'PROTECT' YOU...
...THEN ALL YOU DO IS GIVE UP YOUR OWN RIGHT TO DEFEND YOURSELF!
THEN IF YOU DEFEND YOURSELF, THEY CALL YOU A VIGILANTE! IMAGINE THAT!
AS IF I CAN'T TAKE CARE OF MYSELF! AS IF THEY CAN DEFEND ANYTHING!
WATCH THIS! I HAVE A MILLION TRAPS--ONE MUST BE PREPARED FOR THE DAY WHEN THOUSANDS ARE TRYING TO GET INTO YOUR FALLOUT SHELTER!
LET'S TAKE OFF!
SNAG!
YAOWZA! FOOLS. WE NOW HAVE LEAD TIME.
13

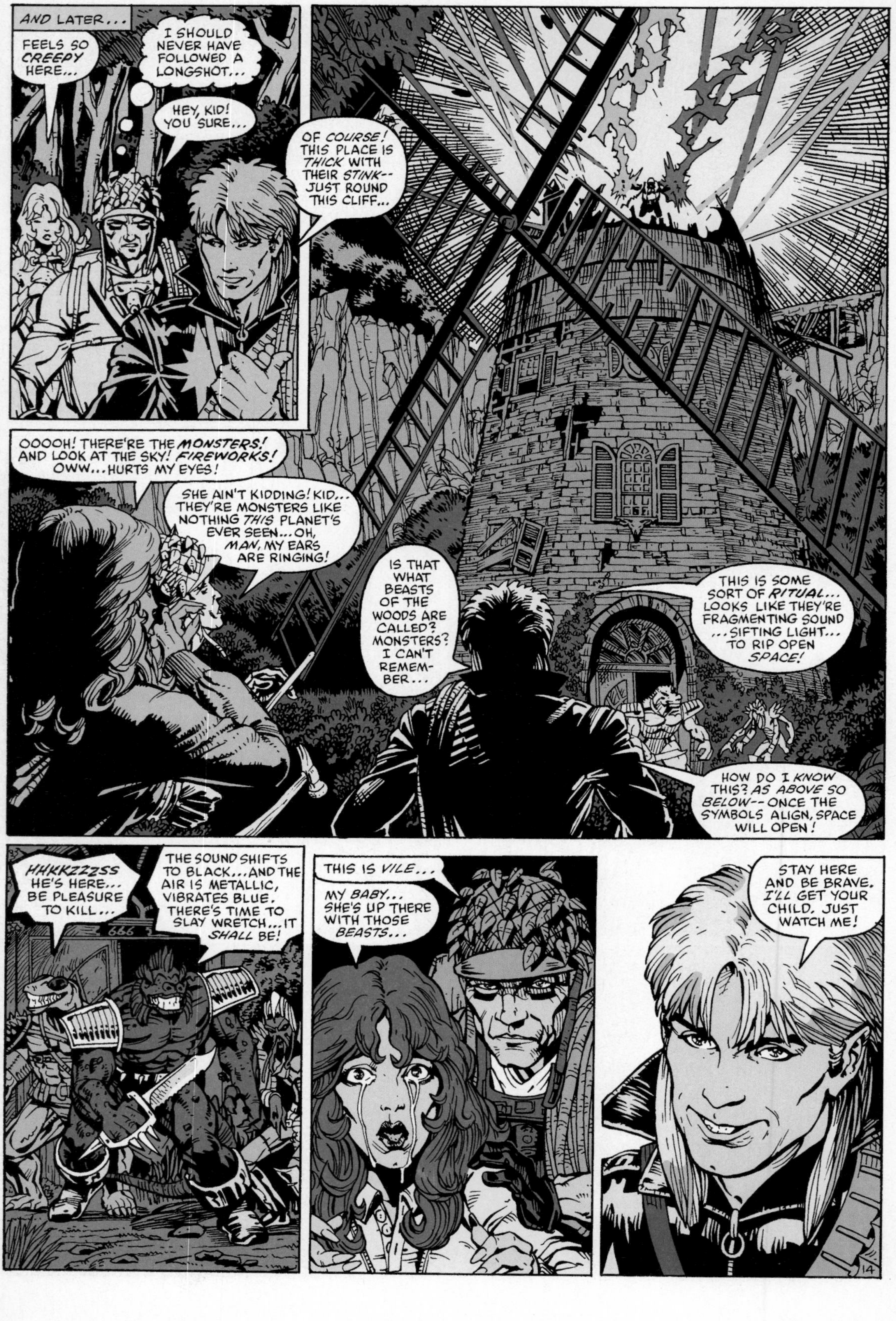
AND LATER...
FEELS SO CREEPY HERE...
I SHOULD NEVER HAVE FOLLOWED A LONGSHOT...
HEY, KID! YOU SURE...
OF COURSE! THIS PLACE IS THICK WITH THEIR STINK-- JUST ROUND THIS CLIFF...
OOOOH! THERE'RE THE MONSTERS! AND LOOK AT THE SKY! FIREWORKS! OWW... HURTS MY EYES!
SHE AIN'T KIDDING! KID... THEY'RE MONSTERS LIKE NOTHING THIS PLANET'S EVER SEEN... OH, MAN, MY EARS ARE RINGING!
IS THAT WHAT BEASTS OF THE WOODS ARE CALLED? MONSTERS? I CAN'T REMEMBER...
THIS IS SOME SORT OF RITUAL... LOOKS LIKE THEY'RE FRAGMENTING SOUND ...SIFTING LIGHT... TO RIP OPEN SPACE!
HOW DO I KNOW THIS? AS ABOVE SO BELOW-- ONCE THE SYMBOLS ALIGN, SPACE WILL OPEN!
HHKKZZZZSS HE'S HERE... BE PLEASURE TO KILL...
THE SOUND SHIFTS TO BLACK... AND THE AIR IS METALLIC, VIBRATES BLUE. THERE'S TIME TO SLAY WRETCH... IT SHALL BE!
666
THIS IS VILE...
MY BABY... SHE'S UP THERE WITH THOSE BEASTS...
STAY HERE AND BE BRAVE. I'LL GET YOUR CHILD. JUST WATCH ME!
14

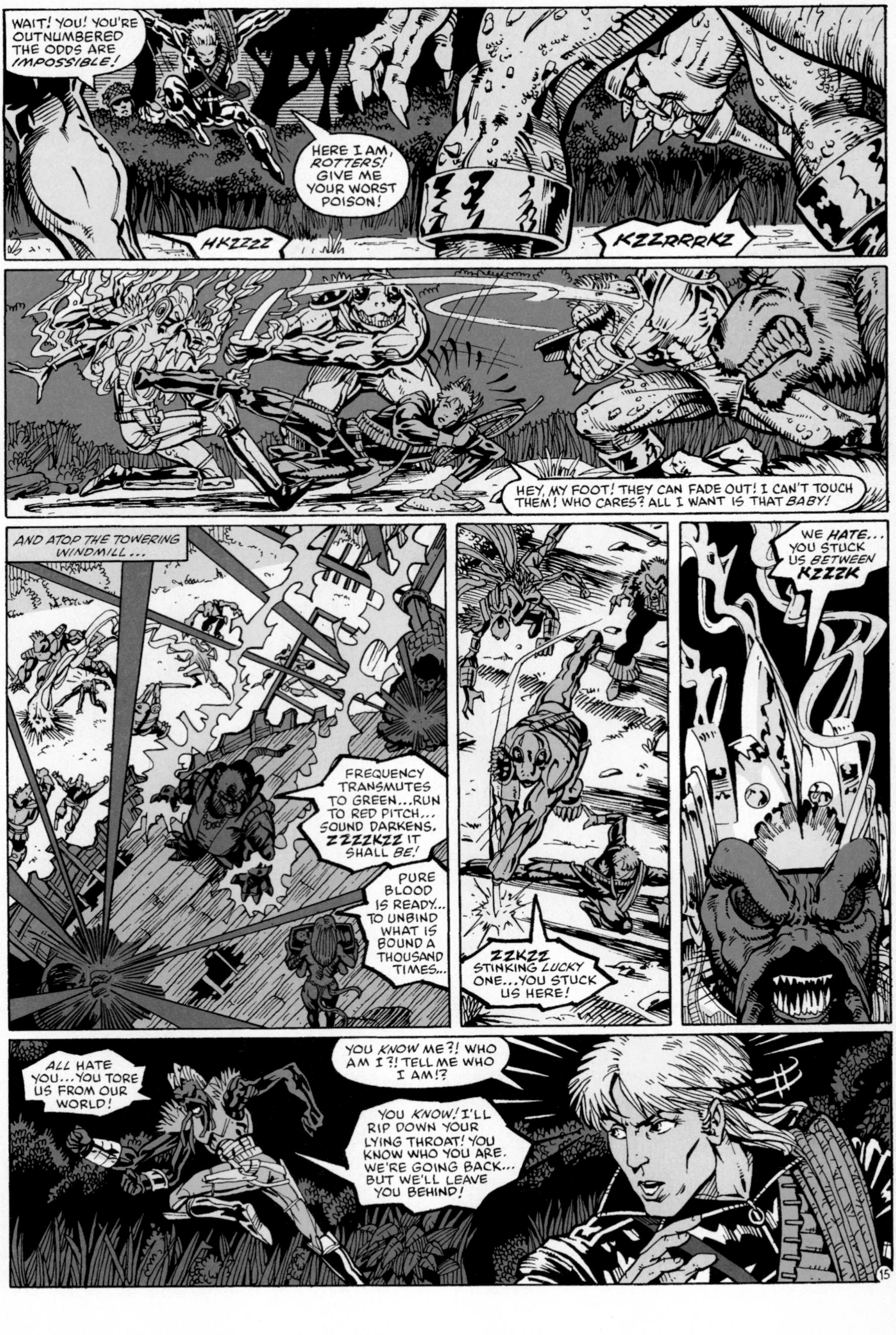
WAIT! YOU! YOU'RE OUTNUMBERED THE ODDS ARE *IMPOSSIBLE!*
HERE I AM, *ROTTERS!* GIVE ME YOUR WORST POISON!
HKZZZZ
KZZRRRKZ
HEY, MY FOOT! THEY CAN FADE OUT! I CAN'T TOUCH THEM! WHO CARES? ALL I WANT IS THAT *BABY!*
AND ATOP THE TOWERING WINDMILL...
FREQUENCY TRANSMUTES TO GREEN...RUN TO RED PITCH... SOUND DARKENS. **ZZZZKZZ** IT SHALL *BE!*
PURE BLOOD IS READY... TO UNBIND WHAT IS BOUND A THOUSAND TIMES...
ZZKZZ STINKING *LUCKY* ONE...YOU STUCK US HERE!
WE *HATE*... YOU STUCK US *BETWEEN* **KZZZK**
ALL HATE YOU...YOU TORE US FROM OUR WORLD!
YOU *KNOW* ME?! WHO AM I?! TELL ME WHO I AM!?
YOU *KNOW!* I'LL RIP DOWN YOUR LYING THROAT! YOU KNOW WHO YOU ARE. WE'RE GOING BACK... BUT WE'LL LEAVE YOU BEHIND!
15

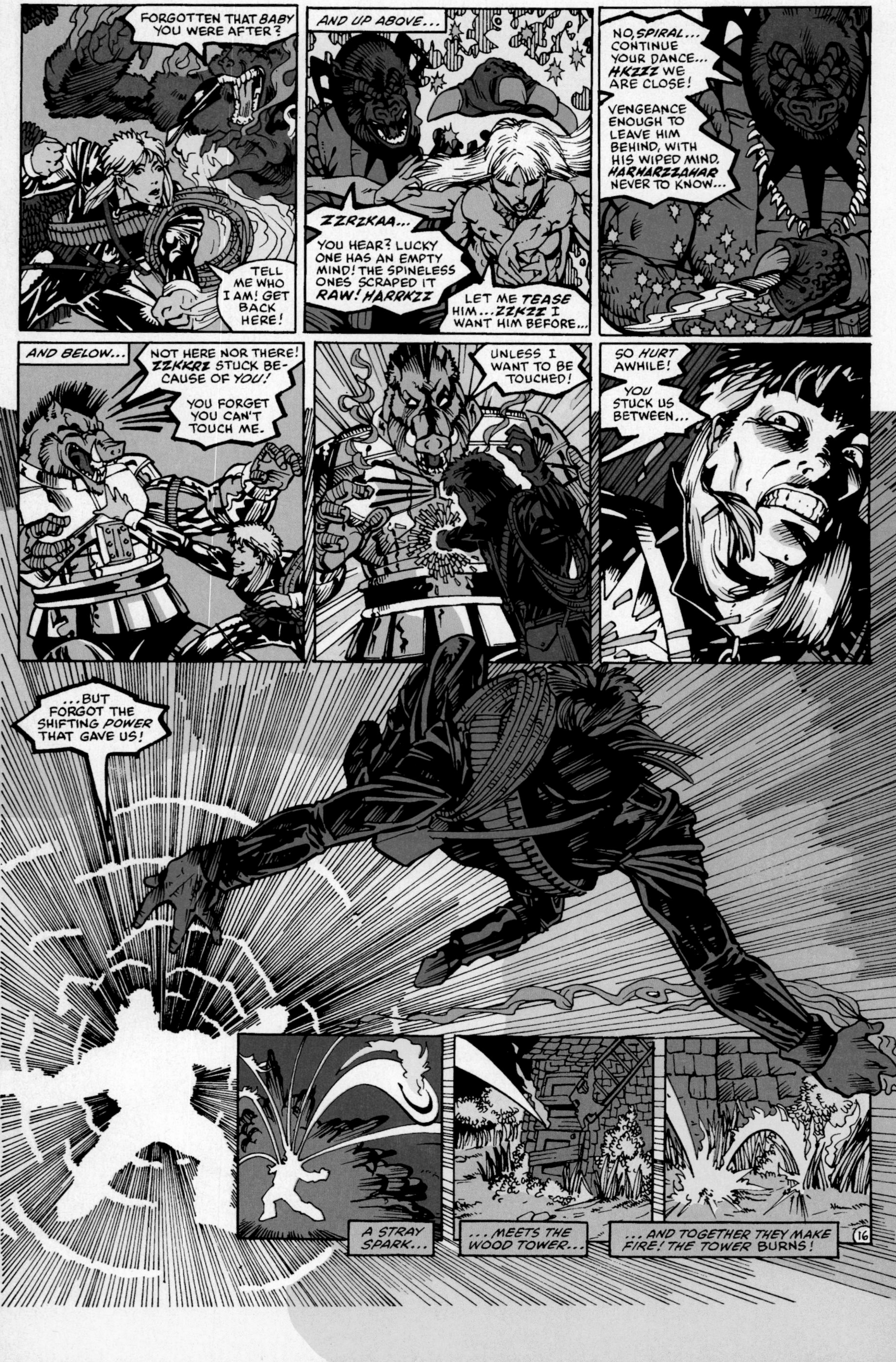
FORGOTTEN THAT BABY YOU WERE AFTER?
TELL ME WHO I AM! GET BACK HERE!
AND UP ABOVE...
ZZRZKAA...
YOU HEAR? LUCKY ONE HAS AN EMPTY MIND! THE SPINELESS ONES SCRAPED IT RAW! HARRKZZ
LET ME TEASE HIM...ZZKZZ I WANT HIM BEFORE...
NO, SPIRAL... CONTINUE YOUR DANCE... HKZZZ WE ARE CLOSE!
VENGEANCE ENOUGH TO LEAVE HIM BEHIND, WITH HIS WIPED MIND, HARHARZZAHAR NEVER TO KNOW...
AND BELOW...
NOT HERE NOR THERE! ZZKKRZ STUCK BECAUSE OF YOU!
YOU FORGET YOU CAN'T TOUCH ME.
UNLESS I WANT TO BE TOUCHED!
SO HURT AWHILE!
YOU STUCK US BETWEEN...
...BUT FORGOT THE SHIFTING POWER THAT GAVE US!
A STRAY SPARK...
...MEETS THE WOOD TOWER...
...AND TOGETHER THEY MAKE FIRE! THE TOWER BURNS!
16

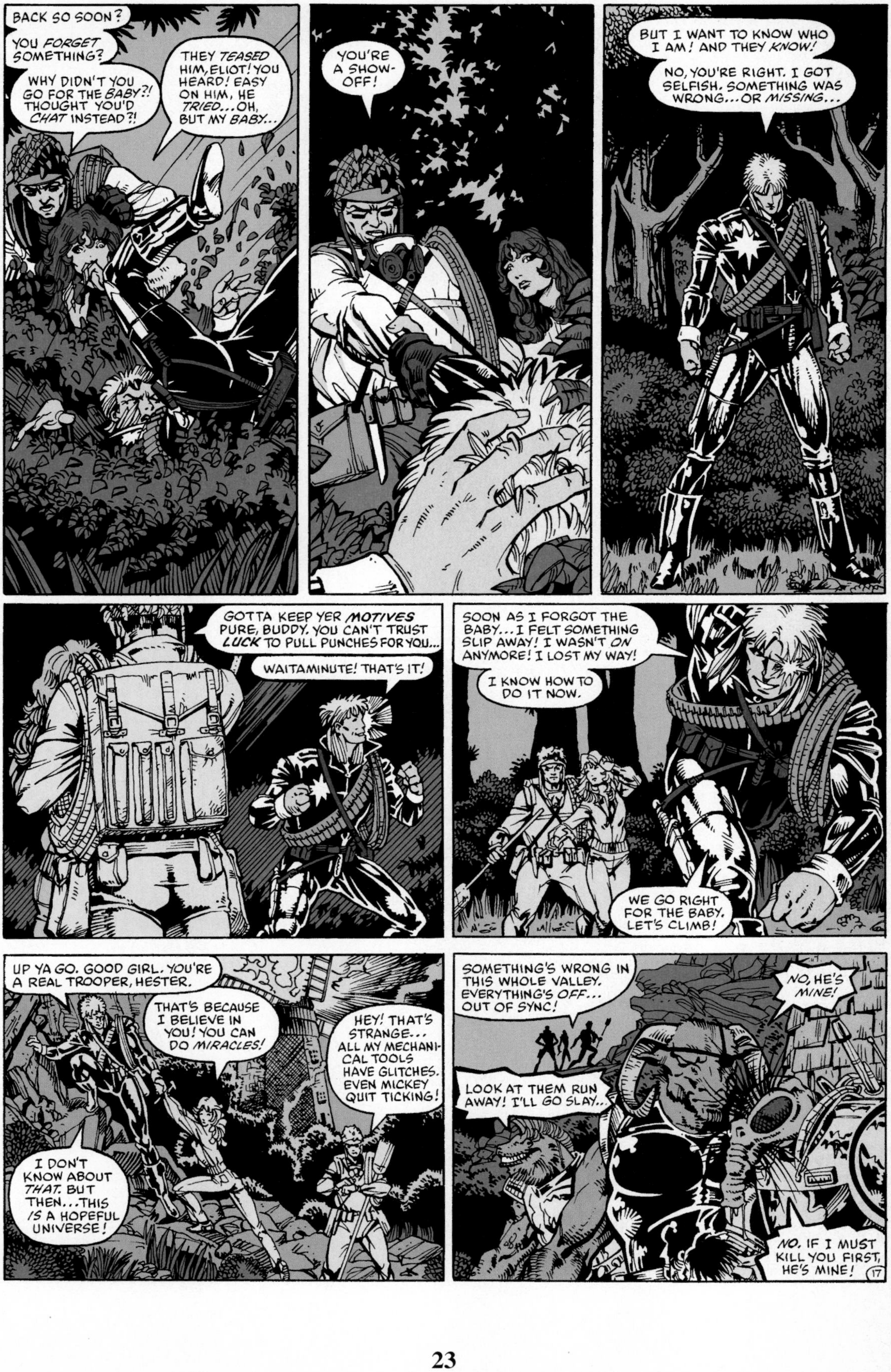
BACK SO SOON? YOU FORGET SOMETHING?
WHY DIDN'T YOU GO FOR THE BABY?! THOUGHT YOU'D CHAT INSTEAD?!
THEY TEASED HIM, ELIOT! YOU HEARD! EASY ON HIM, HE TRIED... OH, BUT MY BABY...
YOU'RE A SHOW-OFF!
BUT I WANT TO KNOW WHO I AM! AND THEY KNOW!
NO, YOU'RE RIGHT. I GOT SELFISH. SOMETHING WAS WRONG... OR MISSING...
GOTTA KEEP YER MOTIVES PURE, BUDDY. YOU CAN'T TRUST LUCK TO PULL PUNCHES FOR YOU...
WAITAMINUTE! THAT'S IT!
SOON AS I FORGOT THE BABY... I FELT SOMETHING SLIP AWAY! I WASN'T ON ANYMORE! I LOST MY WAY!
I KNOW HOW TO DO IT NOW.
WE GO RIGHT FOR THE BABY. LET'S CLIMB!
UP YA GO. GOOD GIRL. YOU'RE A REAL TROOPER, HESTER.
THAT'S BECAUSE I BELIEVE IN YOU! YOU CAN DO MIRACLES!
HEY! THAT'S STRANGE... ALL MY MECHANICAL TOOLS HAVE GLITCHES. EVEN MICKEY QUIT TICKING!
I DON'T KNOW ABOUT THAT. BUT THEN... THIS IS A HOPEFUL UNIVERSE!
SOMETHING'S WRONG IN THIS WHOLE VALLEY. EVERYTHING'S OFF... OUT OF SYNC!
NO, HE'S MINE!
LOOK AT THEM RUN AWAY! I'LL GO SLAY...
NO. IF I MUST KILL YOU FIRST, HE'S MINE!
17

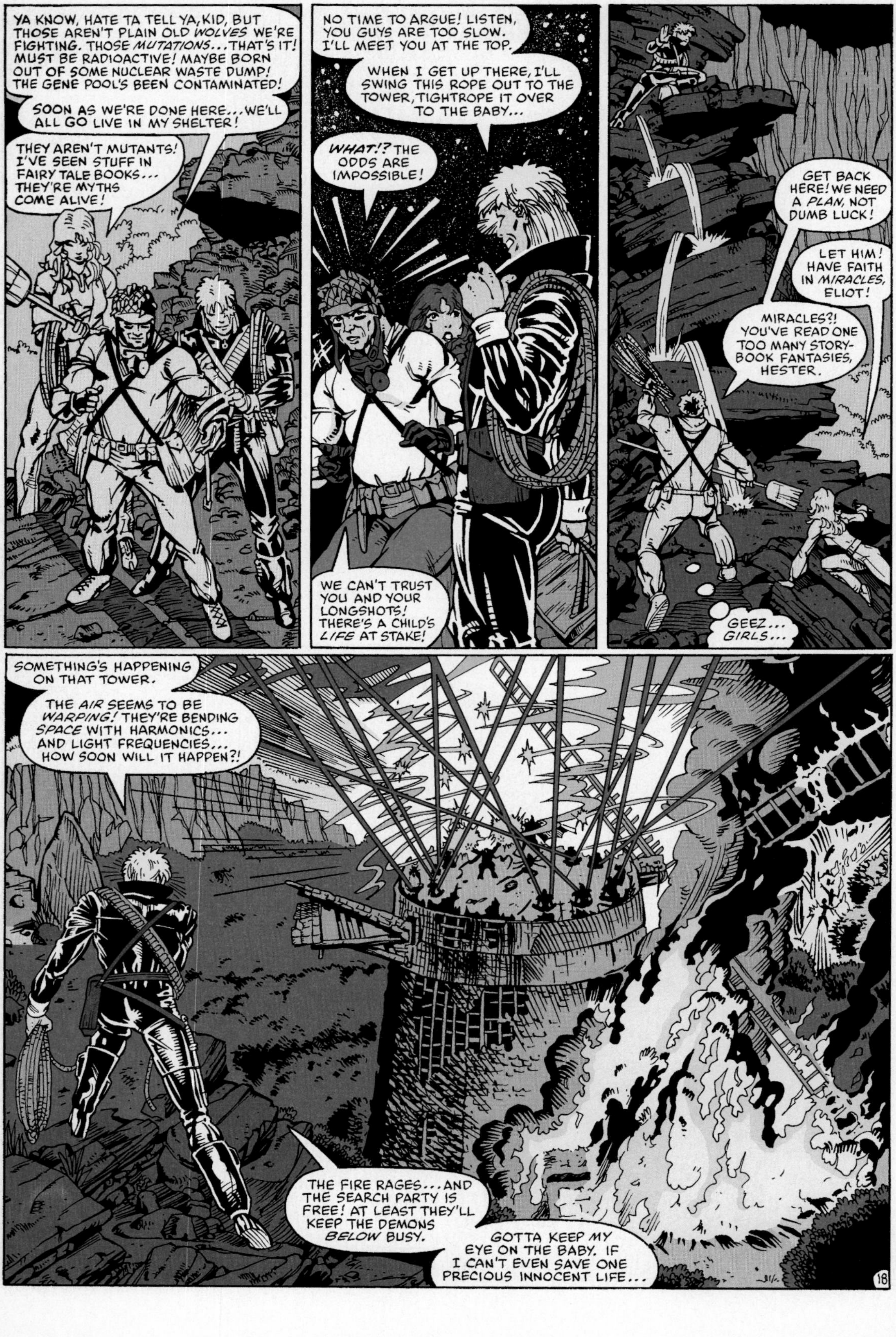
YA KNOW, HATE TA TELL YA, KID, BUT THOSE AREN'T PLAIN OLD WOLVES WE'RE FIGHTING. THOSE MUTATIONS... THAT'S IT! MUST BE RADIOACTIVE! MAYBE BORN OUT OF SOME NUCLEAR WASTE DUMP! THE GENE POOL'S BEEN CONTAMINATED!
SOON AS WE'RE DONE HERE... WE'LL ALL GO LIVE IN MY SHELTER!
THEY AREN'T MUTANTS! I'VE SEEN STUFF IN FAIRY TALE BOOKS... THEY'RE MYTHS COME ALIVE!
NO TIME TO ARGUE! LISTEN, YOU GUYS ARE TOO SLOW. I'LL MEET YOU AT THE TOP.
WHEN I GET UP THERE, I'LL SWING THIS ROPE OUT TO THE TOWER, TIGHTROPE IT OVER TO THE BABY...
WHAT!? THE ODDS ARE IMPOSSIBLE!
WE CAN'T TRUST YOU AND YOUR LONGSHOTS! THERE'S A CHILD'S LIFE AT STAKE!
GET BACK HERE! WE NEED A PLAN, NOT DUMB LUCK!
LET HIM! HAVE FAITH IN MIRACLES, ELIOT!
MIRACLES?! YOU'VE READ ONE TOO MANY STORY-BOOK FANTASIES, HESTER.
GEEZ... GIRLS...
SOMETHING'S HAPPENING ON THAT TOWER.
THE AIR SEEMS TO BE WARPING! THEY'RE BENDING SPACE WITH HARMONICS... AND LIGHT FREQUENCIES... HOW SOON WILL IT HAPPEN?!
THE FIRE RAGES... AND THE SEARCH PARTY IS FREE! AT LEAST THEY'LL KEEP THE DEMONS BELOW BUSY.
GOTTA KEEP MY EYE ON THE BABY. IF I CAN'T EVEN SAVE ONE PRECIOUS INNOCENT LIFE...
18

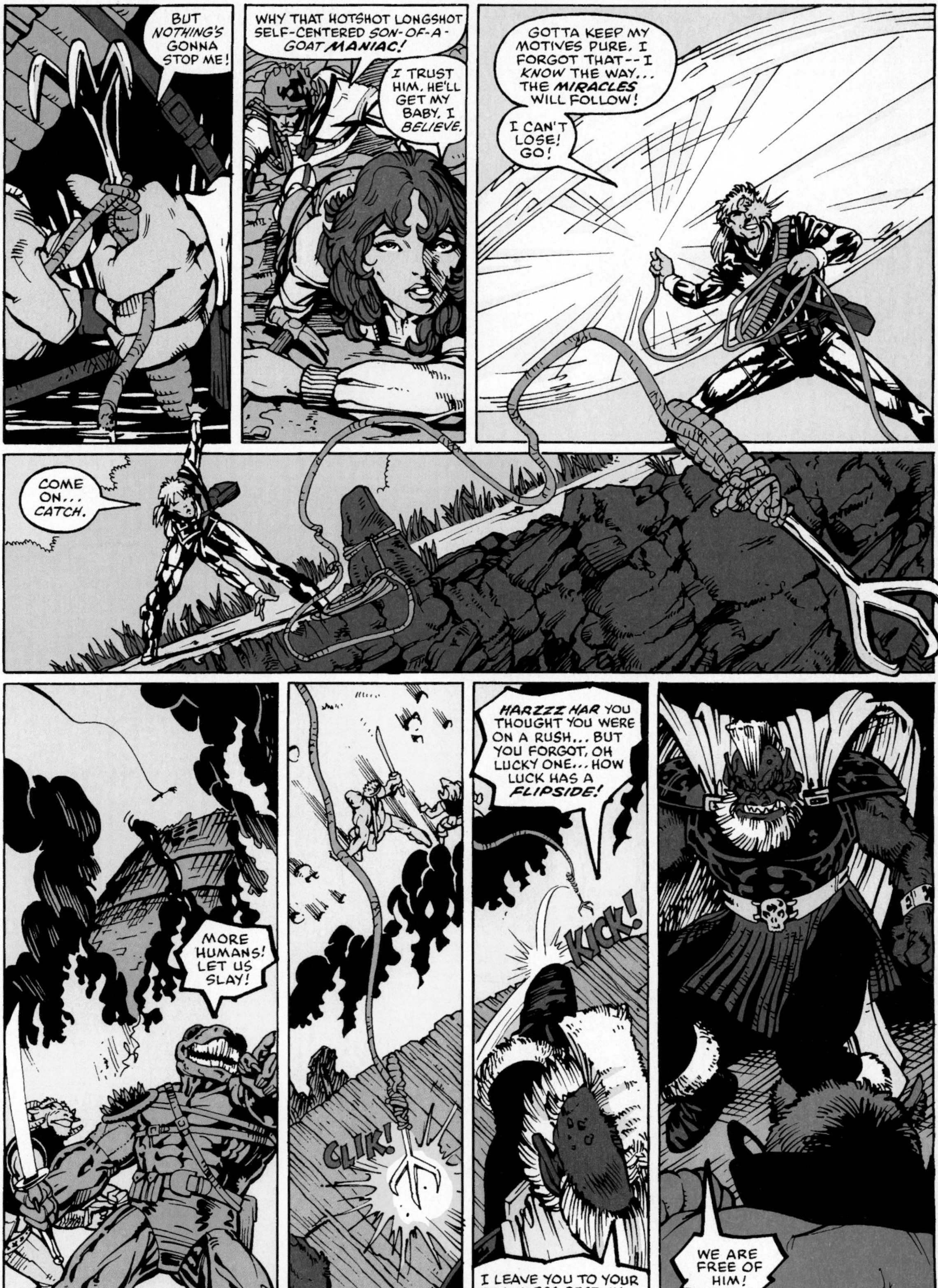
BUT NOTHING'S GONNA STOP ME!
WHY THAT HOTSHOT LONGSHOT SELF-CENTERED SON-OF-A-GOAT MANIAC!
I TRUST HIM. HE'LL GET MY BABY. I BELIEVE.
GOTTA KEEP MY MOTIVES PURE. I FORGOT THAT-- I KNOW THE WAY... THE MIRACLES WILL FOLLOW!
I CAN'T LOSE! GO!
COME ON... CATCH.
MORE HUMANS! LET US SLAY!
CLIK!
HARZZZ HAR YOU THOUGHT YOU WERE ON A RUSH... BUT YOU FORGOT, OH LUCKY ONE... HOW LUCK HAS A FLIPSIDE!
KICK!
I LEAVE YOU TO YOUR BRAINLESS DESTINY, STINKING ONE... THE FATE OF NEVER KNOWING!
WE ARE FREE OF HIM!
ALL FOCUS FOR FINAL RITUAL!
19

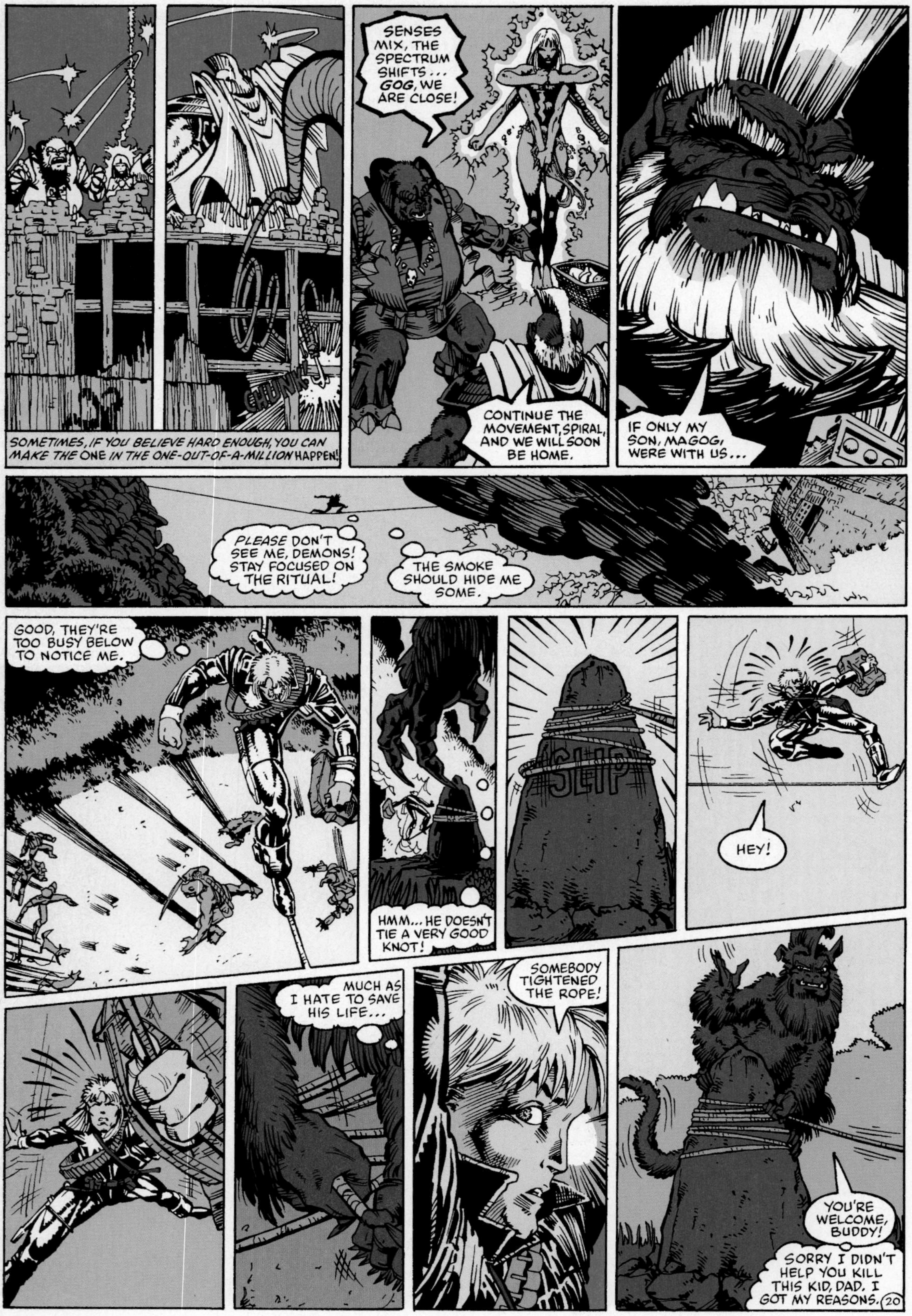

CHUNK!
SOMETIMES, IF YOU BELIEVE HARD ENOUGH, YOU CAN MAKE THE ONE IN THE ONE-OUT-OF-A-MILLION HAPPEN!
SENSES MIX, THE SPECTRUM SHIFTS... GOG, WE ARE CLOSE!
CONTINUE THE MOVEMENT, SPIRAL, AND WE WILL SOON BE HOME.
IF ONLY MY SON, MAGOG, WERE WITH US...
PLEASE DON'T SEE ME, DEMONS! STAY FOCUSED ON THE RITUAL!
THE SMOKE SHOULD HIDE ME SOME.
GOOD, THEY'RE TOO BUSY BELOW TO NOTICE ME.
HMM... HE DOESN'T TIE A VERY GOOD KNOT!
SLIP
HEY!
MUCH AS I HATE TO SAVE HIS LIFE...
SOMEBODY TIGHTENED THE ROPE!
YOU'RE WELCOME, BUDDY!
SORRY I DIDN'T HELP YOU KILL THIS KID, DAD. I GOT MY REASONS.
20

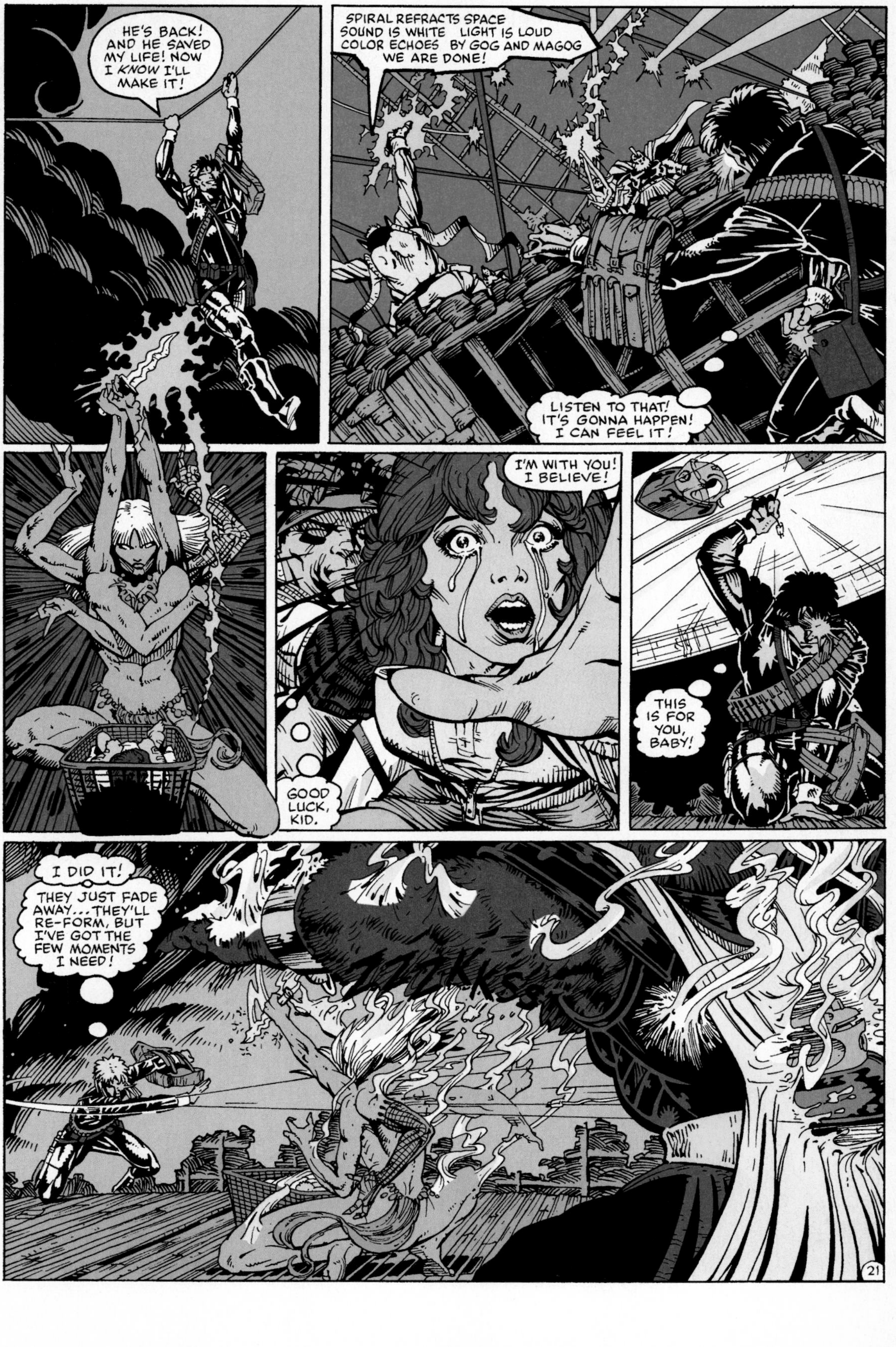
HE'S BACK! AND HE SAVED MY LIFE! NOW I KNOW I'LL MAKE IT!
SPIRAL REFRACTS SPACE SOUND IS WHITE LIGHT IS LOUD COLOR ECHOES BY GOG AND MAGOG WE ARE DONE!
LISTEN TO THAT! IT'S GONNA HAPPEN! I CAN FEEL IT!
I'M WITH YOU! I BELIEVE!
GOOD LUCK, KID.
THIS IS FOR YOU, BABY!
I DID IT!
THEY JUST FADE AWAY... THEY'LL RE-FORM, BUT I'VE GOT THE FEW MOMENTS I NEED!
ZZZKKSS
21

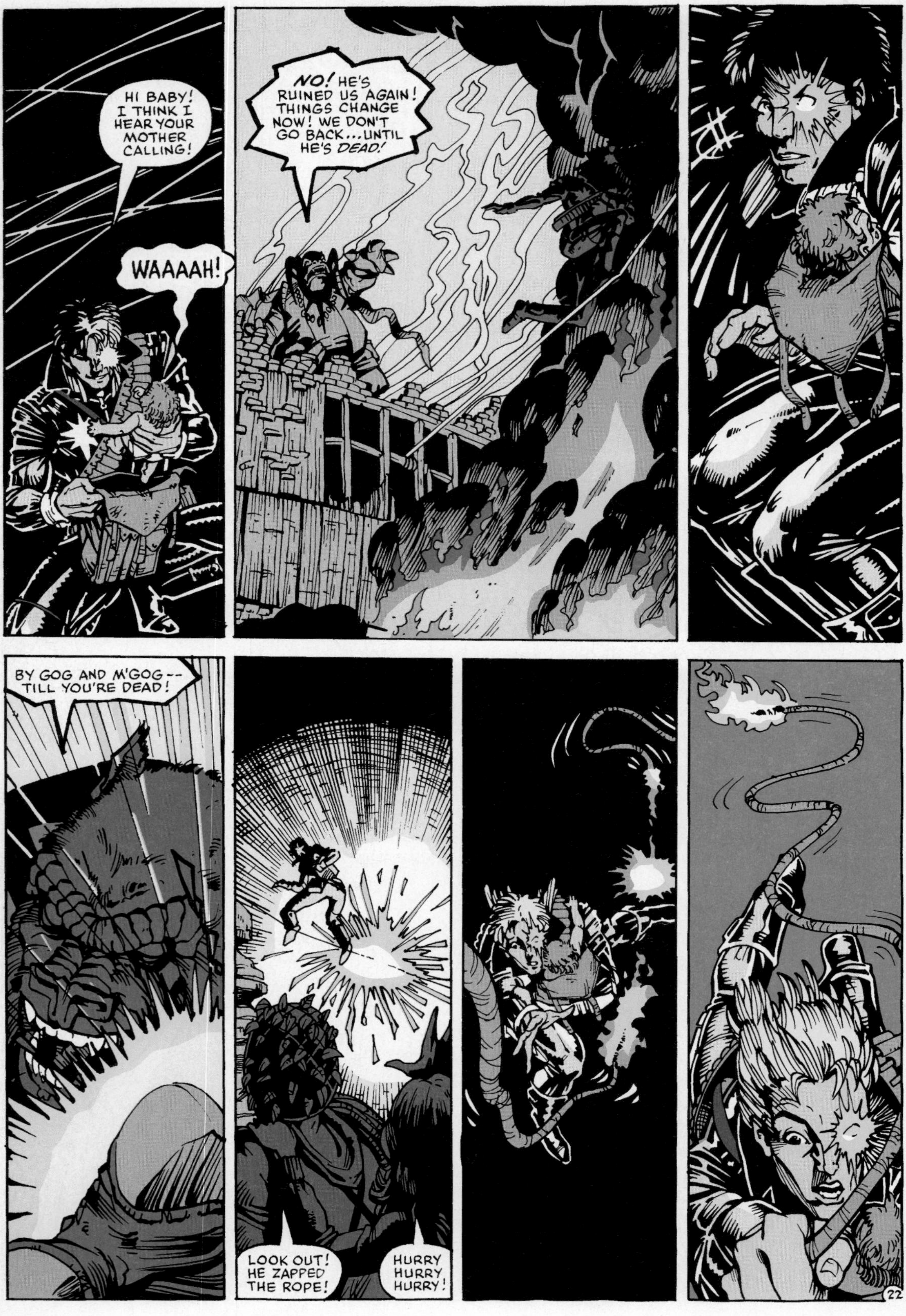
HI BABY! I THINK I HEAR YOUR MOTHER CALLING!
WAAAAH!
NO! HE'S RUINED US AGAIN! THINGS CHANGE NOW! WE DON'T GO BACK...UNTIL HE'S DEAD!
BY GOG AND M'GOG-- TILL YOU'RE DEAD!
LOOK OUT! HE ZAPPED THE ROPE!
HURRY HURRY HURRY!
22

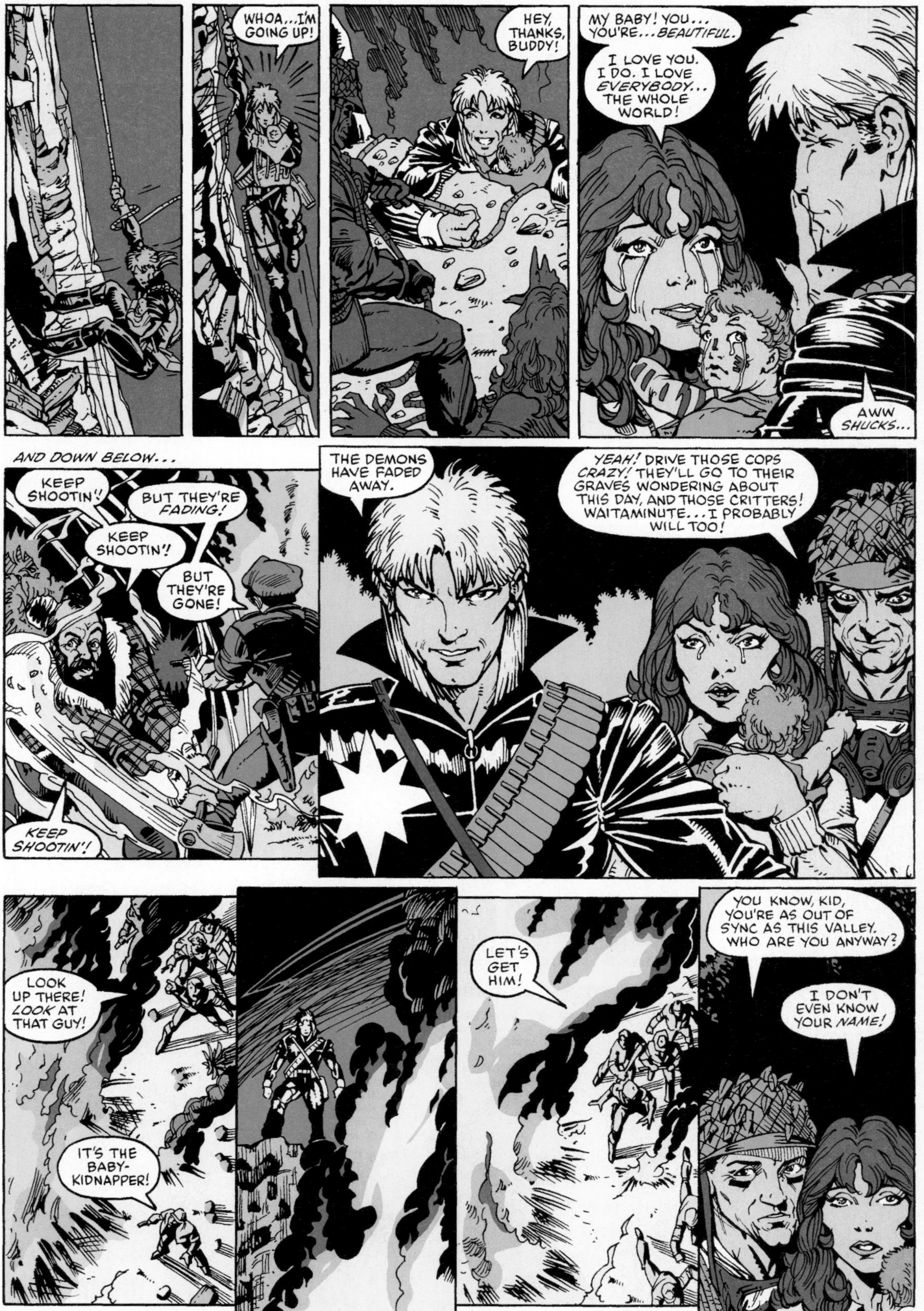
WHOA...I'M GOING UP!
HEY, THANKS, BUDDY!
MY BABY! YOU... YOU'RE...BEAUTIFUL.
I LOVE YOU. I DO. I LOVE EVERYBODY... THE WHOLE WORLD!
AWW SHUCKS...
AND DOWN BELOW...
KEEP SHOOTIN'!
BUT THEY'RE FADING!
KEEP SHOOTIN'!
BUT THEY'RE GONE!
KEEP SHOOTIN'!
THE DEMONS HAVE FADED AWAY.
YEAH! DRIVE THOSE COPS CRAZY! THEY'LL GO TO THEIR GRAVES WONDERING ABOUT THIS DAY, AND THOSE CRITTERS! WAITAMINUTE...I PROBABLY WILL TOO!
LOOK UP THERE! LOOK AT THAT GUY!
IT'S THE BABY-KIDNAPPER!
LET'S GET HIM!
YOU KNOW, KID, YOU'RE AS OUT OF SYNC AS THIS VALLEY. WHO ARE YOU ANYWAY?
I DON'T EVEN KNOW YOUR NAME!
23

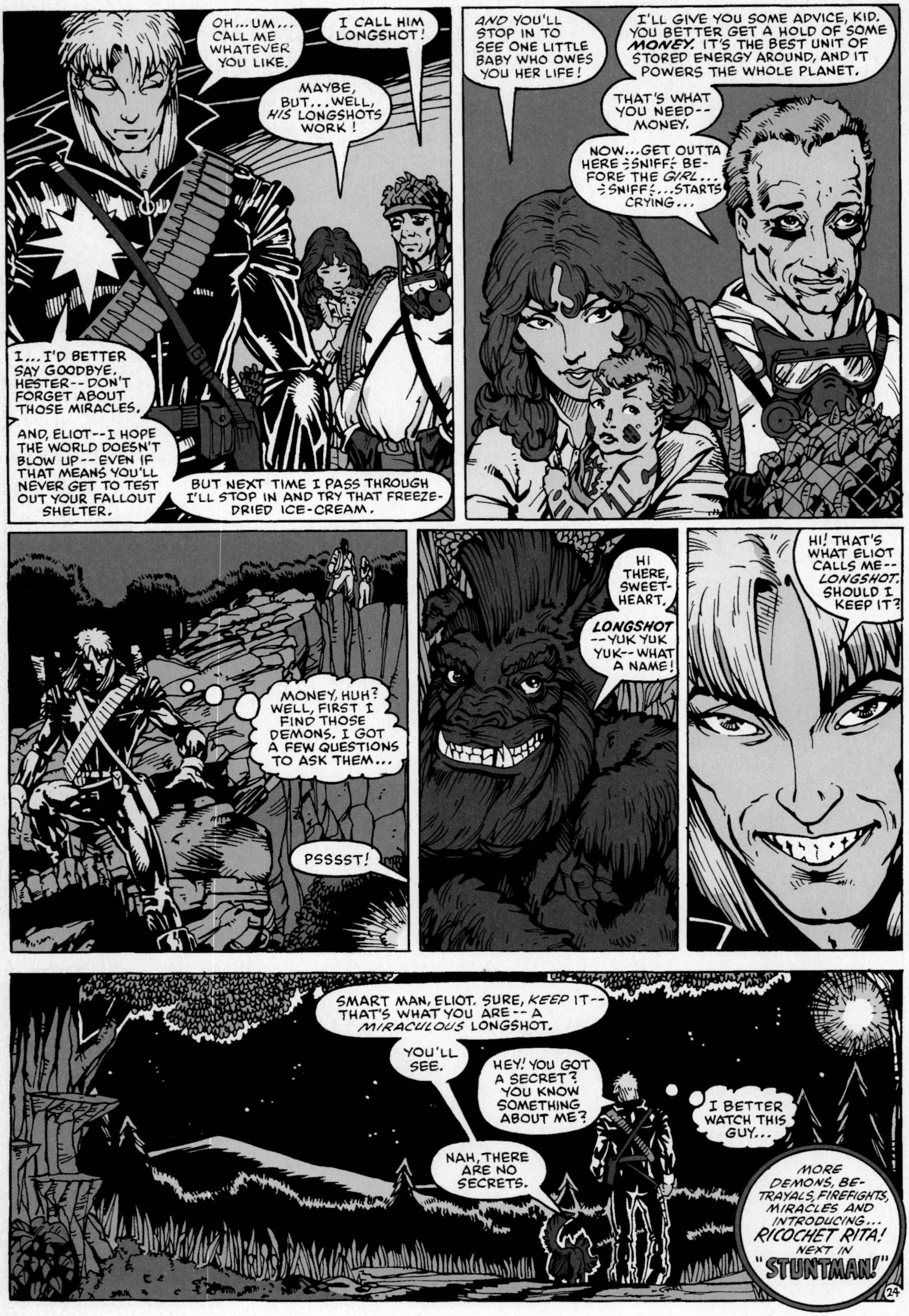

OH...UM... CALL ME WHATEVER YOU LIKE.
I CALL HIM LONGSHOT!
MAYBE, BUT...WELL, HIS LONGSHOTS WORK!
I... I'D BETTER SAY GOODBYE. HESTER--DON'T FORGET ABOUT THOSE MIRACLES.
AND, ELIOT--I HOPE THE WORLD DOESN'T BLOW UP--EVEN IF THAT MEANS YOU'LL NEVER GET TO TEST OUT YOUR FALLOUT SHELTER.
BUT NEXT TIME I PASS THROUGH I'LL STOP IN AND TRY THAT FREEZE-DRIED ICE-CREAM.
AND YOU'LL STOP IN TO SEE ONE LITTLE BABY WHO OWES YOU HER LIFE!
I'LL GIVE YOU SOME ADVICE, KID. YOU BETTER GET A HOLD OF SOME MONEY. IT'S THE BEST UNIT OF STORED ENERGY AROUND, AND IT POWERS THE WHOLE PLANET.
THAT'S WHAT YOU NEED--MONEY.
NOW...GET OUTTA HERE ≑SNIFF≑ BEFORE THE GIRL... ≑SNIFF≑...STARTS CRYING...
MONEY, HUH? WELL, FIRST I FIND THOSE DEMONS. I GOT A FEW QUESTIONS TO ASK THEM...
PSSSST!
HI THERE, SWEET-HEART.
LONGSHOT--YUK YUK YUK--WHAT A NAME!
HI! THAT'S WHAT ELIOT CALLS ME--LONGSHOT. SHOULD I KEEP IT?
SMART MAN, ELIOT. SURE, KEEP IT--THAT'S WHAT YOU ARE--A MIRACULOUS LONGSHOT.
YOU'LL SEE.
HEY! YOU GOT A SECRET? YOU KNOW SOMETHING ABOUT ME?
NAH, THERE ARE NO SECRETS.
I BETTER WATCH THIS GUY...
MORE DEMONS, BETRAYALS, FIREFIGHTS, MIRACLES AND INTRODUCING... RICOCHET RITA! NEXT IN "STUNTMAN!"
24

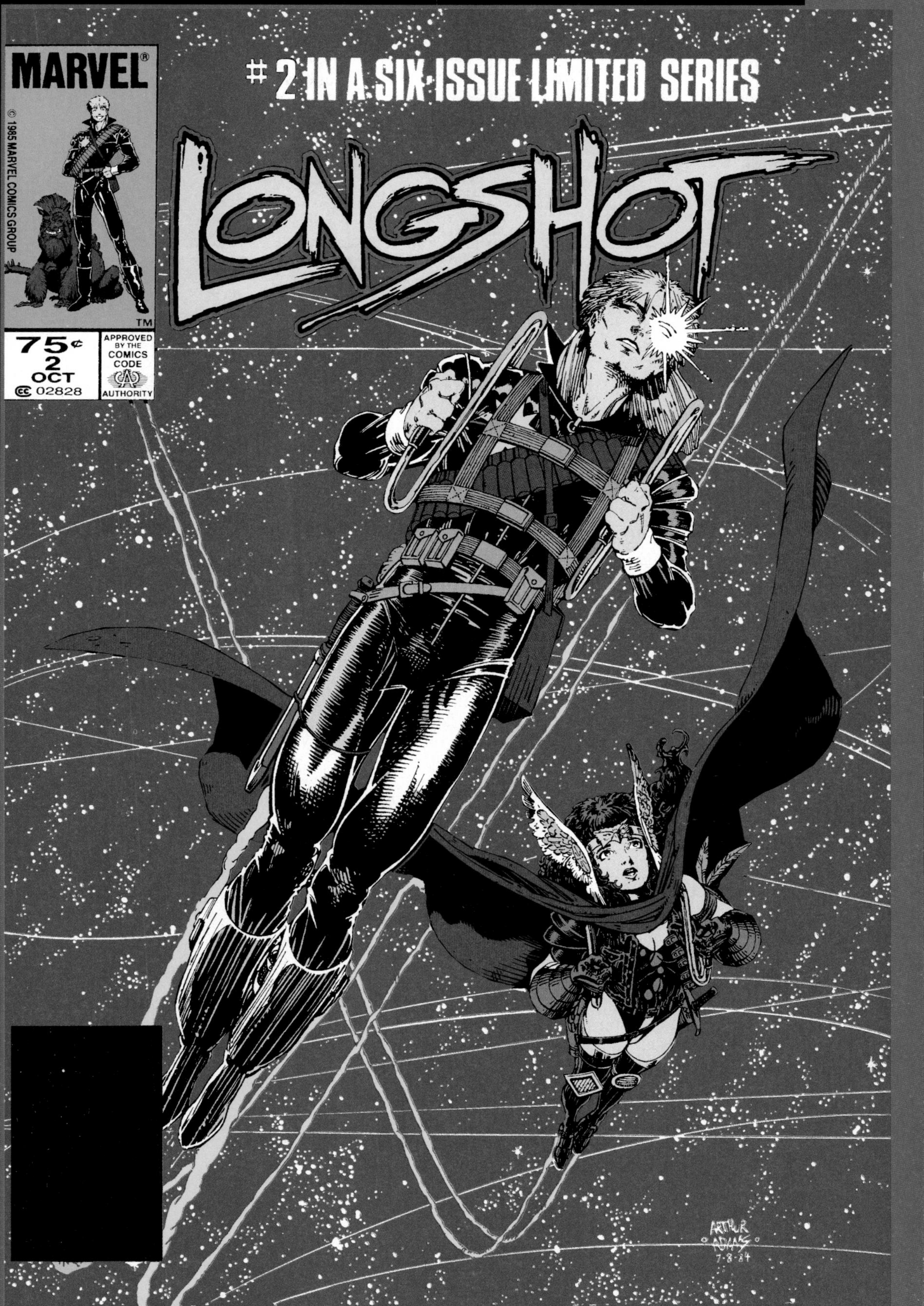
MARVEL®
2 IN A SIX-ISSUE LIMITED SERIES
© 1985 MARVEL COMICS GROUP
LONGSHOT
TM
75¢
2
OCT
CC 02828
APPROVED BY THE COMICS CODE AUTHORITY
ARTHUR ADAMS 7-8-84

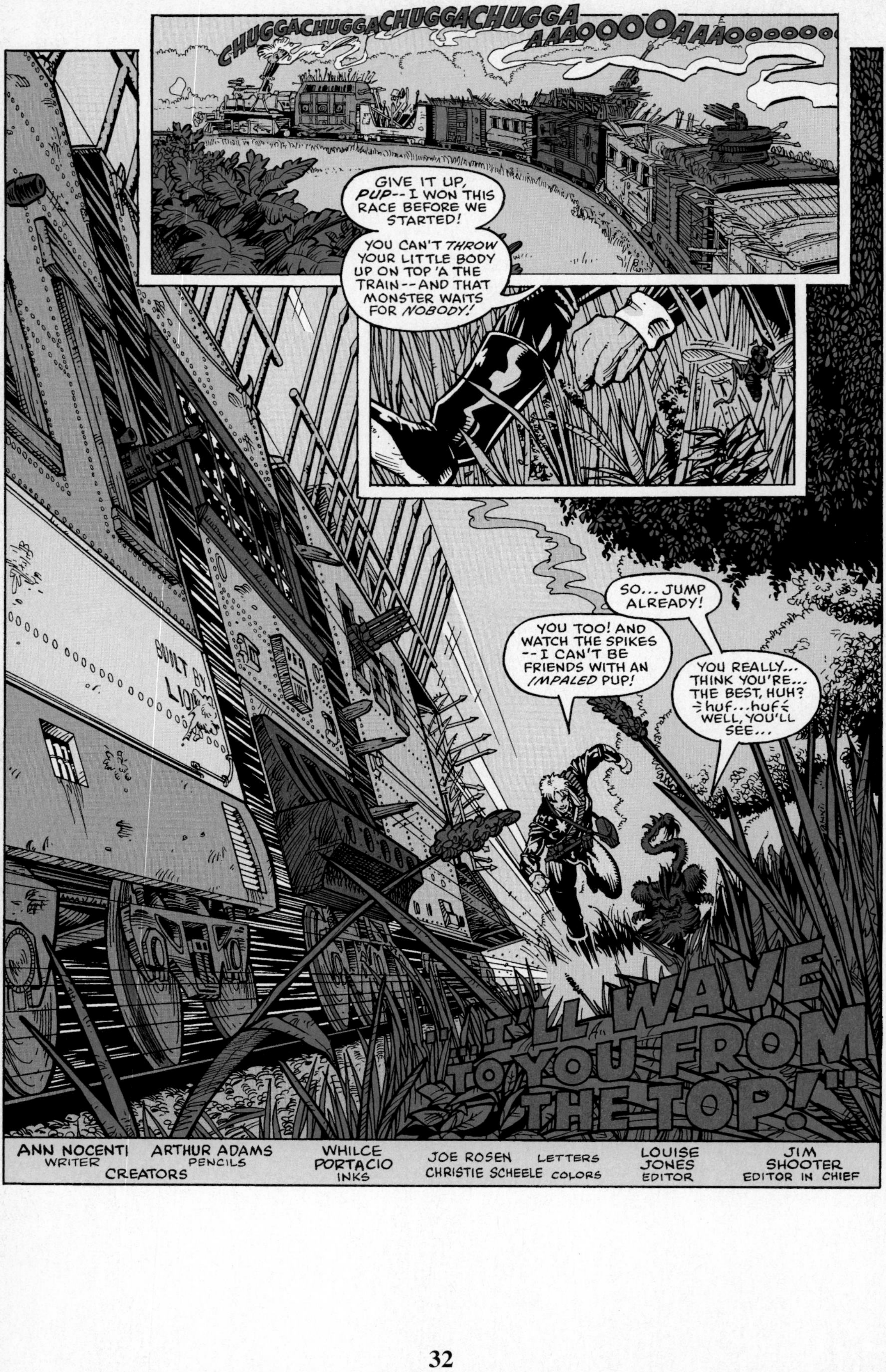
CHUGGACHUGGACHUGGACHUGGA
AAAOOOOOAAAOoooooo
GIVE IT UP, PUP-- I WON THIS RACE BEFORE WE STARTED!
YOU CAN'T THROW YOUR LITTLE BODY UP ON TOP 'A THE TRAIN--AND THAT MONSTER WAITS FOR NOBODY!
SO... JUMP ALREADY!
YOU TOO! AND WATCH THE SPIKES --I CAN'T BE FRIENDS WITH AN IMPALED PUP!
YOU REALLY... THINK YOU'RE... THE BEST, HUH? huf...huf WELL, YOU'LL SEE...
"...I'LL WAVE TO YOU FROM THE TOP!"
BUILT BY LIO
ANN NOCENTI WRITER
ARTHUR ADAMS PENCILS
CREATORS
WHILCE PORTACIO INKS
JOE ROSEN LETTERS
CHRISTIE SCHEELE COLORS
LOUISE JONES EDITOR
JIM SHOOTER EDITOR IN CHIEF

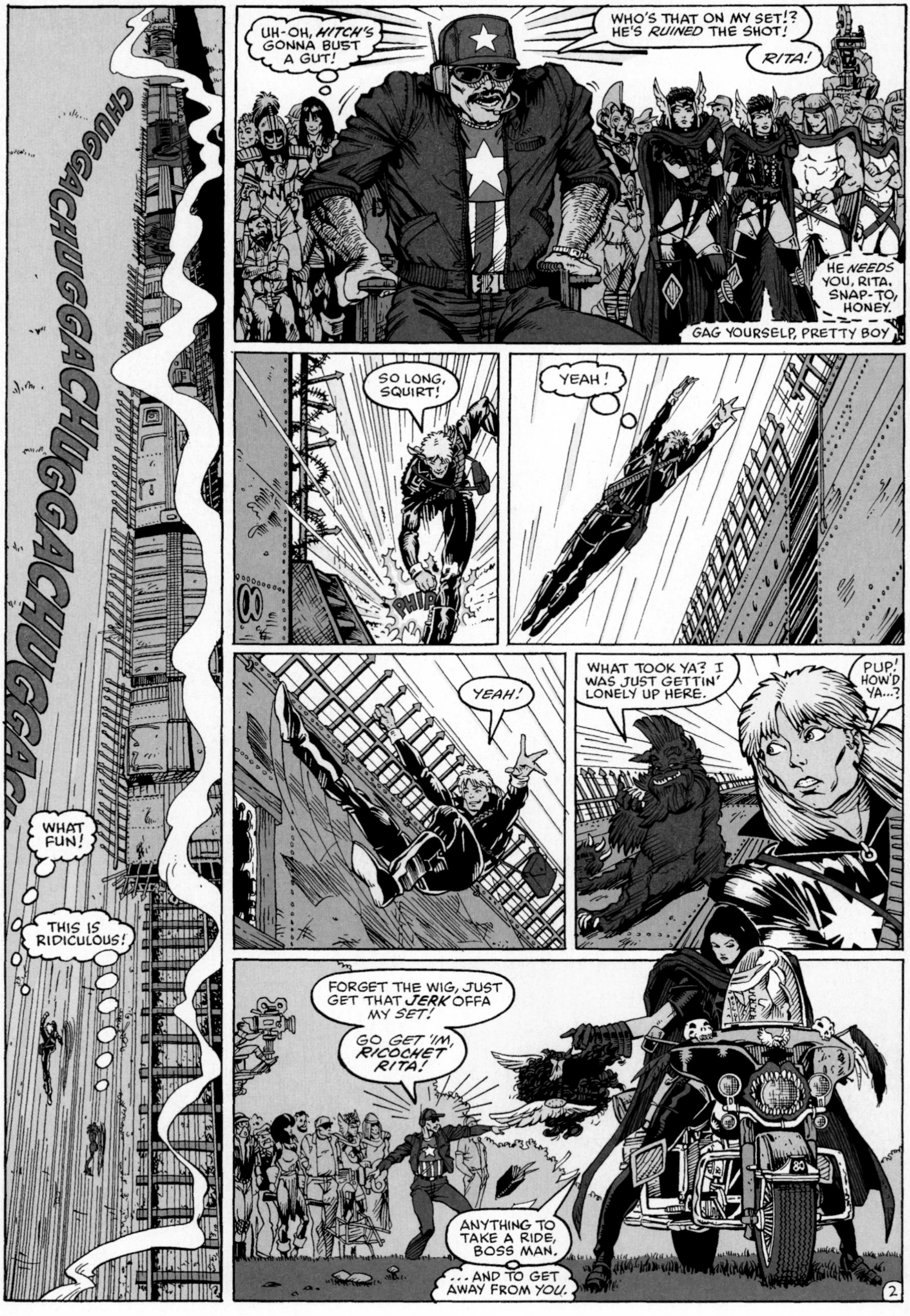
CHUGGACHUGGACHUGGACHUGGA...
WHAT FUN!
THIS IS RIDICULOUS!
UH-OH, HITCH'S GONNA BUST A GUT!
WHO'S THAT ON MY SET!? HE'S RUINED THE SHOT!
RITA!
HE NEEDS YOU, RITA. SNAP-TO, HONEY.
GAG YOURSELF, PRETTY BOY
SO LONG, SQUIRT!
PHIP
YEAH!
YEAH!
WHAT TOOK YA? I WAS JUST GETTIN' LONELY UP HERE.
PUP! HOW'D YA...?
FORGET THE WIG, JUST GET THAT JERK OFFA MY SET!
GO GET 'IM, RICOCHET RITA!
ANYTHING TO TAKE A RIDE, BOSS MAN.
...AND TO GET AWAY FROM YOU.
2

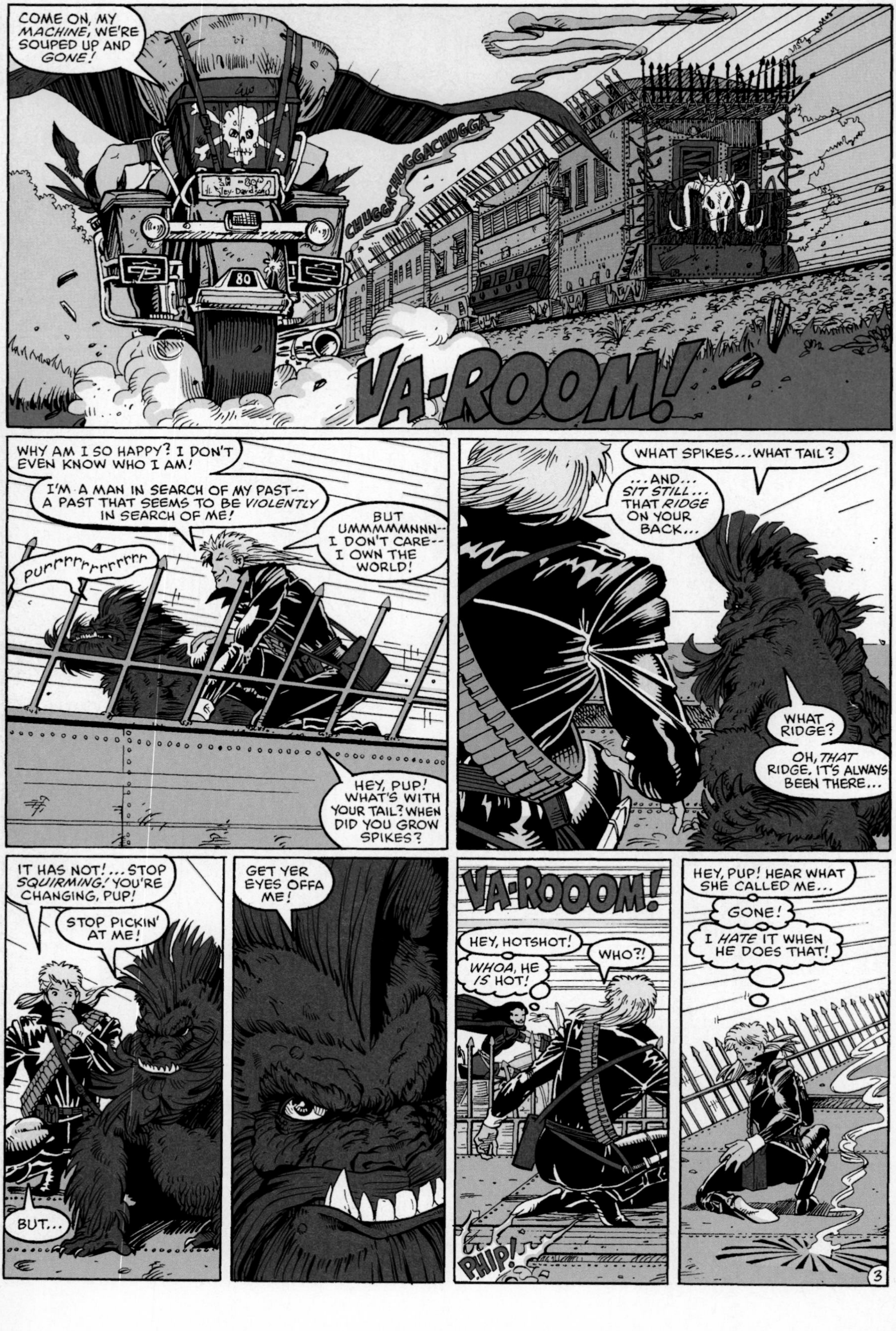
COME ON, MY MACHINE, WE'RE SOUPED UP AND GONE!
CHUGGACHUGGACHUGGA
VA-ROOM!
WHY AM I SO HAPPY? I DON'T EVEN KNOW WHO I AM!
I'M A MAN IN SEARCH OF MY PAST-- A PAST THAT SEEMS TO BE VIOLENTLY IN SEARCH OF ME!
BUT UMMMMMMNN-- I DON'T CARE-- I OWN THE WORLD!
purrrrrrrrrrrr
HEY, PUP! WHAT'S WITH YOUR TAIL? WHEN DID YOU GROW SPIKES?
WHAT SPIKES...WHAT TAIL?
...AND... SIT STILL... THAT RIDGE ON YOUR BACK...
WHAT RIDGE?
OH, THAT RIDGE. IT'S ALWAYS BEEN THERE...
IT HAS NOT! ...STOP SQUIRMING! YOU'RE CHANGING, PUP!
STOP PICKIN' AT ME!
BUT...
GET YER EYES OFFA ME!
VA-ROOOM!
HEY, HOTSHOT!
WHOA, HE IS HOT!
WHO?!
PHIP!
HEY, PUP! HEAR WHAT SHE CALLED ME...
GONE!
I HATE IT WHEN HE DOES THAT!
3

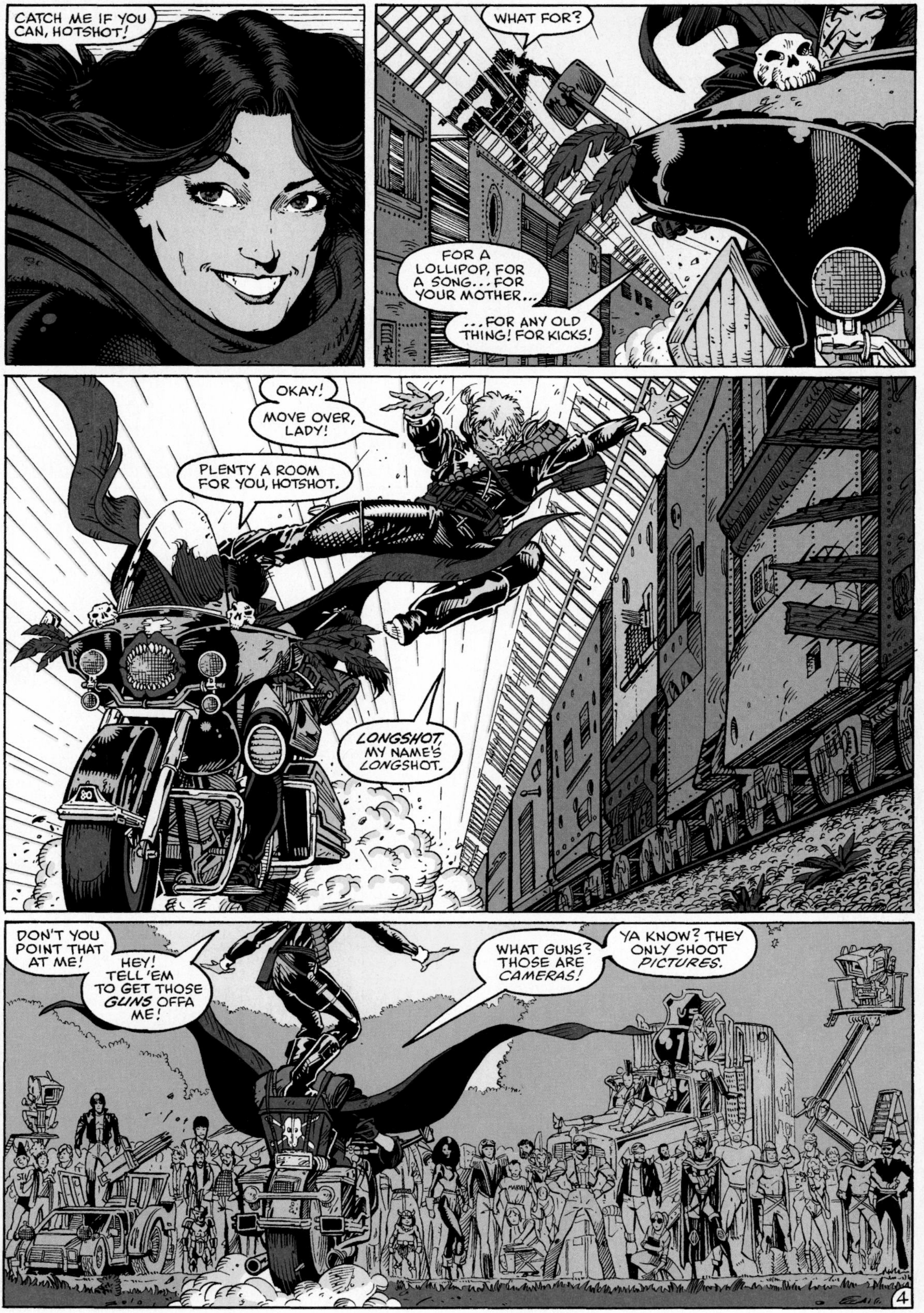
CATCH ME IF YOU CAN, HOTSHOT!
WHAT FOR?
FOR A LOLLIPOP, FOR A SONG... FOR YOUR MOTHER...
...FOR ANY OLD THING! FOR KICKS!
OKAY! MOVE OVER, LADY!
PLENTY A ROOM FOR YOU, HOTSHOT.
LONGSHOT, MY NAME'S LONGSHOT.
DON'T YOU POINT THAT AT ME!
HEY! TELL 'EM TO GET THOSE GUNS OFFA ME!
WHAT GUNS? THOSE ARE CAMERAS!
YA KNOW? THEY ONLY SHOOT PICTURES.
4

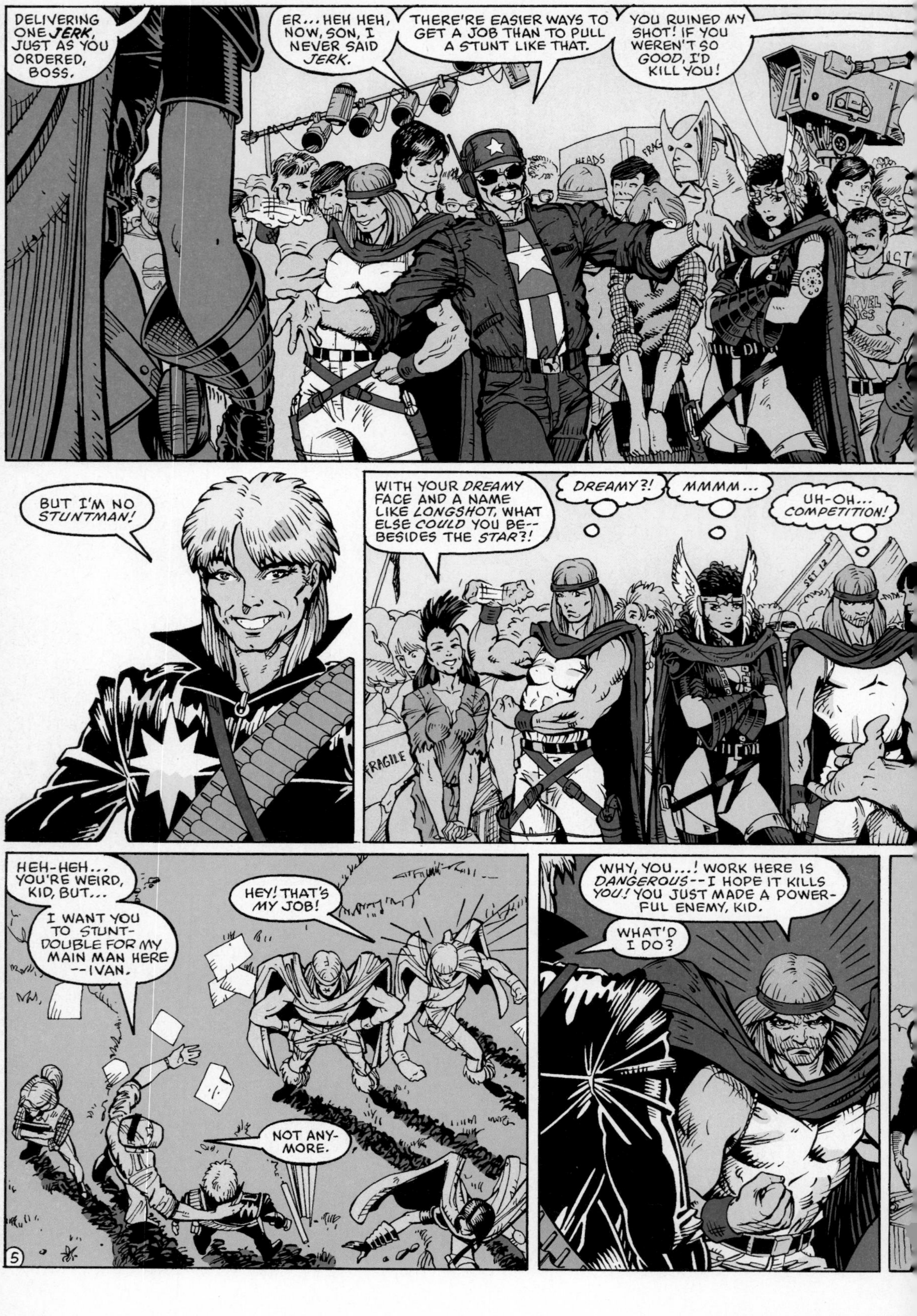
DELIVERING ONE JERK, JUST AS YOU ORDERED, BOSS.
ER... HEH HEH, NOW, SON, I NEVER SAID JERK.
THERE'RE EASIER WAYS TO GET A JOB THAN TO PULL A STUNT LIKE THAT.
YOU RUINED MY SHOT! IF YOU WEREN'T SO GOOD, I'D KILL YOU!
BUT I'M NO STUNTMAN!
WITH YOUR DREAMY FACE AND A NAME LIKE LONGSHOT, WHAT ELSE COULD YOU BE-- BESIDES THE STAR?!
DREAMY?!
MMMM...
UH-OH... COMPETITION!
FRAGILE
HEH-HEH... YOU'RE WEIRD, KID, BUT...
I WANT YOU TO STUNT-DOUBLE FOR MY MAIN MAN HERE --IVAN.
HEY! THAT'S MY JOB!
NOT ANY-MORE.
WHY, YOU...! WORK HERE IS DANGEROUS--I HOPE IT KILLS YOU! YOU JUST MADE A POWERFUL ENEMY, KID.
WHAT'D I DO?
5

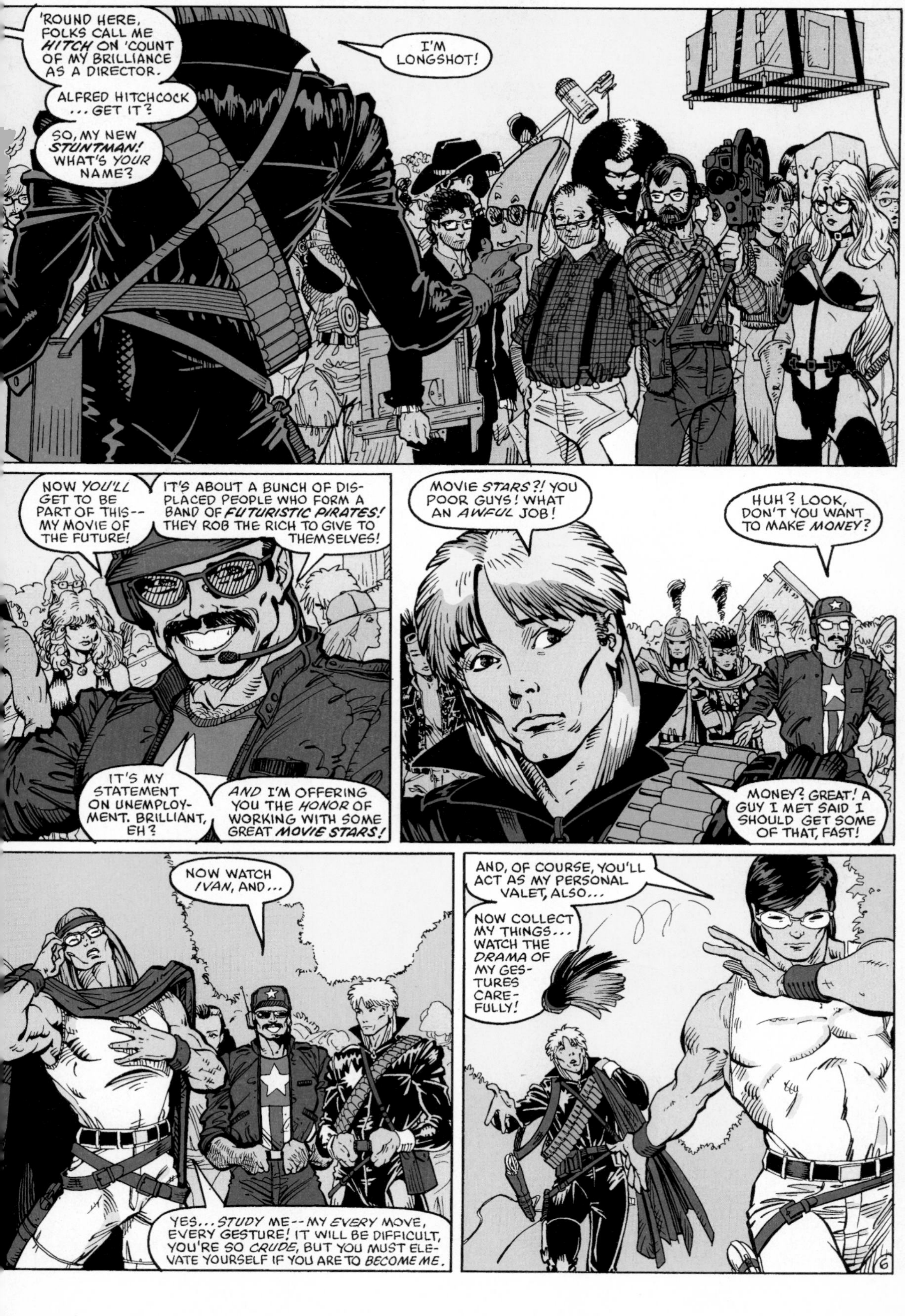
'ROUND HERE, FOLKS CALL ME *HITCH* ON 'COUNT OF MY BRILLIANCE AS A DIRECTOR.
ALFRED HITCHCOCK ...GET IT?
SO, MY NEW *STUNTMAN!* WHAT'S *YOUR* NAME?
I'M LONGSHOT!
NOW *YOU'LL* GET TO BE PART OF THIS-- MY MOVIE OF THE FUTURE!
IT'S ABOUT A BUNCH OF DIS-PLACED PEOPLE WHO FORM A BAND OF *FUTURISTIC PIRATES!* THEY ROB THE RICH TO GIVE TO THEMSELVES!
IT'S MY STATEMENT ON UNEMPLOY-MENT. BRILLIANT, EH?
AND I'M OFFERING YOU THE *HONOR* OF WORKING WITH SOME GREAT *MOVIE STARS!*
MOVIE *STARS?!* YOU POOR GUYS! WHAT AN *AWFUL* JOB!
HUH? LOOK, DON'T YOU WANT TO MAKE *MONEY*?
MONEY? GREAT! A GUY I MET SAID I SHOULD GET SOME OF THAT, FAST!
NOW WATCH *IVAN*, AND...
YES... *STUDY* ME--MY *EVERY* MOVE, EVERY GESTURE! IT WILL BE DIFFICULT, YOU'RE SO *CRUDE*, BUT YOU MUST ELE-VATE YOURSELF IF YOU ARE TO *BECOME ME*.
AND, OF COURSE, YOU'LL ACT AS MY PERSONAL VALET, ALSO...
NOW COLLECT MY THINGS... WATCH THE *DRAMA* OF MY GES-TURES CARE-FULLY!
6

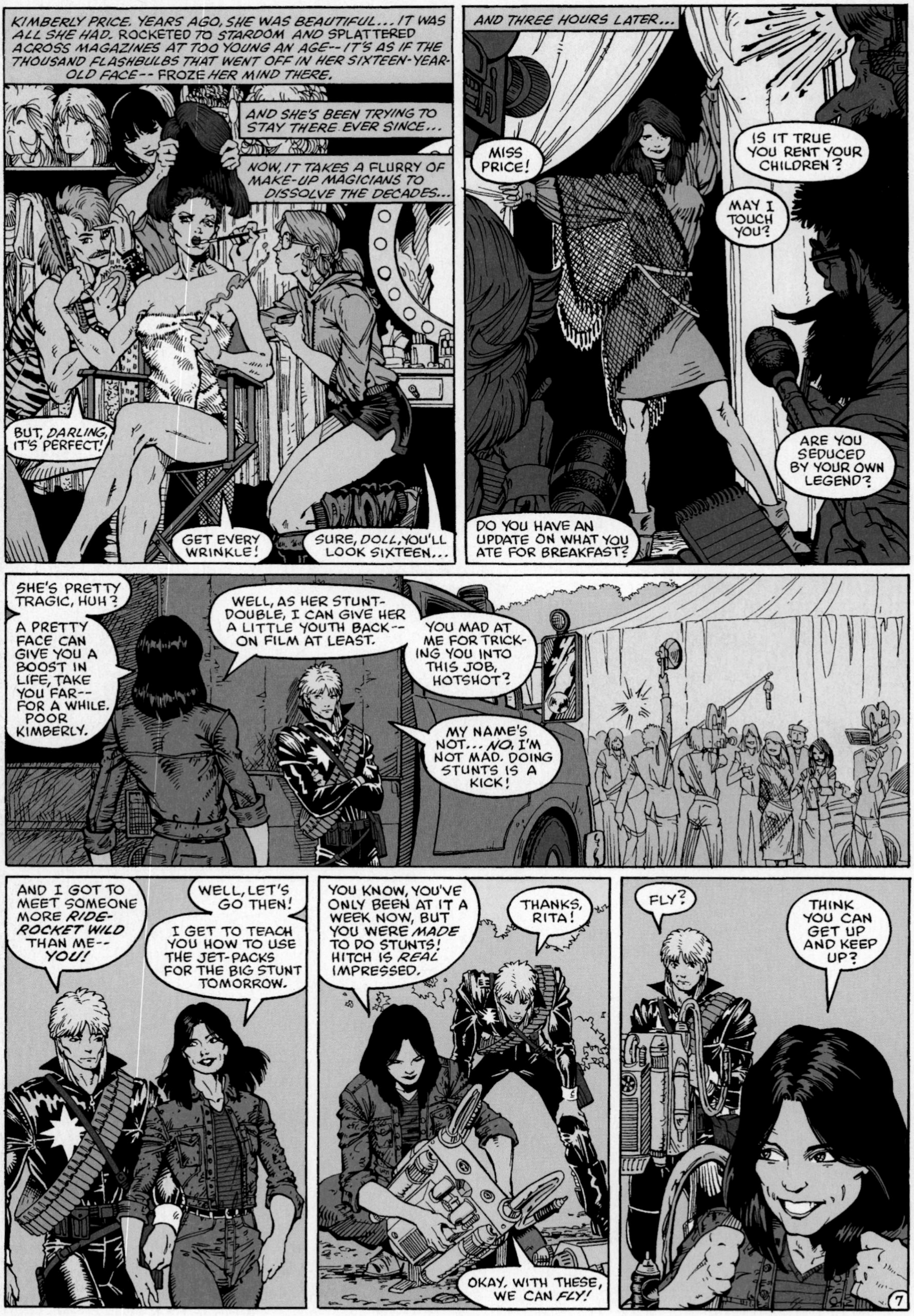
KIMBERLY PRICE. YEARS AGO, SHE WAS BEAUTIFUL... IT WAS ALL SHE HAD. ROCKETED TO STARDOM AND SPLATTERED ACROSS MAGAZINES AT TOO YOUNG AN AGE-- IT'S AS IF THE THOUSAND FLASHBULBS THAT WENT OFF IN HER SIXTEEN-YEAR-OLD FACE-- FROZE HER MIND THERE.
AND SHE'S BEEN TRYING TO STAY THERE EVER SINCE...
NOW, IT TAKES A FLURRY OF MAKE-UP MAGICIANS TO DISSOLVE THE DECADES...
BUT, DARLING, IT'S PERFECT!
GET EVERY WRINKLE!
SURE, DOLL, YOU'LL LOOK SIXTEEN...
AND THREE HOURS LATER...
MISS PRICE!
IS IT TRUE YOU RENT YOUR CHILDREN?
MAY I TOUCH YOU?
ARE YOU SEDUCED BY YOUR OWN LEGEND?
DO YOU HAVE AN UPDATE ON WHAT YOU ATE FOR BREAKFAST?
SHE'S PRETTY TRAGIC, HUH?
A PRETTY FACE CAN GIVE YOU A BOOST IN LIFE, TAKE YOU FAR-- FOR A WHILE. POOR KIMBERLY.
WELL, AS HER STUNT-DOUBLE, I CAN GIVE HER A LITTLE YOUTH BACK-- ON FILM AT LEAST.
YOU MAD AT ME FOR TRICKING YOU INTO THIS JOB, HOTSHOT?
MY NAME'S NOT... NO, I'M NOT MAD. DOING STUNTS IS A KICK!
AND I GOT TO MEET SOMEONE MORE RIDE-ROCKET WILD THAN ME-- YOU!
WELL, LET'S GO THEN!
I GET TO TEACH YOU HOW TO USE THE JET-PACKS FOR THE BIG STUNT TOMORROW.
YOU KNOW, YOU'VE ONLY BEEN AT IT A WEEK NOW, BUT YOU WERE MADE TO DO STUNTS! HITCH IS REAL IMPRESSED.
THANKS, RITA!
OKAY, WITH THESE, WE CAN FLY!
FLY?
THINK YOU CAN GET UP AND KEEP UP?
7

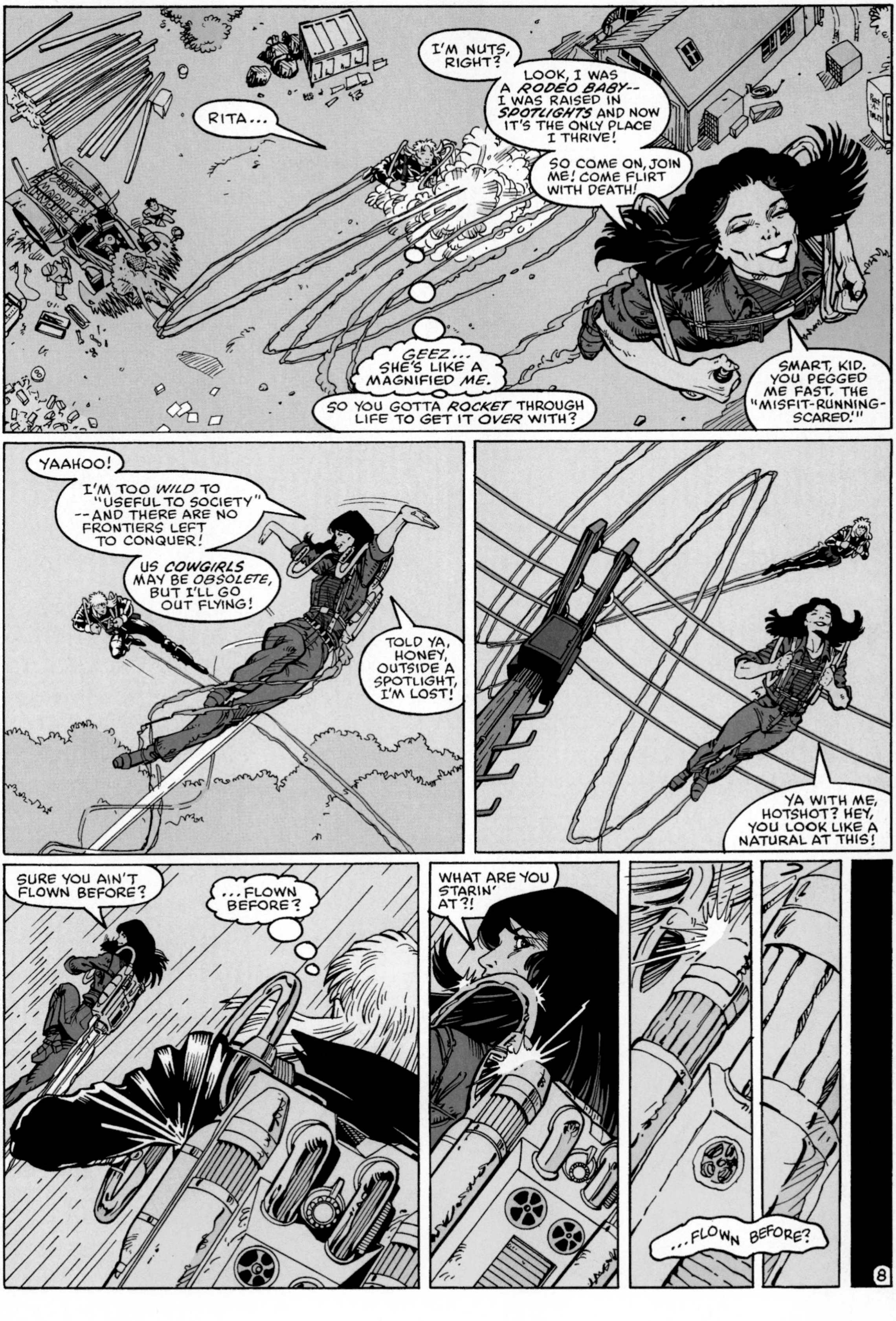
RITA...
I'M NUTS, RIGHT?
LOOK, I WAS A RODEO BABY-- I WAS RAISED IN SPOTLIGHTS AND NOW IT'S THE ONLY PLACE I THRIVE!
SO COME ON, JOIN ME! COME FLIRT WITH DEATH!
GEEZ... SHE'S LIKE A MAGNIFIED ME.
SO YOU GOTTA ROCKET THROUGH LIFE TO GET IT OVER WITH?
SMART, KID. YOU PEGGED ME FAST. THE "MISFIT-RUNNING-SCARED!"
YAAHOO!
I'M TOO WILD TO "USEFUL TO SOCIETY" --AND THERE ARE NO FRONTIERS LEFT TO CONQUER!
US COWGIRLS MAY BE OBSOLETE, BUT I'LL GO OUT FLYING!
TOLD YA, HONEY, OUTSIDE A SPOTLIGHT, I'M LOST!
YA WITH ME, HOTSHOT? HEY, YOU LOOK LIKE A NATURAL AT THIS!
SURE YOU AIN'T FLOWN BEFORE?
...FLOWN BEFORE?
WHAT ARE YOU STARIN' AT?!
...FLOWN BEFORE?
8

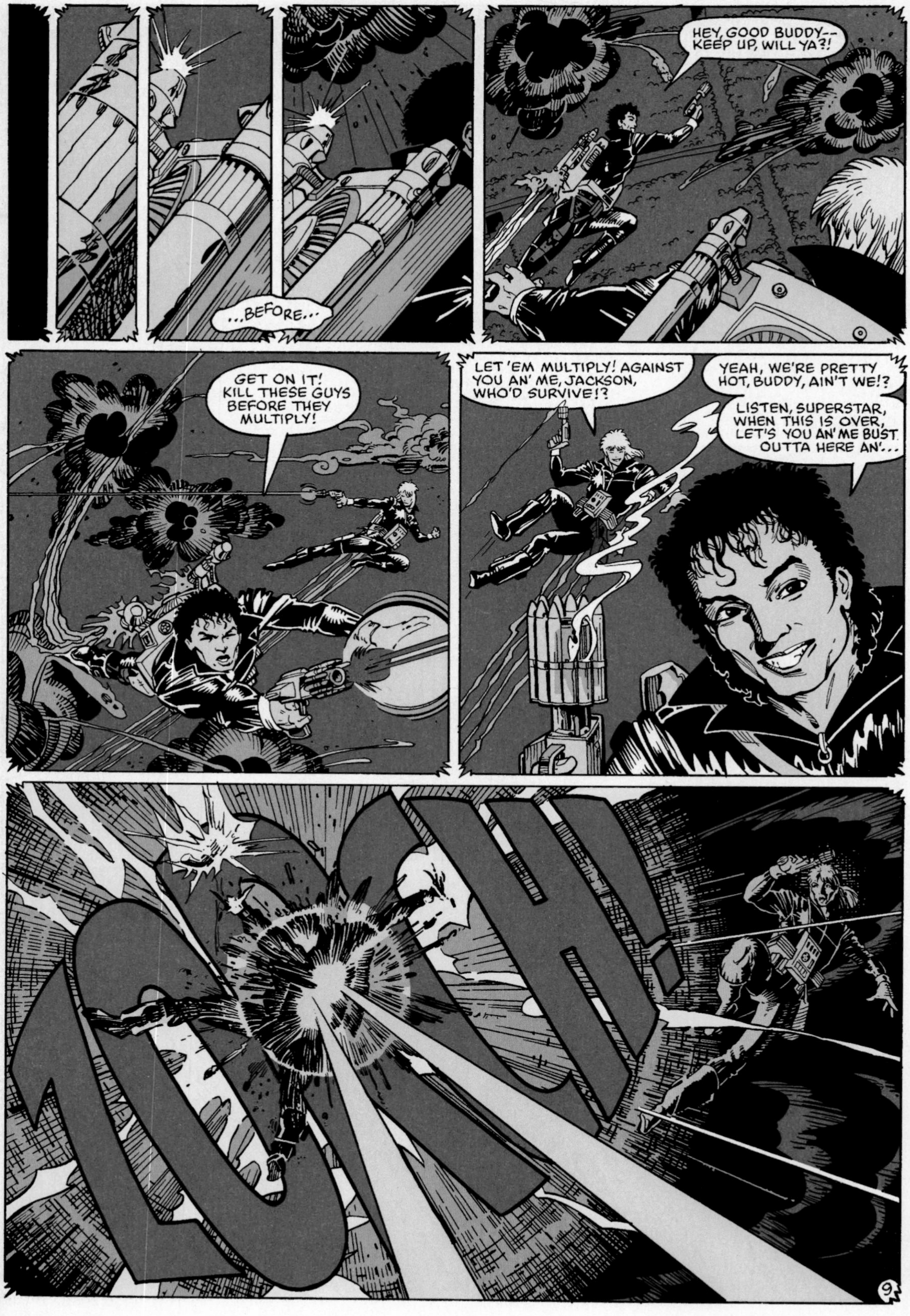
...BEFORE...
HEY, GOOD BUDDY-- KEEP UP, WILL YA?!
GET ON IT! KILL THESE GUYS BEFORE THEY MULTIPLY!
LET 'EM MULTIPLY! AGAINST YOU AN' ME, JACKSON, WHO'D SURVIVE!?
YEAH, WE'RE PRETTY HOT, BUDDY, AIN'T WE!?
LISTEN, SUPERSTAR, WHEN THIS IS OVER, LET'S YOU AN' ME BUST OUTTA HERE AN'...
9

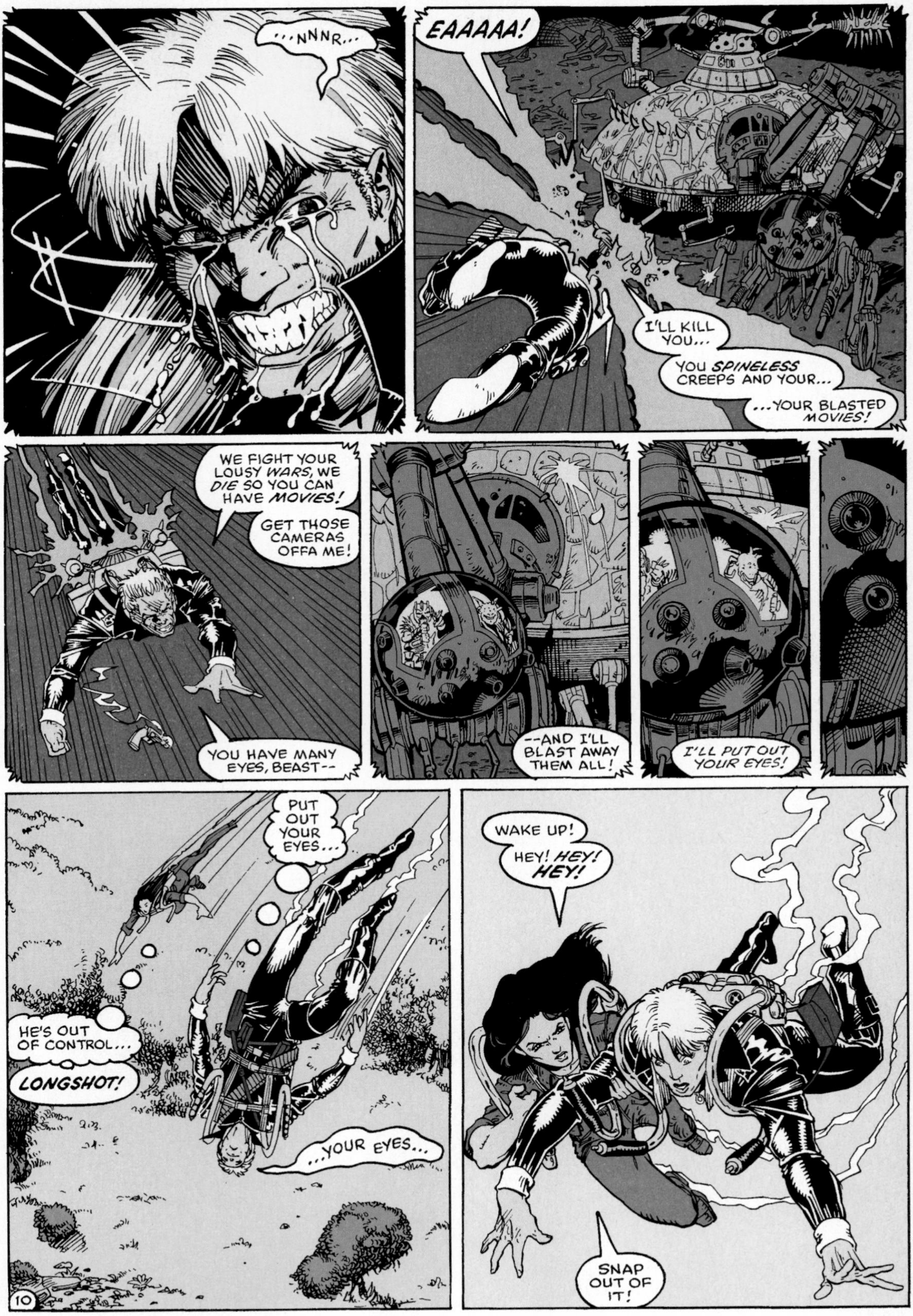

...NNNR...
EAAAAA!
I'LL KILL YOU...
YOU SPINELESS CREEPS AND YOUR...
...YOUR BLASTED MOVIES!
WE FIGHT YOUR LOUSY WARS, WE DIE SO YOU CAN HAVE MOVIES!
GET THOSE CAMERAS OFFA ME!
YOU HAVE MANY EYES, BEAST--
--AND I'LL BLAST AWAY THEM ALL!
I'LL PUT OUT YOUR EYES!
PUT OUT YOUR EYES...
HE'S OUT OF CONTROL...
LONGSHOT!
...YOUR EYES...
10
WAKE UP!
HEY! HEY! HEY!
SNAP OUT OF IT!

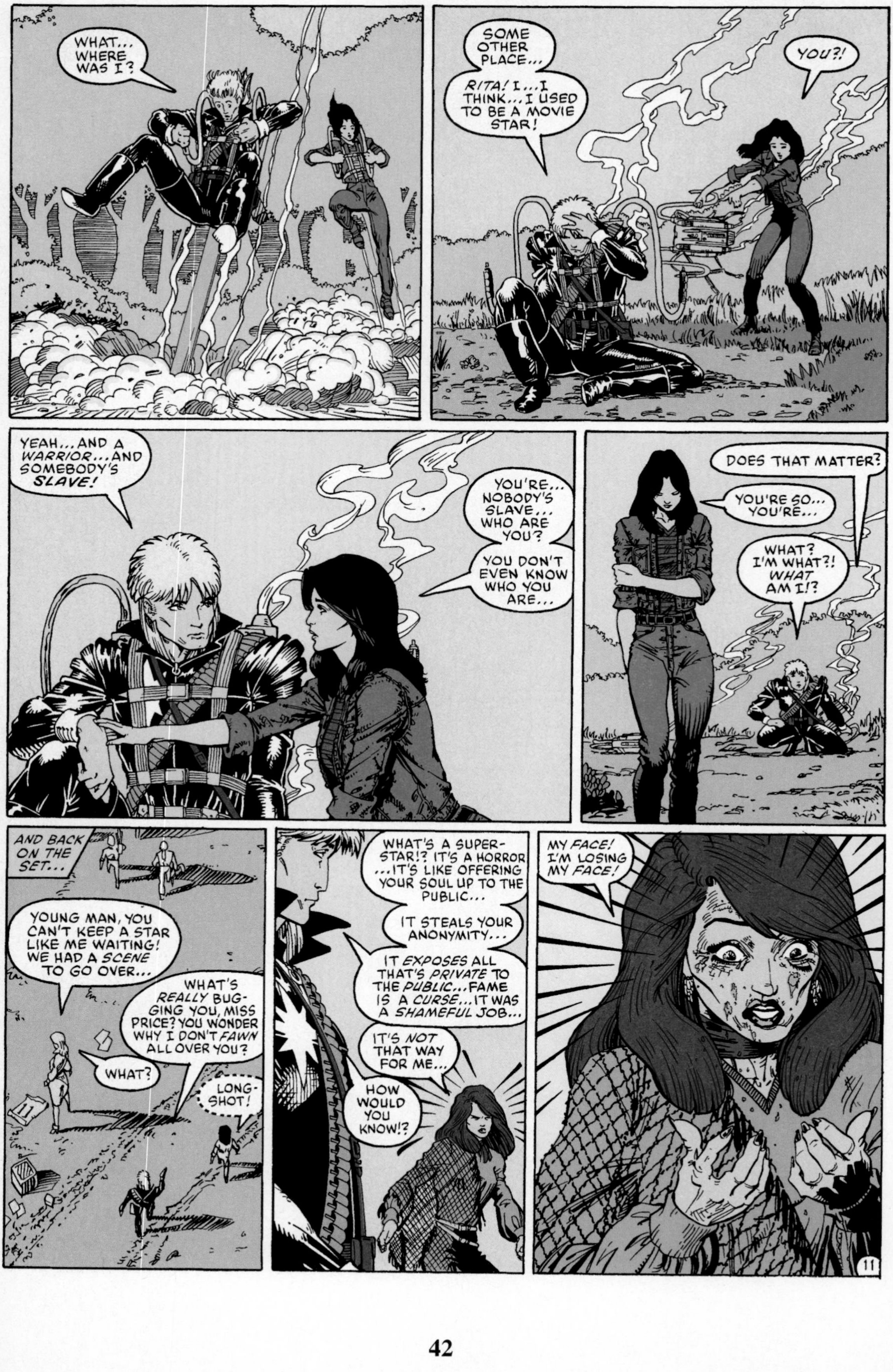

WHAT... WHERE WAS I?
SOME OTHER PLACE...
RITA! I...I THINK...I USED TO BE A MOVIE STAR!
YOU?!
YEAH...AND A WARRIOR...AND SOMEBODY'S SLAVE!
YOU'RE... NOBODY'S SLAVE... WHO ARE YOU?
YOU DON'T EVEN KNOW WHO YOU ARE...
DOES THAT MATTER?
YOU'RE SO... YOU'RE...
WHAT? I'M WHAT?! WHAT AM I!?
AND BACK ON THE SET...
YOUNG MAN, YOU CAN'T KEEP A STAR LIKE ME WAITING! WE HAD A SCENE TO GO OVER...
WHAT'S REALLY BUGGING YOU, MISS PRICE? YOU WONDER WHY I DON'T FAWN ALL OVER YOU?
WHAT?
LONGSHOT!
WHAT'S A SUPERSTAR!? IT'S A HORROR ...IT'S LIKE OFFERING YOUR SOUL UP TO THE PUBLIC...
IT STEALS YOUR ANONYMITY...
IT EXPOSES ALL THAT'S PRIVATE TO THE PUBLIC...FAME IS A CURSE...IT WAS A SHAMEFUL JOB...
IT'S NOT THAT WAY FOR ME...
HOW WOULD YOU KNOW!?
MY FACE! I'M LOSING MY FACE!
11

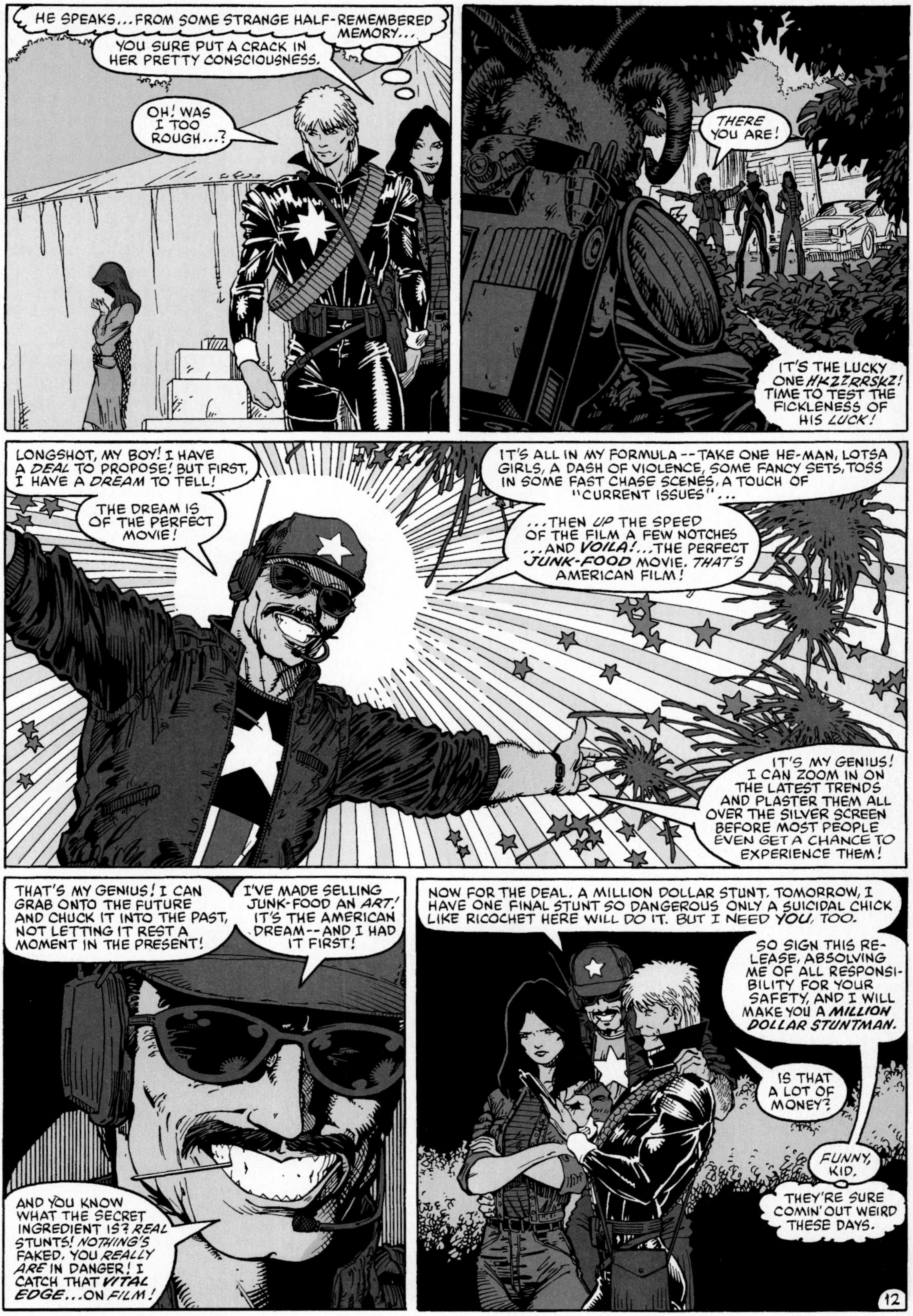
HE SPEAKS... FROM SOME STRANGE HALF-REMEMBERED MEMORY...
YOU SURE PUT A CRACK IN HER PRETTY CONSCIOUSNESS.
OH! WAS I TOO ROUGH...?
THERE YOU ARE!
IT'S THE LUCKY ONE HKZZRRSKZ! TIME TO TEST THE FICKLENESS OF HIS LUCK!
LONGSHOT, MY BOY! I HAVE A DEAL TO PROPOSE! BUT FIRST, I HAVE A DREAM TO TELL!
THE DREAM IS OF THE PERFECT MOVIE!
IT'S ALL IN MY FORMULA -- TAKE ONE HE-MAN, LOTSA GIRLS, A DASH OF VIOLENCE, SOME FANCY SETS, TOSS IN SOME FAST CHASE SCENES, A TOUCH OF "CURRENT ISSUES"...
...THEN UP THE SPEED OF THE FILM A FEW NOTCHES ...AND VOILA!...THE PERFECT JUNK-FOOD MOVIE. THAT'S AMERICAN FILM!
IT'S MY GENIUS! I CAN ZOOM IN ON THE LATEST TRENDS AND PLASTER THEM ALL OVER THE SILVER SCREEN BEFORE MOST PEOPLE EVEN GET A CHANCE TO EXPERIENCE THEM!
THAT'S MY GENIUS! I CAN GRAB ONTO THE FUTURE AND CHUCK IT INTO THE PAST, NOT LETTING IT REST A MOMENT IN THE PRESENT!
I'VE MADE SELLING JUNK-FOOD AN ART! IT'S THE AMERICAN DREAM--AND I HAD IT FIRST!
AND YOU KNOW WHAT THE SECRET INGREDIENT IS? REAL STUNTS! NOTHING'S FAKED. YOU REALLY ARE IN DANGER! I CATCH THAT VITAL EDGE...ON FILM!
NOW FOR THE DEAL. A MILLION DOLLAR STUNT. TOMORROW, I HAVE ONE FINAL STUNT SO DANGEROUS ONLY A SUICIDAL CHICK LIKE RICOCHET HERE WILL DO IT. BUT I NEED YOU, TOO.
SO SIGN THIS RELEASE, ABSOLVING ME OF ALL RESPONSIBILITY FOR YOUR SAFETY, AND I WILL MAKE YOU A MILLION DOLLAR STUNTMAN.
IS THAT A LOT OF MONEY?
FUNNY, KID.
THEY'RE SURE COMIN' OUT WEIRD THESE DAYS.
12

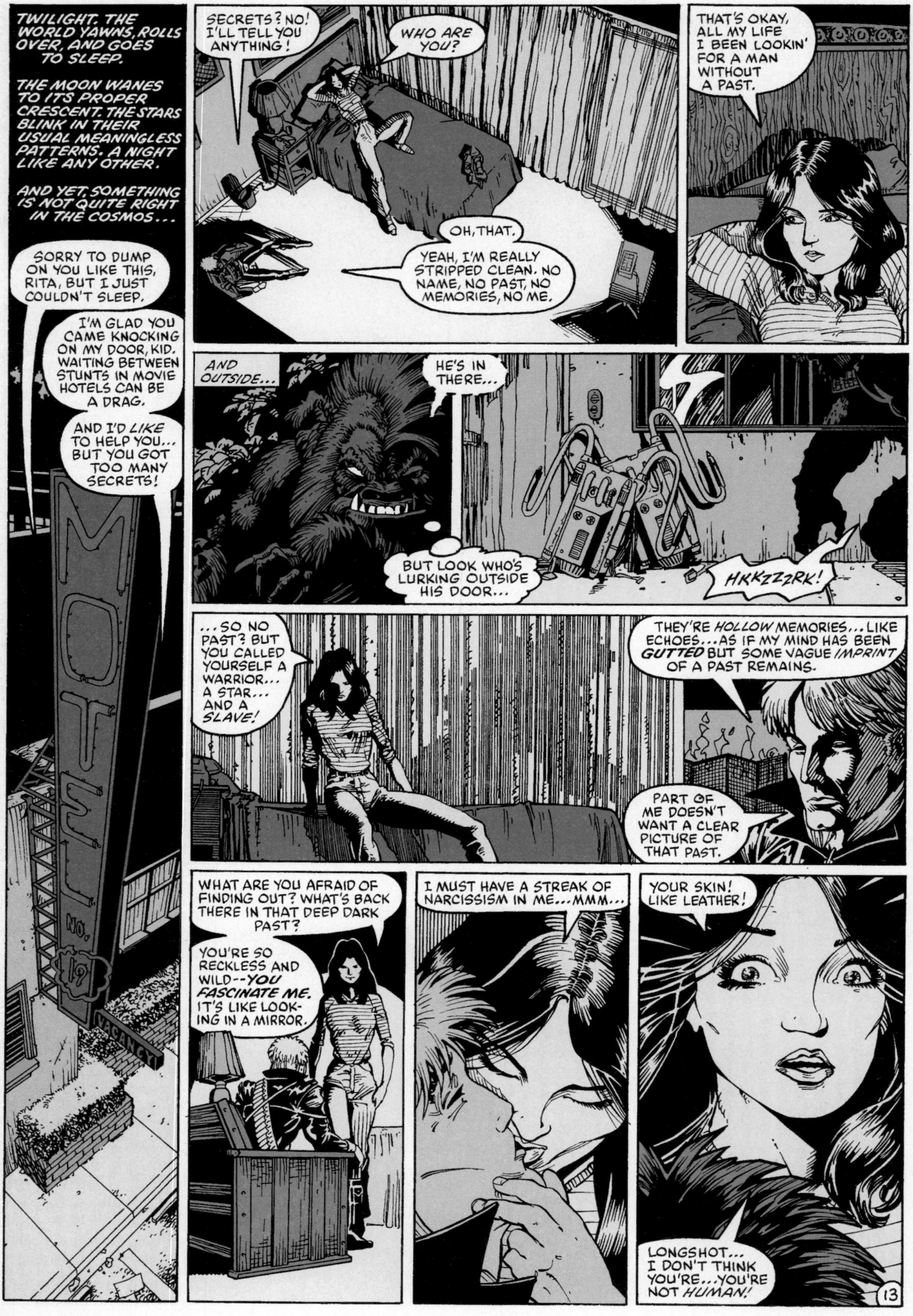
TWILIGHT. THE WORLD YAWNS, ROLLS OVER, AND GOES TO SLEEP.
THE MOON WANES TO ITS PROPER CRESCENT. THE STARS BLINK IN THEIR USUAL MEANINGLESS PATTERNS. A NIGHT LIKE ANY OTHER.
AND YET, SOMETHING IS NOT QUITE RIGHT IN THE COSMOS...
SORRY TO DUMP ON YOU LIKE THIS, RITA, BUT I JUST COULDN'T SLEEP.
I'M GLAD YOU CAME KNOCKING ON MY DOOR, KID. WAITING BETWEEN STUNTS IN MOVIE HOTELS CAN BE A DRAG.
AND I'D LIKE TO HELP YOU... BUT YOU GOT TOO MANY SECRETS!
MOTEL
NO. 19
VACANCY
SECRETS? NO! I'LL TELL YOU ANYTHING!
WHO ARE YOU?
OH, THAT.
YEAH, I'M REALLY STRIPPED CLEAN. NO NAME, NO PAST, NO MEMORIES, NO ME.
THAT'S OKAY, ALL MY LIFE I BEEN LOOKIN' FOR A MAN WITHOUT A PAST.
AND OUTSIDE...
HE'S IN THERE...
BUT LOOK WHO'S LURKING OUTSIDE HIS DOOR...
HKKZZZRK!
...SO NO PAST? BUT YOU CALLED YOURSELF A WARRIOR... A STAR... AND A SLAVE!
THEY'RE HOLLOW MEMORIES... LIKE ECHOES... AS IF MY MIND HAS BEEN GUTTED BUT SOME VAGUE IMPRINT OF A PAST REMAINS.
PART OF ME DOESN'T WANT A CLEAR PICTURE OF THAT PAST.
WHAT ARE YOU AFRAID OF FINDING OUT? WHAT'S BACK THERE IN THAT DEEP DARK PAST?
YOU'RE SO RECKLESS AND WILD--YOU FASCINATE ME. IT'S LIKE LOOKING IN A MIRROR.
I MUST HAVE A STREAK OF NARCISSISM IN ME...MMM...
YOUR SKIN! LIKE LEATHER!
LONGSHOT... I DON'T THINK YOU'RE...YOU'RE NOT HUMAN!
13

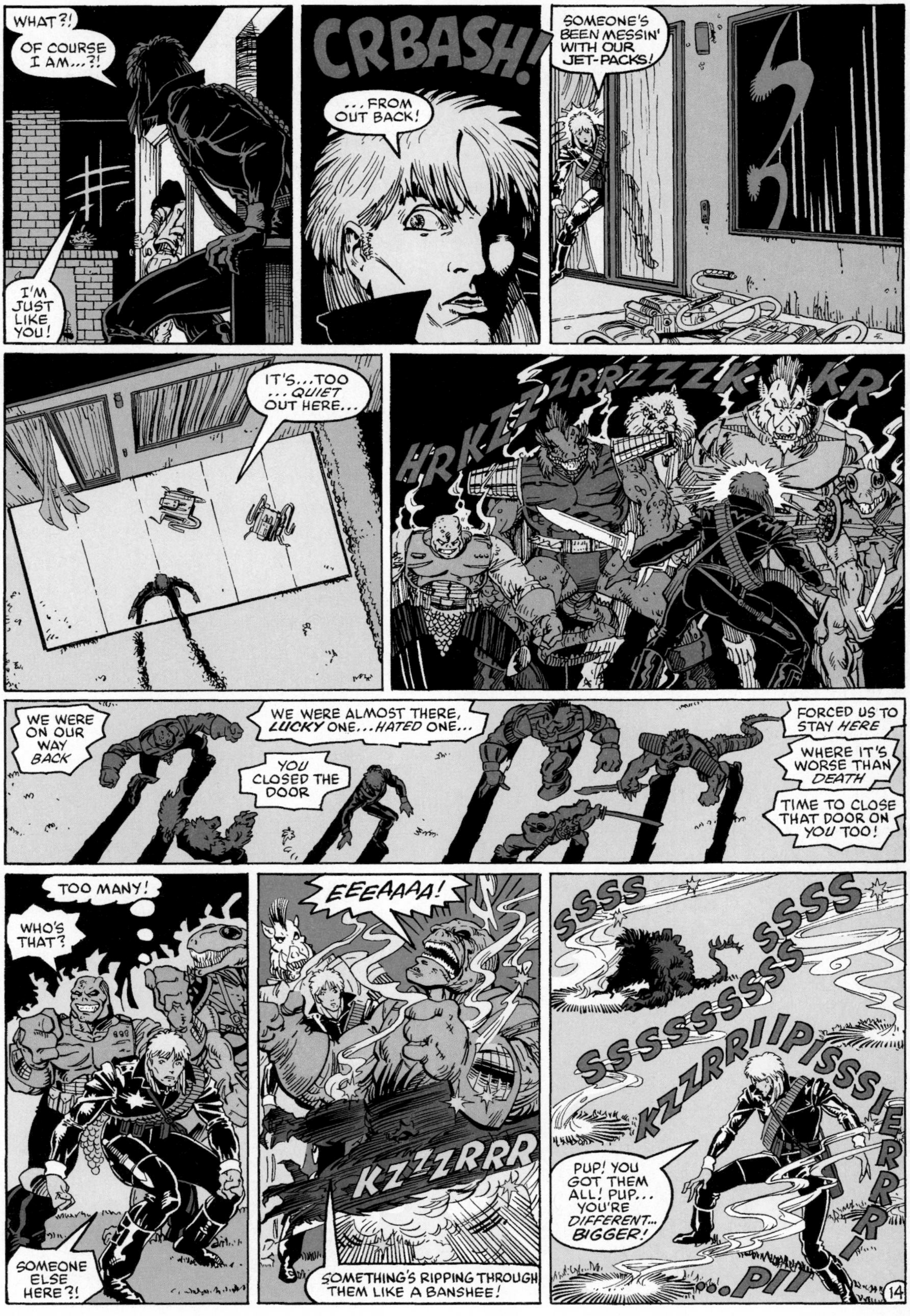
WHAT?! OF COURSE I AM...?!
I'M JUST LIKE YOU!
CRBASH!
...FROM OUT BACK!
SOMEONE'S BEEN MESSIN' WITH OUR JET-PACKS!
IT'S...TOO ...QUIET OUT HERE...
HRKZZZZRRRZZZZK-KR
WE WERE ON OUR WAY BACK
WE WERE ALMOST THERE, LUCKY ONE...HATED ONE...
YOU CLOSED THE DOOR
FORCED US TO STAY HERE
WHERE IT'S WORSE THAN DEATH
TIME TO CLOSE THAT DOOR ON YOU TOO!
TOO MANY!
WHO'S THAT?
SOMEONE ELSE HERE?!
EEEAAAA!
KZZZRRR
SOMETHING'S RIPPING THROUGH THEM LIKE A BANSHEE!
SSSS
SSSS
SSSSSSSS
SSSSSSSSSS
KZZZRRIIPISSSSIERRRRI
PUP! YOU GOT THEM ALL! PUP... YOU'RE DIFFERENT... BIGGER!
...PII
14

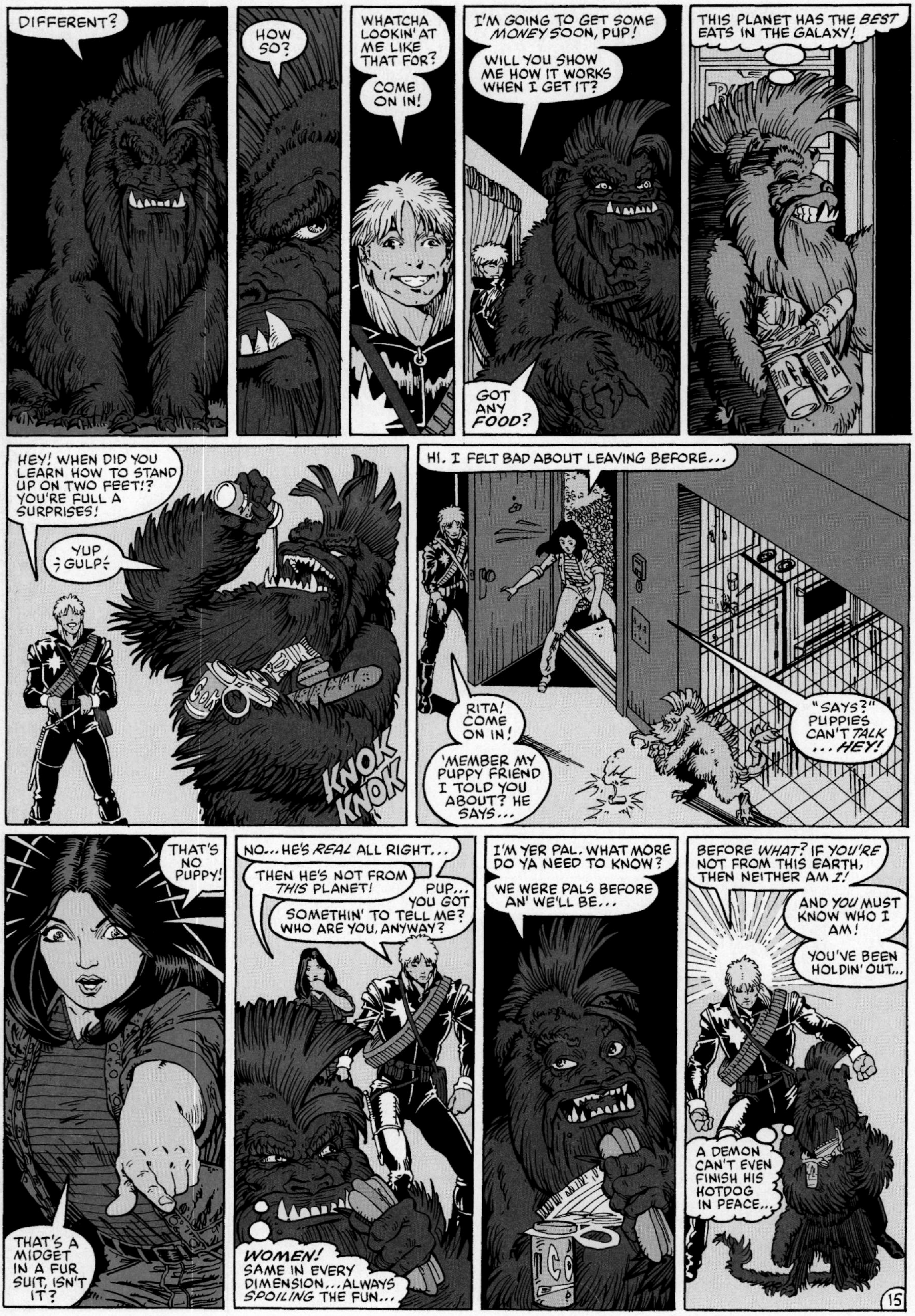

DIFFERENT?
HOW SO?
WHATCHA LOOKIN' AT ME LIKE THAT FOR?
COME ON IN!
I'M GOING TO GET SOME MONEY SOON, PUP!
WILL YOU SHOW ME HOW IT WORKS WHEN I GET IT?
GOT ANY FOOD?
THIS PLANET HAS THE BEST EATS IN THE GALAXY!
HEY! WHEN DID YOU LEARN HOW TO STAND UP ON TWO FEET!? YOU'RE FULL A SURPRISES!
YUP GULP
KNOK KNOK
HI. I FELT BAD ABOUT LEAVING BEFORE...
RITA! COME ON IN!
'MEMBER MY PUPPY FRIEND I TOLD YOU ABOUT? HE SAYS...
"SAYS?" PUPPIES CAN'T TALK ...HEY!
THAT'S NO PUPPY!
THAT'S A MIDGET IN A FUR SUIT, ISN'T IT?
NO...HE'S REAL ALL RIGHT...
THEN HE'S NOT FROM THIS PLANET!
PUP... YOU GOT SOMETHIN' TO TELL ME? WHO ARE YOU, ANYWAY?
WOMEN! SAME IN EVERY DIMENSION...ALWAYS SPOILING THE FUN...
I'M YER PAL. WHAT MORE DO YA NEED TO KNOW?
WE WERE PALS BEFORE AN' WE'LL BE...
BEFORE WHAT? IF YOU'RE NOT FROM THIS EARTH, THEN NEITHER AM I!
AND YOU MUST KNOW WHO I AM!
YOU'VE BEEN HOLDIN' OUT...
A DEMON CAN'T EVEN FINISH HIS HOTDOG IN PEACE...
15

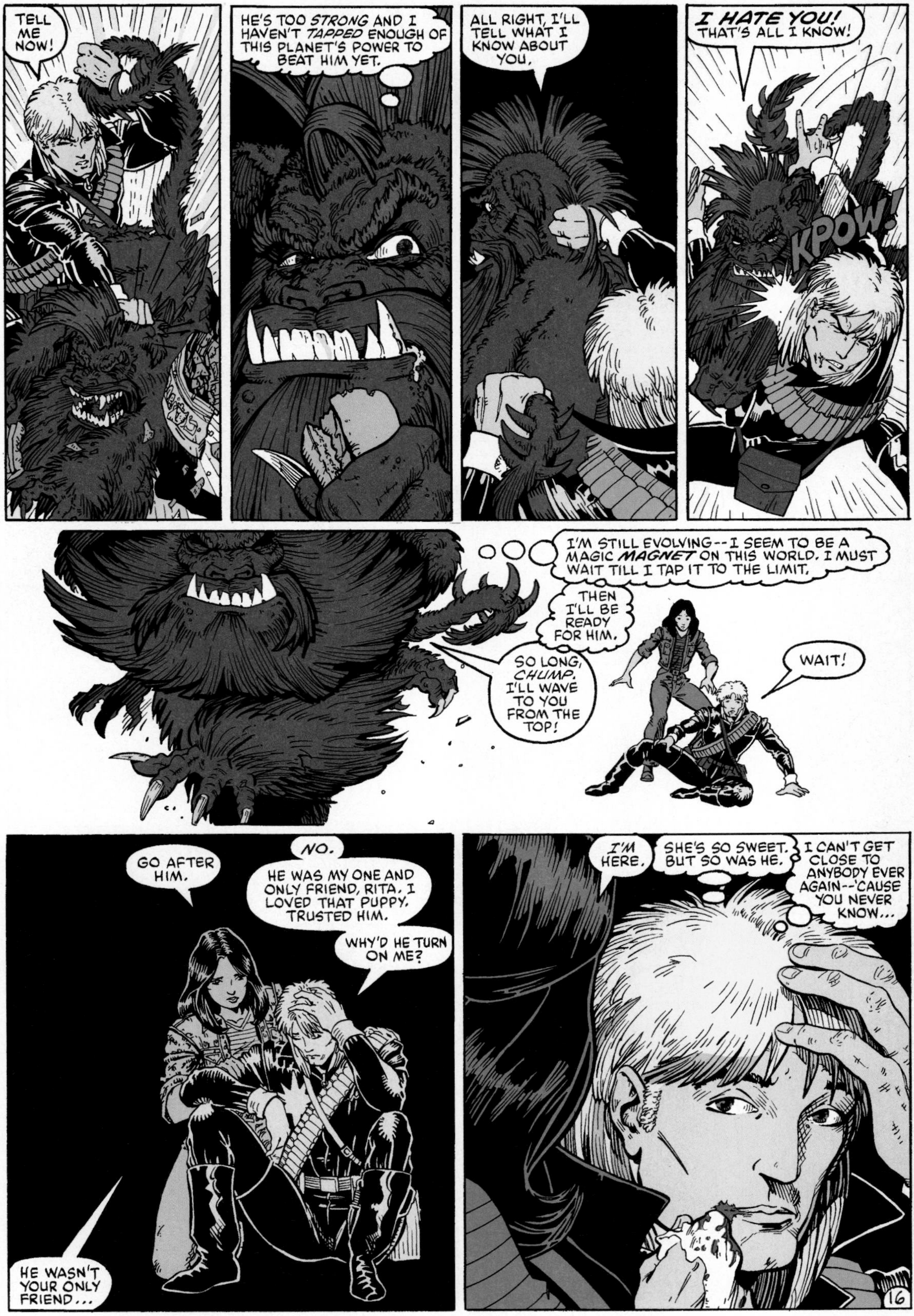
TELL ME NOW!
HE'S TOO *STRONG* AND I HAVEN'T *TAPPED* ENOUGH OF THIS PLANET'S POWER TO BEAT HIM YET.
ALL RIGHT, I'LL TELL WHAT I KNOW ABOUT YOU.
I HATE YOU! THAT'S ALL I KNOW!
KPOW!
I'M STILL EVOLVING--I SEEM TO BE A MAGIC *MAGNET* ON THIS WORLD. I MUST WAIT TILL I TAP IT TO THE LIMIT.
THEN I'LL BE READY FOR HIM.
SO LONG, *CHUMP*. I'LL WAVE TO YOU FROM THE TOP!
WAIT!
GO AFTER HIM.
NO.
HE WAS MY ONE AND ONLY FRIEND, RITA. I LOVED THAT PUPPY. TRUSTED HIM.
WHY'D HE TURN ON ME?
HE WASN'T YOUR ONLY FRIEND...
I'M HERE.
SHE'S SO SWEET. BUT SO WAS HE.
I CAN'T GET CLOSE TO ANYBODY EVER AGAIN--'CAUSE YOU NEVER KNOW...
16

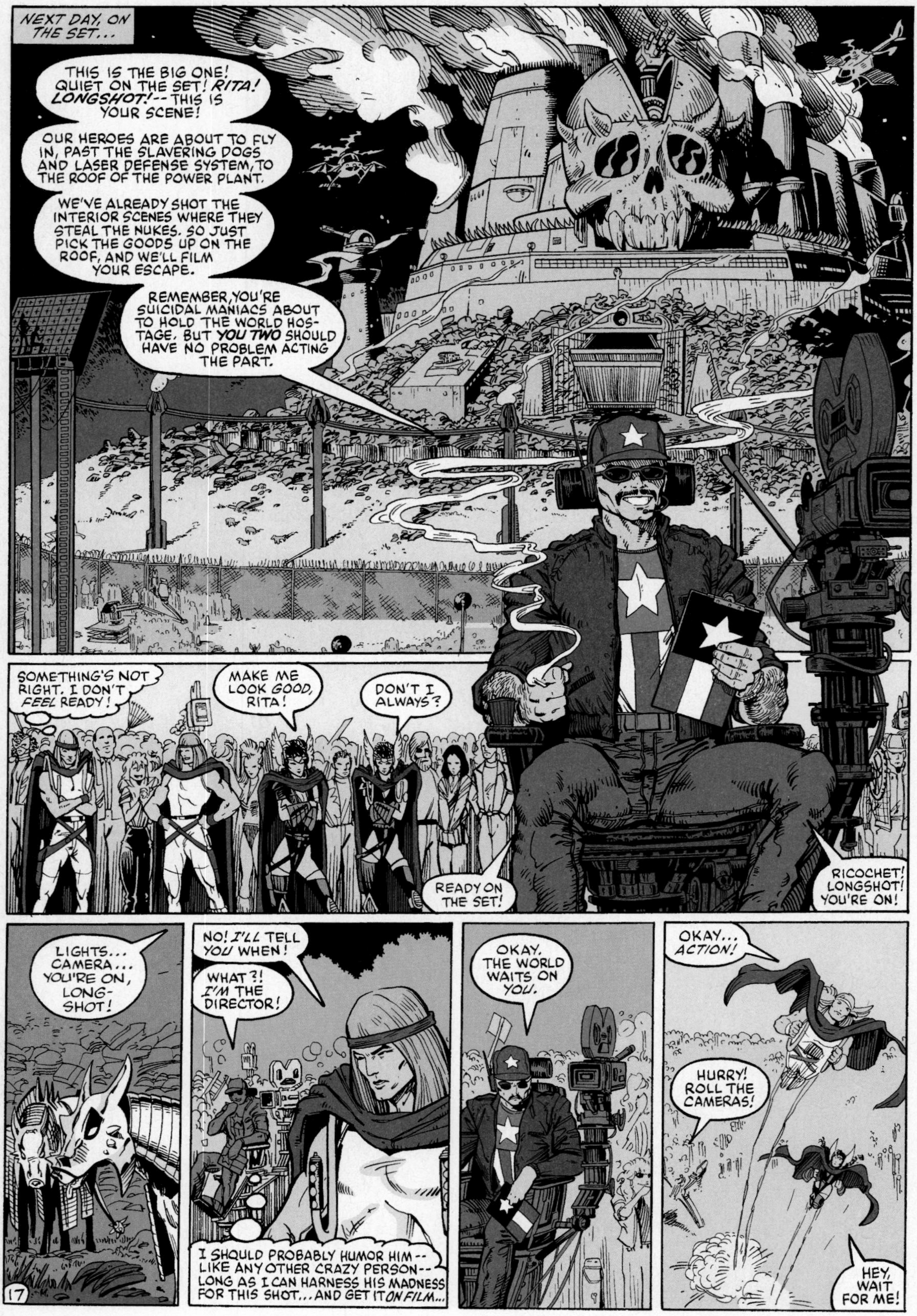
NEXT DAY, ON THE SET...
THIS IS THE BIG ONE! QUIET ON THE SET! RITA! LONGSHOT!-- THIS IS YOUR SCENE!
OUR HEROES ARE ABOUT TO FLY IN, PAST THE SLAVERING DOGS AND LASER DEFENSE SYSTEM, TO THE ROOF OF THE POWER PLANT.
WE'VE ALREADY SHOT THE INTERIOR SCENES WHERE THEY STEAL THE NUKES. SO JUST PICK THE GOODS UP ON THE ROOF, AND WE'LL FILM YOUR ESCAPE.
REMEMBER, YOU'RE SUICIDAL MANIACS ABOUT TO HOLD THE WORLD HOSTAGE. BUT YOU TWO SHOULD HAVE NO PROBLEM ACTING THE PART.
SOMETHING'S NOT RIGHT. I DON'T FEEL READY!
MAKE ME LOOK GOOD, RITA!
DON'T I ALWAYS?
READY ON THE SET!
RICOCHET! LONGSHOT! YOU'RE ON!
LIGHTS... CAMERA... YOU'RE ON, LONG-SHOT!
17
NO! I'LL TELL YOU WHEN!
WHAT?! I'M THE DIRECTOR!
I SHOULD PROBABLY HUMOR HIM-- LIKE ANY OTHER CRAZY PERSON-- LONG AS I CAN HARNESS HIS MADNESS FOR THIS SHOT... AND GET IT ON FILM...
OKAY. THE WORLD WAITS ON YOU.
OKAY... ACTION!
HURRY! ROLL THE CAMERAS!
HEY, WAIT FOR ME!

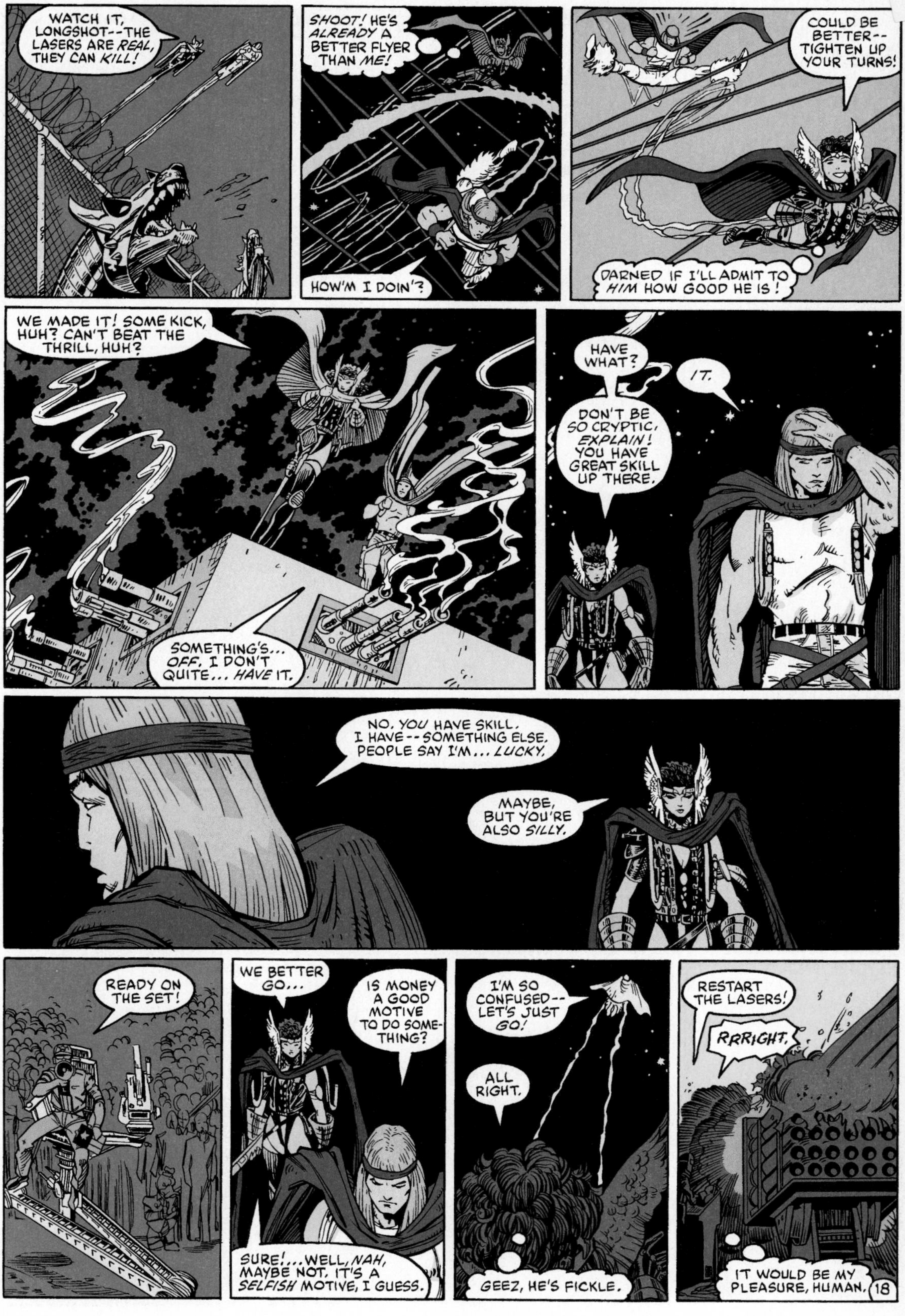
WATCH IT, LONGSHOT--THE LASERS ARE *REAL*, THEY CAN *KILL*!
SHOOT! HE'S *ALREADY* A BETTER FLYER THAN *ME*!
HOW'M I DOIN'?
COULD BE BETTER--TIGHTEN UP YOUR TURNS!
DARNED IF I'LL ADMIT TO *HIM* HOW GOOD HE IS!
WE MADE IT! SOME KICK, HUH? CAN'T BEAT THE THRILL, HUH?
SOMETHING'S... *OFF*, I DON'T QUITE... *HAVE* IT.
HAVE WHAT?
IT.
DON'T BE SO CRYPTIC, *EXPLAIN*! YOU HAVE GREAT SKILL UP THERE.
NO. *YOU* HAVE SKILL. I HAVE--SOMETHING ELSE. PEOPLE SAY I'M... *LUCKY.*
MAYBE, BUT YOU'RE ALSO *SILLY.*
READY ON THE SET!
WE BETTER GO...
IS MONEY A GOOD MOTIVE TO DO SOME-THING?
SURE!... WELL, *NAH*, MAYBE NOT, IT'S A *SELFISH* MOTIVE, I GUESS.
I'M SO CONFUSED--LET'S JUST *GO!*
ALL RIGHT.
GEEZ, HE'S FICKLE.
RESTART THE LASERS!
RRRIGHT.
IT WOULD BE MY PLEASURE, HUMAN.
18

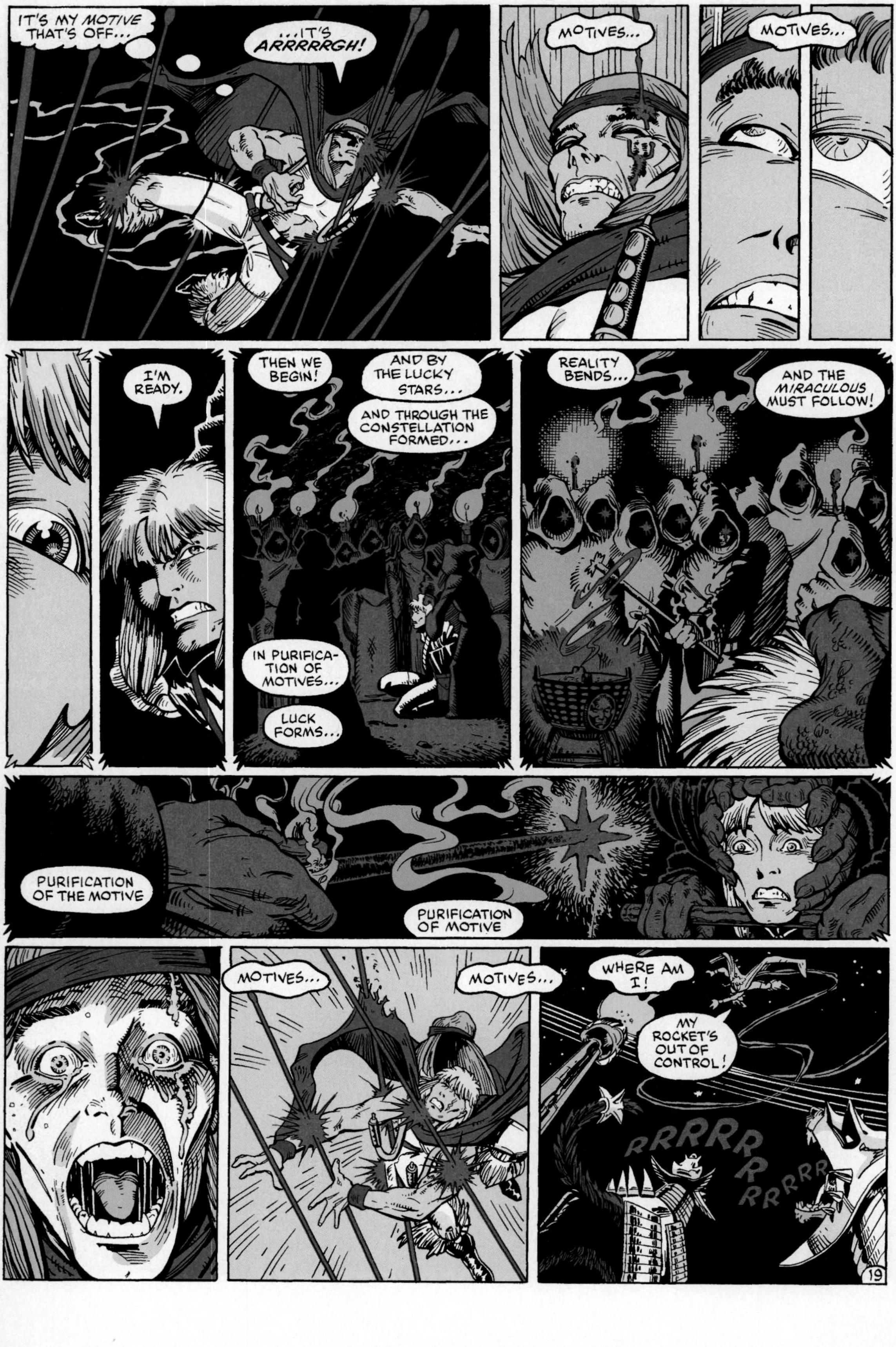
IT'S MY MOTIVE THAT'S OFF...
...IT'S ARRRRRGH!
MOTIVES...
MOTIVES...
I'M READY.
THEN WE BEGIN!
AND BY THE LUCKY STARS...
AND THROUGH THE CONSTELLATION FORMED...
IN PURIFICATION OF MOTIVES...
LUCK FORMS...
REALITY BENDS...
AND THE MIRACULOUS MUST FOLLOW!
PURIFICATION OF THE MOTIVE
PURIFICATION OF MOTIVE
MOTIVES...
MOTIVES...
WHERE AM I!
MY ROCKET'S OUT OF CONTROL!
RRRRRRRRRRRR
19

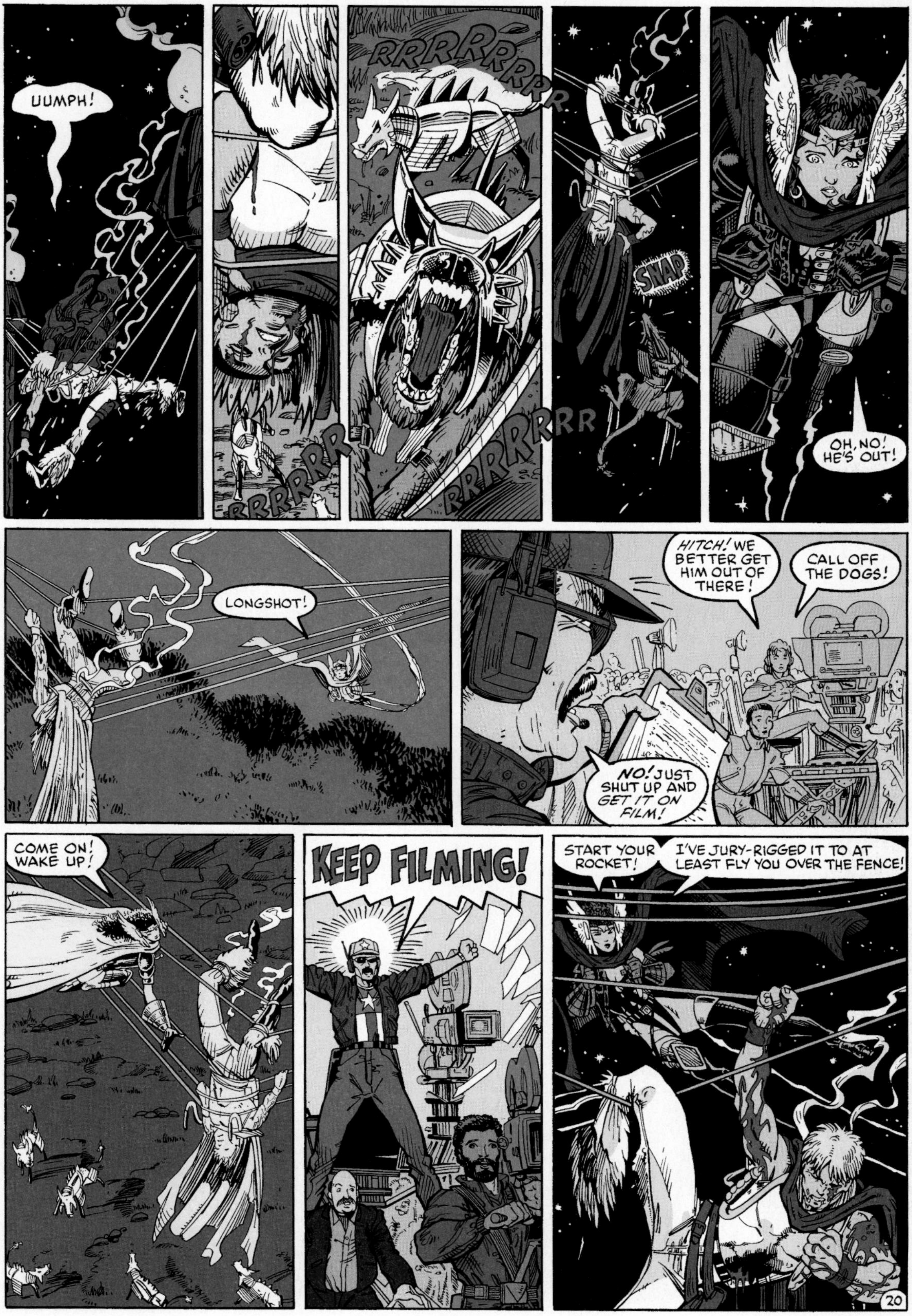

UUMPH!
RRRRRR
RRRRRRRRR
SNAP
RRRRRRRRRR
OH, NO! HE'S OUT!
LONGSHOT!
HITCH! WE BETTER GET HIM OUT OF THERE!
CALL OFF THE DOGS!
NO! JUST SHUT UP AND GET IT ON FILM!
COME ON! WAKE UP!
KEEP FILMING!
START YOUR ROCKET!
I'VE JURY-RIGGED IT TO AT LEAST FLY YOU OVER THE FENCE!
20

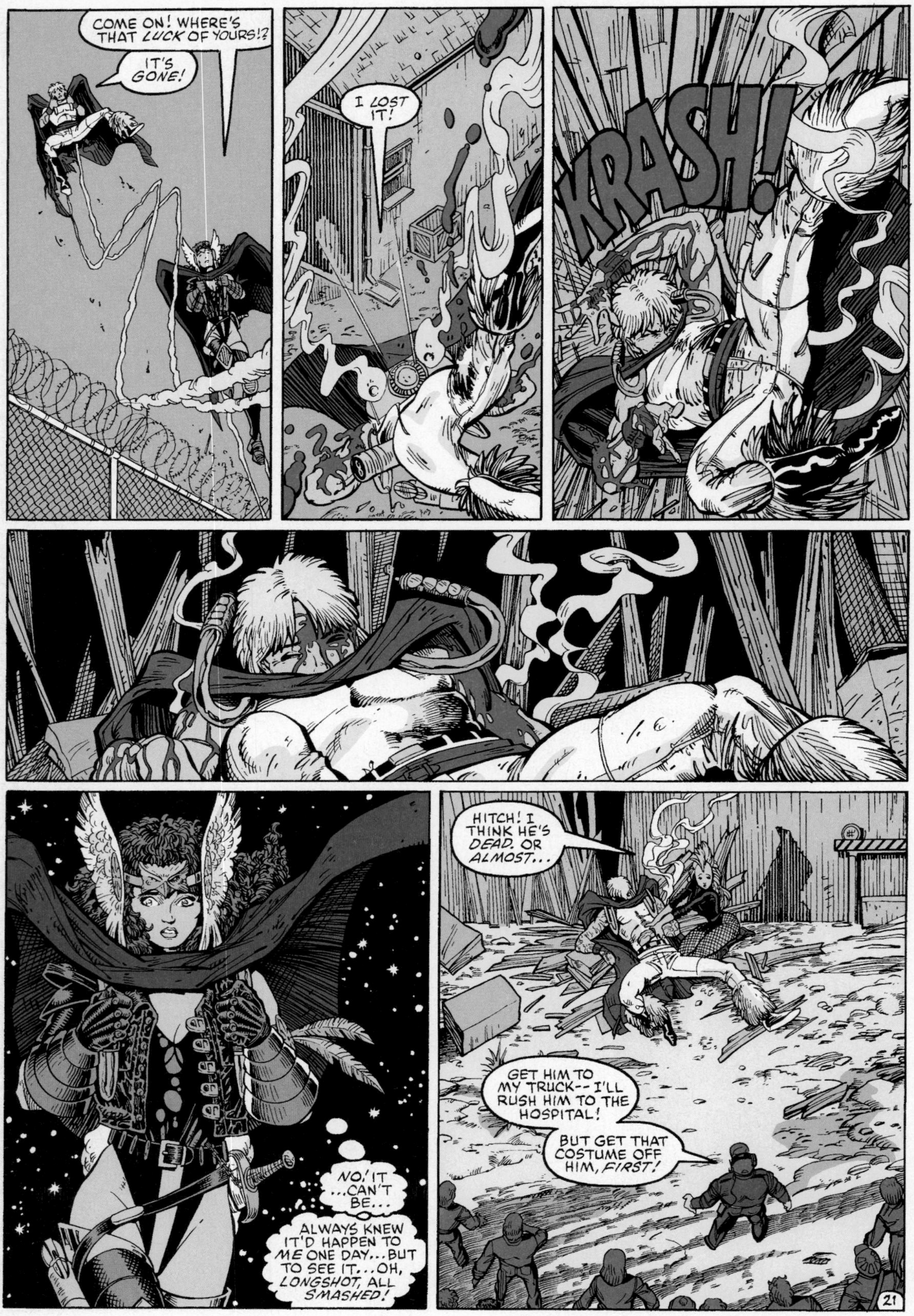
COME ON! WHERE'S THAT LUCK OF YOURS!?
IT'S GONE!
I LOST IT!
KRASH!
NO! IT ...CAN'T BE...
ALWAYS KNEW IT'D HAPPEN TO ME ONE DAY...BUT TO SEE IT...OH, LONGSHOT, ALL SMASHED!
HITCH! I THINK HE'S DEAD. OR ALMOST...
GET HIM TO MY TRUCK-- I'LL RUSH HIM TO THE HOSPITAL!
BUT GET THAT COSTUME OFF HIM, FIRST!
21

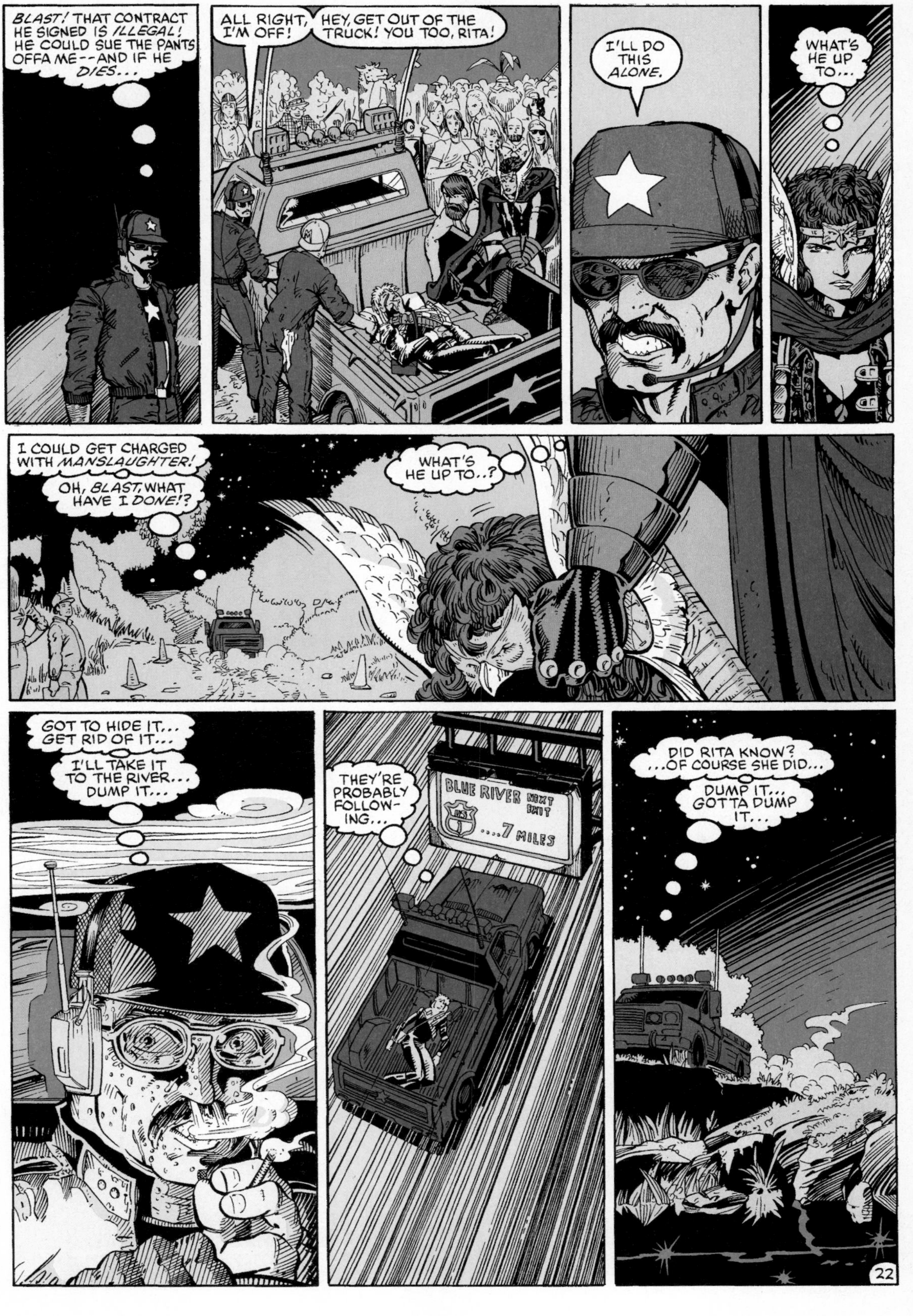
BLAST! THAT CONTRACT HE SIGNED IS ILLEGAL! HE COULD SUE THE PANTS OFFA ME--AND IF HE DIES...
ALL RIGHT, I'M OFF!
HEY, GET OUT OF THE TRUCK! YOU TOO, RITA!
I'LL DO THIS ALONE.
WHAT'S HE UP TO...
I COULD GET CHARGED WITH MANSLAUGHTER!
OH, BLAST, WHAT HAVE I DONE!?
WHAT'S HE UP TO..?
GOT TO HIDE IT... GET RID OF IT...
I'LL TAKE IT TO THE RIVER... DUMP IT...
THEY'RE PROBABLY FOLLOW-ING...
BLUE RIVER NEXT EXIT
....7 MILES
DID RITA KNOW? ...OF COURSE SHE DID...
DUMP IT... GOTTA DUMP IT...
22

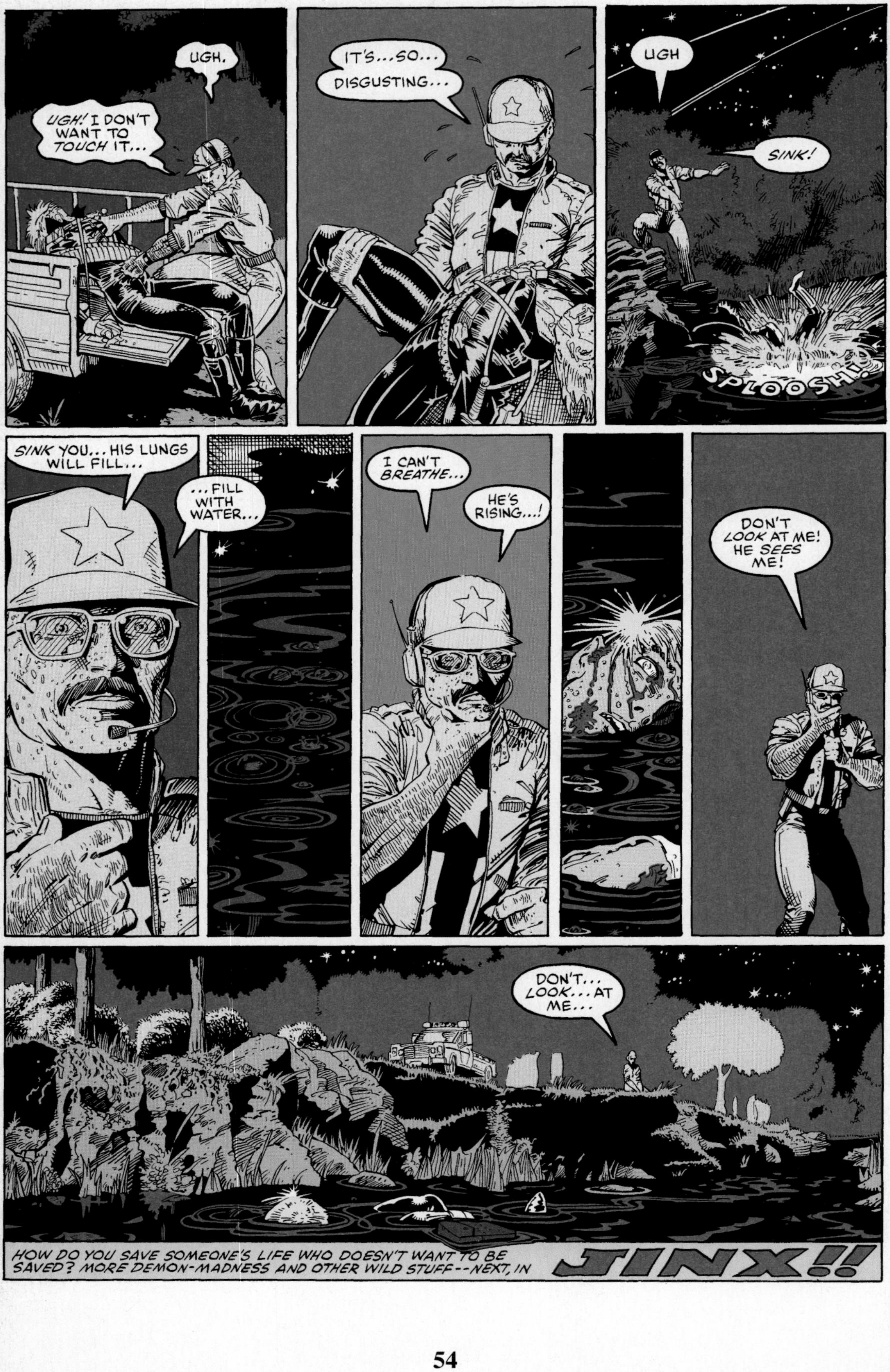
UGH.
UGH! I DON'T WANT TO TOUCH IT...
IT'S...SO... DISGUSTING...
UGH
SINK!
SPLOOSH!
SINK YOU... HIS LUNGS WILL FILL...
...FILL WITH WATER...
I CAN'T BREATHE...
HE'S RISING...!
DON'T LOOK AT ME! HE SEES ME!
DON'T... LOOK... AT ME...
HOW DO YOU SAVE SOMEONE'S LIFE WHO DOESN'T WANT TO BE SAVED? MORE DEMON-MADNESS AND OTHER WILD STUFF--NEXT, IN
JINX!!

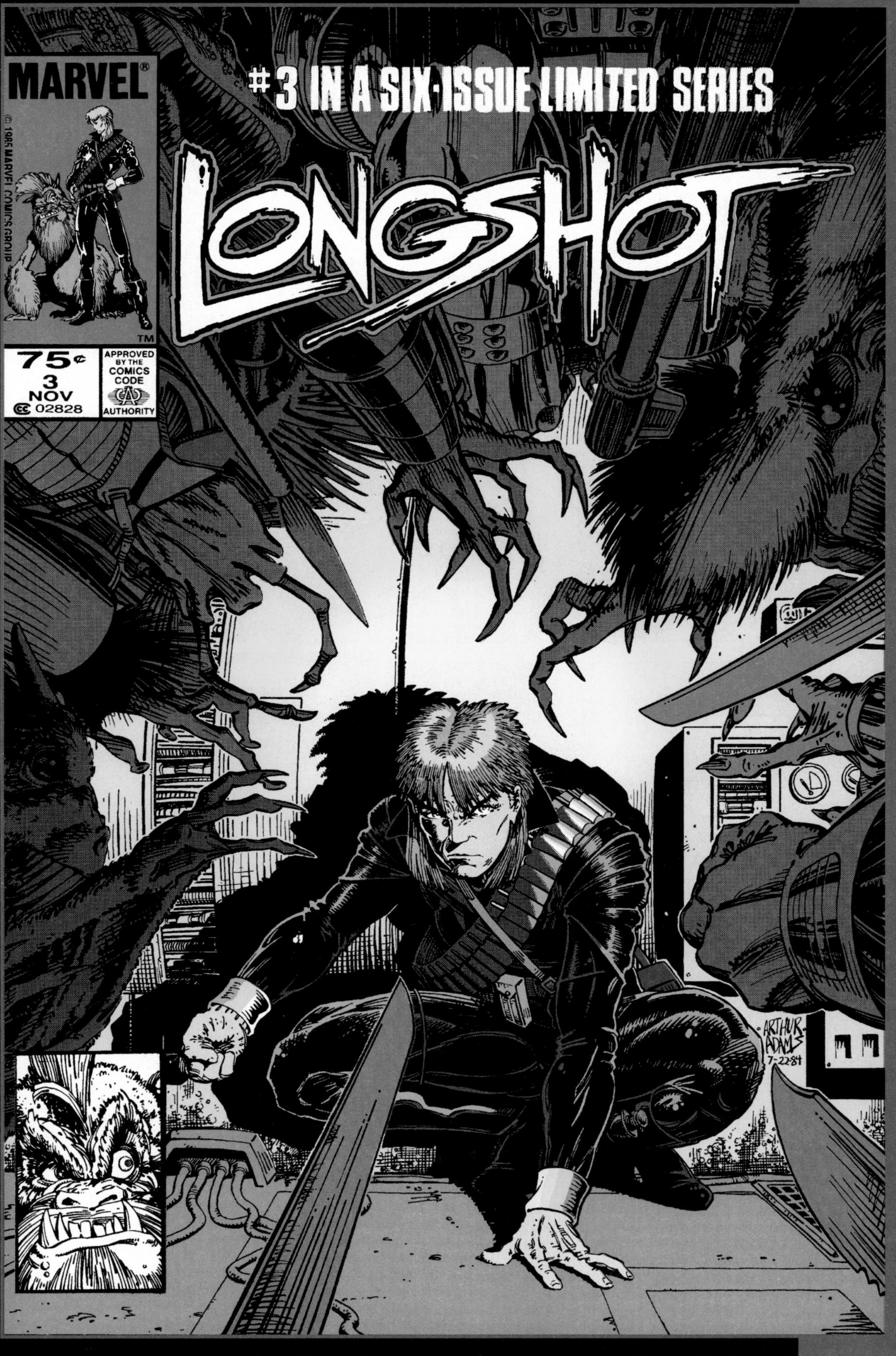
MARVEL®
© 1985 MARVEL COMICS GROUP
#3 IN A SIX-ISSUE LIMITED SERIES
LONGSHOT™
75¢
3
NOV
02828
APPROVED BY THE COMICS CODE AUTHORITY
ARTHUR ADAMS 7-22-84

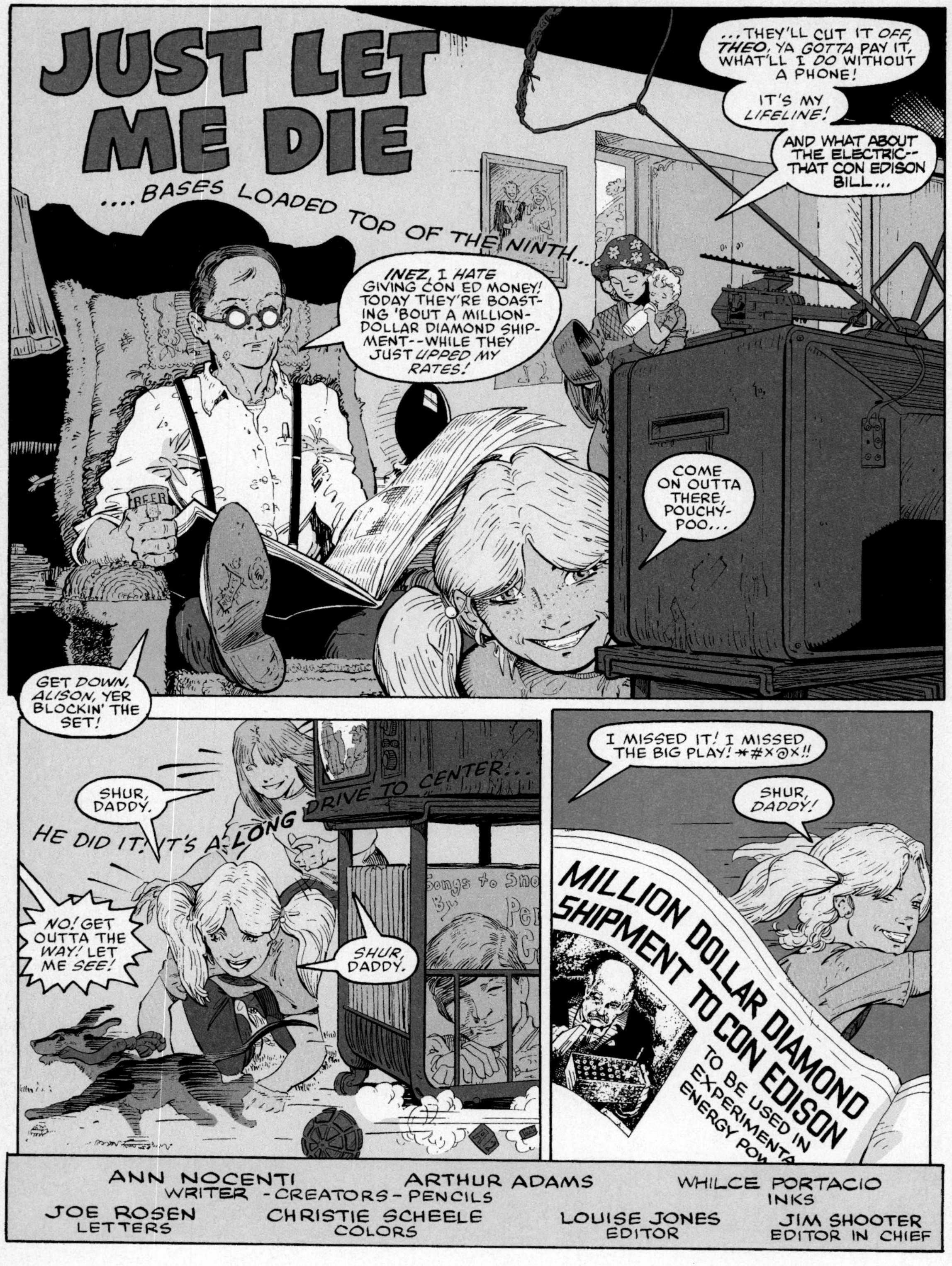
JUST LET ME DIE
....BASES LOADED TOP OF THE NINTH...
...THEY'LL CUT IT OFF, THEO, YA GOTTA PAY IT. WHAT'LL I DO WITHOUT A PHONE!
IT'S MY LIFELINE!
AND WHAT ABOUT THE ELECTRIC-- THAT CON EDISON BILL...
INEZ, I HATE GIVING CON ED MONEY! TODAY THEY'RE BOASTING 'BOUT A MILLION-DOLLAR DIAMOND SHIPMENT--WHILE THEY JUST UPPED MY RATES!
COME ON OUTTA THERE, POUCHY-POO...
BEER
GET DOWN, ALISON, YER BLOCKIN' THE SET!
SHUR, DADDY.
HE DID IT! IT'S A LONG DRIVE TO CENTER...
NO! GET OUTTA THE WAY! LET ME SEE!
SHUR, DADDY.
I MISSED IT! I MISSED THE BIG PLAY! *#x@x!!
SHUR, DADDY!
MILLION DOLLAR DIAMOND SHIPMENT TO CON EDISON
TO BE USED IN EXPERIMENTA ENERGY POW

ANN NOCENTI WRITER - CREATORS - ARTHUR ADAMS PENCILS
WHILCE PORTACIO INKS
JOE ROSEN LETTERS
CHRISTIE SCHEELE COLORS
LOUISE JONES EDITOR
JIM SHOOTER EDITOR IN CHIEF

GET 'IM! HE'S GOT MY GUMBY!

I HOPE HE *CHEWS* IT!

...ROUND HERE I GOTTA FIND MY ENTERTAINMENT *CHEAP*. TELEPHONE'S MY ONLY...

THEODORE, DID YOU HEAR ME?

HEHEEHEEE HEEEE

HEHEHEEHEE

I'M INVISIBLE. I DON'T EXIST. I MIGHT AS WELL BE DEAD.

LISTEN TO HER ROOF-BRAINCHATTER. BLAH BLAH BLAH RATTLE RATTLE RATTLE.

...I WORK MY FINGERS TO THE...

RATTLE RATTLE RATTLE

THEO! SOMETIMES I THINK YOU DON'T LISTEN TO ME!

PEACE AT LAST. I HAVE TO GO TO THE BATHROOM TO GET PEACE.

IT AIN'T FAIR.

I'M UGLY. AN' DUMB.

AN' THEY TOLD ME MAN WAS CREATED *EQUAL*. HA!

GOTTA BRUSH MY TEETH.

YET AGAIN.

LIKE I DO EVERY DAY.

AND EVERY NITE.

FOR THE REST OF ALL MY BORN DAYS.

BRUSHING MY TEETH OVER AND OVER...

FOR THE REST OF MY...

...TO THE *BONE* I WORK SO HARD...AN' WATTABOUT ALL THESE DIAPERS...

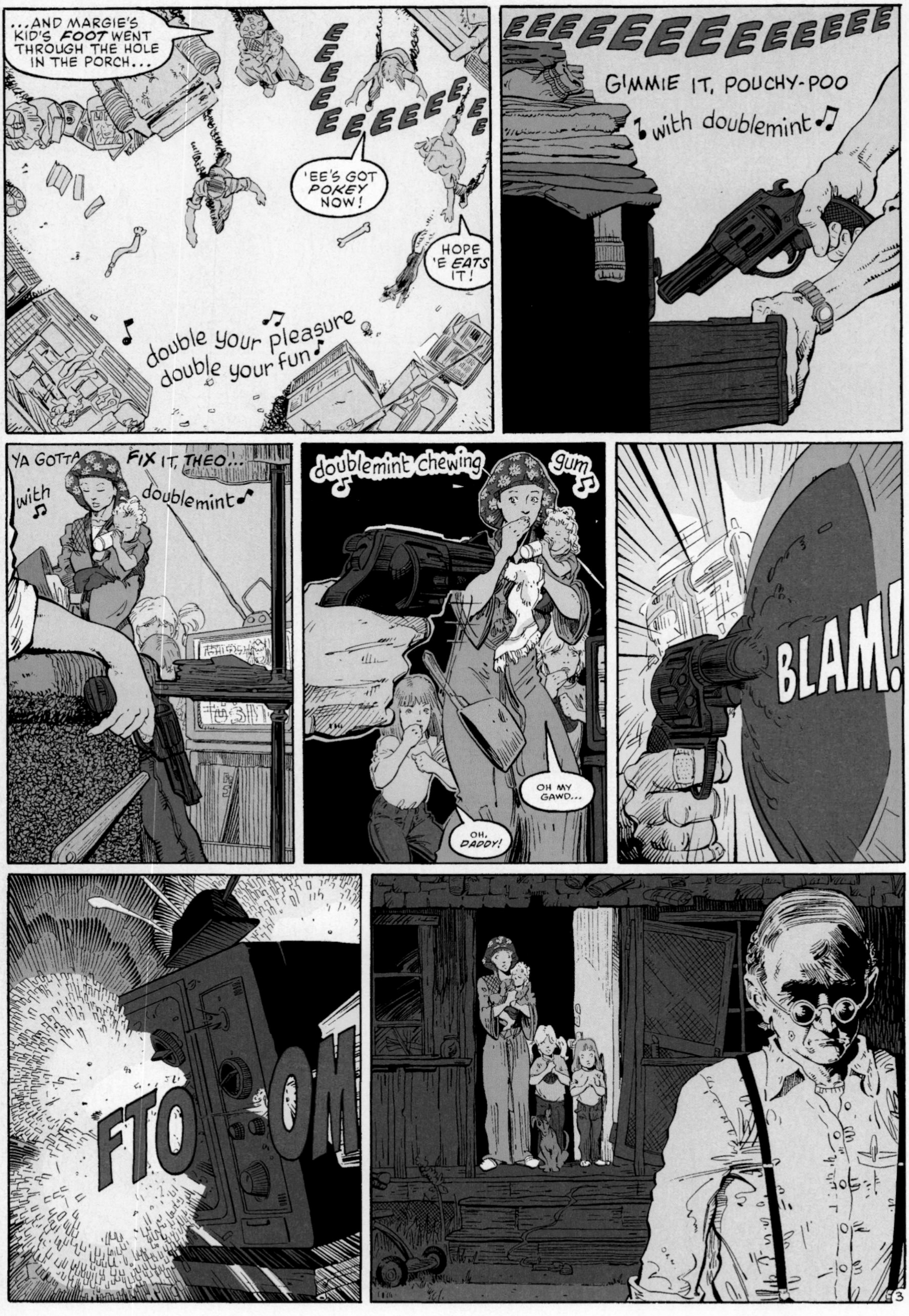
...AND MARGIE'S KID'S FOOT WENT THROUGH THE HOLE IN THE PORCH...
EEEEEEEEEEEE
'EE'S GOT POKEY NOW!
HOPE 'E EATS IT!
double your pleasure double your fun
EEEEEEEEEEEEE
GIMMIE IT, POUCHY-POO
with doublemint
YA GOTTA FIX IT, THEO...
with doublemint
doublemint chewing gum
OH MY GAWD...
OH, DADDY!
BLAM!
FTOOM

AND SOON...

WELL, HERE'S A BRIDGE TO JUMP OFF OF.

GOTTA HAVE SOME LAST THOUGHTS.

MY BACK HURTS. BETTER HOLD MY NOSE.

MAYBE I SHOULDN'T DO THIS.

BUT...NO MORE PISSING PUPPIES ...NO MORE BILLS... NO MORE NAGGING... NO MORE TV JINGLES...

HERE'S TO NEVER HAVING TO BRUSH MY TEETH AGAIN!

SPLOOSH!

DIDN'T WORK! CAN'T EVEN KILL MYSELF RIGHT.

OH MY, EXCUSE ME! WHO AM I SITTING ON!?

ANOTHER SUICIDE! AT LEAST HE MANAGED TO LAND RIGHT!

I THINK HE'S STILL ALIVE!

SHOULD I SAVE HIS LIFE?

WHAT IF ⸮UGH⸮ HE DOESN'T WANT ⸮HUF⸮ TO BE SAVED?

HE'LL PROBABLY KILL ME FOR THIS.

4

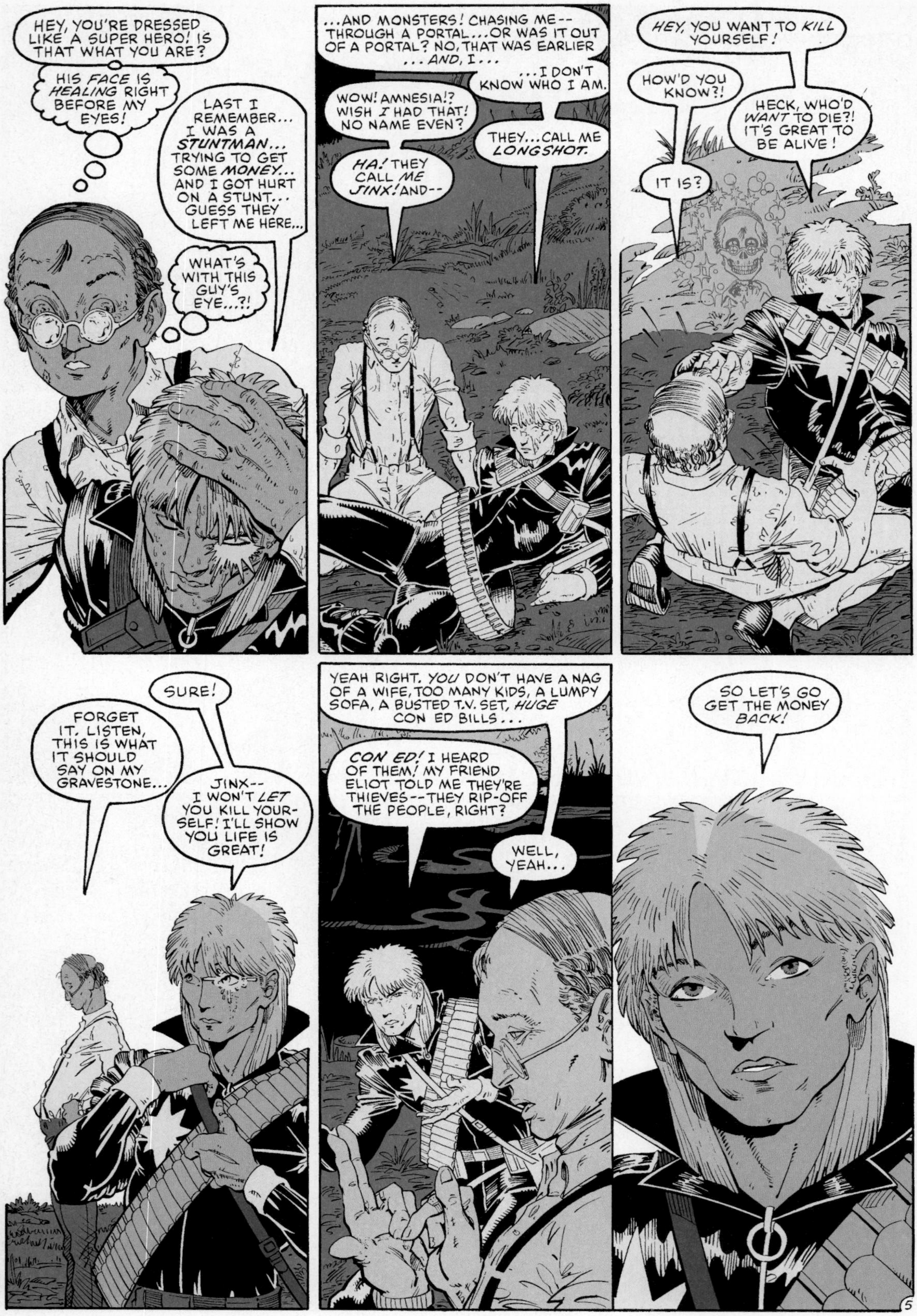
HEY, YOU'RE DRESSED LIKE A SUPER HERO! IS THAT WHAT YOU ARE?
HIS FACE IS HEALING RIGHT BEFORE MY EYES!
LAST I REMEMBER... I WAS A STUNTMAN... TRYING TO GET SOME MONEY... AND I GOT HURT ON A STUNT... GUESS THEY LEFT ME HERE...
WHAT'S WITH THIS GUY'S EYE...?!
...AND MONSTERS! CHASING ME-- THROUGH A PORTAL... OR WAS IT OUT OF A PORTAL? NO, THAT WAS EARLIER ...AND, I...
...I DON'T KNOW WHO I AM.
WOW! AMNESIA!? WISH I HAD THAT! NO NAME EVEN?
THEY... CALL ME LONGSHOT.
HA! THEY CALL ME JINX! AND--
HEY, YOU WANT TO KILL YOURSELF!
HOW'D YOU KNOW?!
HECK, WHO'D WANT TO DIE?! IT'S GREAT TO BE ALIVE!
IT IS?
FORGET IT. LISTEN, THIS IS WHAT IT SHOULD SAY ON MY GRAVESTONE...
SURE!
JINX-- I WON'T LET YOU KILL YOURSELF! I'LL SHOW YOU LIFE IS GREAT!
YEAH RIGHT. YOU DON'T HAVE A NAG OF A WIFE, TOO MANY KIDS, A LUMPY SOFA, A BUSTED T.V. SET, HUGE CON ED BILLS...
CON ED! I HEARD OF THEM! MY FRIEND ELIOT TOLD ME THEY'RE THIEVES--THEY RIP-OFF THE PEOPLE, RIGHT?
WELL, YEAH...
SO LET'S GO GET THE MONEY BACK!
5

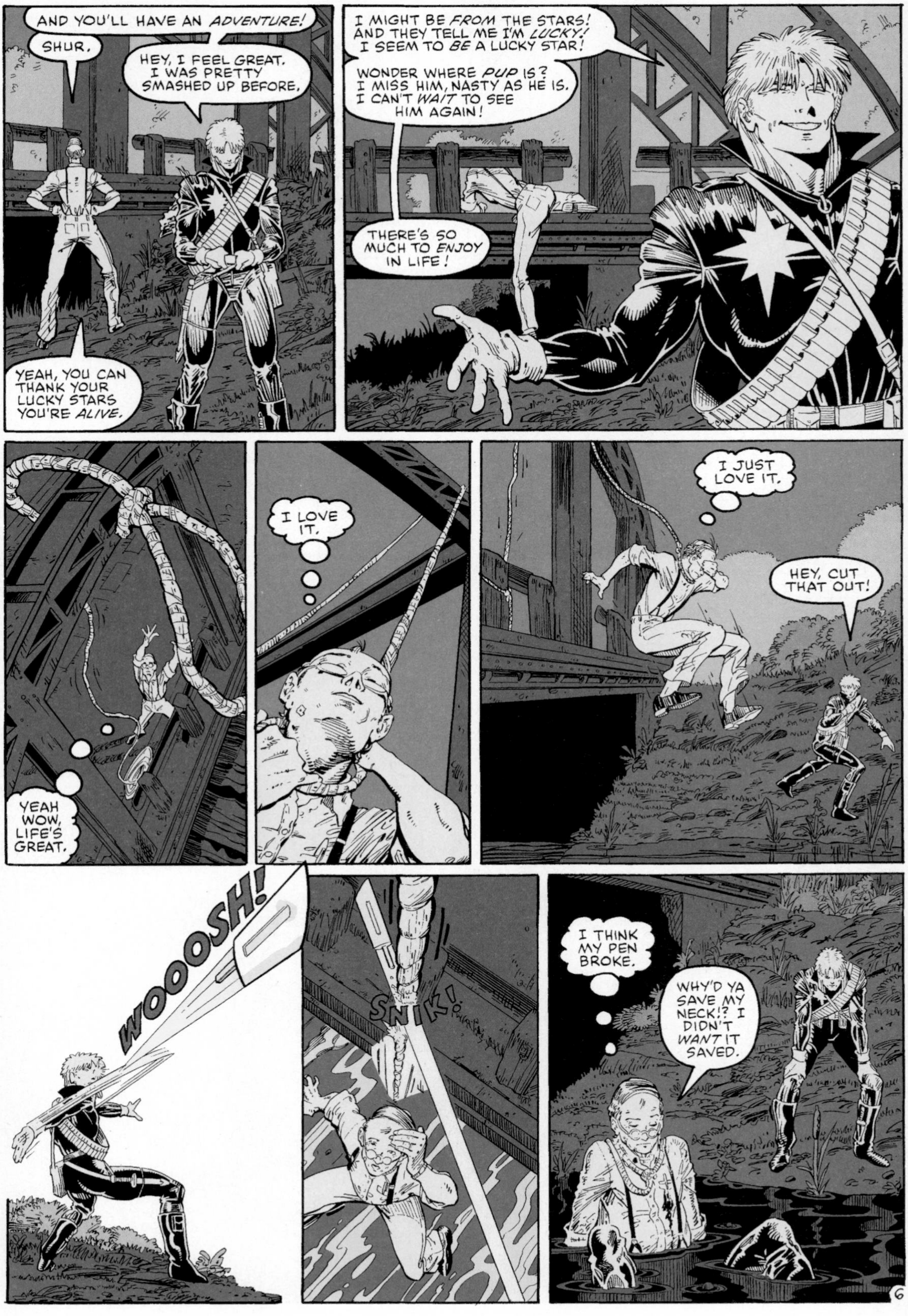
AND YOU'LL HAVE AN ADVENTURE!
SHUR.
HEY, I FEEL GREAT. I WAS PRETTY SMASHED UP BEFORE.
YEAH, YOU CAN THANK YOUR LUCKY STARS YOU'RE ALIVE.
I MIGHT BE FROM THE STARS! AND THEY TELL ME I'M LUCKY! I SEEM TO BE A LUCKY STAR!
WONDER WHERE PUP IS? I MISS HIM, NASTY AS HE IS. I CAN'T WAIT TO SEE HIM AGAIN!
THERE'S SO MUCH TO ENJOY IN LIFE!
YEAH WOW, LIFE'S GREAT.
I LOVE IT.
I JUST LOVE IT.
HEY, CUT THAT OUT!
WOOOSH!
SNIK!
I THINK MY PEN BROKE.
WHY'D YA SAVE MY NECK!? I DIDN'T WANT IT SAVED.
6

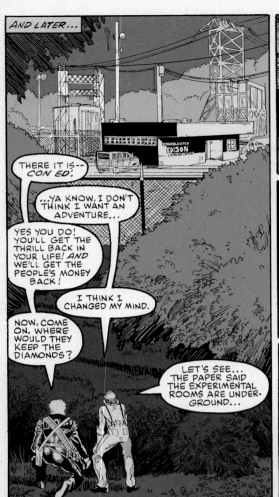

AND LATER...

THERE IT IS-- CON ED!

...YA KNOW, I DON'T THINK I WANT AN ADVENTURE...

YES YOU DO! YOU'LL GET THE THRILL BACK IN YOUR LIFE! AND WE'LL GET THE PEOPLE'S MONEY BACK!

I THINK I CHANGED MY MIND.

NOW, COME ON, WHERE WOULD THEY KEEP THE DIAMONDS?

LET'S SEE... THE PAPER SAID THE EXPERIMENTAL ROOMS ARE UNDER-GROUND...

GOOD. NOW BLACKEN YOUR FACE FOR CAMOUFLAGE...

OKAY.

...AND WE'LL LEAVE THE REST TO LUCK.

LUCK! YOU CAN'T TRUST SOMETHING AS FICKLE AND SNEAKY AS LUCK!

I CAN, AND SO CAN YOU!

WAITAMINUTE, WHY DO YOU THINK THEY CALL ME JINX!

I GOT THIS BLACK CLOUD FOLLOWING ME! HEY!

NO! YOU CAN DO ANYTHING IF YOU TRY!

JUST KEEP YOUR MOTIVES PURE, AND BELIEVE!

YEAH! WOW! YA JUST GOTTA BELIEVE!

OKAY, THAT'S THE SPIRIT. NOW QUIET, LET'S GO!

AN' KEEP YOUR BUTT DOWN.

I'M TRYING!

7

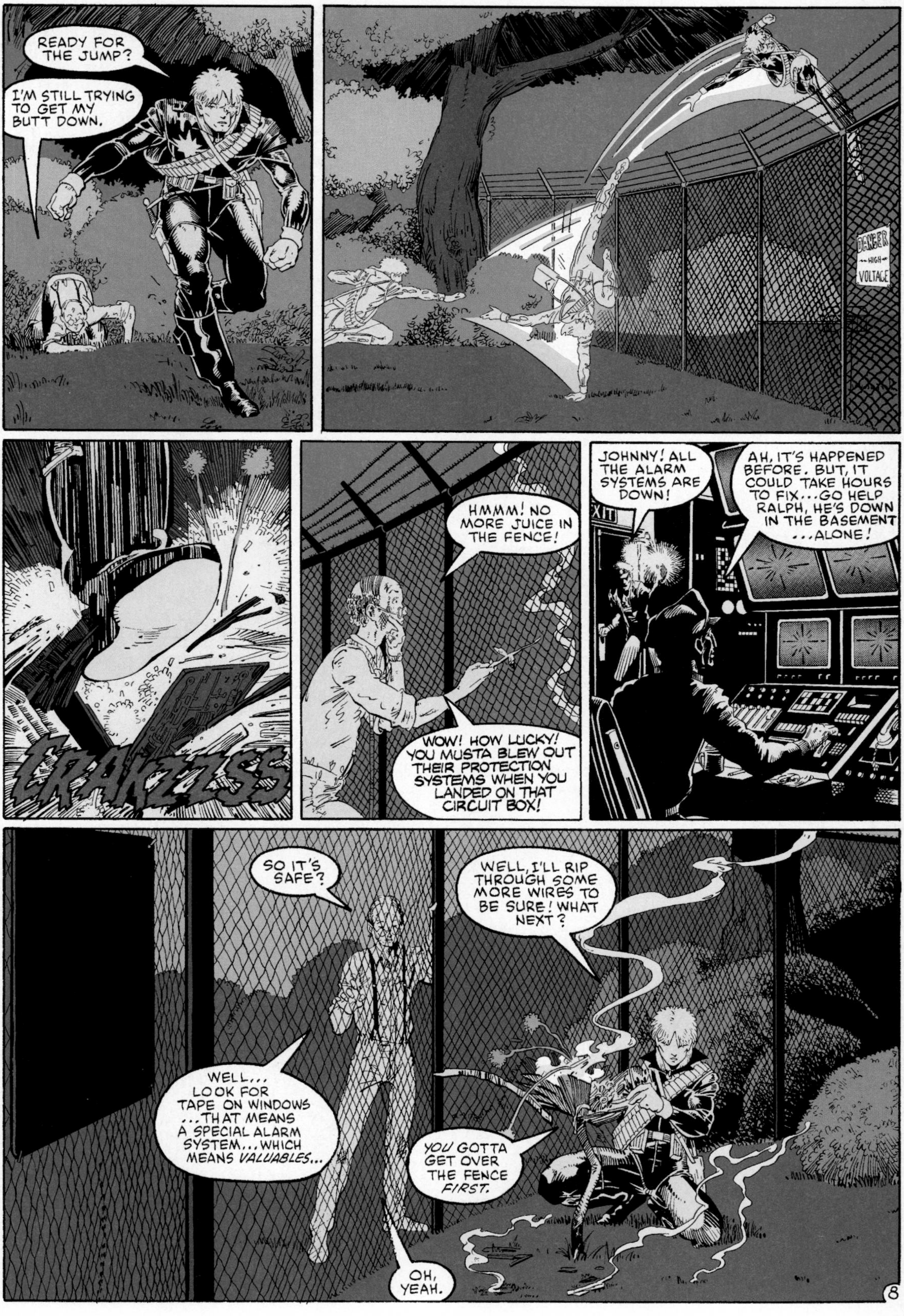

READY FOR THE JUMP?
I'M STILL TRYING TO GET MY BUTT DOWN.
DANGER HIGH VOLTAGE
CRAKZZSS
HMMM! NO MORE JUICE IN THE FENCE!
WOW! HOW LUCKY! YOU MUSTA BLEW OUT THEIR PROTECTION SYSTEMS WHEN YOU LANDED ON THAT CIRCUIT BOX!
JOHNNY! ALL THE ALARM SYSTEMS ARE DOWN!
AH, IT'S HAPPENED BEFORE. BUT, IT COULD TAKE HOURS TO FIX...GO HELP RALPH, HE'S DOWN IN THE BASEMENT ...ALONE!
SO IT'S SAFE?
WELL, I'LL RIP THROUGH SOME MORE WIRES TO BE SURE! WHAT NEXT?
WELL... LOOK FOR TAPE ON WINDOWS ...THAT MEANS A SPECIAL ALARM SYSTEM...WHICH MEANS *VALUABLES*...
YOU GOTTA GET OVER THE FENCE *FIRST.*
OH, YEAH.
8

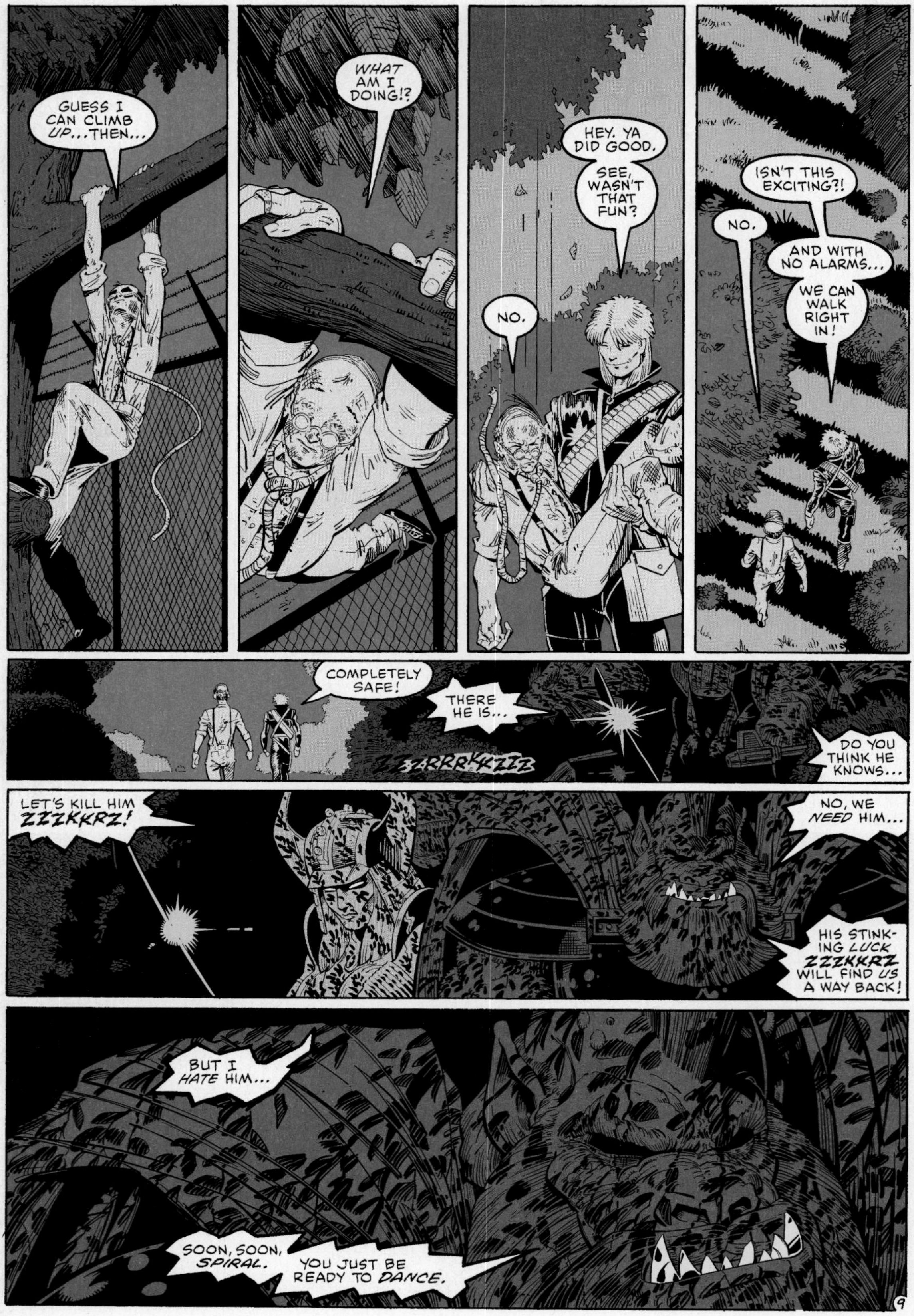
GUESS I CAN CLIMB UP...THEN...
WHAT AM I DOING!?
HEY. YA DID GOOD.
SEE, WASN'T THAT FUN?
NO.
ISN'T THIS EXCITING?!
NO.
AND WITH NO ALARMS...
WE CAN WALK RIGHT IN!
COMPLETELY SAFE!
THERE HE IS...
ZZRRRKKZZZ
DO YOU THINK HE KNOWS...
LET'S KILL HIM ZZZKKRZ!
NO, WE NEED HIM...
HIS STINKING LUCK ZZZKKRZ WILL FIND US A WAY BACK!
BUT I HATE HIM...
SOON, SOON, SPIRAL.
YOU JUST BE READY TO DANCE.
9

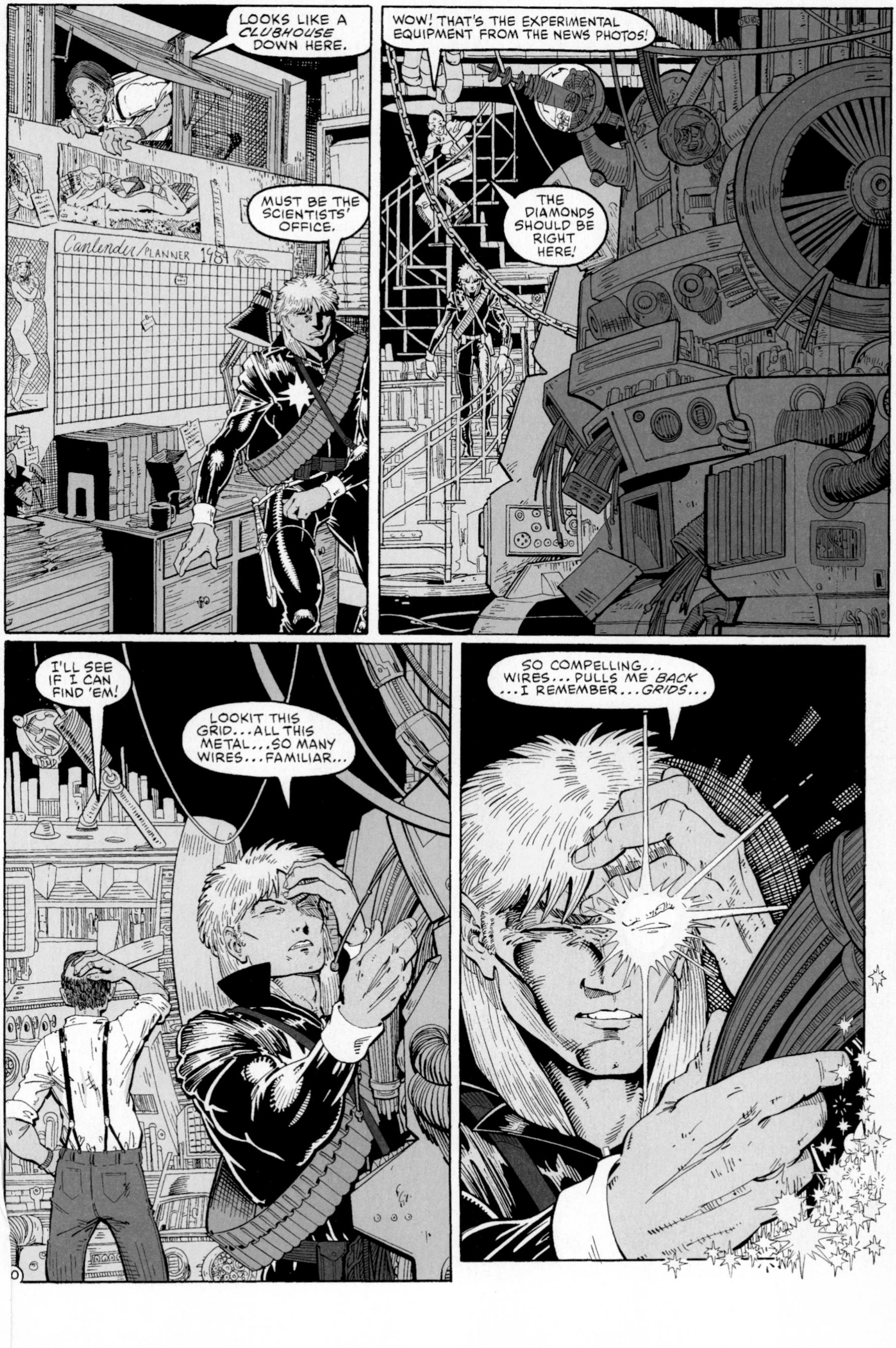
LOOKS LIKE A *CLUBHOUSE* DOWN HERE.
Canlender/PLANNER 1984
MUST BE THE SCIENTISTS' OFFICE.
WOW! THAT'S THE EXPERIMENTAL EQUIPMENT FROM THE NEWS PHOTOS!
THE DIAMONDS SHOULD BE RIGHT HERE!
I'LL SEE IF I CAN FIND 'EM!
LOOKIT THIS GRID...ALL THIS METAL...SO MANY WIRES...FAMILIAR...
SO COMPELLING... WIRES... PULLS ME *BACK* ...I REMEMBER... *GRIDS*...

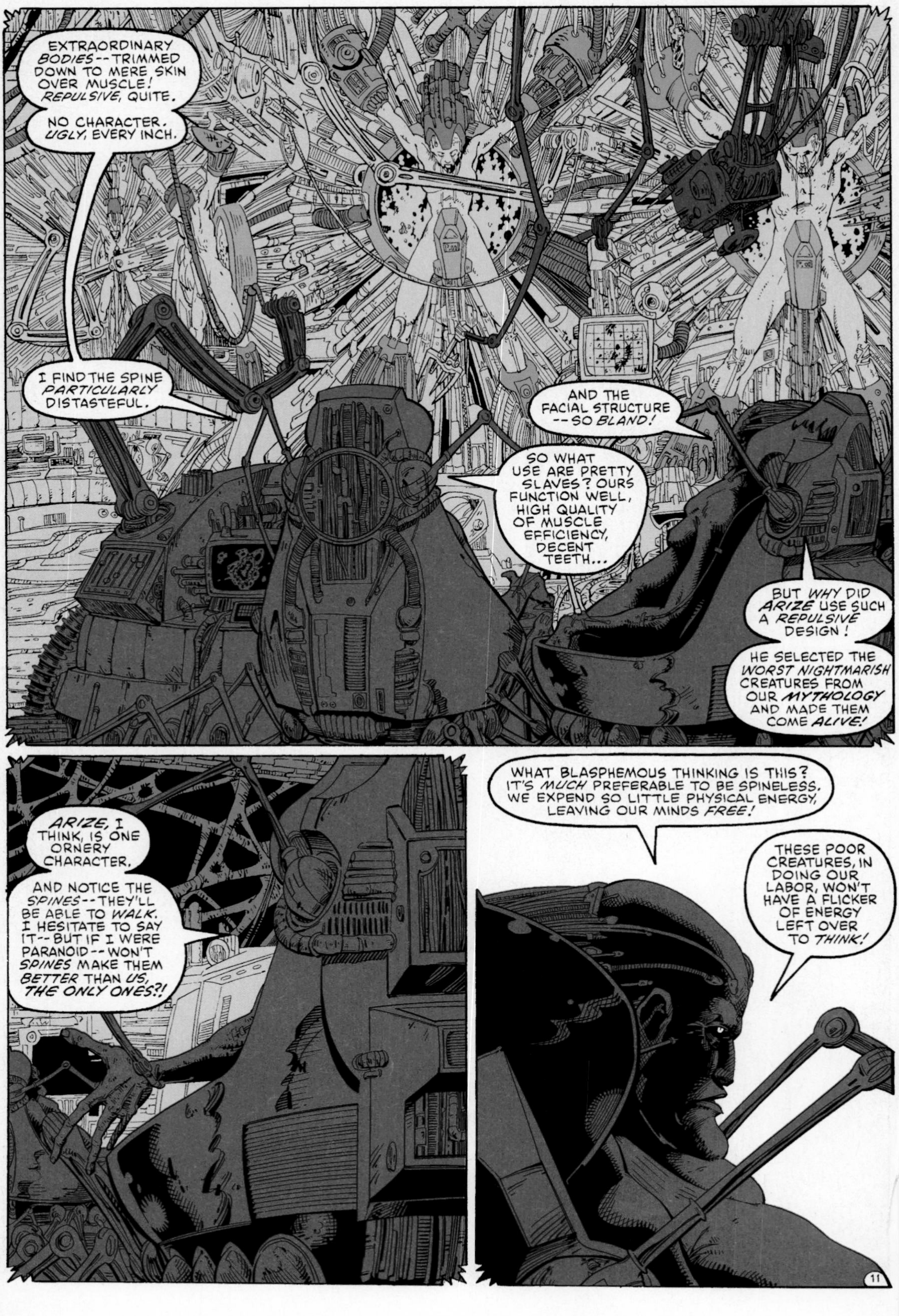
EXTRAORDINARY BODIES--TRIMMED DOWN TO MERE SKIN OVER MUSCLE! REPULSIVE, QUITE.
NO CHARACTER. UGLY, EVERY INCH.
I FIND THE SPINE PARTICULARLY DISTASTEFUL.
AND THE FACIAL STRUCTURE --SO BLAND!
SO WHAT USE ARE PRETTY SLAVES? OURS FUNCTION WELL, HIGH QUALITY OF MUSCLE EFFICIENCY, DECENT TEETH...
BUT WHY DID ARIZE USE SUCH A REPULSIVE DESIGN!
HE SELECTED THE WORST NIGHTMARISH CREATURES FROM OUR MYTHOLOGY AND MADE THEM COME ALIVE!
ARIZE, I THINK, IS ONE ORNERY CHARACTER.
AND NOTICE THE SPINES--THEY'LL BE ABLE TO WALK. I HESITATE TO SAY IT--BUT IF I WERE PARANOID--WON'T SPINES MAKE THEM BETTER THAN US, THE ONLY ONES?!
WHAT BLASPHEMOUS THINKING IS THIS? IT'S MUCH PREFERABLE TO BE SPINELESS. WE EXPEND SO LITTLE PHYSICAL ENERGY, LEAVING OUR MINDS FREE!
THESE POOR CREATURES, IN DOING OUR LABOR, WON'T HAVE A FLICKER OF ENERGY LEFT OVER TO THINK!
11

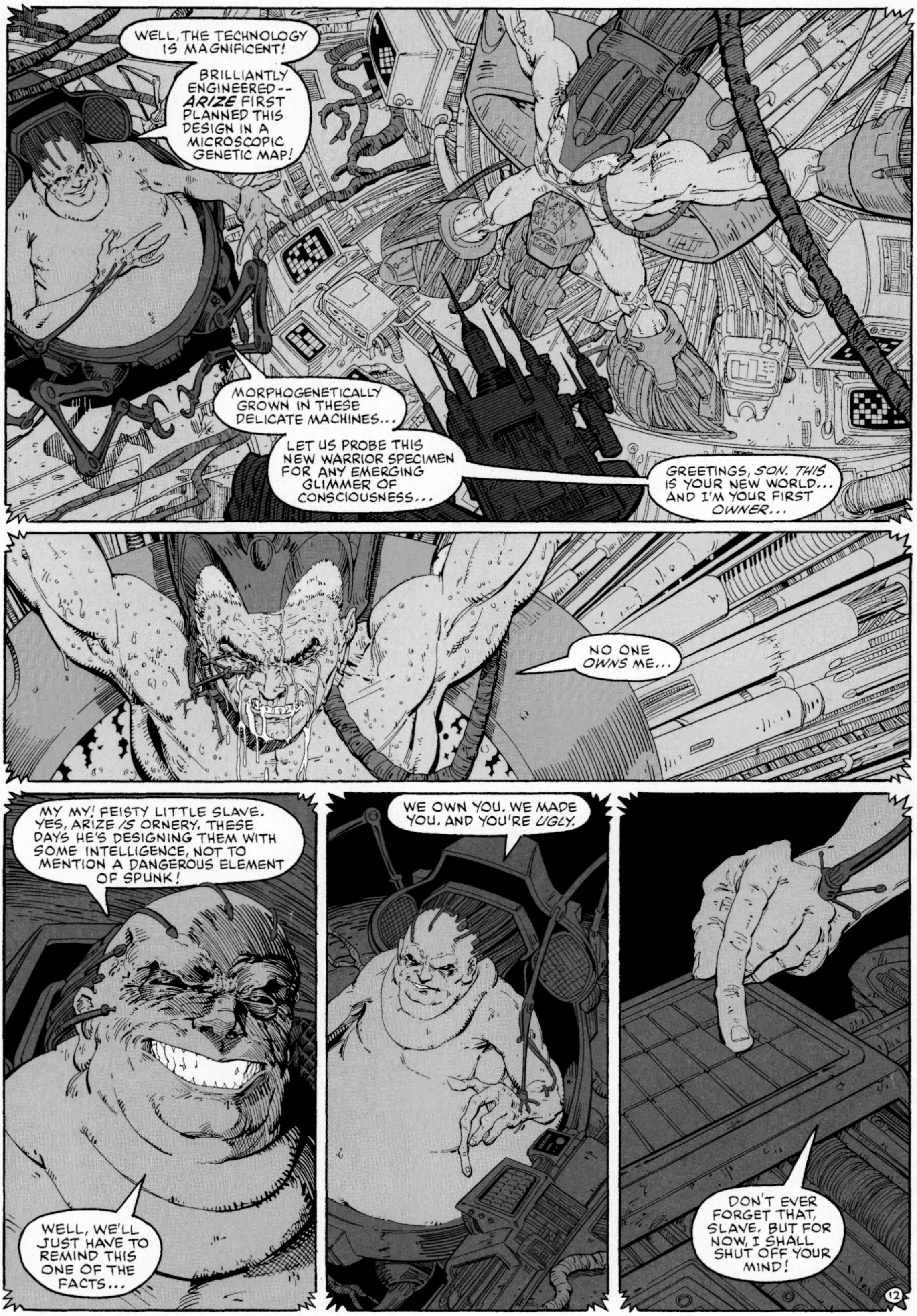
WELL, THE TECHNOLOGY IS MAGNIFICENT!
BRILLIANTLY ENGINEERED-- ARIZE FIRST PLANNED THIS DESIGN IN A MICROSCOPIC GENETIC MAP!
MORPHOGENETICALLY GROWN IN THESE DELICATE MACHINES...
LET US PROBE THIS NEW WARRIOR SPECIMEN FOR ANY EMERGING GLIMMER OF CONSCIOUSNESS...
GREETINGS, SON. THIS IS YOUR NEW WORLD... AND I'M YOUR FIRST OWNER...
NO ONE OWNS ME...
MY MY! FEISTY LITTLE SLAVE. YES, ARIZE IS ORNERY. THESE DAYS HE'S DESIGNING THEM WITH SOME INTELLIGENCE, NOT TO MENTION A DANGEROUS ELEMENT OF SPUNK!
WELL, WE'LL JUST HAVE TO REMIND THIS ONE OF THE FACTS...
WE OWN YOU. WE MADE YOU. AND YOU'RE UGLY.
DON'T EVER FORGET THAT, SLAVE. BUT FOR NOW, I SHALL SHUT OFF YOUR MIND!
12

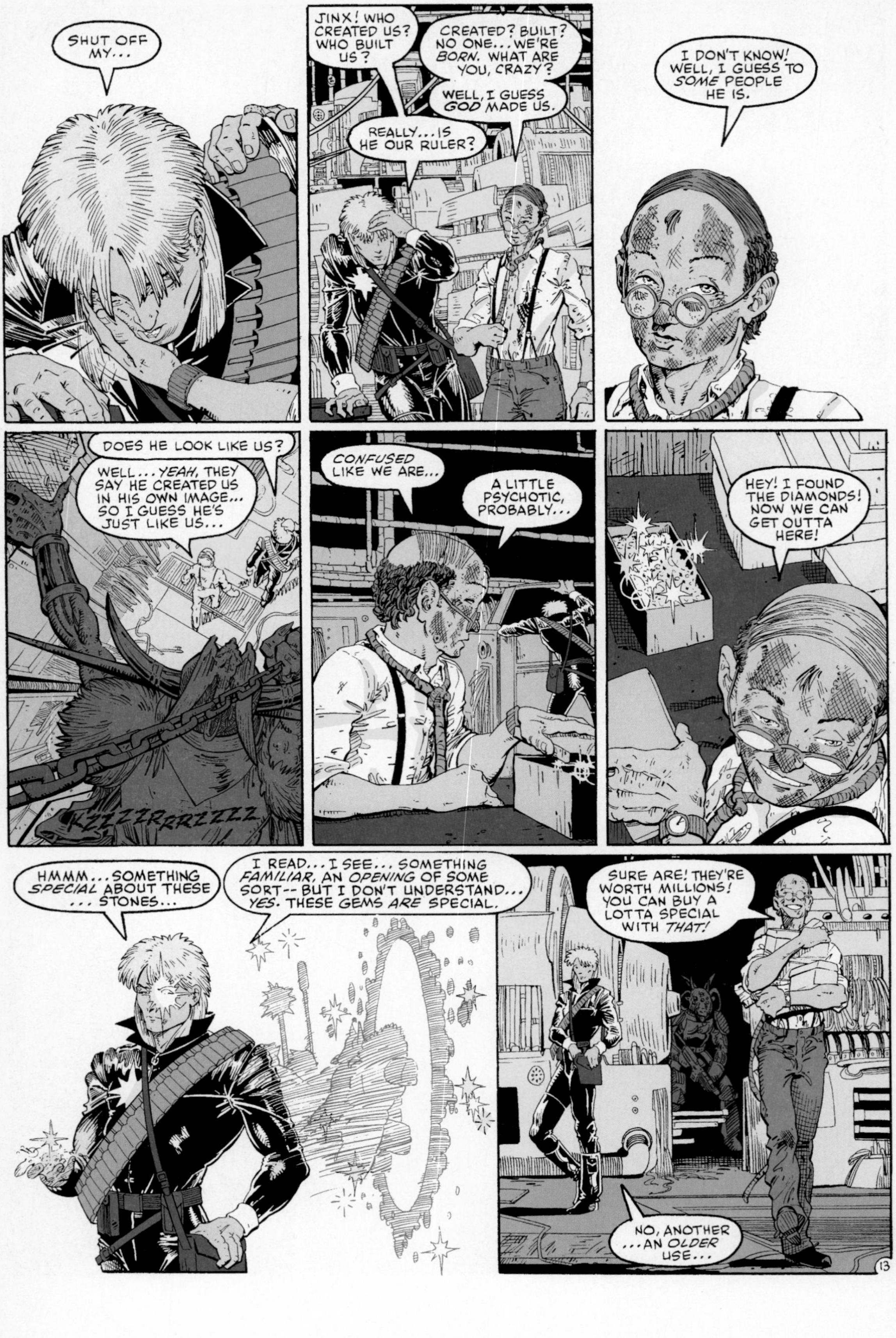
SHUT OFF MY...
JINX! WHO CREATED US? WHO BUILT US?
CREATED? BUILT? NO ONE... WE'RE BORN. WHAT ARE YOU, CRAZY?
WELL, I GUESS GOD MADE US.
REALLY... IS HE OUR RULER?
I DON'T KNOW! WELL, I GUESS TO SOME PEOPLE HE IS.
DOES HE LOOK LIKE US?
WELL... YEAH, THEY SAY HE CREATED US IN HIS OWN IMAGE... SO I GUESS HE'S JUST LIKE US...
KZZZZRRRRZZZZZ
CONFUSED LIKE WE ARE...
A LITTLE PSYCHOTIC, PROBABLY...
HEY! I FOUND THE DIAMONDS! NOW WE CAN GET OUTTA HERE!
HMMM... SOMETHING SPECIAL ABOUT THESE ... STONES...
I READ... I SEE... SOMETHING FAMILIAR, AN OPENING OF SOME SORT-- BUT I DON'T UNDERSTAND... YES. THESE GEMS ARE SPECIAL.
SURE ARE! THEY'RE WORTH MILLIONS! YOU CAN BUY A LOTTA SPECIAL WITH THAT!
NO, ANOTHER ...AN OLDER USE...
13

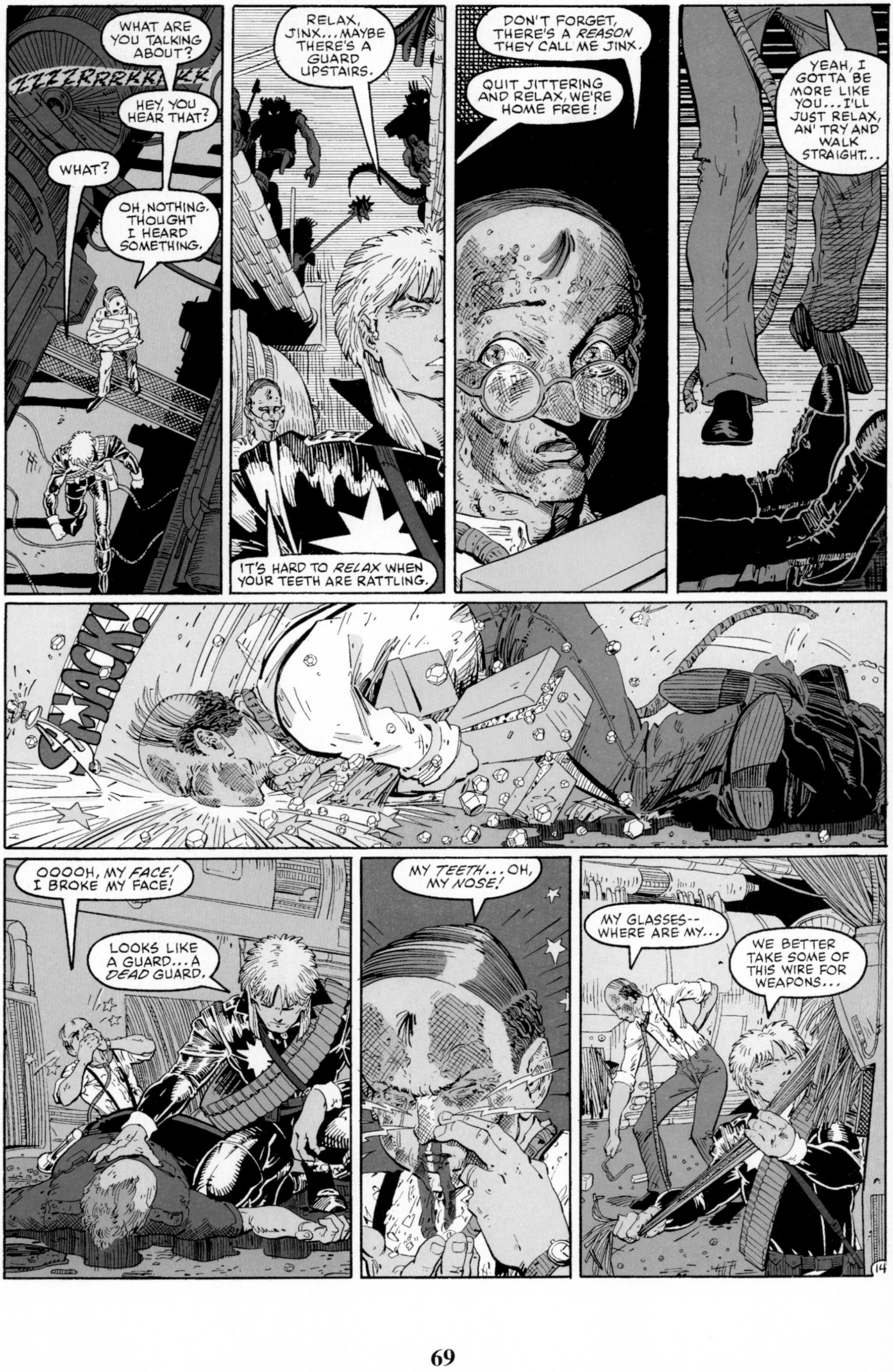
WHAT ARE YOU TALKING ABOUT?
ZZZZRRRRKKK KK
HEY, YOU HEAR THAT?
WHAT?
OH, NOTHING. THOUGHT I HEARD SOMETHING.
RELAX, JINX... MAYBE THERE'S A GUARD UPSTAIRS.
IT'S HARD TO RELAX WHEN YOUR TEETH ARE RATTLING.
DON'T FORGET, THERE'S A REASON THEY CALL ME JINX.
QUIT JITTERING AND RELAX, WE'RE HOME FREE!
YEAH, I GOTTA BE MORE LIKE YOU... I'LL JUST RELAX, AN' TRY AND WALK STRAIGHT...
CHACK!
OOOOH, MY FACE! I BROKE MY FACE!
LOOKS LIKE A GUARD... A DEAD GUARD.
MY TEETH... OH, MY NOSE!
MY GLASSES-- WHERE ARE MY...
WE BETTER TAKE SOME OF THIS WIRE FOR WEAPONS...
14

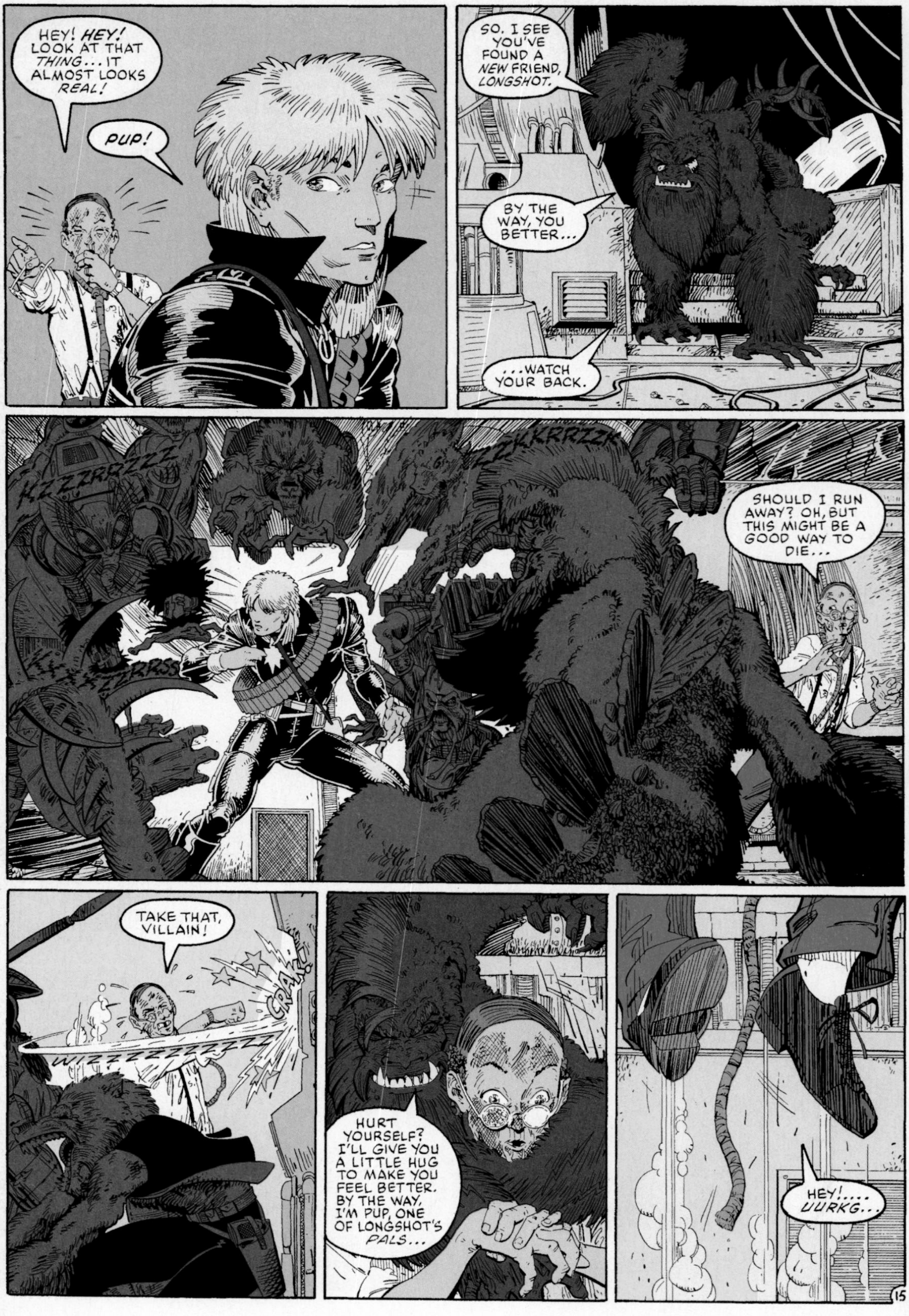
HEY! HEY! LOOK AT THAT THING... IT ALMOST LOOKS REAL!
PUP!
SO. I SEE YOU'VE FOUND A NEW FRIEND, LONGSHOT.
BY THE WAY, YOU BETTER...
...WATCH YOUR BACK.
KZZZRRZZZ
ZZZKRRZZK
SHOULD I RUN AWAY? OH, BUT THIS MIGHT BE A GOOD WAY TO DIE...
TAKE THAT, VILLAIN!
CRAK!
WIZZZZZZZZZZZ
HURT YOURSELF? I'LL GIVE YOU A LITTLE HUG TO MAKE YOU FEEL BETTER. BY THE WAY, I'M PUP, ONE OF LONGSHOT'S PALS...
HEY!.... UURKG...
15

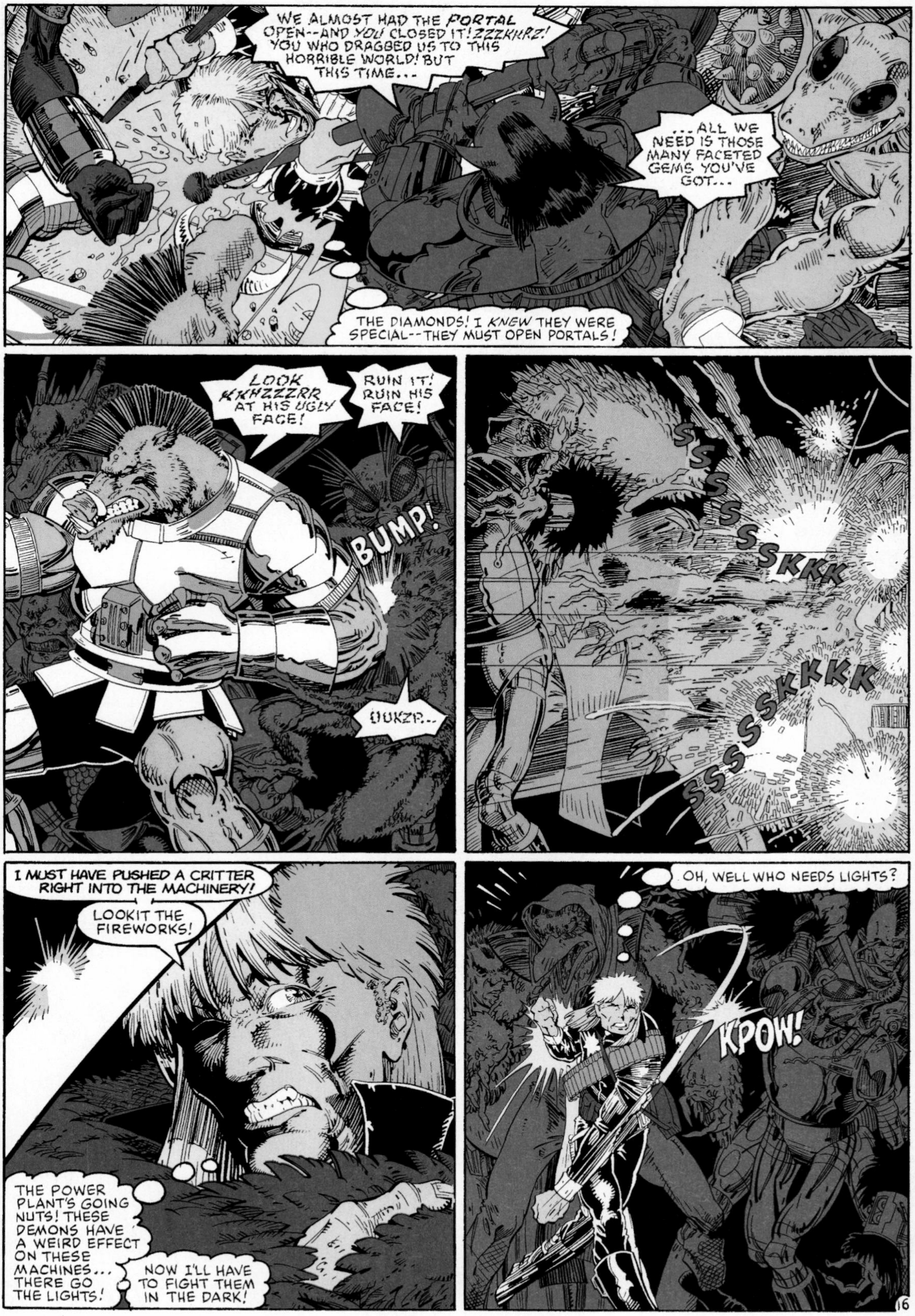

WE ALMOST HAD THE PORTAL OPEN--AND YOU CLOSED IT! ZZZKKRZ! YOU WHO DRAGGED US TO THIS HORRIBLE WORLD! BUT THIS TIME...
...ALL WE NEED IS THOSE MANY FACETED GEMS YOU'VE GOT...
THE DIAMONDS! I KNEW THEY WERE SPECIAL--THEY MUST OPEN PORTALS!
LOOK KKHZZZRR AT HIS UGLY FACE!
RUIN IT! RUIN HIS FACE!
BUMP!
UUKZP...
SSSSSKKK
SSSSSSKKKKK
I MUST HAVE PUSHED A CRITTER RIGHT INTO THE MACHINERY!
LOOKIT THE FIREWORKS!
THE POWER PLANT'S GOING NUTS! THESE DEMONS HAVE A WEIRD EFFECT ON THESE MACHINES... THERE GO THE LIGHTS!
NOW I'LL HAVE TO FIGHT THEM IN THE DARK!
OH, WELL WHO NEEDS LIGHTS?
KPOW!
16

LOOK, LET ME SHOW YOU...

SWITCH CHANNELS! I WANT TO WATCH...

LET'S SEE THOSE LOVELY FLOWERS...

WHEN I FINISH PAINTING THIS...

...THE LIGHTS...

OH, NO!

HARRY, WATCH OUT!

...WHAT'S FLICKERING...

EEEEEEEEEEE!

I'M BLIND!

STOP IT!

OUCH!

CRBASH!

GET OUT OF MY WAY!

NO!   DON'T!

CITY-WIDE BLACKOUT!

MANHATTAN'S IN THE DARK! IT'LL BE CHAOS! CRIME-RATE'S GONNA SKYROCKET!

GO AHEAD, JAMESON, SAY IT.

MUST BE SPIDER-MAN'S FAULT!

SSK

SSSSHK

SSSSHK

SSSSHK

COME ON, LONGSHOT, GET LUCKY!

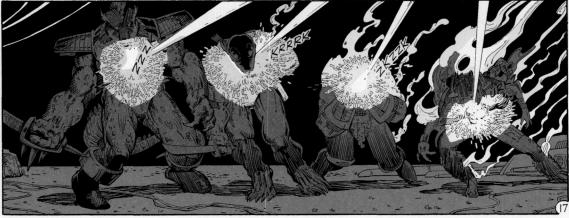

ZZZ

KRRRK

ZZZK

ZZZK

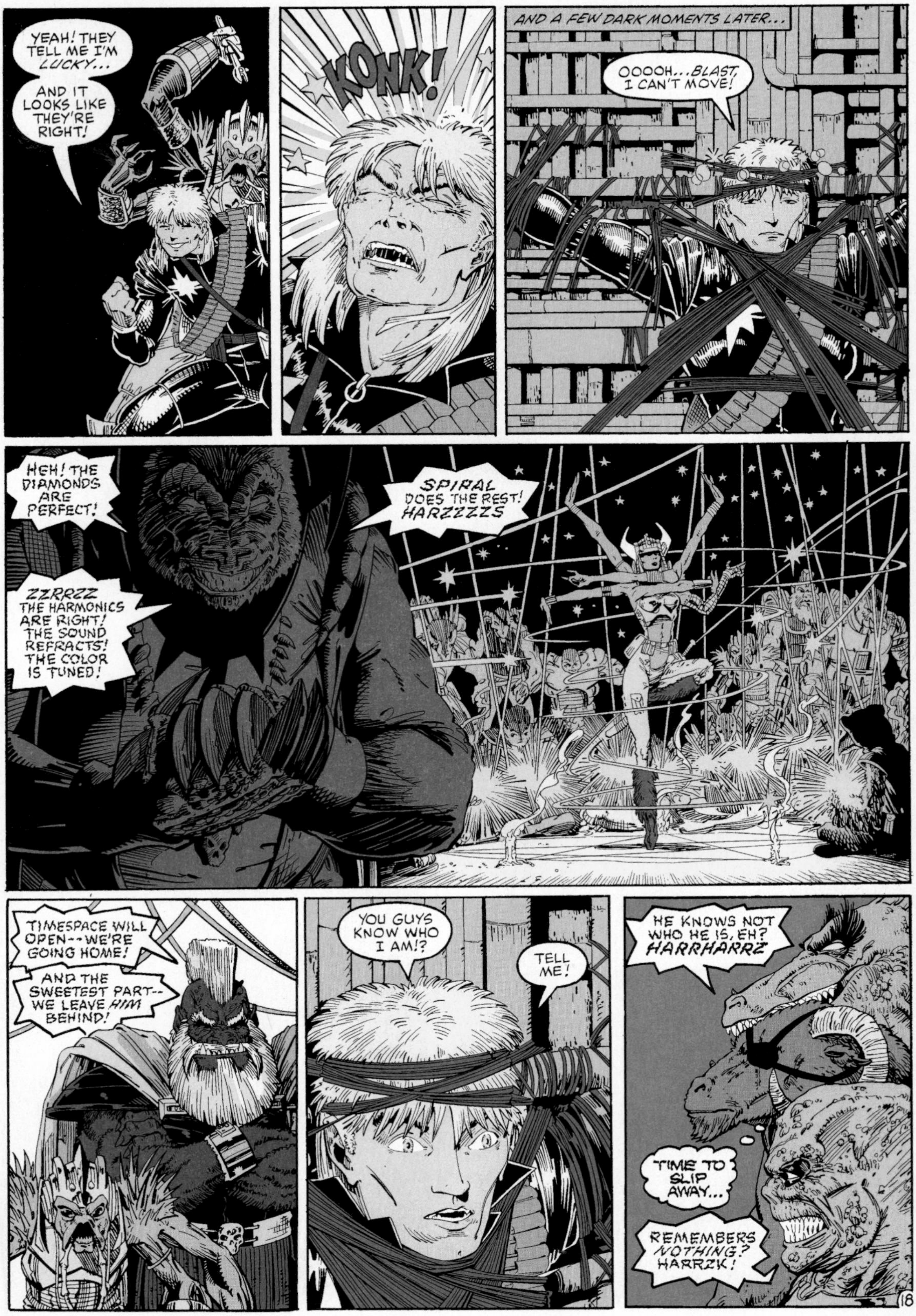
YEAH! THEY TELL ME I'M LUCKY...
AND IT LOOKS LIKE THEY'RE RIGHT!
KONK!
AND A FEW DARK MOMENTS LATER...
OOOOH... BLAST, I CAN'T MOVE!
HEH! THE DIAMONDS ARE PERFECT!
ZZRRZZ THE HARMONICS ARE RIGHT! THE SOUND REFRACTS! THE COLOR IS TUNED!
SPIRAL DOES THE REST! HARZZZZS
TIMESPACE WILL OPEN--WE'RE GOING HOME!
AND THE SWEETEST PART--WE LEAVE HIM BEHIND!
YOU GUYS KNOW WHO I AM!?
TELL ME!
HE KNOWS NOT WHO HE IS, EH? HARRHARRZ
TIME TO SLIP AWAY...
REMEMBERS NOTHING? HARRZK!
18

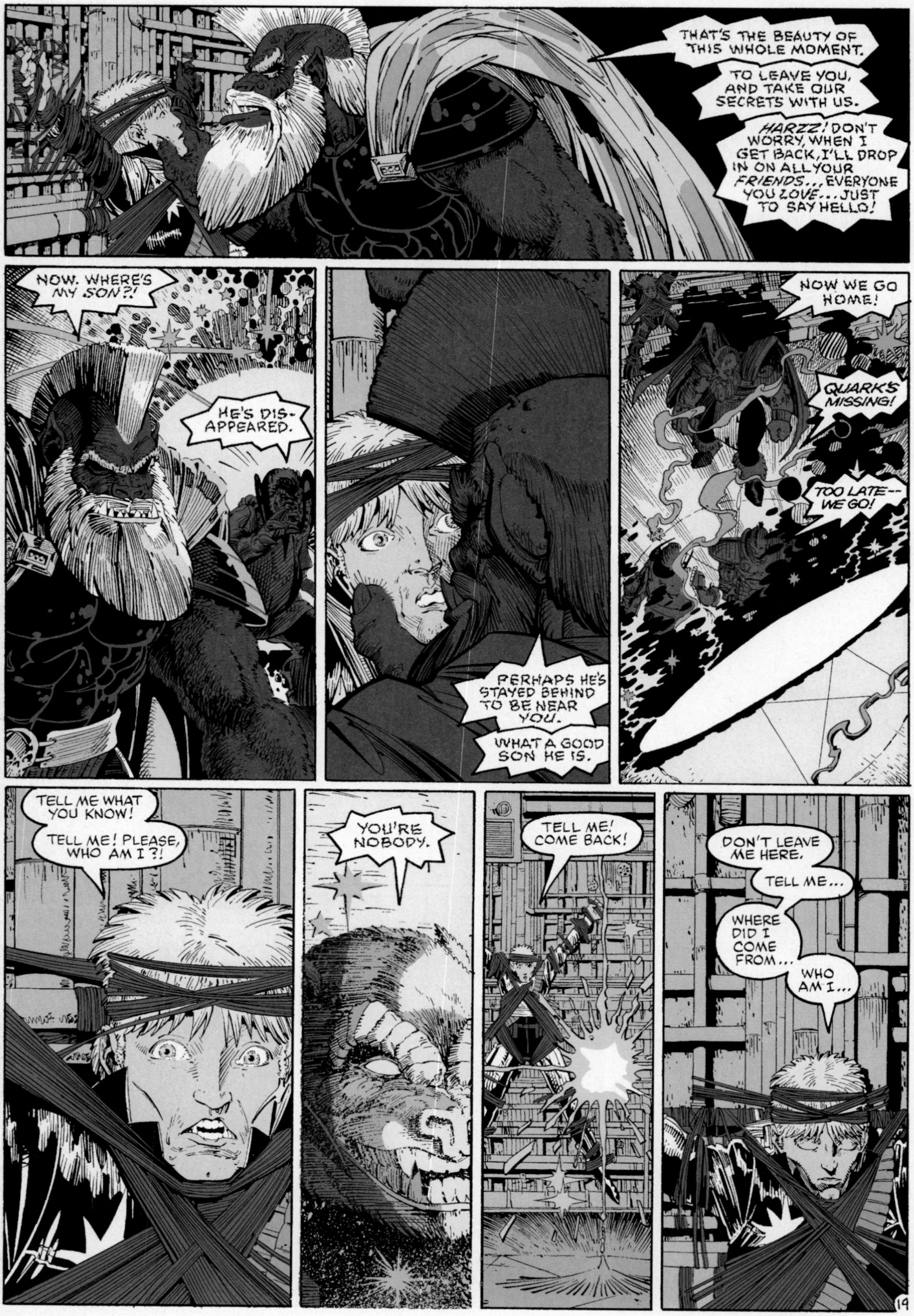
THAT'S THE BEAUTY OF THIS WHOLE MOMENT.
TO LEAVE YOU, AND TAKE OUR SECRETS WITH US.
HARZZ! DON'T WORRY, WHEN I GET BACK, I'LL DROP IN ON ALL YOUR FRIENDS... EVERYONE YOU LOVE... JUST TO SAY HELLO!
NOW. WHERE'S MY SON?!
HE'S DIS-APPEARED.
PERHAPS HE'S STAYED BEHIND TO BE NEAR YOU.
WHAT A GOOD SON HE IS.
NOW WE GO HOME!
QUARK'S MISSING!
TOO LATE-- WE GO!
TELL ME WHAT YOU KNOW!
TELL ME! PLEASE, WHO AM I?!
YOU'RE NOBODY.
TELL ME! COME BACK!
DON'T LEAVE ME HERE.
TELL ME...
WHERE DID I COME FROM...
WHO AM I...
19

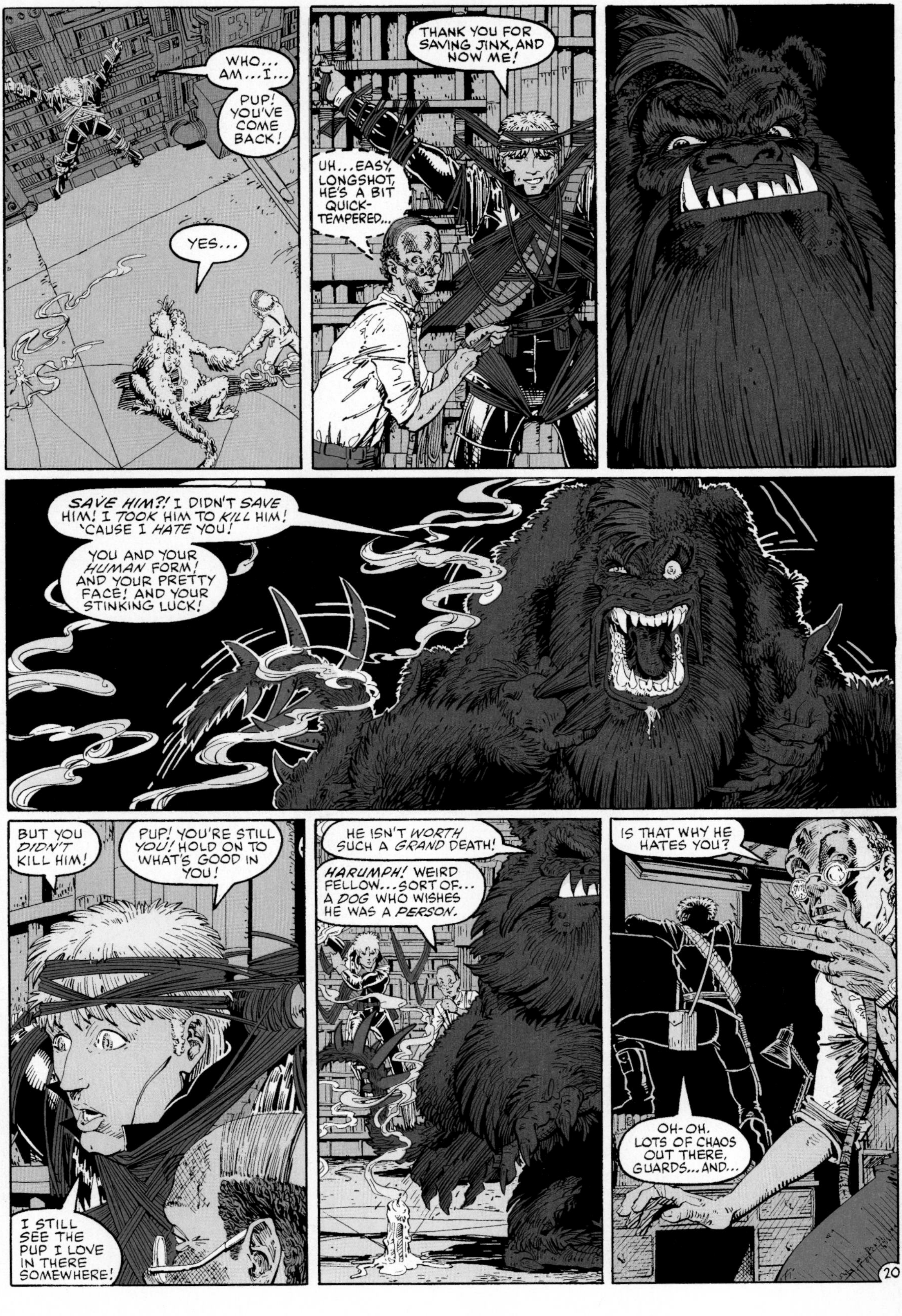
WHO... AM...I...
PUP! YOU'VE COME BACK!
YES...
THANK YOU FOR SAVING JINX, AND NOW ME!
UH...EASY, LONGSHOT, HE'S A BIT QUICK-TEMPERED...
SAVE HIM?! I DIDN'T SAVE HIM! I TOOK HIM TO KILL HIM! 'CAUSE I HATE YOU!
YOU AND YOUR HUMAN FORM! AND YOUR PRETTY FACE! AND YOUR STINKING LUCK!
BUT YOU DIDN'T KILL HIM!
PUP! YOU'RE STILL YOU! HOLD ON TO WHAT'S GOOD IN YOU!
I STILL SEE THE PUP I LOVE IN THERE SOMEWHERE!
HE ISN'T WORTH SUCH A GRAND DEATH!
HARUMPH! WEIRD FELLOW...SORT OF... A DOG WHO WISHES HE WAS A PERSON.
IS THAT WHY HE HATES YOU?
OH-OH. LOTS OF CHAOS OUT THERE, GUARDS...AND...
20

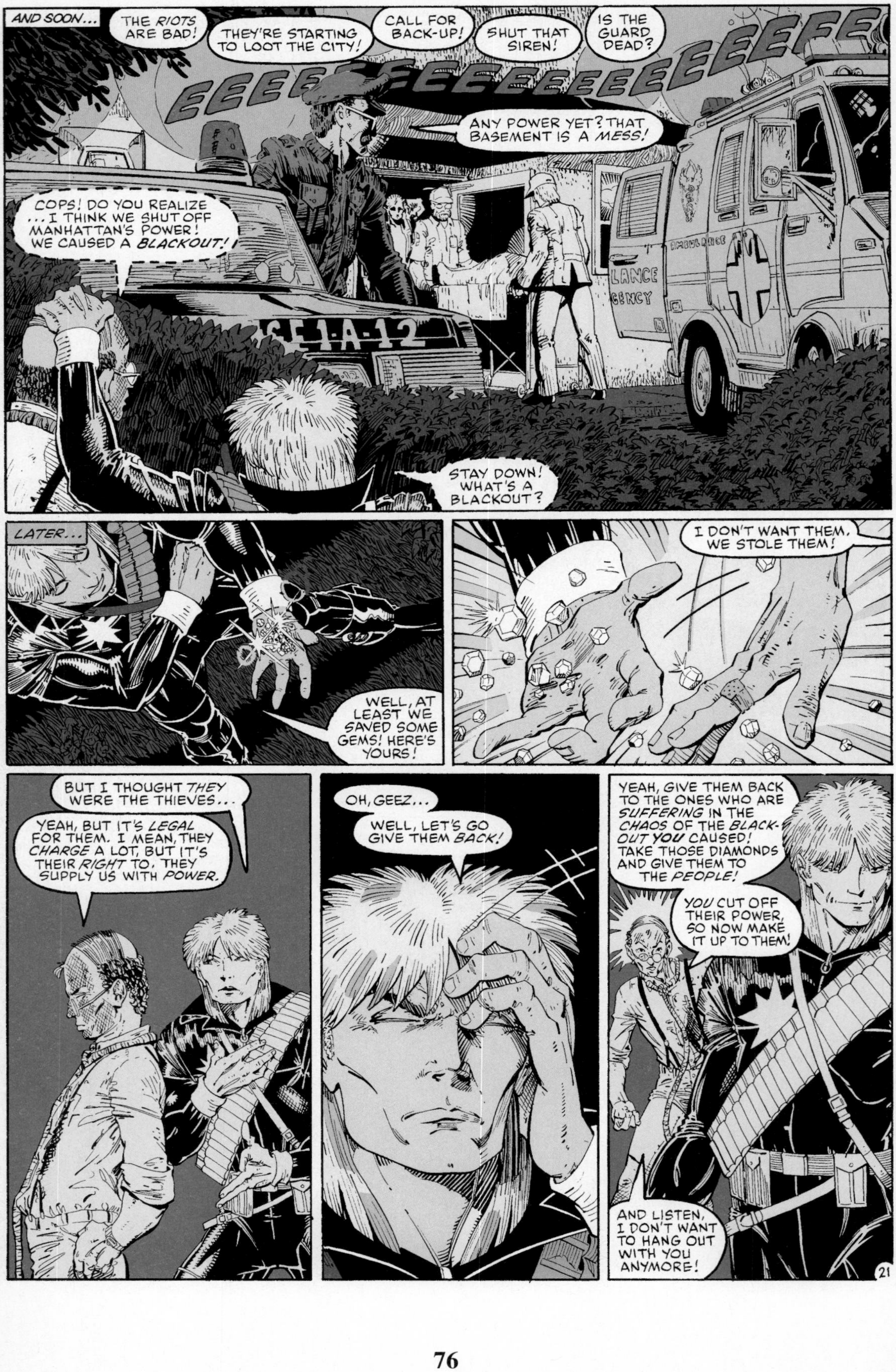
AND SOON...
THE RIOTS ARE BAD!
THEY'RE STARTING TO LOOT THE CITY!
CALL FOR BACK-UP!
SHUT THAT SIREN!
IS THE GUARD DEAD?
EEEEEEEEEEEEEEEEEEFE
ANY POWER YET? THAT BASEMENT IS A MESS!
COPS! DO YOU REALIZE ...I THINK WE SHUT OFF MANHATTAN'S POWER! WE CAUSED A BLACKOUT!
STAY DOWN! WHAT'S A BLACKOUT?
LATER...
WELL, AT LEAST WE SAVED SOME GEMS! HERE'S YOURS!
I DON'T WANT THEM. WE STOLE THEM!
BUT I THOUGHT THEY WERE THE THIEVES...
YEAH, BUT IT'S LEGAL FOR THEM. I MEAN, THEY CHARGE A LOT, BUT IT'S THEIR RIGHT TO. THEY SUPPLY US WITH POWER.
OH, GEEZ...
WELL, LET'S GO GIVE THEM BACK!
YEAH, GIVE THEM BACK TO THE ONES WHO ARE SUFFERING IN THE CHAOS OF THE BLACK-OUT YOU CAUSED! TAKE THOSE DIAMONDS AND GIVE THEM TO THE PEOPLE!
YOU CUT OFF THEIR POWER, SO NOW MAKE IT UP TO THEM!
AND LISTEN, I DON'T WANT TO HANG OUT WITH YOU ANYMORE!
21

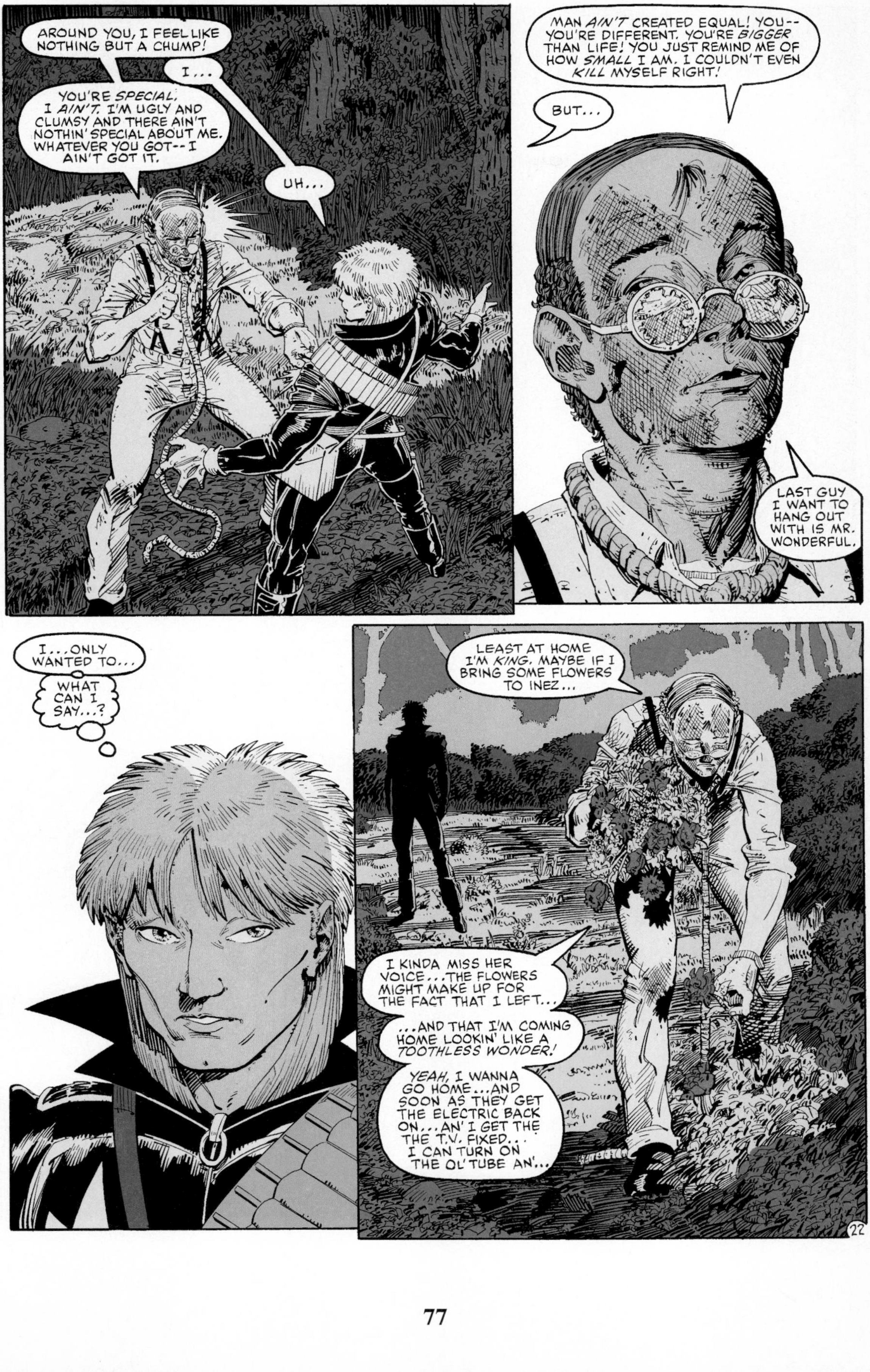
AROUND YOU, I FEEL LIKE NOTHING BUT A CHUMP!
I...
YOU'RE SPECIAL, I AIN'T. I'M UGLY AND CLUMSY AND THERE AIN'T NOTHIN' SPECIAL ABOUT ME. WHATEVER YOU GOT-- I AIN'T GOT IT.
UH...
MAN AIN'T CREATED EQUAL! YOU-- YOU'RE DIFFERENT. YOU'RE BIGGER THAN LIFE! YOU JUST REMIND ME OF HOW SMALL I AM. I COULDN'T EVEN KILL MYSELF RIGHT!
BUT...
LAST GUY I WANT TO HANG OUT WITH IS MR. WONDERFUL.
I...ONLY WANTED TO...
WHAT CAN I SAY...?
LEAST AT HOME I'M KING. MAYBE IF I BRING SOME FLOWERS TO INEZ...
I KINDA MISS HER VOICE...THE FLOWERS MIGHT MAKE UP FOR THE FACT THAT I LEFT...
...AND THAT I'M COMING HOME LOOKIN' LIKE A TOOTHLESS WONDER!
YEAH, I WANNA GO HOME...AND SOON AS THEY GET THE ELECTRIC BACK ON...AN' I GET THE THE T.V. FIXED... I CAN TURN ON THE OL' TUBE AN'...
22

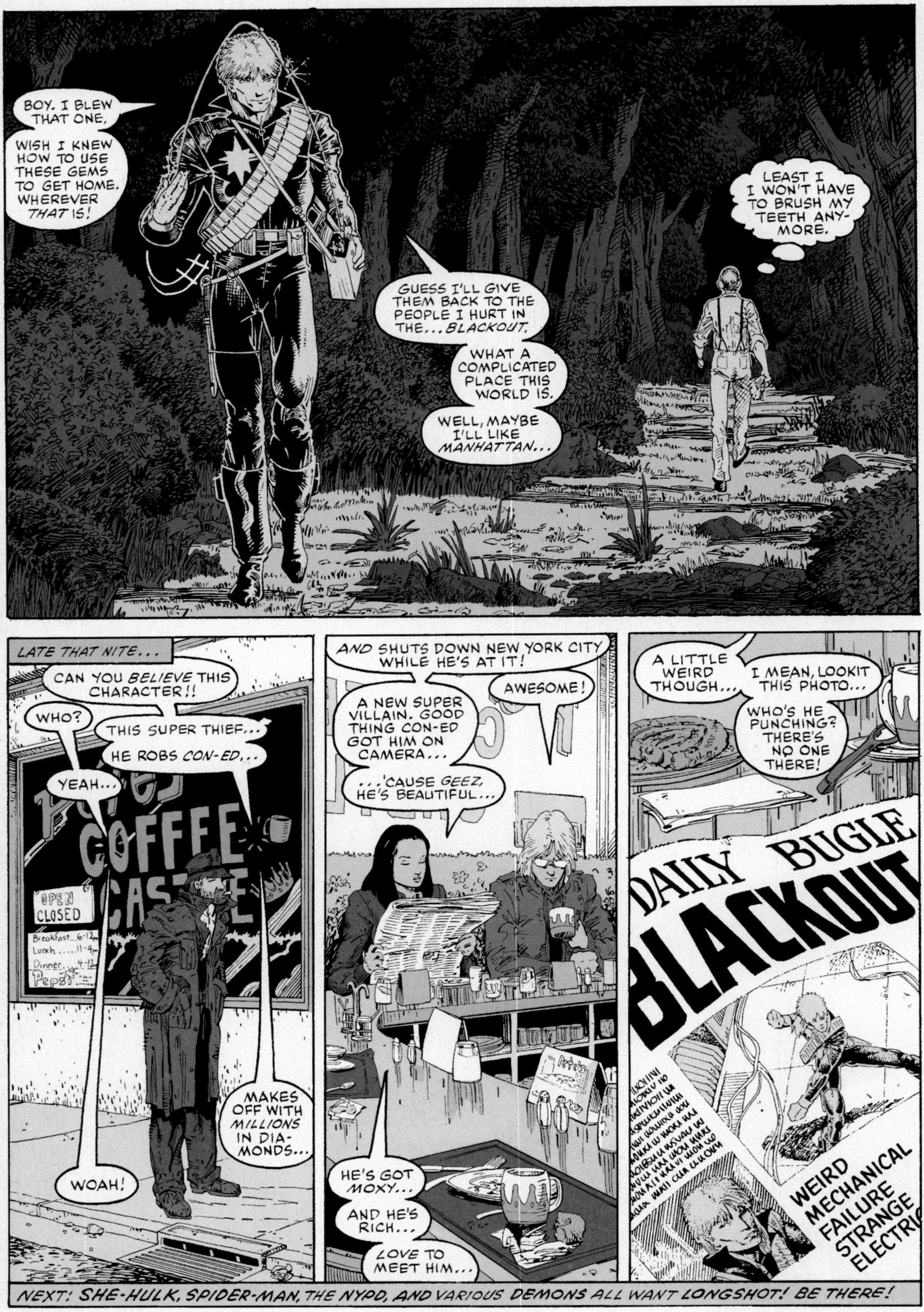
BOY. I BLEW THAT ONE.
WISH I KNEW HOW TO USE THESE GEMS TO GET HOME. WHEREVER *THAT* IS!
GUESS I'LL GIVE THEM BACK TO THE PEOPLE I HURT IN THE... *BLACKOUT*.
WHAT A COMPLICATED PLACE THIS WORLD IS.
WELL, MAYBE I'LL LIKE *MANHATTAN*...
LEAST I I WON'T HAVE TO BRUSH MY TEETH ANY-MORE.
LATE THAT NITE...
CAN YOU *BELIEVE* THIS CHARACTER!!
WHO?
THIS SUPER THIEF...
HE ROBS *CON-ED*...
YEAH...
COFFEE
OPEN
CLOSED
Breakfast...6-12
Lunch.....11-4
Dinner...4-12
Pepsi
MAKES OFF WITH *MILLIONS* IN DIA-MONDS...
WOAH!
AND SHUTS DOWN NEW YORK CITY WHILE HE'S AT IT!
A NEW SUPER VILLAIN. GOOD THING CON-ED GOT HIM ON CAMERA...
AWESOME!
...'CAUSE *GEEZ*, HE'S BEAUTIFUL...
HE'S GOT *MOXY*...
AND HE'S RICH...
LOVE TO MEET HIM...
A LITTLE WEIRD THOUGH...
I MEAN, LOOKIT THIS PHOTO...
WHO'S HE PUNCHING? THERE'S NO ONE THERE!
DAILY BUGLE
BLACKOUT
WEIRD MECHANICAL FAILURE STRANGE ELECTRI
NEXT: SHE-HULK, SPIDER-MAN, THE NYPD, AND VARIOUS DEMONS ALL WANT LONGSHOT! BE THERE!

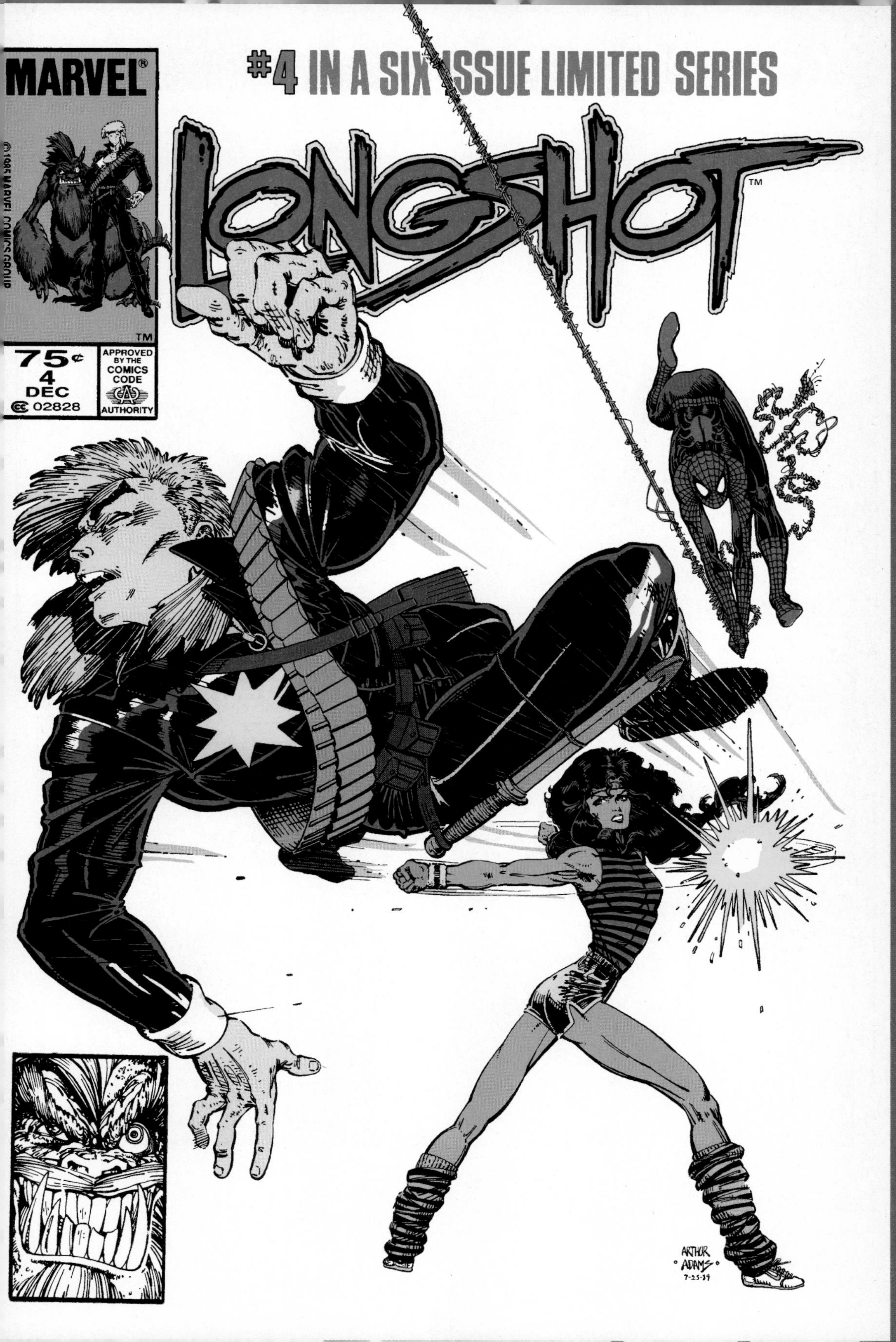
#4 IN A SIX ISSUE LIMITED SERIES
MARVEL®
© 1985 MARVEL COMICS GROUP
TM
75¢
4
DEC
02828
APPROVED BY THE COMICS CODE AUTHORITY
LONGSHOT™
ARTHUR ADAMS
7-25-84

STAN LEE PRESENTS:

CAN'T GIVE IT ALL AWAY!

CREATED BY:
☆ ANN NOCENTI ☆ ARTHUR ADAMS ☆ WHILCE PORTOCIO ☆ JOE ROSEN ☆ CHRISTIE SCHEELE ☆ LOUISE JONES ☆ JIM SHOOTER ☆
WRITER · PENCILS · INKS · LETTERS · COLORS · EDITOR · EDITOR IN CHIEF

...GOT AWAY WITH 3 MILLION DOLLARS WORTH OF *DIAMONDS,* AND CAUSED A CITY-WIDE *BLACKOUT,* LEAVING MANHATTAN CRIPPLED FOR HOURS.

...BUT THIS WAS NO ORDINARY ROBBERY!

STRANGE ELECTRICAL AND PARA-NORMAL ACTIVITY REGISTERED ON THE POWER COMPANY'S SENSITIVE EQUIPMENT ALONG WITH EVIDENCE OF FOREIGN METALS AND A SULPHUR RESIDUE...

LUCKILY, CON ED'S CAMERAS GOT EXCELLENT SHOTS OF THE THIEF...

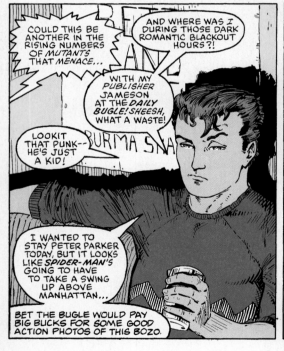

COULD THIS BE ANOTHER IN THE RISING NUMBERS OF *MUTANTS* THAT MENACE...

AND WHERE WAS *I* DURING THOSE DARK ROMANTIC BLACKOUT HOURS?!

WITH MY *PUBLISHER* JAMESON AT THE *DAILY BUGLE!* SHEESH, WHAT A WASTE!

LOOKIT THAT PUNK-- HE'S JUST A KID!

I WANTED TO STAY PETER PARKER TODAY, BUT IT LOOKS LIKE *SPIDER-MAN'S* GOING TO HAVE TO TAKE A SWING UP ABOVE MANHATTAN...

BET THE BUGLE WOULD PAY BIG BUCKS FOR SOME GOOD ACTION PHOTOS OF THIS BOZO.

AND ACROSS TOWN...

JUST WHEN YOU THINK THE WORLD HAS ENOUGH VILLAINS...!

STILL...I WOULDN'T MIND CHASING *HIS* TAIL!

I SHOULD LET THE REST OF THE *FANTASTIC FOUR* KNOW-- IF THEY SEE THAT LOOKER-- PASS HIM ON TO OL' *SHE-HULK!*

THOUGH, WITH THESE MYSTICAL ALIEN TYPES IT'S BEST TO KNOCK THEM OUT FAST BEFORE THEY TRY ANY WIERDO MAGICKS ON YOU.

CAN'T HURT TO JOG ACROSS THE PARK UP TO WHERE HE WAS LAST SEEN, WAY UP IN--

1

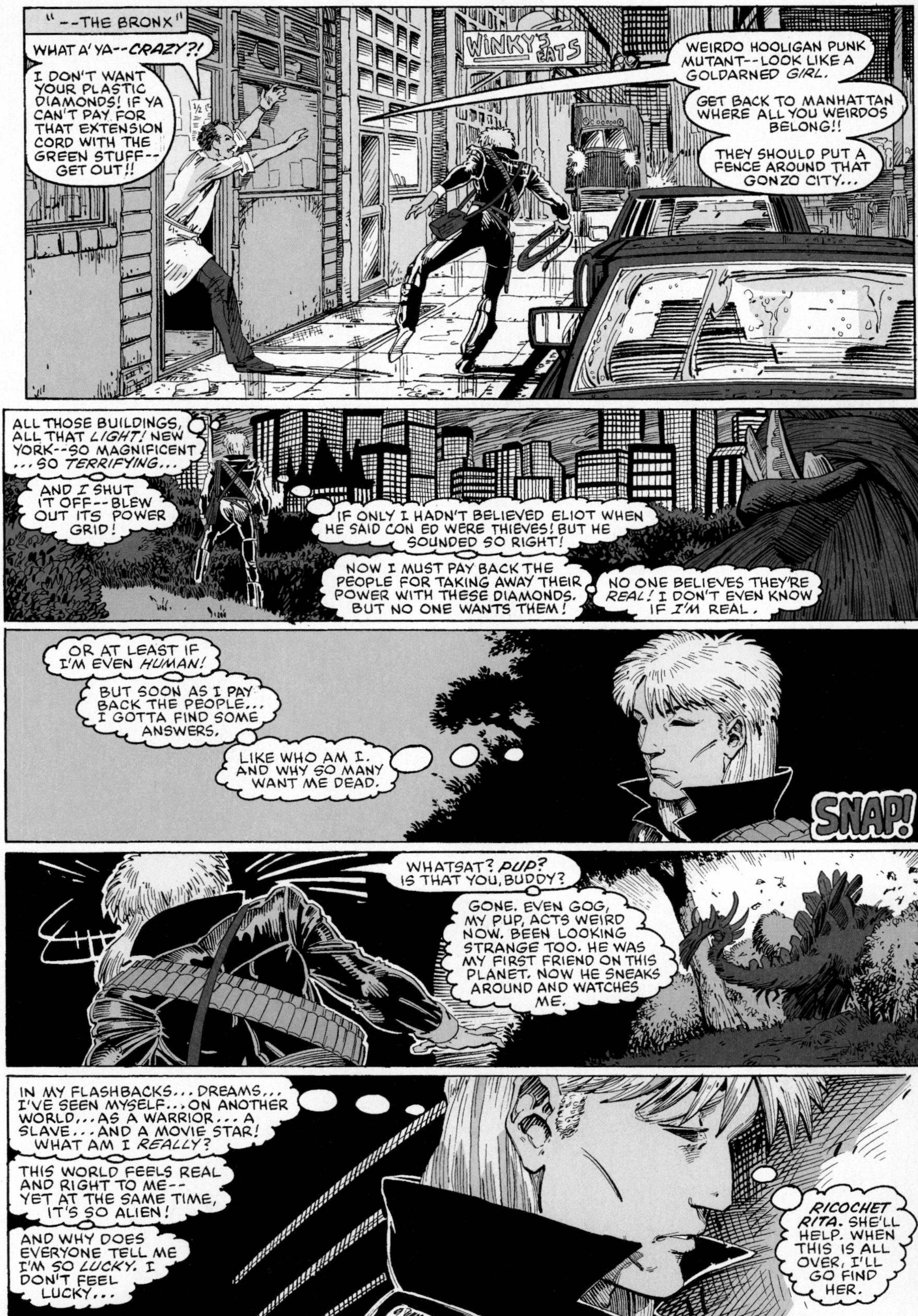
"--THE BRONX"
WHAT A' YA--CRAZY?! I DON'T WANT YOUR PLASTIC DIAMONDS! IF YA CAN'T PAY FOR THAT EXTENSION CORD WITH THE GREEN STUFF--GET OUT!!
WINKY'S EATS
WEIRDO HOOLIGAN PUNK MUTANT--LOOK LIKE A GOLDARNED GIRL.
GET BACK TO MANHATTAN WHERE ALL YOU WEIRDOS BELONG!!
THEY SHOULD PUT A FENCE AROUND THAT GONZO CITY...
ALL THOSE BUILDINGS, ALL THAT LIGHT! NEW YORK--SO MAGNIFICENT ...SO TERRIFYING...
AND I SHUT IT OFF--BLEW OUT ITS POWER GRID!
IF ONLY I HADN'T BELIEVED ELIOT WHEN HE SAID CON ED WERE THIEVES! BUT HE SOUNDED SO RIGHT!
NOW I MUST PAY BACK THE PEOPLE FOR TAKING AWAY THEIR POWER WITH THESE DIAMONDS. BUT NO ONE WANTS THEM!
NO ONE BELIEVES THEY'RE REAL! I DON'T EVEN KNOW IF I'M REAL.
OR AT LEAST IF I'M EVEN HUMAN!
BUT SOON AS I PAY BACK THE PEOPLE... I GOTTA FIND SOME ANSWERS.
LIKE WHO AM I. AND WHY SO MANY WANT ME DEAD.
SNAP!
WHATSAT? PUP? IS THAT YOU, BUDDY?
GONE. EVEN GOG, MY PUP, ACTS WEIRD NOW. BEEN LOOKING STRANGE TOO. HE WAS MY FIRST FRIEND ON THIS PLANET. NOW HE SNEAKS AROUND AND WATCHES ME.
IN MY FLASHBACKS... DREAMS... I'VE SEEN MYSELF... ON ANOTHER WORLD... AS A WARRIOR... A SLAVE... AND A MOVIE STAR! WHAT AM I REALLY?
THIS WORLD FEELS REAL AND RIGHT TO ME--YET AT THE SAME TIME, IT'S SO ALIEN!
AND WHY DOES EVERYONE TELL ME I'M SO LUCKY. I DON'T FEEL LUCKY...
RICOCHET RITA. SHE'LL HELP. WHEN THIS IS ALL OVER, I'LL GO FIND HER.
2

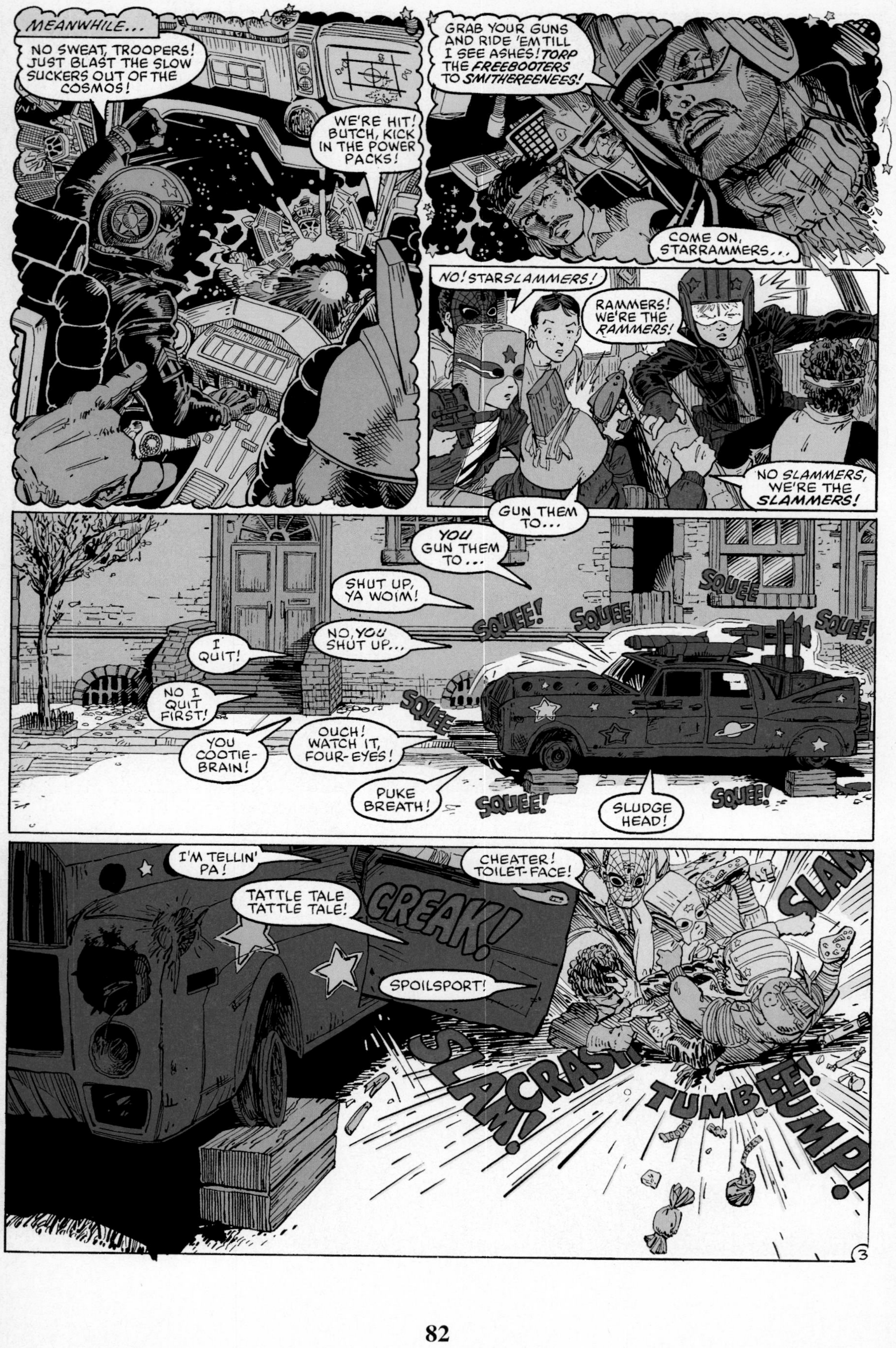
MEANWHILE...
NO SWEAT, TROOPERS! JUST BLAST THE SLOW SUCKERS OUT OF THE COSMOS!
WE'RE HIT! BUTCH, KICK IN THE POWER PACKS!
GRAB YOUR GUNS AND RIDE 'EM TILL I SEE ASHES! TORP THE FREEBOOTERS TO SMITHEREENEES!
COME ON, STARRAMMERS...
NO! STARSLAMMERS!
RAMMERS! WE'RE THE RAMMERS!
NO SLAMMERS, WE'RE THE SLAMMERS!
GUN THEM TO...
YOU GUN THEM TO...
SHUT UP, YA WOIM!
NO, YOU SHUT UP...
I QUIT!
NO I QUIT FIRST!
YOU COOTIE-BRAIN!
OUCH! WATCH IT, FOUR-EYES!
PUKE BREATH!
SLUDGE HEAD!
SQUEE!
SQUEE
SQUEE
SQUEE!
SQUEE
SQUEE!
SQUEE!
I'M TELLIN' PA!
TATTLE TALE TATTLE TALE!
CHEATER! TOILET-FACE!
SPOILSPORT!
CREAK!
SLAM!
CRASH
TUMBLE!
THUMP!
3

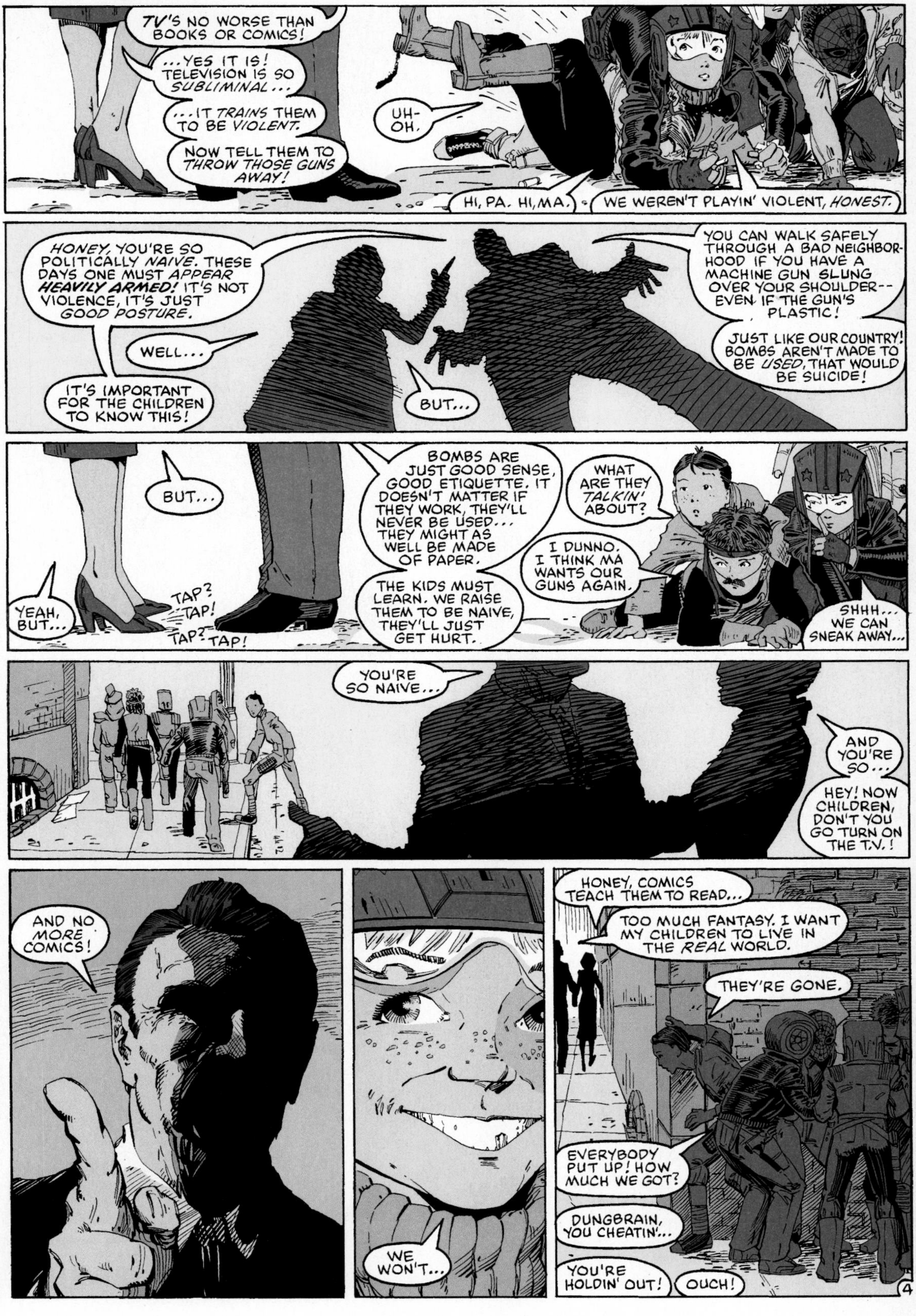
TV'S NO WORSE THAN BOOKS OR COMICS!
...YES IT IS! TELEVISION IS SO SUBLIMINAL...
...IT TRAINS THEM TO BE VIOLENT.
NOW TELL THEM TO THROW THOSE GUNS AWAY!
UH-OH.
HI, PA. HI, MA.
WE WEREN'T PLAYIN' VIOLENT, HONEST.
HONEY, YOU'RE SO POLITICALLY NAIVE. THESE DAYS ONE MUST APPEAR HEAVILY ARMED! IT'S NOT VIOLENCE, IT'S JUST GOOD POSTURE.
WELL...
IT'S IMPORTANT FOR THE CHILDREN TO KNOW THIS!
BUT...
YOU CAN WALK SAFELY THROUGH A BAD NEIGHBORHOOD IF YOU HAVE A MACHINE GUN SLUNG OVER YOUR SHOULDER-- EVEN IF THE GUN'S PLASTIC!
JUST LIKE OUR COUNTRY! BOMBS AREN'T MADE TO BE USED, THAT WOULD BE SUICIDE!
BUT...
YEAH, BUT...
TAP? TAP! TAP? TAP!
BOMBS ARE JUST GOOD SENSE, GOOD ETIQUETTE. IT DOESN'T MATTER IF THEY WORK, THEY'LL NEVER BE USED... THEY MIGHT AS WELL BE MADE OF PAPER.
THE KIDS MUST LEARN. WE RAISE THEM TO BE NAIVE, THEY'LL JUST GET HURT.
WHAT ARE THEY TALKIN' ABOUT?
I DUNNO. I THINK MA WANTS OUR GUNS AGAIN.
SHHH... WE CAN SNEAK AWAY...
YOU'RE SO NAIVE...
AND YOU'RE SO...
HEY! NOW CHILDREN, DON'T YOU GO TURN ON THE T.V.!
AND NO MORE COMICS!
WE WON'T...
HONEY, COMICS TEACH THEM TO READ...
TOO MUCH FANTASY. I WANT MY CHILDREN TO LIVE IN THE REAL WORLD.
THEY'RE GONE.
EVERYBODY PUT UP! HOW MUCH WE GOT?
DUNGBRAIN, YOU CHEATIN'...
YOU'RE HOLDIN' OUT!
OUCH!
4

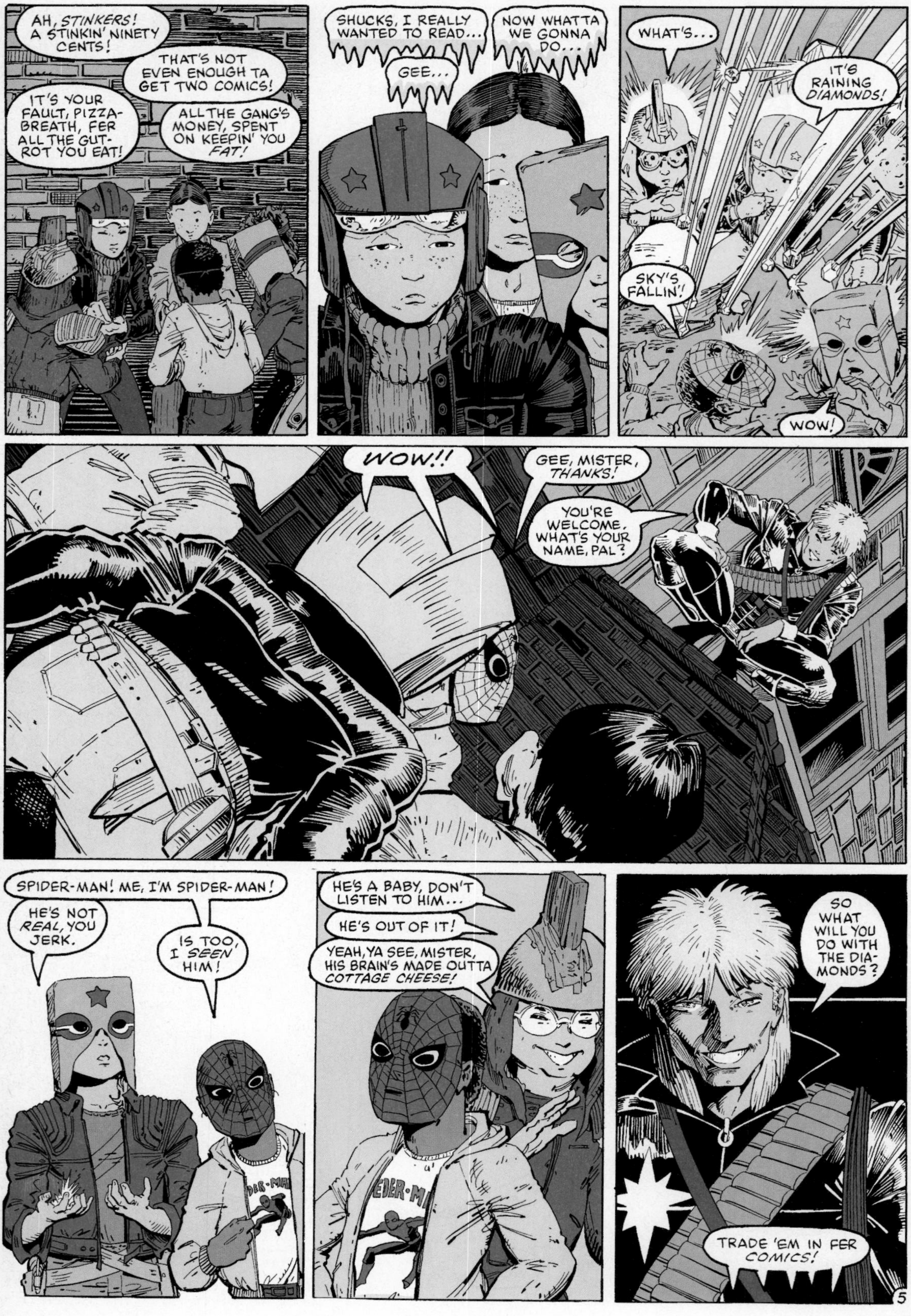
AH, STINKERS! A STINKIN' NINETY CENTS!
THAT'S NOT EVEN ENOUGH TA GET TWO COMICS!
IT'S YOUR FAULT, PIZZA-BREATH, FER ALL THE GUT-ROT YOU EAT!
ALL THE GANG'S MONEY, SPENT ON KEEPIN' YOU FAT!
SHUCKS, I REALLY WANTED TO READ...
NOW WHATTA WE GONNA DO...
GEE...
WHAT'S...
IT'S RAINING DIAMONDS!
SKY'S FALLIN'!
WOW!
WOW!!
GEE, MISTER, THANKS!
YOU'RE WELCOME. WHAT'S YOUR NAME, PAL?
SPIDER-MAN! ME, I'M SPIDER-MAN!
HE'S NOT REAL, YOU JERK.
IS TOO, I SEEN HIM!
HE'S A BABY, DON'T LISTEN TO HIM...
HE'S OUT OF IT!
YEAH, YA SEE, MISTER, HIS BRAIN'S MADE OUTTA COTTAGE CHEESE!
SO WHAT WILL YOU DO WITH THE DIAMONDS?
TRADE 'EM IN FER COMICS!
5

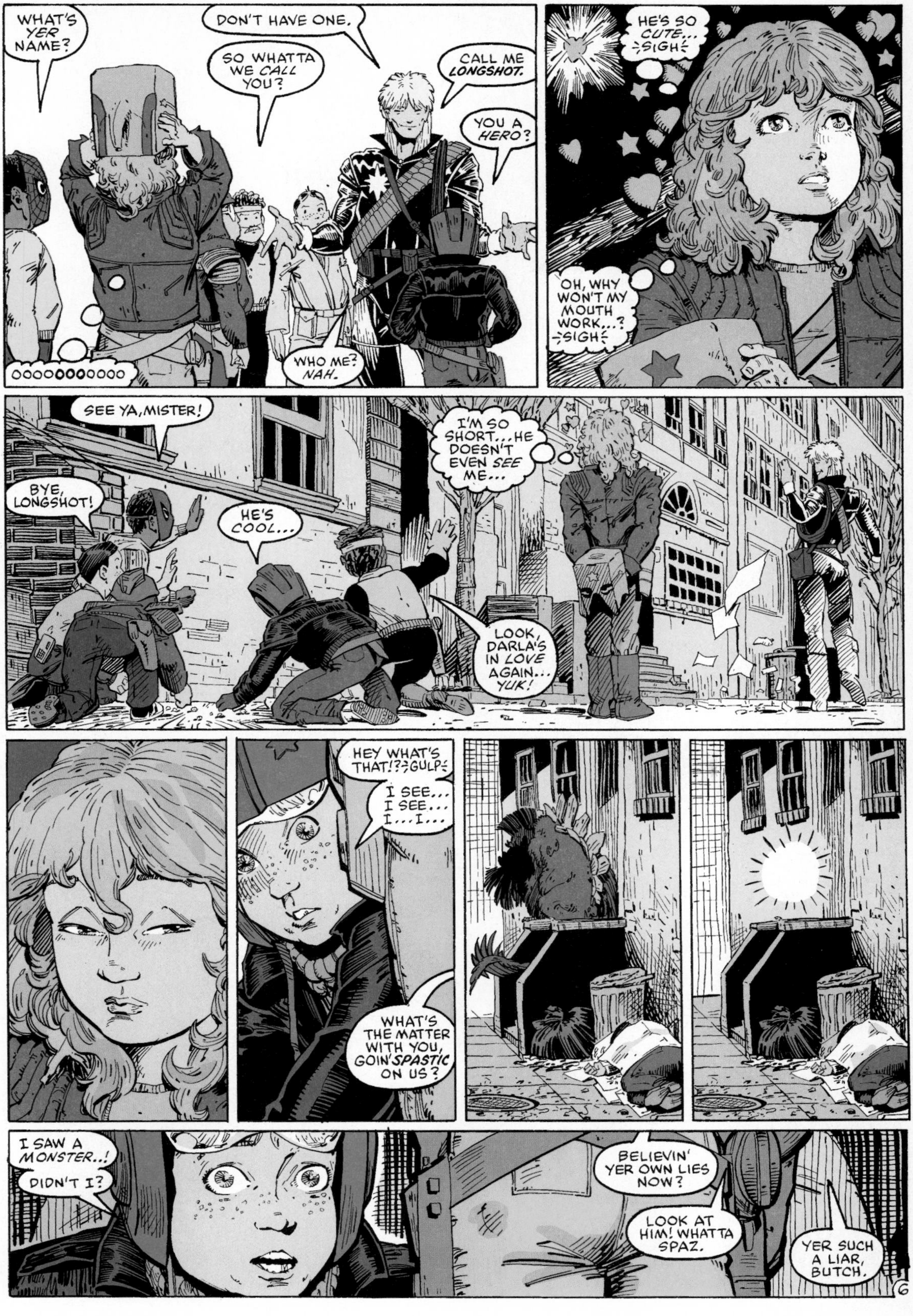
WHAT'S YER NAME?
DON'T HAVE ONE.
SO WHATTA WE CALL YOU?
CALL ME LONGSHOT.
YOU A HERO?
OOOOOOOOOOOO
WHO ME? NAH.
HE'S SO CUTE... SIGH
OH, WHY WON'T MY MOUTH WORK...? SIGH
SEE YA, MISTER!
BYE, LONGSHOT!
HE'S COOL...
I'M SO SHORT... HE DOESN'T EVEN SEE ME...
LOOK, DARLA'S IN LOVE AGAIN... YUK!
HEY WHAT'S THAT!? GULP
I SEE... I SEE... I... I...
WHAT'S THE MATTER WITH YOU, GOIN' SPASTIC ON US?
I SAW A MONSTER..!
DIDN'T I?
BELIEVIN' YER OWN LIES NOW?
LOOK AT HIM! WHATTA SPAZ.
YER SUCH A LIAR, BUTCH.
6

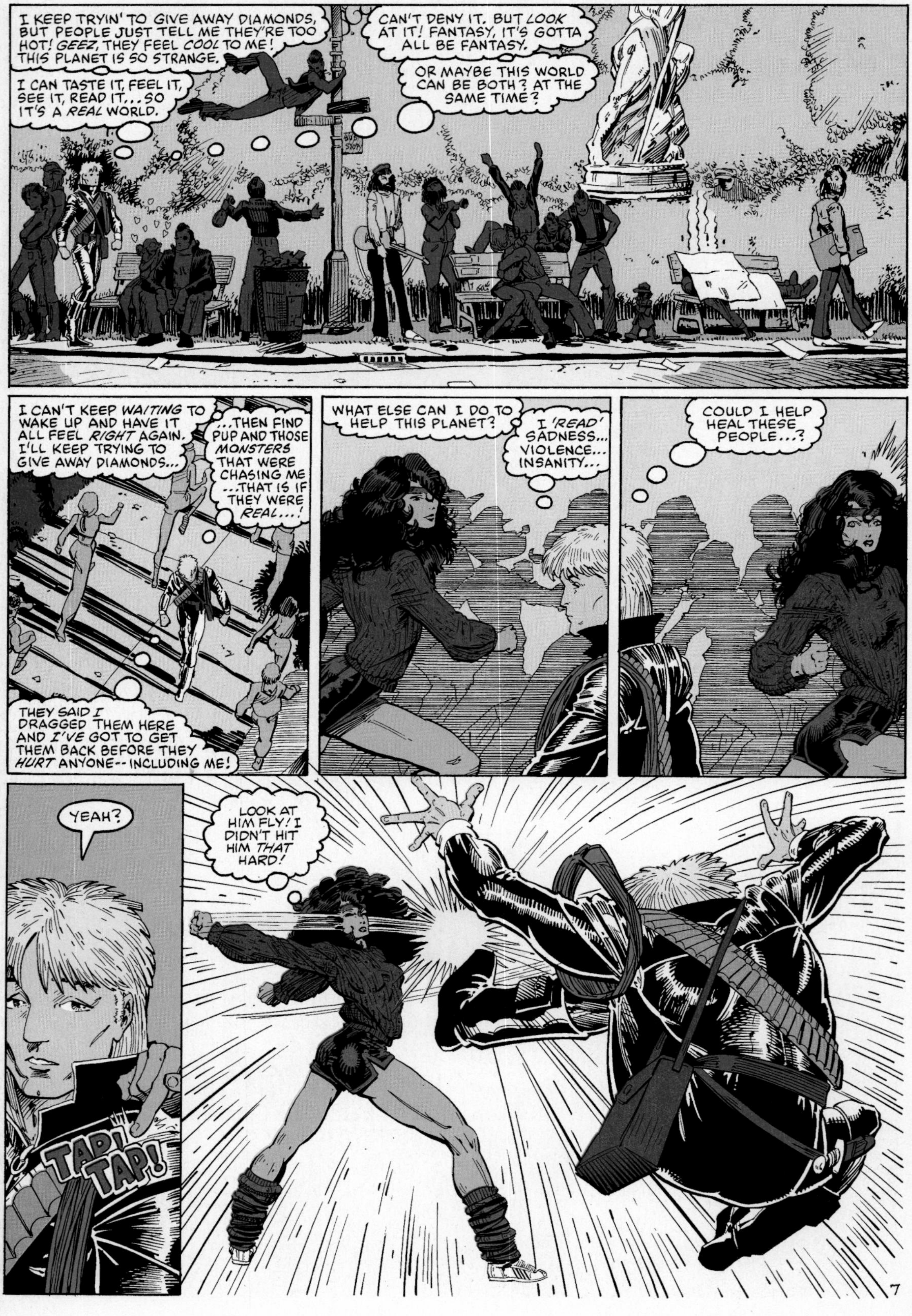
I KEEP TRYIN' TO GIVE AWAY DIAMONDS, BUT PEOPLE JUST TELL ME THEY'RE TOO HOT! GEEZ, THEY FEEL COOL TO ME! THIS PLANET IS SO STRANGE.
I CAN TASTE IT, FEEL IT, SEE IT, READ IT... SO IT'S A REAL WORLD.
CAN'T DENY IT. BUT LOOK AT IT! FANTASY, IT'S GOTTA ALL BE FANTASY.
OR MAYBE THIS WORLD CAN BE BOTH? AT THE SAME TIME?
BUS STOP
I CAN'T KEEP WAITING TO WAKE UP AND HAVE IT ALL FEEL RIGHT AGAIN. I'LL KEEP TRYING TO GIVE AWAY DIAMONDS...
...THEN FIND PUP AND THOSE MONSTERS THAT WERE CHASING ME ...THAT IS IF THEY WERE REAL...!
THEY SAID I DRAGGED THEM HERE AND I'VE GOT TO GET THEM BACK BEFORE THEY HURT ANYONE-- INCLUDING ME!
WHAT ELSE CAN I DO TO HELP THIS PLANET?
I 'READ' SADNESS... VIOLENCE... INSANITY...
COULD I HELP HEAL THESE PEOPLE...?
YEAH?
TAP! TAP!
LOOK AT HIM FLY! I DIDN'T HIT HIM THAT HARD!
7

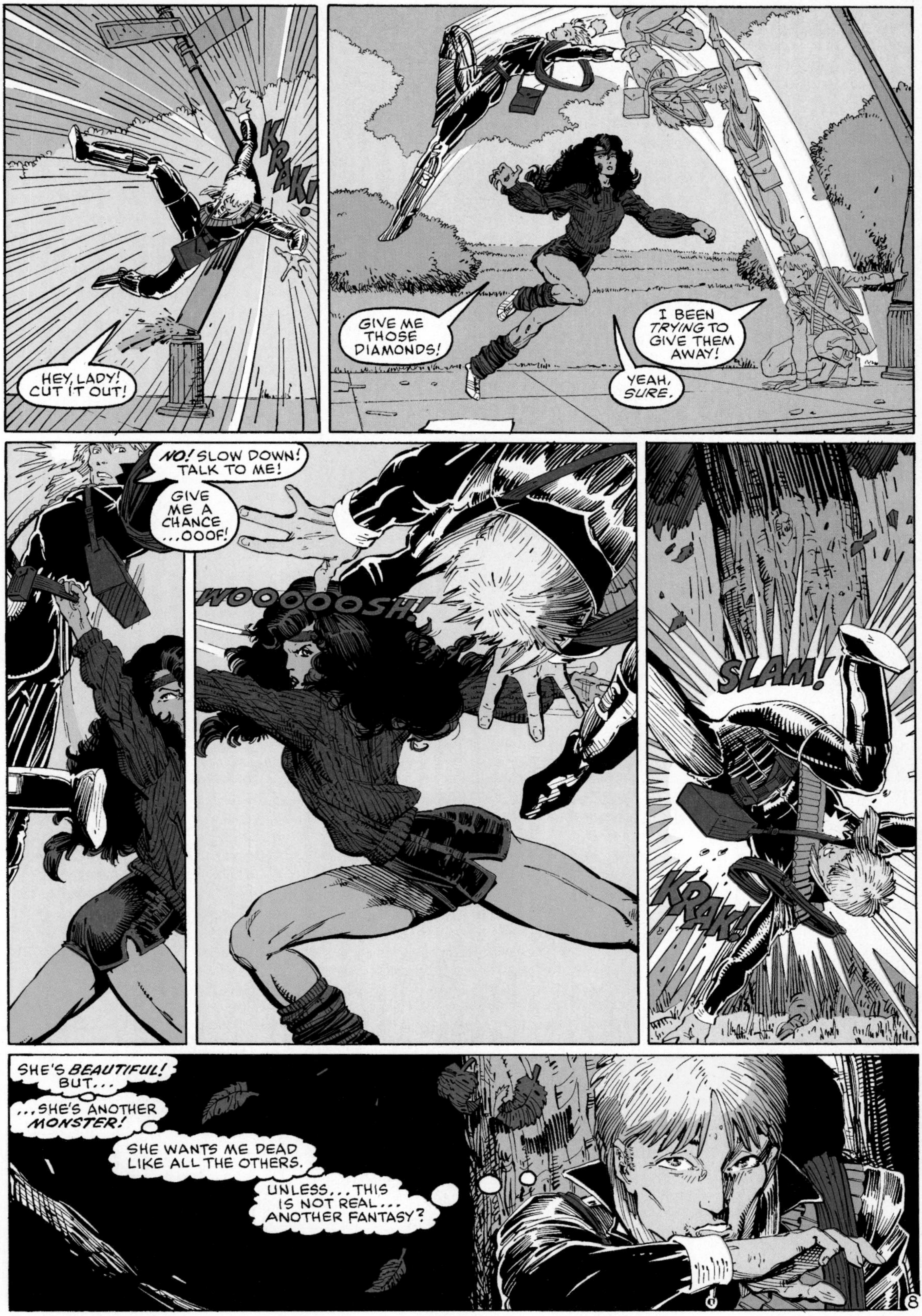
KRAK!
HEY, LADY! CUT IT OUT!
GIVE ME THOSE DIAMONDS!
I BEEN TRYING TO GIVE THEM AWAY!
YEAH, SURE.
NO! SLOW DOWN! TALK TO ME!
GIVE ME A CHANCE ...OOOF!
WOOOOOOSH!
SLAM!
KRAK!
SHE'S BEAUTIFUL! BUT...
...SHE'S ANOTHER MONSTER!
SHE WANTS ME DEAD LIKE ALL THE OTHERS.
UNLESS...THIS IS NOT REAL... ANOTHER FANTASY?
8

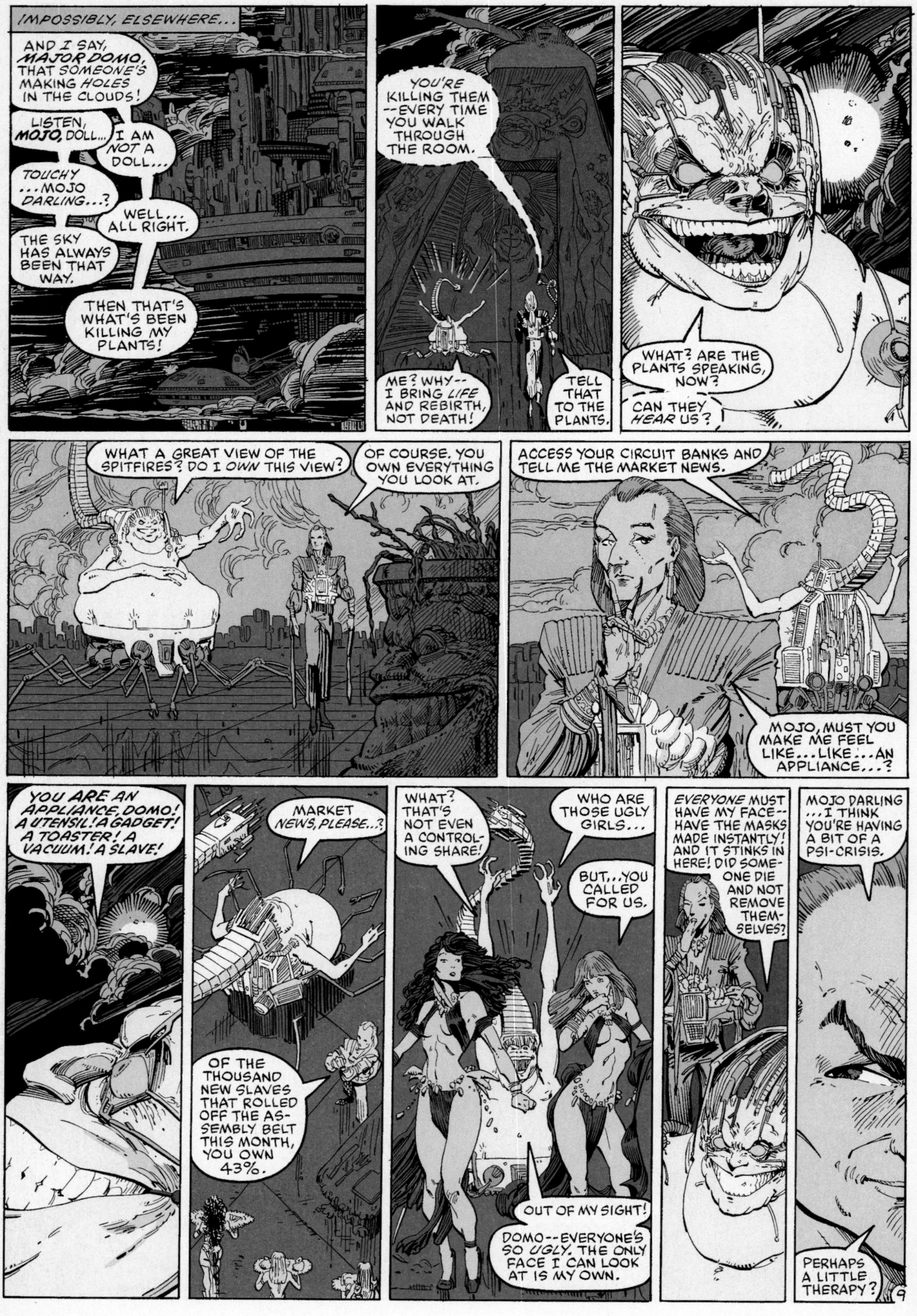
IMPOSSIBLY, ELSEWHERE...
AND I SAY, MAJOR DOMO, THAT SOMEONE'S MAKING HOLES IN THE CLOUDS!
LISTEN, MOJO, DOLL...
I AM NOT A DOLL...
TOUCHY ...MOJO DARLING...?
WELL... ALL RIGHT.
THE SKY HAS ALWAYS BEEN THAT WAY.
THEN THAT'S WHAT'S BEEN KILLING MY PLANTS!
YOU'RE KILLING THEM --EVERY TIME YOU WALK THROUGH THE ROOM.
ME? WHY-- I BRING LIFE AND REBIRTH, NOT DEATH!
TELL THAT TO THE PLANTS.
WHAT? ARE THE PLANTS SPEAKING, NOW?
CAN THEY HEAR US?
WHAT A GREAT VIEW OF THE SPITFIRES? DO I OWN THIS VIEW?
OF COURSE. YOU OWN EVERYTHING YOU LOOK AT.
ACCESS YOUR CIRCUIT BANKS AND TELL ME THE MARKET NEWS.
MOJO, MUST YOU MAKE ME FEEL LIKE...LIKE...AN APPLIANCE...?
YOU ARE AN APPLIANCE, DOMO! A UTENSIL! A GADGET! A TOASTER! A VACUUM! A SLAVE!
MARKET NEWS, PLEASE...?
OF THE THOUSAND NEW SLAVES THAT ROLLED OFF THE AS-SEMBLY BELT THIS MONTH, YOU OWN 43%.
WHAT? THAT'S NOT EVEN A CONTROL-LING SHARE!
WHO ARE THOSE UGLY GIRLS...
BUT...YOU CALLED FOR US.
OUT OF MY SIGHT!
DOMO--EVERYONE'S SO UGLY. THE ONLY FACE I CAN LOOK AT IS MY OWN.
EVERYONE MUST HAVE MY FACE-- HAVE THE MASKS MADE INSTANTLY! AND IT STINKS IN HERE! DID SOME-ONE DIE AND NOT REMOVE THEM-SELVES?
MOJO DARLING ...I THINK YOU'RE HAVING A BIT OF A PSI-CRISIS.
PERHAPS A LITTLE THERAPY?
9

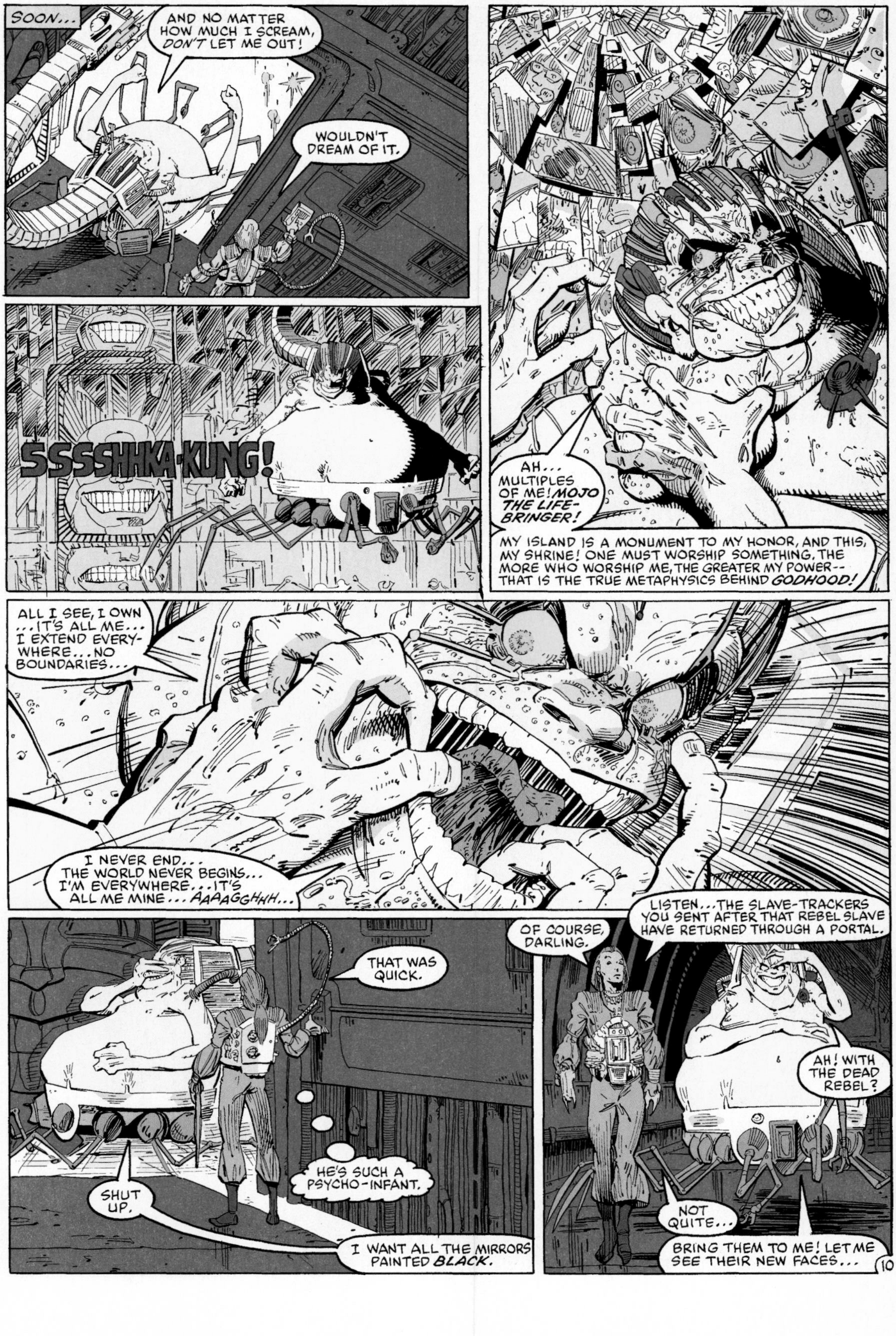
SOON...
AND NO MATTER HOW MUCH I SCREAM, DON'T LET ME OUT!
WOULDN'T DREAM OF IT.
SSSSHHKA-KUNG!
AH... MULTIPLES OF ME! MOJO THE LIFE-BRINGER!
MY ISLAND IS A MONUMENT TO MY HONOR, AND THIS, MY SHRINE! ONE MUST WORSHIP SOMETHING. THE MORE WHO WORSHIP ME, THE GREATER MY POWER-- THAT IS THE TRUE METAPHYSICS BEHIND GODHOOD!
ALL I SEE, I OWN ...IT'S ALL ME... I EXTEND EVERYWHERE... NO BOUNDARIES...
I NEVER END... THE WORLD NEVER BEGINS... I'M EVERYWHERE... IT'S ALL ME MINE... AAAAGGHHH...
THAT WAS QUICK.
HE'S SUCH A PSYCHO-INFANT.
SHUT UP.
I WANT ALL THE MIRRORS PAINTED BLACK.
OF COURSE, DARLING.
LISTEN... THE SLAVE-TRACKERS YOU SENT AFTER THAT REBEL SLAVE HAVE RETURNED THROUGH A PORTAL.
AH! WITH THE DEAD REBEL?
NOT QUITE...
BRING THEM TO ME! LET ME SEE THEIR NEW FACES...
10

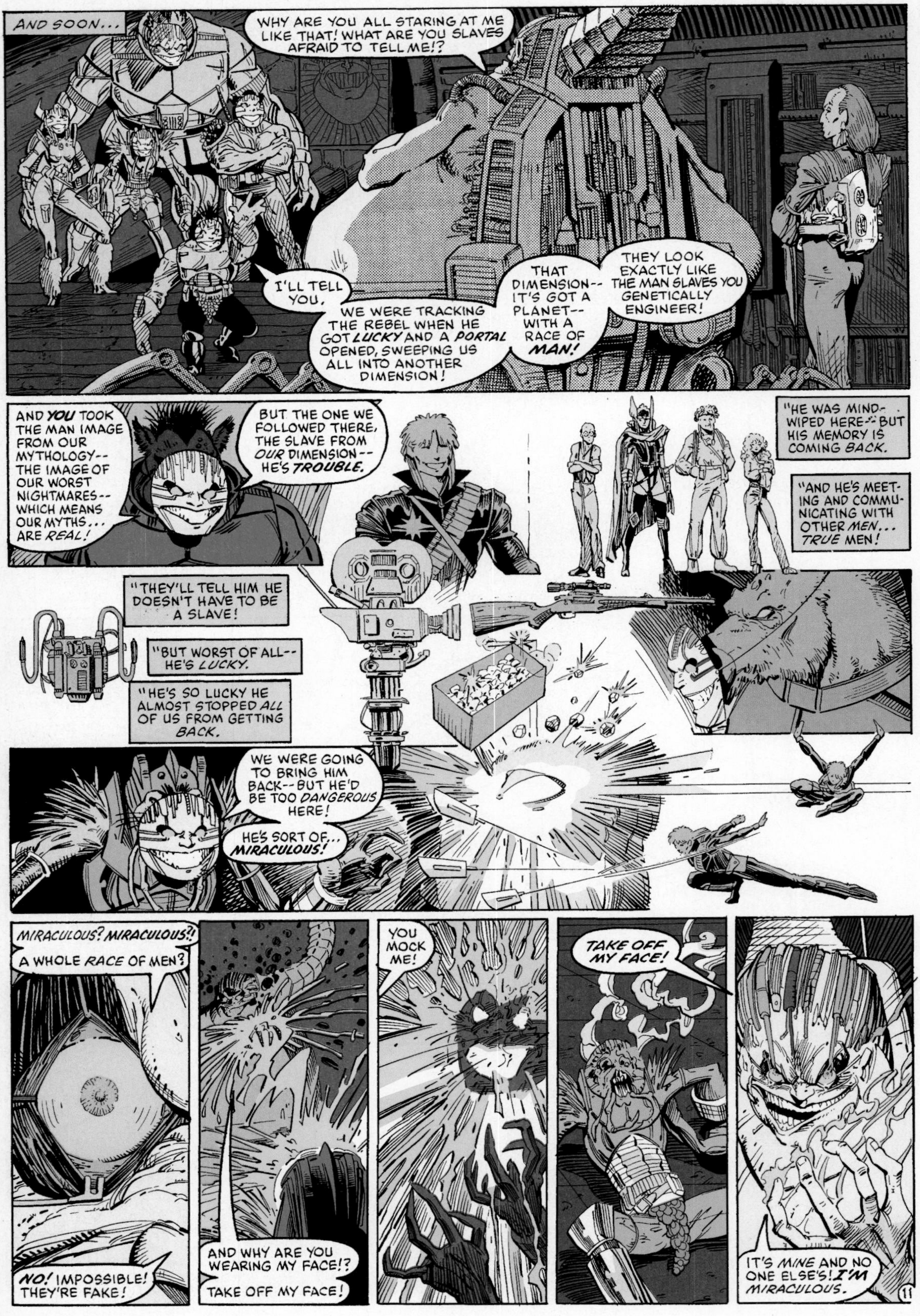

AND SOON...
WHY ARE YOU ALL STARING AT ME LIKE THAT! WHAT ARE YOU SLAVES AFRAID TO TELL ME!?
I'LL TELL YOU.
WE WERE TRACKING THE REBEL WHEN HE GOT LUCKY AND A PORTAL OPENED, SWEEPING US ALL INTO ANOTHER DIMENSION!
THAT DIMENSION-- IT'S GOT A PLANET-- WITH A RACE OF MAN!
THEY LOOK EXACTLY LIKE THE MAN SLAVES YOU GENETICALLY ENGINEER!
AND YOU TOOK THE MAN IMAGE FROM OUR MYTHOLOGY-- THE IMAGE OF OUR WORST NIGHTMARES-- WHICH MEANS OUR MYTHS... ARE REAL!
BUT THE ONE WE FOLLOWED THERE, THE SLAVE FROM OUR DIMENSION-- HE'S TROUBLE.
"HE WAS MIND-WIPED HERE-- BUT HIS MEMORY IS COMING BACK.
"AND HE'S MEETING AND COMMUNICATING WITH OTHER MEN... TRUE MEN!
"THEY'LL TELL HIM HE DOESN'T HAVE TO BE A SLAVE!
"BUT WORST OF ALL-- HE'S LUCKY.
"HE'S SO LUCKY HE ALMOST STOPPED ALL OF US FROM GETTING BACK.
WE WERE GOING TO BRING HIM BACK--BUT HE'D BE TOO DANGEROUS HERE!
HE'S SORT OF... MIRACULOUS!
MIRACULOUS? MIRACULOUS?! A WHOLE RACE OF MEN?
NO! IMPOSSIBLE! THEY'RE FAKE!
AND WHY ARE YOU WEARING MY FACE!?
TAKE OFF MY FACE!
YOU MOCK ME!
TAKE OFF MY FACE!
IT'S MINE AND NO ONE ELSE'S! I'M MIRACULOUS.
11

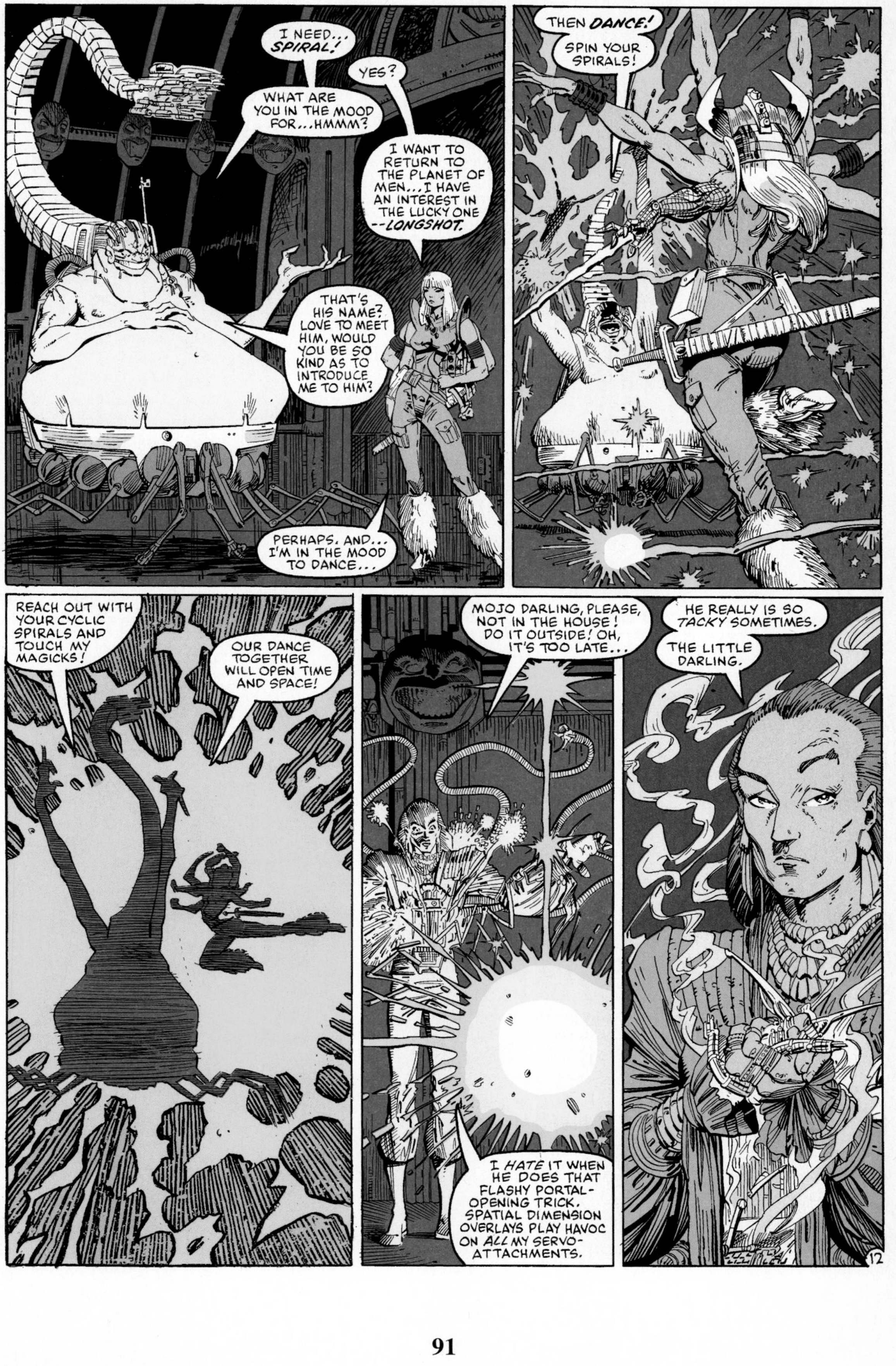
I NEED... SPIRAL!
WHAT ARE YOU IN THE MOOD FOR...HMMM?
YES?
I WANT TO RETURN TO THE PLANET OF MEN...I HAVE AN INTEREST IN THE LUCKY ONE --LONGSHOT.
THAT'S HIS NAME? LOVE TO MEET HIM, WOULD YOU BE SO KIND AS TO INTRODUCE ME TO HIM?
PERHAPS. AND... I'M IN THE MOOD TO DANCE...
THEN DANCE!
SPIN YOUR SPIRALS!
REACH OUT WITH YOUR CYCLIC SPIRALS AND TOUCH MY MAGICKS!
OUR DANCE TOGETHER WILL OPEN TIME AND SPACE!
MOJO DARLING, PLEASE, NOT IN THE HOUSE! DO IT OUTSIDE! OH, IT'S TOO LATE...
I HATE IT WHEN HE DOES THAT FLASHY PORTAL-OPENING TRICK. SPATIAL DIMENSION OVERLAYS PLAY HAVOC ON ALL MY SERVO-ATTACHMENTS.
HE REALLY IS SO TACKY SOMETIMES.
THE LITTLE DARLING.
12

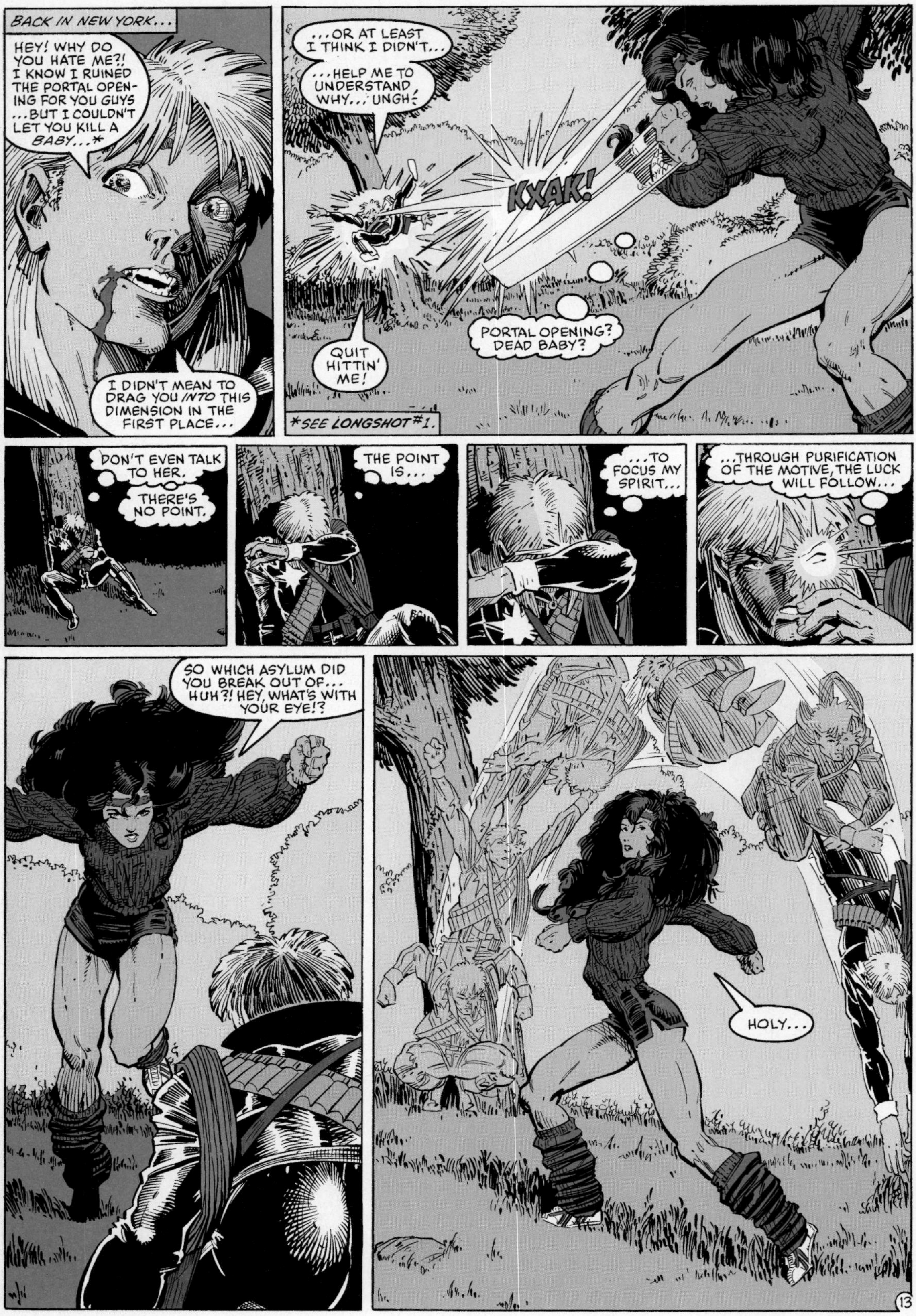

BACK IN NEW YORK...
HEY! WHY DO YOU HATE ME?! I KNOW I RUINED THE PORTAL OPENING FOR YOU GUYS ...BUT I COULDN'T LET YOU KILL A BABY...*
I DIDN'T MEAN TO DRAG YOU INTO THIS DIMENSION IN THE FIRST PLACE...
...OR AT LEAST I THINK I DIDN'T...
...HELP ME TO UNDERSTAND WHY... UNGH!
KXAK!
QUIT HITTIN' ME!
PORTAL OPENING? DEAD BABY?
*SEE LONGSHOT #1.
DON'T EVEN TALK TO HER.
THERE'S NO POINT.
THE POINT IS...
...TO FOCUS MY SPIRIT...
...THROUGH PURIFICATION OF THE MOTIVE, THE LUCK WILL FOLLOW...
SO WHICH ASYLUM DID YOU BREAK OUT OF... HUH?! HEY, WHAT'S WITH YOUR EYE!?
HOLY...
13

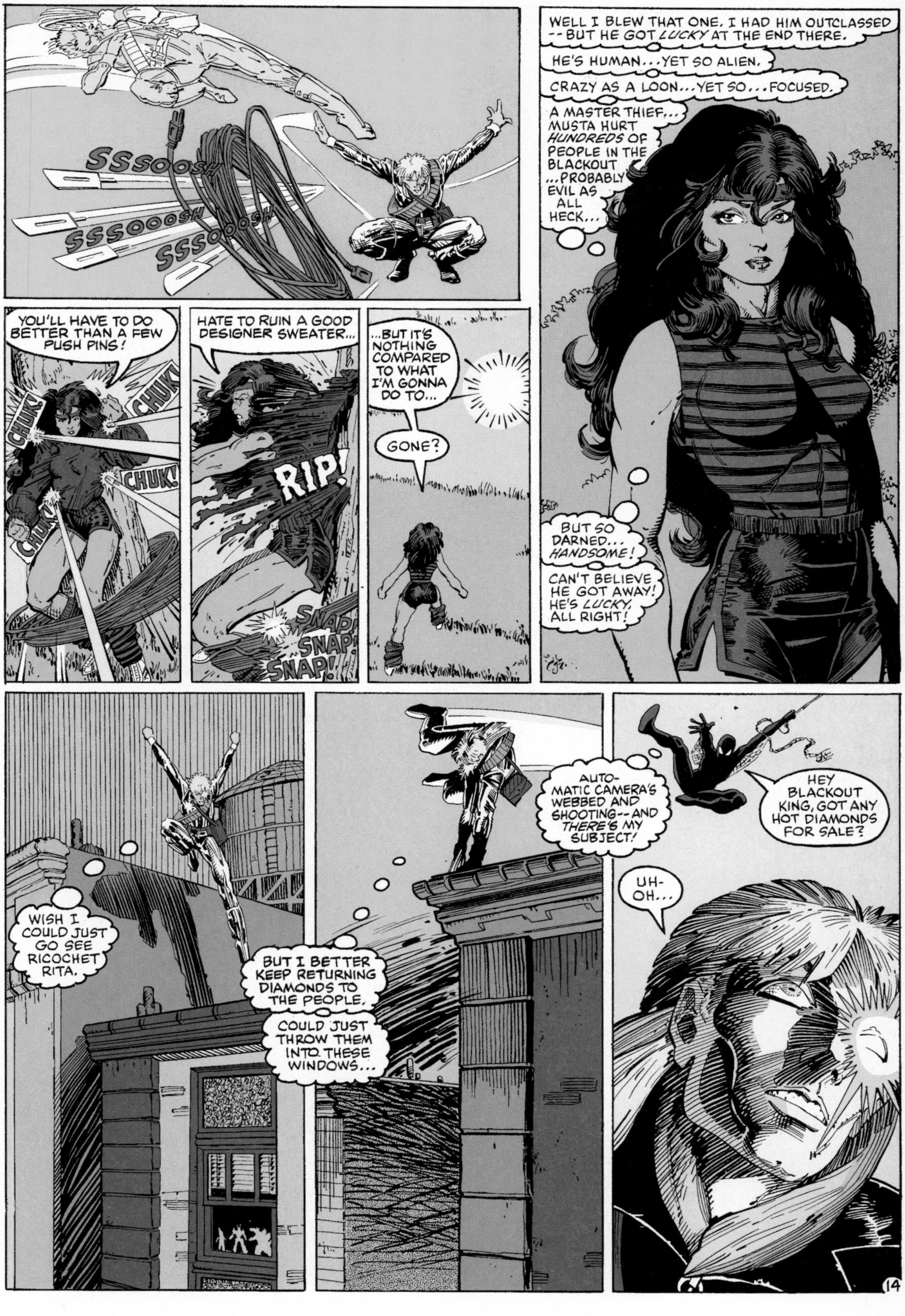
SSSOOSH
SSSOOOOSH
SSSOOOOSH
YOU'LL HAVE TO DO BETTER THAN A FEW PUSH PINS!
CHUK!
CHUK!
CHUK!
CHUK!
HATE TO RUIN A GOOD DESIGNER SWEATER...
RIP!
SNAP!
SNAP!
SNAP!
...BUT IT'S NOTHING COMPARED TO WHAT I'M GONNA DO TO...
GONE?
WELL I BLEW THAT ONE. I HAD HIM OUTCLASSED -- BUT HE GOT *LUCKY* AT THE END THERE.
HE'S HUMAN...YET SO ALIEN.
CRAZY AS A LOON...YET SO...FOCUSED.
A MASTER THIEF... MUSTA HURT *HUNDREDS* OF PEOPLE IN THE BLACKOUT ...PROBABLY EVIL AS ALL HECK...
BUT SO DARNED... *HANDSOME*!
CAN'T BELIEVE HE GOT AWAY! HE'S *LUCKY*, ALL RIGHT!
WISH I COULD JUST GO SEE RICOCHET RITA.
BUT I BETTER KEEP RETURNING DIAMONDS TO THE PEOPLE.
COULD JUST THROW THEM INTO THESE WINDOWS...
AUTO-MATIC CAMERA'S WEBBED AND SHOOTING--AND *THERE'S* MY SUBJECT!
HEY BLACKOUT KING, GOT ANY HOT DIAMONDS FOR SALE?
UH-OH...
14

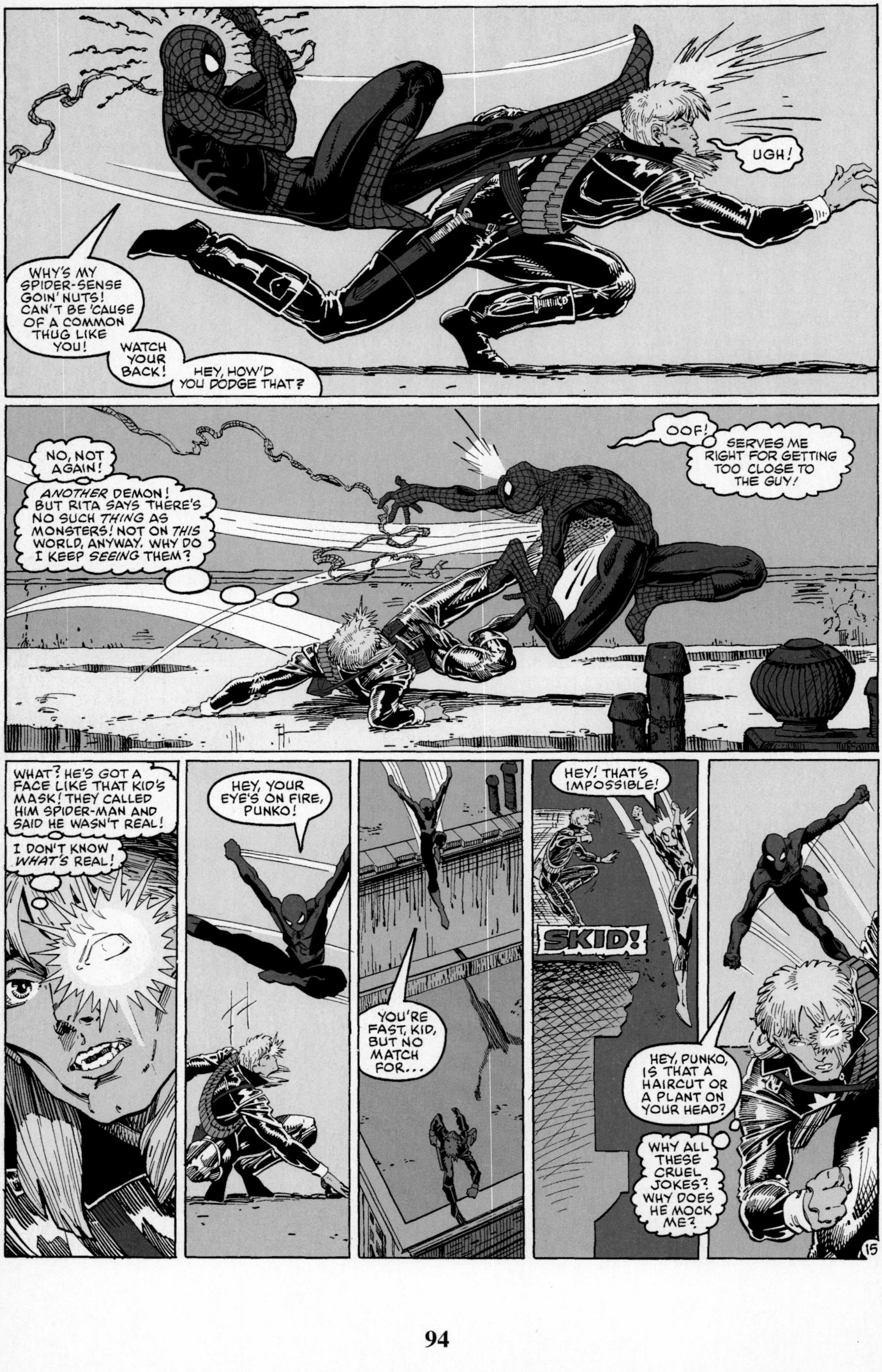
UGH!
WHY'S MY SPIDER-SENSE GOIN' NUTS! CAN'T BE 'CAUSE OF A COMMON THUG LIKE YOU!
WATCH YOUR BACK!
HEY, HOW'D YOU DODGE THAT?
NO, NOT AGAIN!
ANOTHER DEMON! BUT RITA SAYS THERE'S NO SUCH THING AS MONSTERS! NOT ON THIS WORLD, ANYWAY. WHY DO I KEEP SEEING THEM?
OOF!
SERVES ME RIGHT FOR GETTING TOO CLOSE TO THE GUY!
WHAT? HE'S GOT A FACE LIKE THAT KID'S MASK! THEY CALLED HIM SPIDER-MAN AND SAID HE WASN'T REAL!
I DON'T KNOW WHAT'S REAL!
HEY, YOUR EYE'S ON FIRE, PUNKO!
YOU'RE FAST, KID, BUT NO MATCH FOR...
HEY! THAT'S IMPOSSIBLE!
SKID!
HEY, PUNKO, IS THAT A HAIRCUT OR A PLANT ON YOUR HEAD?
WHY ALL THESE CRUEL JOKES? WHY DOES HE MOCK ME?
15

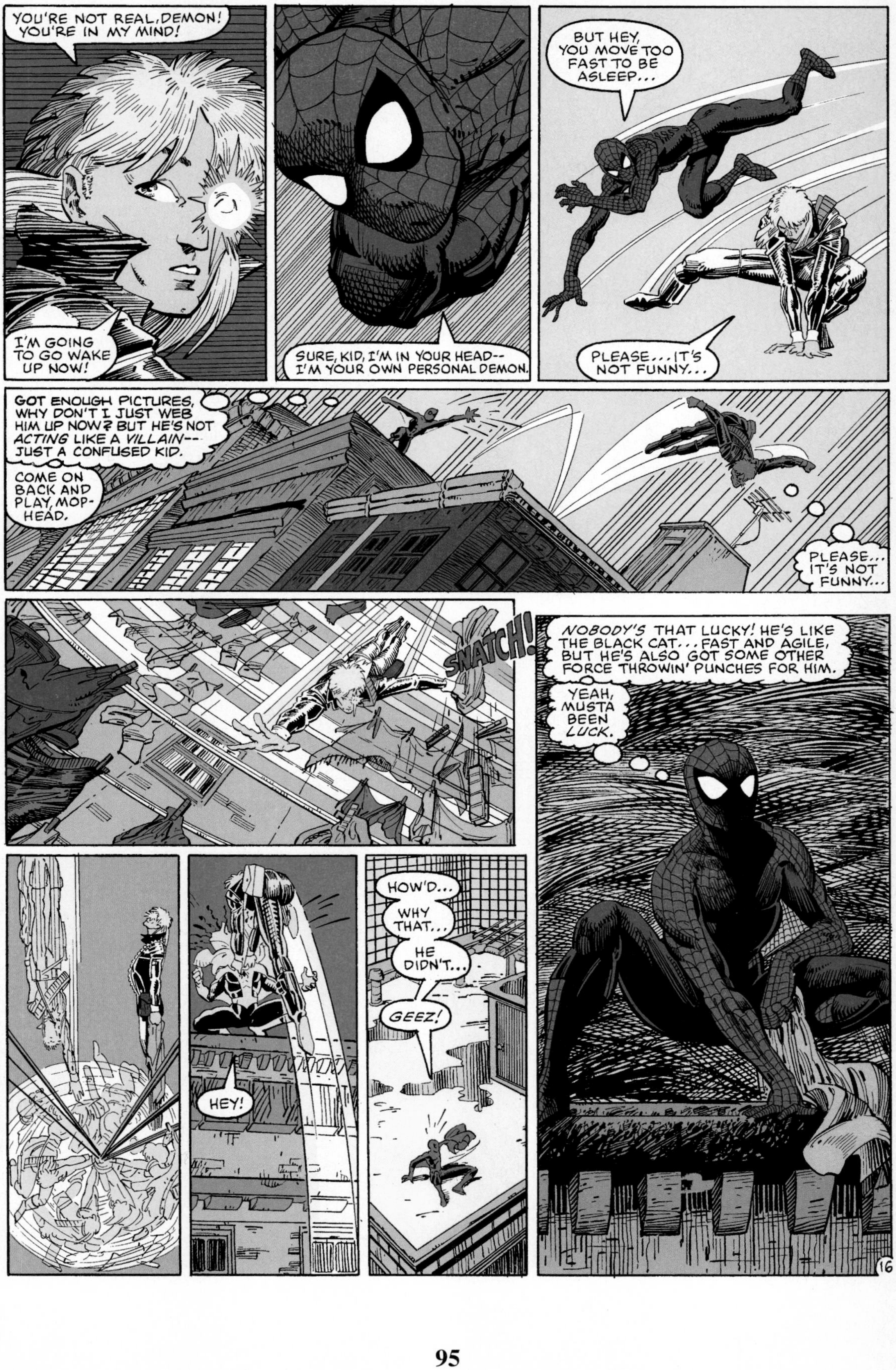

YOU'RE NOT REAL, DEMON! YOU'RE IN MY MIND!
I'M GOING TO GO WAKE UP NOW!
SURE, KID, I'M IN YOUR HEAD-- I'M YOUR OWN PERSONAL DEMON.
BUT HEY, YOU MOVE TOO FAST TO BE ASLEEP...
PLEASE... IT'S NOT FUNNY...
GOT ENOUGH PICTURES, WHY DON'T I JUST WEB HIM UP NOW? BUT HE'S NOT ACTING LIKE A VILLAIN-- JUST A CONFUSED KID.
COME ON BACK AND PLAY, MOP-HEAD.
PLEASE... IT'S NOT FUNNY...
SNATCH!
NOBODY'S THAT LUCKY! HE'S LIKE THE BLACK CAT... FAST AND AGILE, BUT HE'S ALSO GOT SOME OTHER FORCE THROWIN' PUNCHES FOR HIM.
YEAH, MUSTA BEEN LUCK.
HEY!
HOW'D...
WHY THAT...
HE DIDN'T...
GEEZ!
16

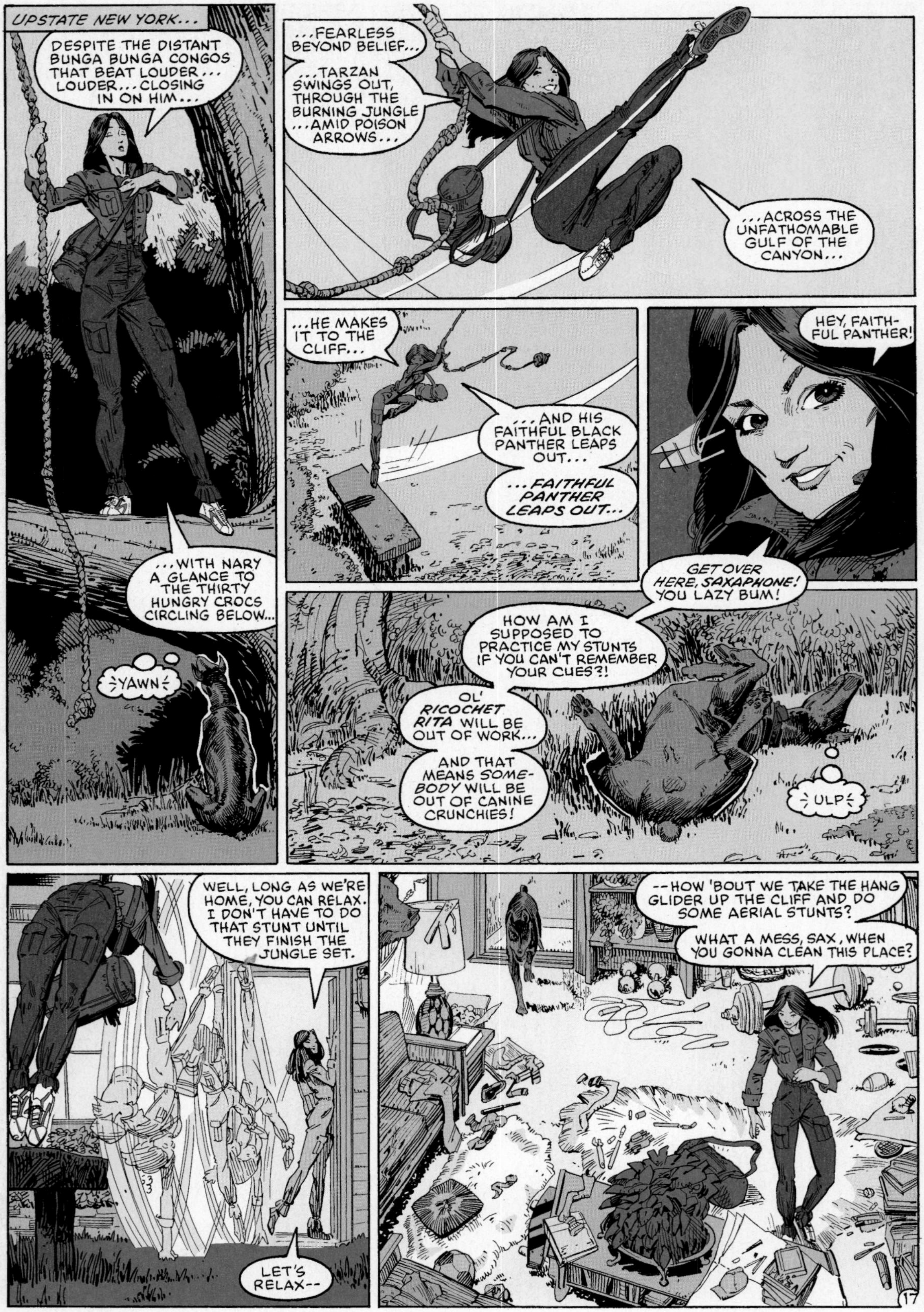
UPSTATE NEW YORK...
DESPITE THE DISTANT BUNGA BUNGA CONGOS THAT BEAT LOUDER... LOUDER... CLOSING IN ON HIM...
...WITH NARY A GLANCE TO THE THIRTY HUNGRY CROCS CIRCLING BELOW...
YAWN
...FEARLESS BEYOND BELIEF...
...TARZAN SWINGS OUT, THROUGH THE BURNING JUNGLE ...AMID POISON ARROWS...
...ACROSS THE UNFATHOMABLE GULF OF THE CANYON...
...HE MAKES IT TO THE CLIFF...
...AND HIS FAITHFUL BLACK PANTHER LEAPS OUT...
...*FAITHFUL PANTHER LEAPS OUT*...
HEY, FAITHFUL PANTHER!
GET OVER HERE, SAXAPHONE! YOU LAZY BUM!
HOW AM I SUPPOSED TO PRACTICE MY STUNTS IF YOU CAN'T REMEMBER YOUR CUES?!
OL' *RICOCHET RITA* WILL BE OUT OF WORK...
AND THAT MEANS *SOME-BODY* WILL BE OUT OF CANINE CRUNCHIES!
ULP
WELL, LONG AS WE'RE HOME, YOU CAN RELAX. I DON'T HAVE TO DO THAT STUNT UNTIL THEY FINISH THE JUNGLE SET.
LET'S RELAX--
--HOW 'BOUT WE TAKE THE HANG GLIDER UP THE CLIFF AND DO SOME AERIAL STUNTS?
WHAT A MESS, SAX, WHEN YOU GONNA CLEAN THIS PLACE?
17

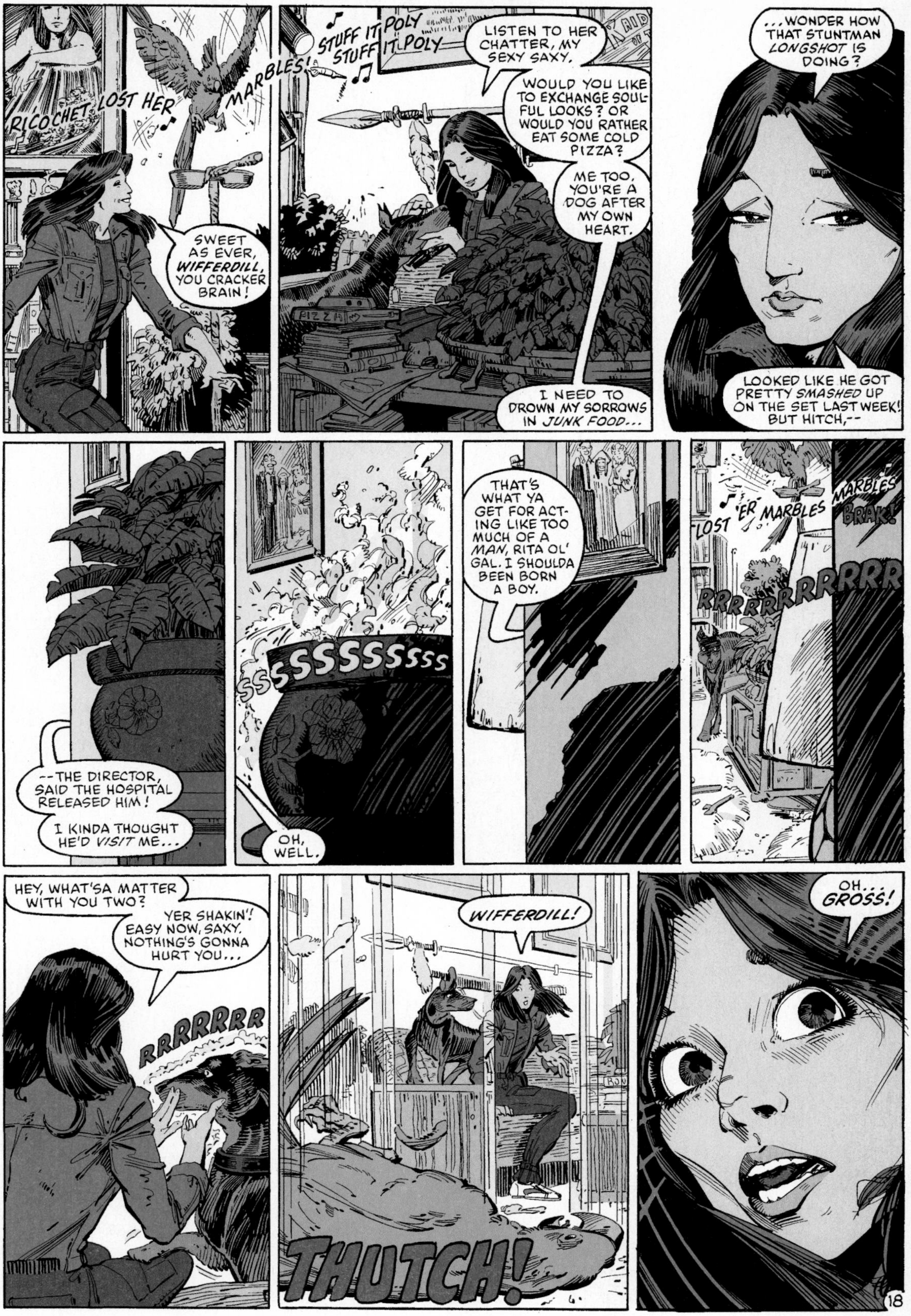
RICOCHET LOST HER MARBLES!
SWEET AS EVER, WIFFERDILL, YOU CRACKER BRAIN!
STUFF IT POLY STUFF IT POLY
LISTEN TO HER CHATTER, MY SEXY SAXY.
WOULD YOU LIKE TO EXCHANGE SOULFUL LOOKS? OR WOULD YOU RATHER EAT SOME COLD PIZZA?
ME TOO, YOU'RE A DOG AFTER MY OWN HEART.
I NEED TO DROWN MY SORROWS IN JUNK FOOD...
...WONDER HOW THAT STUNTMAN LONGSHOT IS DOING?
LOOKED LIKE HE GOT PRETTY SMASHED UP ON THE SET LAST WEEK! BUT HITCH,--
--THE DIRECTOR, SAID THE HOSPITAL RELEASED HIM!
I KINDA THOUGHT HE'D VISIT ME...
SSSSSSSSSSSS
OH, WELL.
THAT'S WHAT YA GET FOR ACTING LIKE TOO MUCH OF A MAN, RITA OL' GAL. I SHOULDA BEEN BORN A BOY.
LOST 'ER MARBLES MARBLES
BRAK!
RRRRRRRRRRRR
HEY, WHAT'SA MATTER WITH YOU TWO?
YER SHAKIN'! EASY NOW, SAXY. NOTHING'S GONNA HURT YOU...
RRRRRRRR
WIFFERDILL!
THUTCH!
OH... GROSS!
18

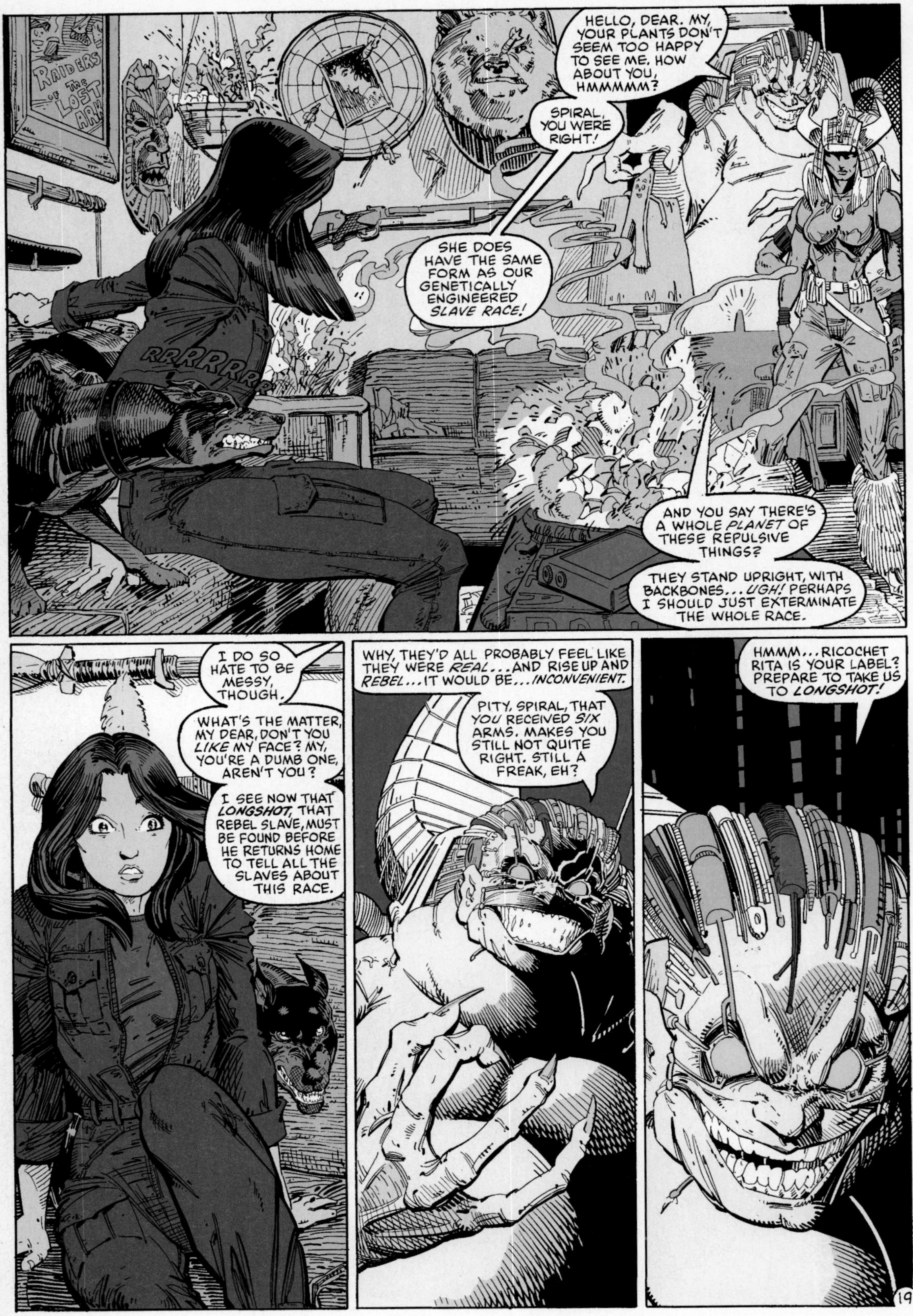
HELLO, DEAR. MY, YOUR PLANTS DON'T SEEM TOO HAPPY TO SEE ME. HOW ABOUT YOU, HMMMMM?
SPIRAL, YOU WERE RIGHT!
SHE DOES HAVE THE SAME FORM AS OUR GENETICALLY ENGINEERED *SLAVE RACE!*
RRRRRRRR
AND YOU SAY THERE'S A WHOLE *PLANET* OF THESE REPULSIVE THINGS?
THEY STAND UPRIGHT, WITH BACKBONES... *UGH!* PERHAPS I SHOULD JUST EXTERMINATE THE WHOLE RACE.
I DO SO HATE TO BE MESSY, THOUGH.
WHAT'S THE MATTER, MY DEAR, DON'T YOU *LIKE* MY FACE? MY, YOU'RE A DUMB ONE, AREN'T YOU?
I SEE NOW THAT *LONGSHOT,* THAT REBEL SLAVE, MUST BE FOUND BEFORE HE RETURNS HOME TO TELL ALL THE SLAVES ABOUT THIS RACE.
WHY, THEY'D ALL PROBABLY FEEL LIKE THEY WERE *REAL*...AND RISE UP AND *REBEL*...IT WOULD BE...*INCONVENIENT.*
PITY, SPIRAL, THAT *YOU* RECEIVED *SIX* ARMS. MAKES YOU STILL NOT QUITE RIGHT. STILL A FREAK, EH?
HMMM...RICOCHET RITA IS YOUR LABEL? PREPARE TO TAKE US TO *LONGSHOT!*
19

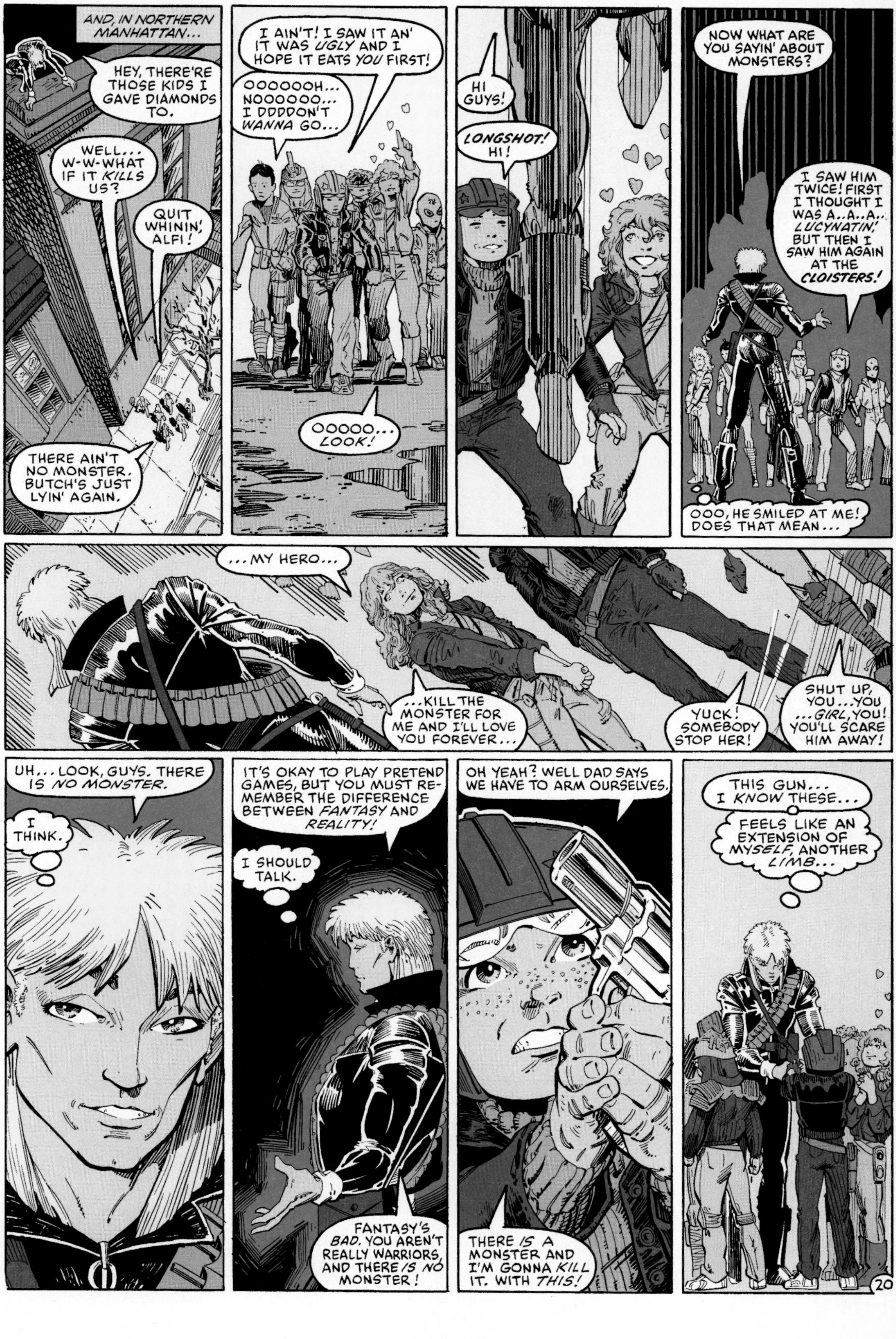
AND, IN NORTHERN MANHATTAN...
HEY, THERE'RE THOSE KIDS I GAVE DIAMONDS TO.
WELL... W-W-WHAT IF IT KILLS US?
QUIT WHININ', ALFI!
THERE AIN'T NO MONSTER. BUTCH'S JUST LYIN' AGAIN.
I AIN'T! I SAW IT AN' IT WAS UGLY AND I HOPE IT EATS YOU FIRST!
OOOOOOH... NOOOOOO... I DDDDON'T WANNA GO...
OOOOO... LOOK!
HI GUYS!
LONGSHOT! HI!
NOW WHAT ARE YOU SAYIN' ABOUT MONSTERS?
I SAW HIM TWICE! FIRST I THOUGHT I WAS A..A..A.. LUCYNATIN', BUT THEN I SAW HIM AGAIN AT THE CLOISTERS!
OOO, HE SMILED AT ME! DOES THAT MEAN...
...MY HERO...
...KILL THE MONSTER FOR ME AND I'LL LOVE YOU FOREVER...
YUCK! SOMEBODY STOP HER!
SHUT UP, YOU...YOU ...GIRL, YOU! YOU'LL SCARE HIM AWAY!
UH... LOOK, GUYS. THERE IS NO MONSTER.
I THINK.
IT'S OKAY TO PLAY PRETEND GAMES, BUT YOU MUST REMEMBER THE DIFFERENCE BETWEEN FANTASY AND REALITY!
I SHOULD TALK.
FANTASY'S BAD. YOU AREN'T REALLY WARRIORS, AND THERE IS NO MONSTER!
OH YEAH? WELL DAD SAYS WE HAVE TO ARM OURSELVES.
THERE IS A MONSTER AND I'M GONNA KILL IT. WITH THIS!
THIS GUN... I KNOW THESE...
FEELS LIKE AN EXTENSION OF MYSELF, ANOTHER LIMB...
20

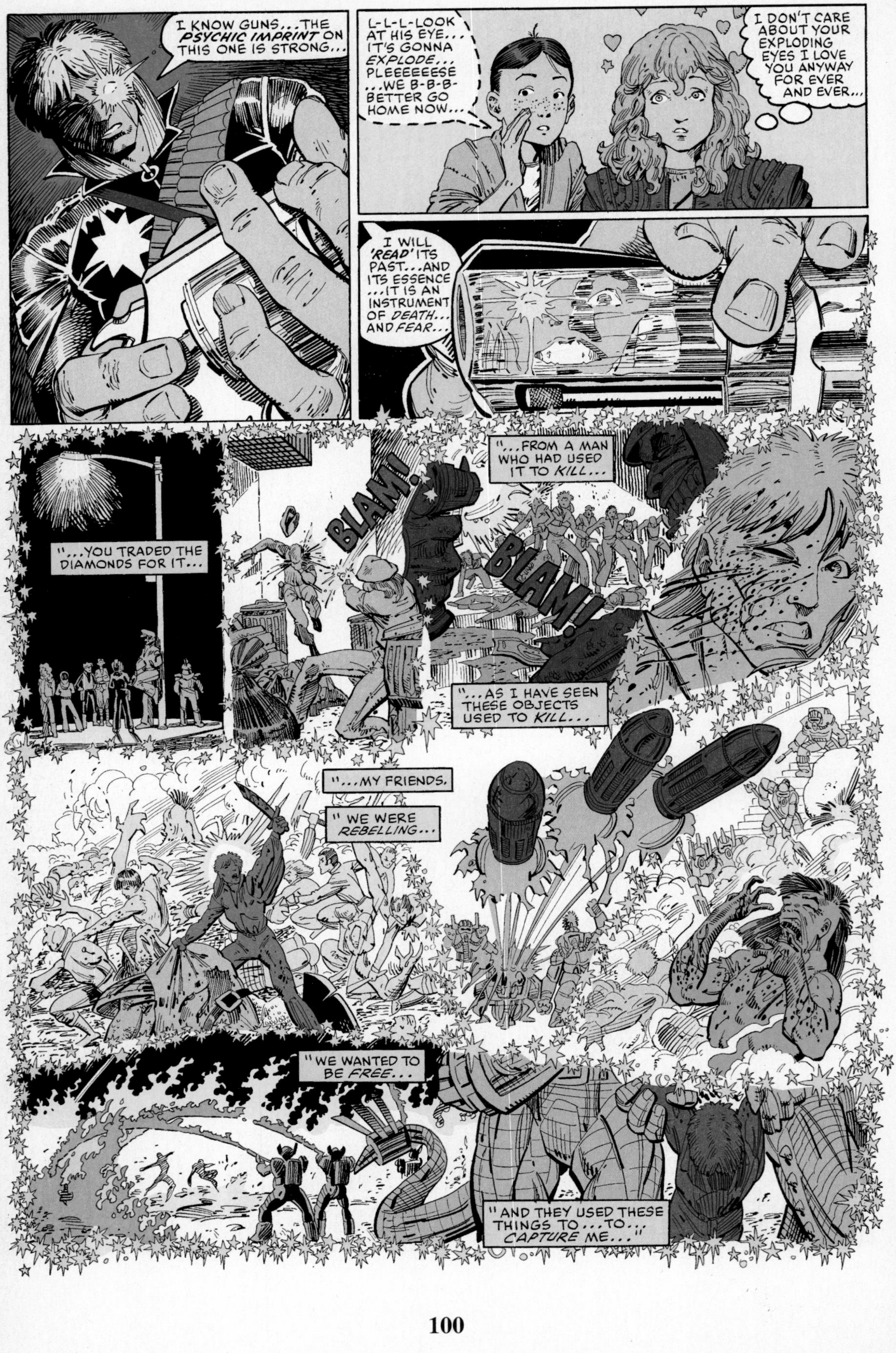

I KNOW GUNS... THE PSYCHIC IMPRINT ON THIS ONE IS STRONG...
L-L-L-LOOK AT HIS EYE... IT'S GONNA EXPLODE... PLEEEEEESE ...WE B-B-B-BETTER GO HOME NOW...
I DON'T CARE ABOUT YOUR EXPLODING EYES I LOVE YOU ANYWAY FOR EVER AND EVER...
I WILL 'READ' ITS PAST...AND ITS ESSENCE ...IT IS AN INSTRUMENT OF DEATH... AND FEAR...
"...YOU TRADED THE DIAMONDS FOR IT...
"...FROM A MAN WHO HAD USED IT TO KILL...
BLAM!
BLAM!
"...AS I HAVE SEEN THESE OBJECTS USED TO KILL...
"...MY FRIENDS.
" WE WERE REBELLING...
"WE WANTED TO BE FREE...
"AND THEY USED THESE THINGS TO...TO... CAPTURE ME..."

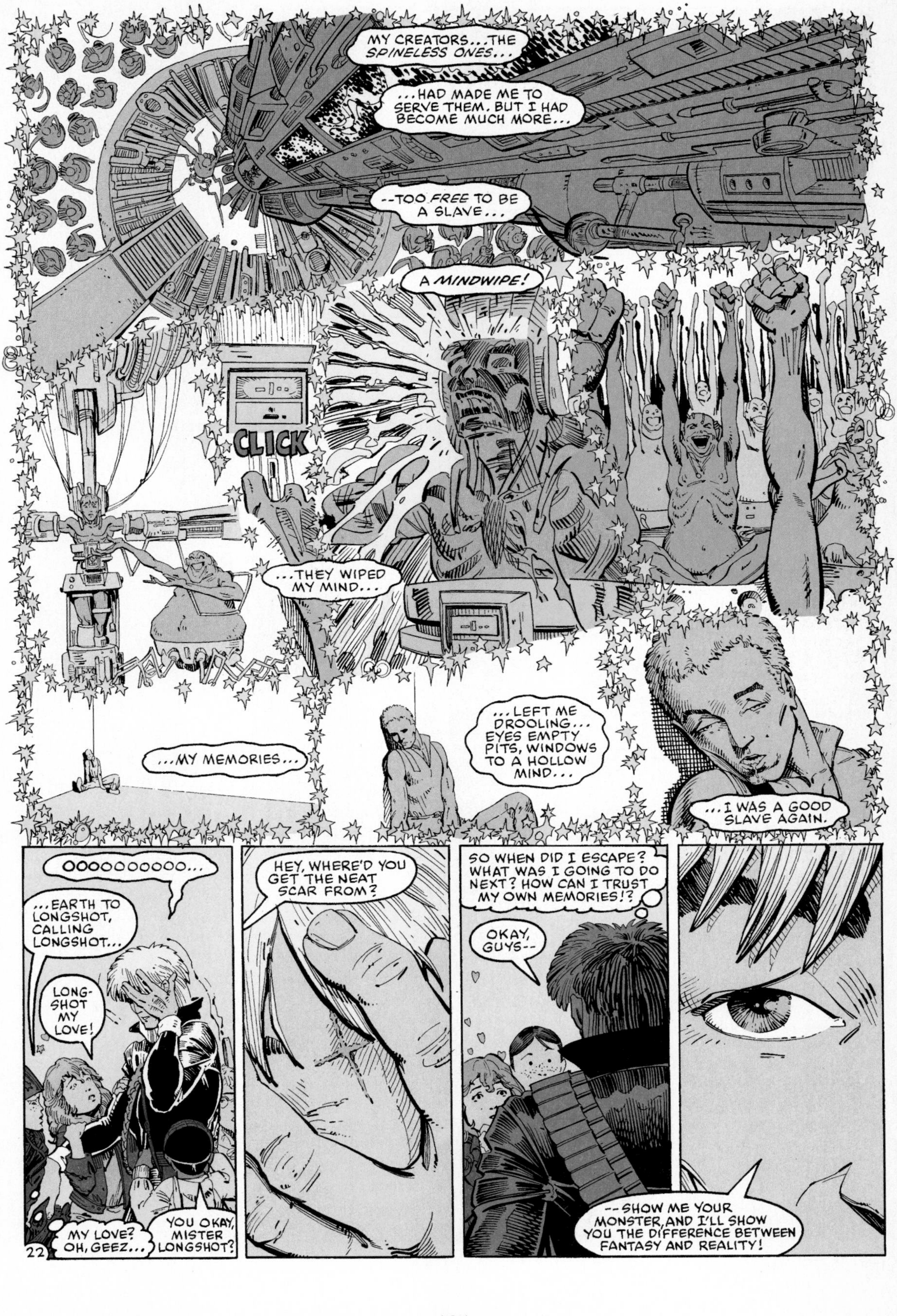
MY CREATORS... THE SPINELESS ONES...
...HAD MADE ME TO SERVE THEM. BUT I HAD BECOME MUCH MORE...
--TOO FREE TO BE A SLAVE...
A MINDWIPE!
CLICK
...THEY WIPED MY MIND...
...MY MEMORIES...
...LEFT ME DROOLING... EYES EMPTY PITS, WINDOWS TO A HOLLOW MIND...
...I WAS A GOOD SLAVE AGAIN.
OOOOOOOOOO...
...EARTH TO LONGSHOT, CALLING LONGSHOT...
LONGSHOT MY LOVE!
MY LOVE? OH, GEEZ...
YOU OKAY, MISTER LONGSHOT?
22
HEY, WHERE'D YOU GET THE NEAT SCAR FROM?
SO WHEN DID I ESCAPE? WHAT WAS I GOING TO DO NEXT? HOW CAN I TRUST MY OWN MEMORIES!?
OKAY, GUYS--
--SHOW ME YOUR MONSTER, AND I'LL SHOW YOU THE DIFFERENCE BETWEEN FANTASY AND REALITY!

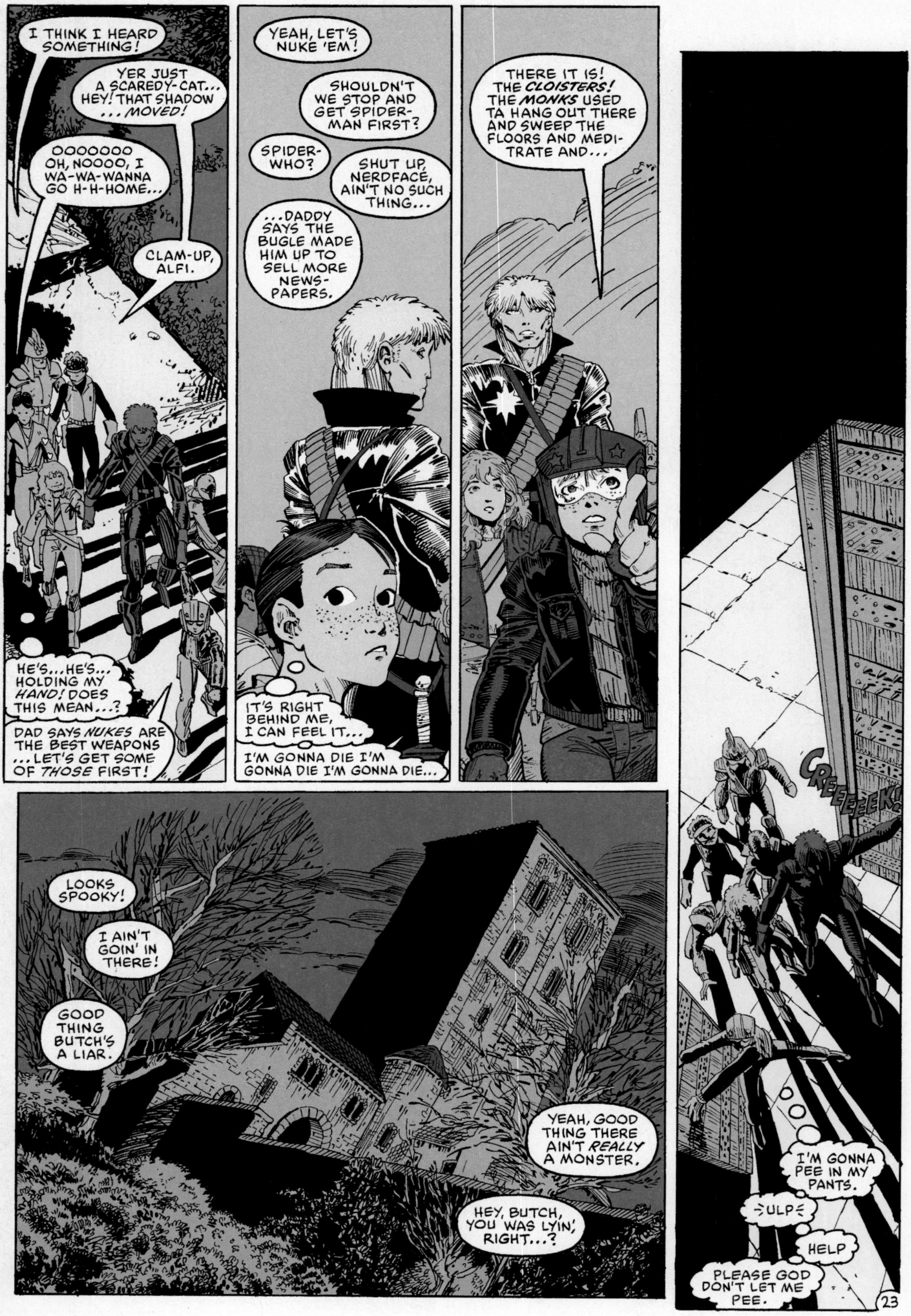

I THINK I HEARD SOMETHING!
YER JUST A SCAREDY-CAT... HEY! THAT SHADOW ...*MOVED!*
OOOOOOO OH, NOOOO, I WA-WA-WANNA GO H-H-HOME...
CLAM-UP, ALFI.
HE'S...HE'S... HOLDING MY *HAND!* DOES THIS MEAN...?
DAD SAYS *NUKES* ARE THE BEST WEAPONS ...LET'S GET SOME OF *THOSE* FIRST!
YEAH, LET'S NUKE 'EM!
SHOULDN'T WE STOP AND GET SPIDER-MAN FIRST?
SPIDER-WHO?
SHUT UP, NERDFACE, AIN'T NO SUCH THING...
...DADDY SAYS THE BUGLE MADE HIM UP TO SELL MORE NEWS-PAPERS.
IT'S RIGHT BEHIND ME, I CAN FEEL IT...
I'M GONNA DIE I'M GONNA DIE I'M GONNA DIE...
THERE IT IS! THE *CLOISTERS!* THE *MONKS* USED TA HANG OUT THERE AND SWEEP THE FLOORS AND MEDI-TATE AND...
LOOKS SPOOKY!
I AIN'T GOIN' IN THERE!
GOOD THING BUTCH'S A LIAR.
YEAH, GOOD THING THERE AIN'T *REALLY* A MONSTER.
HEY, BUTCH, YOU WAS LYIN', RIGHT...?
CREEEEEK!
I'M GONNA PEE IN MY PANTS.
ULP
HELP
PLEASE GOD DON'T LET ME PEE.
23

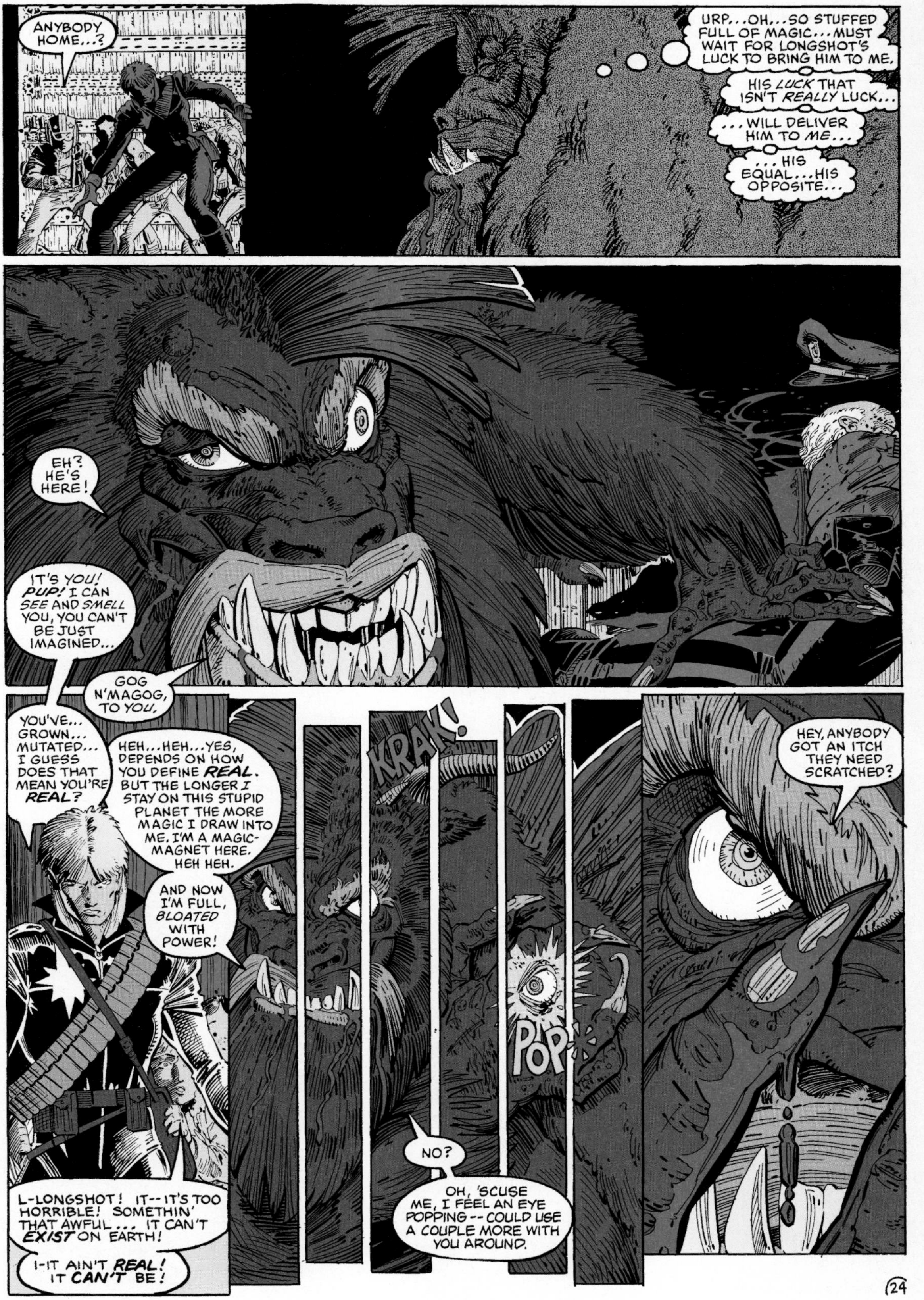
ANYBODY HOME...?
URP...OH...SO STUFFED FULL OF MAGIC...MUST WAIT FOR LONGSHOT'S LUCK TO BRING HIM TO ME.
HIS *LUCK* THAT ISN'T *REALLY* LUCK...
...WILL DELIVER HIM TO *ME*...
...HIS EQUAL...HIS OPPOSITE...
EH? HE'S HERE!
IT'S *YOU! PUP!* I CAN *SEE* AND *SMELL* YOU, YOU CAN'T BE JUST IMAGINED...
GOG N'MAGOG, TO *YOU*.
YOU'VE... GROWN... MUTATED... I GUESS DOES THAT MEAN YOU'RE ***REAL***?
HEH...HEH...YES, DEPENDS ON HOW YOU DEFINE ***REAL***. BUT THE LONGER *I* STAY ON THIS STUPID PLANET THE MORE MAGIC I DRAW INTO ME. I'M A MAGIC-MAGNET HERE. HEH HEH.
AND NOW I'M FULL, *BLOATED* WITH POWER!
L-LONGSHOT! IT--IT'S TOO HORRIBLE! SOMETHIN' THAT AWFUL... IT CAN'T ***EXIST*** ON EARTH!
I-IT AIN'T ***REAL***! IT ***CAN'T*** BE!
KRAK!
NO?
OH, 'SCUSE ME, I FEEL AN EYE POPPING -- COULD USE A COUPLE MORE WITH YOU AROUND.
POP
HEY, ANYBODY GOT AN ITCH THEY NEED SCRATCHED?
24

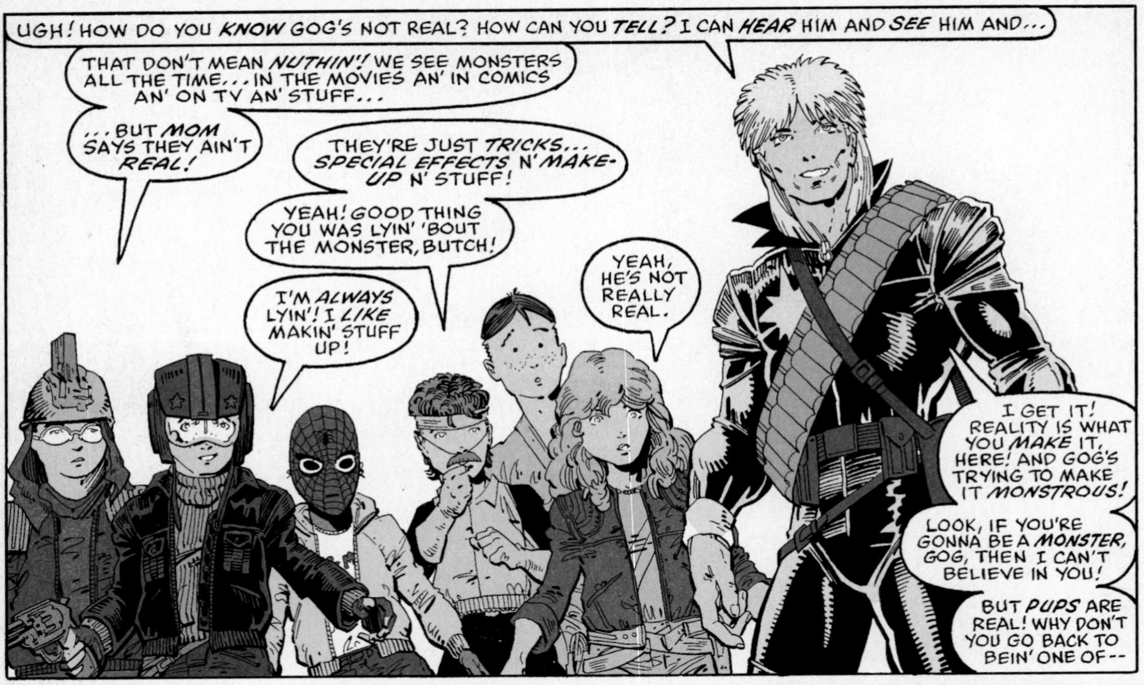
UGH! HOW DO YOU KNOW GOG'S NOT REAL? HOW CAN YOU TELL? I CAN HEAR HIM AND SEE HIM AND...
THAT DON'T MEAN NUTHIN'! WE SEE MONSTERS ALL THE TIME... IN THE MOVIES AN' IN COMICS AN' ON TV AN' STUFF...
...BUT MOM SAYS THEY AIN'T REAL!
THEY'RE JUST TRICKS... SPECIAL EFFECTS N' MAKE-UP N' STUFF!
YEAH! GOOD THING YOU WAS LYIN' 'BOUT THE MONSTER, BUTCH!
I'M ALWAYS LYIN'! I LIKE MAKIN' STUFF UP!
YEAH, HE'S NOT REALLY REAL.
I GET IT! REALITY IS WHAT YOU MAKE IT, HERE! AND GOG'S TRYING TO MAKE IT MONSTROUS!
LOOK, IF YOU'RE GONNA BE A MONSTER, GOG, THEN I CAN'T BELIEVE IN YOU!
BUT PUPS ARE REAL! WHY DON'T YOU GO BACK TO BEIN' ONE OF--

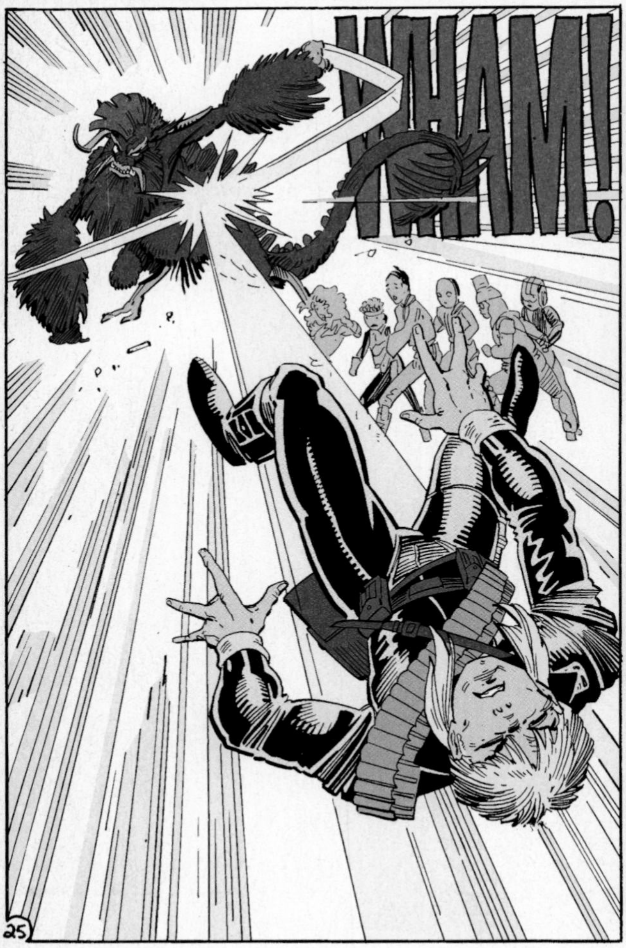
WHAM!
25

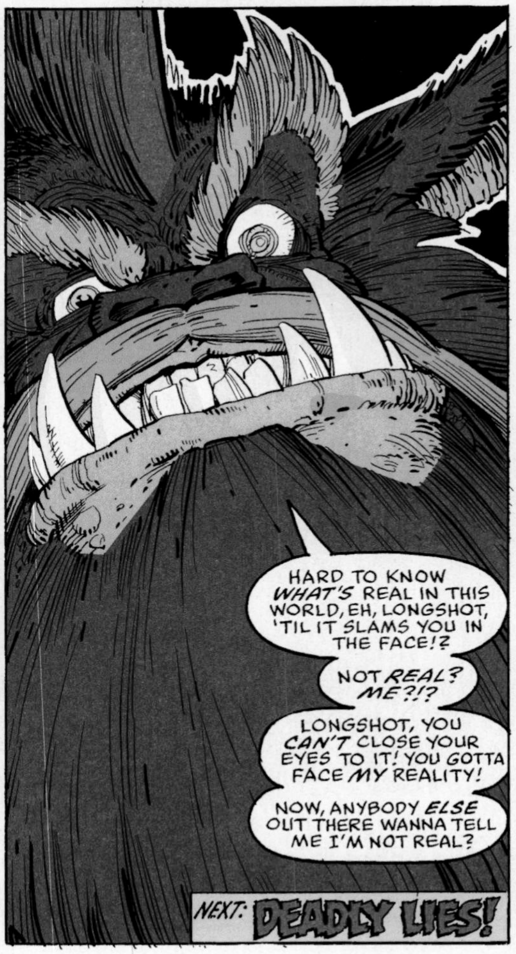
HARD TO KNOW WHAT'S REAL IN THIS WORLD, EH, LONGSHOT, 'TIL IT SLAMS YOU IN THE FACE!?
NOT REAL? ME?!?
LONGSHOT, YOU CAN'T CLOSE YOUR EYES TO IT! YOU GOTTA FACE MY REALITY!
NOW, ANYBODY ELSE OUT THERE WANNA TELL ME I'M NOT REAL?
NEXT: DEADLY LIES!

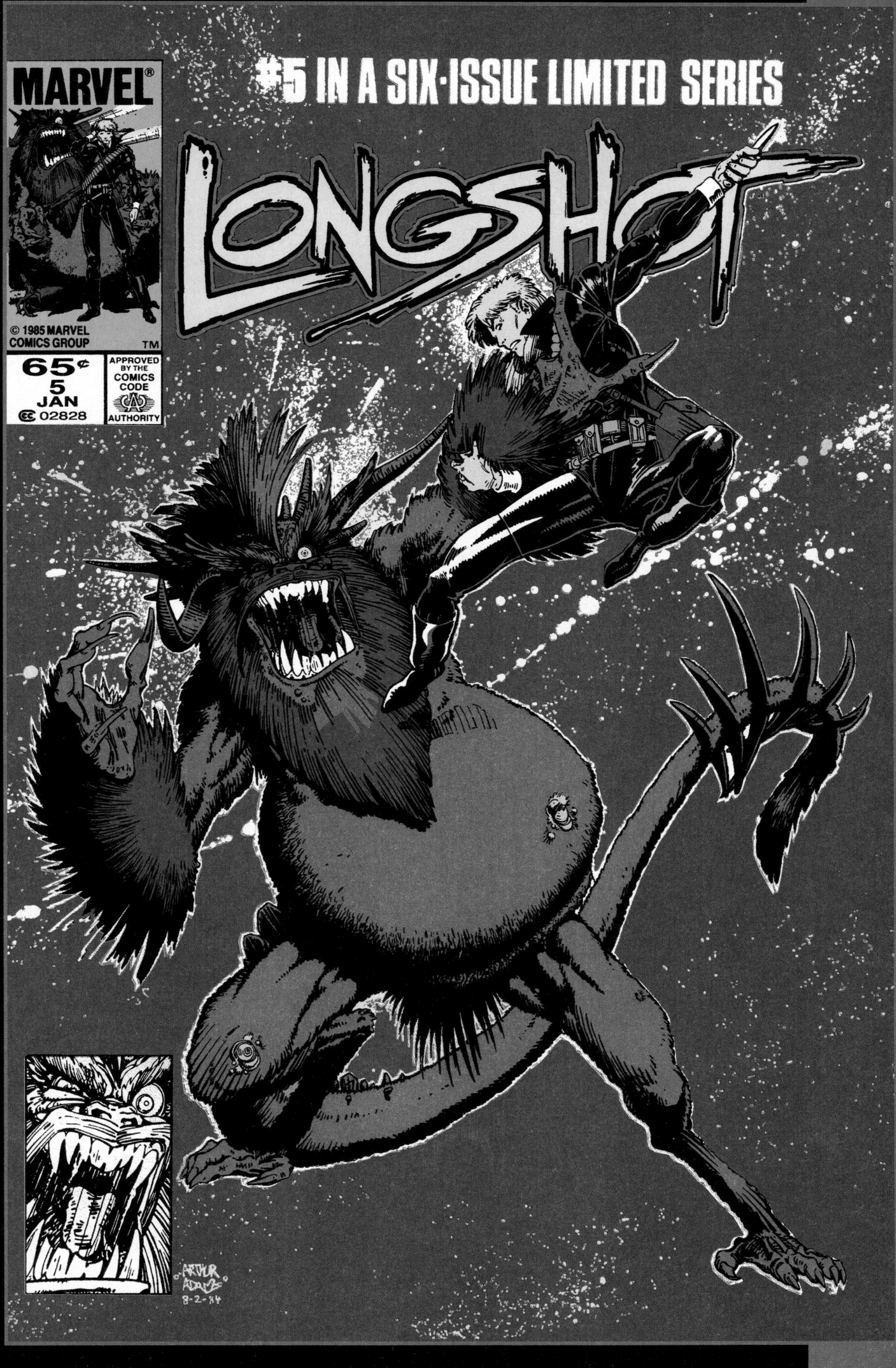

MARVEL®
#5 IN A SIX-ISSUE LIMITED SERIES
LONGSHOT
© 1985 MARVEL COMICS GROUP
TM
65¢
5
JAN
02828
APPROVED BY THE COMICS CODE AUTHORITY
ARTHUR ADAMS
8-2-84

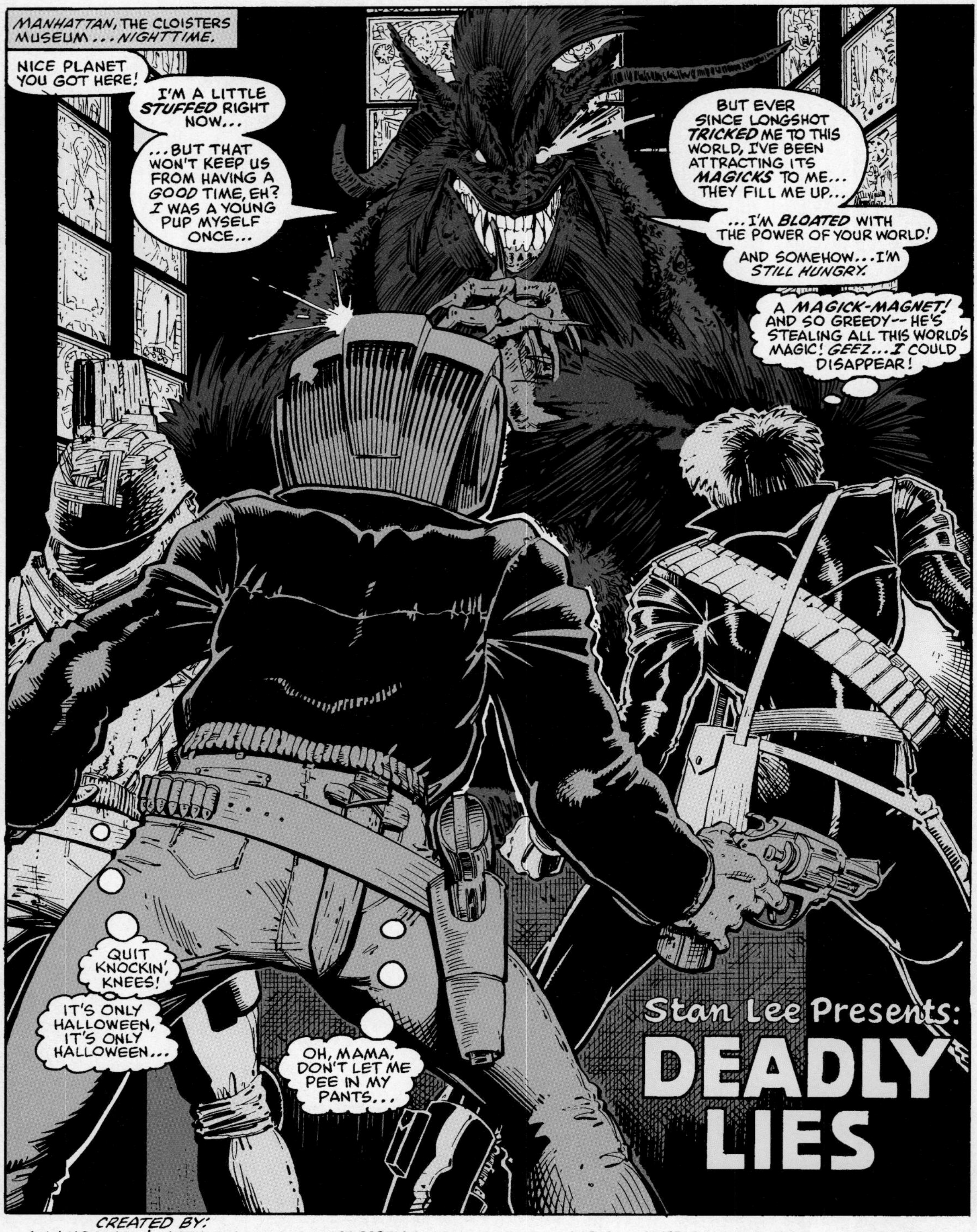
MANHATTAN, THE CLOISTERS MUSEUM... NIGHTTIME.
NICE PLANET YOU GOT HERE!
I'M A LITTLE STUFFED RIGHT NOW...
...BUT THAT WON'T KEEP US FROM HAVING A GOOD TIME, EH? I WAS A YOUNG PUP MYSELF ONCE...
BUT EVER SINCE LONGSHOT TRICKED ME TO THIS WORLD, I'VE BEEN ATTRACTING ITS MAGICKS TO ME... THEY FILL ME UP...
...I'M BLOATED WITH THE POWER OF YOUR WORLD!
AND SOMEHOW...I'M STILL HUNGRY.
A MAGICK-MAGNET! AND SO GREEDY-- HE'S STEALING ALL THIS WORLD'S MAGIC! GEEZ...I COULD DISAPPEAR!
QUIT KNOCKIN' KNEES!
IT'S ONLY HALLOWEEN, IT'S ONLY HALLOWEEN...
OH, MAMA, DON'T LET ME PEE IN MY PANTS...
Stan Lee Presents:
DEADLY LIES

CREATED BY: ANN NOCENTI & ARTHUR ADAMS · WHILCE PORTACIO · JOE ROSEN · CHRISTIE SCHEELE · LOUISE JONES · JIM SHOOTER

WRITER · PENCILER · INKER · LETTERS · COLORS · EDITOR · EDITOR IN CHIEF

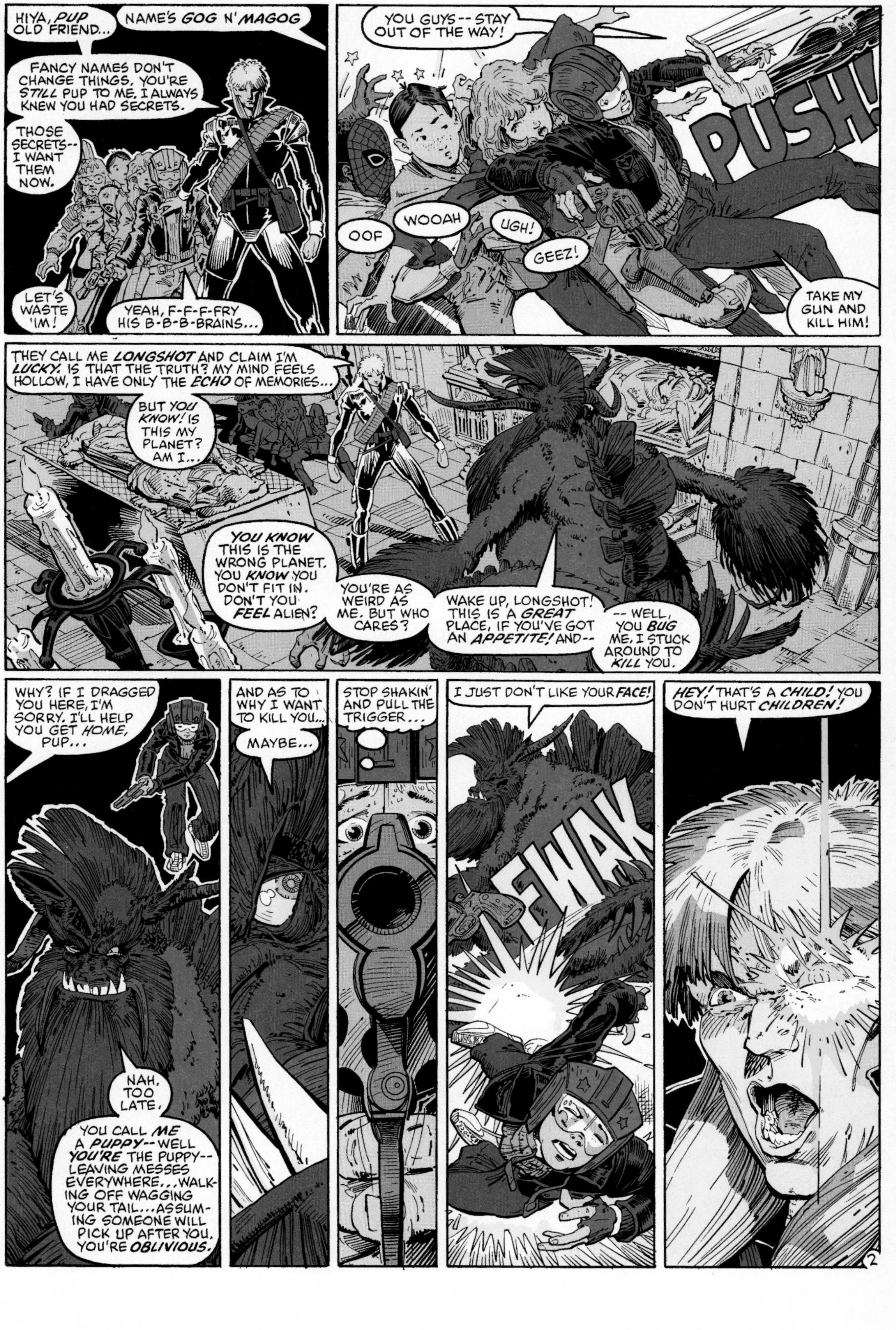
HIYA, PUP OLD FRIEND...
NAME'S GOG N' MAGOG
FANCY NAMES DON'T CHANGE THINGS. YOU'RE STILL PUP TO ME. I ALWAYS KNEW YOU HAD SECRETS.
THOSE SECRETS-- I WANT THEM NOW.
LET'S WASTE 'IM!
YEAH, F-F-F-FRY HIS B-B-B-BRAINS...
YOU GUYS -- STAY OUT OF THE WAY!
PUSH!
OOF
WOOAH
UGH!
GEEZ!
TAKE MY GUN AND KILL HIM!
THEY CALL ME LONGSHOT AND CLAIM I'M LUCKY. IS THAT THE TRUTH? MY MIND FEELS HOLLOW, I HAVE ONLY THE ECHO OF MEMORIES...
BUT YOU KNOW! IS THIS MY PLANET? AM I...
YOU KNOW THIS IS THE WRONG PLANET. YOU KNOW YOU DON'T FIT IN. DON'T YOU FEEL ALIEN?
YOU'RE AS WEIRD AS ME. BUT WHO CARES?
WAKE UP, LONGSHOT! THIS IS A GREAT PLACE, IF YOU'VE GOT AN APPETITE! AND--
-- WELL, YOU BUG ME. I STUCK AROUND TO KILL YOU.
WHY? IF I DRAGGED YOU HERE, I'M SORRY. I'LL HELP YOU GET HOME, PUP...
NAH, TOO LATE.
YOU CALL ME A PUPPY-- WELL YOU'RE THE PUPPY-- LEAVING MESSES EVERYWHERE... WALKING OFF WAGGING YOUR TAIL... ASSUMING SOMEONE WILL PICK UP AFTER YOU. YOU'RE OBLIVIOUS.
AND AS TO WHY I WANT TO KILL YOU...
MAYBE...
STOP SHAKIN' AND PULL THE TRIGGER...
I JUST DON'T LIKE YOUR FACE!
FWAK
HEY! THAT'S A CHILD! YOU DON'T HURT CHILDREN!
2

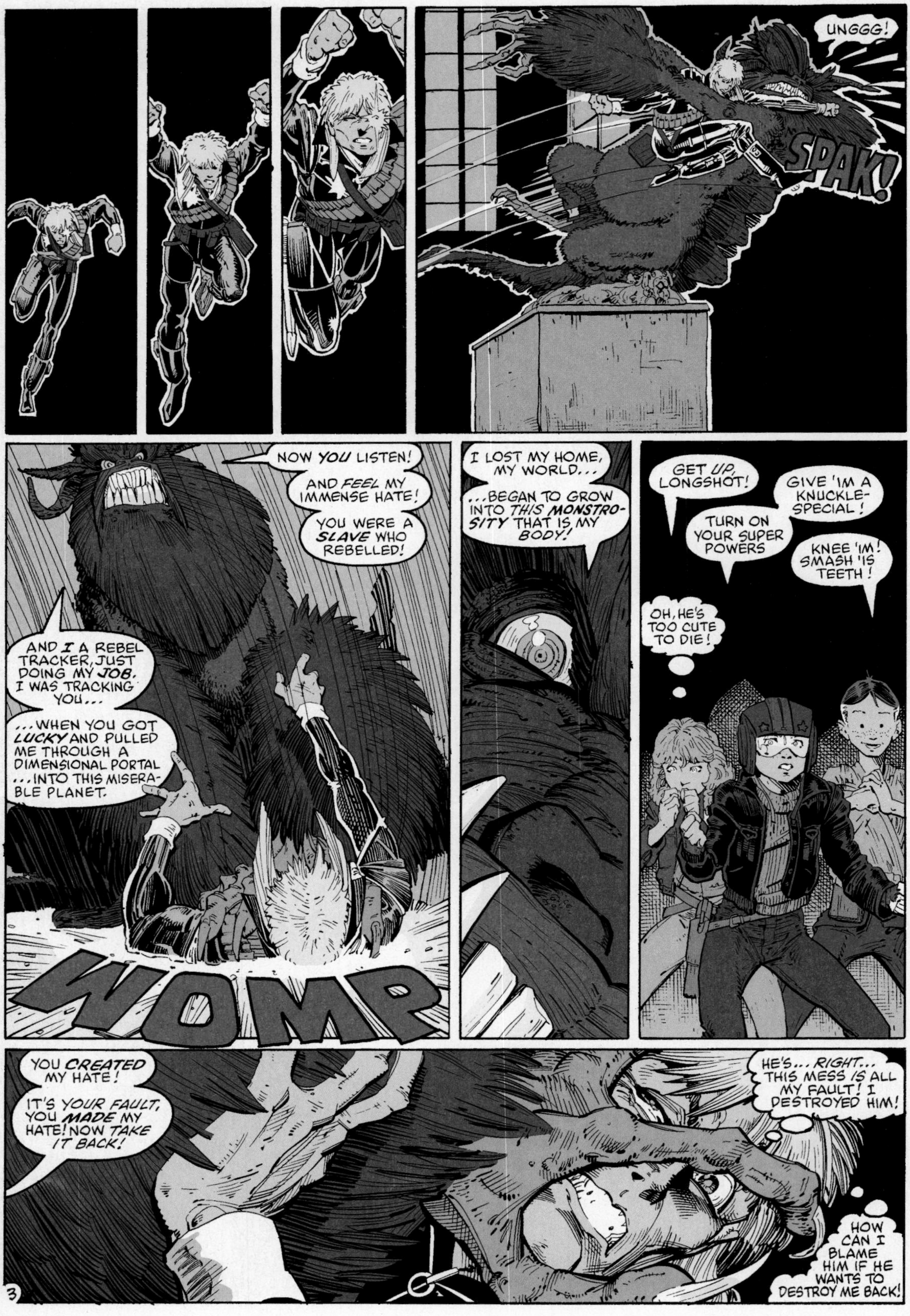
UNGGG!
SPAK!
NOW YOU LISTEN!
AND FEEL MY IMMENSE HATE!
YOU WERE A SLAVE WHO REBELLED!
AND I A REBEL TRACKER, JUST DOING MY JOB. I WAS TRACKING YOU...
...WHEN YOU GOT LUCKY AND PULLED ME THROUGH A DIMENSIONAL PORTAL ...INTO THIS MISERABLE PLANET.
WOMP
I LOST MY HOME, MY WORLD...
...BEGAN TO GROW INTO THIS MONSTROSITY THAT IS MY BODY!
GET UP, LONGSHOT!
GIVE 'IM A KNUCKLE-SPECIAL!
TURN ON YOUR SUPER POWERS
KNEE 'IM! SMASH 'IS TEETH!
OH, HE'S TOO CUTE TO DIE!
YOU CREATED MY HATE!
IT'S YOUR FAULT, YOU MADE MY HATE! NOW TAKE IT BACK!
HE'S... RIGHT... THIS MESS IS ALL MY FAULT! I DESTROYED HIM!
HOW CAN I BLAME HIM IF HE WANTS TO DESTROY ME BACK!
3

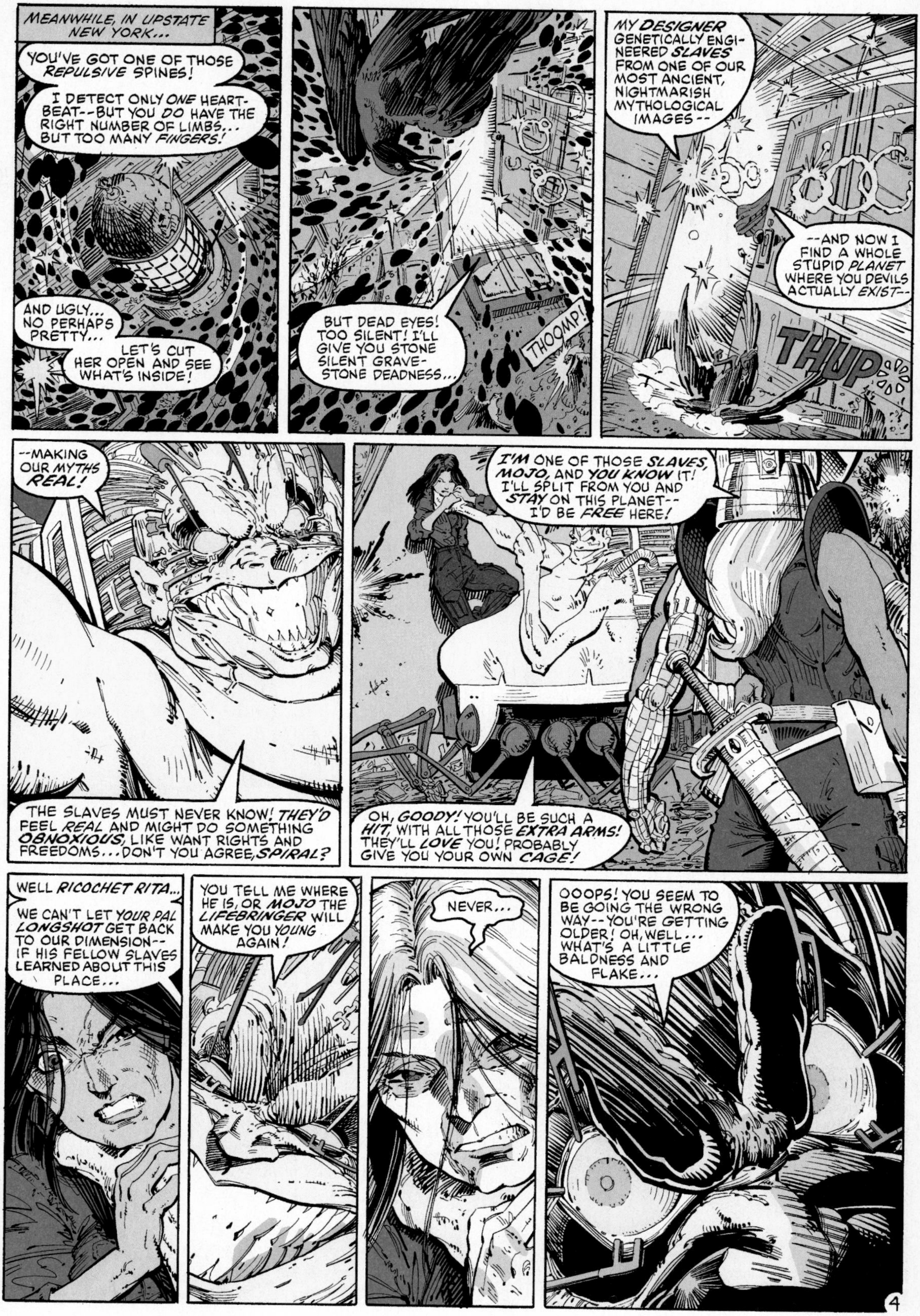
MEANWHILE, IN UPSTATE NEW YORK...
YOU'VE GOT ONE OF THOSE REPULSIVE SPINES!
I DETECT ONLY ONE HEART-BEAT--BUT YOU DO HAVE THE RIGHT NUMBER OF LIMBS... BUT TOO MANY FINGERS!
AND UGLY... NO PERHAPS PRETTY...
LET'S CUT HER OPEN AND SEE WHAT'S INSIDE!
BUT DEAD EYES! TOO SILENT! I'LL GIVE YOU STONE SILENT GRAVE-STONE DEADNESS...
THOOMP!
MY DESIGNER GENETICALLY ENGI-NEERED SLAVES FROM ONE OF OUR MOST ANCIENT, NIGHTMARISH MYTHOLOGICAL IMAGES--
--AND NOW I FIND A WHOLE STUPID PLANET WHERE YOU DEVILS ACTUALLY EXIST--
THUP
--MAKING OUR MYTHS REAL!
THE SLAVES MUST NEVER KNOW! THEY'D FEEL REAL AND MIGHT DO SOMETHING OBNOXIOUS, LIKE WANT RIGHTS AND FREEDOMS...DON'T YOU AGREE, SPIRAL?
I'M ONE OF THOSE SLAVES, MOJO, AND YOU KNOW IT! I'LL SPLIT FROM YOU AND STAY ON THIS PLANET--I'D BE FREE HERE!
OH, GOODY! YOU'LL BE SUCH A HIT, WITH ALL THOSE EXTRA ARMS! THEY'LL LOVE YOU! PROBABLY GIVE YOU YOUR OWN CAGE!
WELL RICOCHET RITA...
WE CAN'T LET YOUR PAL LONGSHOT GET BACK TO OUR DIMENSION--IF HIS FELLOW SLAVES LEARNED ABOUT THIS PLACE...
YOU TELL ME WHERE HE IS, OR MOJO THE LIFEBRINGER WILL MAKE YOU YOUNG AGAIN!
NEVER...
OOOPS! YOU SEEM TO BE GOING THE WRONG WAY--YOU'RE GETTING OLDER! OH, WELL... WHAT'S A LITTLE BALDNESS AND FLAKE...
4

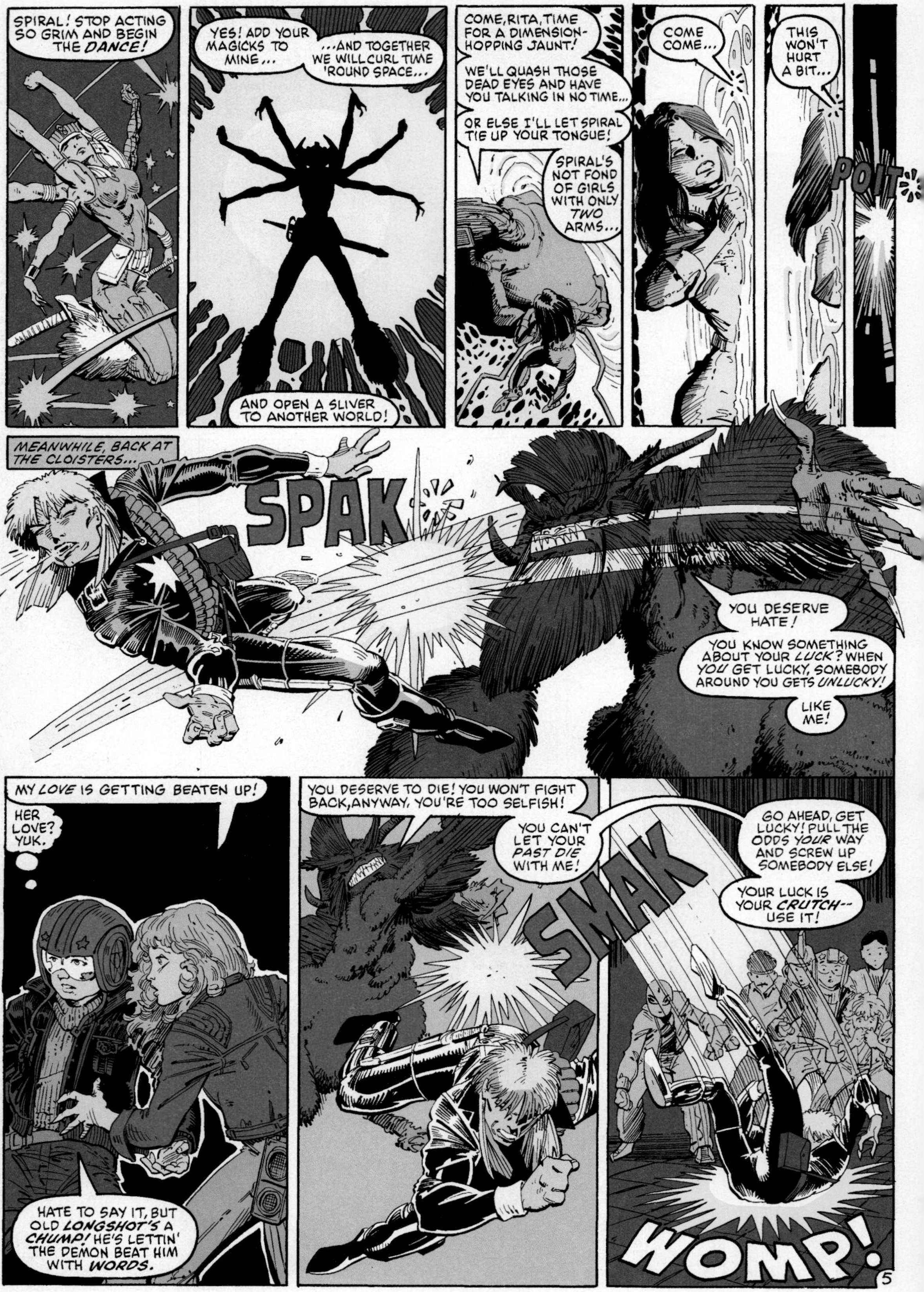
SPIRAL! STOP ACTING SO GRIM AND BEGIN THE DANCE!
YES! ADD YOUR MAGICKS TO MINE...
...AND TOGETHER WE WILL CURL TIME 'ROUND SPACE...
AND OPEN A SLIVER TO ANOTHER WORLD!
COME, RITA, TIME FOR A DIMENSION-HOPPING JAUNT!
WE'LL QUASH THOSE DEAD EYES AND HAVE YOU TALKING IN NO TIME...
OR ELSE I'LL LET SPIRAL TIE UP YOUR TONGUE!
SPIRAL'S NOT FOND OF GIRLS WITH ONLY TWO ARMS...
COME COME...
THIS WON'T HURT A BIT...
POIT
MEANWHILE, BACK AT THE CLOISTERS...
SPAK
YOU DESERVE HATE!
YOU KNOW SOMETHING ABOUT YOUR LUCK? WHEN YOU GET LUCKY, SOMEBODY AROUND YOU GETS UNLUCKY!
LIKE ME!
MY LOVE IS GETTING BEATEN UP!
HER LOVE? YUK.
HATE TO SAY IT, BUT OLD LONGSHOT'S A CHUMP! HE'S LETTIN' THE DEMON BEAT HIM WITH WORDS.
YOU DESERVE TO DIE! YOU WON'T FIGHT BACK, ANYWAY. YOU'RE TOO SELFISH!
YOU CAN'T LET YOUR PAST DIE WITH ME!
SMAK
GO AHEAD, GET LUCKY! PULL THE ODDS YOUR WAY AND SCREW UP SOMEBODY ELSE!
YOUR LUCK IS YOUR CRUTCH-- USE IT!
WOMP!
5

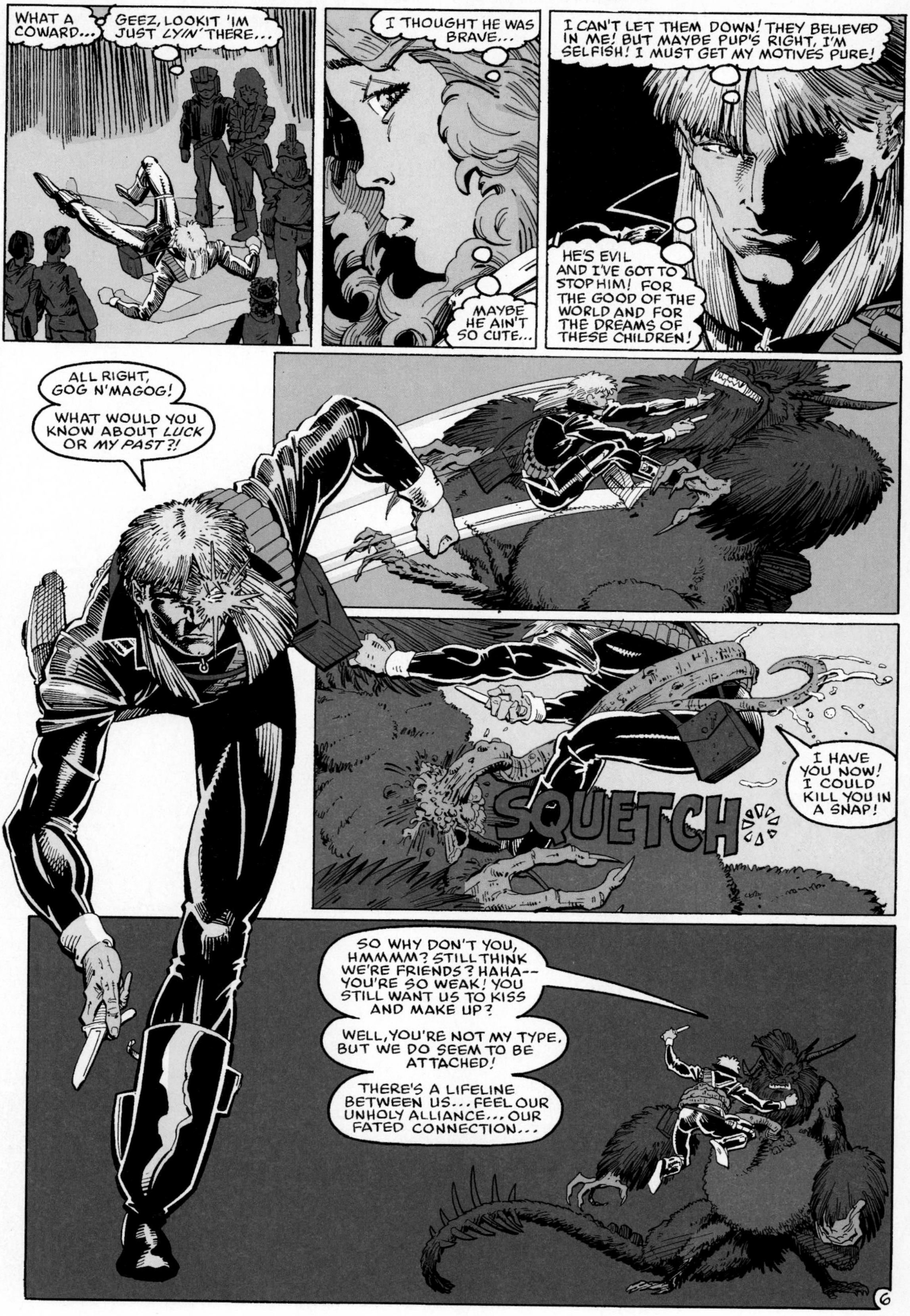
WHAT A COWARD...
GEEZ, LOOKIT 'IM JUST LYIN' THERE...
I THOUGHT HE WAS BRAVE...
MAYBE HE AIN'T SO CUTE...
I CAN'T LET THEM DOWN! THEY BELIEVED IN ME! BUT MAYBE PUP'S RIGHT, I'M SELFISH! I MUST GET MY MOTIVES PURE!
HE'S EVIL AND I'VE GOT TO STOP HIM! FOR THE GOOD OF THE WORLD AND FOR THE DREAMS OF THESE CHILDREN!
ALL RIGHT, GOG N'MAGOG!
WHAT WOULD YOU KNOW ABOUT LUCK OR MY PAST?!
SQUETCH
I HAVE YOU NOW! I COULD KILL YOU IN A SNAP!
SO WHY DON'T YOU, HMMMM? STILL THINK WE'RE FRIENDS? HAHA-- YOU'RE SO WEAK! YOU STILL WANT US TO KISS AND MAKE UP?
WELL, YOU'RE NOT MY TYPE, BUT WE DO SEEM TO BE ATTACHED!
THERE'S A LIFELINE BETWEEN US... FEEL OUR UNHOLY ALLIANCE... OUR FATED CONNECTION...
6

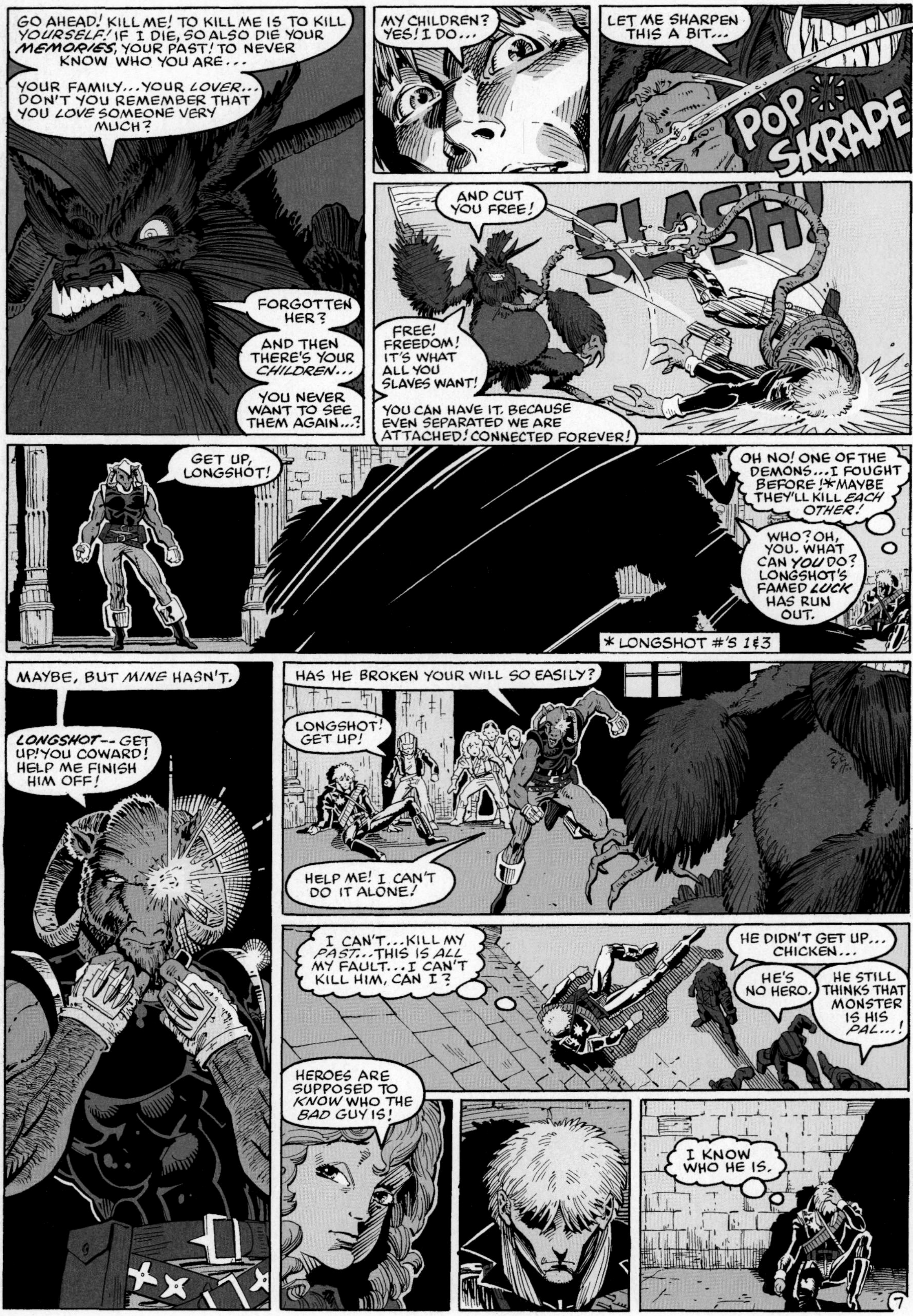
GO AHEAD! KILL ME! TO KILL ME IS TO KILL YOURSELF! IF I DIE, SO ALSO DIE YOUR MEMORIES, YOUR PAST! TO NEVER KNOW WHO YOU ARE...
YOUR FAMILY... YOUR LOVER... DON'T YOU REMEMBER THAT YOU LOVE SOMEONE VERY MUCH?
FORGOTTEN HER?
AND THEN THERE'S YOUR CHILDREN...
YOU NEVER WANT TO SEE THEM AGAIN...?
MY CHILDREN? YES! I DO...
LET ME SHARPEN THIS A BIT...
POP
SKRAPE
AND CUT YOU FREE!
SLASH
FREE! FREEDOM! IT'S WHAT ALL YOU SLAVES WANT!
YOU CAN HAVE IT. BECAUSE EVEN SEPARATED WE ARE ATTACHED! CONNECTED FOREVER!
GET UP, LONGSHOT!
OH NO! ONE OF THE DEMONS... I FOUGHT BEFORE!* MAYBE THEY'LL KILL EACH OTHER!
WHO? OH, YOU. WHAT CAN YOU DO? LONGSHOT'S FAMED LUCK HAS RUN OUT.
* LONGSHOT #'S 1 & 3
MAYBE, BUT MINE HASN'T.
LONGSHOT-- GET UP! YOU COWARD! HELP ME FINISH HIM OFF!
HAS HE BROKEN YOUR WILL SO EASILY?
LONGSHOT! GET UP!
HELP ME! I CAN'T DO IT ALONE!
I CAN'T... KILL MY PAST... THIS IS ALL MY FAULT... I CAN'T KILL HIM, CAN I?
HE DIDN'T GET UP... CHICKEN...
HE'S NO HERO.
HE STILL THINKS THAT MONSTER IS HIS PAL...!
HEROES ARE SUPPOSED TO KNOW WHO THE BAD GUY IS!
I KNOW WHO HE IS.
7

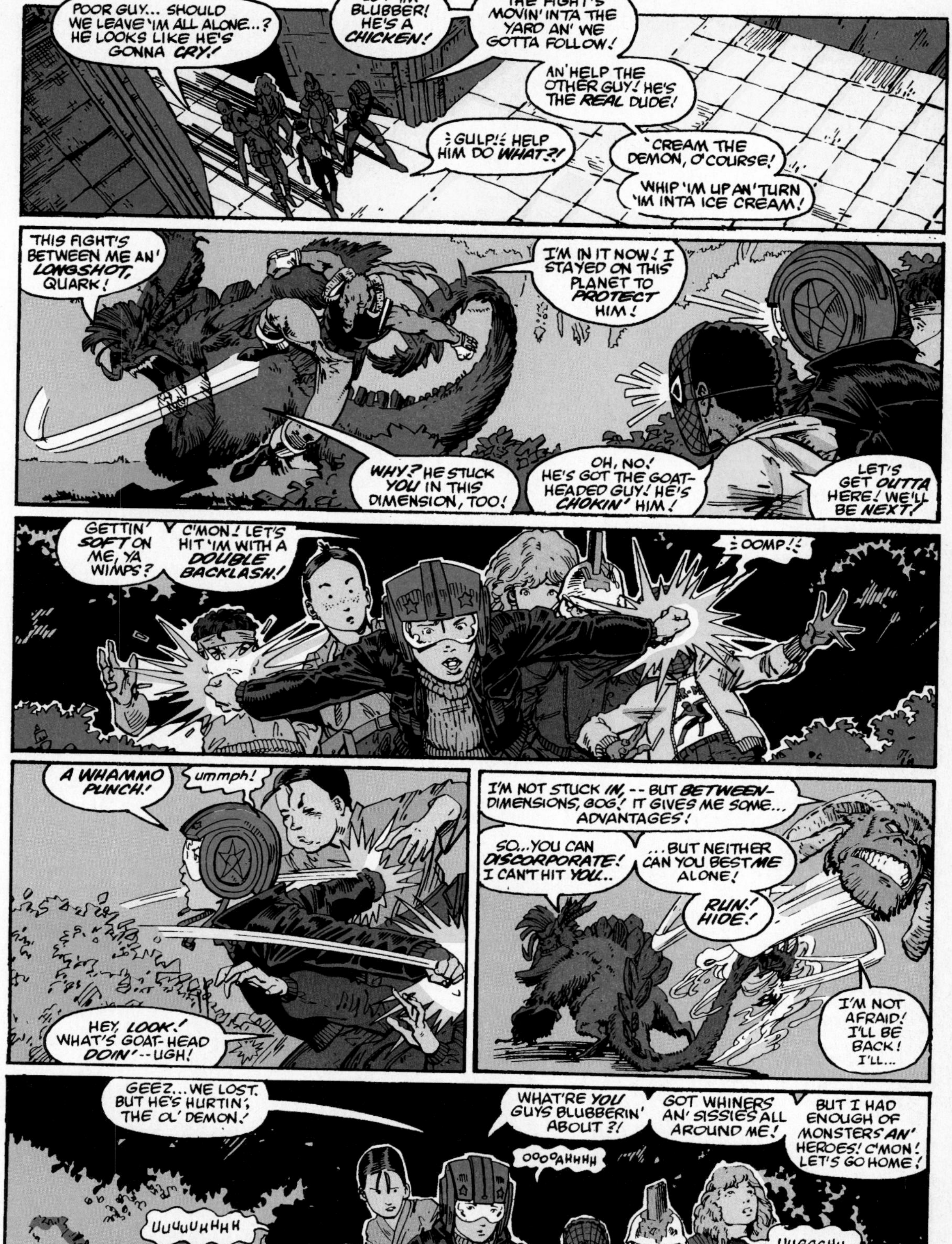
POOR GUY... SHOULD WE LEAVE 'IM ALL ALONE...? HE LOOKS LIKE HE'S GONNA CRY!
LET 'IM BLUBBER! HE'S A CHICKEN!
THE FIGHT'S MOVIN' INTA THE YARD AN' WE GOTTA FOLLOW!
AN' HELP THE OTHER GUY! HE'S THE REAL DUDE!
GULP! HELP HIM DO WHAT?!
CREAM THE DEMON, O'COURSE!
WHIP 'IM UP AN' TURN 'IM INTA ICE CREAM!
THIS FIGHT'S BETWEEN ME AN' LONGSHOT, QUARK!
I'M IN IT NOW! I STAYED ON THIS PLANET TO PROTECT HIM!
WHY? HE STUCK YOU IN THIS DIMENSION, TOO!
OH, NO! HE'S GOT THE GOAT-HEADED GUY! HE'S CHOKIN' HIM!
LET'S GET OUTTA HERE! WE'LL BE NEXT!
GETTIN' SOFT ON ME, YA WIMPS?
C'MON! LET'S HIT 'IM WITH A DOUBLE BACKLASH!
OOMP!
A WHAMMO PUNCH!
ummph!
HEY, LOOK! WHAT'S GOAT-HEAD DOIN' -- UGH!
I'M NOT STUCK IN, -- BUT BETWEEN-DIMENSIONS, GOG! IT GIVES ME SOME... ADVANTAGES!
SO...YOU CAN DISCORPORATE! I CAN'T HIT YOU..
...BUT NEITHER CAN YOU BEST ME ALONE!
RUN! HIDE!
I'M NOT AFRAID! I'LL BE BACK! I'LL...
GEEZ...WE LOST. BUT HE'S HURTIN', THE OL' DEMON!
WHAT'RE YOU GUYS BLUBBERIN' ABOUT?!
GOT WHINERS AN' SISSIES ALL AROUND ME!
BUT I HAD ENOUGH OF MONSTERS AN' HEROES! C'MON! LET'S GO HOME!
OOOOAHHHH
UUUUUHHHH
UUGGGHU
8

ELSEWHERE... THE ULTIMATE, UNFATHOMABLE PARADOX IS THAT, TUCKED WITHIN TIMESPACE AS WE KNOW IT, LIE ALL THESE MYRIAD DIMENSIONS!

QUITE, MASTER!

TURNING MY GAZE INTO THIS REALM IS NOT WITHOUT ITS DANGERS, WONG.

OH, NO, MASTER.

THE HORRIFYING *BEAUTY*...THE RIVETING, SEDUCTIVE *POWER* OF THIS WORLD...

...CAN TRANSFIX ONE'S EVERY SENSE.

TRANSFIX...

WONG! KEEP A LUCID MIND! ONE WOULD MISTAKE YOU FOR A NOVICE.

IT IS JUST SO WONDROUS! FORGIVE THE CHILD IN ME, MASTER.

FORGIVEN. LOOK THERE! A PORTAL OPENS....AND EARTH HAS SOME VISITORS!

THERE THEY TRY TO LEAVE! AN ARCANE RITUAL WARPS TIME AND SPACE--BUT FAILS TO CREATE A DOORWAY!

AGAIN! THIS TIME SUCCESS--FOR MOST! WHAT MANNER OF CREATURE ARE THESE? AH! I'VE SEEN ENOUGH!

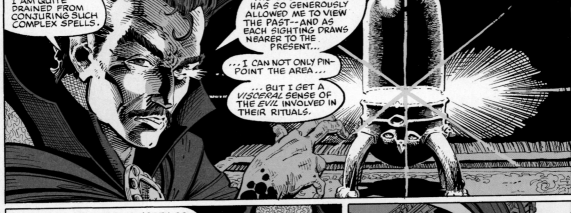

I AM QUITE DRAINED FROM CONJURING SUCH COMPLEX SPELLS.

THE ORB OF AGAMOTTO HAS SO GENEROUSLY ALLOWED ME TO VIEW THE PAST--AND AS EACH SIGHTING DRAWS NEARER TO THE PRESENT...

...I CAN NOT ONLY PIN-POINT THE AREA...

...BUT I GET A *VISCERAL* SENSE OF THE *EVIL* INVOLVED IN THEIR RITUALS.

THE LAST PORTAL OPENED NORTH OF NEW YORK CITY. MORE OTHERWORLDLY BEINGS ENTERED THIS DIMENSION A MERE HOUR AGO!

GUARD OUR HOME, WONG.

I FEAR OUR ALIEN VISITORS MEAN TO DO THIS PLANET HARM!

BUT THEY HAVE NOT PREPARED TO MEET *DOCTOR STRANGE.* 9

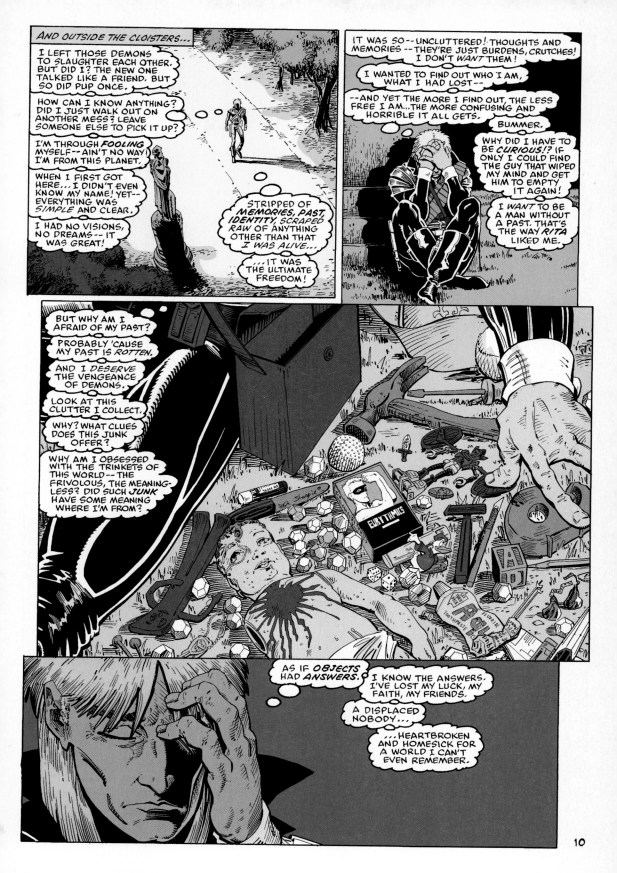

AND OUTSIDE THE CLOISTERS...

I LEFT THOSE DEMONS TO SLAUGHTER EACH OTHER. BUT DID I? THE NEW ONE TALKED LIKE A FRIEND, BUT SO DID PUP ONCE.

HOW CAN I KNOW ANYTHING? DID I JUST WALK OUT ON ANOTHER MESS? LEAVE SOMEONE ELSE TO PICK IT UP?

I'M THROUGH *FOOLING* MYSELF--AIN'T NO WAY I'M FROM THIS PLANET.

WHEN I FIRST GOT HERE... I DIDN'T EVEN KNOW MY NAME! YET-- EVERYTHING WAS *SIMPLE* AND CLEAR.

I HAD NO VISIONS, NO DREAMS-- IT WAS GREAT!

STRIPPED OF *MEMORIES, PAST, IDENTITY,* SCRAPED *RAW* OF ANYTHING OTHER THAN THAT I WAS ALIVE...

....IT WAS THE ULTIMATE FREEDOM!

IT WAS SO-- UNCLUTTERED! THOUGHTS AND MEMORIES --THEY'RE JUST BURDENS, CRUTCHES! I DON'T *WANT* THEM!

I WANTED TO FIND OUT WHO I AM, WHAT I HAD LOST--

--AND YET THE MORE I FIND OUT, THE LESS FREE I AM...THE MORE CONFUSING AND HORRIBLE IT ALL GETS.

BUMMER.

WHY DID I HAVE TO BE *CURIOUS!?* IF ONLY I COULD FIND THE GUY THAT WIPED MY MIND AND GET HIM TO EMPTY IT AGAIN!

I *WANT* TO BE A MAN WITHOUT A PAST. THAT'S THE WAY *RITA* LIKED ME.

BUT WHY AM I AFRAID OF MY PAST?

PROBABLY 'CAUSE MY PAST IS *ROTTEN.*

AND I *DESERVE* THE VENGEANCE OF DEMONS.

LOOK AT THIS CLUTTER I COLLECT.

WHY? WHAT CLUES DOES THIS JUNK OFFER?

WHY AM I OBSESSED WITH THE TRINKETS OF THIS WORLD-- THE FRIVOLOUS, THE MEANING- LESS? DID SUCH JUNK HAVE SOME MEANING WHERE I'M FROM?

AS IF *OBJECTS* HAD *ANSWERS.*

I KNOW THE ANSWERS. I'VE LOST MY LUCK, MY FAITH, MY FRIENDS.

A DISPLACED NOBODY...

....HEARTBROKEN AND HOMESICK FOR A WORLD I CAN'T EVEN REMEMBER.

10

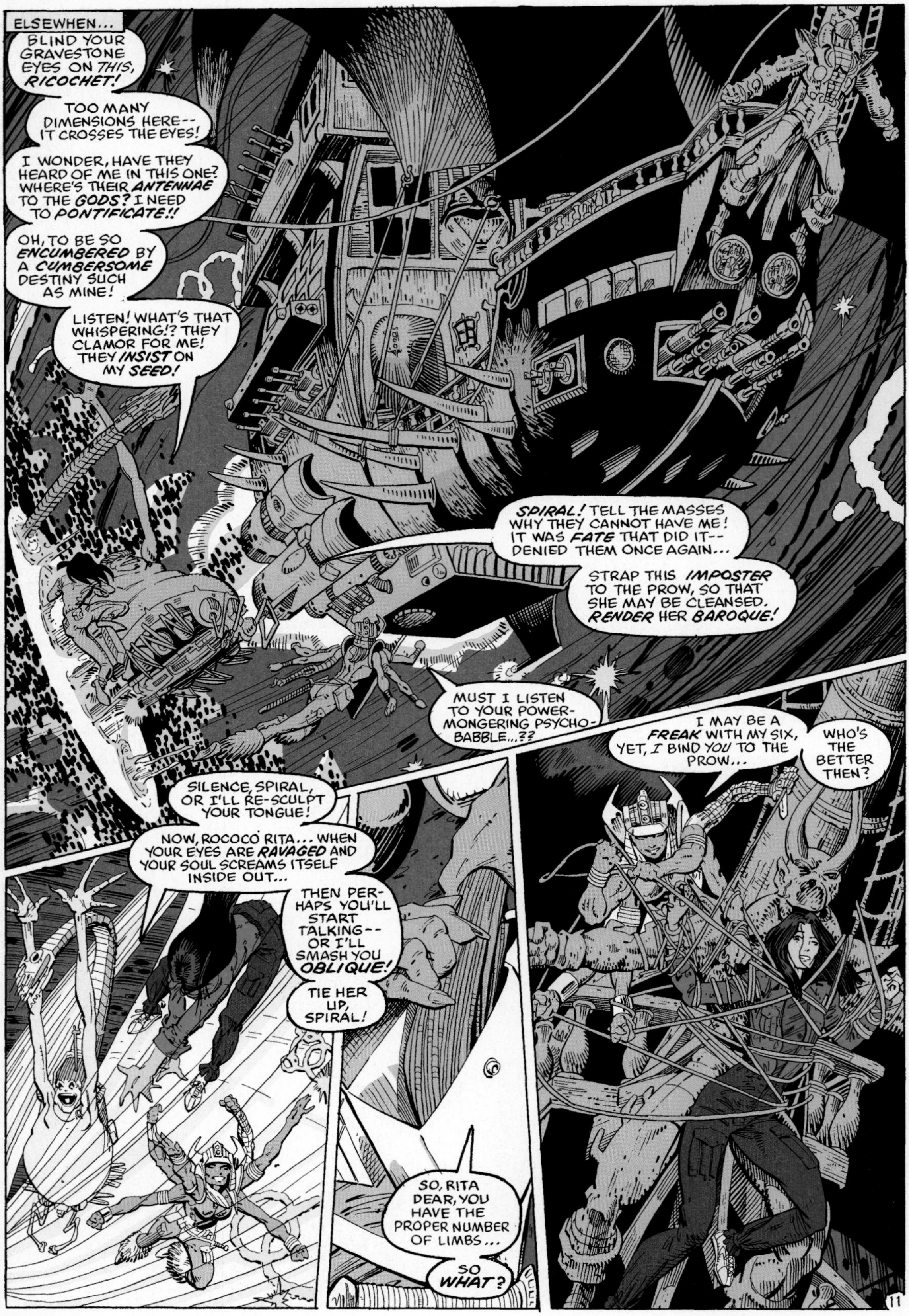

ELSEWHEN...
BLIND YOUR GRAVESTONE EYES ON THIS, RICOCHET!
TOO MANY DIMENSIONS HERE-- IT CROSSES THE EYES!
I WONDER, HAVE THEY HEARD OF ME IN THIS ONE? WHERE'S THEIR ANTENNAE TO THE GODS? I NEED TO PONTIFICATE!!
OH, TO BE SO ENCUMBERED BY A CUMBERSOME DESTINY SUCH AS MINE!
LISTEN! WHAT'S THAT WHISPERING!? THEY CLAMOR FOR ME! THEY INSIST ON MY SEED!
SPIRAL! TELL THE MASSES WHY THEY CANNOT HAVE ME! IT WAS FATE THAT DID IT-- DENIED THEM ONCE AGAIN...
STRAP THIS IMPOSTER TO THE PROW, SO THAT SHE MAY BE CLEANSED. RENDER HER BAROQUE!
MUST I LISTEN TO YOUR POWER-MONGERING PSYCHO-BABBLE...??
SILENCE, SPIRAL, OR I'LL RE-SCULPT YOUR TONGUE!
NOW, ROCOCO RITA... WHEN YOUR EYES ARE RAVAGED AND YOUR SOUL SCREAMS ITSELF INSIDE OUT...
THEN PERHAPS YOU'LL START TALKING-- OR I'LL SMASH YOU OBLIQUE!
TIE HER UP, SPIRAL!
SO, RITA DEAR, YOU HAVE THE PROPER NUMBER OF LIMBS...
SO WHAT?
I MAY BE A FREAK WITH MY SIX, YET, I BIND YOU TO THE PROW...
WHO'S THE BETTER THEN?
11

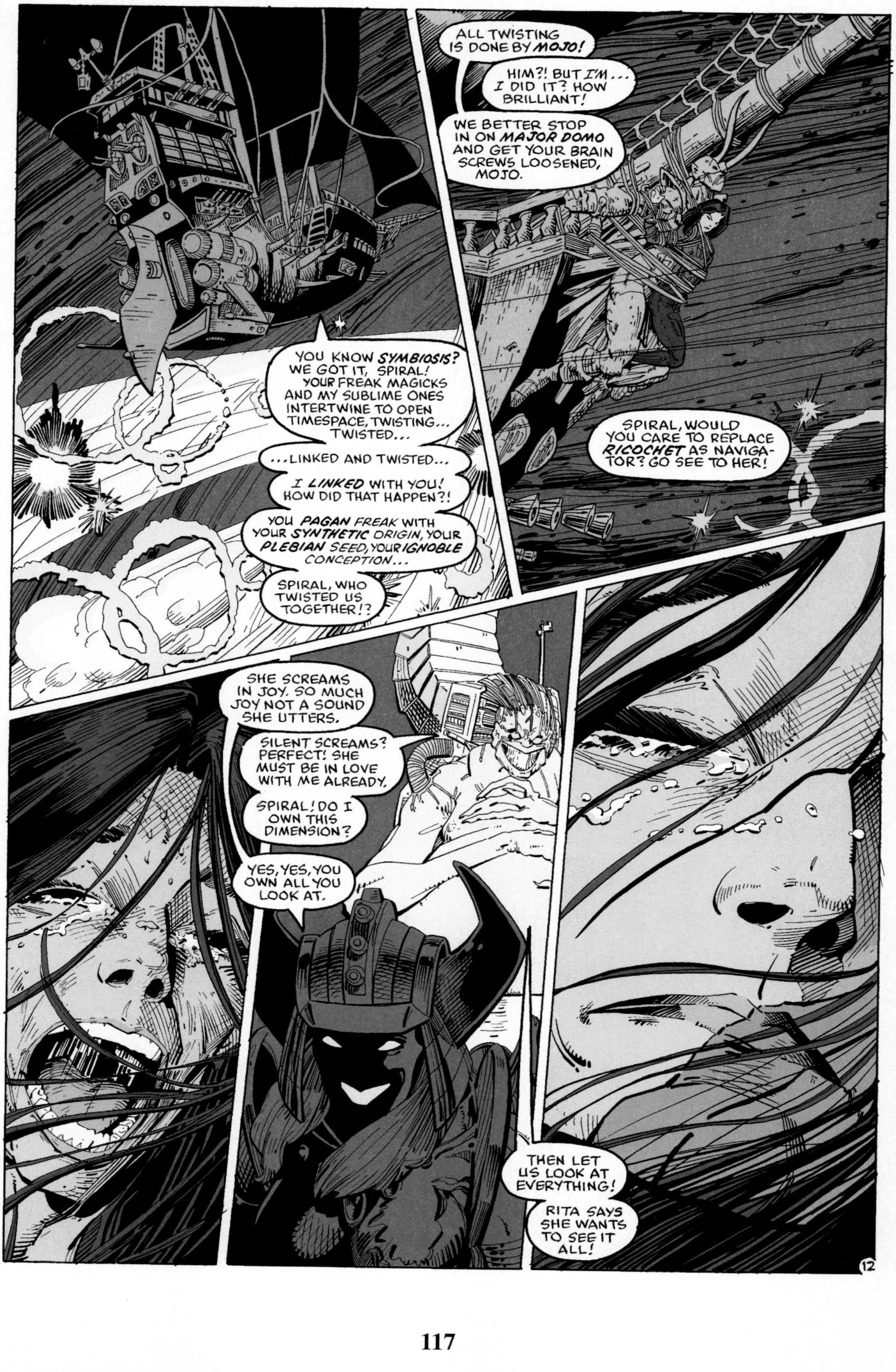
YOU KNOW SYMBIOSIS? WE GOT IT, SPIRAL! YOUR FREAK MAGICKS AND MY SUBLIME ONES INTERTWINE TO OPEN TIMESPACE, TWISTING... TWISTED...
...LINKED AND TWISTED...
I LINKED WITH YOU! HOW DID THAT HAPPEN?!
YOU PAGAN FREAK WITH YOUR SYNTHETIC ORIGIN, YOUR PLEBIAN SEED, YOUR IGNOBLE CONCEPTION...
SPIRAL, WHO TWISTED US TOGETHER!?
ALL TWISTING IS DONE BY MOJO!
HIM?! BUT I'M... I DID IT? HOW BRILLIANT!
WE BETTER STOP IN ON MAJOR DOMO AND GET YOUR BRAIN SCREWS LOOSENED, MOJO.
SPIRAL, WOULD YOU CARE TO REPLACE RICOCHET AS NAVIGATOR? GO SEE TO HER!
SHE SCREAMS IN JOY. SO MUCH JOY NOT A SOUND SHE UTTERS.
SILENT SCREAMS? PERFECT! SHE MUST BE IN LOVE WITH ME ALREADY.
SPIRAL! DO I OWN THIS DIMENSION?
YES, YES, YOU OWN ALL YOU LOOK AT.
THEN LET US LOOK AT EVERYTHING!
RITA SAYS SHE WANTS TO SEE IT ALL!
12

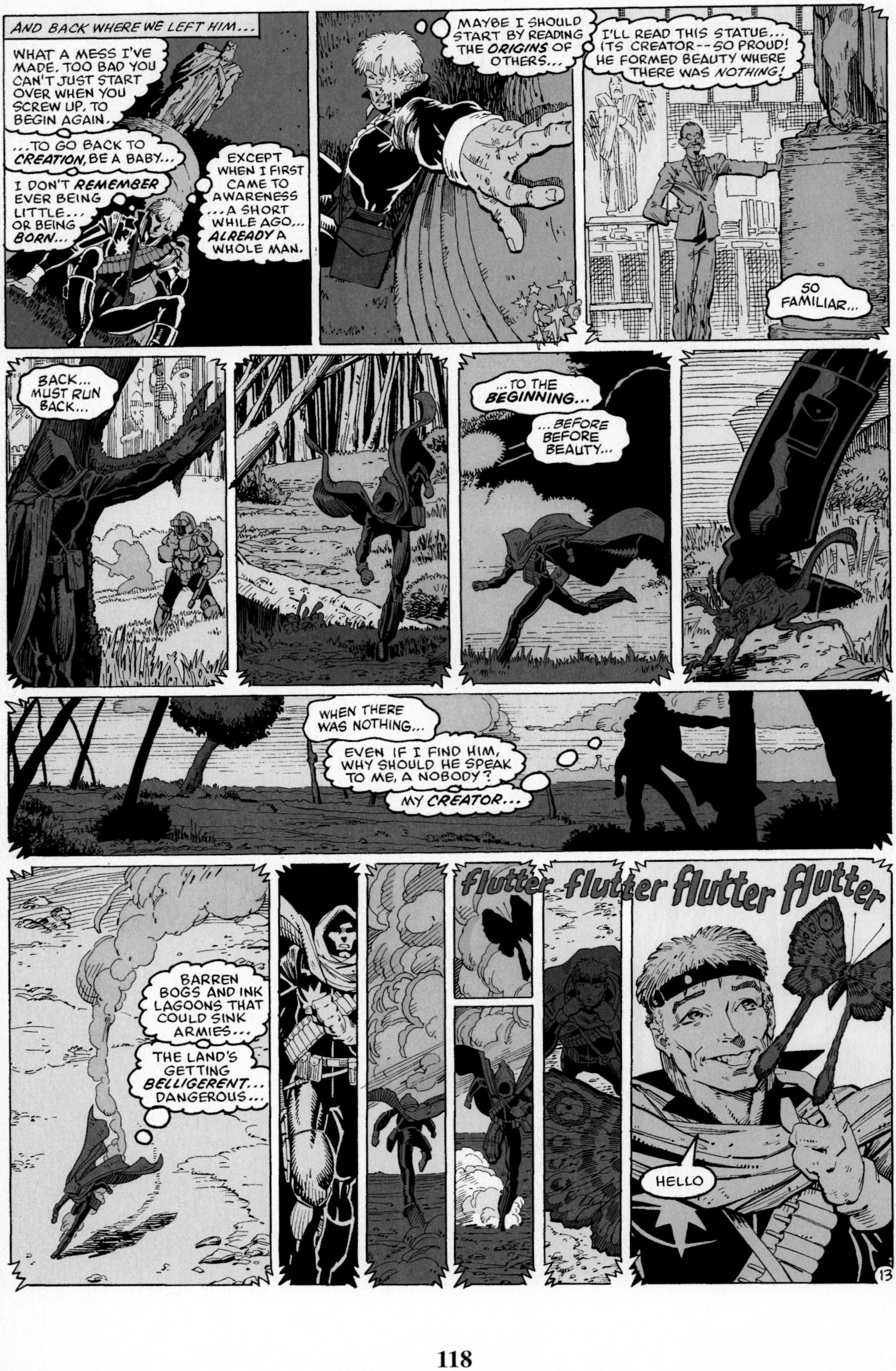
AND BACK WHERE WE LEFT HIM...
WHAT A MESS I'VE MADE. TOO BAD YOU CAN'T JUST START OVER WHEN YOU SCREW UP, TO BEGIN AGAIN.
...TO GO BACK TO CREATION, BE A BABY...
I DON'T REMEMBER EVER BEING LITTLE... OR BEING BORN...
EXCEPT WHEN I FIRST CAME TO AWARENESS ...A SHORT WHILE AGO... ALREADY A WHOLE MAN.
MAYBE I SHOULD START BY READING THE ORIGINS OF OTHERS...
I'LL READ THIS STATUE... ITS CREATOR--SO PROUD! HE FORMED BEAUTY WHERE THERE WAS NOTHING!
SO FAMILIAR...
BACK... MUST RUN BACK...
...TO THE BEGINNING...
...BEFORE BEFORE BEAUTY...
WHEN THERE WAS NOTHING...
EVEN IF I FIND HIM, WHY SHOULD HE SPEAK TO ME, A NOBODY?
MY CREATOR...
BARREN BOGS AND INK LAGOONS THAT COULD SINK ARMIES...
THE LAND'S GETTING BELLIGERENT... DANGEROUS...
flutter flutter flutter flutter
HELLO
13

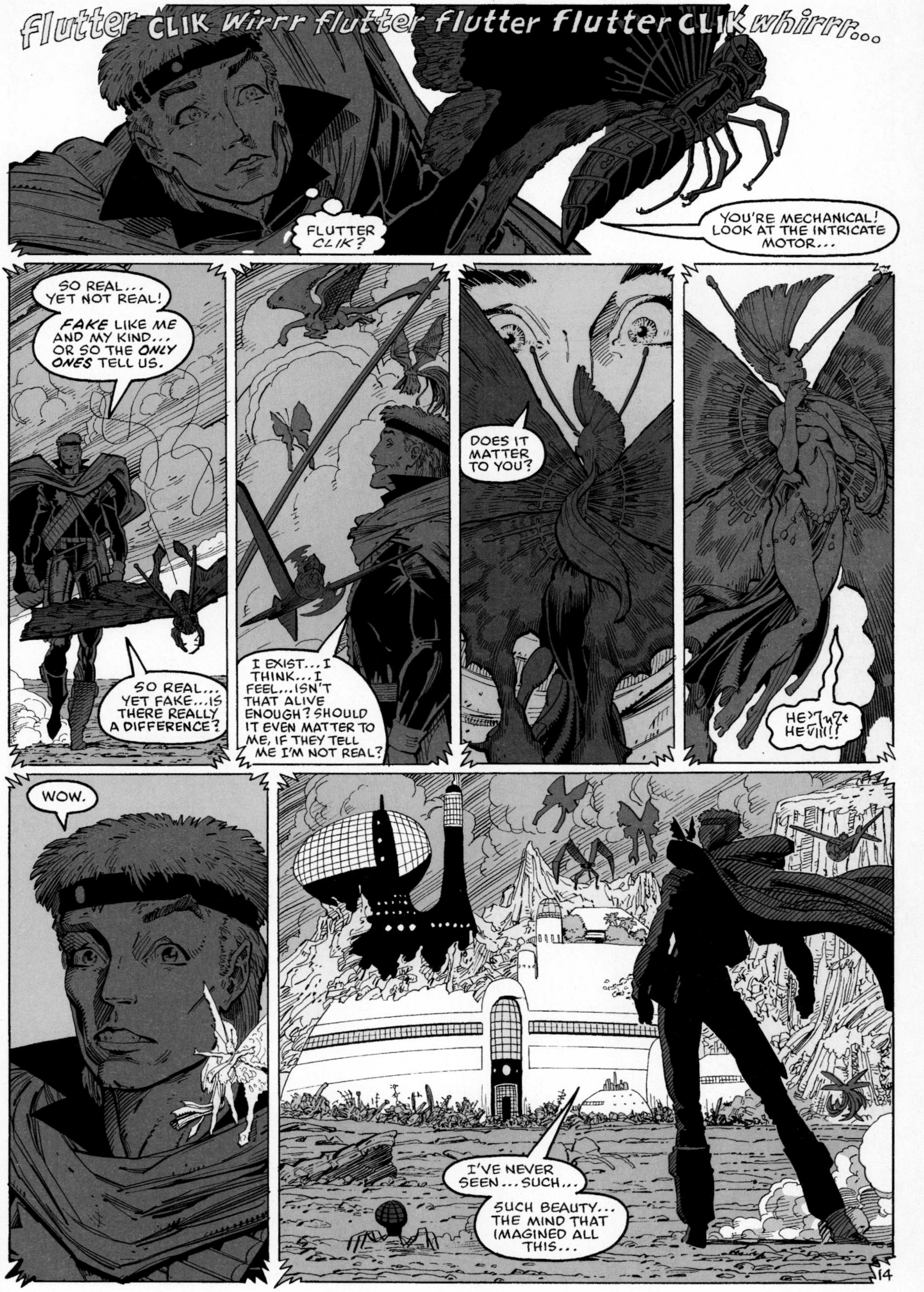
flutter CLIK wirrr flutter flutter flutter CLIK whirrr...
FLUTTER CLIK?
YOU'RE MECHANICAL! LOOK AT THE INTRICATE MOTOR...
SO REAL... YET NOT REAL!
FAKE LIKE ME AND MY KIND... OR SO THE ONLY ONES TELL US.
SO REAL... YET FAKE...IS THERE REALLY A DIFFERENCE?
I EXIST... I THINK... I FEEL...ISN'T THAT ALIVE ENOUGH? SHOULD IT EVEN MATTER TO ME, IF THEY TELL ME I'M NOT REAL?
DOES IT MATTER TO YOU?
WOW.
I'VE NEVER SEEN... SUCH...
SUCH BEAUTY... THE MIND THAT IMAGINED ALL THIS...
14

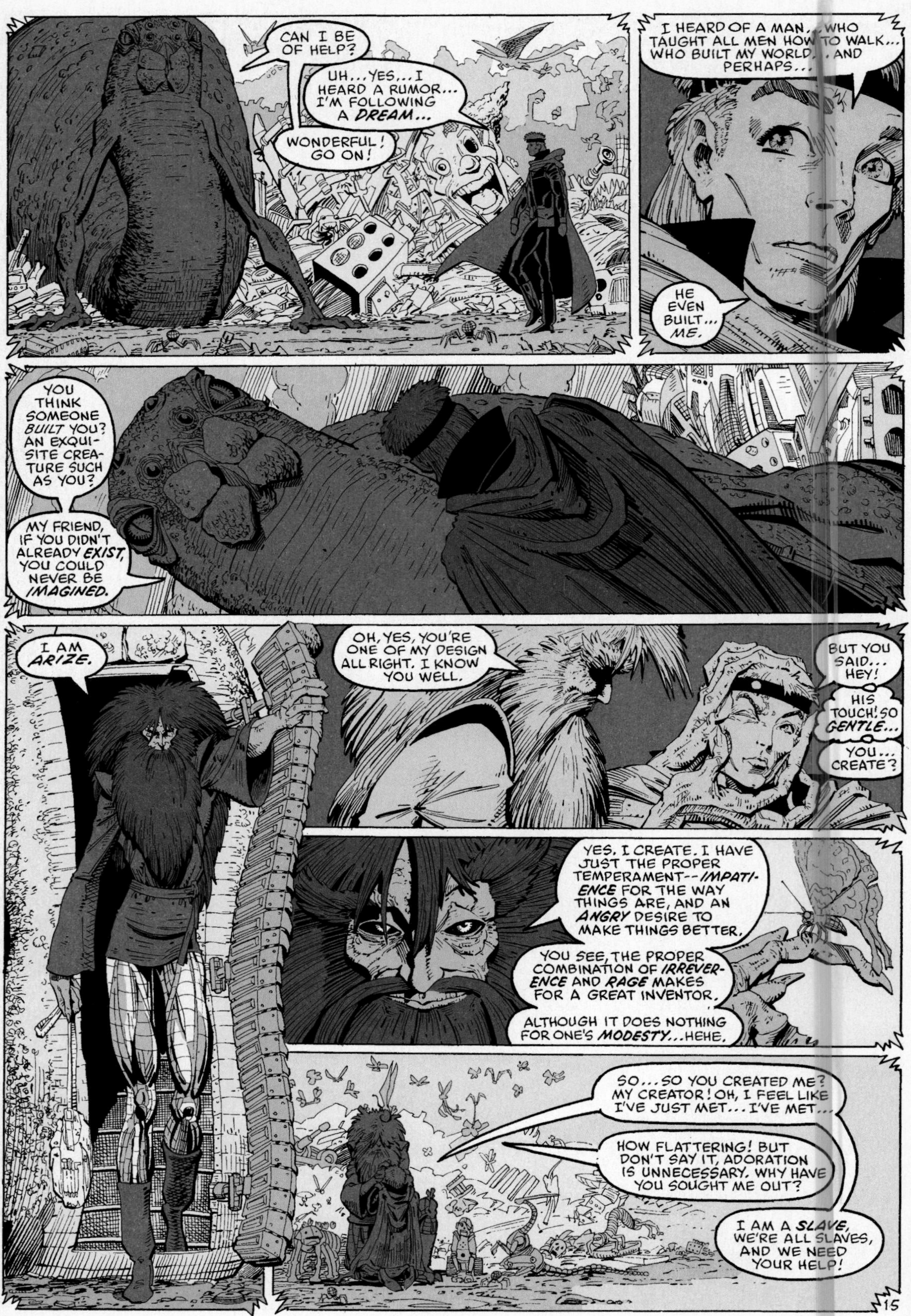
CAN I BE OF HELP?
UH... YES... I HEARD A RUMOR... I'M FOLLOWING A DREAM...
WONDERFUL! GO ON!
I HEARD OF A MAN... WHO TAUGHT ALL MEN HOW TO WALK... WHO BUILT MY WORLD... AND PERHAPS...
HE EVEN BUILT... ME.
YOU THINK SOMEONE BUILT YOU? AN EXQUISITE CREATURE SUCH AS YOU?
MY FRIEND, IF YOU DIDN'T ALREADY EXIST, YOU COULD NEVER BE IMAGINED.
I AM ARIZE.
OH, YES, YOU'RE ONE OF MY DESIGN ALL RIGHT. I KNOW YOU WELL.
BUT YOU SAID... HEY!
HIS TOUCH! SO GENTLE...
YOU... CREATE?
YES. I CREATE. I HAVE JUST THE PROPER TEMPERAMENT--IMPATIENCE FOR THE WAY THINGS ARE, AND AN ANGRY DESIRE TO MAKE THINGS BETTER.
YOU SEE, THE PROPER COMBINATION OF IRREVERENCE AND RAGE MAKES FOR A GREAT INVENTOR.
ALTHOUGH IT DOES NOTHING FOR ONE'S MODESTY... HEHE.
SO... SO YOU CREATED ME? MY CREATOR! OH, I FEEL LIKE I'VE JUST MET... I'VE MET...
HOW FLATTERING! BUT DON'T SAY IT, ADORATION IS UNNECESSARY. WHY HAVE YOU SOUGHT ME OUT?
I AM A SLAVE, WE'RE ALL SLAVES, AND WE NEED YOUR HELP!
15

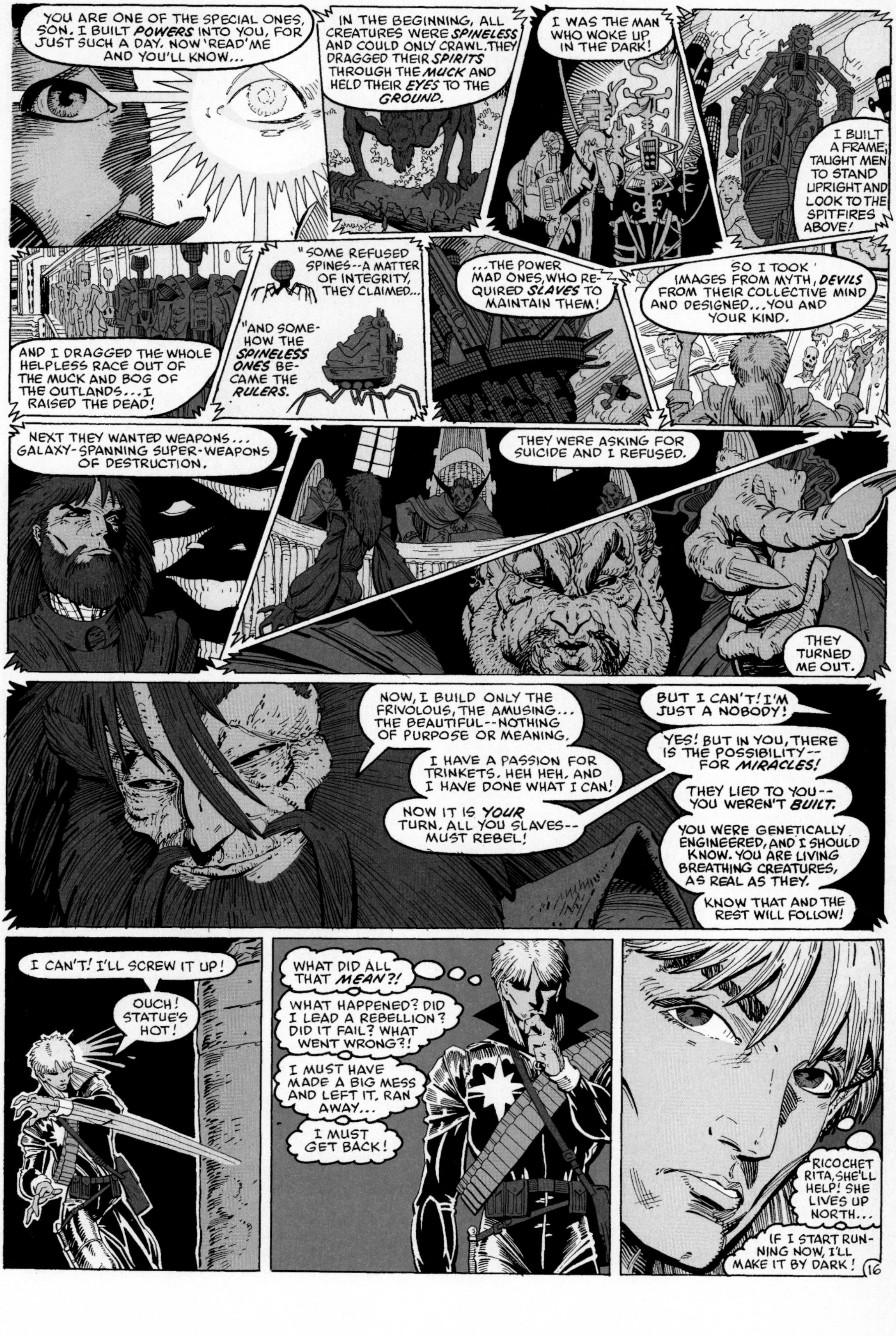
YOU ARE ONE OF THE SPECIAL ONES, SON. I BUILT POWERS INTO YOU, FOR JUST SUCH A DAY. NOW 'READ' ME AND YOU'LL KNOW...
IN THE BEGINNING, ALL CREATURES WERE SPINELESS AND COULD ONLY CRAWL. THEY DRAGGED THEIR SPIRITS THROUGH THE MUCK AND HELD THEIR EYES TO THE GROUND.
I WAS THE MAN WHO WOKE UP IN THE DARK!
I BUILT A FRAME; TAUGHT MEN TO STAND UPRIGHT AND LOOK TO THE SPITFIRES ABOVE!
AND I DRAGGED THE WHOLE HELPLESS RACE OUT OF THE MUCK AND BOG OF THE OUTLANDS... I RAISED THE DEAD!
"SOME REFUSED SPINES--A MATTER OF INTEGRITY, THEY CLAIMED...
"AND SOMEHOW THE SPINELESS ONES BECAME THE RULERS.
...THE POWER MAD ONES, WHO REQUIRED SLAVES TO MAINTAIN THEM!
SO I TOOK IMAGES FROM MYTH, DEVILS FROM THEIR COLLECTIVE MIND AND DESIGNED... YOU AND YOUR KIND.
NEXT THEY WANTED WEAPONS... GALAXY-SPANNING SUPER-WEAPONS OF DESTRUCTION.
THEY WERE ASKING FOR SUICIDE AND I REFUSED.
THEY TURNED ME OUT.
NOW, I BUILD ONLY THE FRIVOLOUS, THE AMUSING... THE BEAUTIFUL--NOTHING OF PURPOSE OR MEANING.
I HAVE A PASSION FOR TRINKETS. HEH HEH. AND I HAVE DONE WHAT I CAN!
NOW IT IS YOUR TURN. ALL YOU SLAVES--MUST REBEL!
BUT I CAN'T! I'M JUST A NOBODY!
YES! BUT IN YOU, THERE IS THE POSSIBILITY--FOR MIRACLES!
THEY LIED TO YOU--YOU WEREN'T BUILT.
YOU WERE GENETICALLY ENGINEERED, AND I SHOULD KNOW. YOU ARE LIVING BREATHING CREATURES, AS REAL AS THEY.
KNOW THAT AND THE REST WILL FOLLOW!
I CAN'T! I'LL SCREW IT UP!
OUCH! STATUE'S HOT!
WHAT DID ALL THAT MEAN?!
WHAT HAPPENED? DID I LEAD A REBELLION? DID IT FAIL? WHAT WENT WRONG?!
I MUST HAVE MADE A BIG MESS AND LEFT IT. RAN AWAY...
I MUST GET BACK!
RICOCHET RITA, SHE'LL HELP! SHE LIVES UP NORTH...
IF I START RUNNING NOW, I'LL MAKE IT BY DARK!
16

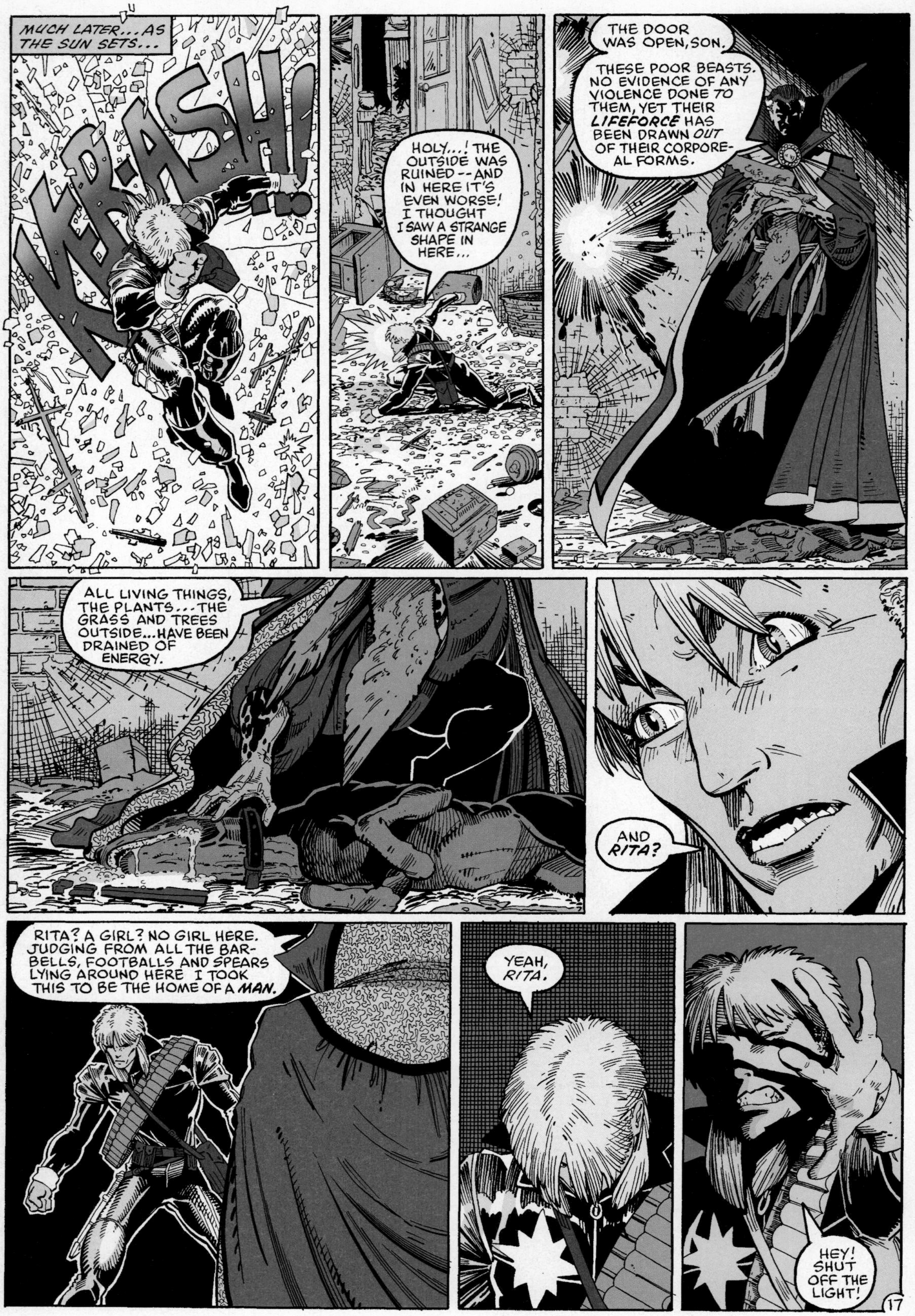
MUCH LATER... AS THE SUN SETS...
K-RA-ASH!
HOLY...! THE OUTSIDE WAS RUINED--AND IN HERE IT'S EVEN WORSE! I THOUGHT I SAW A STRANGE SHAPE IN HERE...
THE DOOR WAS OPEN, SON.
THESE POOR BEASTS. NO EVIDENCE OF ANY VIOLENCE DONE TO THEM, YET THEIR LIFEFORCE HAS BEEN DRAWN OUT OF THEIR CORPOREAL FORMS.
ALL LIVING THINGS, THE PLANTS... THE GRASS AND TREES OUTSIDE... HAVE BEEN DRAINED OF ENERGY.
AND RITA?
RITA? A GIRL? NO GIRL HERE. JUDGING FROM ALL THE BARBELLS, FOOTBALLS AND SPEARS LYING AROUND HERE I TOOK THIS TO BE THE HOME OF A MAN.
YEAH, RITA.
HEY! SHUT OFF THE LIGHT!
17

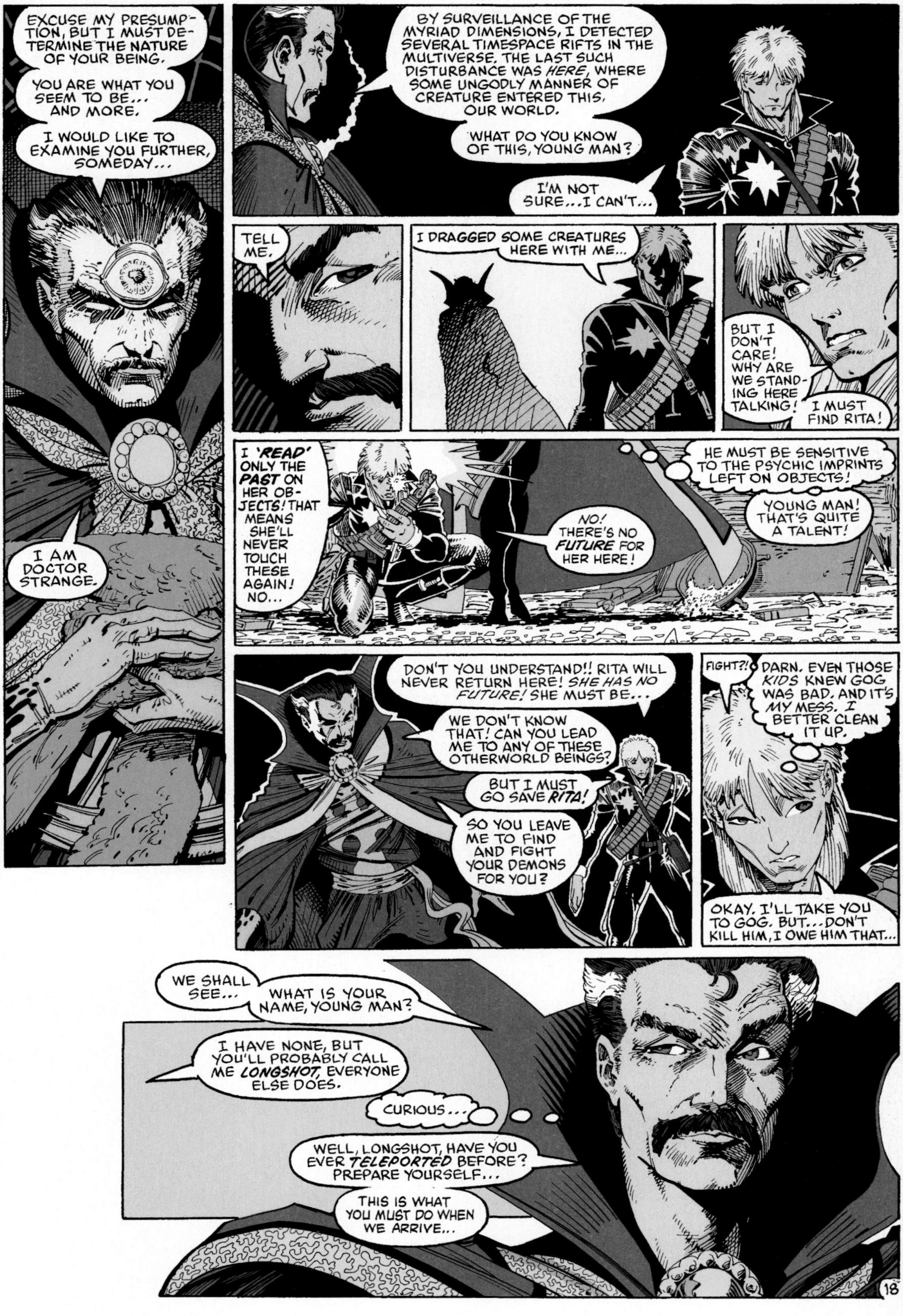
EXCUSE MY PRESUMPTION, BUT I MUST DETERMINE THE NATURE OF YOUR BEING.
YOU ARE WHAT YOU SEEM TO BE... AND MORE.
I WOULD LIKE TO EXAMINE YOU FURTHER, SOMEDAY...
I AM DOCTOR STRANGE.
BY SURVEILLANCE OF THE MYRIAD DIMENSIONS, I DETECTED SEVERAL TIMESPACE RIFTS IN THE MULTIVERSE. THE LAST SUCH DISTURBANCE WAS HERE, WHERE SOME UNGODLY MANNER OF CREATURE ENTERED THIS, OUR WORLD.
WHAT DO YOU KNOW OF THIS, YOUNG MAN?
I'M NOT SURE... I CAN'T...
TELL ME.
I DRAGGED SOME CREATURES HERE WITH ME...
BUT I DON'T CARE! WHY ARE WE STANDING HERE TALKING!
I MUST FIND RITA!
I 'READ' ONLY THE PAST ON HER OBJECTS! THAT MEANS SHE'LL NEVER TOUCH THESE AGAIN! NO...
NO! THERE'S NO FUTURE FOR HER HERE!
HE MUST BE SENSITIVE TO THE PSYCHIC IMPRINTS LEFT ON OBJECTS!
YOUNG MAN! THAT'S QUITE A TALENT!
DON'T YOU UNDERSTAND!! RITA WILL NEVER RETURN HERE! SHE HAS NO FUTURE! SHE MUST BE...
WE DON'T KNOW THAT! CAN YOU LEAD ME TO ANY OF THESE OTHERWORLD BEINGS?
BUT I MUST GO SAVE RITA!
SO YOU LEAVE ME TO FIND AND FIGHT YOUR DEMONS FOR YOU?
FIGHT?!
DARN. EVEN THOSE KIDS KNEW GOG WAS BAD. AND IT'S MY MESS. I BETTER CLEAN IT UP.
OKAY. I'LL TAKE YOU TO GOG. BUT... DON'T KILL HIM, I OWE HIM THAT...
WE SHALL SEE...
WHAT IS YOUR NAME, YOUNG MAN?
I HAVE NONE, BUT YOU'LL PROBABLY CALL ME LONGSHOT, EVERYONE ELSE DOES.
CURIOUS...
WELL, LONGSHOT, HAVE YOU EVER TELEPORTED BEFORE? PREPARE YOURSELF...
THIS IS WHAT YOU MUST DO WHEN WE ARRIVE...
18

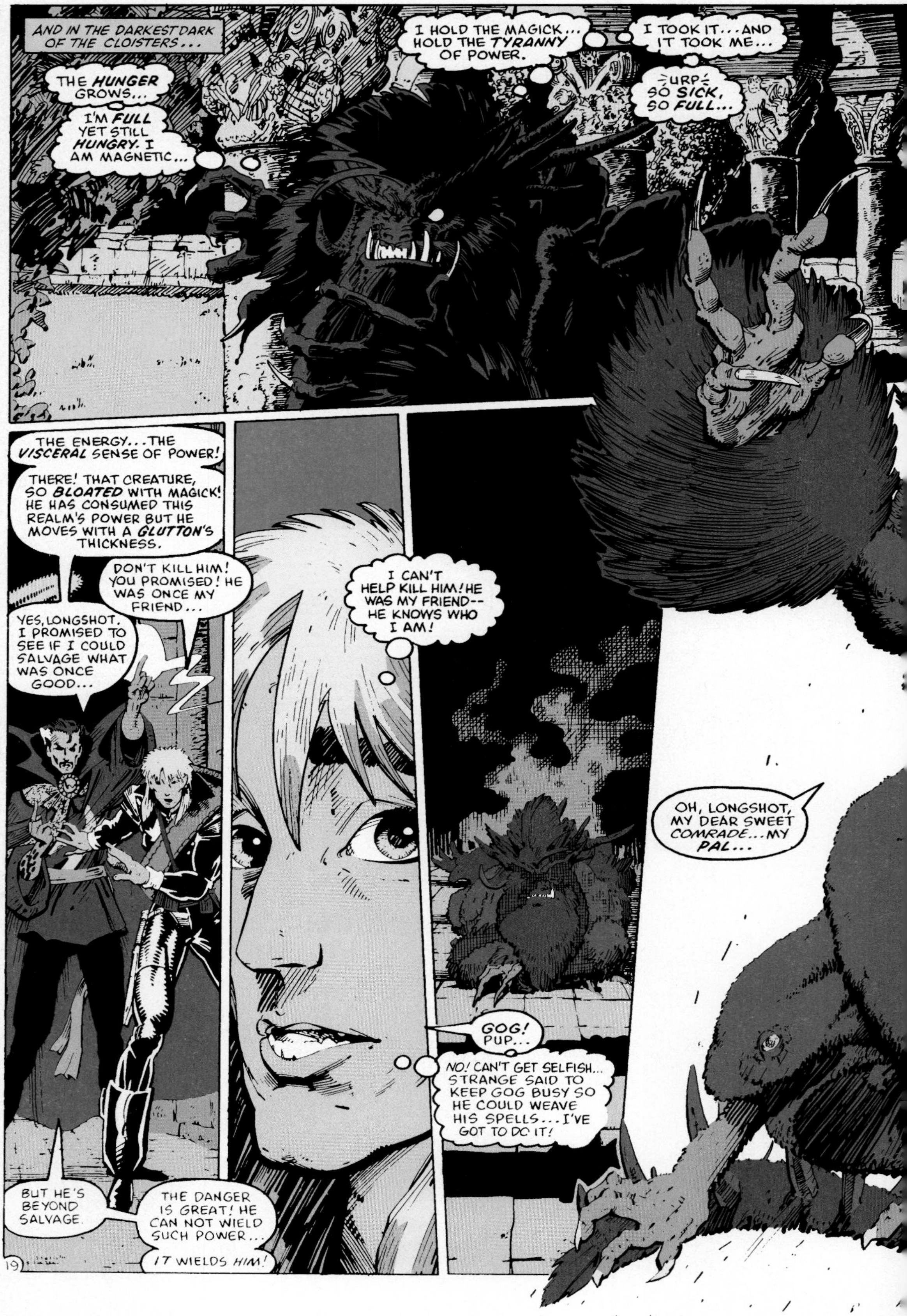
AND IN THE DARKEST DARK OF THE CLOISTERS...
THE HUNGER GROWS...
I'M FULL YET STILL HUNGRY. I AM MAGNETIC...
I HOLD THE MAGICK... HOLD THE TYRANNY OF POWER.
I TOOK IT... AND IT TOOK ME...
URP SO SICK, SO FULL...
THE ENERGY... THE VISCERAL SENSE OF POWER!
THERE! THAT CREATURE, SO BLOATED WITH MAGICK! HE HAS CONSUMED THIS REALM'S POWER BUT HE MOVES WITH A GLUTTON'S THICKNESS.
DON'T KILL HIM! YOU PROMISED! HE WAS ONCE MY FRIEND...
YES, LONGSHOT. I PROMISED TO SEE IF I COULD SALVAGE WHAT WAS ONCE GOOD...
BUT HE'S BEYOND SALVAGE.
THE DANGER IS GREAT! HE CAN NOT WIELD SUCH POWER...
IT WIELDS HIM!
I CAN'T HELP KILL HIM! HE WAS MY FRIEND-- HE KNOWS WHO I AM!
GOG! PUP...
NO! CAN'T GET SELFISH... STRANGE SAID TO KEEP GOG BUSY SO HE COULD WEAVE HIS SPELLS... I'VE GOT TO DO IT!
OH, LONGSHOT, MY DEAR SWEET COMRADE... MY PAL...

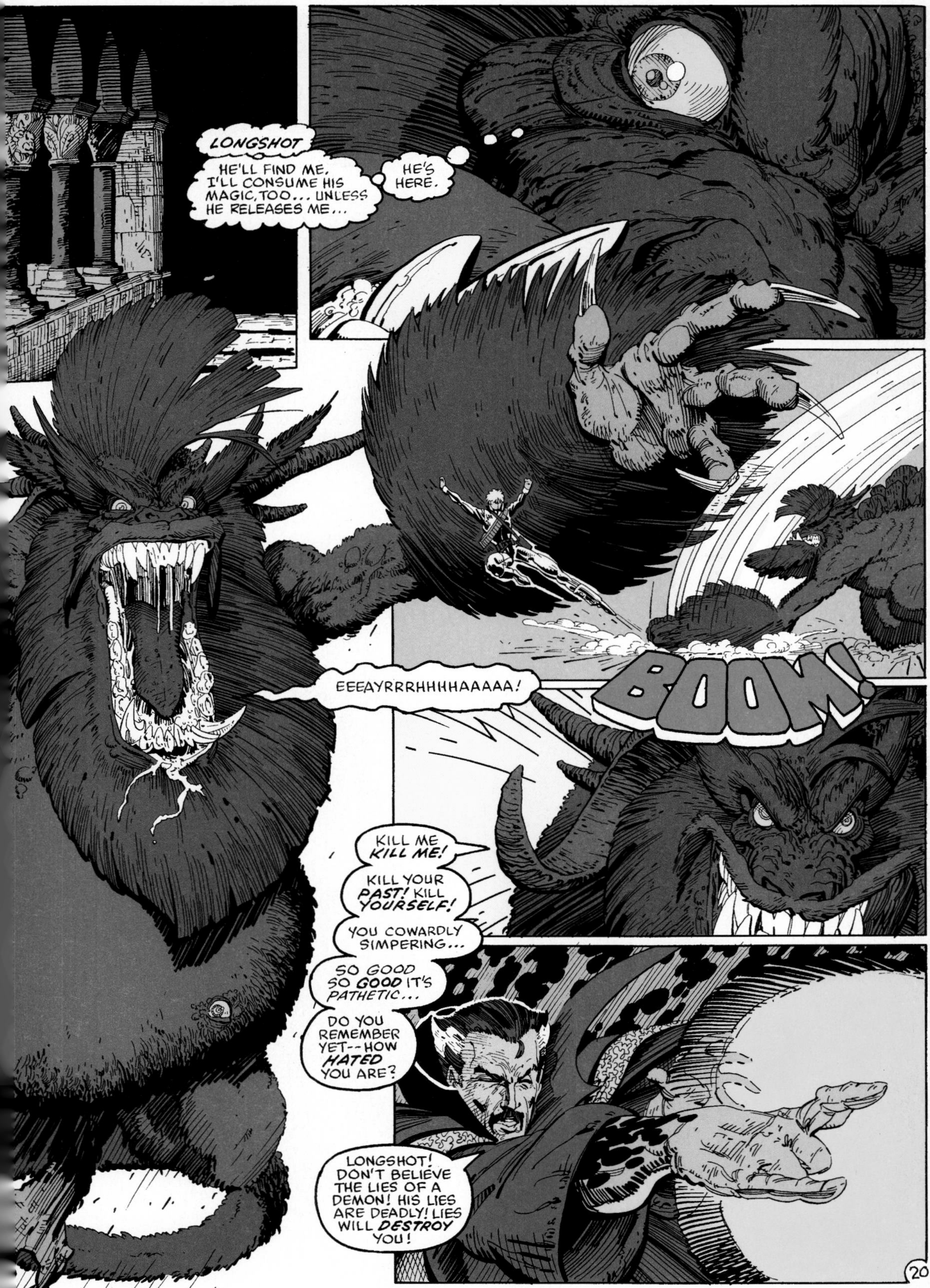
LONGSHOT
HE'LL FIND ME. I'LL CONSUME HIS MAGIC, TOO... UNLESS HE RELEASES ME...
HE'S HERE.
EEEAYRRRHHHHAAAAA!
BOOM!
KILL ME KILL ME!
KILL YOUR PAST! KILL YOURSELF!
YOU COWARDLY SIMPERING...
SO GOOD SO GOOD IT'S PATHETIC...
DO YOU REMEMBER YET--HOW HATED YOU ARE?
LONGSHOT! DON'T BELIEVE THE LIES OF A DEMON! HIS LIES ARE DEADLY! LIES WILL DESTROY YOU!
20

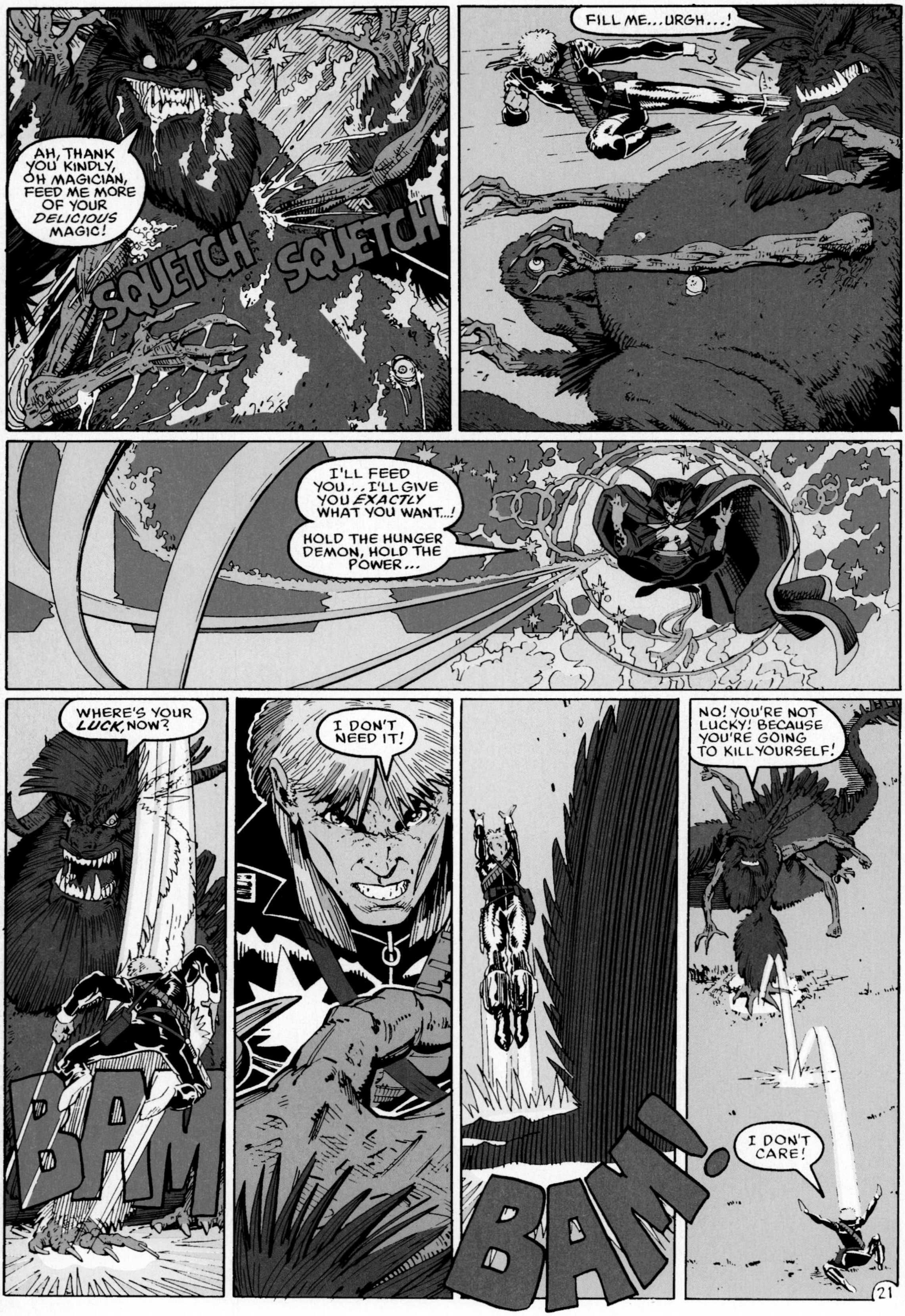
AH, THANK YOU KINDLY, OH MAGICIAN, FEED ME MORE OF YOUR *DELICIOUS* MAGIC!
SQUETCH
SQUETCH
FILL ME... URGH...!
I'LL FEED YOU... I'LL GIVE YOU *EXACTLY* WHAT YOU WANT...!
HOLD THE HUNGER DEMON, HOLD THE POWER...
WHERE'S YOUR ***LUCK***, NOW?
BAM
I DON'T NEED IT!
BAM!
NO! YOU'RE NOT LUCKY! BECAUSE YOU'RE GOING TO KILL YOURSELF!
I DON'T CARE!
21

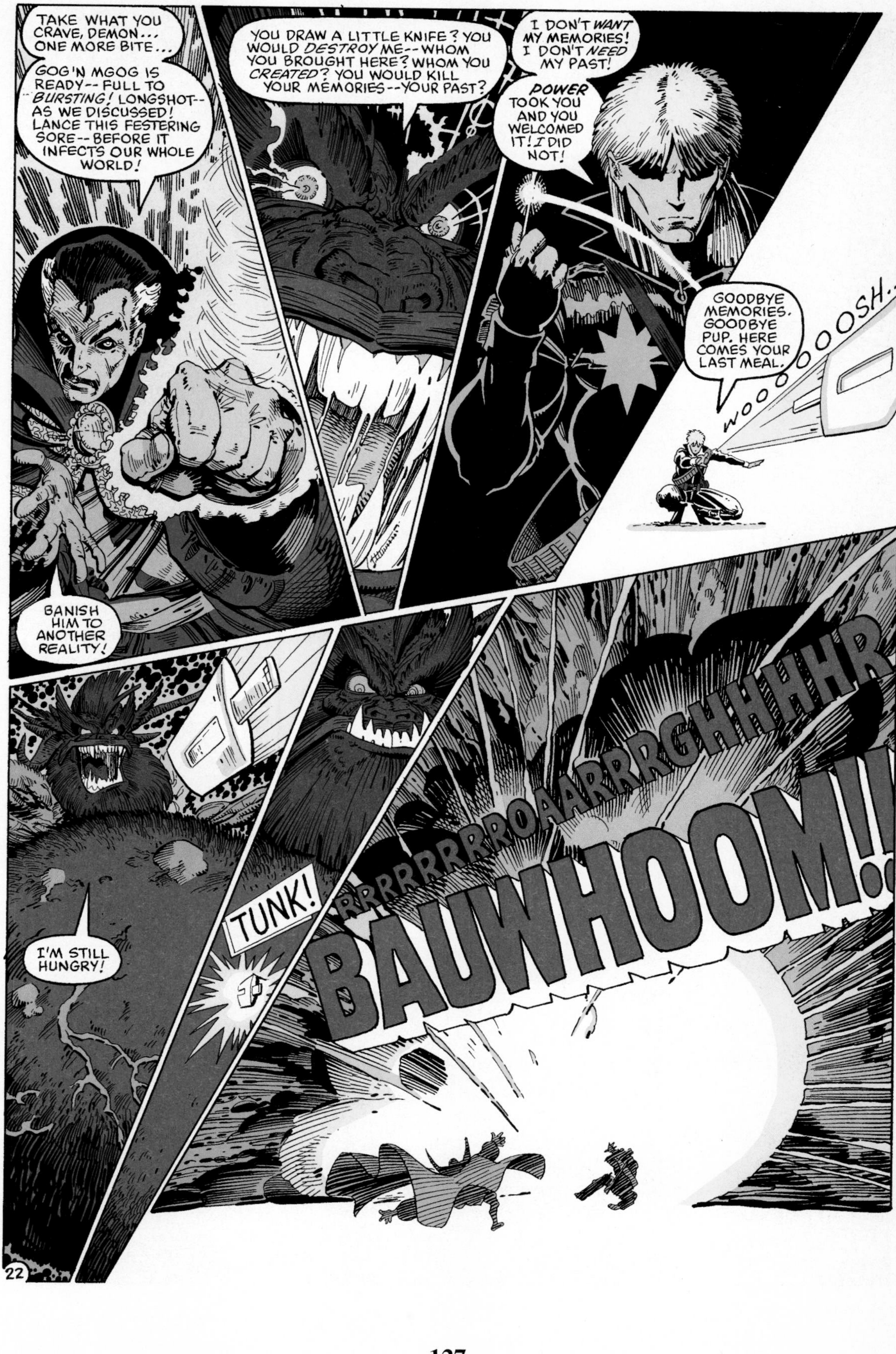
TAKE WHAT YOU CRAVE, DEMON... ONE MORE BITE...
GOG'N MGOG IS READY--FULL TO BURSTING! LONGSHOT--AS WE DISCUSSED! LANCE THIS FESTERING SORE--BEFORE IT INFECTS OUR WHOLE WORLD!
BANISH HIM TO ANOTHER REALITY!
YOU DRAW A LITTLE KNIFE? YOU WOULD DESTROY ME--WHOM YOU BROUGHT HERE? WHOM YOU CREATED? YOU WOULD KILL YOUR MEMORIES--YOUR PAST?
I DON'T WANT MY MEMORIES! I DON'T NEED MY PAST!
POWER TOOK YOU AND YOU WELCOMED IT! I DID NOT!
GOODBYE MEMORIES. GOODBYE PUP. HERE COMES YOUR LAST MEAL.
WOOOOOOOSH...
I'M STILL HUNGRY!
TUNK!
RRRRRRRROAARRRGHHHHR
BAUWHOOM!!
22

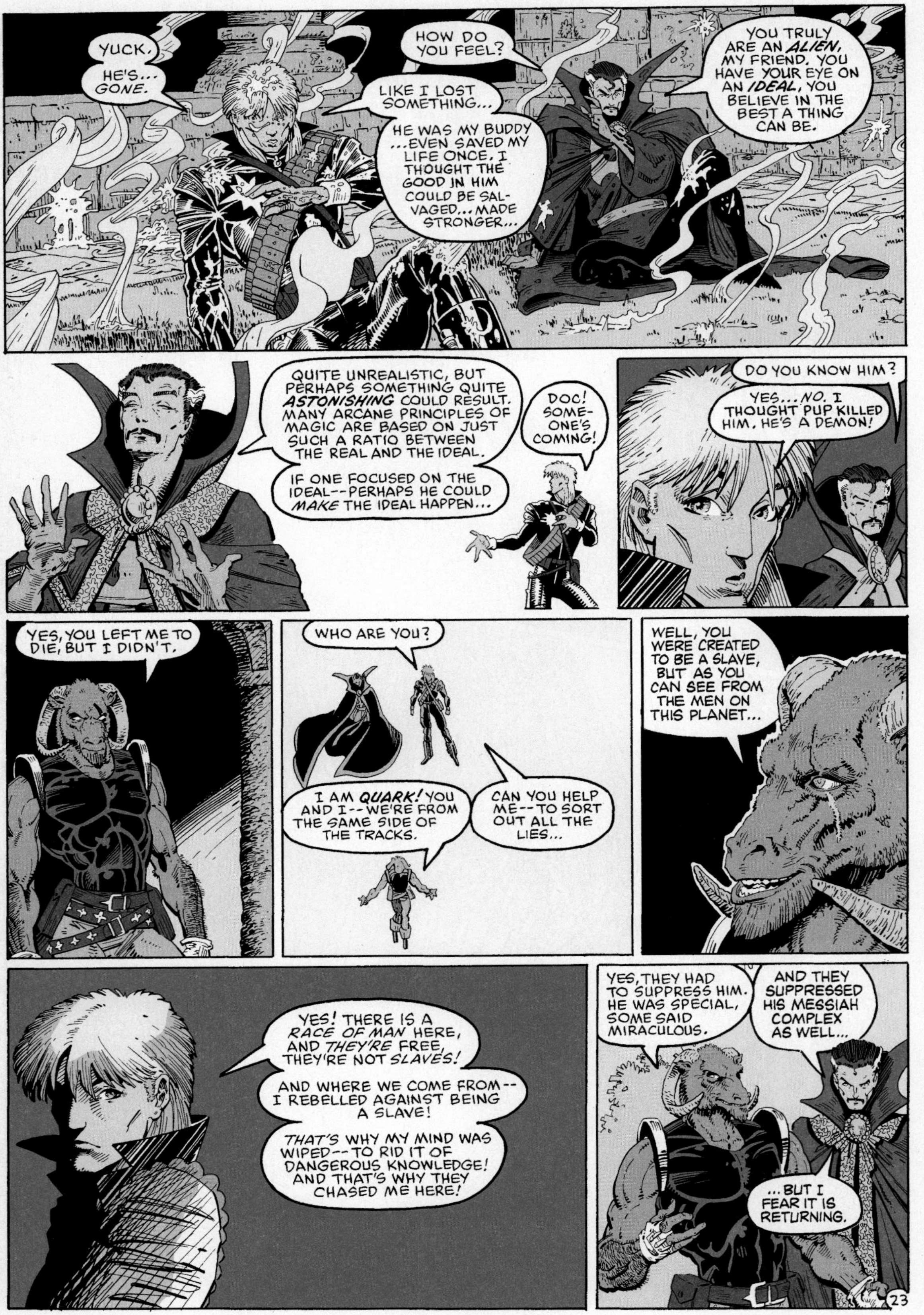
YUCK, HE'S... GONE.
HOW DO YOU FEEL?
LIKE I LOST SOMETHING...
HE WAS MY BUDDY ...EVEN SAVED MY LIFE ONCE. I THOUGHT THE GOOD IN HIM COULD BE SALVAGED... MADE STRONGER...
YOU TRULY ARE AN ALIEN, MY FRIEND. YOU HAVE YOUR EYE ON AN IDEAL, YOU BELIEVE IN THE BEST A THING CAN BE.
QUITE UNREALISTIC, BUT PERHAPS SOMETHING QUITE ASTONISHING COULD RESULT. MANY ARCANE PRINCIPLES OF MAGIC ARE BASED ON JUST SUCH A RATIO BETWEEN THE REAL AND THE IDEAL.
IF ONE FOCUSED ON THE IDEAL--PERHAPS HE COULD MAKE THE IDEAL HAPPEN...
DOC! SOMEONE'S COMING!
DO YOU KNOW HIM?
YES... NO. I THOUGHT PUP KILLED HIM. HE'S A DEMON!
YES, YOU LEFT ME TO DIE, BUT I DIDN'T.
WHO ARE YOU?
I AM QUARK! YOU AND I--WE'RE FROM THE SAME SIDE OF THE TRACKS.
CAN YOU HELP ME--TO SORT OUT ALL THE LIES...
WELL, YOU WERE CREATED TO BE A SLAVE, BUT AS YOU CAN SEE FROM THE MEN ON THIS PLANET...
YES! THERE IS A RACE OF MAN HERE, AND THEY'RE FREE, THEY'RE NOT SLAVES!
AND WHERE WE COME FROM-- I REBELLED AGAINST BEING A SLAVE!
THAT'S WHY MY MIND WAS WIPED--TO RID IT OF DANGEROUS KNOWLEDGE! AND THAT'S WHY THEY CHASED ME HERE!
YES, THEY HAD TO SUPPRESS HIM. HE WAS SPECIAL, SOME SAID MIRACULOUS.
AND THEY SUPPRESSED HIS MESSIAH COMPLEX AS WELL...
...BUT I FEAR IT IS RETURNING.
23

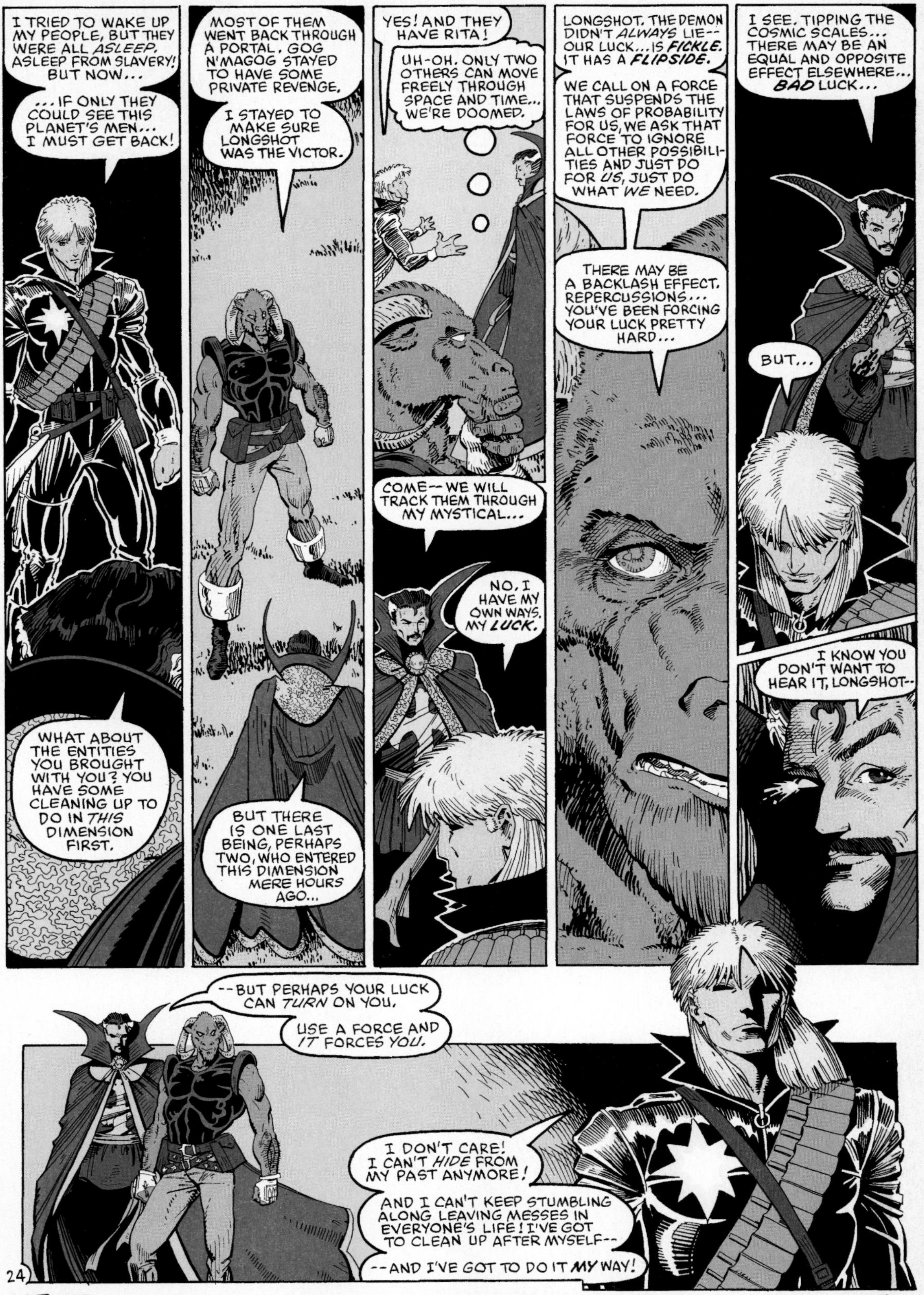
I TRIED TO WAKE UP MY PEOPLE, BUT THEY WERE ALL *ASLEEP*. ASLEEP FROM SLAVERY! BUT NOW...
...IF ONLY THEY COULD SEE THIS PLANET'S MEN... I MUST GET BACK!
WHAT ABOUT THE ENTITIES YOU BROUGHT WITH YOU? YOU HAVE SOME CLEANING UP TO DO IN *THIS* DIMENSION FIRST.
MOST OF THEM WENT BACK THROUGH A PORTAL. GOG N'MAGOG STAYED TO HAVE SOME PRIVATE REVENGE.
I STAYED TO MAKE SURE LONGSHOT WAS THE VICTOR.
BUT THERE IS ONE LAST BEING, PERHAPS TWO, WHO ENTERED THIS DIMENSION MERE HOURS AGO...
YES! AND THEY HAVE RITA!
UH-OH. ONLY TWO OTHERS CAN MOVE FREELY THROUGH SPACE AND TIME... WE'RE DOOMED.
COME-- WE WILL TRACK THEM THROUGH MY MYSTICAL...
NO. I HAVE MY OWN WAYS. MY **LUCK**.
LONGSHOT. THE DEMON DIDN'T *ALWAYS* LIE-- OUR LUCK...IS ***FICKLE***. IT HAS A ***FLIPSIDE***.
WE CALL ON A FORCE THAT SUSPENDS THE LAWS OF PROBABILITY FOR US. WE ASK THAT FORCE TO IGNORE ALL OTHER POSSIBILITIES AND JUST DO FOR *US*, JUST DO WHAT *WE* NEED.
THERE MAY BE A BACKLASH EFFECT. REPERCUSSIONS... YOU'VE BEEN FORCING YOUR LUCK PRETTY HARD...
I SEE. TIPPING THE COSMIC SCALES... THERE MAY BE AN EQUAL AND OPPOSITE EFFECT ELSEWHERE... ***BAD*** LUCK...
BUT...
I KNOW YOU DON'T WANT TO HEAR IT, LONGSHOT--
--BUT PERHAPS YOUR LUCK CAN *TURN* ON YOU.
USE A FORCE AND *IT* FORCES *YOU*.
I DON'T CARE! I CAN'T *HIDE* FROM MY PAST ANYMORE!
AND I CAN'T KEEP STUMBLING ALONG LEAVING MESSES IN EVERYONE'S LIFE! I'VE GOT TO CLEAN UP AFTER MYSELF--
--AND I'VE GOT TO DO IT ***MY*** WAY!
24

NEXT: *GALA DOUBLE-SIZED LAST ISSUE! WITH **SPIRAL, MOJO, RICOCHET RITA, DR. STRANGE,** AND THE WHOLE SICK CREW!*

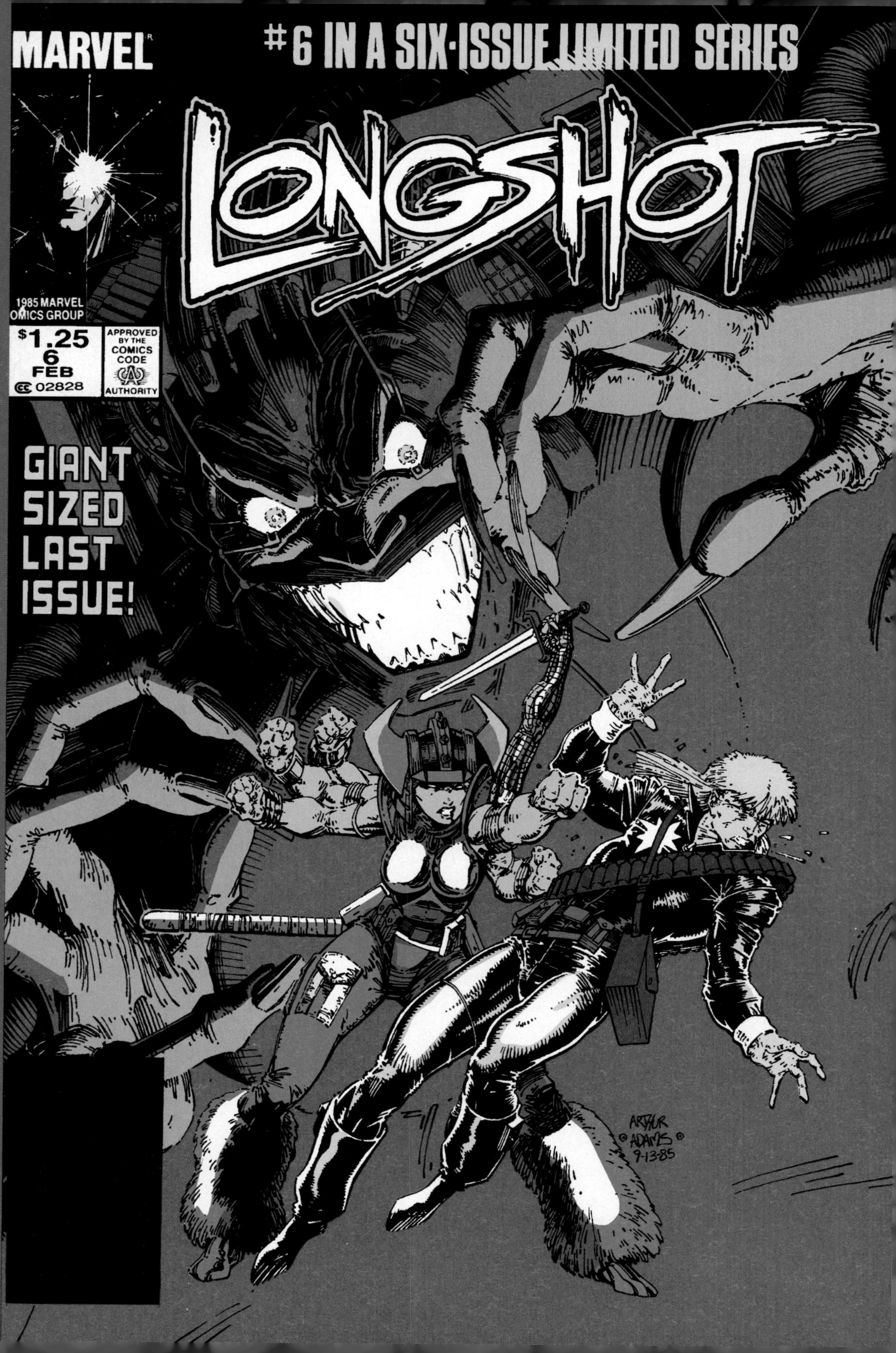
MARVEL
#6 IN A SIX-ISSUE LIMITED SERIES
LONGSHOT
1985 MARVEL COMICS GROUP
$1.25
6
FEB
02828
APPROVED BY THE COMICS CODE AUTHORITY
GIANT SIZED LAST ISSUE!
ARTHUR ADAMS
9-13-85

A SNAKE COILS...

ANN NOCENTI — WRITER * CO-CREATORS * ARTHUR ADAMS — PENCILER
WHILCE PORTACIO — INKER
JOE ROSEN — LETTERS
CHRISTIE SCHEELE — COLORS
LOUISE JONES — EDITOR
JIM SHOOTER — EDITOR IN CHIEF

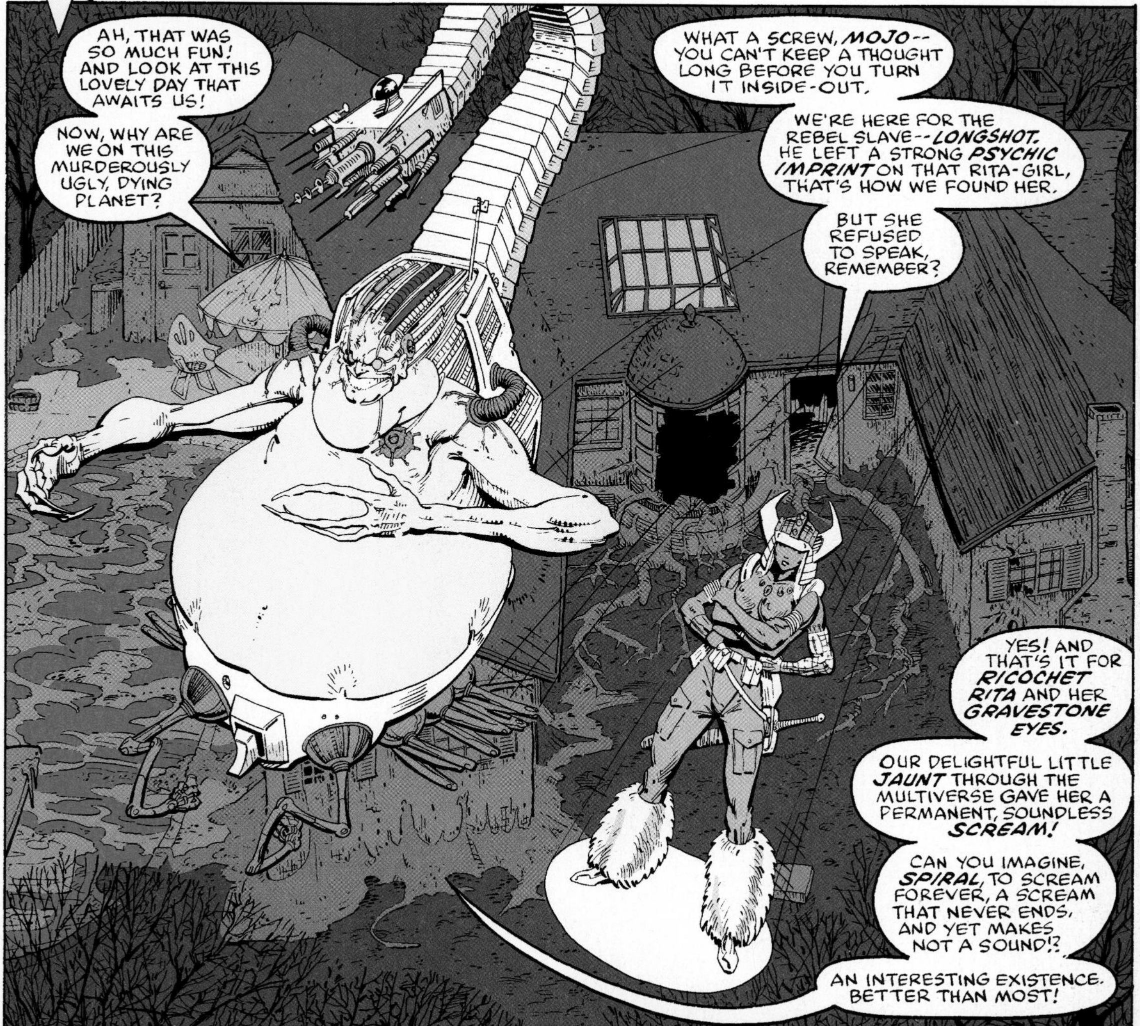
AH, THAT WAS SO MUCH FUN! AND LOOK AT THIS LOVELY DAY THAT AWAITS US!
NOW, WHY ARE WE ON THIS MURDEROUSLY UGLY, DYING PLANET?
WHAT A SCREW, MOJO-- YOU CAN'T KEEP A THOUGHT LONG BEFORE YOU TURN IT INSIDE-OUT.
WE'RE HERE FOR THE REBEL SLAVE--LONGSHOT. HE LEFT A STRONG PSYCHIC IMPRINT ON THAT RITA-GIRL, THAT'S HOW WE FOUND HER.
BUT SHE REFUSED TO SPEAK, REMEMBER?
YES! AND THAT'S IT FOR RICOCHET RITA AND HER GRAVESTONE EYES.
OUR DELIGHTFUL LITTLE JAUNT THROUGH THE MULTIVERSE GAVE HER A PERMANENT, SOUNDLESS SCREAM!
CAN YOU IMAGINE, SPIRAL, TO SCREAM FOREVER, A SCREAM THAT NEVER ENDS, AND YET MAKES NOT A SOUND!?
AN INTERESTING EXISTENCE. BETTER THAN MOST!

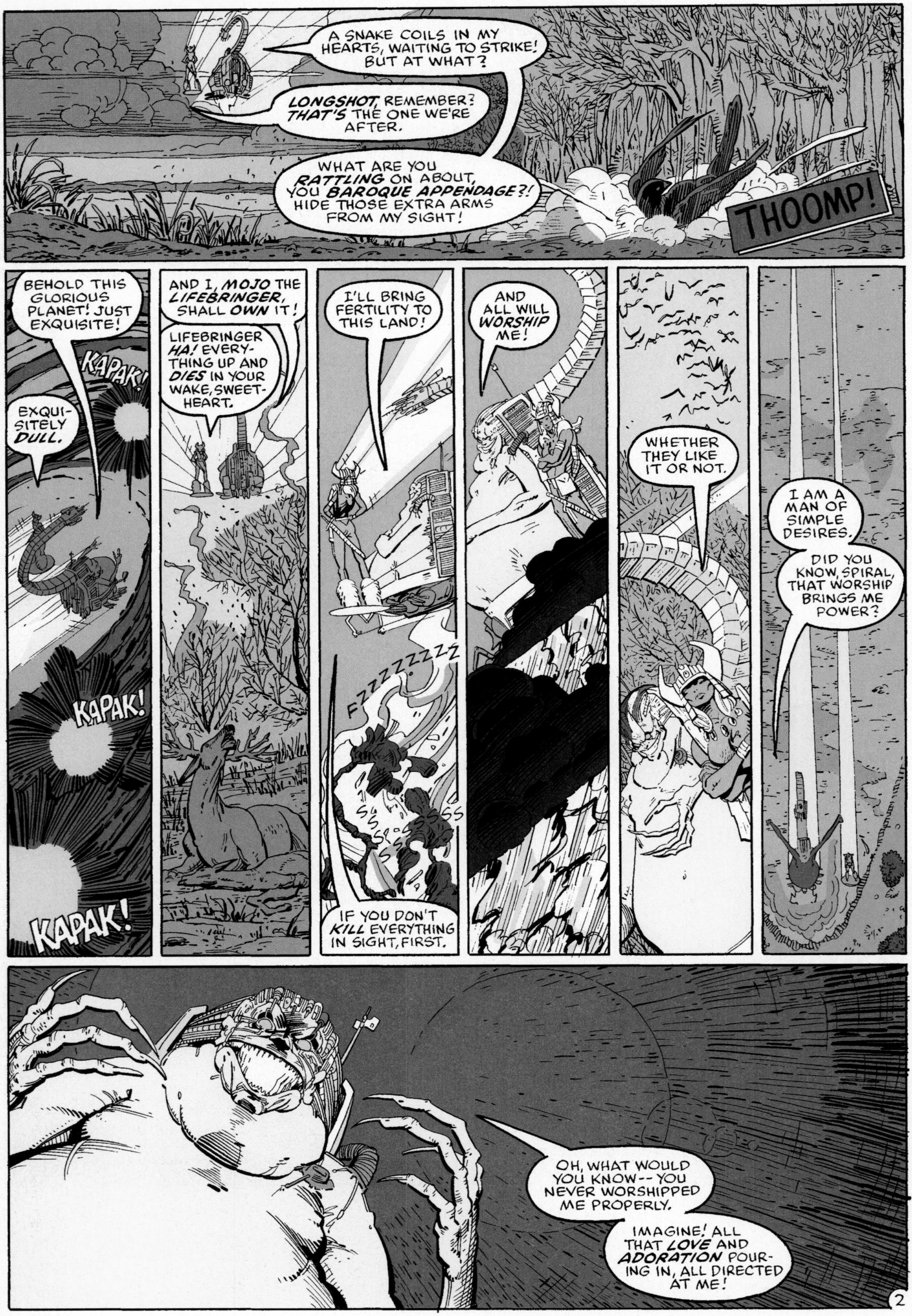
A SNAKE COILS IN MY HEARTS, WAITING TO STRIKE! BUT AT WHAT?
LONGSHOT, REMEMBER? THAT'S THE ONE WE'RE AFTER.
WHAT ARE YOU RATTLING ON ABOUT, YOU BAROQUE APPENDAGE?! HIDE THOSE EXTRA ARMS FROM MY SIGHT!
THOOMP!
BEHOLD THIS GLORIOUS PLANET! JUST EXQUISITE!
KAPAK!
EXQUISITELY DULL.
KAPAK!
KAPAK!
AND I, MOJO THE LIFEBRINGER, SHALL OWN IT!
LIFEBRINGER HA! EVERYTHING UP AND DIES IN YOUR WAKE, SWEETHEART.
I'LL BRING FERTILITY TO THIS LAND!
FZZZZZZZZZ
IF YOU DON'T KILL EVERYTHING IN SIGHT, FIRST.
AND ALL WILL WORSHIP ME!
WHETHER THEY LIKE IT OR NOT.
I AM A MAN OF SIMPLE DESIRES.
DID YOU KNOW, SPIRAL, THAT WORSHIP BRINGS ME POWER?
OH, WHAT WOULD YOU KNOW-- YOU NEVER WORSHIPPED ME PROPERLY.
IMAGINE! ALL THAT LOVE AND ADORATION POURING IN, ALL DIRECTED AT ME!

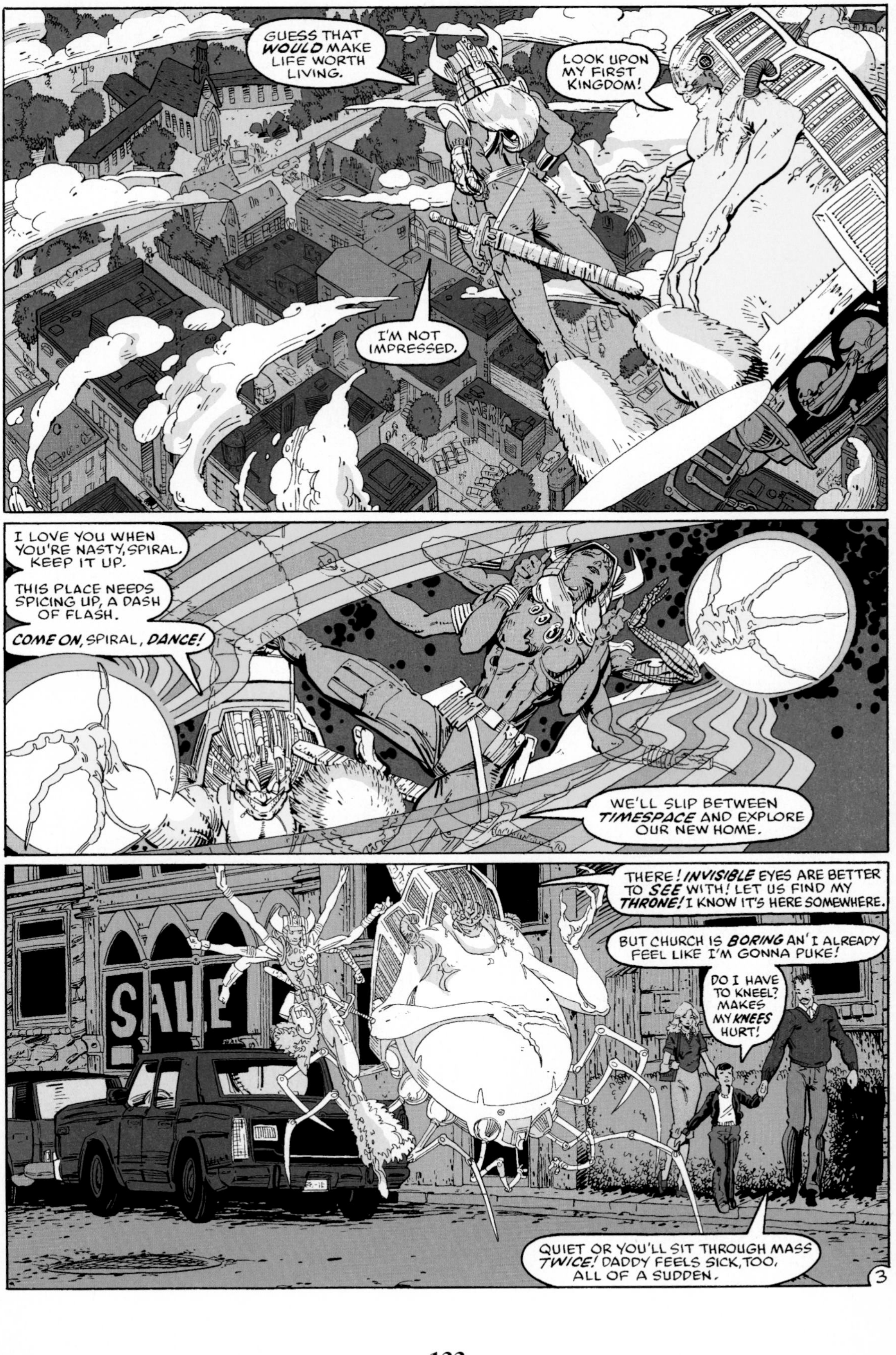
GUESS THAT WOULD MAKE LIFE WORTH LIVING.
LOOK UPON MY FIRST KINGDOM!
I'M NOT IMPRESSED.
I LOVE YOU WHEN YOU'RE NASTY, SPIRAL. KEEP IT UP.
THIS PLACE NEEDS SPICING UP, A DASH OF FLASH.
COME ON, SPIRAL, DANCE!
WE'LL SLIP BETWEEN TIMESPACE AND EXPLORE OUR NEW HOME.
SALE
THERE! INVISIBLE EYES ARE BETTER TO SEE WITH! LET US FIND MY THRONE! I KNOW IT'S HERE SOMEWHERE.
BUT CHURCH IS BORING AN' I ALREADY FEEL LIKE I'M GONNA PUKE!
DO I HAVE TO KNEEL? MAKES MY KNEES HURT!
QUIET OR YOU'LL SIT THROUGH MASS TWICE! DADDY FEELS SICK, TOO, ALL OF A SUDDEN.
3

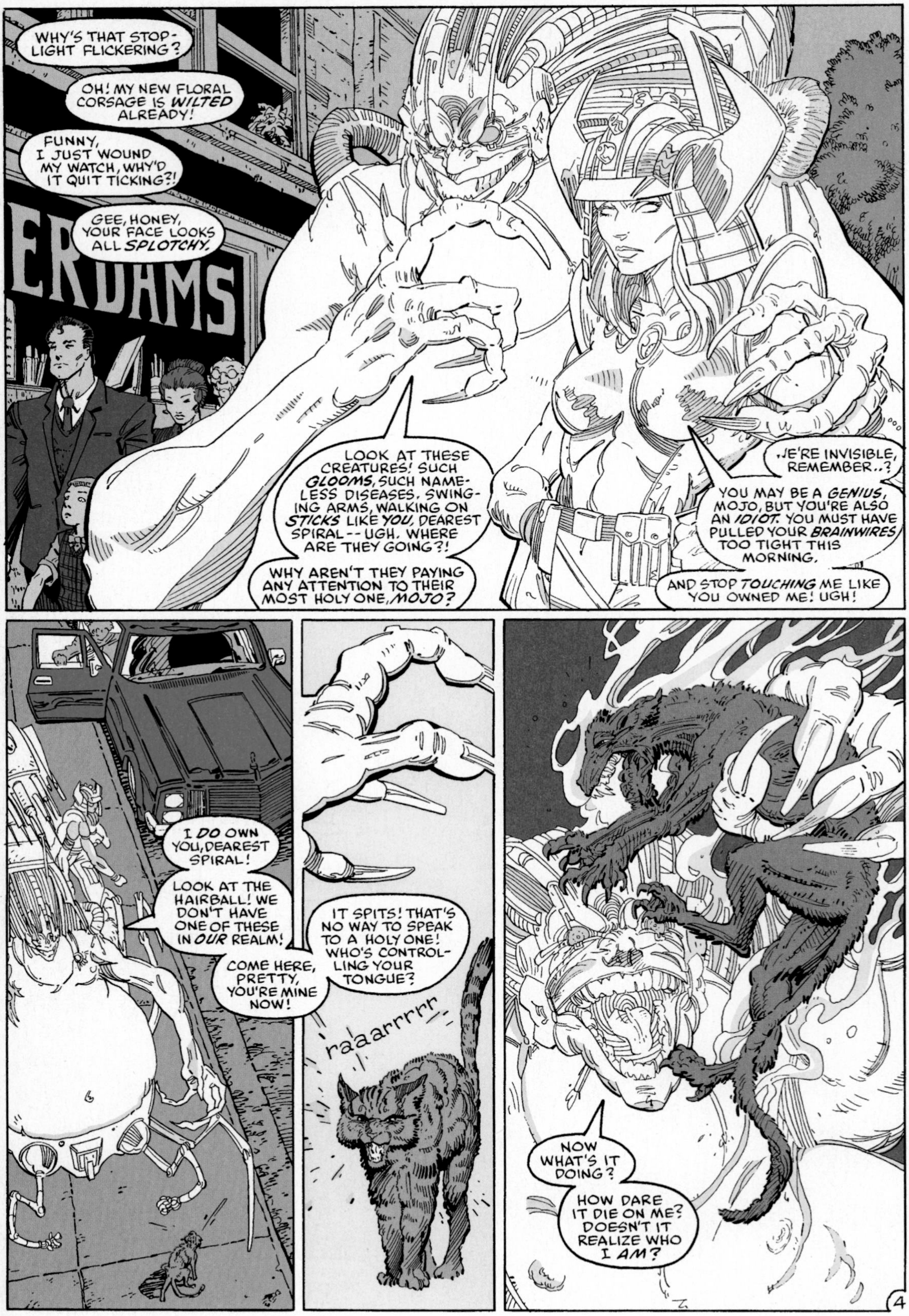
WHY'S THAT STOP-LIGHT FLICKERING?
OH! MY NEW FLORAL CORSAGE IS WILTED ALREADY!
FUNNY, I JUST WOUND MY WATCH, WHY'D IT QUIT TICKING?!
GEE, HONEY, YOUR FACE LOOKS ALL SPLOTCHY.
ERDAMS
LOOK AT THESE CREATURES! SUCH GLOOMS, SUCH NAMELESS DISEASES. SWINGING ARMS, WALKING ON STICKS LIKE YOU, DEAREST SPIRAL -- UGH. WHERE ARE THEY GOING?!
WHY AREN'T THEY PAYING ANY ATTENTION TO THEIR MOST HOLY ONE, MOJO?
WE'RE INVISIBLE, REMEMBER..?
YOU MAY BE A GENIUS, MOJO, BUT YOU'RE ALSO AN IDIOT. YOU MUST HAVE PULLED YOUR BRAINWIRES TOO TIGHT THIS MORNING.
AND STOP TOUCHING ME LIKE YOU OWNED ME! UGH!
I DO OWN YOU, DEAREST SPIRAL!
LOOK AT THE HAIRBALL! WE DON'T HAVE ONE OF THESE IN OUR REALM!
COME HERE, PRETTY, YOU'RE MINE NOW!
IT SPITS! THAT'S NO WAY TO SPEAK TO A HOLY ONE! WHO'S CONTROLLING YOUR TONGUE?
raaarrrrr
NOW WHAT'S IT DOING?
HOW DARE IT DIE ON ME? DOESN'T IT REALIZE WHO I AM?
4

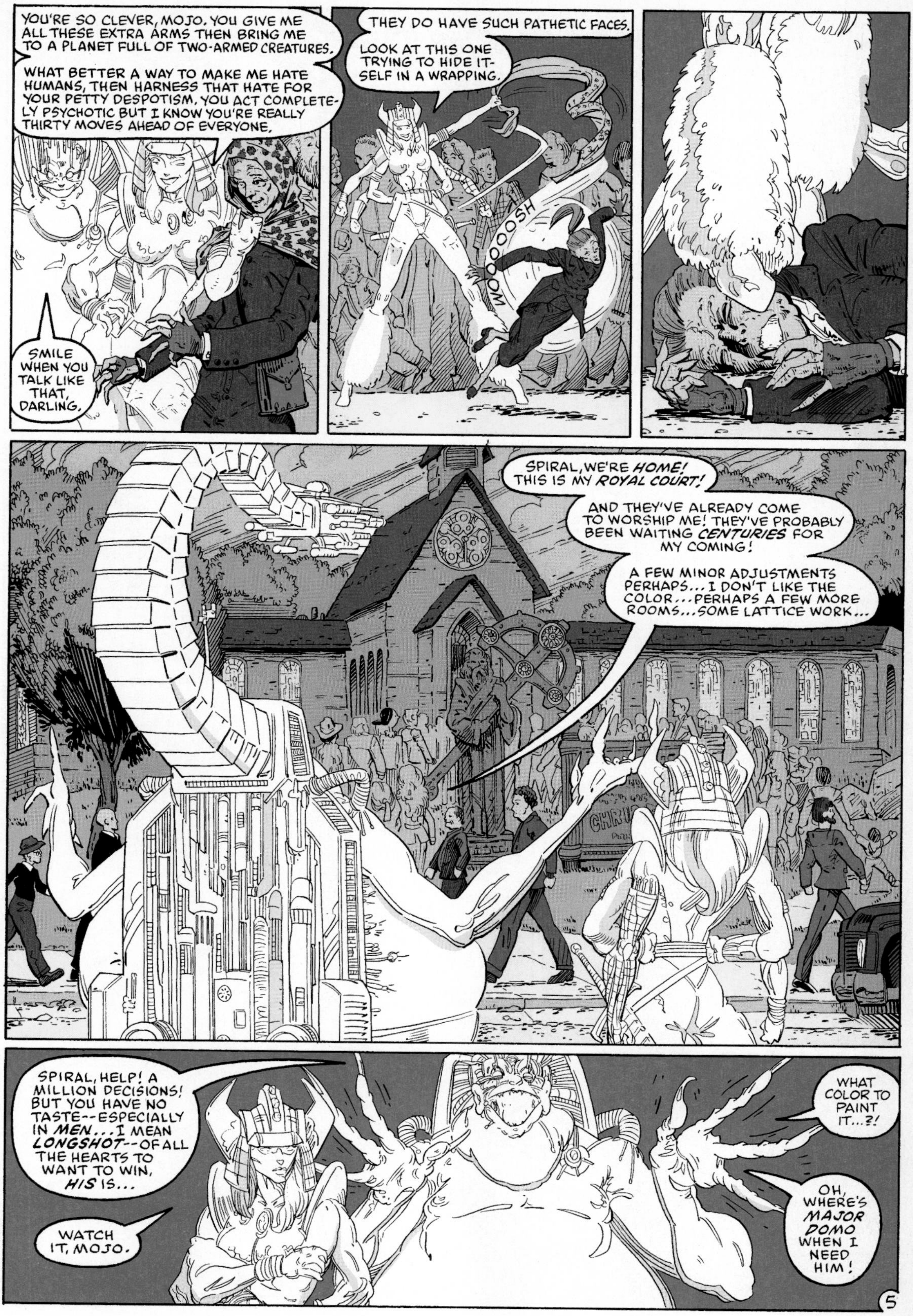

YOU'RE SO CLEVER, MOJO. YOU GIVE ME ALL THESE EXTRA ARMS THEN BRING ME TO A PLANET FULL OF TWO-ARMED CREATURES.
WHAT BETTER A WAY TO MAKE ME HATE HUMANS, THEN HARNESS THAT HATE FOR YOUR PETTY DESPOTISM, YOU ACT COMPLETELY PSYCHOTIC BUT I KNOW YOU'RE REALLY THIRTY MOVES AHEAD OF EVERYONE.
SMILE WHEN YOU TALK LIKE THAT, DARLING.
THEY DO HAVE SUCH PATHETIC FACES.
LOOK AT THIS ONE TRYING TO HIDE ITSELF IN A WRAPPING.
WOOOOOSH
SPIRAL, WE'RE *HOME!* THIS IS MY *ROYAL COURT!*
AND THEY'VE ALREADY COME TO WORSHIP ME! THEY'VE PROBABLY BEEN WAITING *CENTURIES* FOR MY COMING!
A FEW MINOR ADJUSTMENTS PERHAPS... I DON'T LIKE THE COLOR... PERHAPS A FEW MORE ROOMS... SOME LATTICE WORK...
SPIRAL, HELP! A MILLION DECISIONS! BUT YOU HAVE NO TASTE--ESPECIALLY IN *MEN*... I MEAN *LONGSHOT*--OF ALL THE HEARTS TO WANT TO WIN, *HIS* IS...
WATCH IT, MOJO.
WHAT COLOR TO PAINT IT...?!
OH, WHERE'S *MAJOR DOMO* WHEN I NEED HIM!
5

NOW WHAT WOULD DOMO DO?

HE'D GET THEM IN THE PROPER FRAME OF MIND!

A FEW BRAIN-TWISTS TO THE RIGHT... SOT THEM BAWDY!

THERE!

MOJO!

OUR LORD MOJO, WHO ART MOST HOLY!

HALLOWED BE HIS FAME!

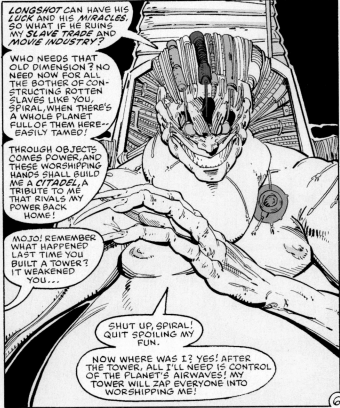

LONGSHOT CAN HAVE HIS LUCK AND HIS MIRACLES, SO WHAT IF HE RUINS MY SLAVE TRADE AND MOVIE INDUSTRY?

WHO NEEDS THAT OLD DIMENSION? NO NEED NOW FOR ALL THE BOTHER OF CONSTRUCTING ROTTEN SLAVES LIKE YOU, SPIRAL, WHEN THERE'S A WHOLE PLANET FULL OF THEM HERE-- EASILY TAMED!

THROUGH OBJECTS COMES POWER, AND THESE WORSHIPPING HANDS SHALL BUILD ME A CITADEL, A TRIBUTE TO ME THAT RIVALS MY POWER BACK HOME!

MOJO! REMEMBER WHAT HAPPENED LAST TIME YOU BUILT A TOWER? IT WEAKENED YOU...

SHUT UP, SPIRAL! QUIT SPOILING MY FUN.

NOW WHERE WAS I? YES! AFTER THE TOWER, ALL I'LL NEED IS CONTROL OF THE PLANET'S AIRWAVES! MY TOWER WILL ZAP EVERYONE INTO WORSHIPPING ME!

6

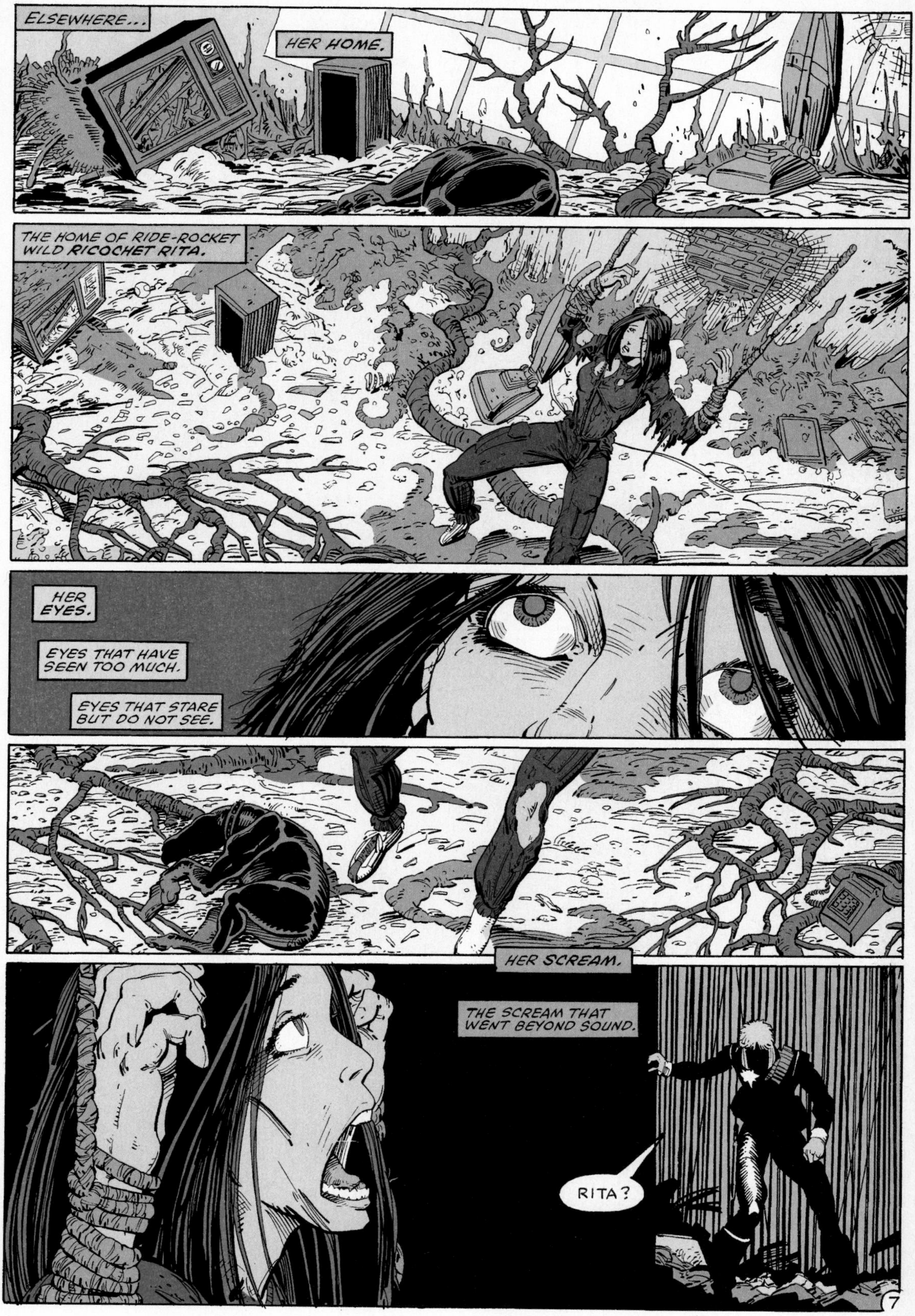
ELSEWHERE...
HER HOME.
THE HOME OF RIDE-ROCKET WILD RICOCHET RITA.
HER EYES.
EYES THAT HAVE SEEN TOO MUCH.
EYES THAT STARE BUT DO NOT SEE.
HER SCREAM.
THE SCREAM THAT WENT BEYOND SOUND.
RITA?
7

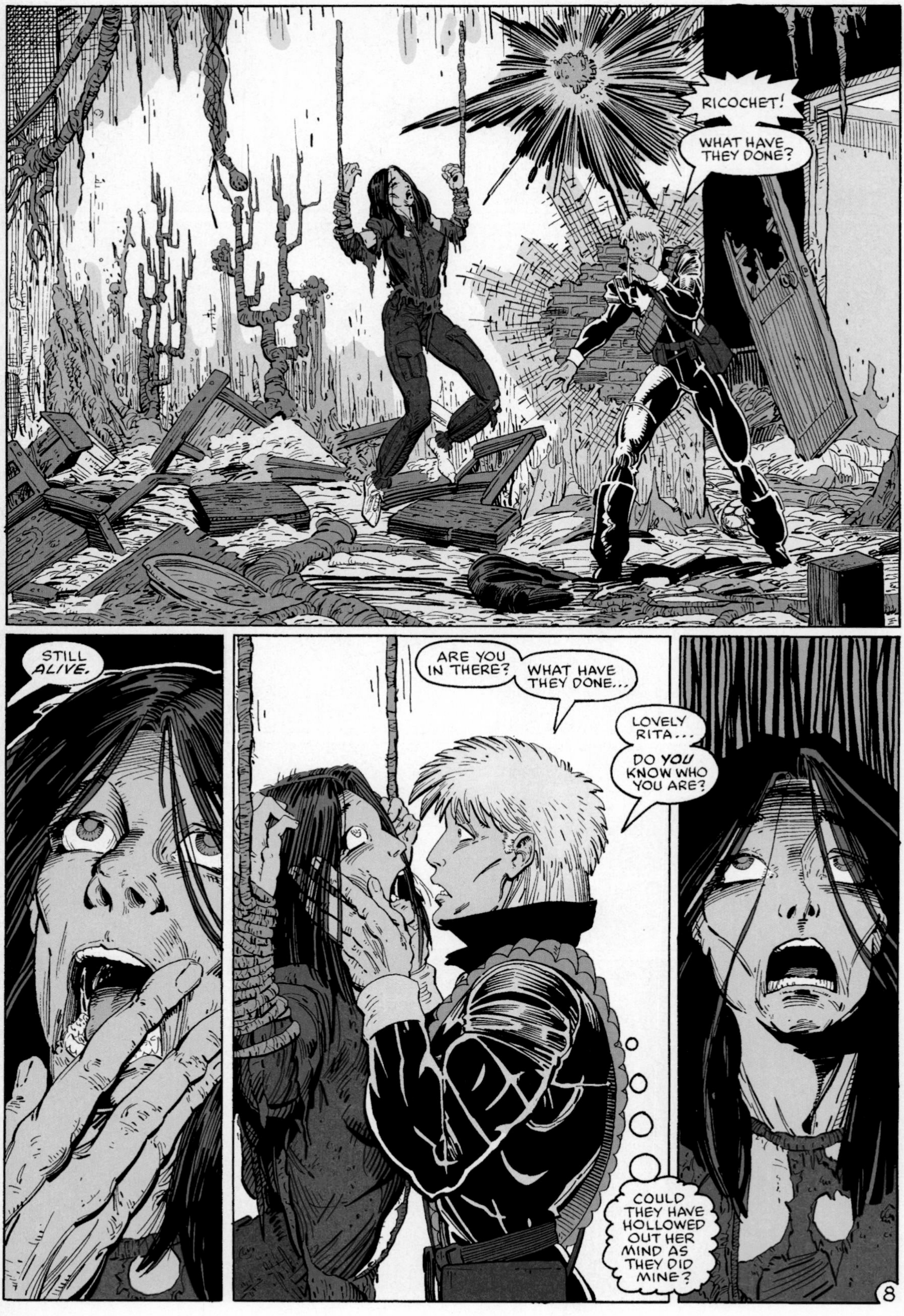
RICOCHET!
WHAT HAVE THEY DONE?
STILL ALIVE.
ARE YOU IN THERE?
WHAT HAVE THEY DONE...
LOVELY RITA...
DO YOU KNOW WHO YOU ARE?
COULD THEY HAVE HOLLOWED OUT HER MIND AS THEY DID MINE?
8

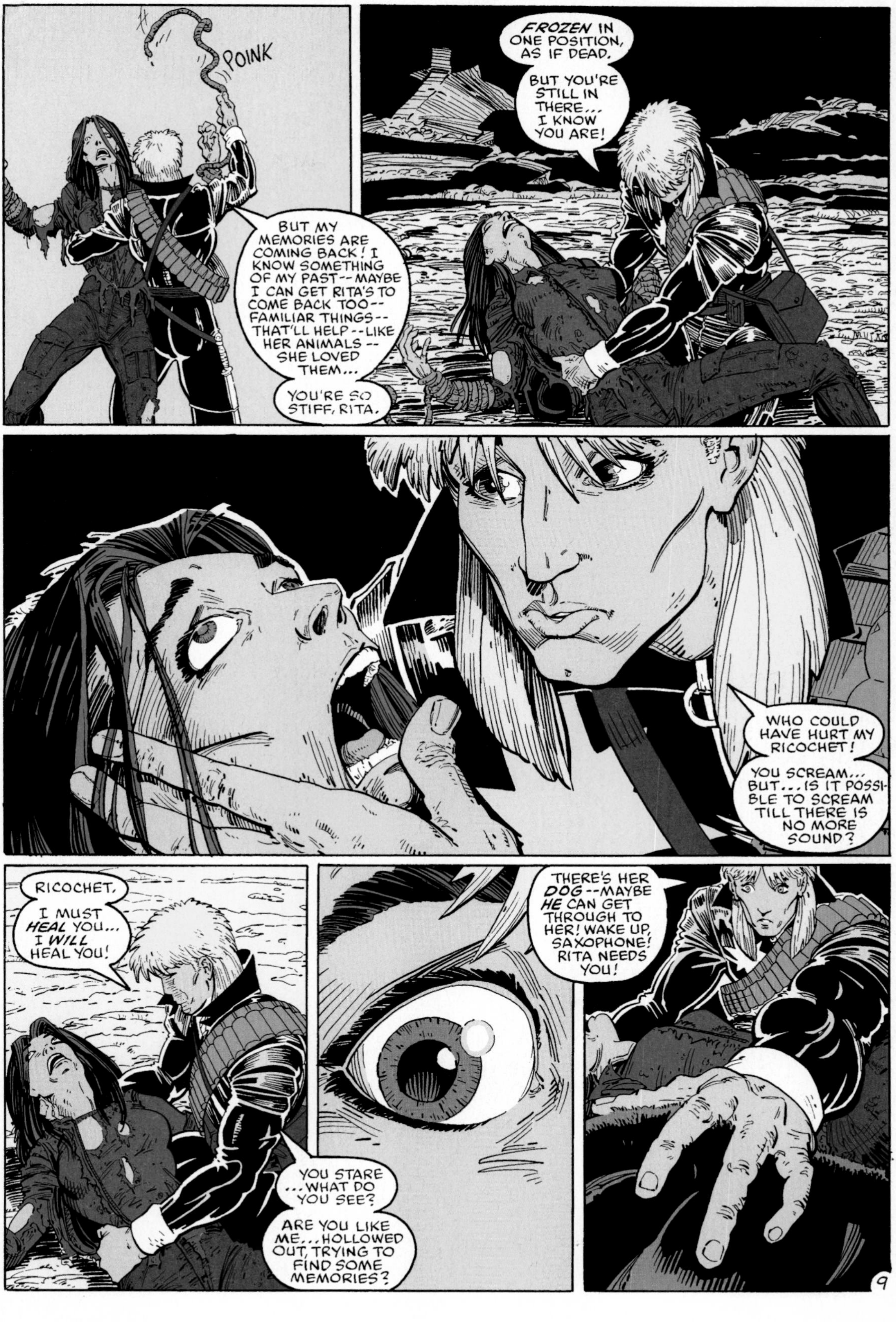
POINK
BUT MY MEMORIES ARE COMING BACK! I KNOW SOMETHING OF MY PAST--MAYBE I CAN GET RITA'S TO COME BACK TOO--FAMILIAR THINGS--THAT'LL HELP--LIKE HER ANIMALS--SHE LOVED THEM...
YOU'RE SO STIFF, RITA.
FROZEN IN ONE POSITION, AS IF DEAD.
BUT YOU'RE STILL IN THERE... I KNOW YOU ARE!
WHO COULD HAVE HURT MY RICOCHET!
YOU SCREAM... BUT... IS IT POSSIBLE TO SCREAM TILL THERE IS NO MORE SOUND?
RICOCHET, I MUST HEAL YOU... I WILL HEAL YOU!
YOU STARE ...WHAT DO YOU SEE?
ARE YOU LIKE ME... HOLLOWED OUT, TRYING TO FIND SOME MEMORIES?
THERE'S HER DOG--MAYBE HE CAN GET THROUGH TO HER! WAKE UP, SAXOPHONE! RITA NEEDS YOU!
9

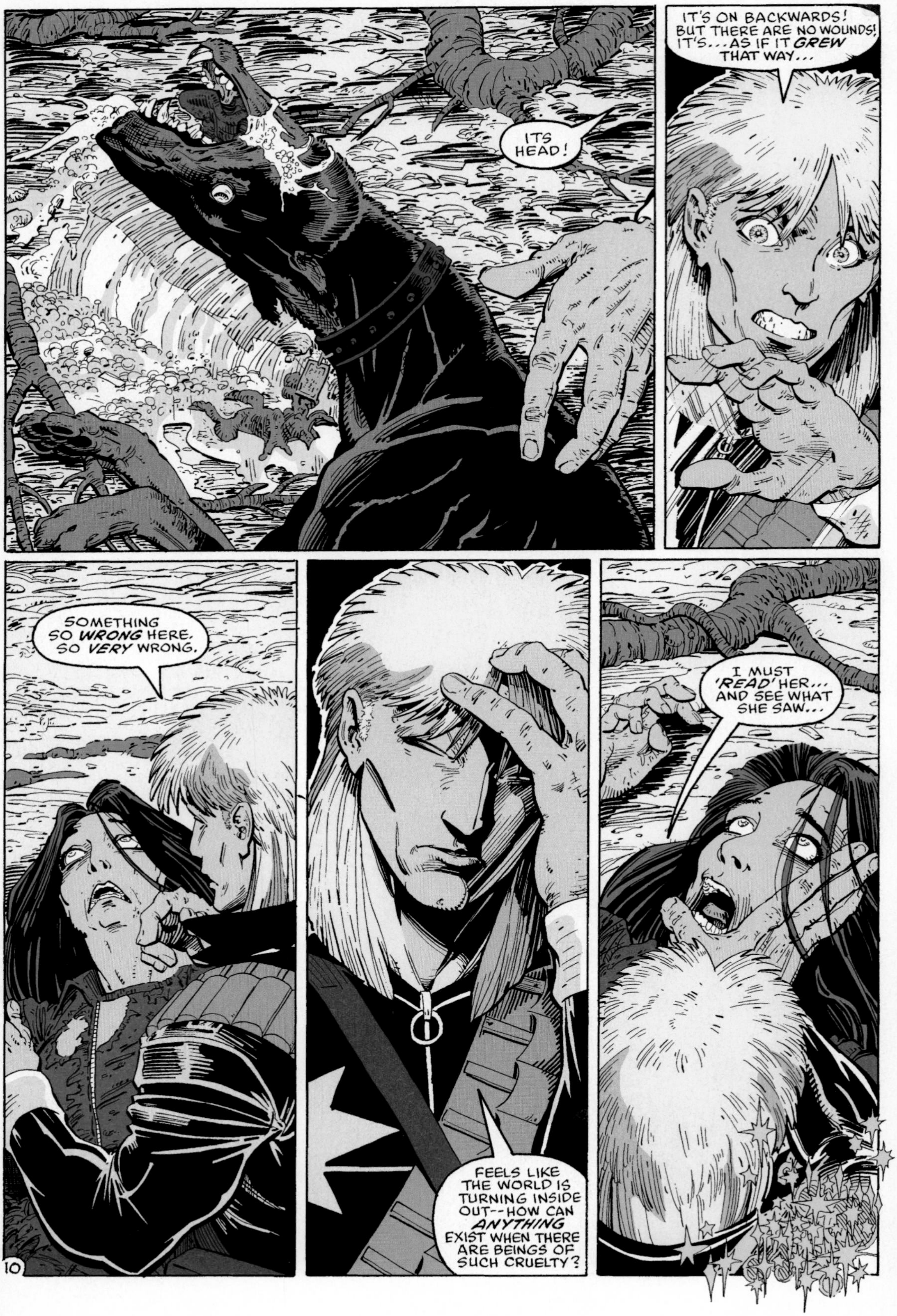
ITS HEAD!
IT'S ON BACKWARDS! BUT THERE ARE NO WOUNDS! IT'S...AS IF IT GREW THAT WAY...
SOMETHING SO WRONG HERE. SO VERY WRONG.
10
FEELS LIKE THE WORLD IS TURNING INSIDE OUT--HOW CAN ANYTHING EXIST WHEN THERE ARE BEINGS OF SUCH CRUELTY?
I MUST 'READ' HER... AND SEE WHAT SHE SAW...

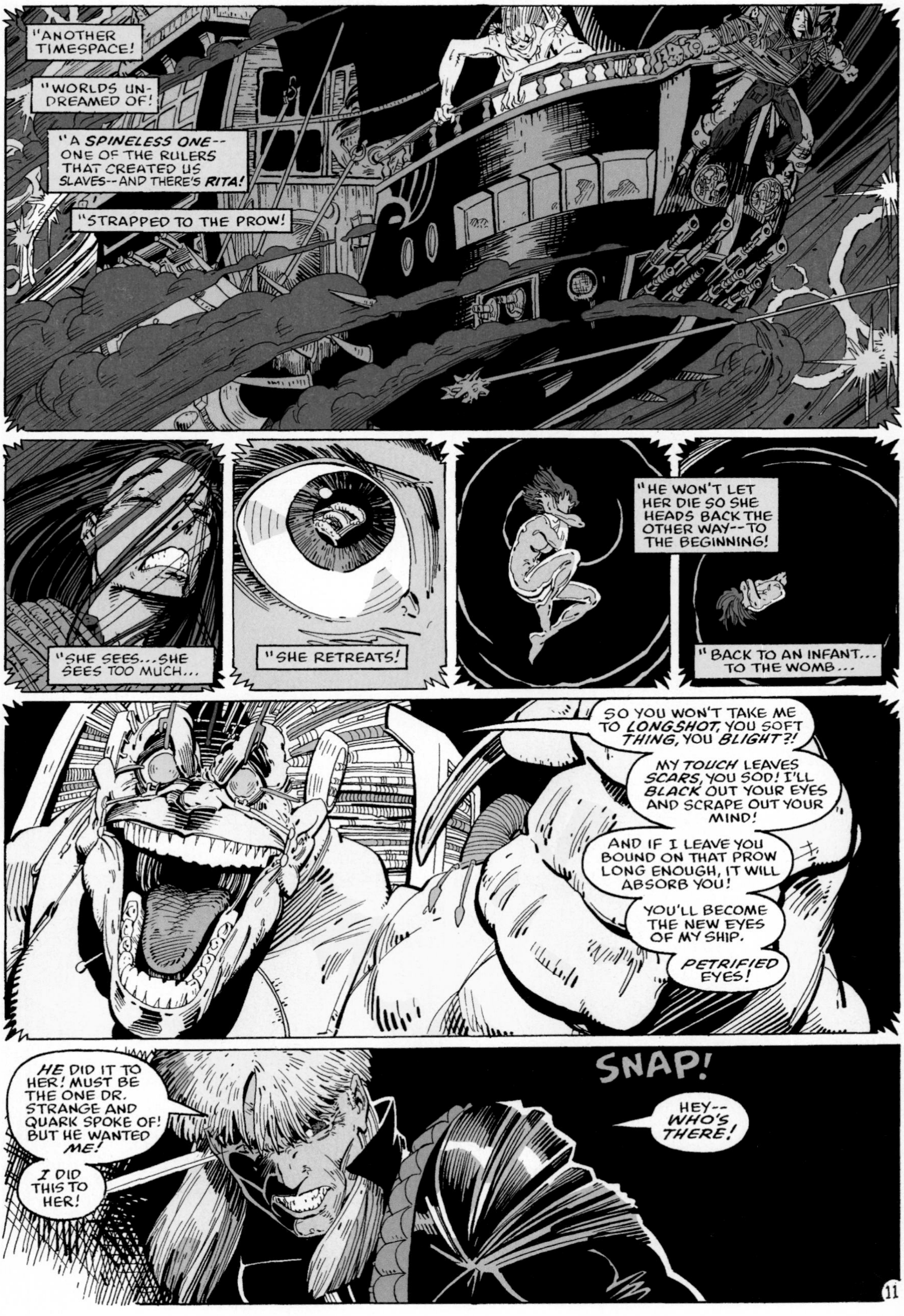
"ANOTHER TIMESPACE!
"WORLDS UNDREAMED OF!
"A SPINELESS ONE-- ONE OF THE RULERS THAT CREATED US SLAVES--AND THERE'S RITA!
"STRAPPED TO THE PROW!
"SHE SEES...SHE SEES TOO MUCH...
"SHE RETREATS!
"HE WON'T LET HER DIE SO SHE HEADS BACK THE OTHER WAY--TO THE BEGINNING!
"BACK TO AN INFANT... TO THE WOMB...
SO YOU WON'T TAKE ME TO LONGSHOT, YOU SOFT THING, YOU BLIGHT?!
MY TOUCH LEAVES SCARS, YOU SOD! I'LL BLACK OUT YOUR EYES AND SCRAPE OUT YOUR MIND!
AND IF I LEAVE YOU BOUND ON THAT PROW LONG ENOUGH, IT WILL ABSORB YOU!
YOU'LL BECOME THE NEW EYES OF MY SHIP.
PETRIFIED EYES!
HE DID IT TO HER! MUST BE THE ONE DR. STRANGE AND QUARK SPOKE OF! BUT HE WANTED ME!
I DID THIS TO HER!
SNAP!
HEY-- WHO'S THERE!
11

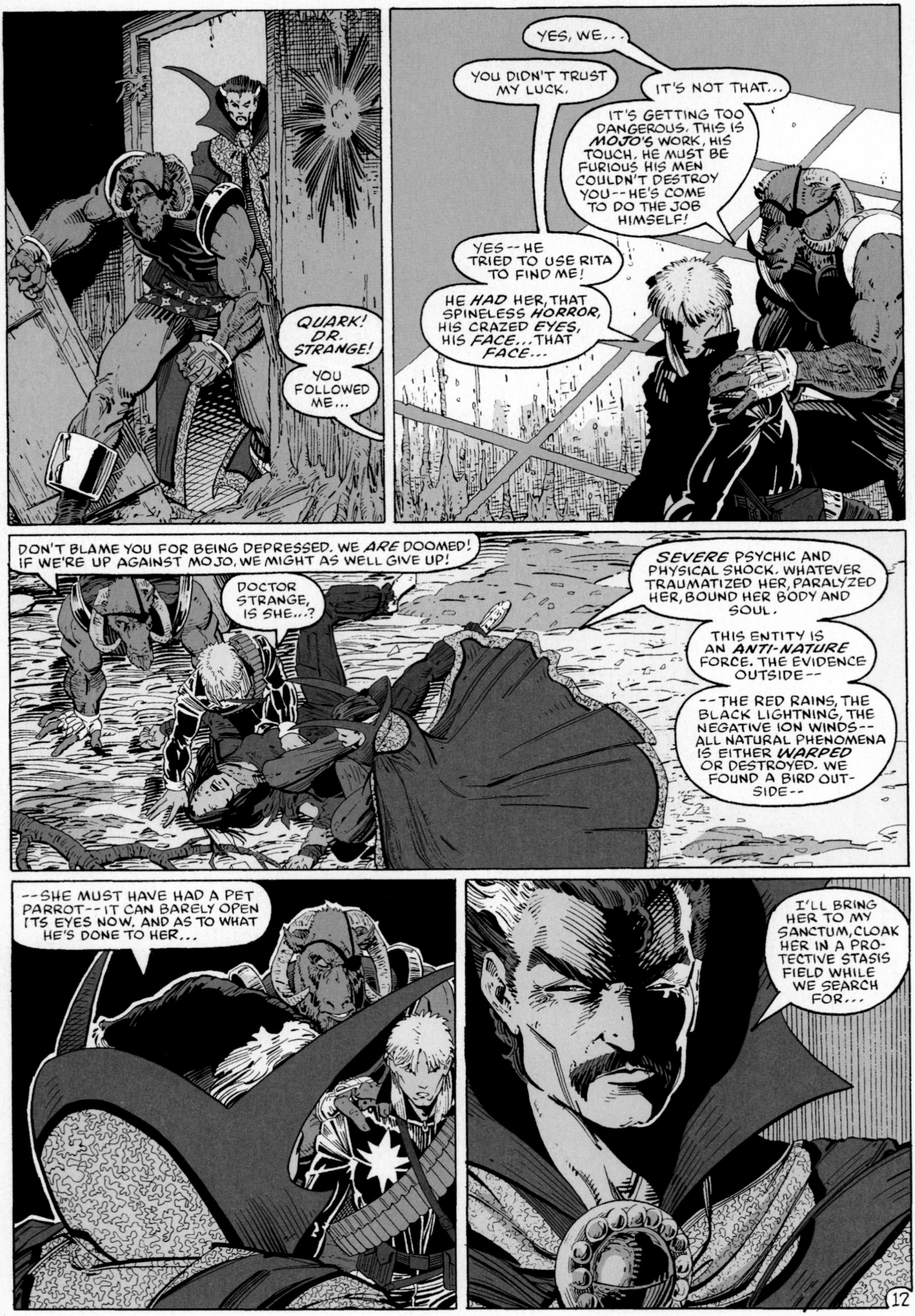
QUARK! DR. STRANGE!
YOU FOLLOWED ME...
YES, WE...
YOU DIDN'T TRUST MY LUCK.
IT'S NOT THAT...
IT'S GETTING TOO DANGEROUS. THIS IS MOJO'S WORK, HIS TOUCH. HE MUST BE FURIOUS HIS MEN COULDN'T DESTROY YOU--HE'S COME TO DO THE JOB HIMSELF!
YES--HE TRIED TO USE RITA TO FIND ME!
HE HAD HER, THAT SPINELESS HORROR, HIS CRAZED EYES, HIS FACE...THAT FACE...
DON'T BLAME YOU FOR BEING DEPRESSED. WE ARE DOOMED! IF WE'RE UP AGAINST MOJO, WE MIGHT AS WELL GIVE UP!
DOCTOR STRANGE, IS SHE...?
SEVERE PSYCHIC AND PHYSICAL SHOCK. WHATEVER TRAUMATIZED HER, PARALYZED HER, BOUND HER BODY AND SOUL.
THIS ENTITY IS AN ANTI-NATURE FORCE. THE EVIDENCE OUTSIDE--
--THE RED RAINS, THE BLACK LIGHTNING, THE NEGATIVE ION WINDS--ALL NATURAL PHENOMENA IS EITHER WARPED OR DESTROYED. WE FOUND A BIRD OUT-SIDE--
--SHE MUST HAVE HAD A PET PARROT--IT CAN BARELY OPEN ITS EYES NOW. AND AS TO WHAT HE'S DONE TO HER...
I'LL BRING HER TO MY SANCTUM, CLOAK HER IN A PROTECTIVE STASIS FIELD WHILE WE SEARCH FOR...
12

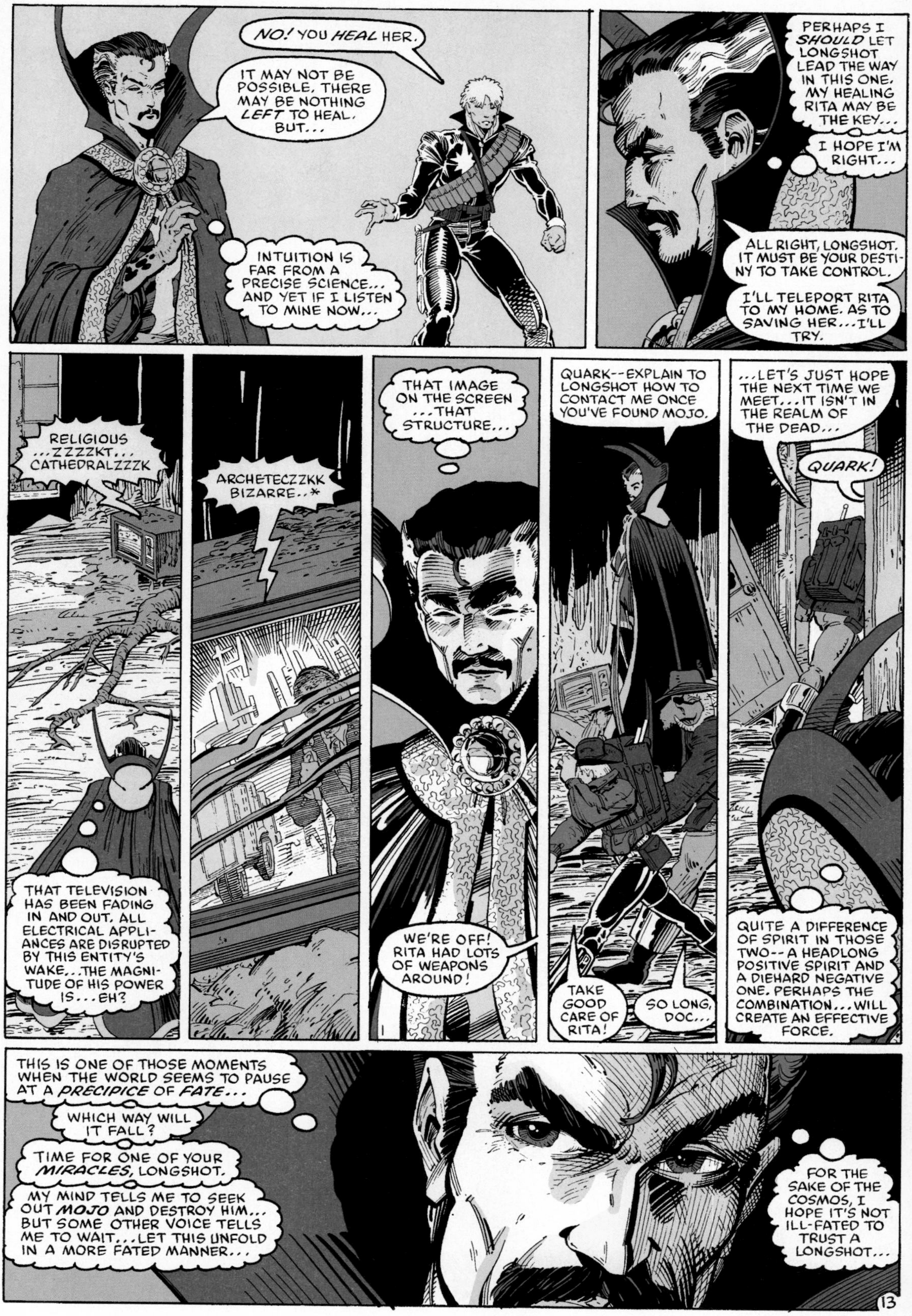
NO! YOU HEAL HER.
IT MAY NOT BE POSSIBLE. THERE MAY BE NOTHING LEFT TO HEAL. BUT...
INTUITION IS FAR FROM A PRECISE SCIENCE... AND YET IF I LISTEN TO MINE NOW...
PERHAPS I SHOULD LET LONGSHOT LEAD THE WAY IN THIS ONE. MY HEALING RITA MAY BE THE KEY...
I HOPE I'M RIGHT...
ALL RIGHT, LONGSHOT. IT MUST BE YOUR DESTINY TO TAKE CONTROL.
I'LL TELEPORT RITA TO MY HOME. AS TO SAVING HER... I'LL TRY.
RELIGIOUS ...ZZZZKT... CATHEDRALZZZK
THAT TELEVISION HAS BEEN FADING IN AND OUT. ALL ELECTRICAL APPLIANCES ARE DISRUPTED BY THIS ENTITY'S WAKE... THE MAGNITUDE OF HIS POWER IS... EH?
ARCHETECZZKK BIZARRE..*
THAT IMAGE ON THE SCREEN ...THAT STRUCTURE...
WE'RE OFF! RITA HAD LOTS OF WEAPONS AROUND!
QUARK--EXPLAIN TO LONGSHOT HOW TO CONTACT ME ONCE YOU'VE FOUND MOJO.
TAKE GOOD CARE OF RITA!
SO LONG, DOC...
...LET'S JUST HOPE THE NEXT TIME WE MEET... IT ISN'T IN THE REALM OF THE DEAD...
QUARK!
QUITE A DIFFERENCE OF SPIRIT IN THOSE TWO-- A HEADLONG POSITIVE SPIRIT AND A DIEHARD NEGATIVE ONE. PERHAPS THE COMBINATION... WILL CREATE AN EFFECTIVE FORCE.
THIS IS ONE OF THOSE MOMENTS WHEN THE WORLD SEEMS TO PAUSE AT A PRECIPICE OF FATE...
WHICH WAY WILL IT FALL?
TIME FOR ONE OF YOUR MIRACLES, LONGSHOT.
MY MIND TELLS ME TO SEEK OUT MOJO AND DESTROY HIM... BUT SOME OTHER VOICE TELLS ME TO WAIT... LET THIS UNFOLD IN A MORE FATED MANNER...
FOR THE SAKE OF THE COSMOS, I HOPE IT'S NOT ILL-FATED TO TRUST A LONGSHOT...
13

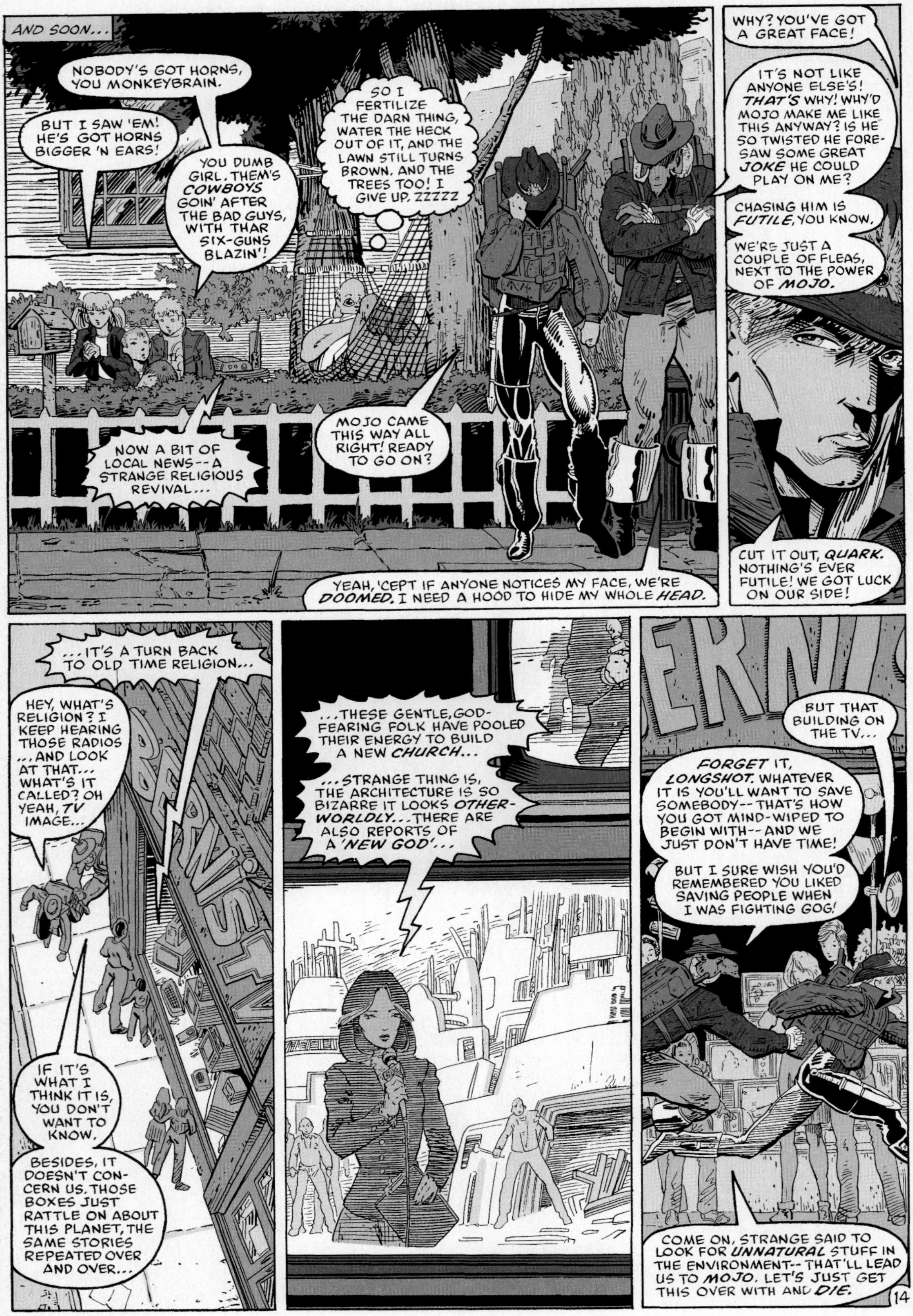
AND SOON...
NOBODY'S GOT HORNS, YOU MONKEYBRAIN.
BUT I SAW 'EM! HE'S GOT HORNS BIGGER 'N EARS!
YOU DUMB GIRL. THEM'S COWBOYS GOIN' AFTER THE BAD GUYS, WITH THAR SIX-GUNS BLAZIN'!
SO I FERTILIZE THE DARN THING, WATER THE HECK OUT OF IT, AND THE LAWN STILL TURNS BROWN, AND THE TREES TOO! I GIVE UP. ZZZZZ
NOW A BIT OF LOCAL NEWS-- A STRANGE RELIGIOUS REVIVAL...
MOJO CAME THIS WAY ALL RIGHT! READY TO GO ON?
YEAH, 'CEPT IF ANYONE NOTICES MY FACE, WE'RE DOOMED. I NEED A HOOD TO HIDE MY WHOLE HEAD.
WHY? YOU'VE GOT A GREAT FACE!
IT'S NOT LIKE ANYONE ELSE'S! THAT'S WHY! WHY'D MOJO MAKE ME LIKE THIS ANYWAY? IS HE SO TWISTED HE FORESAW SOME GREAT JOKE HE COULD PLAY ON ME?
CHASING HIM IS FUTILE, YOU KNOW.
WE'RE JUST A COUPLE OF FLEAS, NEXT TO THE POWER OF MOJO.
CUT IT OUT, QUARK. NOTHING'S EVER FUTILE! WE GOT LUCK ON OUR SIDE!
...IT'S A TURN BACK TO OLD TIME RELIGION...
HEY, WHAT'S RELIGION? I KEEP HEARING THOSE RADIOS ...AND LOOK AT THAT... WHAT'S IT CALLED? OH YEAH, TV IMAGE...
IF IT'S WHAT I THINK IT IS, YOU DON'T WANT TO KNOW.
BESIDES, IT DOESN'T CONCERN US. THOSE BOXES JUST RATTLE ON ABOUT THIS PLANET, THE SAME STORIES REPEATED OVER AND OVER...
...THESE GENTLE, GOD-FEARING FOLK HAVE POOLED THEIR ENERGY TO BUILD A NEW CHURCH...
...STRANGE THING IS, THE ARCHITECTURE IS SO BIZARRE IT LOOKS OTHER-WORLDLY... THERE ARE ALSO REPORTS OF A 'NEW GOD'...
BUT THAT BUILDING ON THE TV...
FORGET IT, LONGSHOT. WHATEVER IT IS YOU'LL WANT TO SAVE SOMEBODY-- THAT'S HOW YOU GOT MIND-WIPED TO BEGIN WITH-- AND WE JUST DON'T HAVE TIME!
BUT I SURE WISH YOU'D REMEMBERED YOU LIKED SAVING PEOPLE WHEN I WAS FIGHTING GOG!
COME ON, STRANGE SAID TO LOOK FOR UNNATURAL STUFF IN THE ENVIRONMENT-- THAT'LL LEAD US TO MOJO. LET'S JUST GET THIS OVER WITH AND DIE.
14

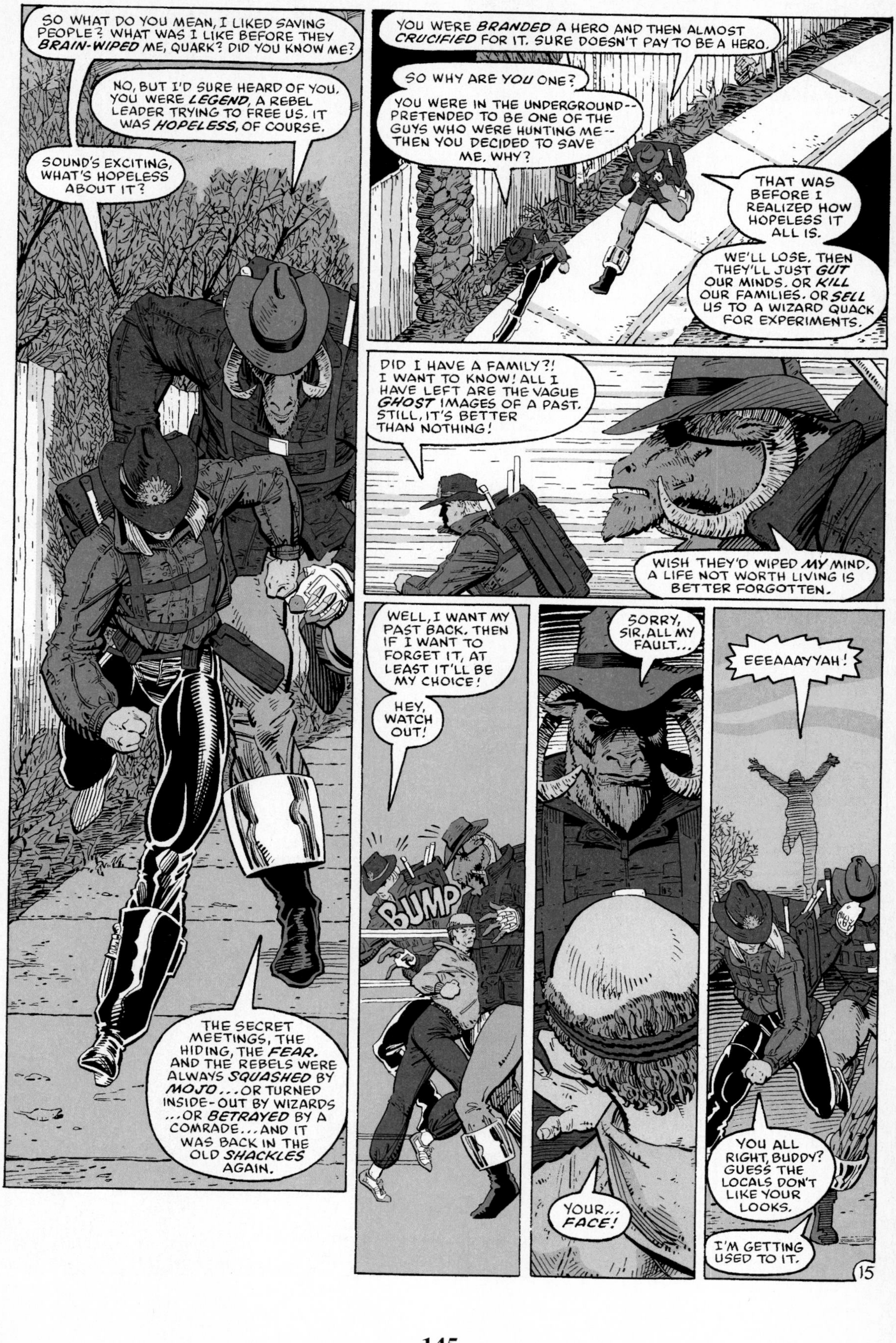

SO WHAT DO YOU MEAN, I LIKED SAVING PEOPLE? WHAT WAS I LIKE BEFORE THEY BRAIN-WIPED ME, QUARK? DID YOU KNOW ME?
NO, BUT I'D SURE HEARD OF YOU. YOU WERE LEGEND, A REBEL LEADER TRYING TO FREE US. IT WAS HOPELESS, OF COURSE.
SOUND'S EXCITING, WHAT'S HOPELESS ABOUT IT?
THE SECRET MEETINGS, THE HIDING, THE FEAR. AND THE REBELS WERE ALWAYS SQUASHED BY MOJO...OR TURNED INSIDE-OUT BY WIZARDS ...OR BETRAYED BY A COMRADE...AND IT WAS BACK IN THE OLD SHACKLES AGAIN.
YOU WERE BRANDED A HERO AND THEN ALMOST CRUCIFIED FOR IT. SURE DOESN'T PAY TO BE A HERO.
SO WHY ARE YOU ONE?
YOU WERE IN THE UNDERGROUND--PRETENDED TO BE ONE OF THE GUYS WHO WERE HUNTING ME--THEN YOU DECIDED TO SAVE ME. WHY?
THAT WAS BEFORE I REALIZED HOW HOPELESS IT ALL IS.
WE'LL LOSE. THEN THEY'LL JUST GUT OUR MINDS. OR KILL OUR FAMILIES. OR SELL US TO A WIZARD QUACK FOR EXPERIMENTS.
DID I HAVE A FAMILY?! I WANT TO KNOW! ALL I HAVE LEFT ARE THE VAGUE GHOST IMAGES OF A PAST. STILL, IT'S BETTER THAN NOTHING!
WISH THEY'D WIPED MY MIND. A LIFE NOT WORTH LIVING IS BETTER FORGOTTEN.
WELL, I WANT MY PAST BACK. THEN IF I WANT TO FORGET IT, AT LEAST IT'LL BE MY CHOICE!
HEY, WATCH OUT!
BUMP
SORRY, SIR, ALL MY FAULT...
YOUR... FACE!
EEEAAAYYAH!
YOU ALL RIGHT, BUDDY? GUESS THE LOCALS DON'T LIKE YOUR LOOKS.
I'M GETTING USED TO IT.
15

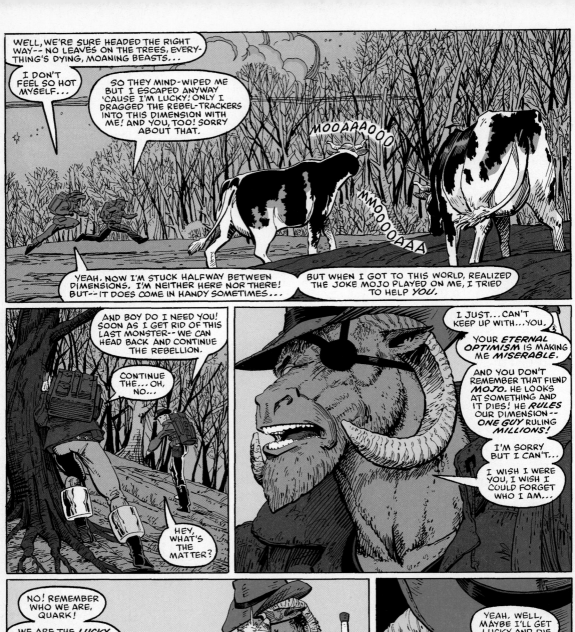

WELL, WE'RE SURE HEADED THE RIGHT WAY-- NO LEAVES ON THE TREES, EVERY-THING'S DYING, MOANING BEASTS...

I DON'T FEEL SO HOT MYSELF...

SO THEY MIND-WIPED ME BUT I ESCAPED ANYWAY 'CAUSE I'M LUCKY! ONLY I DRAGGED THE REBEL-TRACKERS INTO THIS DIMENSION WITH ME! AND YOU, TOO! SORRY ABOUT THAT.

MOOAAAOOO

MMOOOOAAA

YEAH, NOW I'M STUCK HALFWAY BETWEEN DIMENSIONS, I'M NEITHER HERE NOR THERE! BUT-- IT DOES COME IN HANDY SOMETIMES...

BUT WHEN I GOT TO THIS WORLD, REALIZED THE JOKE MOJO PLAYED ON ME, I TRIED TO HELP *YOU.*

AND BOY DO I NEED YOU! SOON AS I GET RID OF THIS LAST MONSTER-- WE CAN HEAD BACK AND CONTINUE THE REBELLION.

CONTINUE THE... OH, NO...

HEY, WHAT'S THE MATTER?

I JUST... CAN'T KEEP UP WITH... YOU.

YOUR *ETERNAL OPTIMISM* IS MAKING ME *MISERABLE.*

AND YOU DON'T REMEMBER THAT FIEND *MOJO.* HE LOOKS AT SOMETHING AND IT DIES! HE *RULES* OUR DIMENSION-- *ONE GUY* RULING *MILLIONS!*

I'M SORRY BUT I CAN'T...

I WISH I WERE YOU, I WISH I COULD FORGET WHO I AM...

NO! REMEMBER WHO WE ARE, QUARK!

WE ARE THE *LUCKY* ONES! IF WE KEEP OUR *MOTIVES PURE* AND OUR *HEARTS HONEST,* WE WILL WIN!

WE'LL SAVE BOTH DIMEN-SIONS! WE WILL! WE'VE NO TIME FOR COWARDICE!

NO, LONGSHOT. SINCE COMING HERE, I'VE *LOST* FAITH. I DON'T BELIEVE IN LUCK ANYMORE. IT'S GOT A FLIPSIDE...

WHY?

WE HOOKED INTO THIS LUCK-FORCE TO HELP THE REBELLION. BUT I THINK THAT'S JUST WHAT THEY WANTED! THEY KNEW THE LUCK WOULD TURN ON US! I FEEL SET-UP...

YOU MOAN AND COMPLAIN, QUARK, BUT YOU KEEP FIGHTING, DESPITE YOURSELF!

YEAH, WELL, MAYBE I'LL GET LUCKY AND DIE TRYING.

16

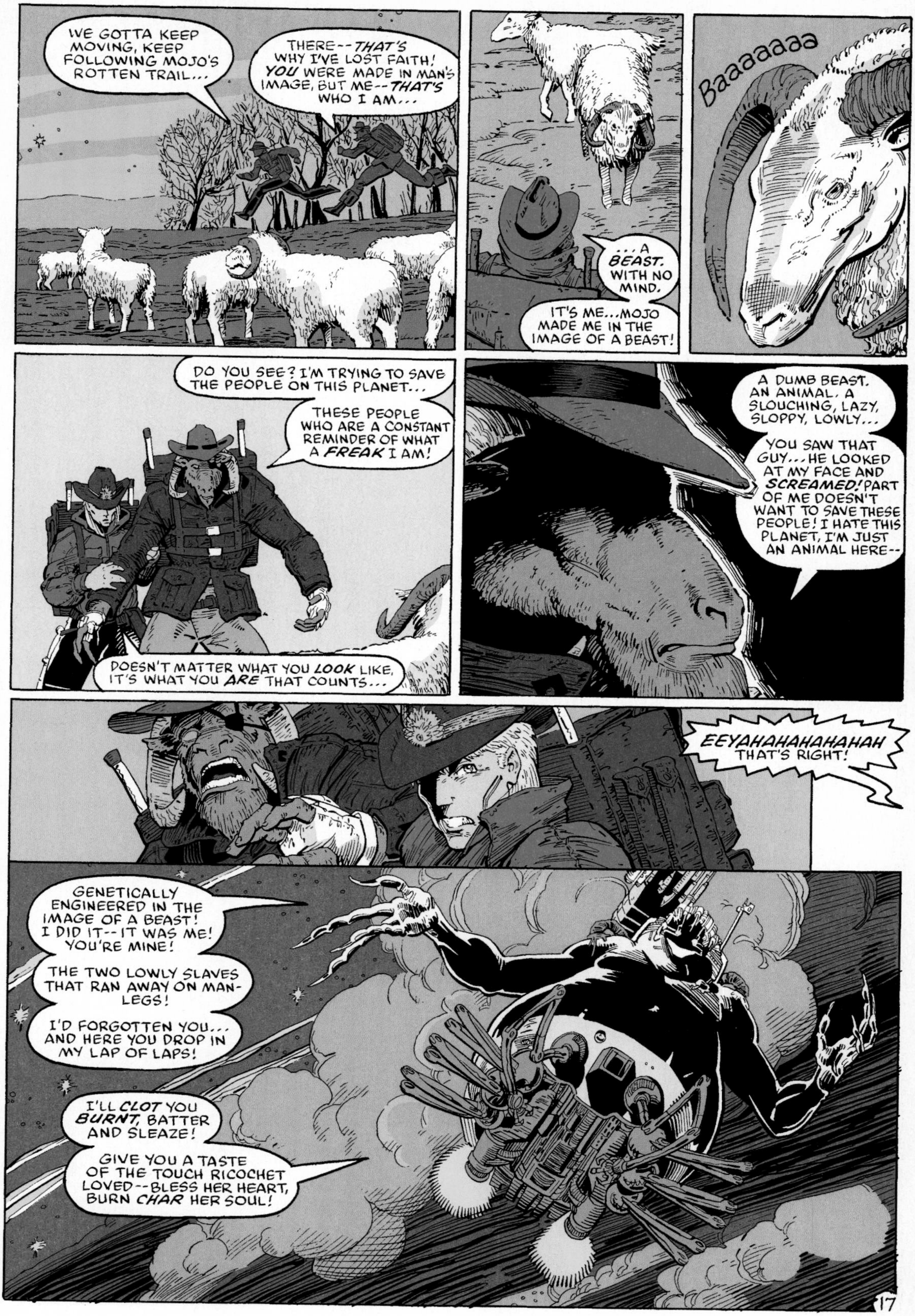
WE GOTTA KEEP MOVING, KEEP FOLLOWING MOJO'S ROTTEN TRAIL...
THERE--THAT'S WHY I'VE LOST FAITH! YOU WERE MADE IN MAN'S IMAGE, BUT ME--THAT'S WHO I AM...
...A BEAST. WITH NO MIND.
IT'S ME...MOJO MADE ME IN THE IMAGE OF A BEAST!
Baaaaaaa
DO YOU SEE? I'M TRYING TO SAVE THE PEOPLE ON THIS PLANET...
THESE PEOPLE WHO ARE A CONSTANT REMINDER OF WHAT A FREAK I AM!
DOESN'T MATTER WHAT YOU LOOK LIKE, IT'S WHAT YOU ARE THAT COUNTS...
A DUMB BEAST. AN ANIMAL. A SLOUCHING, LAZY, SLOPPY, LOWLY...
YOU SAW THAT GUY...HE LOOKED AT MY FACE AND SCREAMED! PART OF ME DOESN'T WANT TO SAVE THESE PEOPLE! I HATE THIS PLANET, I'M JUST AN ANIMAL HERE--
EEYAHAHAHAHAHAHAH THAT'S RIGHT!
GENETICALLY ENGINEERED IN THE IMAGE OF A BEAST! I DID IT--IT WAS ME! YOU'RE MINE!
THE TWO LOWLY SLAVES THAT RAN AWAY ON MAN-LEGS!
I'D FORGOTTEN YOU... AND HERE YOU DROP IN MY LAP OF LAPS!
I'LL CLOT YOU BURNT, BATTER AND SLEAZE!
GIVE YOU A TASTE OF THE TOUCH RICOCHET LOVED--BLESS HER HEART, BURN CHAR HER SOUL!
17

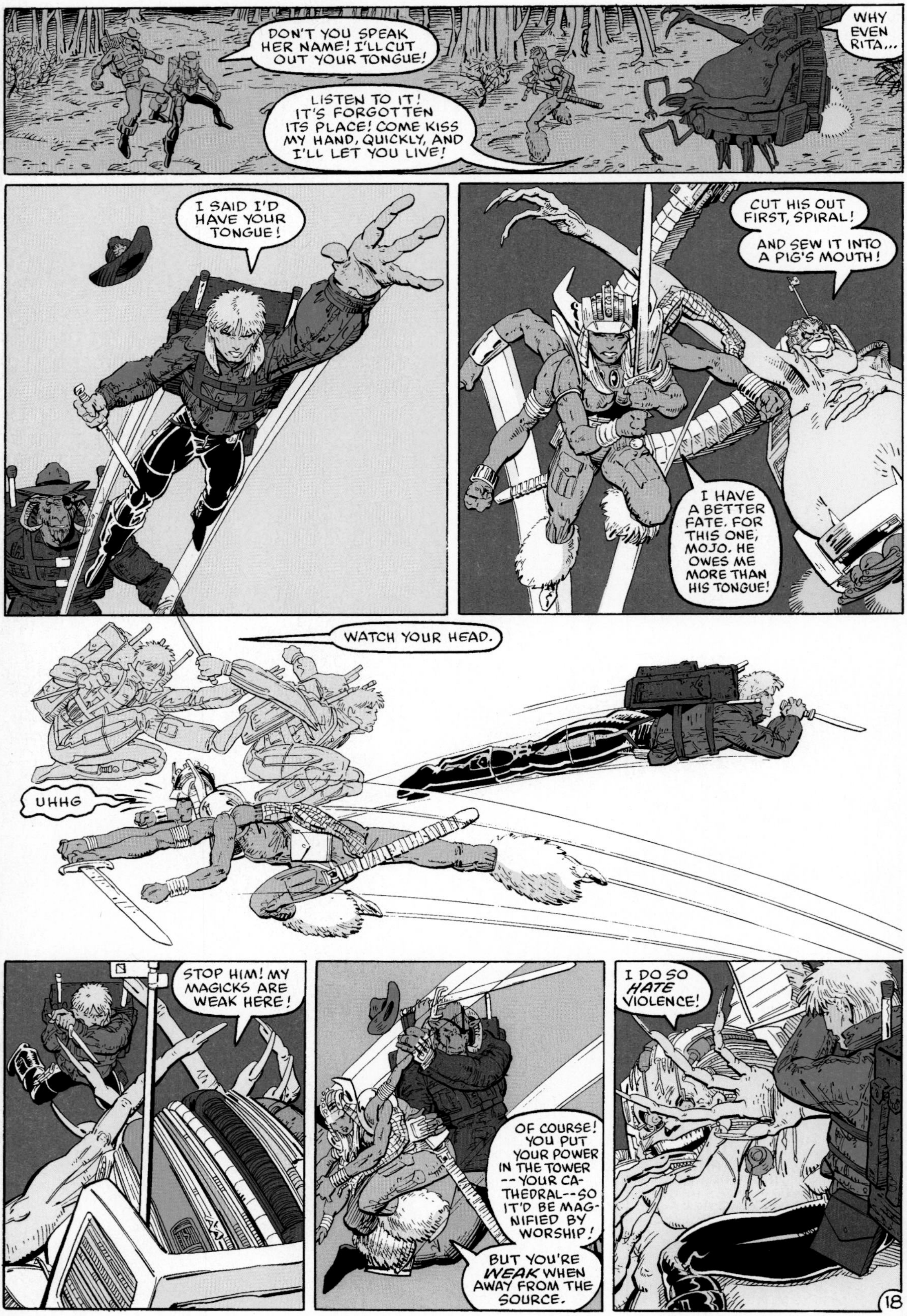
DON'T YOU SPEAK HER NAME! I'LL CUT OUT YOUR TONGUE!
LISTEN TO IT! IT'S FORGOTTEN ITS PLACE! COME KISS MY HAND, QUICKLY, AND I'LL LET YOU LIVE!
WHY EVEN RITA...
I SAID I'D HAVE YOUR TONGUE!
CUT HIS OUT FIRST, SPIRAL!
AND SEW IT INTO A PIG'S MOUTH!
I HAVE A BETTER FATE. FOR THIS ONE, MOJO. HE OWES ME MORE THAN HIS TONGUE!
WATCH YOUR HEAD.
UHHG
STOP HIM! MY MAGICKS ARE WEAK HERE!
OF COURSE! YOU PUT YOUR POWER IN THE TOWER --YOUR CATHEDRAL--SO IT'D BE MAGNIFIED BY WORSHIP!
BUT YOU'RE WEAK WHEN AWAY FROM THE SOURCE.
I DO SO HATE VIOLENCE!
18

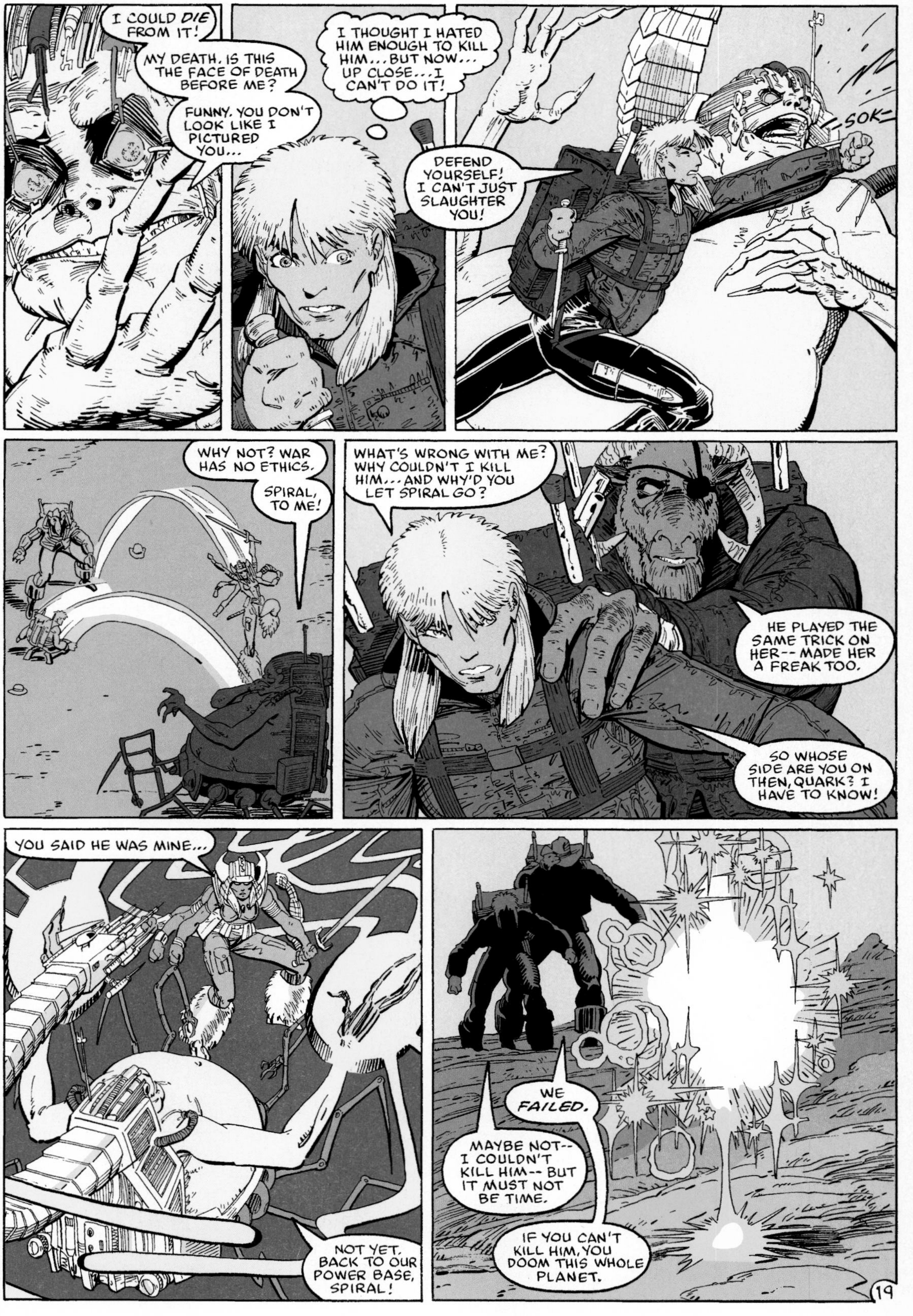
I COULD DIE FROM IT!
MY DEATH. IS THIS THE FACE OF DEATH BEFORE ME?
FUNNY. YOU DON'T LOOK LIKE I PICTURED YOU...
I THOUGHT I HATED HIM ENOUGH TO KILL HIM... BUT NOW... UP CLOSE... I CAN'T DO IT!
DEFEND YOURSELF! I CAN'T JUST SLAUGHTER YOU!
SOK
WHY NOT? WAR HAS NO ETHICS.
SPIRAL, TO ME!
WHAT'S WRONG WITH ME? WHY COULDN'T I KILL HIM... AND WHY'D YOU LET SPIRAL GO?
HE PLAYED THE SAME TRICK ON HER-- MADE HER A FREAK TOO.
SO WHOSE SIDE ARE YOU ON THEN, QUARK? I HAVE TO KNOW!
YOU SAID HE WAS MINE...
NOT YET. BACK TO OUR POWER BASE, SPIRAL!
WE FAILED.
MAYBE NOT-- I COULDN'T KILL HIM-- BUT IT MUST NOT BE TIME.
IF YOU CAN'T KILL HIM, YOU DOOM THIS WHOLE PLANET.
19

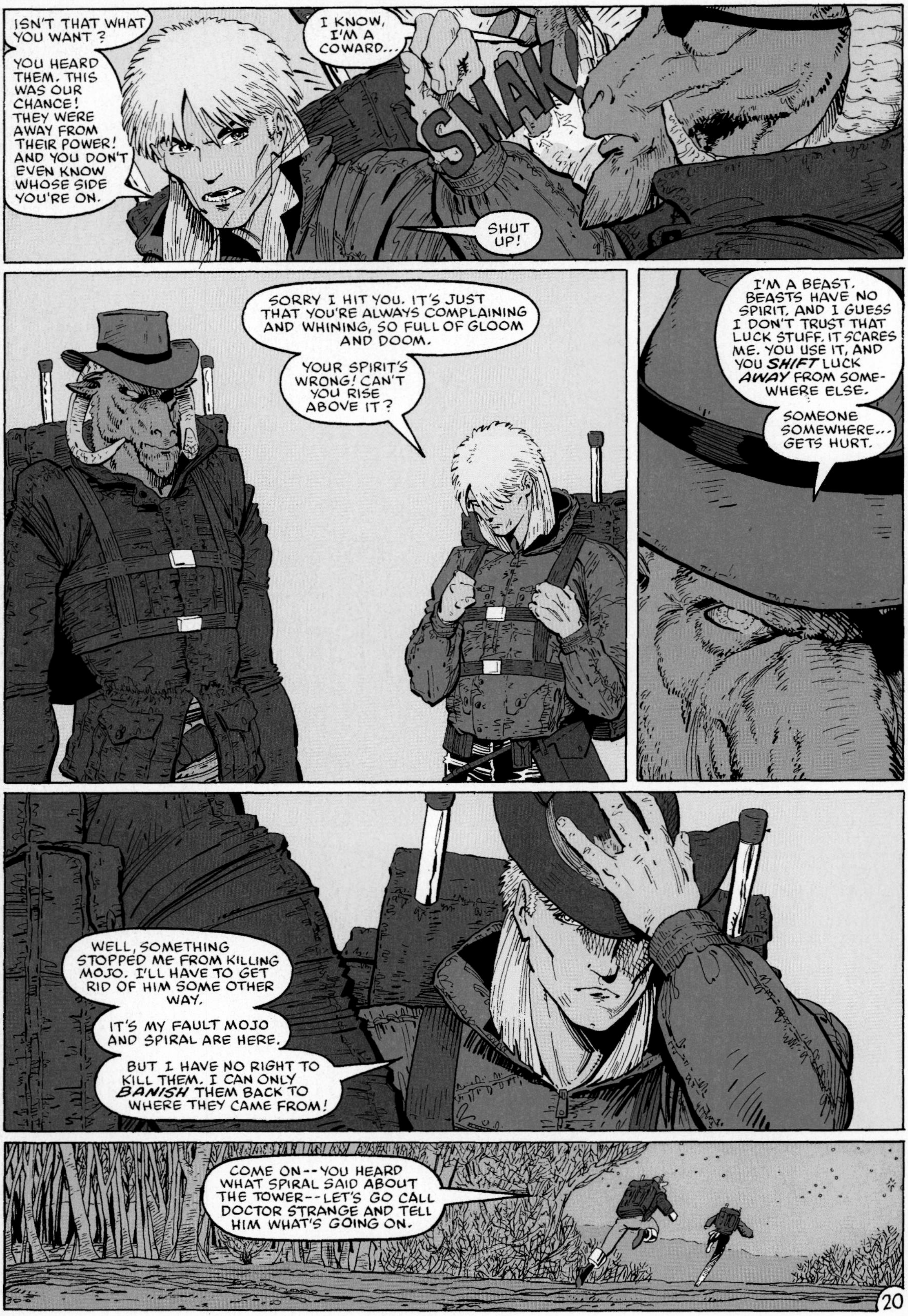
ISN'T THAT WHAT YOU WANT?
YOU HEARD THEM. THIS WAS OUR CHANCE! THEY WERE AWAY FROM THEIR POWER! AND YOU DON'T EVEN KNOW WHOSE SIDE YOU'RE ON.
I KNOW, I'M A COWARD...
SMAK!
SHUT UP!
SORRY I HIT YOU. IT'S JUST THAT YOU'RE ALWAYS COMPLAINING AND WHINING, SO FULL OF GLOOM AND DOOM.
YOUR SPIRIT'S WRONG! CAN'T YOU RISE ABOVE IT?
I'M A BEAST. BEASTS HAVE NO SPIRIT, AND I GUESS I DON'T TRUST THAT LUCK STUFF. IT SCARES ME. YOU USE IT, AND YOU SHIFT LUCK AWAY FROM SOMEWHERE ELSE.
SOMEONE SOMEWHERE... GETS HURT.
WELL, SOMETHING STOPPED ME FROM KILLING MOJO. I'LL HAVE TO GET RID OF HIM SOME OTHER WAY.
IT'S MY FAULT MOJO AND SPIRAL ARE HERE.
BUT I HAVE NO RIGHT TO KILL THEM. I CAN ONLY BANISH THEM BACK TO WHERE THEY CAME FROM!
COME ON--YOU HEARD WHAT SPIRAL SAID ABOUT THE TOWER--LET'S GO CALL DOCTOR STRANGE AND TELL HIM WHAT'S GOING ON.
20

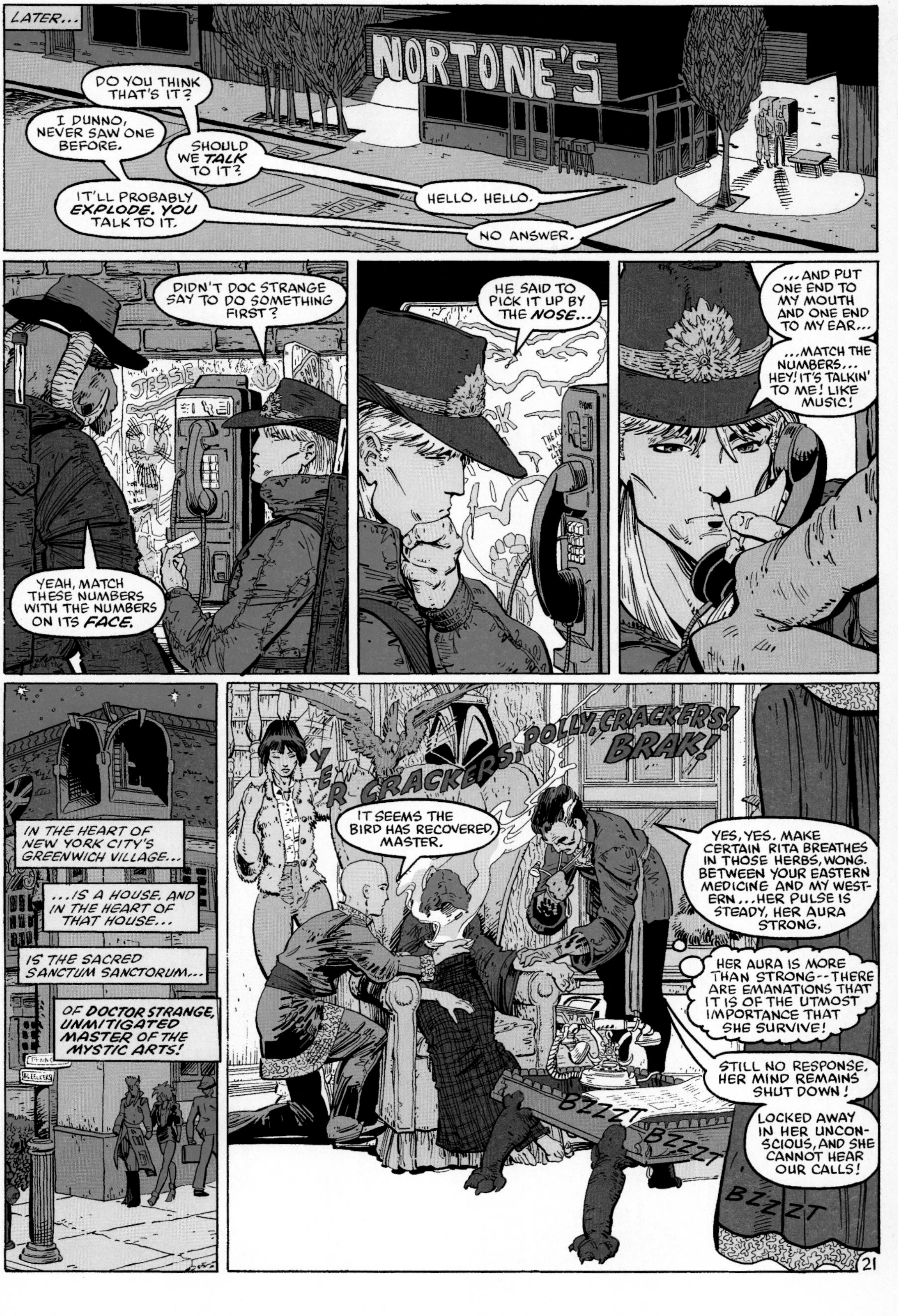
LATER...
NORTONE'S
DO YOU THINK THAT'S IT?
I DUNNO, NEVER SAW ONE BEFORE.
SHOULD WE TALK TO IT?
IT'LL PROBABLY EXPLODE. YOU TALK TO IT.
HELLO. HELLO.
NO ANSWER.
DIDN'T DOC STRANGE SAY TO DO SOMETHING FIRST?
YEAH, MATCH THESE NUMBERS WITH THE NUMBERS ON ITS FACE.
HE SAID TO PICK IT UP BY THE NOSE...
...AND PUT ONE END TO MY MOUTH AND ONE END TO MY EAR...
...MATCH THE NUMBERS... HEY! IT'S TALKIN' TO ME! LIKE MUSIC!
IN THE HEART OF NEW YORK CITY'S GREENWICH VILLAGE...
...IS A HOUSE. AND IN THE HEART OF THAT HOUSE...
IS THE SACRED SANCTUM SANCTORUM...
OF DOCTOR STRANGE, UNMITIGATED MASTER OF THE MYSTIC ARTS!
YER CRACKERS, POLLY, CRACKERS! BRAK!
IT SEEMS THE BIRD HAS RECOVERED, MASTER.
YES, YES. MAKE CERTAIN RITA BREATHES IN THOSE HERBS, WONG. BETWEEN YOUR EASTERN MEDICINE AND MY WEST-ERN ...HER PULSE IS STEADY, HER AURA STRONG.
HER AURA IS MORE THAN STRONG--THERE ARE EMANATIONS THAT IT IS OF THE UTMOST IMPORTANCE THAT SHE SURVIVE!
STILL NO RESPONSE. HER MIND REMAINS SHUT DOWN!
LOCKED AWAY IN HER UNCON-SCIOUS, AND SHE CANNOT HEAR OUR CALLS!
BZZZT
BZZZT
BZZZT
21

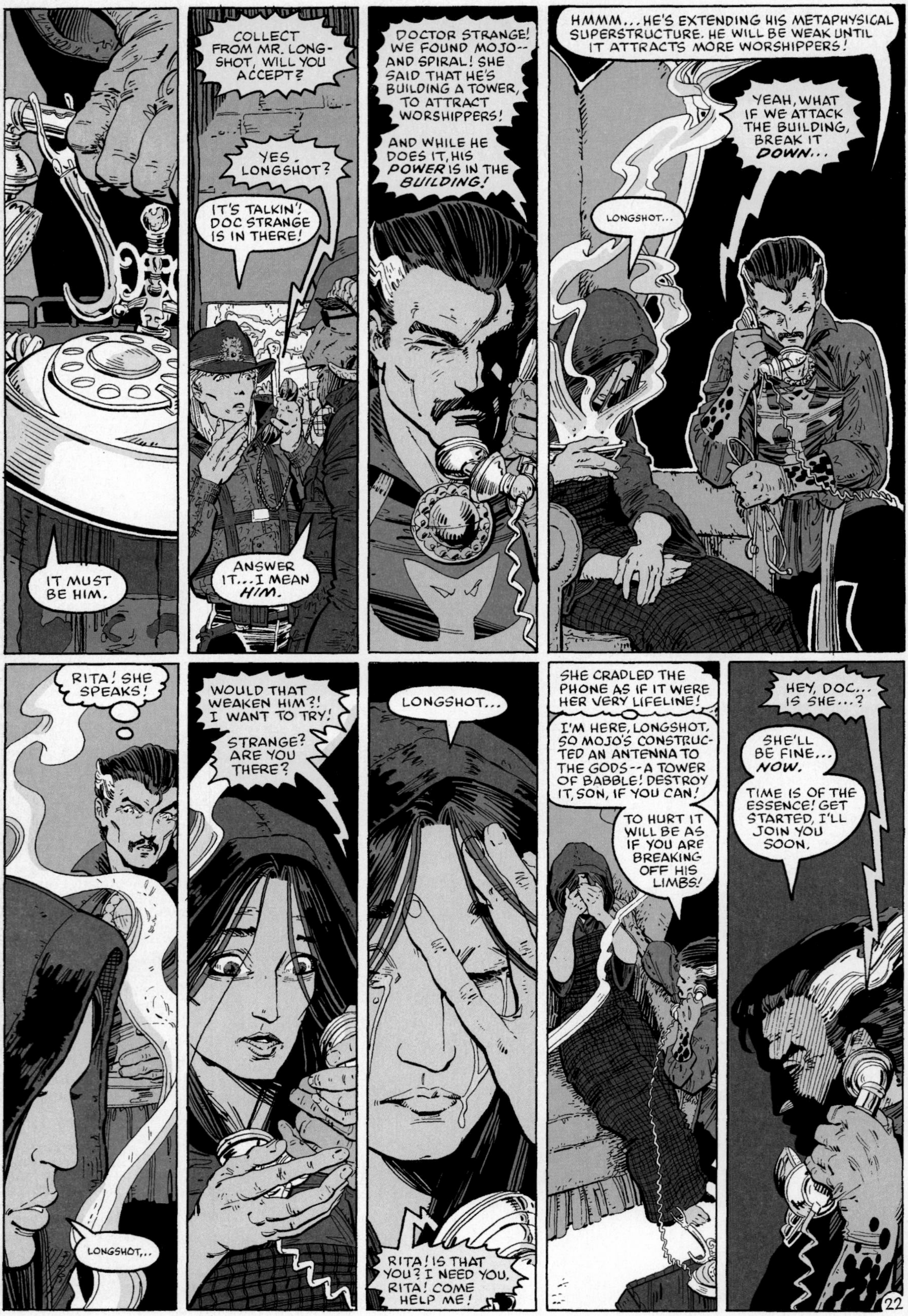
IT MUST BE HIM.
COLLECT FROM MR. LONG-SHOT, WILL YOU ACCEPT?
YES. LONGSHOT?
IT'S TALKIN'! DOC STRANGE IS IN THERE!
ANSWER IT... I MEAN HIM.
DOCTOR STRANGE! WE FOUND MOJO-- AND SPIRAL! SHE SAID THAT HE'S BUILDING A TOWER, TO ATTRACT WORSHIPPERS!
AND WHILE HE DOES IT, HIS POWER IS IN THE BUILDING!
HMMM... HE'S EXTENDING HIS METAPHYSICAL SUPERSTRUCTURE. HE WILL BE WEAK UNTIL IT ATTRACTS MORE WORSHIPPERS!
LONGSHOT...
YEAH, WHAT IF WE ATTACK THE BUILDING, BREAK IT DOWN...
RITA! SHE SPEAKS!
LONGSHOT,..
WOULD THAT WEAKEN HIM?! I WANT TO TRY!
STRANGE? ARE YOU THERE?
LONGSHOT...
RITA! IS THAT YOU? I NEED YOU, RITA! COME HELP ME!
SHE CRADLED THE PHONE AS IF IT WERE HER VERY LIFELINE!
I'M HERE, LONGSHOT, SO MOJO'S CONSTRUCTED AN ANTENNA TO THE GODS--A TOWER OF BABBLE! DESTROY IT, SON, IF YOU CAN!
TO HURT IT WILL BE AS IF YOU ARE BREAKING OFF HIS LIMBS!
HEY, DOC... IS SHE...?
SHE'LL BE FINE... NOW.
TIME IS OF THE ESSENCE! GET STARTED, I'LL JOIN YOU SOON.
22

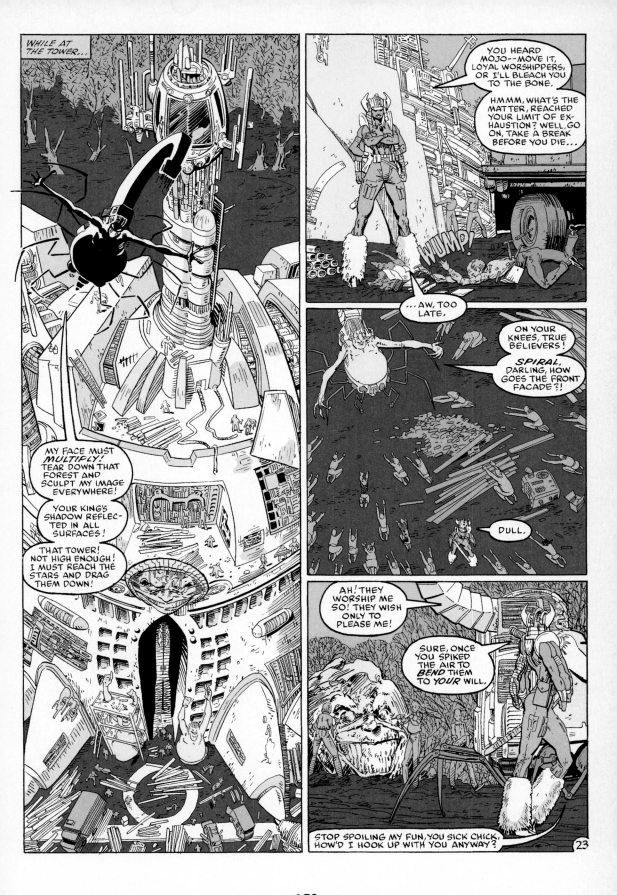

WHILE AT THE TOWER...

MY FACE MUST *MULTIPLY!* TEAR DOWN THAT FOREST AND SCULPT MY IMAGE EVERYWHERE!

YOUR KING'S SHADOW REFLECTED IN ALL SURFACES!

THAT TOWER! NOT HIGH ENOUGH! I MUST REACH THE STARS AND DRAG THEM DOWN!

YOU HEARD MOJO--MOVE IT, LOYAL WORSHIPPERS, OR I'LL BLEACH YOU TO THE BONE.

HMMM, WHAT'S THE MATTER, REACHED YOUR LIMIT OF EX-HAUSTION? WELL, GO ON, TAKE A BREAK BEFORE YOU DIE...

WUMP!

...AW, TOO LATE.

ON YOUR KNEES, TRUE BELIEVERS!

SPIRAL, DARLING, HOW GOES THE FRONT FACADE?!

DULL.

AH! THEY WORSHIP ME SO! THEY WISH ONLY TO PLEASE ME!

SURE, ONCE YOU SPIKED THE AIR TO *BEND* THEM TO *YOUR* WILL.

STOP SPOILING MY FUN, YOU SICK CHICK, HOW'D I HOOK UP WITH YOU ANYWAY?

23

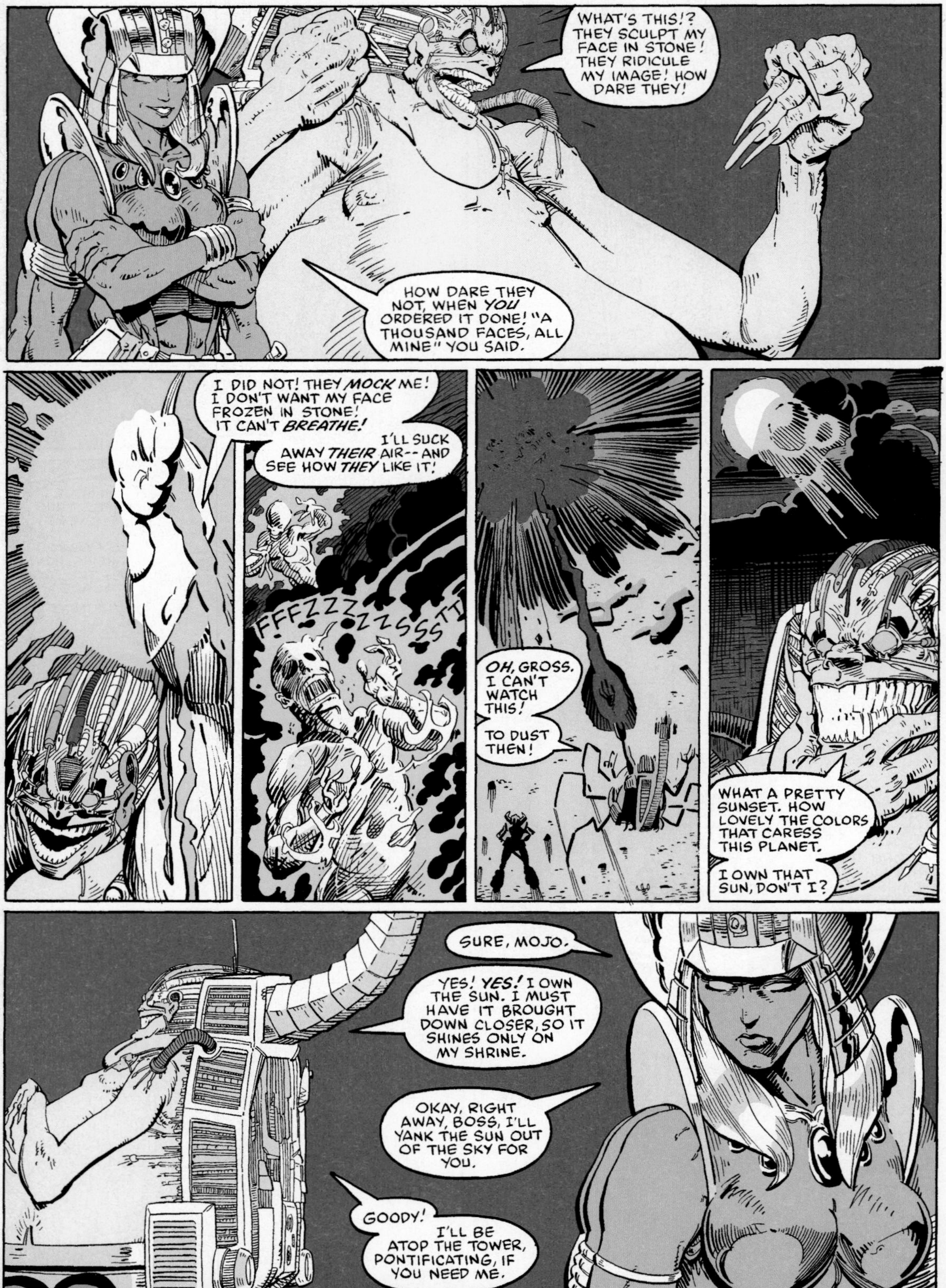
WHAT'S THIS!? THEY SCULPT MY FACE IN STONE! THEY RIDICULE MY IMAGE! HOW DARE THEY!
HOW DARE THEY NOT, WHEN YOU ORDERED IT DONE! "A THOUSAND FACES, ALL MINE" YOU SAID.
I DID NOT! THEY MOCK ME! I DON'T WANT MY FACE FROZEN IN STONE! IT CAN'T BREATHE!
I'LL SUCK AWAY THEIR AIR-- AND SEE HOW THEY LIKE IT!
FFFZZZZZZSSSTT
OH, GROSS. I CAN'T WATCH THIS!
TO DUST THEN!
WHAT A PRETTY SUNSET. HOW LOVELY THE COLORS THAT CARESS THIS PLANET.
I OWN THAT SUN, DON'T I?
SURE, MOJO.
YES! YES! I OWN THE SUN. I MUST HAVE IT BROUGHT DOWN CLOSER, SO IT SHINES ONLY ON MY SHRINE.
OKAY, RIGHT AWAY, BOSS, I'LL YANK THE SUN OUT OF THE SKY FOR YOU.
GOODY!
I'LL BE ATOP THE TOWER, PONTIFICATING, IF YOU NEED ME.
24

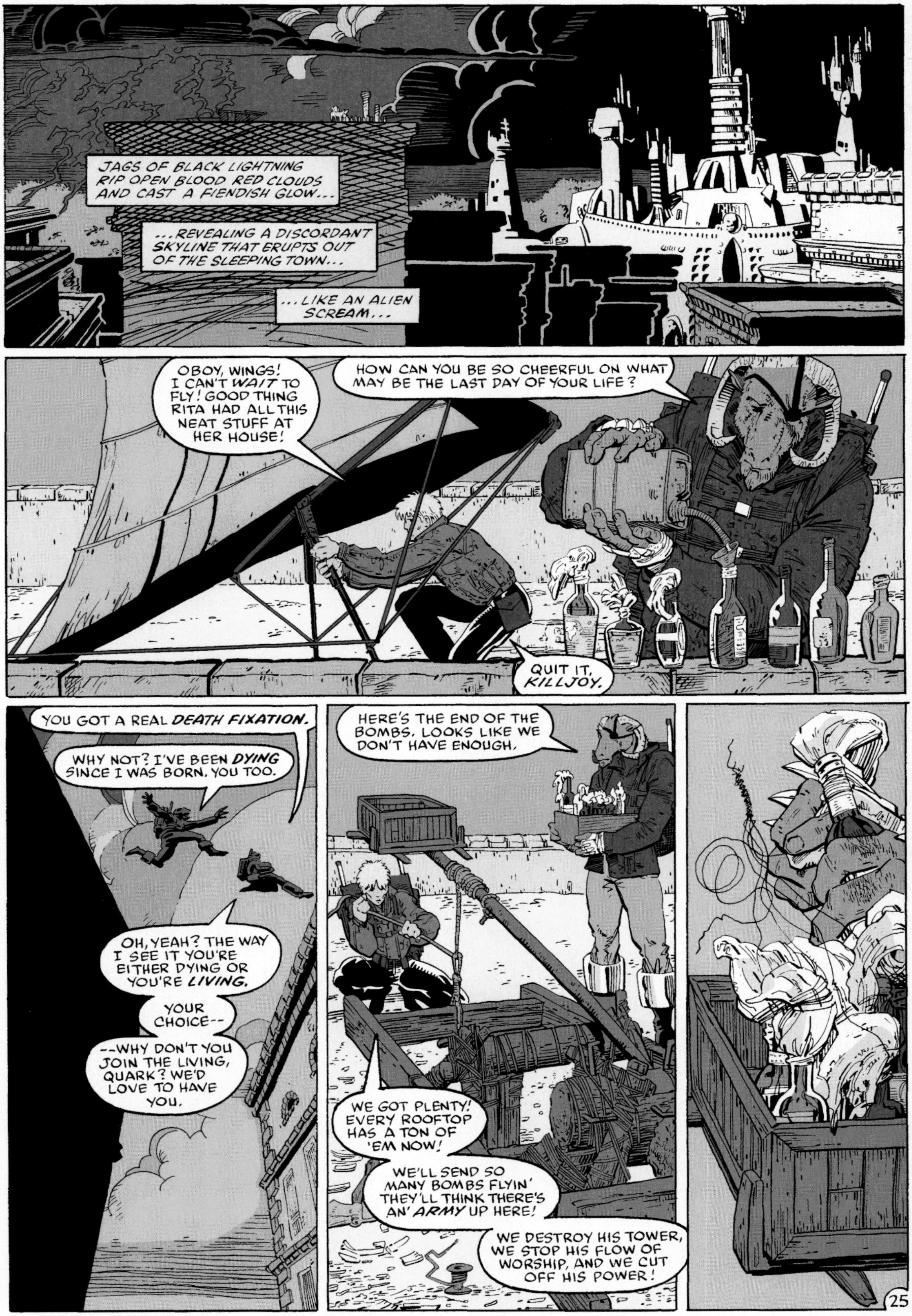
JAGS OF BLACK LIGHTNING RIP OPEN BLOOD RED CLOUDS AND CAST A FIENDISH GLOW...
...REVEALING A DISCORDANT SKYLINE THAT ERUPTS OUT OF THE SLEEPING TOWN...
...LIKE AN ALIEN SCREAM...
OBOY, WINGS! I CAN'T WAIT TO FLY! GOOD THING RITA HAD ALL THIS NEAT STUFF AT HER HOUSE!
HOW CAN YOU BE SO CHEERFUL ON WHAT MAY BE THE LAST DAY OF YOUR LIFE?
QUIT IT, KILLJOY.
YOU GOT A REAL DEATH FIXATION.
WHY NOT? I'VE BEEN DYING SINCE I WAS BORN. YOU TOO.
OH, YEAH? THE WAY I SEE IT YOU'RE EITHER DYING OR YOU'RE LIVING.
YOUR CHOICE--
--WHY DON'T YOU JOIN THE LIVING, QUARK? WE'D LOVE TO HAVE YOU.
HERE'S THE END OF THE BOMBS. LOOKS LIKE WE DON'T HAVE ENOUGH.
WE GOT PLENTY! EVERY ROOFTOP HAS A TON OF 'EM NOW!
WE'LL SEND SO MANY BOMBS FLYIN' THEY'LL THINK THERE'S AN' ARMY UP HERE!
WE DESTROY HIS TOWER, WE STOP HIS FLOW OF WORSHIP, AND WE CUT OFF HIS POWER!
25

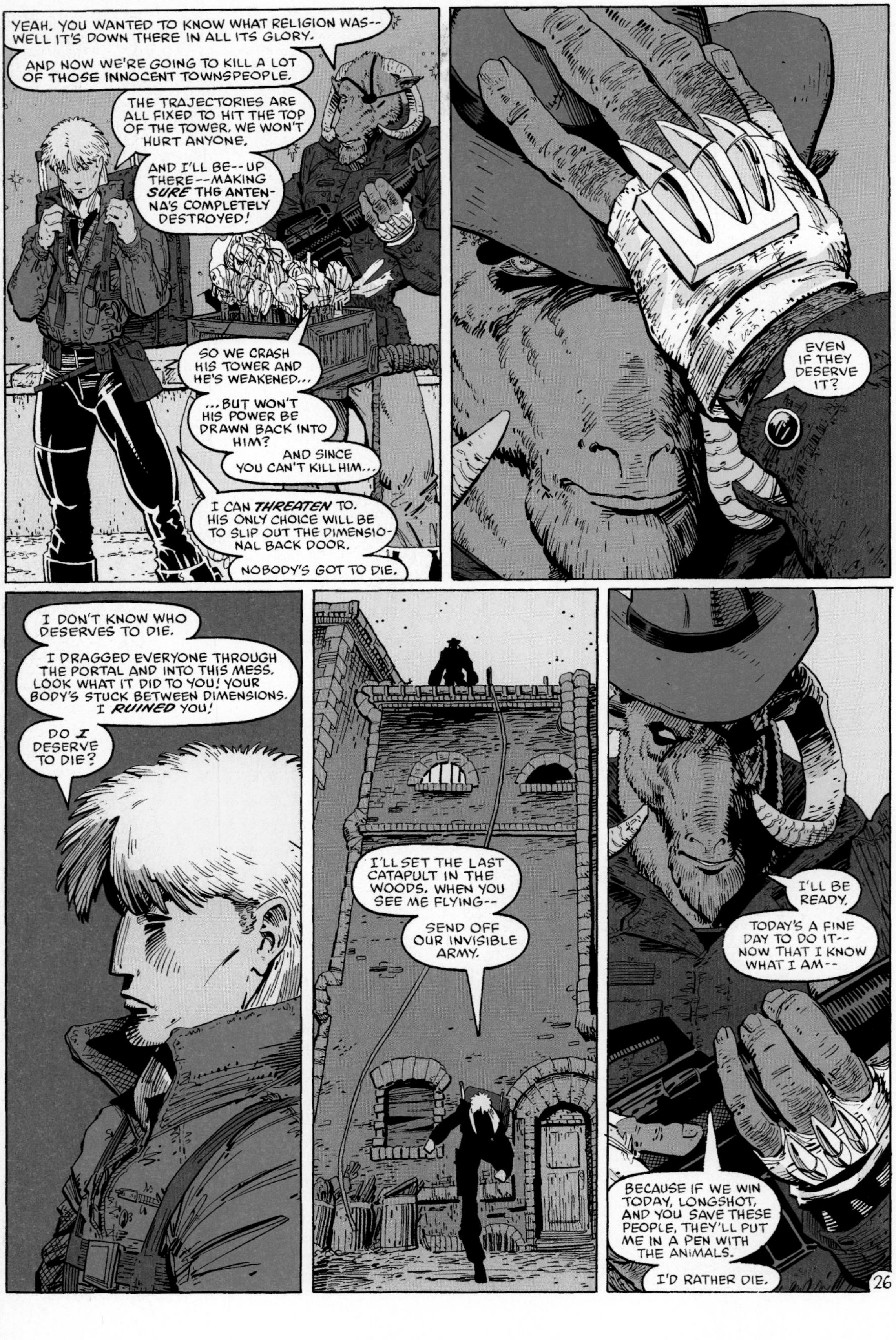
YEAH. YOU WANTED TO KNOW WHAT RELIGION WAS-- WELL IT'S DOWN THERE IN ALL ITS GLORY.
AND NOW WE'RE GOING TO KILL A LOT OF THOSE INNOCENT TOWNSPEOPLE.
THE TRAJECTORIES ARE ALL FIXED TO HIT THE TOP OF THE TOWER. WE WON'T HURT ANYONE.
AND I'LL BE-- UP THERE--MAKING *SURE* THE ANTENNA'S COMPLETELY DESTROYED!
SO WE CRASH HIS TOWER AND HE'S WEAKENED...
...BUT WON'T HIS POWER BE DRAWN BACK INTO HIM?
AND SINCE YOU CAN'T KILL HIM...
I CAN *THREATEN* TO. HIS ONLY CHOICE WILL BE TO SLIP OUT THE DIMENSIONAL BACK DOOR.
NOBODY'S GOT TO DIE.
EVEN IF THEY DESERVE IT?
I DON'T KNOW WHO DESERVES TO DIE.
I DRAGGED EVERYONE THROUGH THE PORTAL AND INTO THIS MESS. LOOK WHAT IT DID TO YOU! YOUR BODY'S STUCK BETWEEN DIMENSIONS. I *RUINED* YOU!
DO *I* DESERVE TO DIE?
I'LL SET THE LAST CATAPULT IN THE WOODS. WHEN YOU SEE ME FLYING--
SEND OFF OUR INVISIBLE ARMY.
I'LL BE READY.
TODAY'S A FINE DAY TO DO IT-- NOW THAT I KNOW WHAT I AM--
BECAUSE IF WE WIN TODAY, LONGSHOT, AND YOU SAVE THESE PEOPLE, THEY'LL PUT ME IN A PEN WITH THE ANIMALS.
I'D RATHER DIE.
26

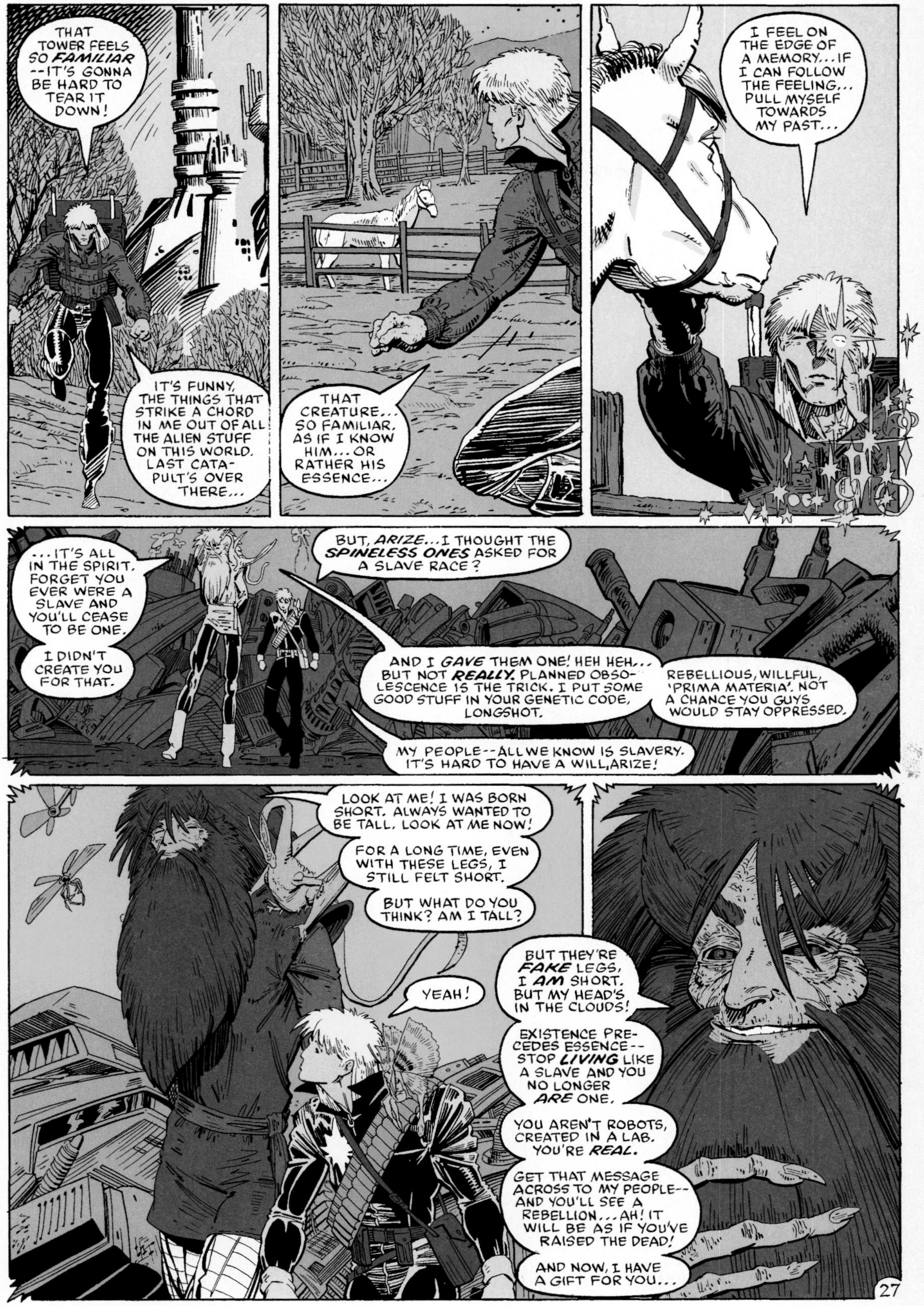
THAT TOWER FEELS SO FAMILIAR --IT'S GONNA BE HARD TO TEAR IT DOWN!
IT'S FUNNY, THE THINGS THAT STRIKE A CHORD IN ME OUT OF ALL THE ALIEN STUFF ON THIS WORLD. LAST CATA-PULT'S OVER THERE...
THAT CREATURE... SO FAMILIAR, AS IF I KNOW HIM... OR RATHER HIS ESSENCE...
I FEEL ON THE EDGE OF A MEMORY... IF I CAN FOLLOW THE FEELING... PULL MYSELF TOWARDS MY PAST...
...IT'S ALL IN THE SPIRIT. FORGET YOU EVER WERE A SLAVE AND YOU'LL CEASE TO BE ONE.
I DIDN'T CREATE YOU FOR THAT.
BUT, ARIZE... I THOUGHT THE SPINELESS ONES ASKED FOR A SLAVE RACE?
AND I GAVE THEM ONE! HEH HEH... BUT NOT REALLY. PLANNED OBSO-LESCENCE IS THE TRICK. I PUT SOME GOOD STUFF IN YOUR GENETIC CODE, LONGSHOT.
REBELLIOUS, WILLFUL, 'PRIMA MATERIA'. NOT A CHANCE YOU GUYS WOULD STAY OPPRESSED.
MY PEOPLE--ALL WE KNOW IS SLAVERY. IT'S HARD TO HAVE A WILL, ARIZE!
LOOK AT ME! I WAS BORN SHORT. ALWAYS WANTED TO BE TALL. LOOK AT ME NOW!
FOR A LONG TIME, EVEN WITH THESE LEGS, I STILL FELT SHORT.
BUT WHAT DO YOU THINK? AM I TALL?
YEAH!
BUT THEY'RE FAKE LEGS, I AM SHORT. BUT MY HEAD'S IN THE CLOUDS!
EXISTENCE PRE-CEDES ESSENCE-- STOP LIVING LIKE A SLAVE AND YOU NO LONGER ARE ONE.
YOU AREN'T ROBOTS, CREATED IN A LAB. YOU'RE REAL.
GET THAT MESSAGE ACROSS TO MY PEOPLE-- AND YOU'LL SEE A REBELLION... AH! IT WILL BE AS IF YOU'VE RAISED THE DEAD!
AND NOW, I HAVE A GIFT FOR YOU...
27

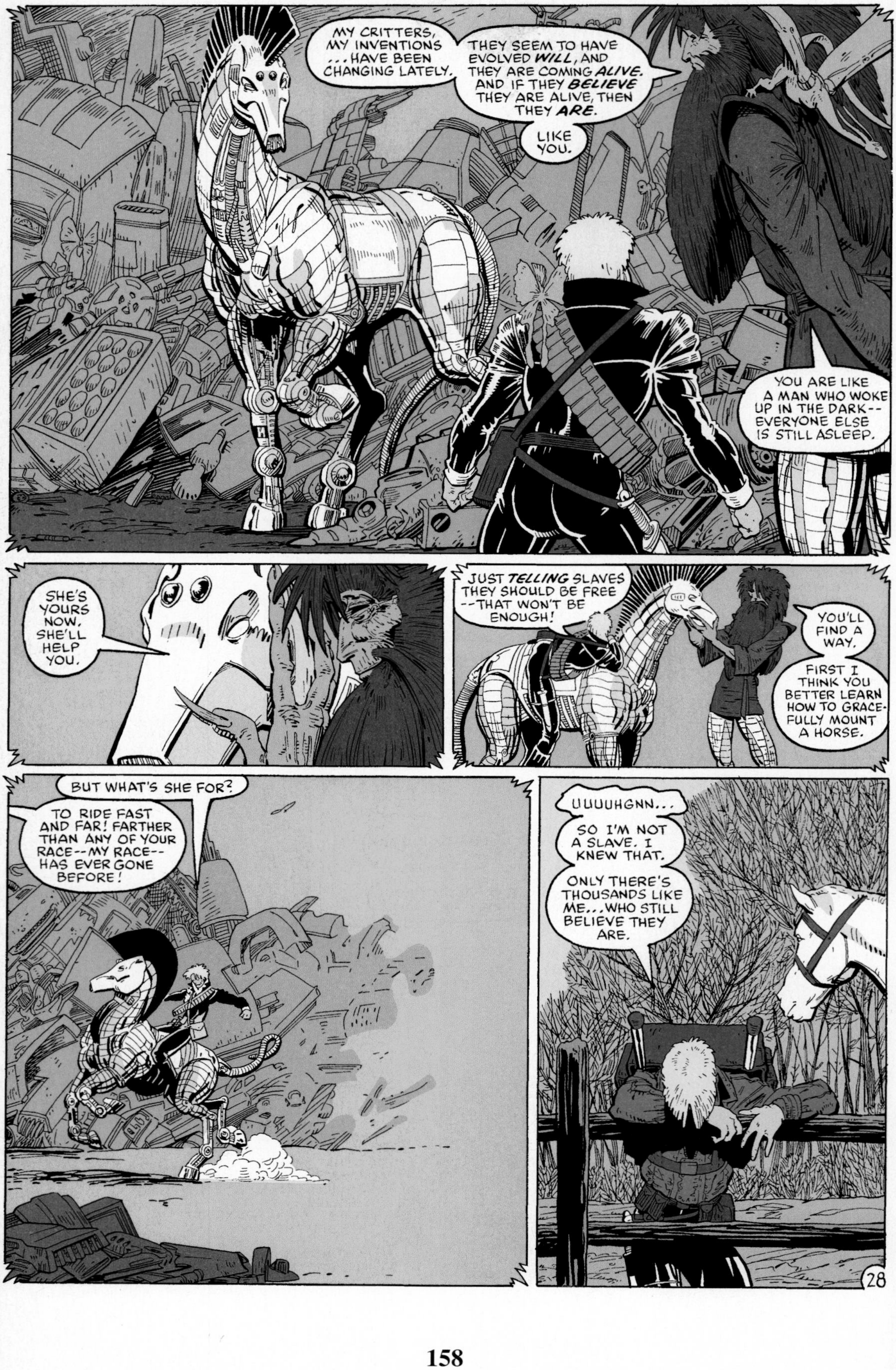
MY CRITTERS, MY INVENTIONS ...HAVE BEEN CHANGING LATELY.
THEY SEEM TO HAVE EVOLVED WILL, AND THEY ARE COMING ALIVE. AND IF THEY BELIEVE THEY ARE ALIVE, THEN THEY ARE.
LIKE YOU.
YOU ARE LIKE A MAN WHO WOKE UP IN THE DARK--EVERYONE ELSE IS STILL ASLEEP.
SHE'S YOURS NOW. SHE'LL HELP YOU.
JUST TELLING SLAVES THEY SHOULD BE FREE --THAT WON'T BE ENOUGH!
YOU'LL FIND A WAY.
FIRST I THINK YOU BETTER LEARN HOW TO GRACEFULLY MOUNT A HORSE.
BUT WHAT'S SHE FOR?
TO RIDE FAST AND FAR! FARTHER THAN ANY OF YOUR RACE--MY RACE--HAS EVER GONE BEFORE!
UUUUHGNN...
SO I'M NOT A SLAVE. I KNEW THAT.
ONLY THERE'S THOUSANDS LIKE ME...WHO STILL BELIEVE THEY ARE.
28

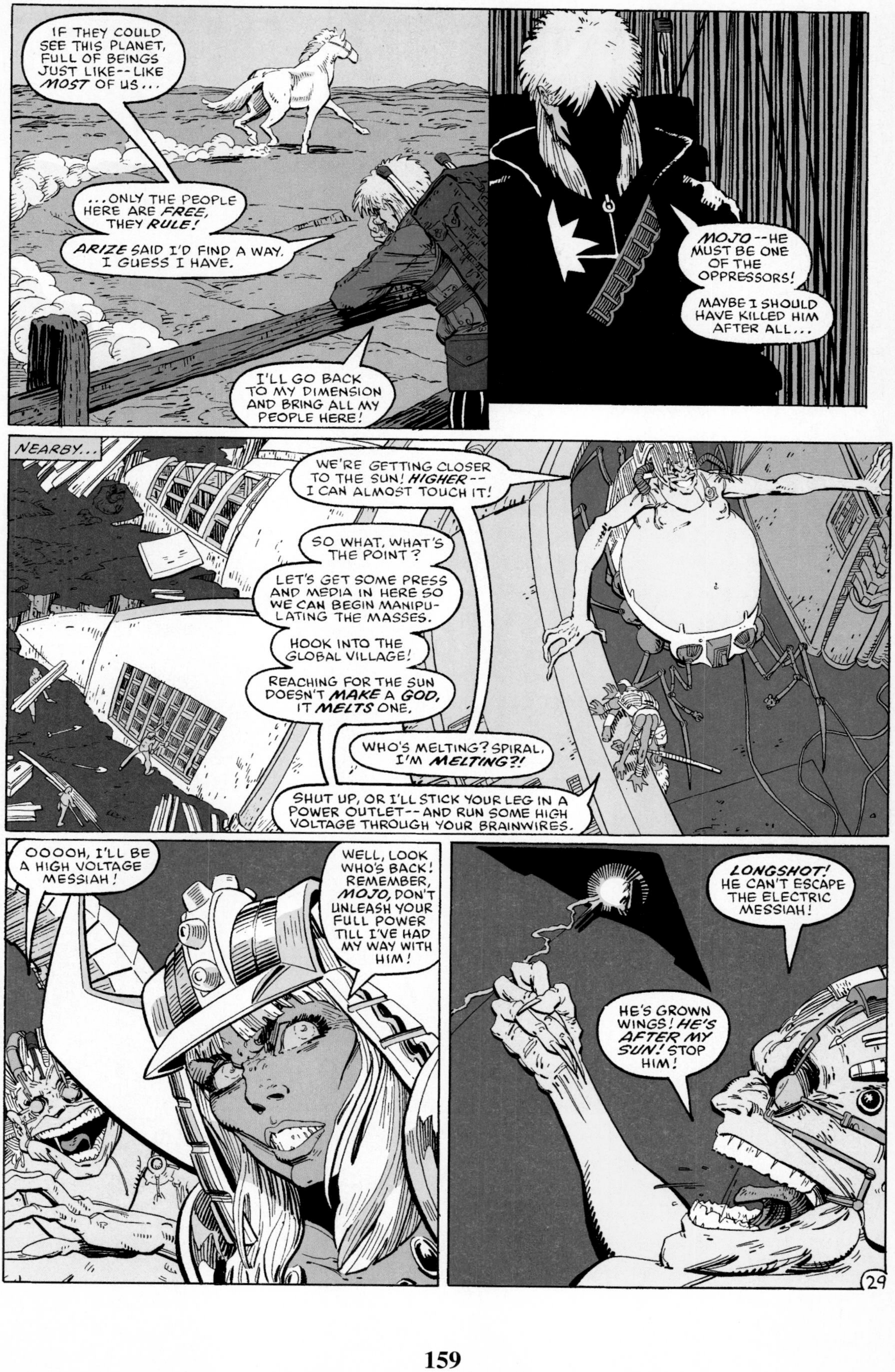
IF THEY COULD SEE THIS PLANET, FULL OF BEINGS JUST LIKE--LIKE MOST OF US...
...ONLY THE PEOPLE HERE ARE FREE, THEY RULE!
ARIZE SAID I'D FIND A WAY. I GUESS I HAVE.
I'LL GO BACK TO MY DIMENSION AND BRING ALL MY PEOPLE HERE!
MOJO--HE MUST BE ONE OF THE OPPRESSORS!
MAYBE I SHOULD HAVE KILLED HIM AFTER ALL...
NEARBY...
WE'RE GETTING CLOSER TO THE SUN! HIGHER-- I CAN ALMOST TOUCH IT!
SO WHAT, WHAT'S THE POINT?
LET'S GET SOME PRESS AND MEDIA IN HERE SO WE CAN BEGIN MANIPULATING THE MASSES.
HOOK INTO THE GLOBAL VILLAGE!
REACHING FOR THE SUN DOESN'T MAKE A GOD, IT MELTS ONE.
WHO'S MELTING? SPIRAL, I'M MELTING?!
SHUT UP, OR I'LL STICK YOUR LEG IN A POWER OUTLET--AND RUN SOME HIGH VOLTAGE THROUGH YOUR BRAINWIRES.
OOOOH, I'LL BE A HIGH VOLTAGE MESSIAH!
WELL, LOOK WHO'S BACK! REMEMBER, MOJO, DON'T UNLEASH YOUR FULL POWER TILL I'VE HAD MY WAY WITH HIM!
LONGSHOT! HE CAN'T ESCAPE THE ELECTRIC MESSIAH!
HE'S GROWN WINGS! HE'S AFTER MY SUN! STOP HIM!
29

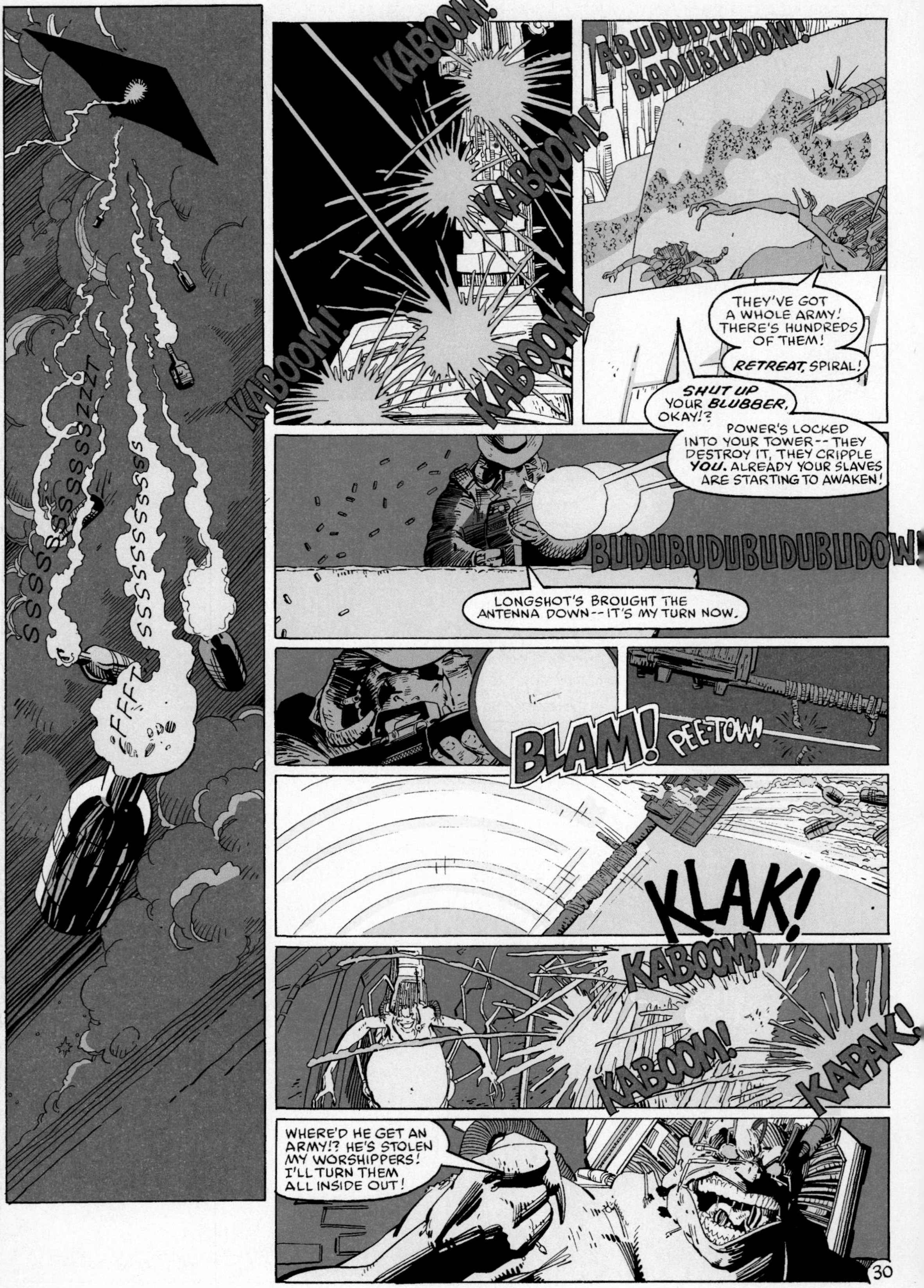
SSSSSSSSSZZZT
SSSSSSSSSSSS
SSSSSSS
FFFT
KABOOM!
KABOOM!
KABOOM!
KABOOM!
KABOOM!
BADUBUDOW!
THEY'VE GOT A WHOLE ARMY! THERE'S HUNDREDS OF THEM!
RETREAT, SPIRAL!
SHUT UP YOUR BLUBBER, OKAY!?
POWER'S LOCKED INTO YOUR TOWER-- THEY DESTROY IT, THEY CRIPPLE YOU. ALREADY YOUR SLAVES ARE STARTING TO AWAKEN!
BUDUBUDUBUDUBUDOW!
LONGSHOT'S BROUGHT THE ANTENNA DOWN-- IT'S MY TURN NOW.
BLAM!
PEE-TOW!
KLAK!
KABOOM!
KABOOM!
KAPAK!
WHERE'D HE GET AN ARMY!? HE'S STOLEN MY WORSHIPPERS! I'LL TURN THEM ALL INSIDE OUT!
30

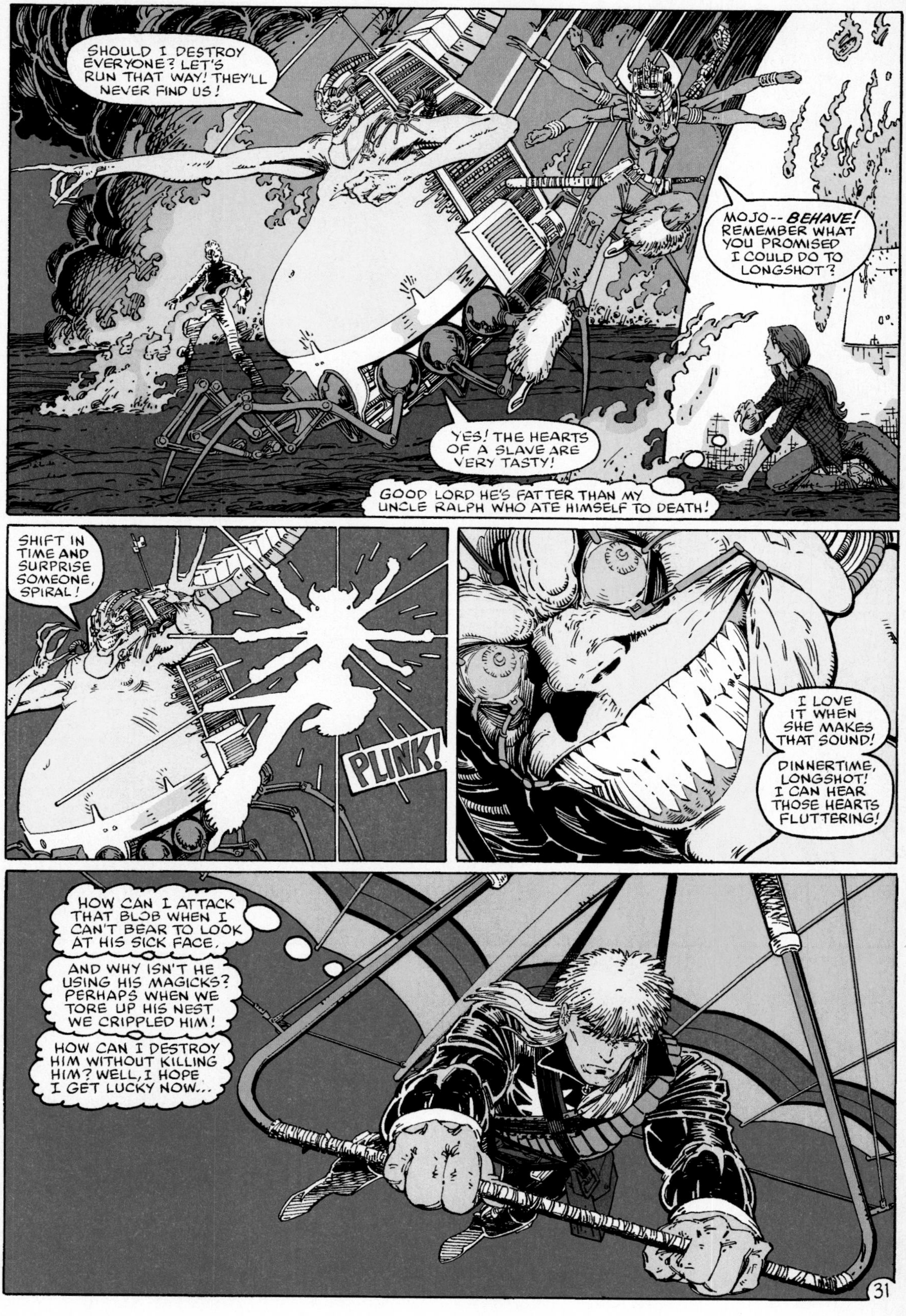
SHOULD I DESTROY EVERYONE? LET'S RUN THAT WAY! THEY'LL NEVER FIND US!
MOJO-- **BEHAVE!** REMEMBER WHAT YOU PROMISED I COULD DO TO LONGSHOT?
YES! THE HEARTS OF A SLAVE ARE VERY TASTY!
GOOD LORD HE'S FATTER THAN MY UNCLE RALPH WHO ATE HIMSELF TO DEATH!
SHIFT IN TIME AND SURPRISE SOMEONE, SPIRAL!
PLINK!
I LOVE IT WHEN SHE MAKES THAT SOUND!
DINNERTIME, LONGSHOT! I CAN HEAR THOSE HEARTS FLUTTERING!
HOW CAN I ATTACK THAT BLOB WHEN I CAN'T BEAR TO LOOK AT HIS SICK FACE.
AND WHY ISN'T HE USING HIS MAGICKS? PERHAPS WHEN WE TORE UP HIS NEST WE CRIPPLED HIM!
HOW CAN I DESTROY HIM WITHOUT KILLING HIM? WELL, I HOPE I GET LUCKY NOW...
31

BETTER USE SOME SKILL TOO-- IF I KEEP FORCING THE ODDS MY WAY--
--NO TELLING WHEN MY LUCK WILL FLIP!
THIS ONE'S FOR YOU, RITA.
HUNGRY? WANT ME FOR DINNER?
FINE-- I'LL HIT THE SPOT!
WUMP
OOOMPH!
PLINK!
CAN'T GET MY SIGHTS ON MOJO WITHOUT RISKING A HIT ON LONGSHOT! I'M NOT EVEN SURE WHICH ONE I SHOULD KILL... EITHER WAY I'M STILL A FREAK.
WHAT DO I CARE?
BUT I DO CARE. I WANT TO DO WHAT IS RIGHT.
LONGSHOT TOLD ME TO BE OPTIMISTIC!
AND I WILL BE! THEY CAN'T STOP US...!
32

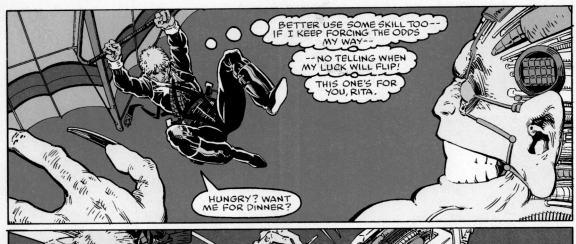

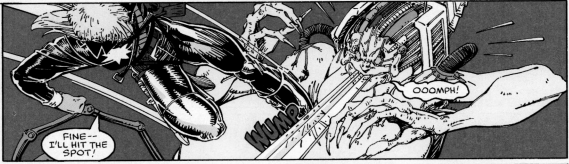

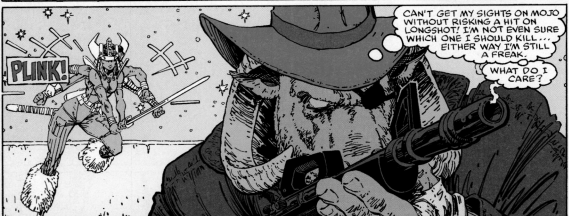

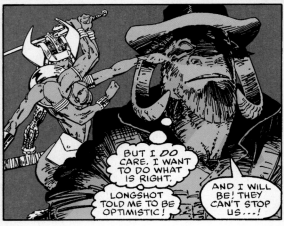

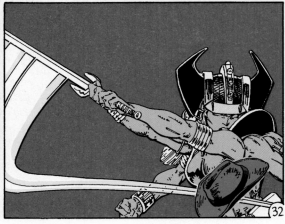

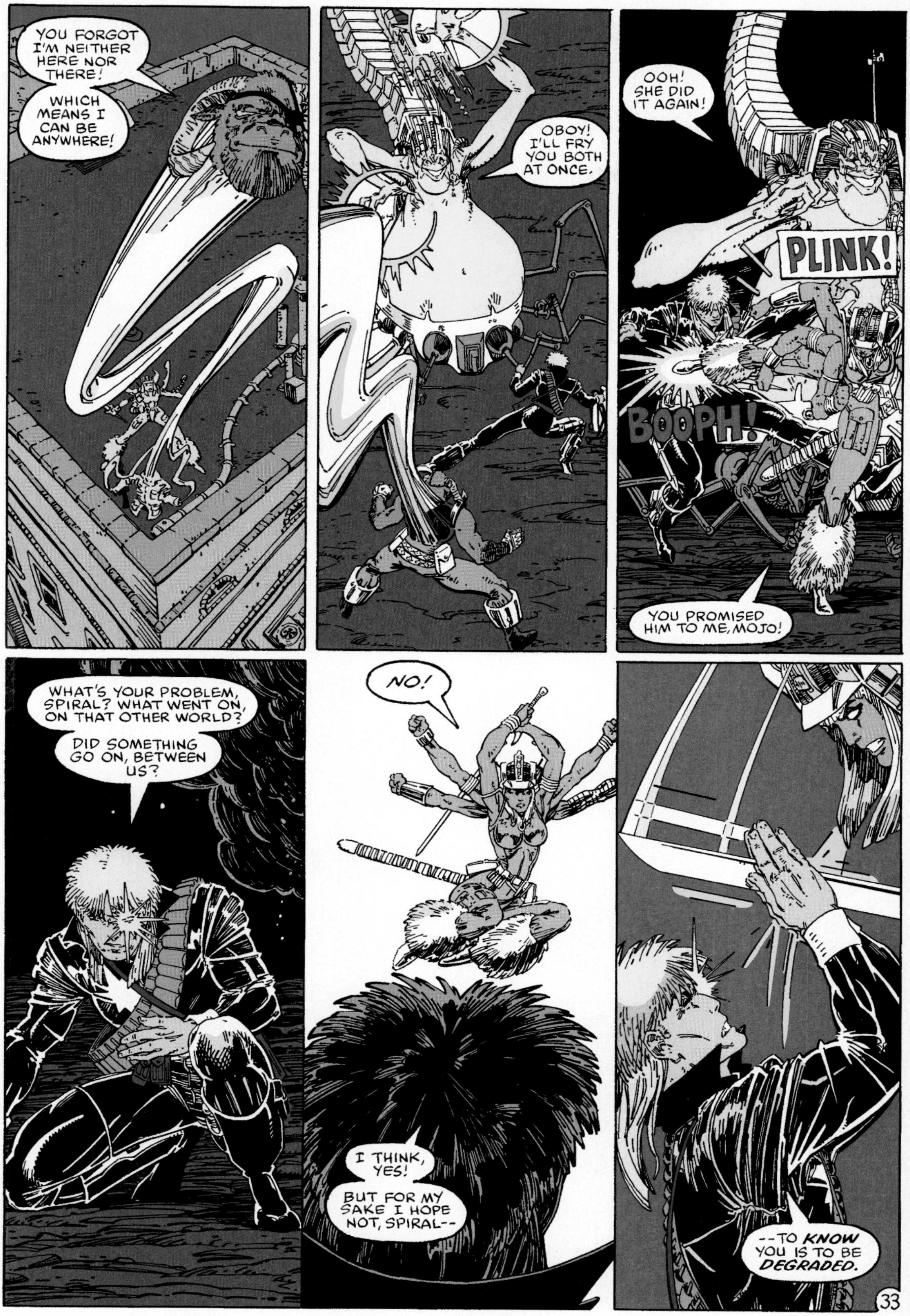
YOU FORGOT I'M NEITHER HERE NOR THERE!
WHICH MEANS I CAN BE ANYWHERE!
OBOY! I'LL FRY YOU BOTH AT ONCE.
OOH! SHE DID IT AGAIN!
PLINK!
BOOPH!
YOU PROMISED HIM TO ME, MOJO!
WHAT'S YOUR PROBLEM, SPIRAL? WHAT WENT ON, ON THAT OTHER WORLD?
DID SOMETHING GO ON, BETWEEN US?
NO!
I THINK, YES!
BUT FOR MY SAKE I HOPE NOT, SPIRAL--
--TO KNOW YOU IS TO BE DEGRADED.
33

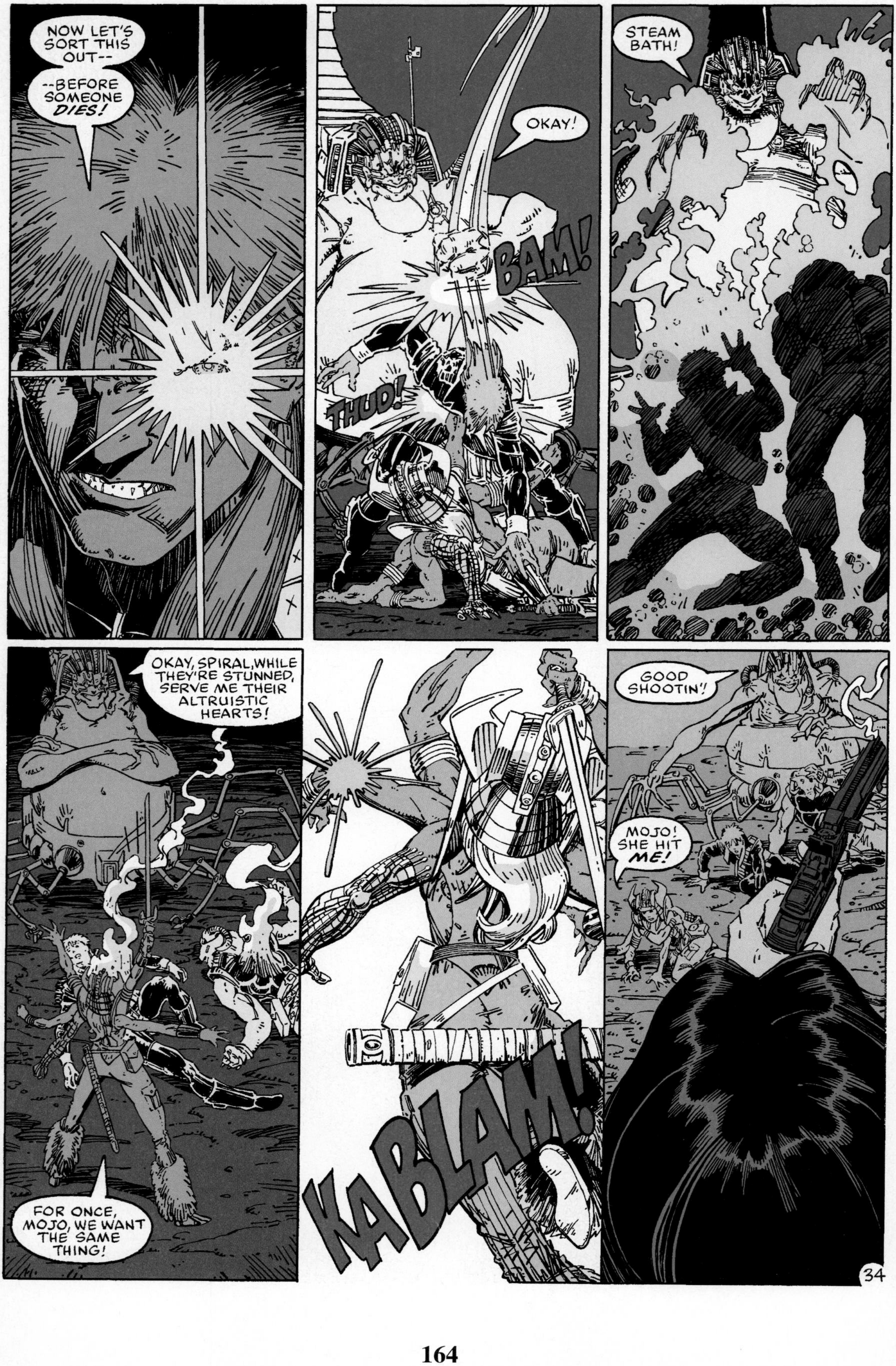
NOW LET'S SORT THIS OUT--
--BEFORE SOMEONE DIES!
OKAY!
BAM!
THUD!
STEAM BATH!
OKAY, SPIRAL, WHILE THEY'RE STUNNED, SERVE ME THEIR ALTRUISTIC HEARTS!
FOR ONCE, MOJO, WE WANT THE SAME THING!
KABLAM!
GOOD SHOOTIN'!
MOJO! SHE HIT ME!
34

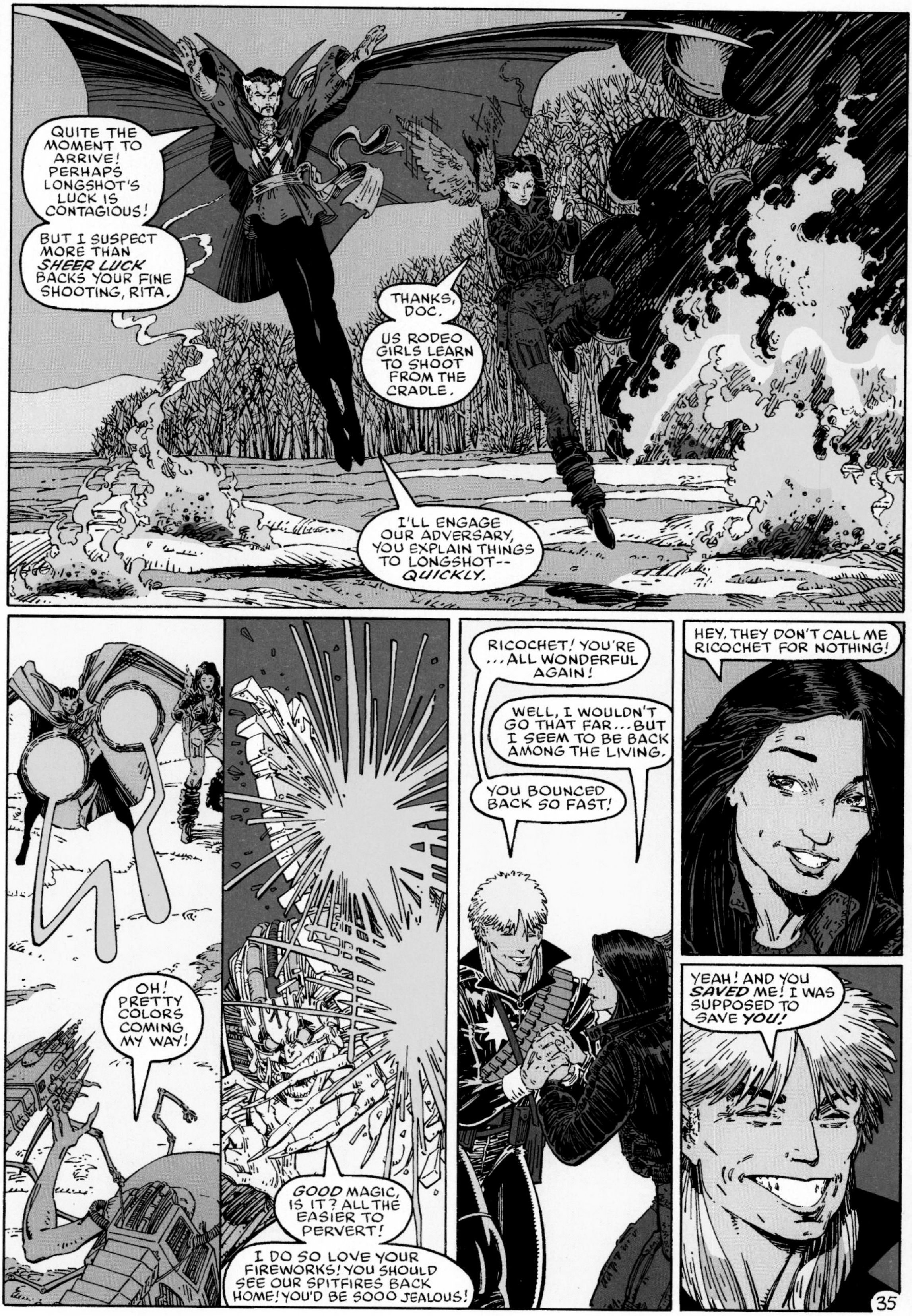
QUITE THE MOMENT TO ARRIVE! PERHAPS LONGSHOT'S LUCK IS CONTAGIOUS!
BUT I SUSPECT MORE THAN *SHEER LUCK* BACKS YOUR FINE SHOOTING, RITA.
THANKS, DOC.
US RODEO GIRLS LEARN TO SHOOT FROM THE CRADLE.
I'LL ENGAGE OUR ADVERSARY, YOU EXPLAIN THINGS TO LONGSHOT-- *QUICKLY.*
OH! PRETTY COLORS COMING MY WAY!
GOOD MAGIC, IS IT? ALL THE EASIER TO PERVERT!
I DO SO LOVE YOUR FIREWORKS! YOU SHOULD SEE OUR SPITFIRES BACK HOME! YOU'D BE SOOO JEALOUS!
RICOCHET! YOU'RE ... ALL WONDERFUL AGAIN!
WELL, I WOULDN'T GO THAT FAR... BUT I SEEM TO BE BACK AMONG THE LIVING.
YOU BOUNCED BACK SO FAST!
HEY, THEY DON'T CALL ME RICOCHET FOR NOTHING!
YEAH! AND YOU *SAVED* ME! I WAS SUPPOSED TO SAVE *YOU!*
35

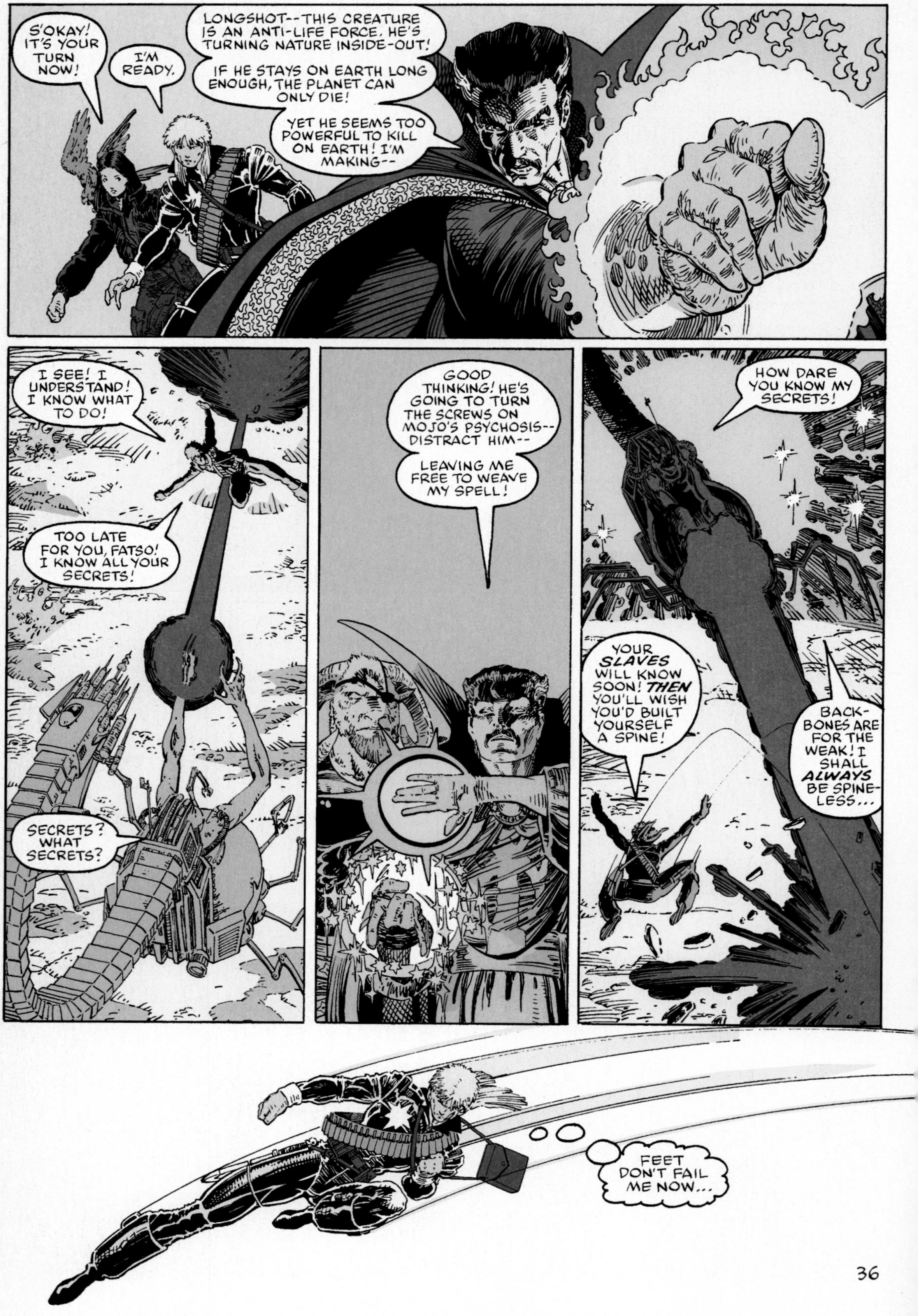
S'OKAY! IT'S YOUR TURN NOW!
I'M READY.
LONGSHOT--THIS CREATURE IS AN ANTI-LIFE FORCE. HE'S TURNING NATURE INSIDE-OUT!
IF HE STAYS ON EARTH LONG ENOUGH, THE PLANET CAN ONLY DIE!
YET HE SEEMS TOO POWERFUL TO KILL ON EARTH! I'M MAKING--
I SEE! I UNDERSTAND! I KNOW WHAT TO DO!
TOO LATE FOR YOU, FATSO! I KNOW ALL YOUR SECRETS!
SECRETS? WHAT SECRETS?
GOOD THINKING! HE'S GOING TO TURN THE SCREWS ON MOJO'S PSYCHOSIS--DISTRACT HIM--
LEAVING ME FREE TO WEAVE MY SPELL!
HOW DARE YOU KNOW MY SECRETS!
YOUR SLAVES WILL KNOW SOON! THEN YOU'LL WISH YOU'D BUILT YOURSELF A SPINE!
BACK-BONES ARE FOR THE WEAK! I SHALL ALWAYS BE SPINE-LESS...
FEET DON'T FAIL ME NOW...
36

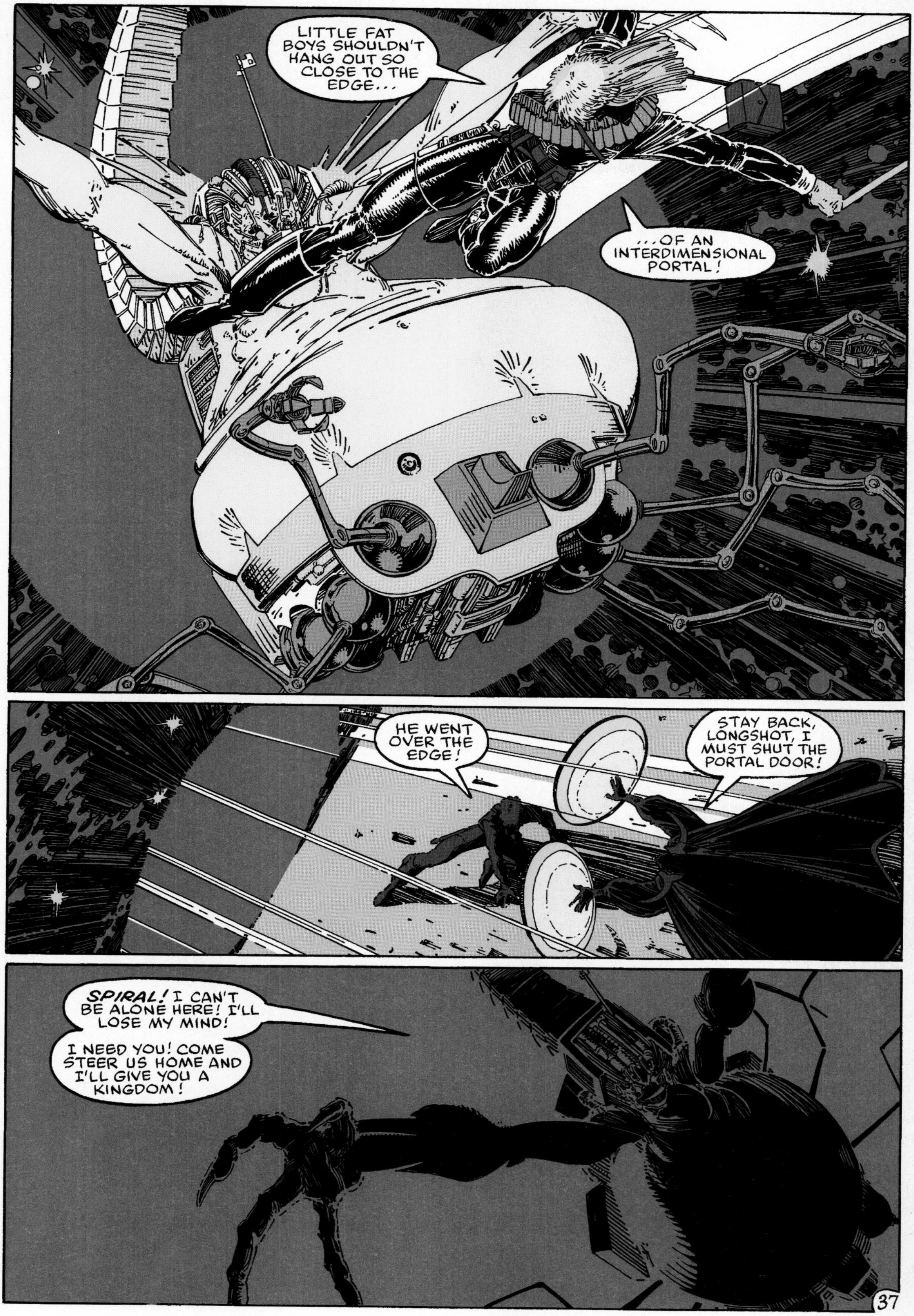
LITTLE FAT BOYS SHOULDN'T HANG OUT SO CLOSE TO THE EDGE...
...OF AN INTERDIMENSIONAL PORTAL!
HE WENT OVER THE EDGE!
STAY BACK, LONGSHOT, I MUST SHUT THE PORTAL DOOR!
SPIRAL! I CAN'T BE ALONE HERE! I'LL LOSE MY MIND!
I NEED YOU! COME STEER US HOME AND I'LL GIVE YOU A KINGDOM!
37

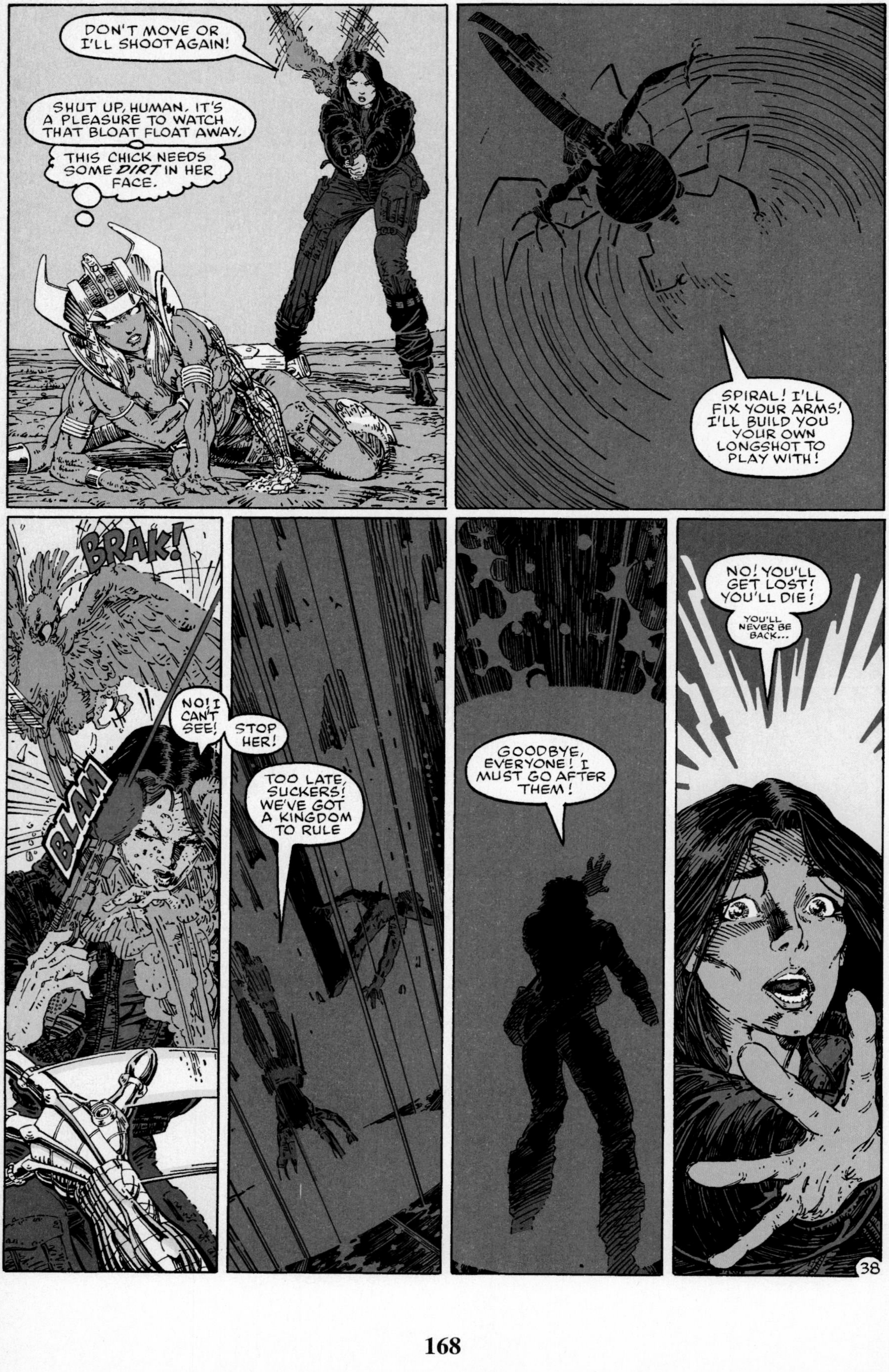
DON'T MOVE OR I'LL SHOOT AGAIN!
SHUT UP, HUMAN. IT'S A PLEASURE TO WATCH THAT BLOAT FLOAT AWAY.
THIS CHICK NEEDS SOME DIRT IN HER FACE.
SPIRAL! I'LL FIX YOUR ARMS! I'LL BUILD YOU YOUR OWN LONGSHOT TO PLAY WITH!
BRAK!
NO! I CAN'T SEE!
STOP HER!
BLAM
TOO LATE, SUCKERS! WE'VE GOT A KINGDOM TO RULE
GOODBYE, EVERYONE! I MUST GO AFTER THEM!
NO! YOU'LL GET LOST! YOU'LL DIE!
YOU'LL NEVER BE BACK...
38

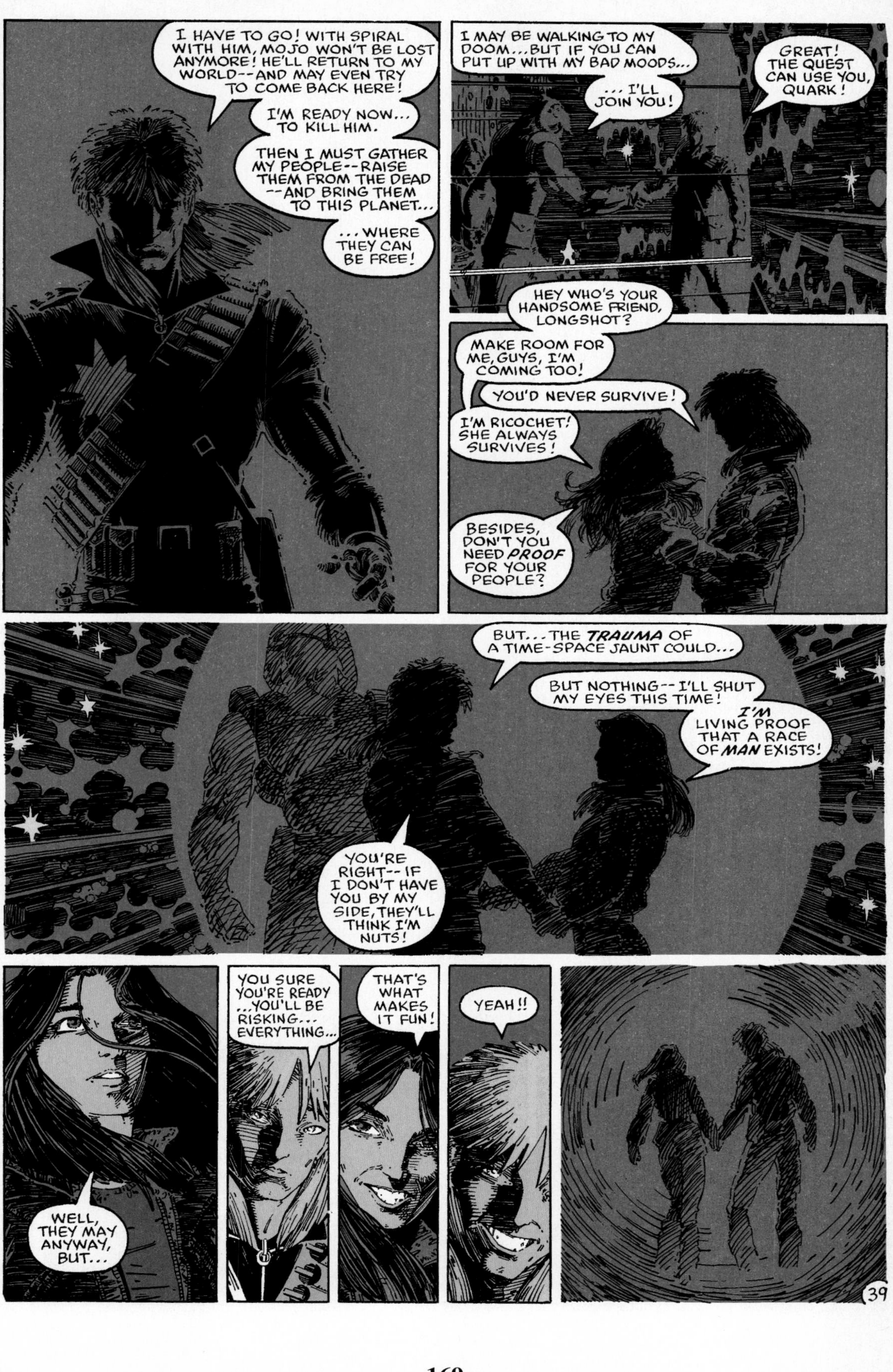
I HAVE TO GO! WITH SPIRAL WITH HIM, MOJO WON'T BE LOST ANYMORE! HE'LL RETURN TO MY WORLD--AND MAY EVEN TRY TO COME BACK HERE!
I'M READY NOW... TO KILL HIM.
THEN I MUST GATHER MY PEOPLE--RAISE THEM FROM THE DEAD --AND BRING THEM TO THIS PLANET...
...WHERE THEY CAN BE FREE!
I MAY BE WALKING TO MY DOOM...BUT IF YOU CAN PUT UP WITH MY BAD MOODS...
...I'LL JOIN YOU!
GREAT! THE QUEST CAN USE YOU, QUARK!
HEY WHO'S YOUR HANDSOME FRIEND, LONGSHOT?
MAKE ROOM FOR ME, GUYS, I'M COMING TOO!
YOU'D NEVER SURVIVE!
I'M RICOCHET! SHE ALWAYS SURVIVES!
BESIDES, DON'T YOU NEED *PROOF* FOR YOUR PEOPLE?
BUT...THE *TRAUMA* OF A TIME-SPACE JAUNT COULD...
BUT NOTHING--I'LL SHUT MY EYES THIS TIME!
I'M LIVING PROOF THAT A RACE OF *MAN* EXISTS!
YOU'RE RIGHT--IF I DON'T HAVE YOU BY MY SIDE, THEY'LL THINK I'M NUTS!
WELL, THEY MAY ANYWAY, BUT...
YOU SURE YOU'RE READY ...YOU'LL BE RISKING... EVERYTHING...
THAT'S WHAT MAKES IT FUN!
YEAH!!
39

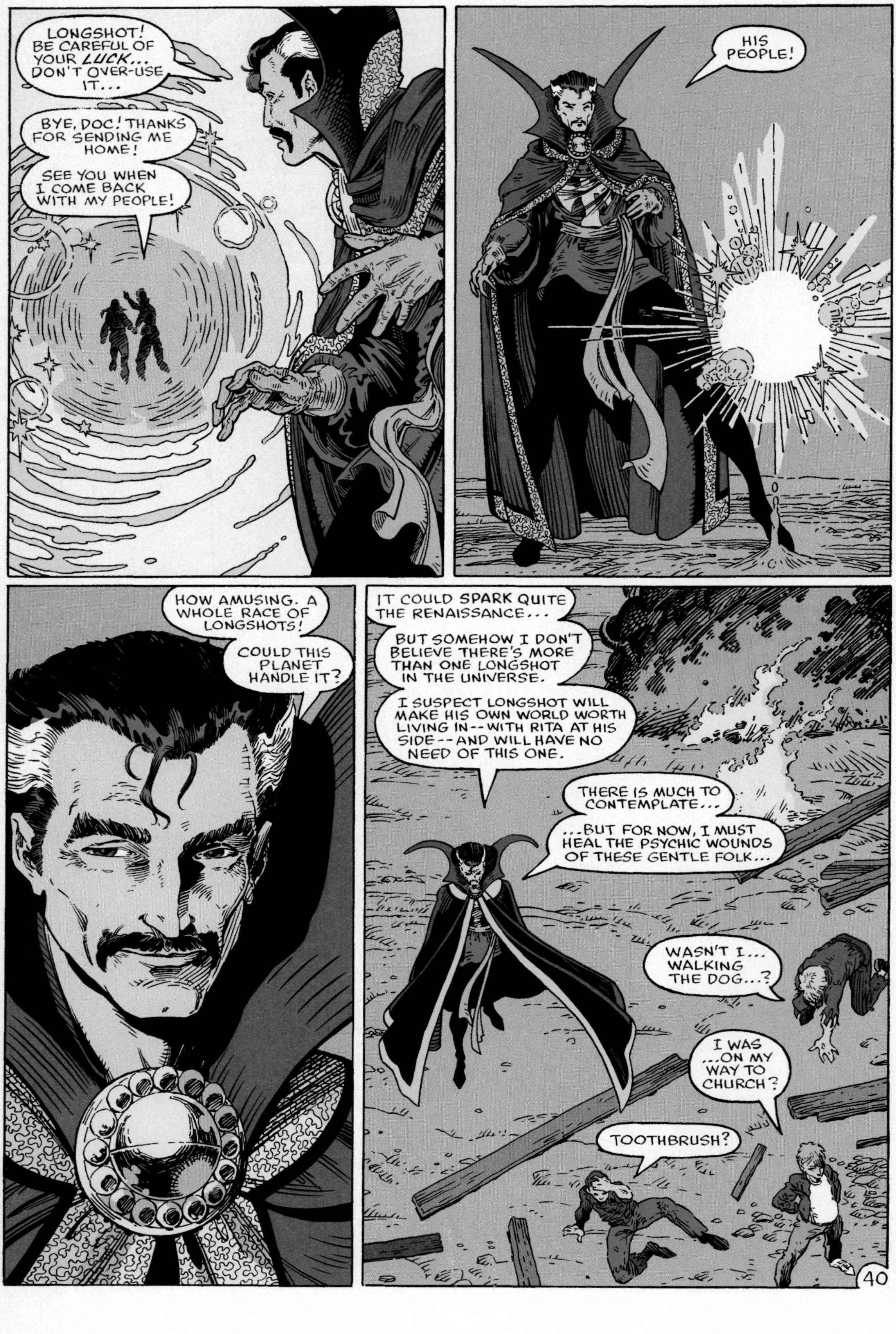
LONGSHOT! BE CAREFUL OF YOUR LUCK... DON'T OVER-USE IT...
BYE, DOC! THANKS FOR SENDING ME HOME!
SEE YOU WHEN I COME BACK WITH MY PEOPLE!
HIS PEOPLE!
HOW AMUSING. A WHOLE RACE OF LONGSHOTS!
COULD THIS PLANET HANDLE IT?
IT COULD SPARK QUITE THE RENAISSANCE...
BUT SOMEHOW I DON'T BELIEVE THERE'S MORE THAN ONE LONGSHOT IN THE UNIVERSE.
I SUSPECT LONGSHOT WILL MAKE HIS OWN WORLD WORTH LIVING IN--WITH RITA AT HIS SIDE--AND WILL HAVE NO NEED OF THIS ONE.
THERE IS MUCH TO CONTEMPLATE...
...BUT FOR NOW, I MUST HEAL THE PSYCHIC WOUNDS OF THESE GENTLE FOLK...
WASN'T I... WALKING THE DOG...?
I WAS ...ON MY WAY TO CHURCH?
TOOTHBRUSH?
40

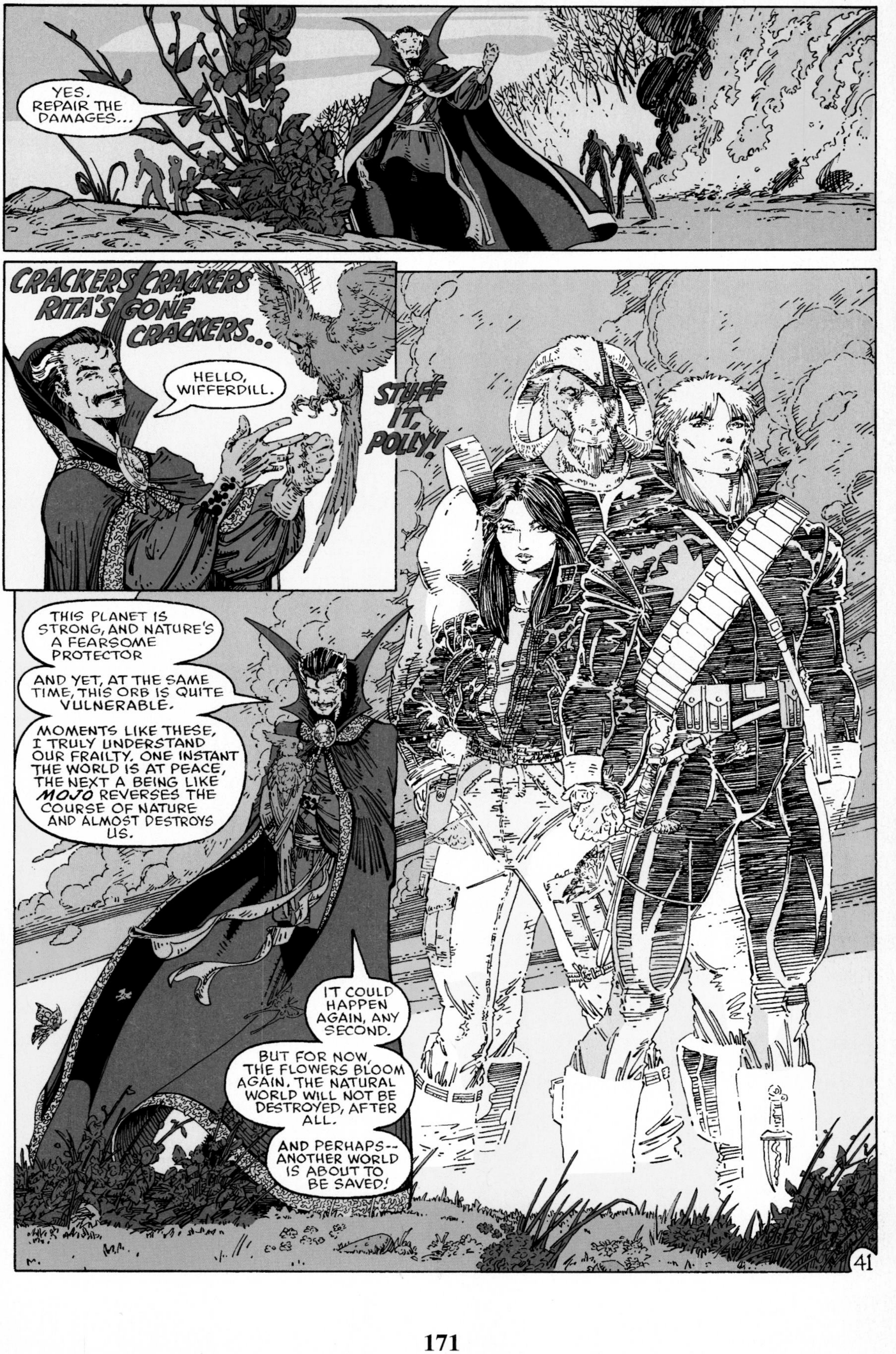
YES. REPAIR THE DAMAGES...
CRACKERS CRACKERS RITA'S GONE CRACKERS...
HELLO, WIFFERDILL.
STUFF IT, POLLY!
THIS PLANET IS STRONG, AND NATURE'S A FEARSOME PROTECTOR
AND YET, AT THE SAME TIME, THIS ORB IS QUITE VULNERABLE.
MOMENTS LIKE THESE, I TRULY UNDERSTAND OUR FRAILTY. ONE INSTANT THE WORLD IS AT PEACE, THE NEXT A BEING LIKE *MOJO* REVERSES THE COURSE OF NATURE AND ALMOST DESTROYS US.
IT COULD HAPPEN AGAIN, ANY SECOND.
BUT FOR NOW, THE FLOWERS BLOOM AGAIN. THE NATURAL WORLD WILL NOT BE DESTROYED, AFTER ALL.
AND PERHAPS-- ANOTHER WORLD IS ABOUT TO BE SAVED!
41

LONGSHOT

Who is Longshot?
That's what he'd like to know!

ORIGIN

We will imply that Longshot comes from a time/space several galaxies removed from Earth, but it will probably turn out that Darkmane 'let him out' of another dimension. His race has a warrior sect that studies and masters luck. Use luck right and it will gush, abuse it and it leaves you. They 'know' when things will run their way, like ESP. When greed comes into play, it masks one's ability to judge when 'luck' is on your side. So, odds go way down in probability. The flip side of this luckyness is that his race is reckless and somewhat weak in character because they let luck decide right and wrong for them. They lean on a collective crutch. It is this 'luck metaphysics' that spit LongShot out, the way a body spits out something foreign. It was because he went too far one day in abusing luck. He has one last lucky streak, where he makes it to earth alive (with the accidental help of Darkmane). He is a fish out of water, out of the fear/luck enviornment he's used to. Without it, he has trouble 'breathing' or getting along. This is his purgatory, where he will learn about himself and the ways of man, and perhaps return to his people to teach them and fix the race.

A true man without a past, Longshot awakens in the world fully-formed. He is mature and worldly yet has no idea why or who he is or where he's from. He is disarmingly niave as to the ways of this particular world. He sees the world anew, with both the wonder and awe of a child, and the cutting insight of a stranger. He has no past to weigh him down. A clean slate. Longshot is wildly lucky, and has a fast-track ride-rocket approach to life cause he can count on his luck to pull punches for him. He 'clicks' into a roll, a hot-streak, and rides it. But if he abuses that luck, it may turn on him. He has a give and take relationship with his power. His luck is ornery and has its own 'morality'. The luck is his morality. As he relies on the 'high metaphysics of luck' to keep him in check, the danger is that it could become a crutch, an addiction, like a gun you whip out so often that when it's out of bullets you find yourself helpless. Longshot's gun is fickle, it only works when his motive is pure. (if he tried to be malicious, or went too far trying to make money with his luck, it would leave him.) He is a flawed hero. His incessent flirting with danger and death often inspires death to flirt back. One of his on-going dilemas is that he tends to get side-tracked and screw up so much while counting on his luck to pull through for him, that he inadvertently hurts people around him. Then he feels awful. As a stranger in a strange land, he is constantly struggling and stumbling thru our complicated and often meaningless taboos and traditions.

He takes life by storm, as with desperate frantic energy
he tries to find out why the hell he's here in the
first place. We get to like him, yet feel on edge cause
this luck can't last. He's grossly deifying   probability
as he has his 'lucky streaks'.

All he remembers of his past is that he was an
inter-galactic warrior; so he likes, needs and may be
addicted to the sense-heightened state of fear.

All he's ever known is war. Life is and was war.
What star-system, what time period, etc., remains
a mystery. From this past existense, he learned to
like fear. Fear is all he's known. It is literally a
way of life. Fear heightened his senses, kept him
on edge. He ever felt more alive than he did on the
front lines. He constantly tries to re-create that
heightened state of living. As a result he throws himself
into dangerous situations. He can be like a fear-junkie.
Then, like a bullfighter, he has to get out of the
danger he himself invoked.

People resent his wild tactics and especially his success.
As a warrior, and just like 'there are no atheists in
foxholes'--he believes in a higher metaphysics, his
'god'. It manifests itself in his luck and his magic.

So we have a lucky alien, desperately searching for
who he is. First issue would be him waking up,
nameless and alone. First five issues would have a
whimsical on-the-road wanderlust type feel to them.
Reader gets to know and love him, then we have an

origin issue where he learns he's from
'out there somewhere'. From then on we slowly
drop clues as to his origin, but the whole picture
may never be revealed. Or by then he may have changed
too much to go back.

He is an alien who misses his people, but doesn't
know who they are.

He also has magic. His magic is an extention of the
powers that are inate in man, that a highly evolved man
could concievably touch on --naturally integrated
magic rather than showy stuff.

In some ways, he is the superman anyman can be.
His magic is an extention of the magical things in
life that man is almost on the edge of believing in.
The things we see glimmers of out of the corners of
our eyes, yet when we try to focus on them, they disappear.
He can extent his mind in 'natural' ways, like seeing
outside our light spectrum, beyond our harmonics. For
example, like this 'sixth sense': Longshot can 'read'
objects and places. He can pick up an object, know the
hands that shaped it, or the machine that stamped it
out. He can feel the tears that fell on it or that it
was passed as a gift. Or that it had killed. He can
sit in a room and 'see' into its past, or feel the
mood of the stranger who just left. He can sit in a
valley and know its people.

Visual

As an alien, he has an exotic, more-than-human
look. He has a star tattoo that appears around his eye
when he clicks into a 'lucky streak'. He has leathery
tough skin and a curving spine so that the spine-bones
stick out, only four fingers....subtle alien differences.
He will be essentially human looking so that he
looks striking yet can still mix in without causing
a stir. He will use strange words, have strange customs,
etc. His costume would have the functional elements
of a soldier, and probably be white. In daylight, his
coloring is lighter, at night he can get darker like
a shadow and reflect the colors around him. So his
costume has a chamelion property.

LONGSHOT'S RACE

What follows is stuff writer/artist/editor need
to know, but reader won't know for a long time.

Longshot comes from a three class society, several
dimensions removed. There is an upper-crust class of
decadent, nasty, amoral parasitic beings. They
have evolved (or devolved) into a spineless race.
They literally have no spines, their bodies long ago
having needed supplementary supports, and now they
have heavy-wire exo-skeletal suits to 'walk' in. (They
find LS's raised-spine quite ugly.) They are a
lazy, sluggy class, physically and morally crippled.
There is a pagen-like demonic-looking middle class that
have less brains but more strength (a sign of lower class)
than the Upper Class. They do have spines. A few of these
are the critters that chase LS to earth.
The third class is bred by the upper class. They are
a slave class bred to fight the wars, farm, make
shelters, do all the work for the planet. They are
highly trained but 'harnessed'--super-beings that are
stabled and controlled like throroughbreds. Genetically
designed to look nothing like the ruleing class (they
even appear ugly to them), they ended up looking like
man. (Some of LS's 'alien' elements are from
the ruling class, the leathery skin, four fingers, etc.)
They got this image of man from their myths, man having
once crossed the dimensions in some time past. LS's

people are like that race's gargoyles or dragons. (this concept of mythical creatures as being imagery from other-dimensional visitations will be one theme of the book. For instance, Darkmane's 2 elemental friends--one type looks like a cherubic angel...the other a little devilish.)

Slaves are also mentally designed to not realize that they are physically superior to the ruling class, so there will be no revolts. They are genetically engineered for subserviance and compliance. When one reaches glimmers of a revolutionary consciousness, they are subject to brain-wipes. (THeir brains also have a built in pain-response trigger to control them...'thought' is painful.)

LS was about to lead a revolt when the ruling class wiped his mind (he has scars on his temples to prove it). With Luck, he escaped, before they managed to chuck him into a black hole. What the ruling class didn't know was that LS was not just your ordinary slave. He belonged to a secret sect--a 'constellation' of luck masters--called Lucky Stars.

They are an underground group that is highly trained and was lying in wait for the right time for a huge revolt. LS got unlucky and was detected. But as he was being chased towards a black hole he got lucky again and made it to earth. He pulled some middle class critters with him. They chase him thru the mini-series cause they think he can get them home. There are many rituals to get one

home. (they try a newborn baby, and in the end LS's luck finds a way to get them home but they leave LS behind, nyah-nyah.)

Now, I know this is all getting complex enough, but there's one more thing you have to know. These critters didn't just happen to be around when LS went thru the portal to earth. They were chasing him. Why did LS get so unlucky as to get himself in this predicament in the first place? Cause his luck turned on him, cause he got greedy. He was gambling with the critters' money to make them and him money. Thus, he was both abusing his power and dangerously exposing his underground sect's discipline to the eyes of the ruling class. That's how he got detected in the firstplace.

As for LS's memories, they were taken by the brain-wipe. There is a theory that when one dies, one leaves an ethereal 'psychic imprint' and that this is what 'ghosts' are. So even though LS's brain was wiped, he still has the residual 'ghosts' of memories. He will have flashbacks on bits of his history till he finally sees the whole picture. These flashbacks will be literally painful to see or hold on to. (remember the built in pain response for control.)

THE VILLAINS

Getting shot thru dimensions affects everyone differently. Our puppy-demon finds he not only has form, but he is a magic-magnet. While where he came from he was a nobody, here he could draw enough magic to be a god. He wants to stay and grow powerful enough to get revenge on LS. For now he just follows LS and watches him and pretends to be innocent. By issue four he is ~~the~~ a huge mega-demon ~~described in proposal~~ of many forms + faces. His shape is inconstant flux + change (nails grow long, curl, drop off, etc for rest of form).

On their world, he was the rebel-tracker who discovered LS and wiped his brain. He hates LS for being stuck in this world. (Remember--he's stuck on a planet made up of humans--the 'devils' of his mythology) Later, he reveals to LS that he knows who LS is. BUt he tells a deadly lie, tells LS a false origin to hurt him. In the final battle, LS must kill him, but if he does kill him he will also be killing all knowledge of his past and self.

The shadow- demons that chase LS are only half-here. They have to concentrate to hold form. They look out of sync, their speech often lapses into garbled sounds. They often move in slow motion or too fast. Just their hands and face may get into crystal clear focus while rest of body fades. (Parts they must use to touch things get more solid and visible.) They are stuck between worlds, neither-here-nor-there. NOt only do they hate LS for pulling them here, they hate the fact that only he made it all the way while they got stuck in-between. Their facial-features shift when they try to hold human form (asian to alien to indian etc.) Their true form shines thru sometimes. They use wrong styles, wrong words, smell funny, make people woosy and nauseous. Skin

goes from hot to cold. World around them seems slightly out of kilter. They make mistakes. For example, they stupidly name themselves from signs (Mr. Burger Woolworth or whatever.) THey say odd things like 'see you back when'. THey drape clothes over their forms to rob banks to get money, or possess people to do things for them, then dump person to wonder what happened.

Not everyone can even see these critters. One must be sensitive to such things. (Some things have to be believed to be seen).

[redacted]

Thru the mini-series LS will coninually be picking up clues, seeing flickers of things out of the corners of his eyes, things trailing him, as it all builds up till the whole picture is revealed. Please refer back to this discription of demons when drawing them thru series.

PORTALS

These high-energy inter-dimensional 'doors' have a distinct character. They are like 'dead' spots. Birds flying thru thump to the ground. Plants won't grow or grow funny. The colors of things are slightly off. Mechanical or electrical gadgets work or work too much--cameras that won't stop clicking, etc. There is a hydrogen sulfide(?) smell. Things fall apart. Clothes tend to unravel, sounds echo or fall flat. Very entropic place. Remember this in plot, as they approach demon-ritual. Hint at wierdness at first, then it gets worse right at the sight of the ritual. As they get near site, they will feel sick from the palpable strangness and notice subtle clues.

LONGSHOT #2

Longshot wants this stuff called MONEY.
His luck gets him a job as a high paid stunt man.
The sleazly director who hired him doesn't care for
LS's safety and starts to use this reckless guy for
more and more dangerous stunts at higher and
higher stakes. He then makes a deal with LS--do
anything I want for this movie and scrap the
'stunt-man-protection-guidlines', and I'll make you
a million-dollar stunt man. Is that a lot of money? asks LS.
LS learns how to click into his luck, throwing himself
into the danger, _liking_ it. He gets carried away, and
since his motive is impure (money) the lucky streak
goes sour and horrific, the luck turns on him
and he is smashed to bits. (Somewhere in there he will
see his tattoo reflected and flash on his home)
Our mischevious demon critters will be lurking around
adding to the chaos.
The director, afraid of being accused of murder, dumps
LS in a river, leaving him for dead.

LONGSHOT #3

We set up a tragic character--an everyman/anyman
regular joe. This guy hates each day each hour, and
especially the inane rattle of his wife and his
constant bill-collectors. He's on a slow treadmill to
nowhere. His only friend is his TV, and even that puts
him to sleep. He goes out to jump off a bridge, but
doesn't fall far enough. He can't even kill himself
right. But he does find something in the river--Longshot--
still alive. LS is a self healer, and when he is
better, the guy tells LS he can thank his 'lucky stars'
he's still alive. LS looks up and wonders--Am I from
the stars? I certainly seem to _be_ a lucky star!
LS revels in life, this guy hides from it. LS
attracts luck like a magnet, whereas the guy's
followed by an unlucky cloud. We juxtapose this as
LS takes it on himself in gratitude to show this
guy life's worth living, it's great to be alive.
Since they both need money, they set off to get some.
Guy says Con-Ed is a big villian, ripping off the people,
we can take some of theirs. LS niavely believes him.
So off they go, LS occasionally haveing to stop this
poor guy from killing himself.
In their big adventure battle fighting advanced con-ed
super-secret guard dog robots or something, with
our lurking demons to add in a wild-card of
chaos, the reader sees how LS is so special he just
dwarfs this guy, makes him look even more like a smuck.

Guy sees this too--whatever it is LS's got, he knows
_he_ ain't got it. All men _weren't_ created equal--sad
but true. But in all the danger and exciement he
starts missing the normalcy of his tired safe little
life and when the adventure is over, he goes home,
even bearing flowers to try again with his wife.
Meanwhile, in the Con-ed battle, LS's shut down
a city-wide energy grid, sees the error of stealing,
and we leave him wondering how to give the money _back_.
In this story we see how in his well-meaning impulsiveness,
LS only manages to royally screw-up.

LONGSHOT #4

Longshot as a modern-day Robin Hood, trying to
return the money to the 'people', with a
string of super heros--Moon Knight, Black Widow,
Cap America and finally Doctor Strange--coming
after him. We switch the perspective here. We
see from LS's (the 'villian's') viewpoint. Super
heroes are seen as pain-in-the-butt bothersome creatures
who mess up your plans.
In sub-plot, LS makes friends with some little kids
he gives money to. They are busy playing war.
("My favorite show is MAGNUM!") etc.
LS has a brief flashback on his days as a warrior, knows
what the kids are emulating is bad, tries to teach them
so. They talk of the 'enemy' they must kill. LS thinks
they've gone too far into the fantasy, and he goes on
this 'ememy-hunt' with them to see that they don't hurt
themselves. In end, we find there really _is_ a
monster, the same one Darkmane meets in _her_ issue #4,
and off we go on the regular comic.

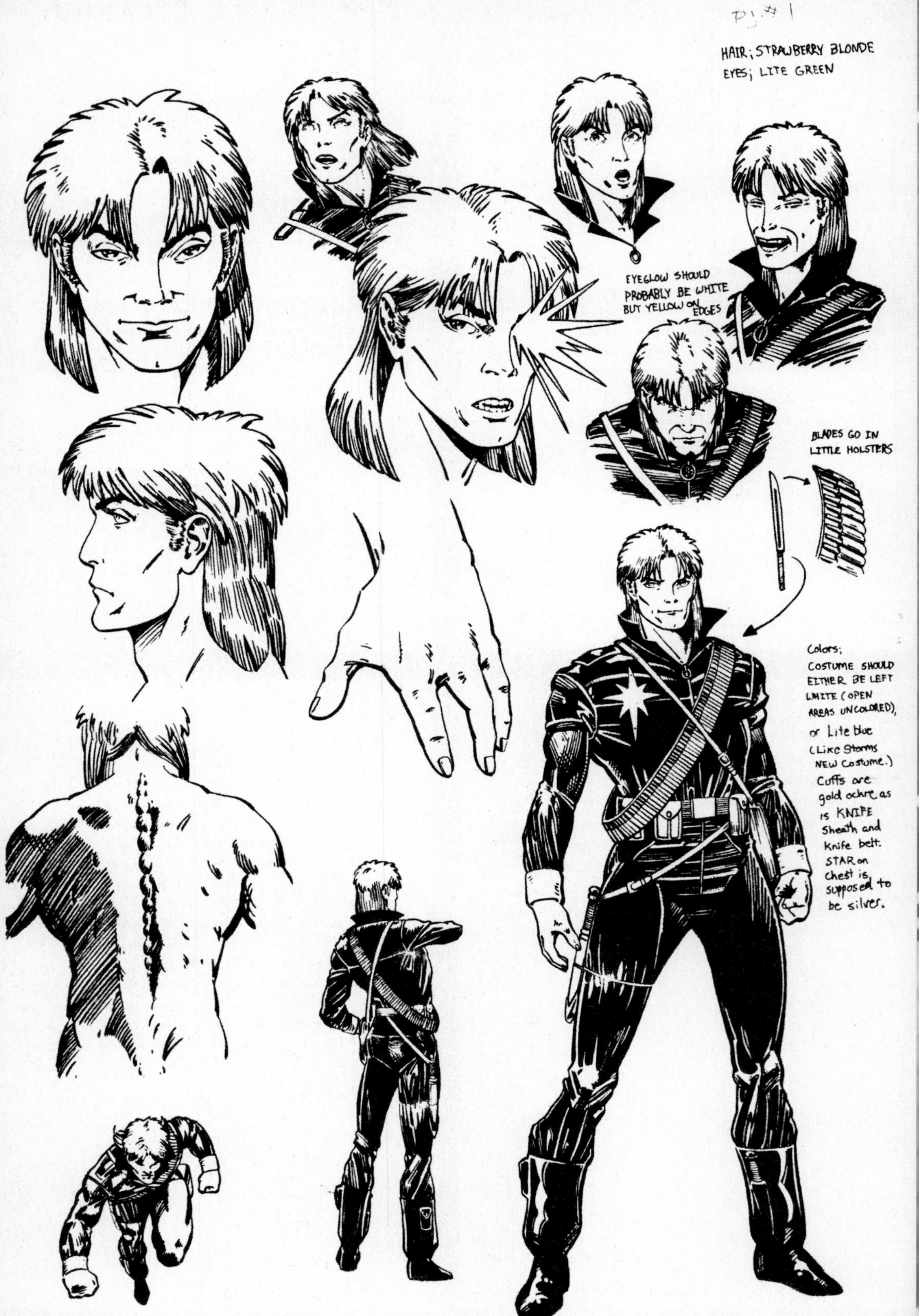
HAIR; STRAWBERRY BLONDE
EYES; LITE GREEN
EYEGLOW SHOULD PROBABLY BE WHITE BUT YELLOW ON EDGES
BLADES GO IN LITTLE HOLSTERS
Colors; COSTUME SHOULD EITHER BE LEFT WHITE (OPEN AREAS UNCOLORED), or Lite blue (Like Storms NEW Costume.) Cuffs are gold ochre as is KNIFE Sheath and Knife belt. STAR on chest is supposed to be silver.
ADAMS 6-83
"LONGSHOT" #1

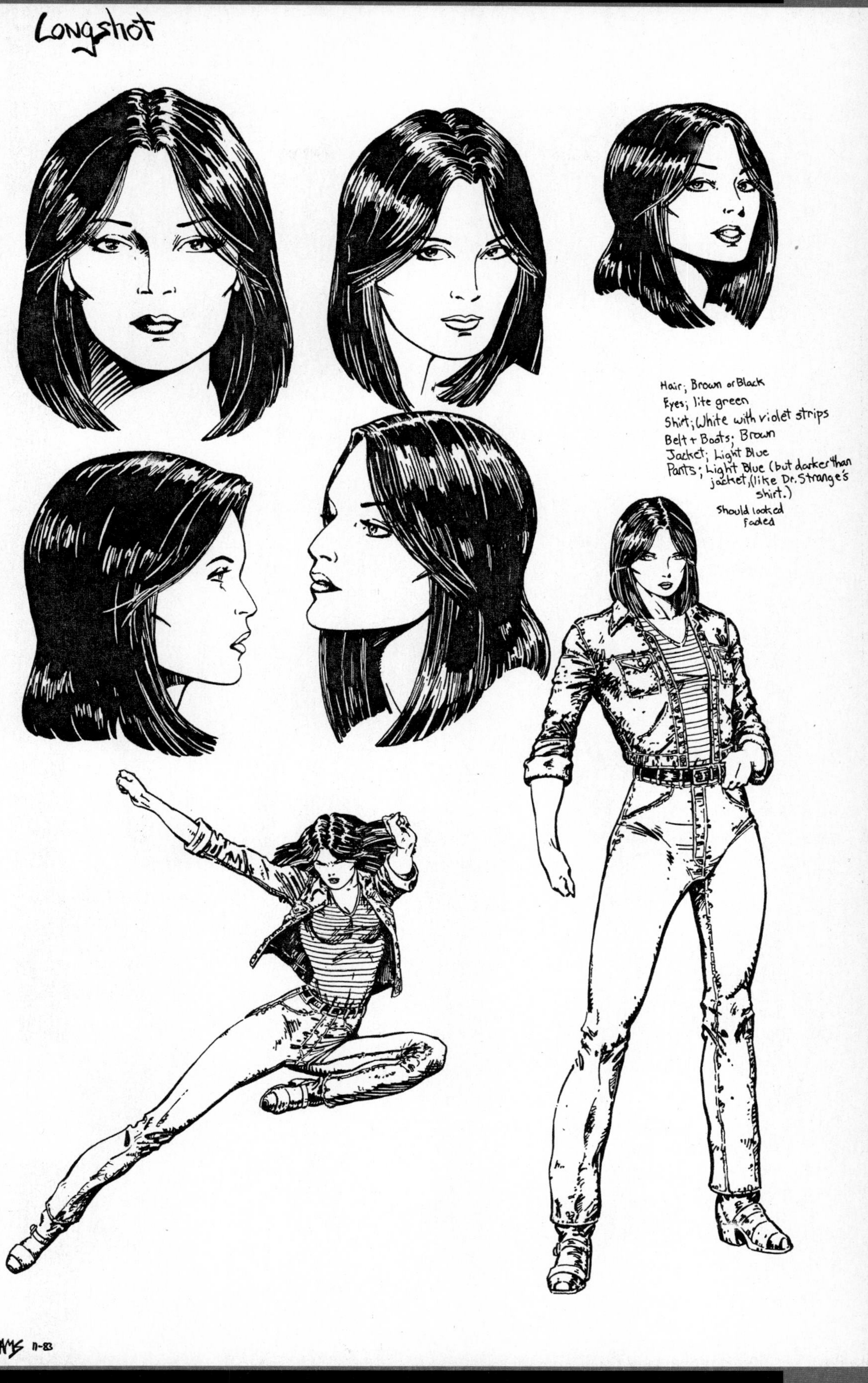
Longshot
Hair; Brown or Black
Eyes; lite green
Shirt; White with violet strips
Belt + Boots; Brown
Jacket; Light Blue
Pants; Light Blue (but darker than jacket, (like Dr. Strange's shirt.)
Should looked faded
ADAMS 11-83

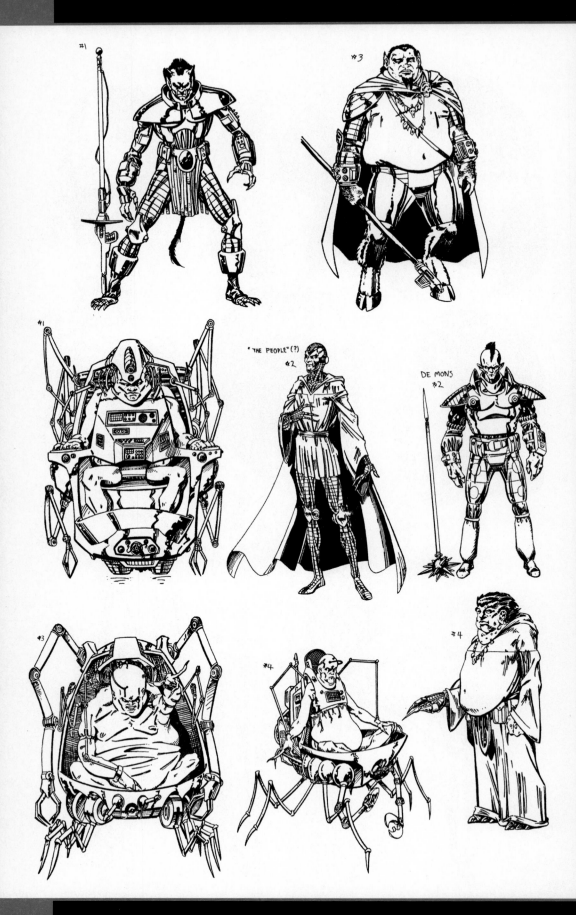

#1

#3

#1

"THE PEOPLE" (?)
#2

DE MONS
#2

#3

#4

#4

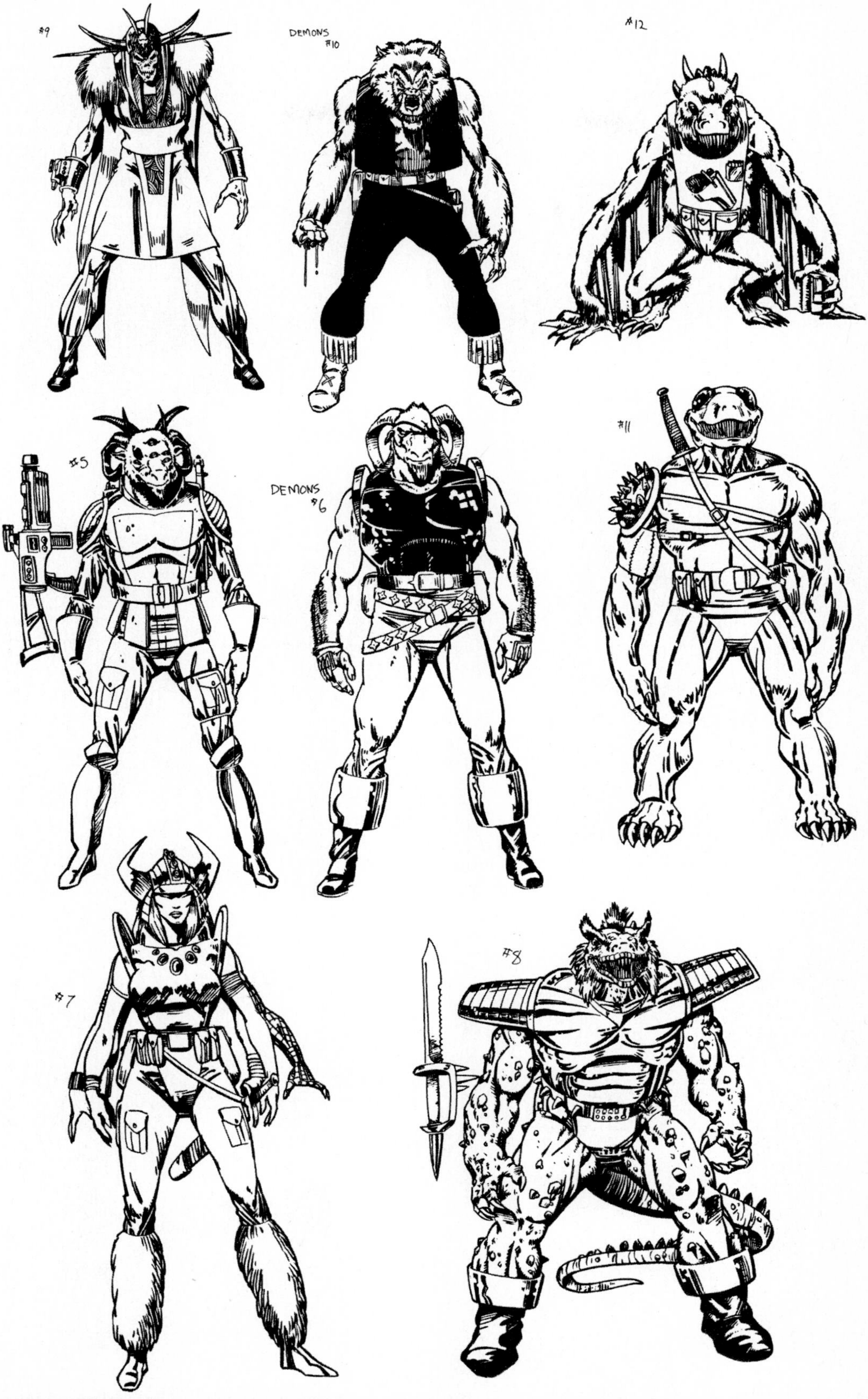
#9
DEMONS #10
#12
#5
DEMONS #6
#11
#7
#8

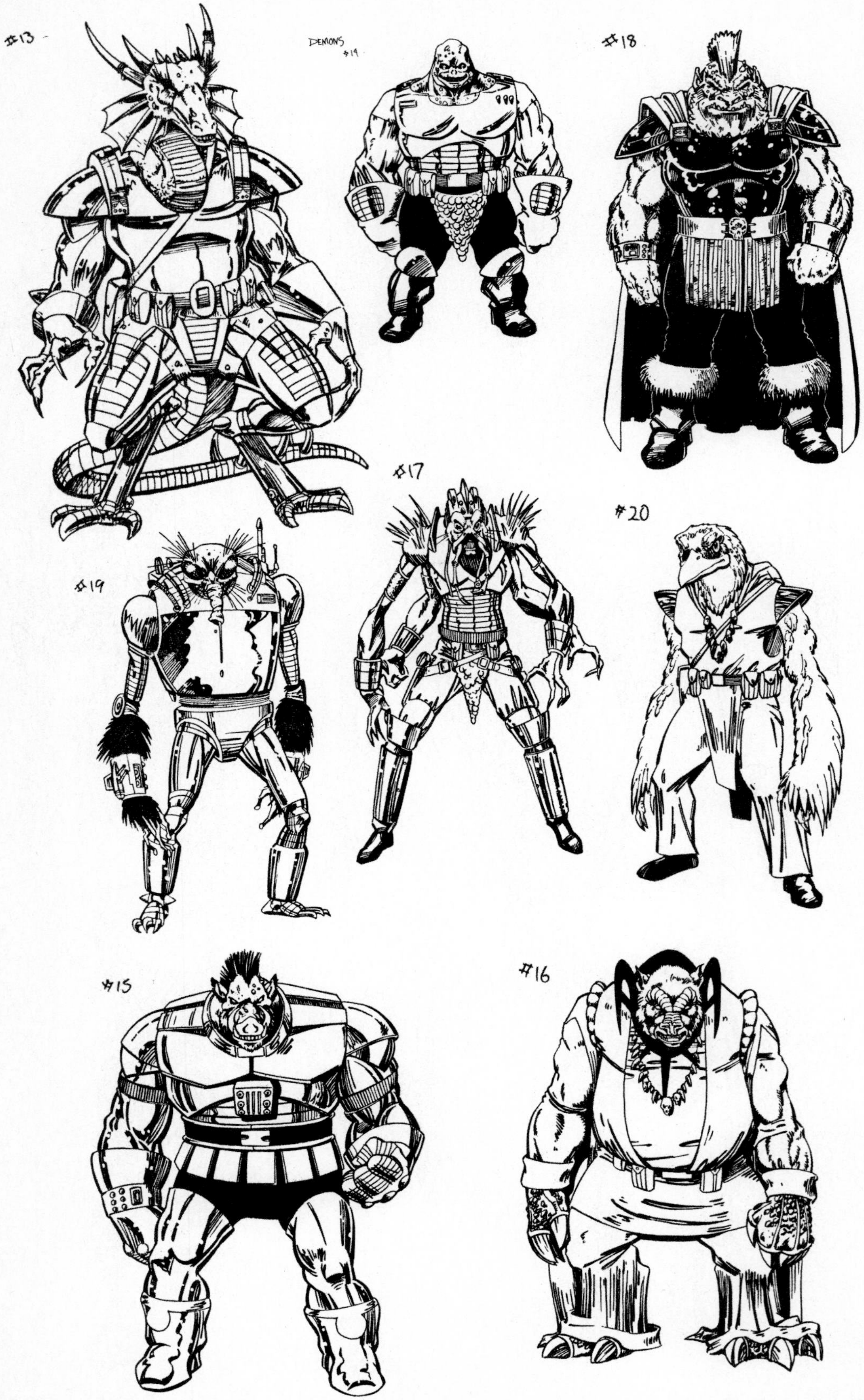
#13
DEMONS
#14
#18
#17
#20
#19
#15
#16

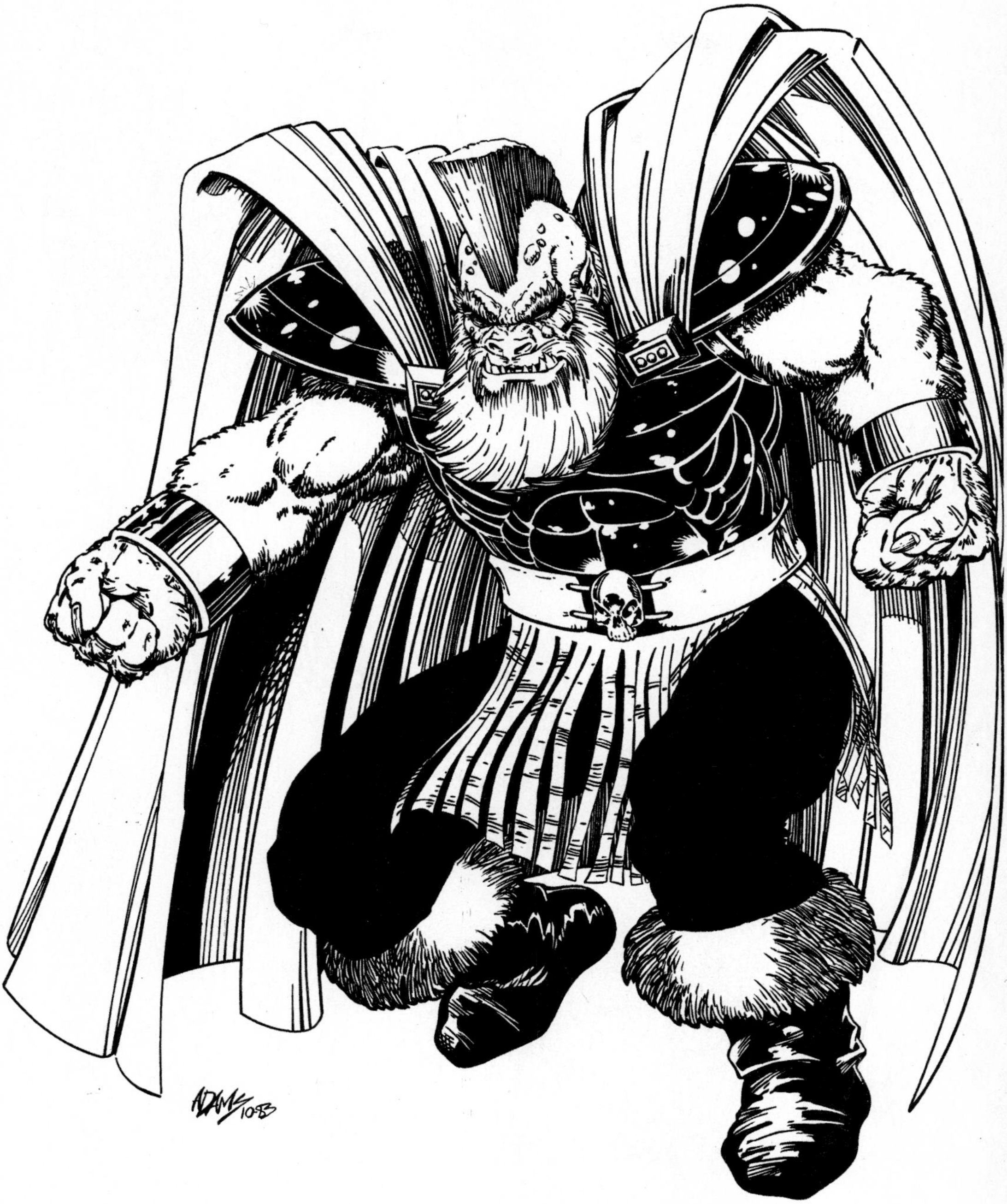
ADAMS 10-83

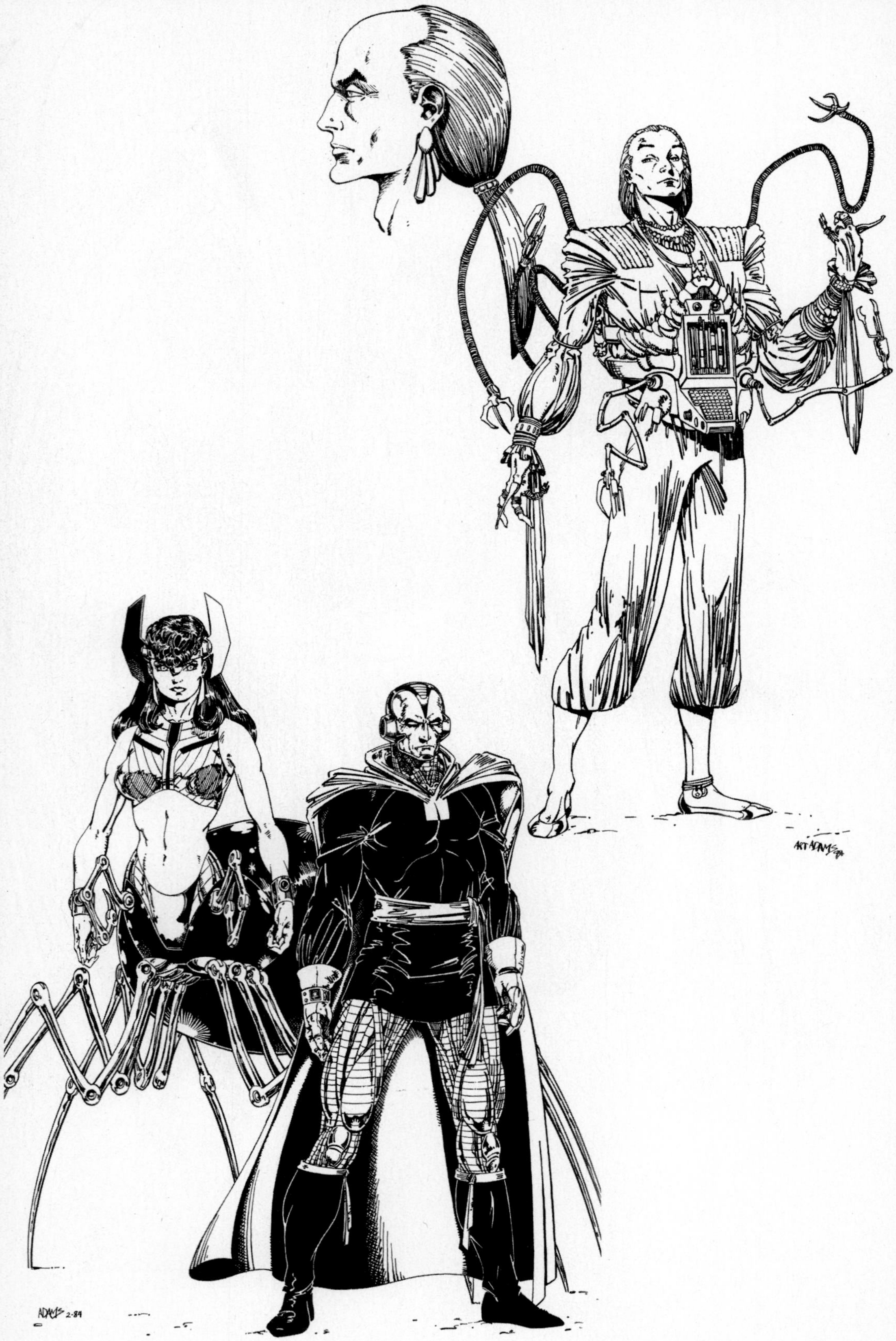
ART ADAMS '84
ADAMS 2-84

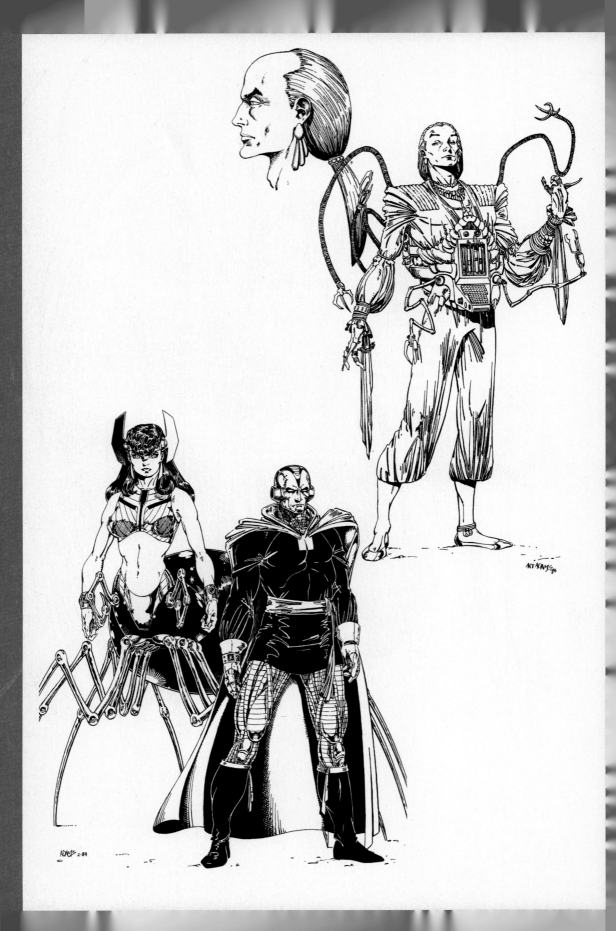

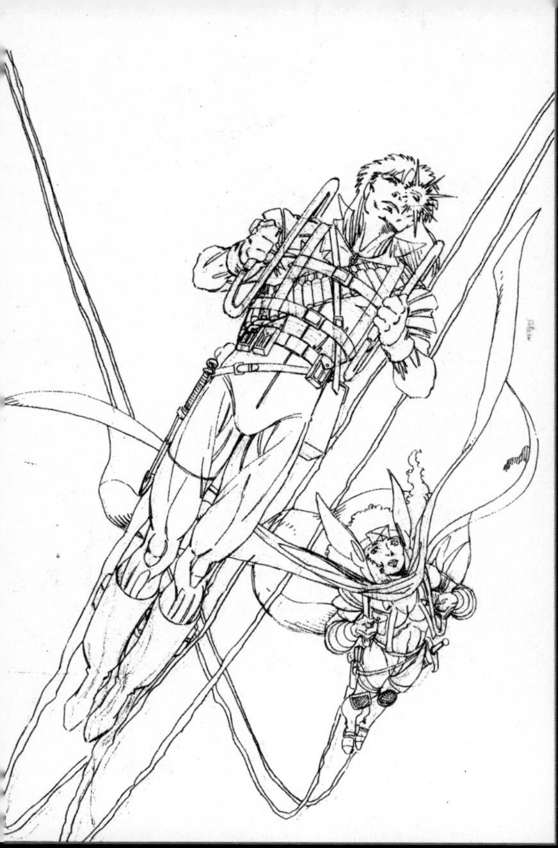

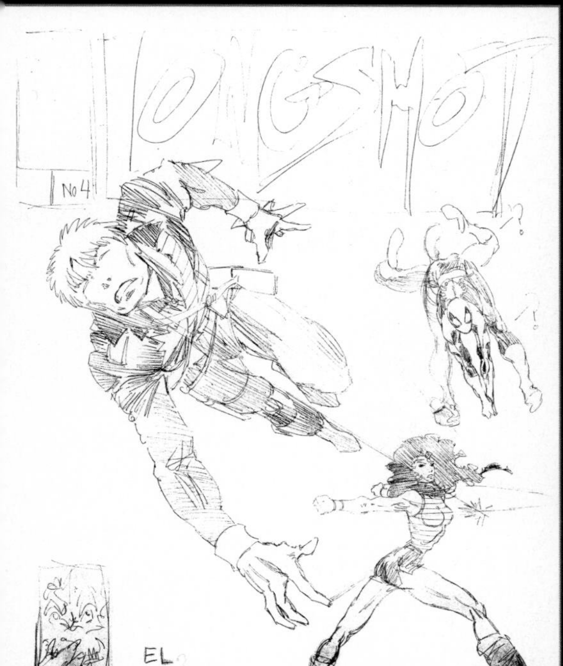
LONGSHOT
No 4
EL COVERO

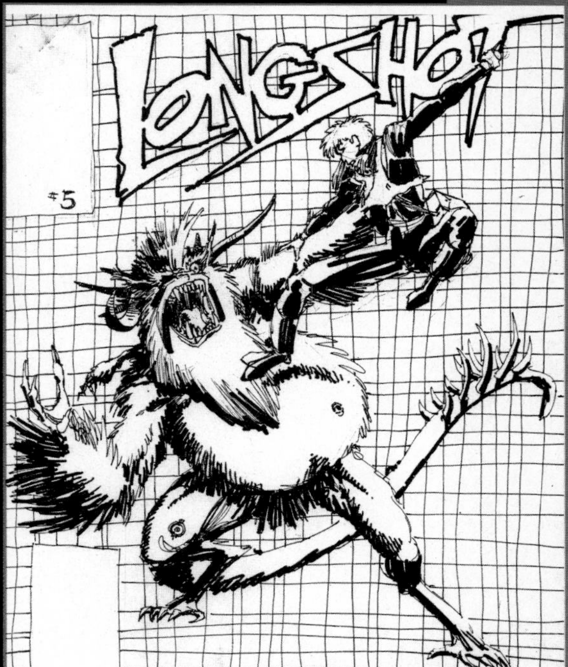
LONGSHOT
#5

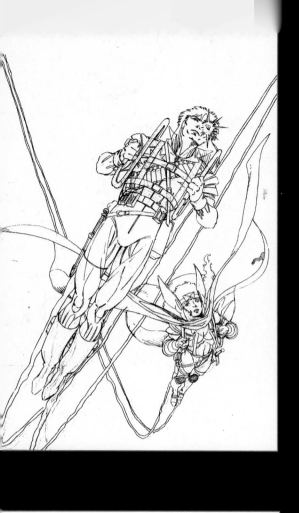

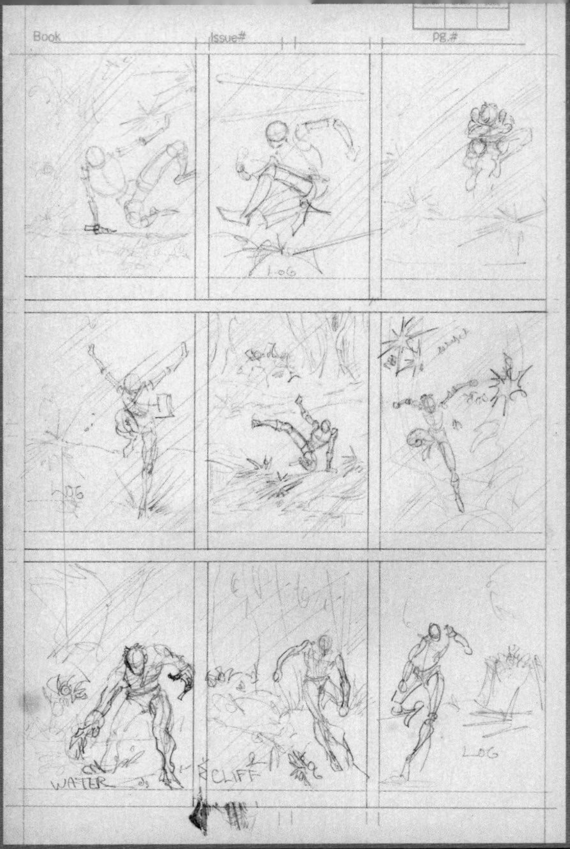
Book
Issue#
pg.#
WATER
CLIFF
LOG

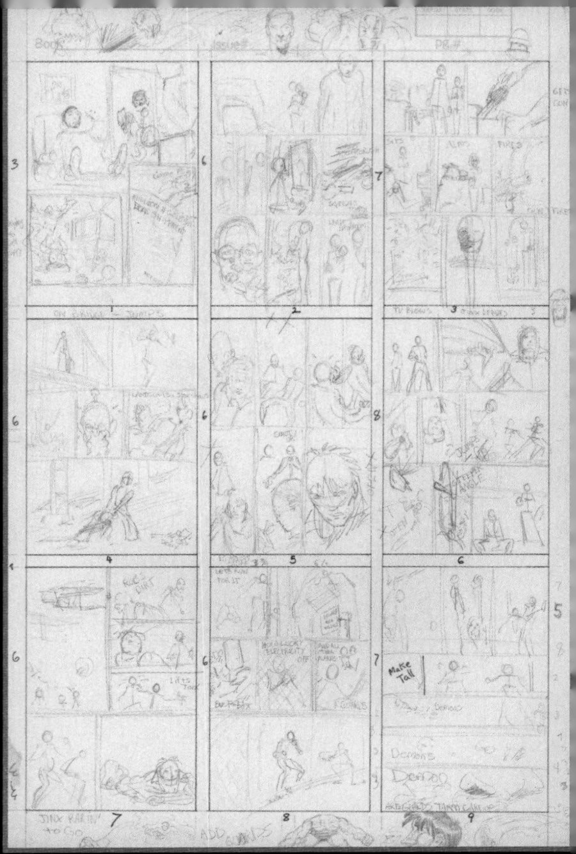
Book
Issue#
pg.#
Make Tall

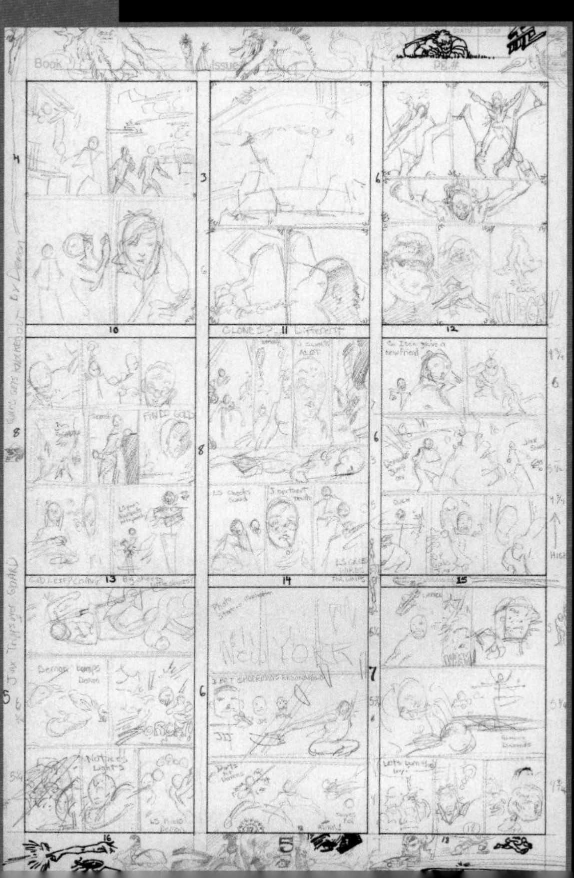
Book
Issue#
pg.#
NEW YORK

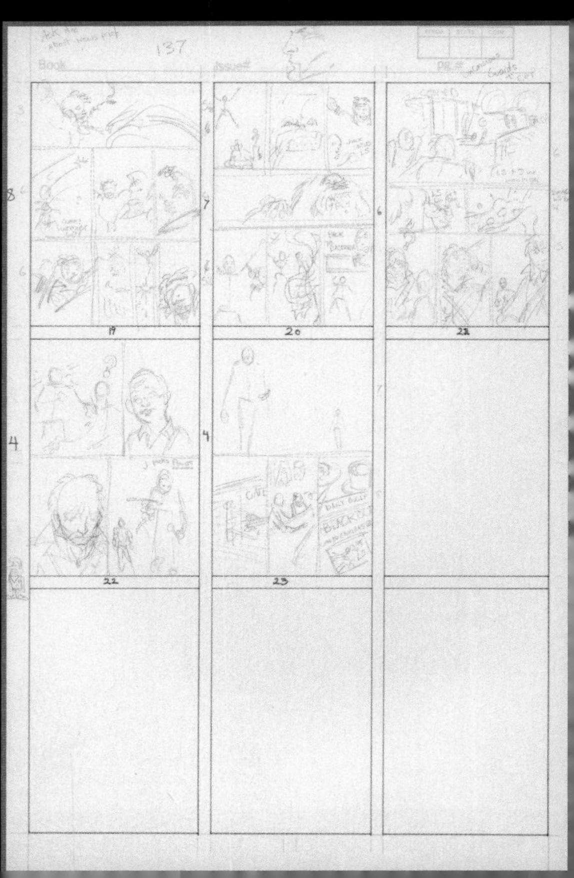
137
Book
Issue#
pg.#

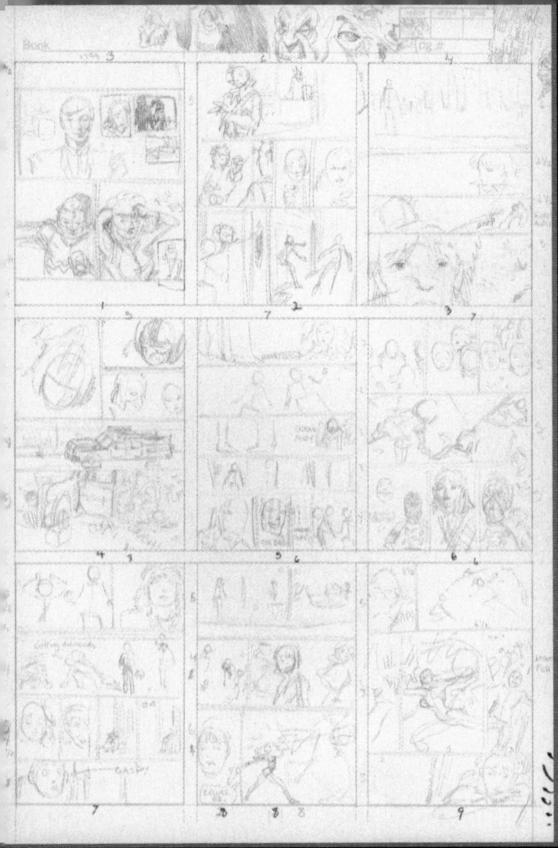
Book
GASP!
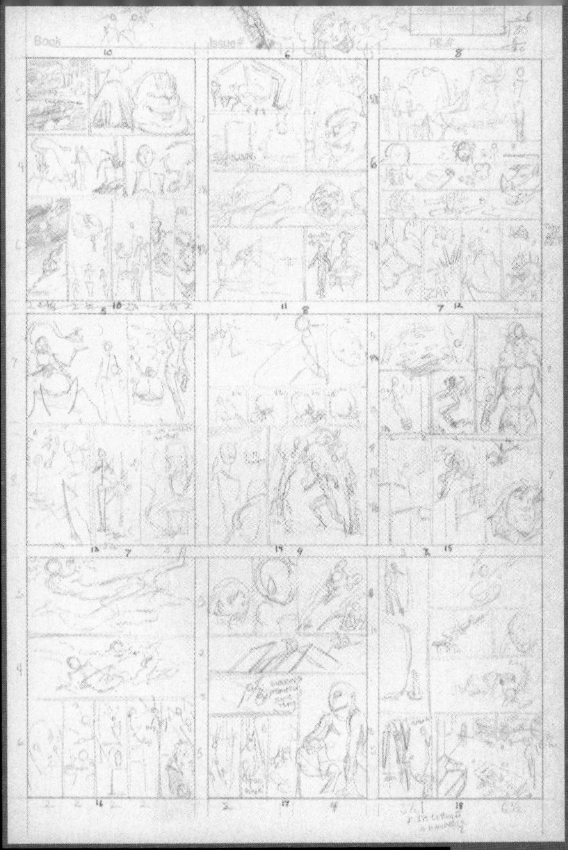
Book
Issue#
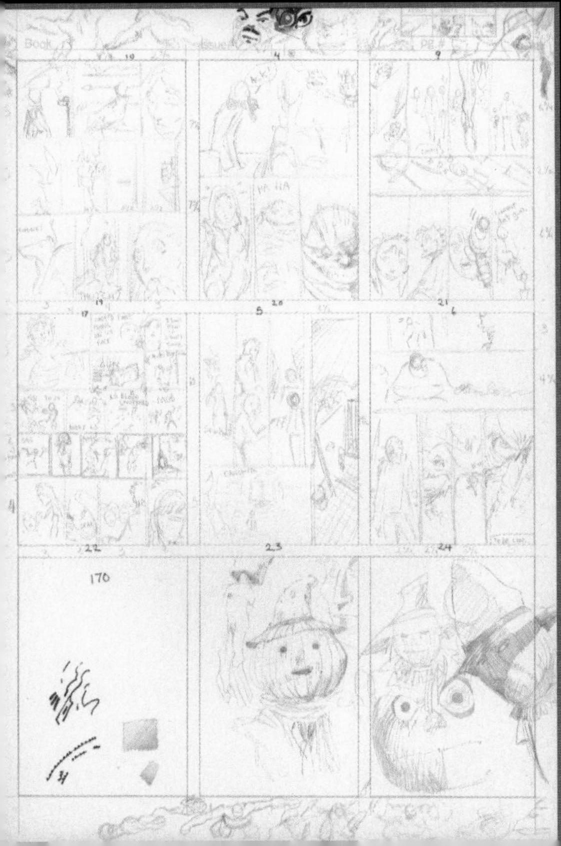
Book
Issue#
HA HA
170
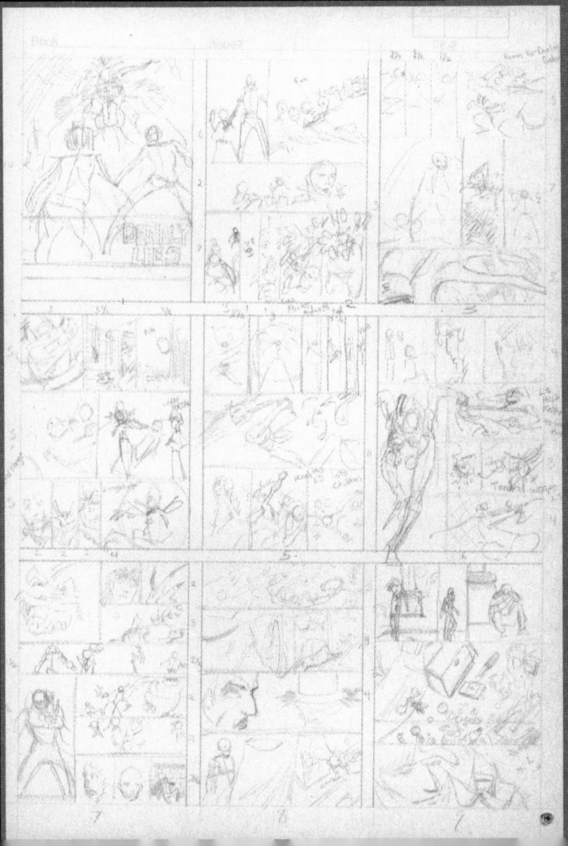
DAILY
LIES

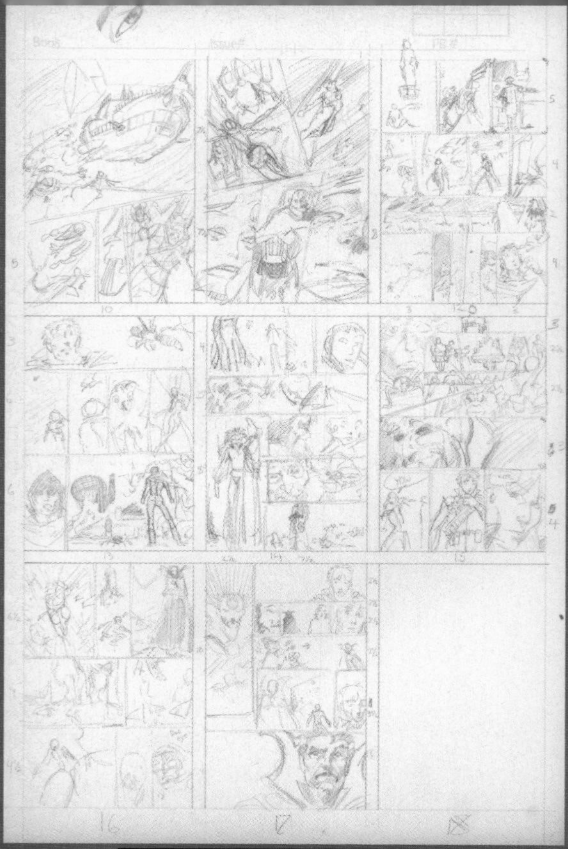

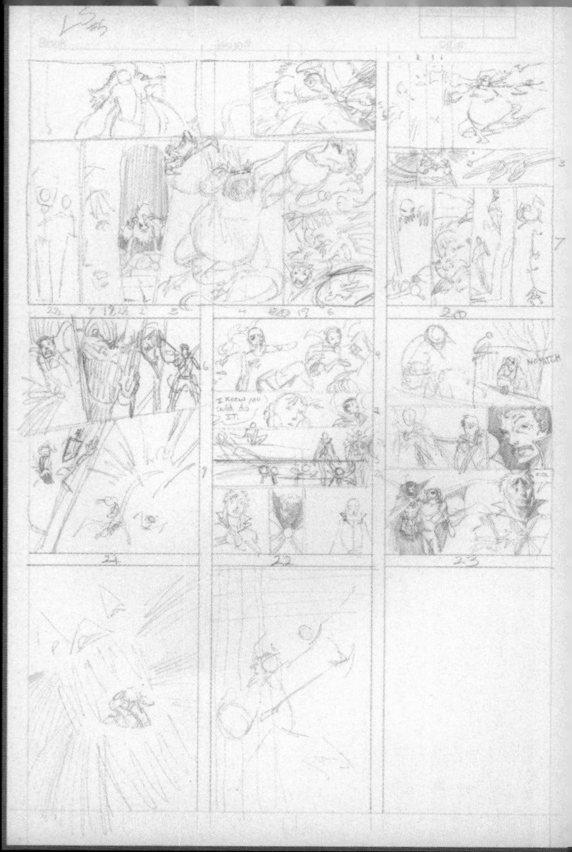

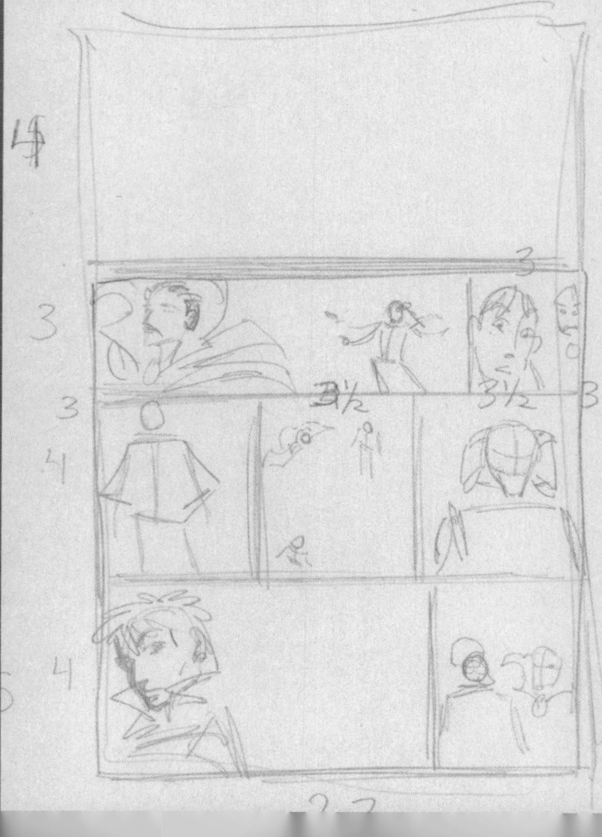

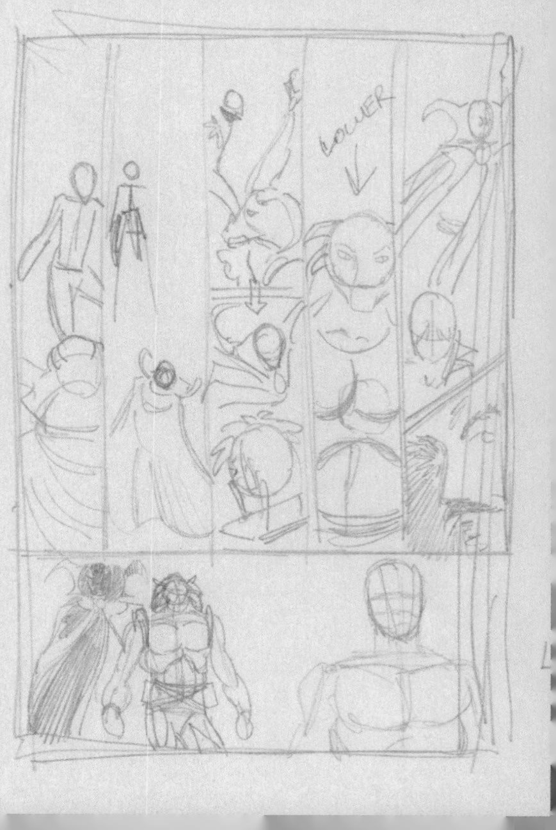
LOWER

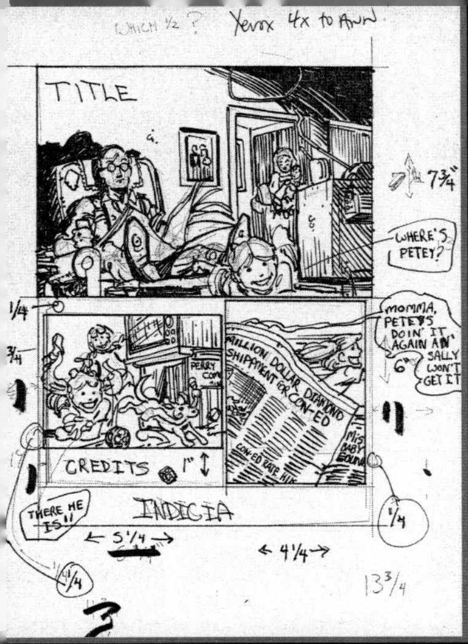
WHICH 1/2 ? Xerox 4x to Awn
TITLE
7 3/4
WHERE'S PETEY?
MOMMA, PETEY'S DOIN' IT AGAIN AN' SALLY WON'T GET IT!
MILLION DOLLAR DIAMOND SHIPMENT CON-ED
CREDITS
INDICIA
THERE HE IS!!
5 1/4
4 1/4
13 3/4

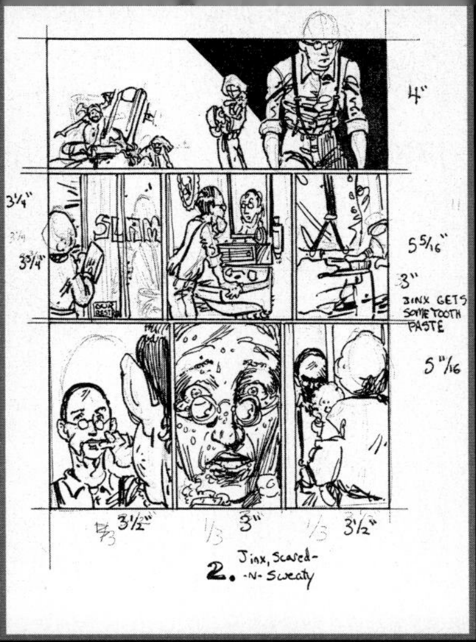
4"
SLAM
5 5/16"
3"
JINX GETS SOME TOOTH PASTE
5 11/16
3 1/2"
3"
3 1/2"
2. Jinx, Scared-N-Sweaty

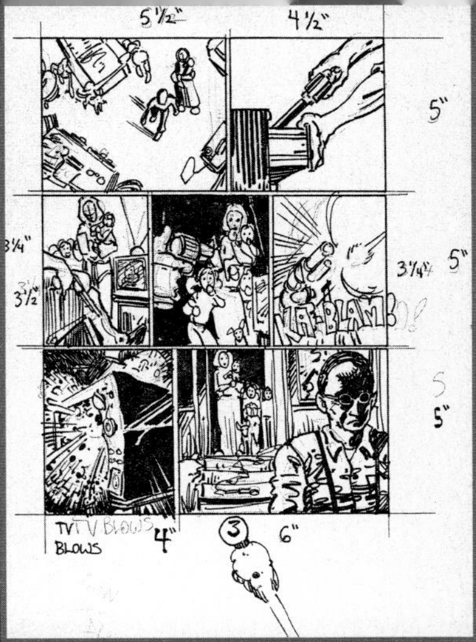
5 1/2"
4 1/2"
5"
KA-BLAM!
5"
5"
TV BLOWS
4"
3
6"

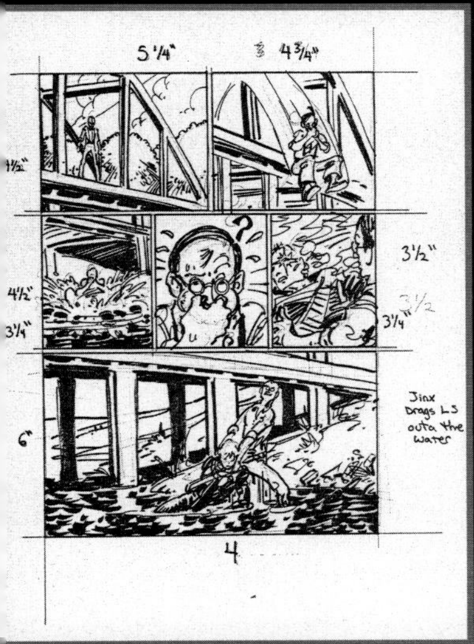
5 1/4"
4 3/4"
3 1/2"
Jinx Drags LS outa the water
6"
4

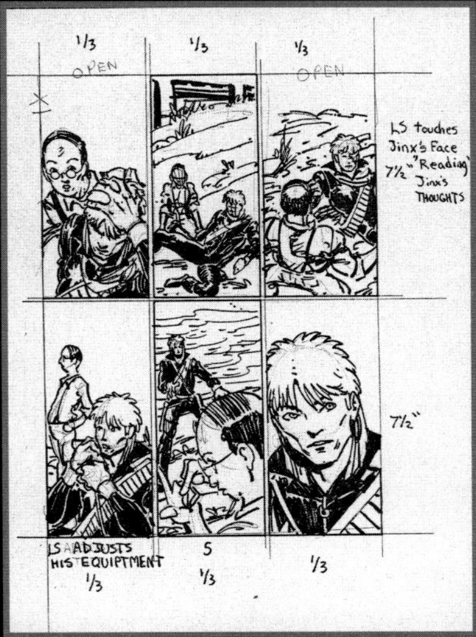
1/3
1/3
1/3
OPEN
OPEN
LS touches Jinx's Face
7 1/2" "Reading" Jinx's THOUGHTS
7 1/2"
LS ADJUSTS HIS EQUIPTMENT
5
1/3
1/3
1/3

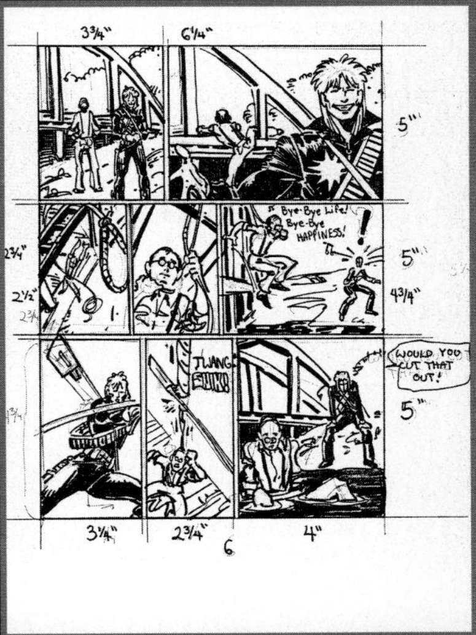
3 3/4"
6 1/4"
5"
"Bye-Bye Life! Bye-Bye HAPPINESS!
5"
4 3/4"
TWANG
WOULD YOU CUT THAT OUT!
5"
3 1/4"
2 3/4"
6
4"

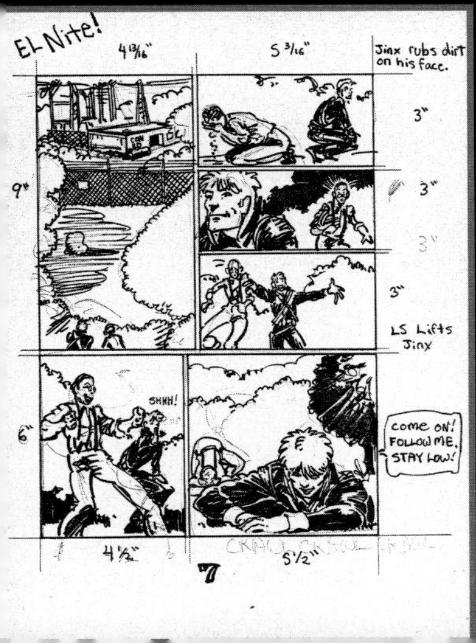
El-Nite!
4 13/16"
5 3/16"
Jinx rubs dirt on his face.
3"
9"
3"
3"
LS Lifts Jinx
SHHH!
6"
come on! FOLLOW ME. STAY LOW!
4 1/2"
7
5 1/2"

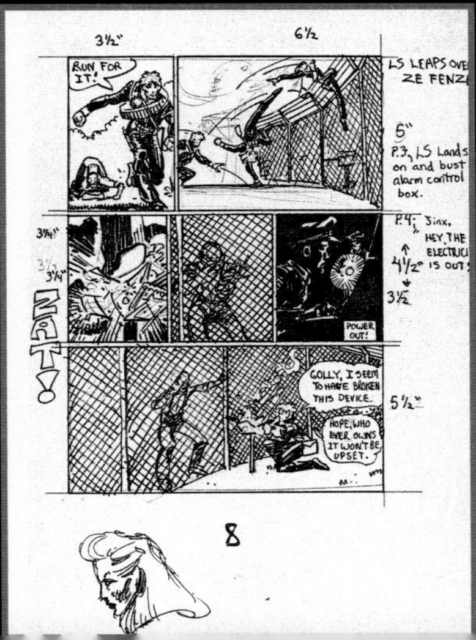
3 1/2"
6 1/2
RUN FOR IT!
LS LEAPS OVER ZE FENZE
5"
P.3, LS Lands on and bust alarm control box.
P.4, Jinx, HEY, THE ELECTRIC IS OUT
4 1/2"
ZOT!
POWER OUT!
GOLLY, I SEEM TO HAVE BROKEN THIS DEVICE.
HOPE WHO EVER OWNS IT WON'T BE UPSET.
5 1/2"
8

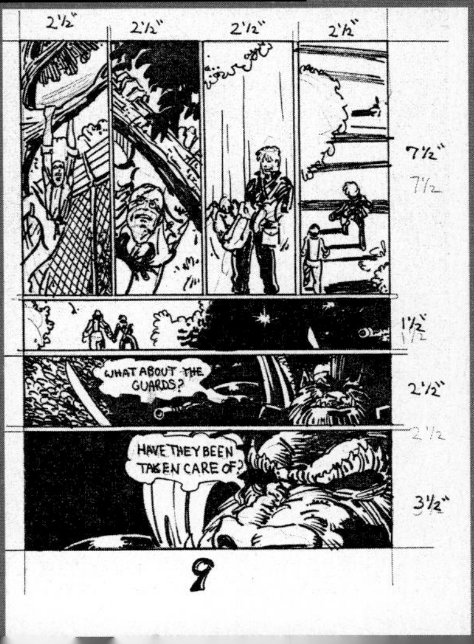
2 1/2"
2 1/2"
2 1/2"
2 1/2"
7 1/2"
1 1/2"
WHAT ABOUT THE GUARDS?
2 1/2"
HAVE THEY BEEN TAKEN CARE OF?
3 1/2"
9

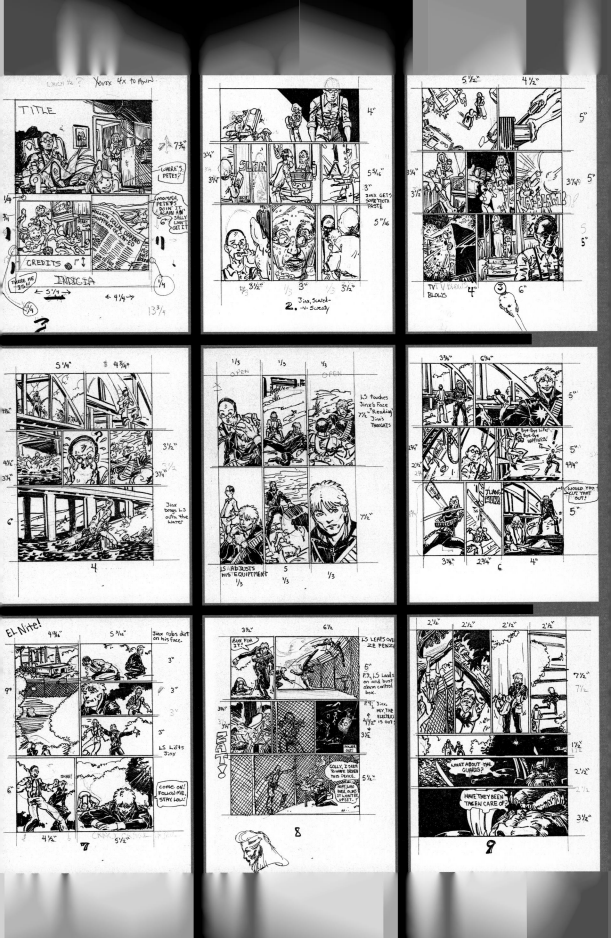

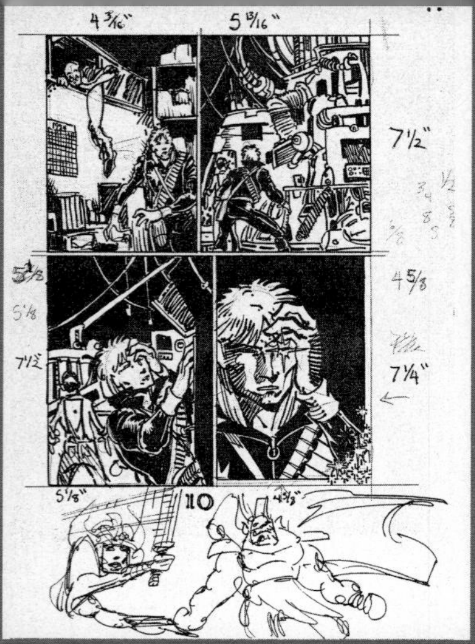
10

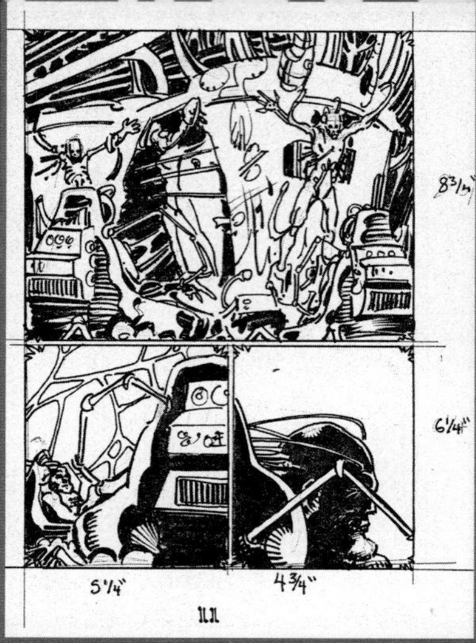
11

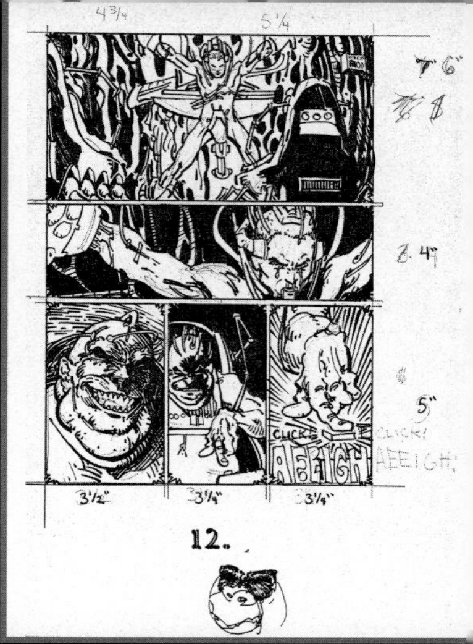
CLICK!
AEEIGH!
12.

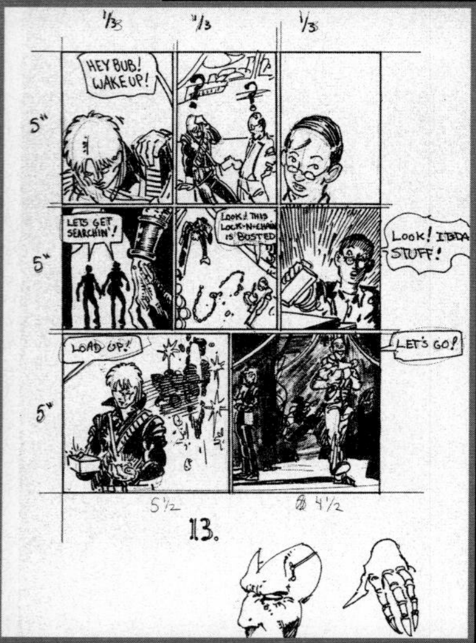
HEY BUB! WAKE UP!
LET'S GET SEARCHIN'!
LOOK! THIS LOCK-N-CHAIN IS BUSTED
LOOK! IBDA STUFF!
LOAD UP!
LET'S GO!
13.

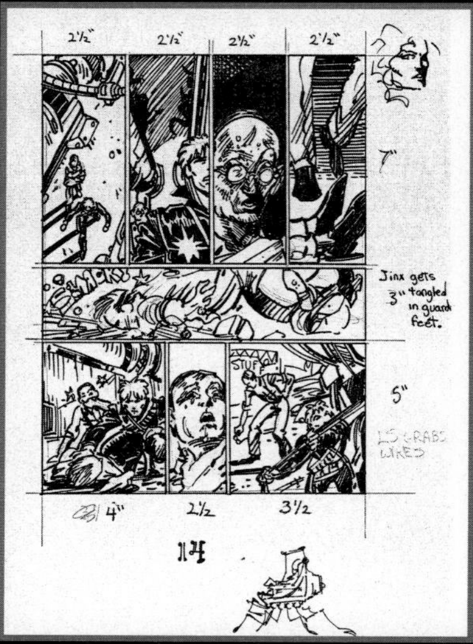
Jinx gets tangled in guard feet.
LS GRABS WIRES
14

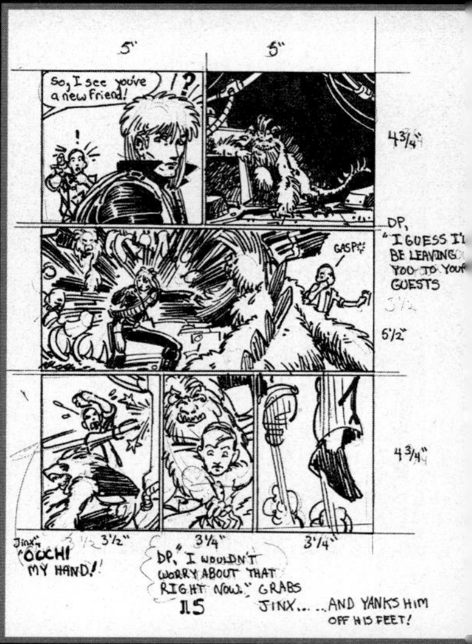
So, I see you've a new friend!
DP, "I GUESS I'LL BE LEAVING YOU TO YOUR GUESTS"
GASP!
Jinx: "OUCH! MY HAND!"
DP, "I WOULDN'T WORRY ABOUT THAT RIGHT NOW." GRABS JINX... AND YANKS HIM OFF HIS FEET!
15

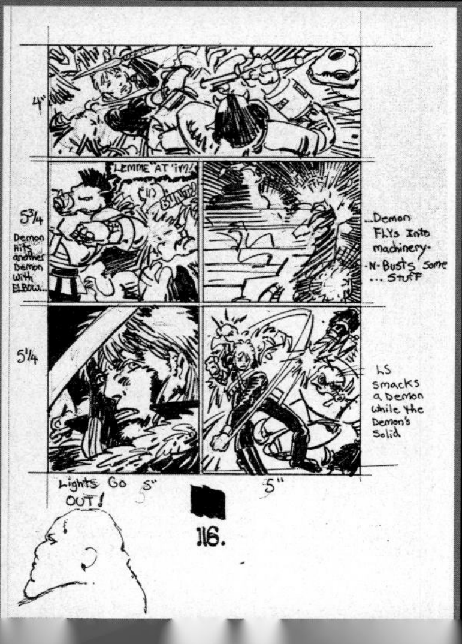
LEMME AT 'IM!
Demon hits another Demon with ELBOW...
...Demon FLYS into machinery-N-Busts some ... STUFF
LS smacks a Demon while the Demon's Solid
Lights Go OUT!
16.

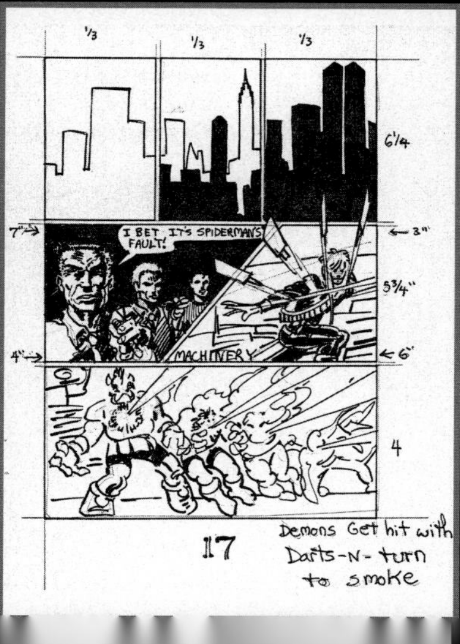
I BET IT'S SPIDERMAN'S FAULT!
MACHINERY
17
Demons Get hit with Darts-N-turn to smoke

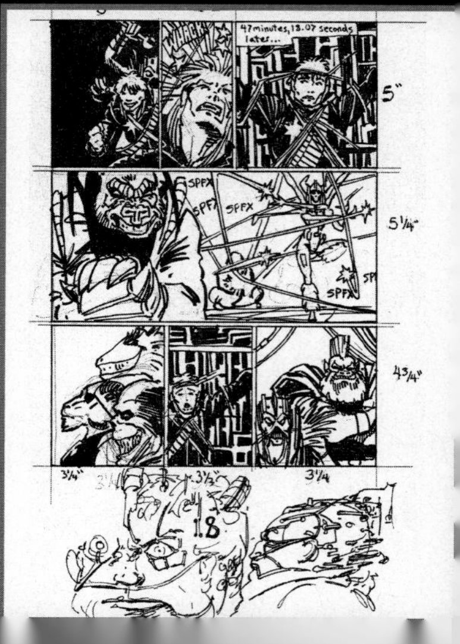
47 minutes, 13.07 seconds later...
SPFX
18

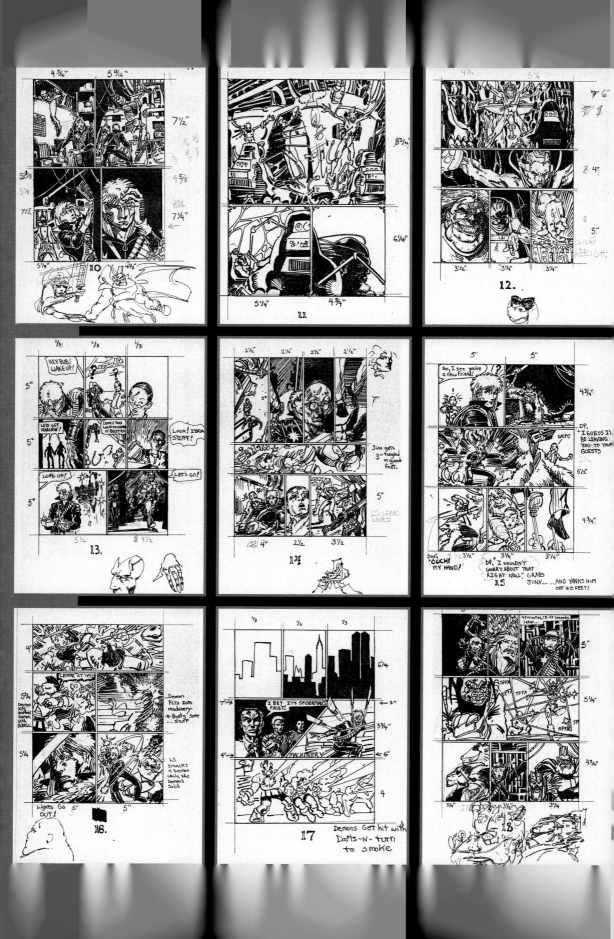

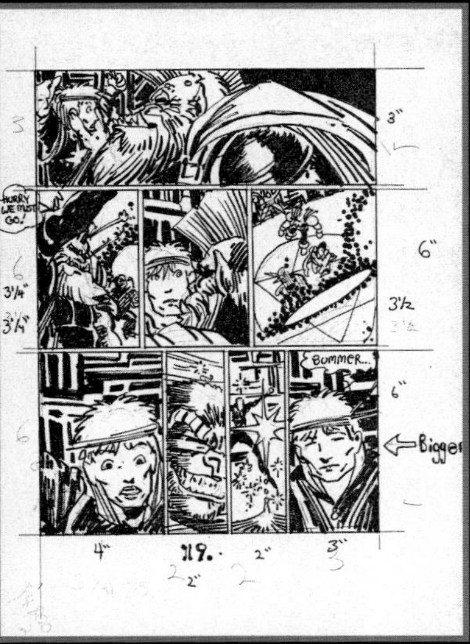
HURRY! WE MUST GO!
BUMMER...
3"
6"
3½
6"
Bigger
4"
2"
3"
19.

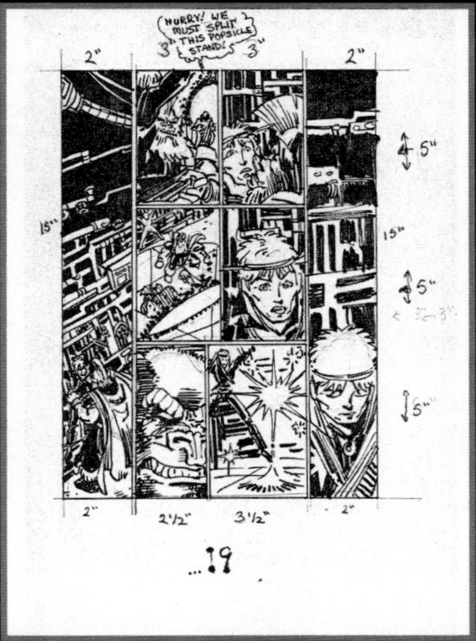
HURRY! WE MUST SPLIT THIS POPSICLE STAND!
2"
3"
3"
2"
5"
15"
5"
5"
2"
2½"
3½"
2"
19

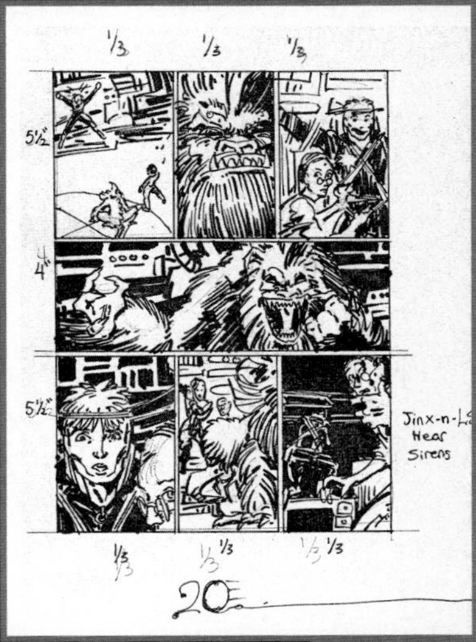
⅓
⅓
⅓
5½"
4"
5½"
Jinx-n-LS Hear Sirens
20

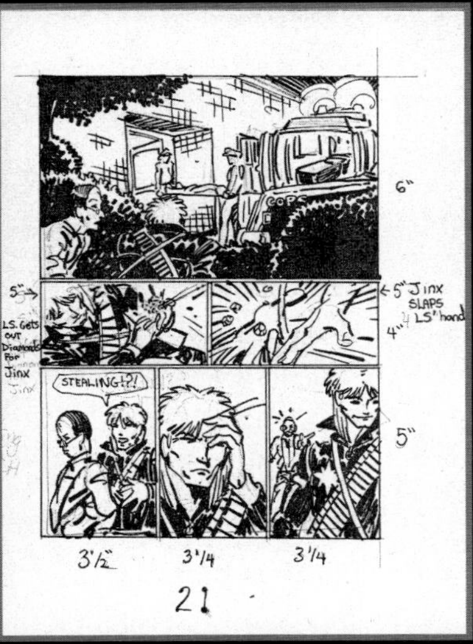
6"
5"
LS Gets out Diamonds For Jinx
Jinx SLAPS LS' hand
4"
STEALING!?!
5"
3½"
3¼
3¼
21

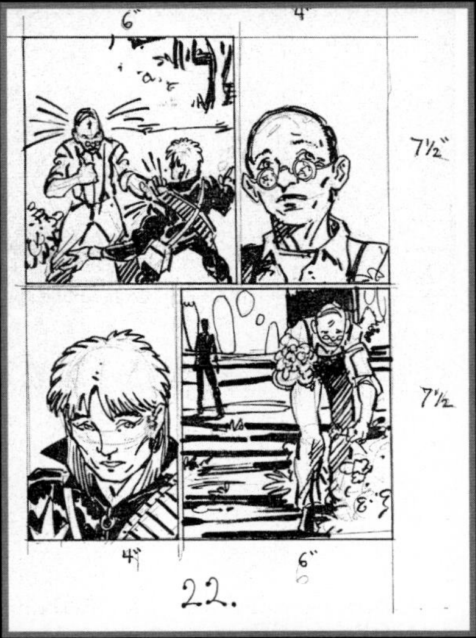
6"
4"
7½"
7½
4"
6"
22.

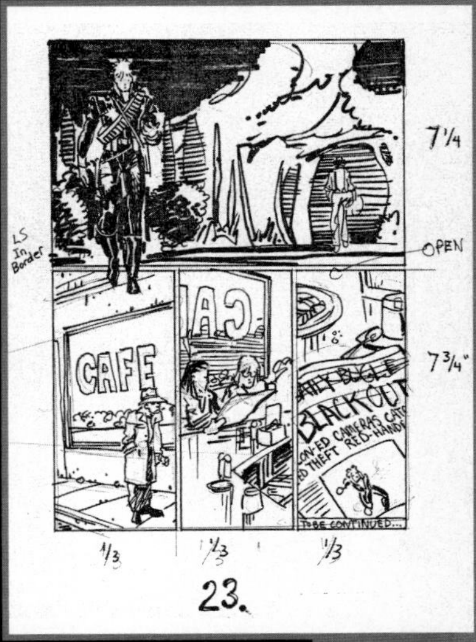
7¼
LS In Border
OPEN
7¾"
CAFE
BLACKOUT
TO BE CONTINUED...
⅓
⅓
⅓
23.

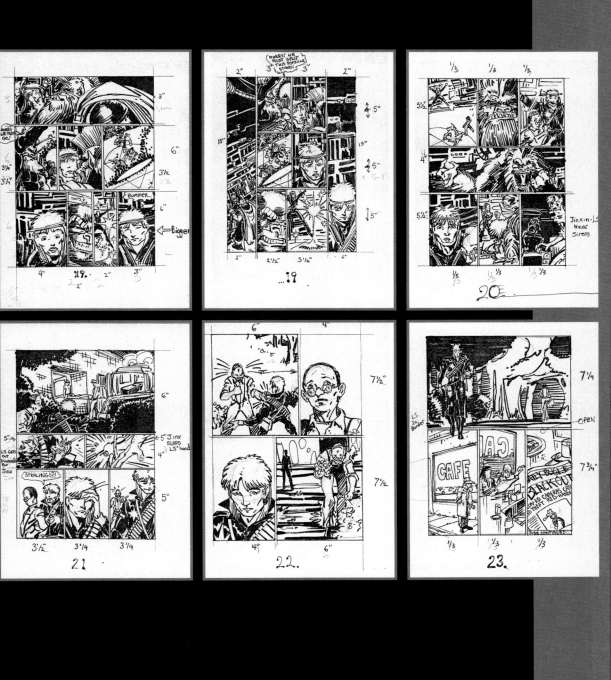

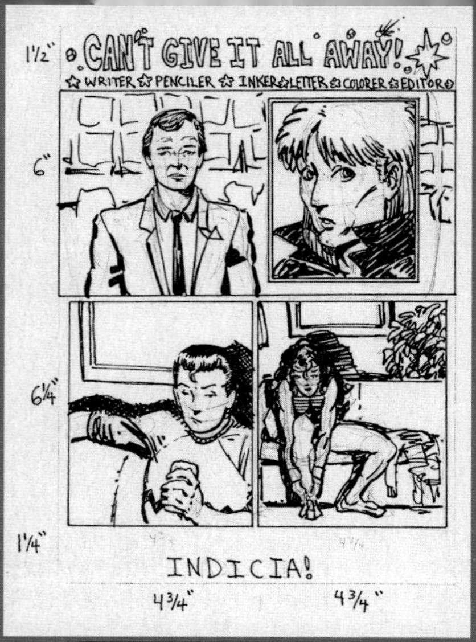
1½"
CAN'T GIVE IT ALL AWAY!
WRITER PENCILER INKER LETTER COLORER EDITOR
6"
6¼"
1¼"
INDICIA!
4¾"
4¾"

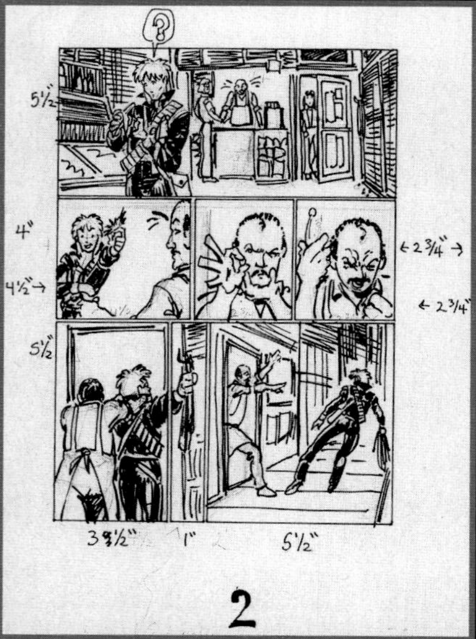
?
5½"
4"
4½"
← 2¾" →
← 2¾"
5½"
3½"
1"
5½"
2

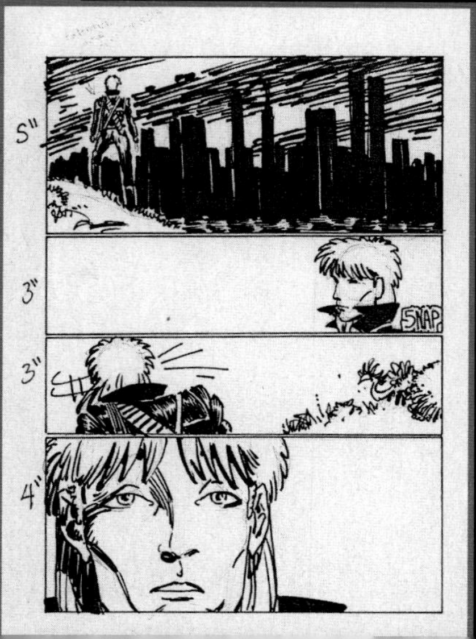
5"
3"
SNAP
3"
4"

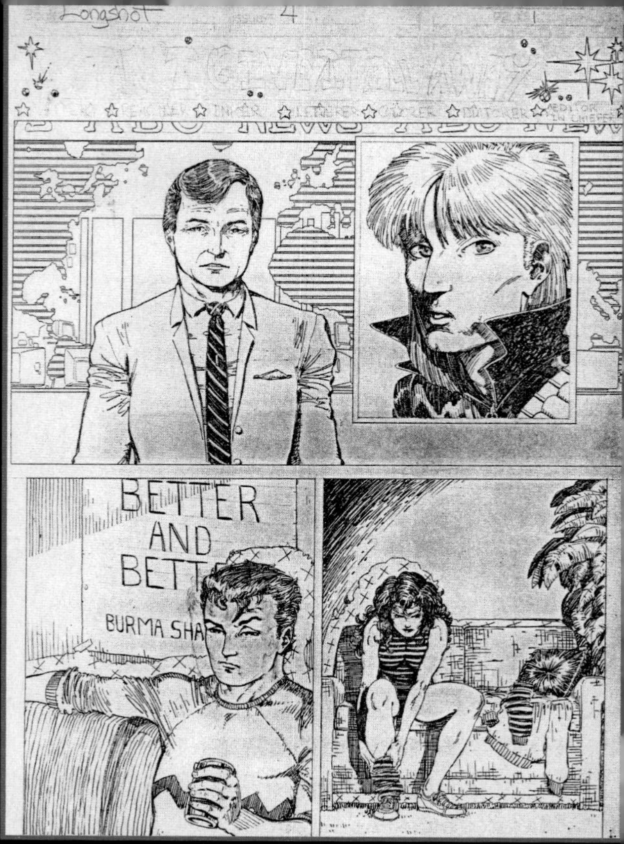
Longshot
4
BETTER AND BETT
BURMA SHA

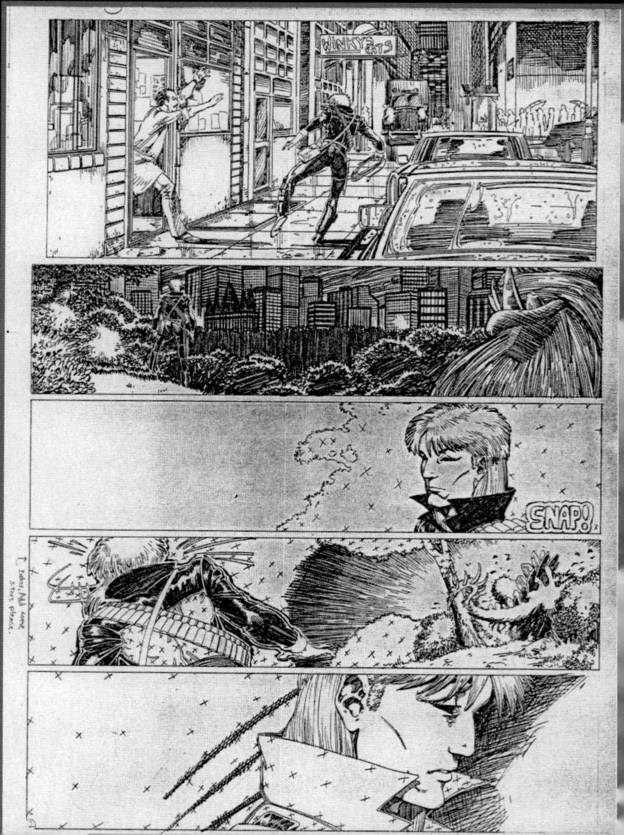
SNAP!

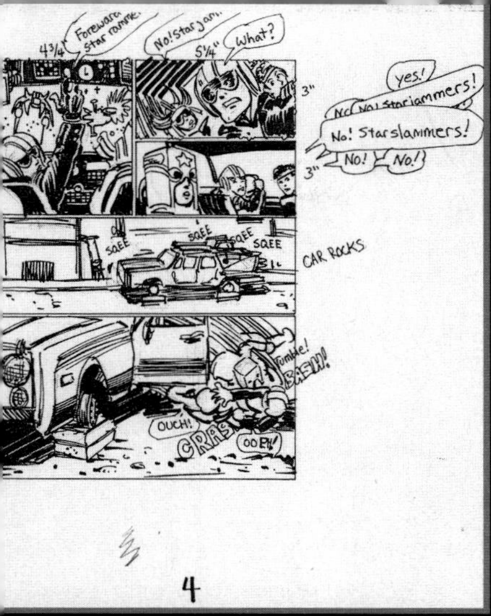
4¾"
Foreward star ramme.
No! Star jam.
5¼"
What?
3"
yes!
No No! Starjammers!
No! Starslammers!
No!
No!
3"
SQEE
SQEE
SQEE
SQEE
CAR ROCKS
Tumble!
OUCH!
CRASH
OOF!!
4

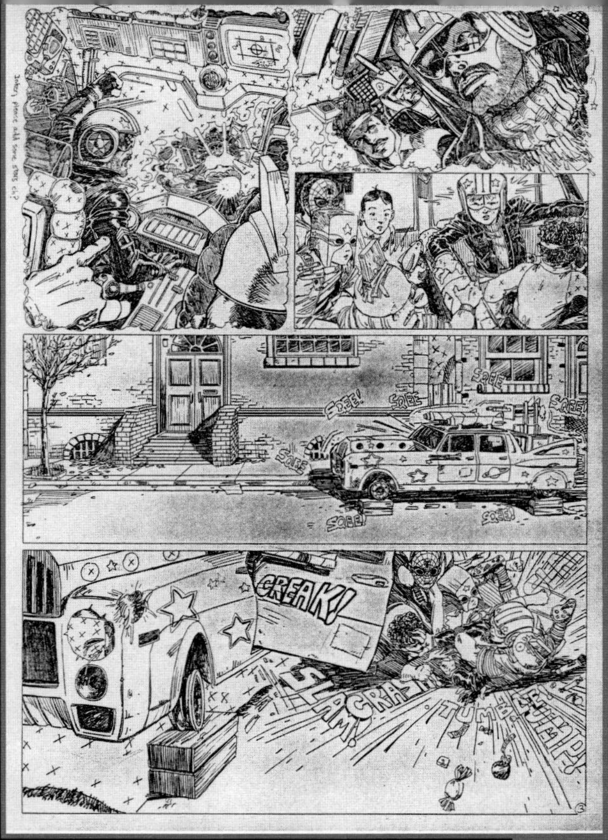
Inker, please add some stars eh?
SQEE!
SQEE
SQEE
SQEE!
CREAK!

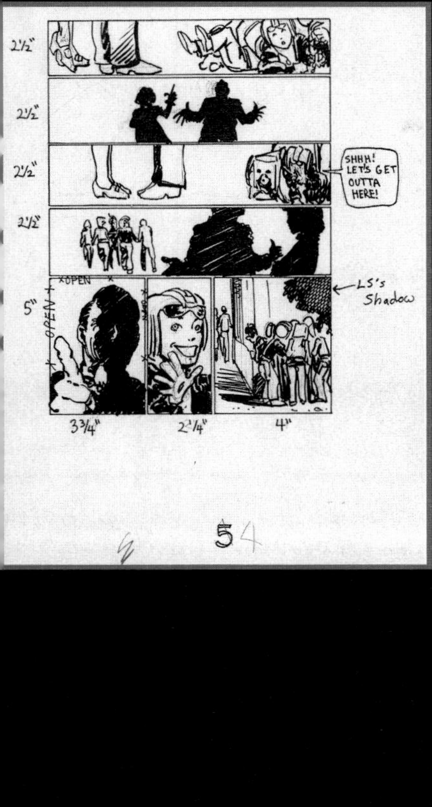
2½"
2½"
2½"
SHHH! LET'S GET OUTTA HERE!
2½"
OPEN
OPEN
5"
LS's Shadow
3¾"
2¼"
4"
54

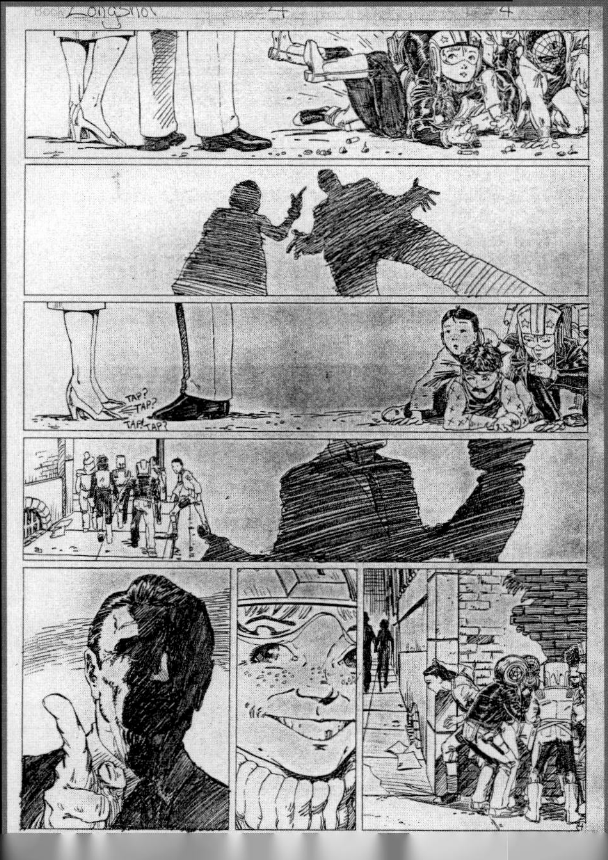
Longshot
4
4
TAP?
TAP?
TAP TAP?

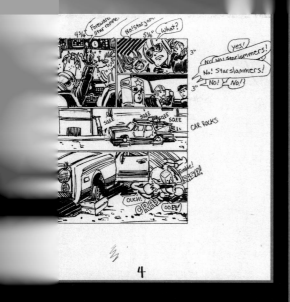

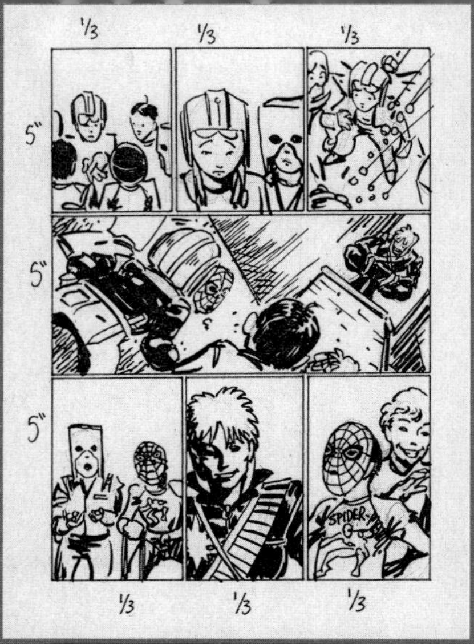
1/3 1/3 1/3
5"
5"
5"
SPIDER
1/3 1/3 1/3

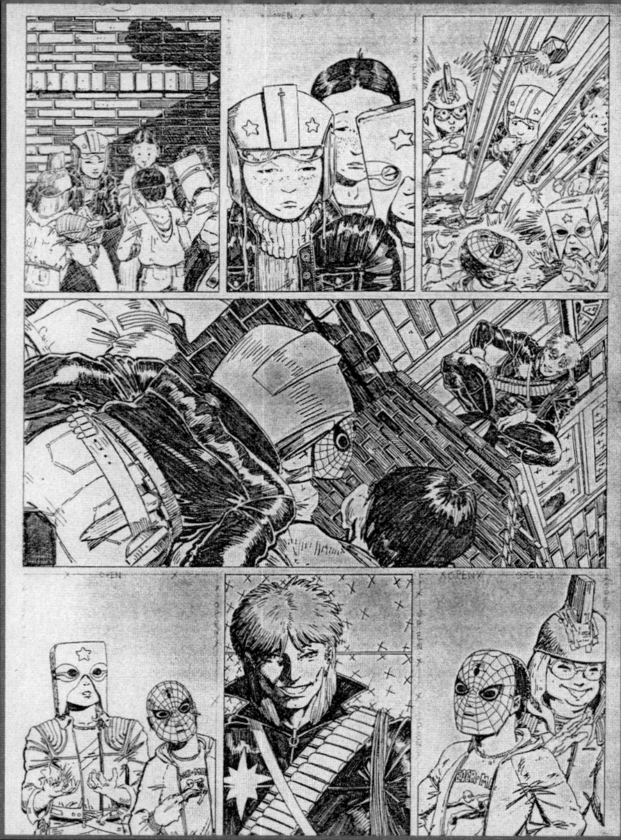

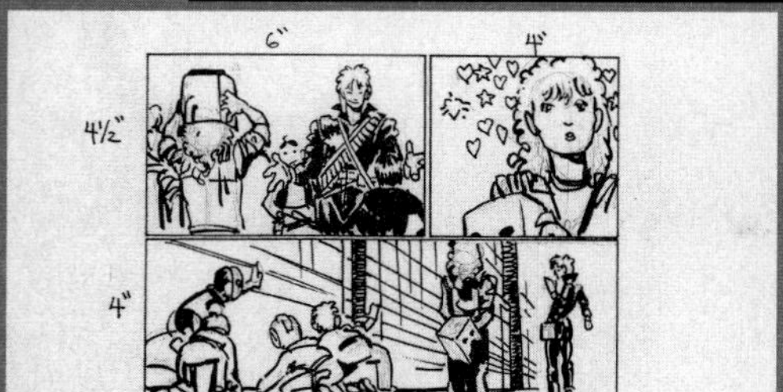
6"
4"
4½"
4"
4½"
GOG
EL STAT
←2½"→
←2½"→
←2½"→
← 2½" →
2"
7

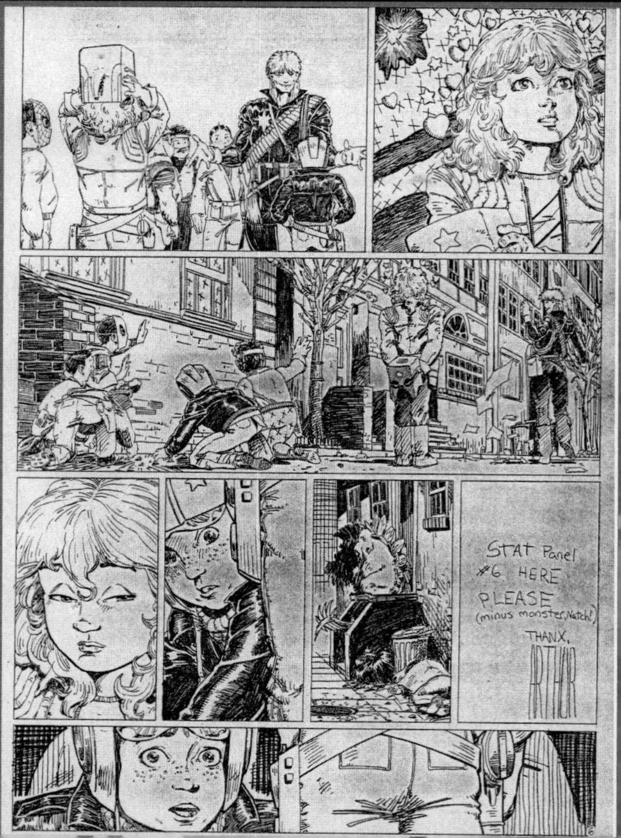
STAT Panel #6 HERE PLEASE
(minus monster, Natch!)
THANX,
ARTHUR

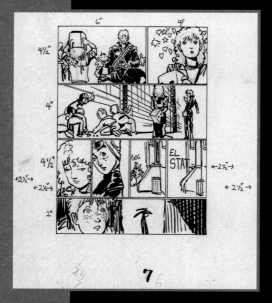

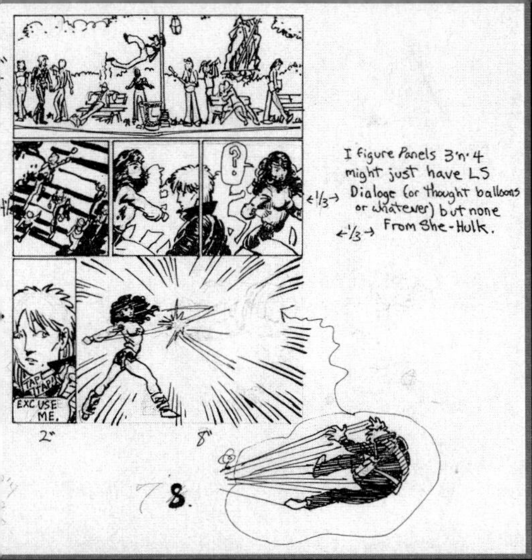
TAP! TAP!
EXCUSE ME.
2"
8"
←1/3→
←1/3→
I figure Panels 3'n' 4 might just have LS Dialoge (or thought balloons or whatever) but none From She-Hulk.
7 8.
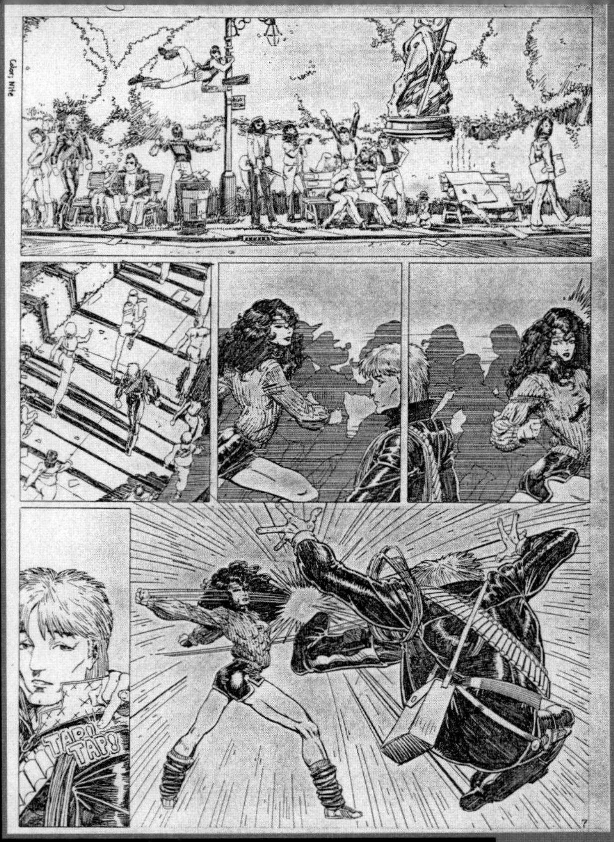
Colors: Nite
TAP! TAP!
7
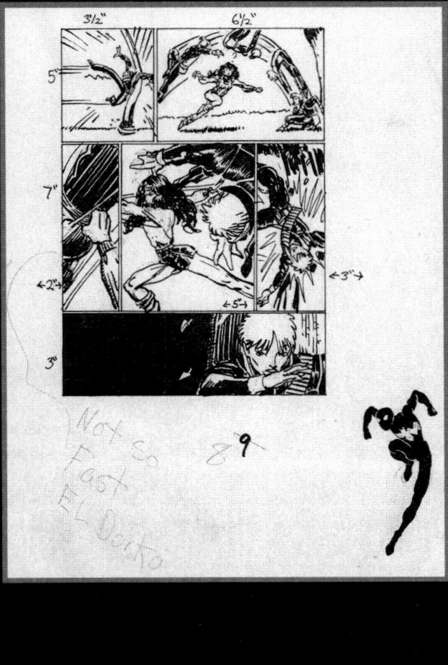
3½"
6½"
5"
7"
←2"→
←5→
←3"→
3"
Not so Fast El Dorko
8 9
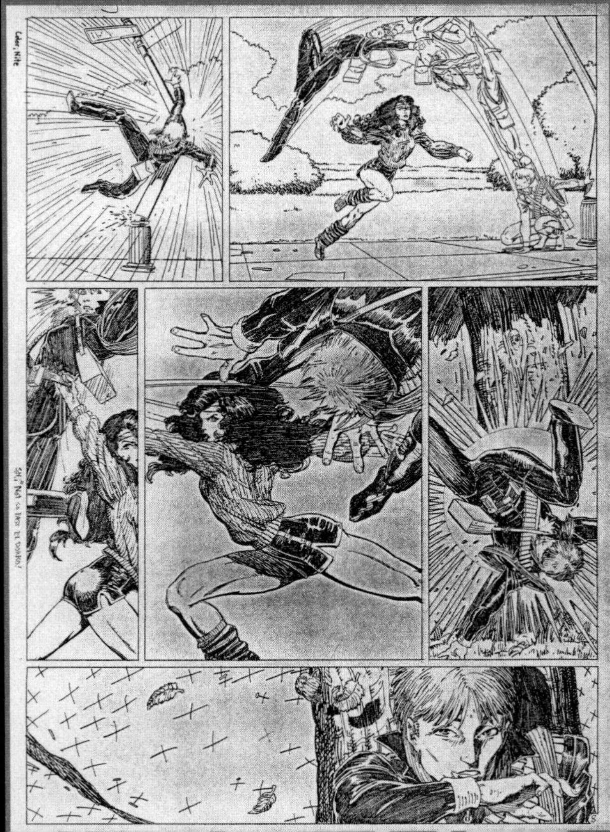
Colors: Nite
SH: "Not so fast El Dorko!"

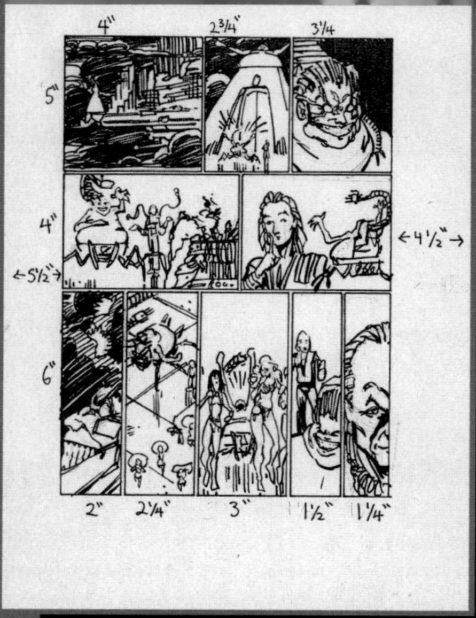
4"
2 3/4"
3 1/4
5"
4"
4 1/2"
5 1/2
6"
2"
2 1/4"
3"
1 1/2"
1 1/4"

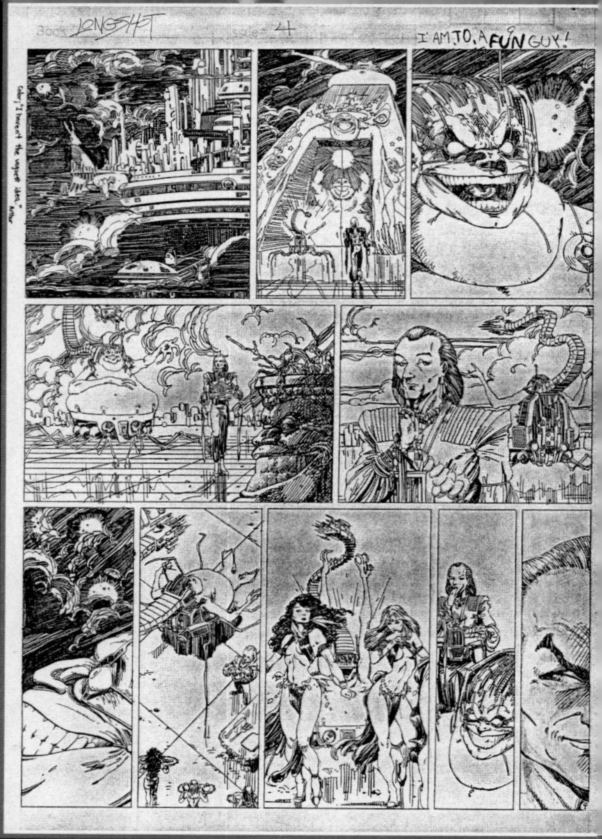
LONGSHOT
4
I AM JO, A FUN GUY!

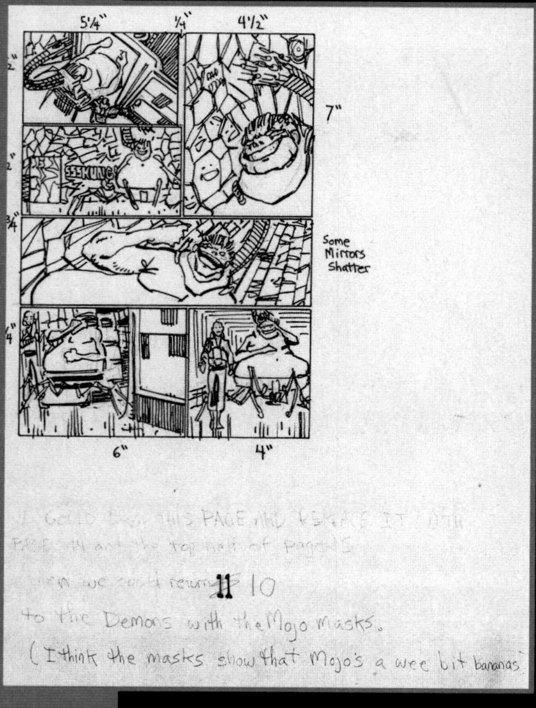
5 1/4"
1/4"
4 1/2"
7"
SSSKUNG!
Some Mirrors Shatter
6"
4"
11 10
to the Demons with the Mojo masks.
(I think the masks show that Mojo's a wee bit bananas

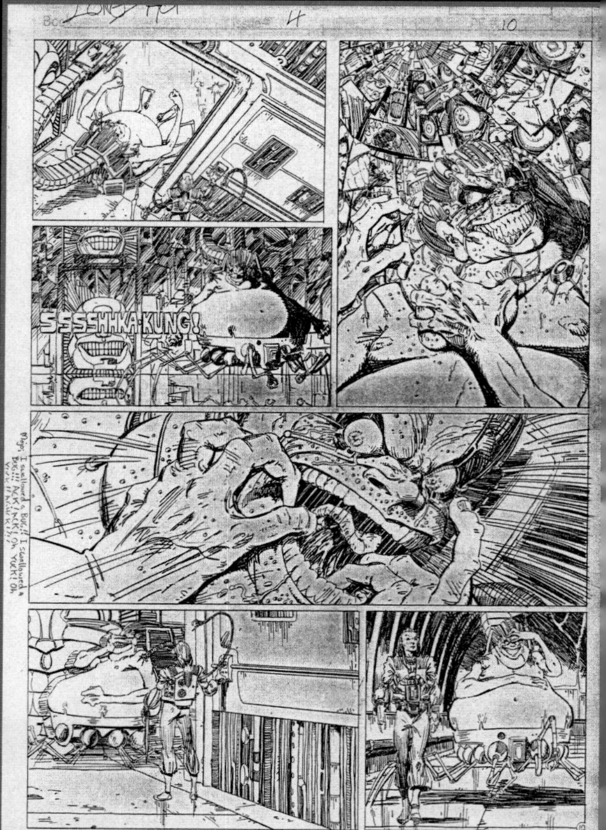
4
10
SSSSHHKA-KUNG!
Mojo: I swallowed a BUG!! I swallowed a BUG!!! ACK! ACK! Oh YUCK! Oh

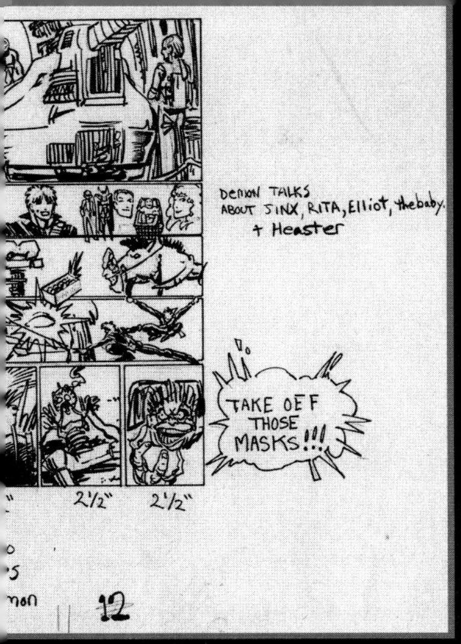
DEMON TALKS
ABOUT JINX, RITA, Elliot, the baby.
+ Heaster
TAKE OFF THOSE MASKS!!!
2 1/2"
2 1/2"
12

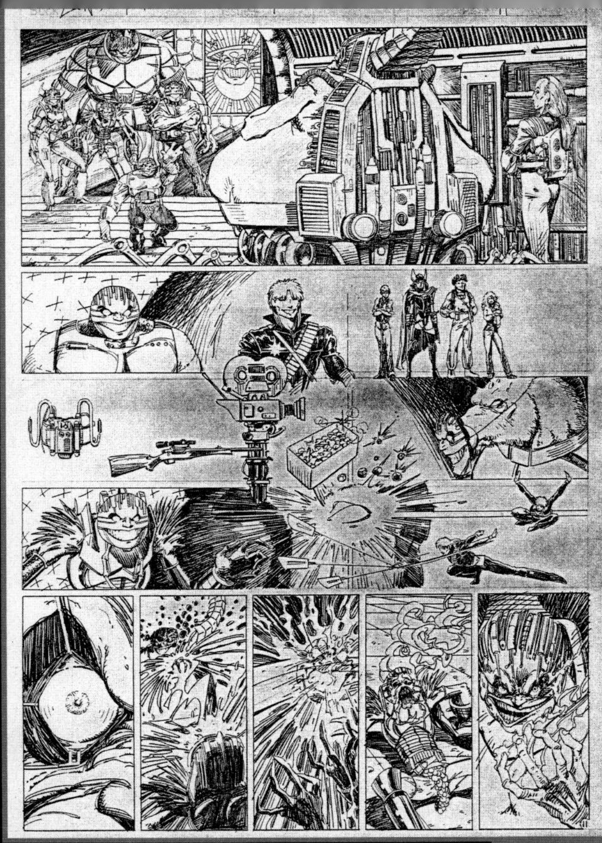
11

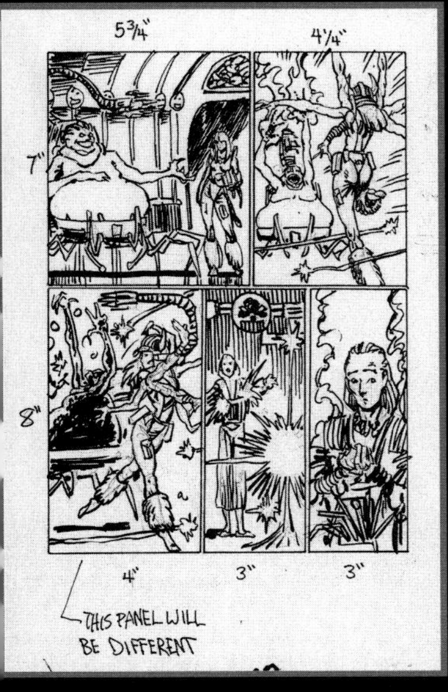
5 3/4"
4 1/4"
7"
8"
4"
3"
3"
THIS PANEL WILL BE DIFFERENT

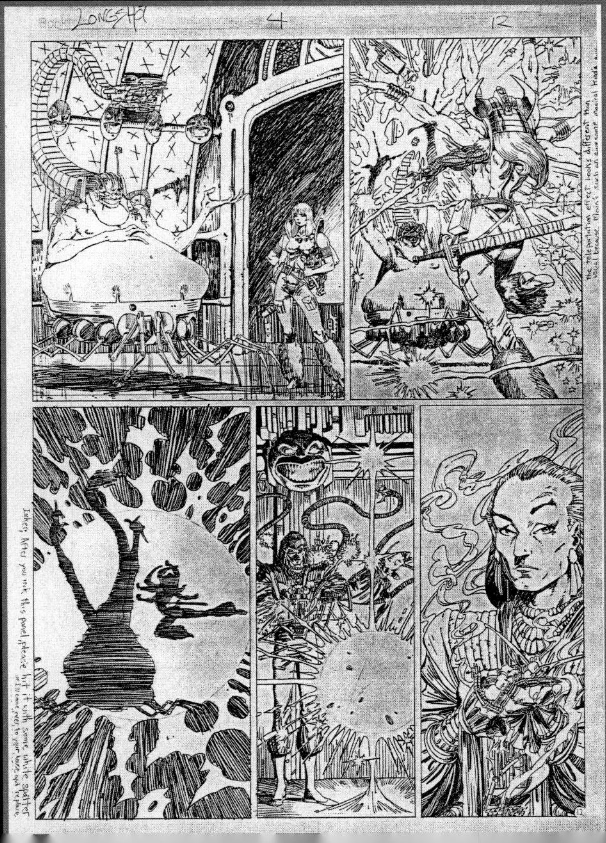
Book Longshot 4 12
The teleportation effect looks different than usual because Mojo's such an awesome magical kind a ...
Inker: After you ink this panel, please hit it with some white spatter

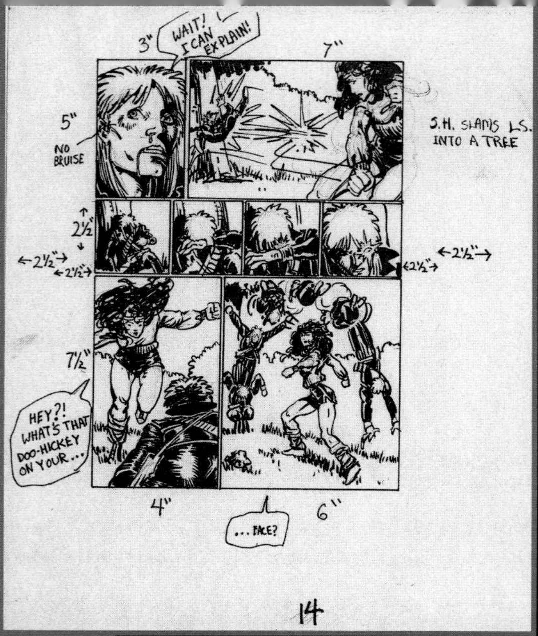
WAIT! I CAN EXPLAIN!
3"
7"
5"
NO BRUISE
S.H. SLAMS L.S. INTO A TREE
2½"
←2½"→
←2½"→
HEY?! WHAT'S THAT DOO-HICKEY ON YOUR...
7½"
4"
...FACE?
6"
14
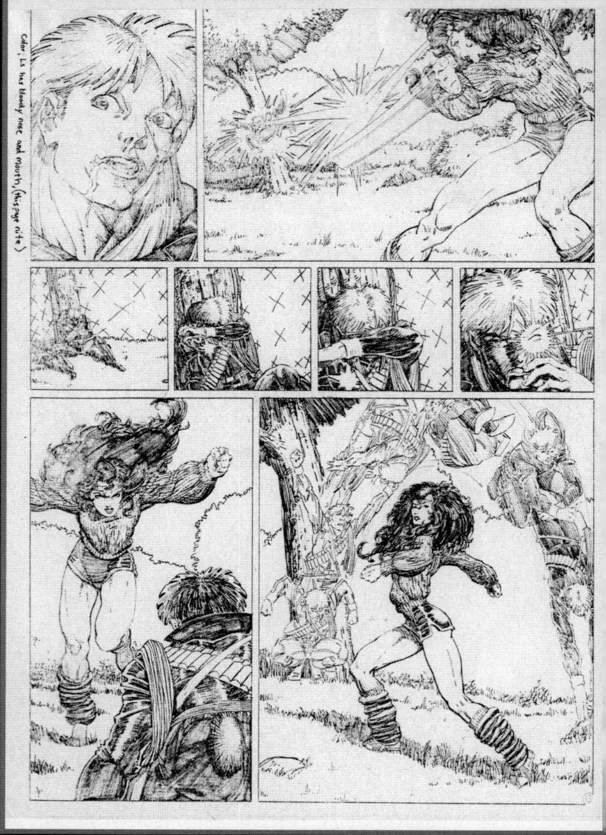
Color: LS has bloody nose and mouth,
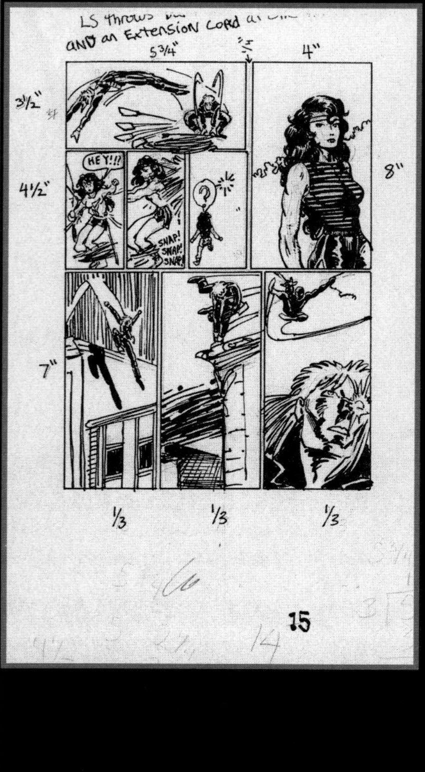
LS throws
AND an Extension Cord
5¾"
4"
3½"
4½"
HEY!!!
SNAP! SNAP! SNAP!
8"
7"
1/3
1/3
1/3
15
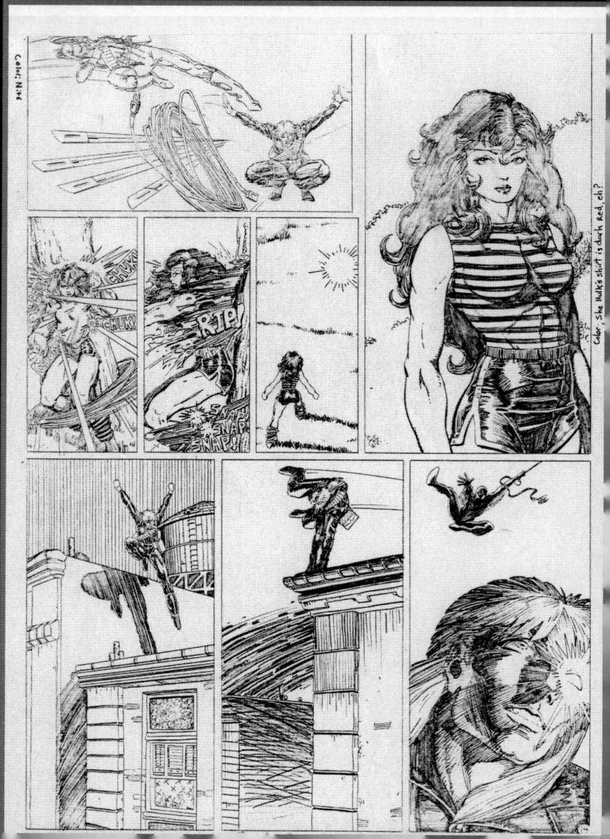
CHUK!
RIP
SNAP! SNAP! SNAP!
Color: She Hulk's shirt is dark red, eh?

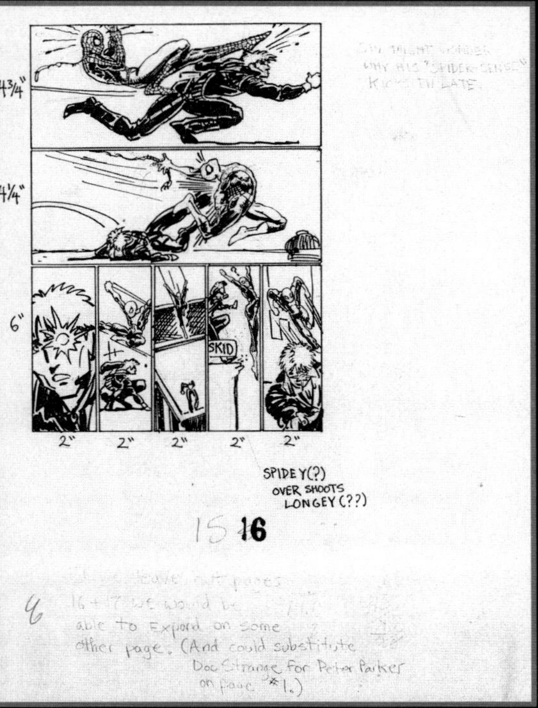
4¾"
4¼"
6"
SKID
2" 2" 2" 2" 2"
SPIDEY(?) OVER SHOOTS LONGEY(??)
15 16
6 16+17 we would be able to Expand on some other page. (And could substitute Doc Strange for Peter Parker on page #1.)
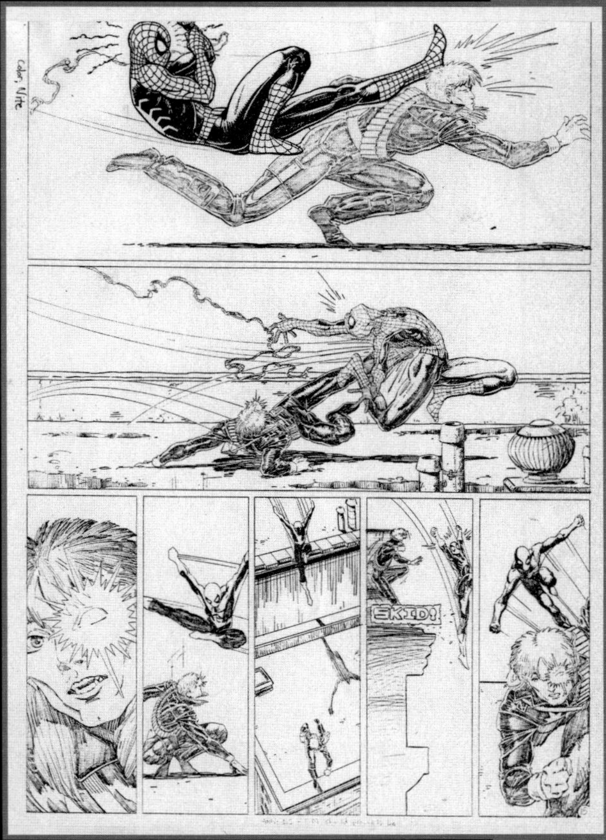
Color, Nite
SKID!
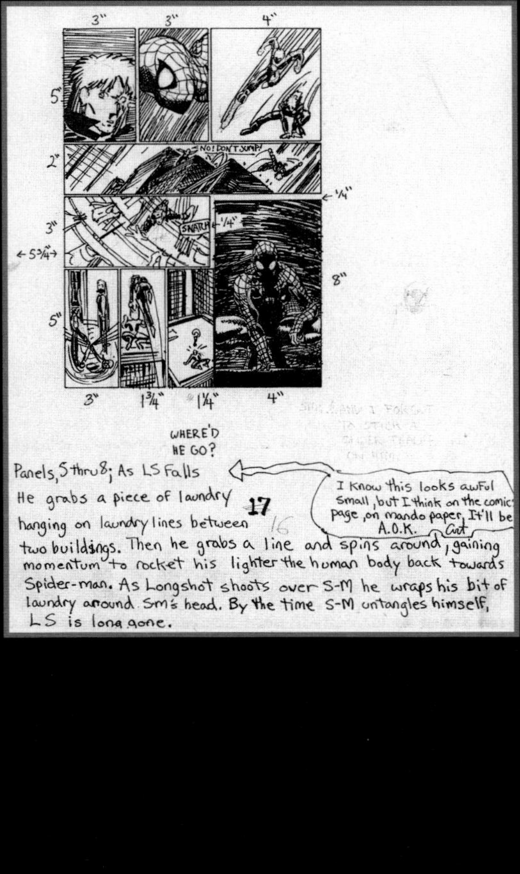
3" 3" 4"
5"
NO! DON'T JUMP!
2"
¼"
3"
SNATCH
←5¾→
8"
5"
3" 1¾" 1¼" 4"
WHERE'D HE GO?
Panels, 5 thru 8; As LS Falls He grabs a piece of laundry hanging on laundry lines between two buildings. Then he grabs a line and spins around, gaining momentum to rocket his lighter the human body back towards Spider-man. As Longshot shoots over S-M he wraps his bit of laundry around Sm's head. By the time S-M untangles himself, LS is long gone.
17 16
I know this looks awful small, but I think on the comic page, on mando paper, It'll be A.O.K. Art
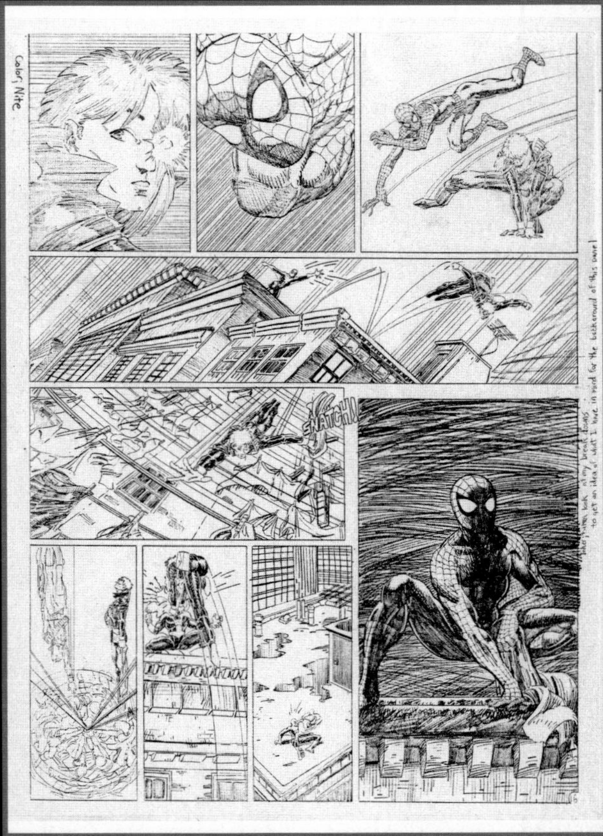
Color, Nite
SNATCH!

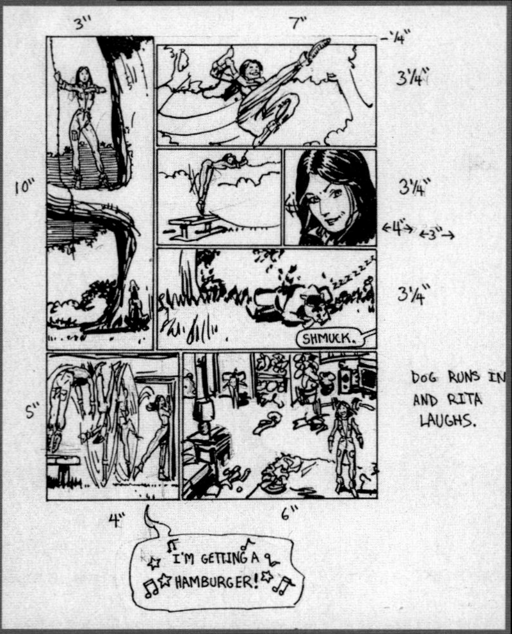
3"
7"
¼"
3¼"
3¼"
10"
←4"→ ←3"→
3¼"
SHMUCK.
5"
DOG RUNS IN AND RITA LAUGHS.
4"
6"
I'M GETTING A HAMBURGER!

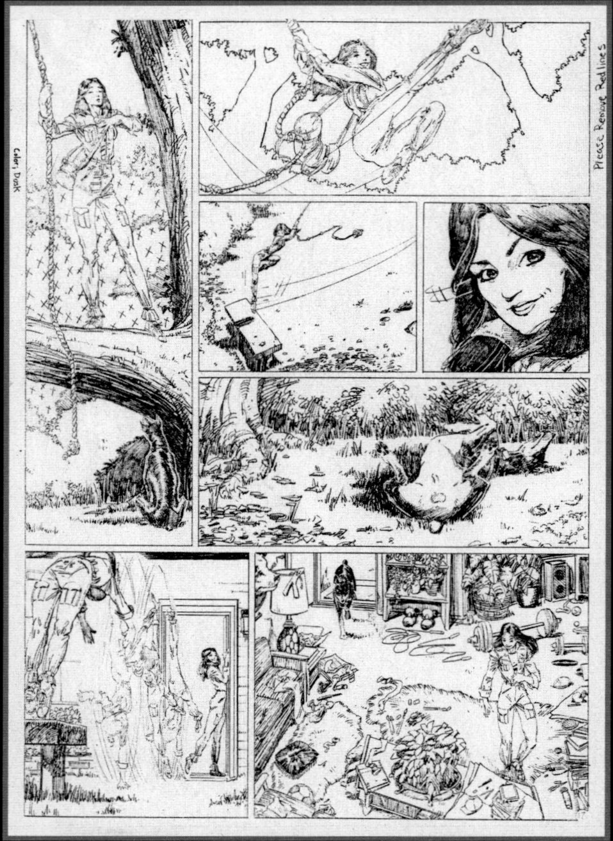
Please Remove Redlines

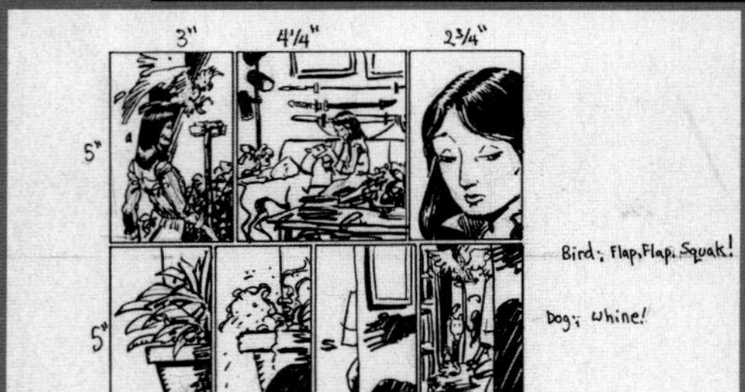
3"
4¼"
2¾"
5"
Bird: Flap. Flap. Squak!
5"
Dog: whine!
←2½"→ each
5"
WHINE!
THUTCH!
3"
4"
3"
19
18

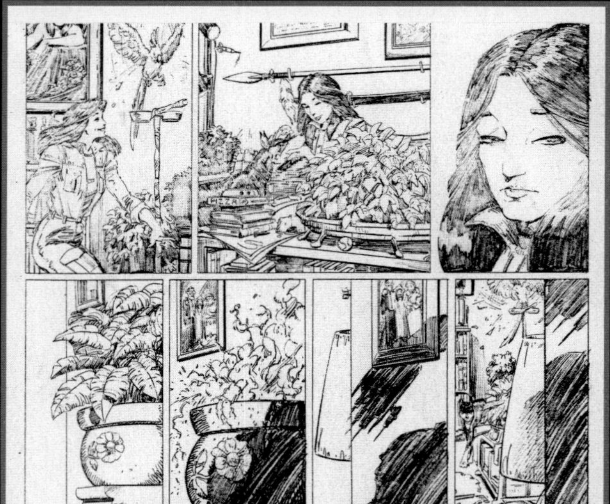
THUTCH!

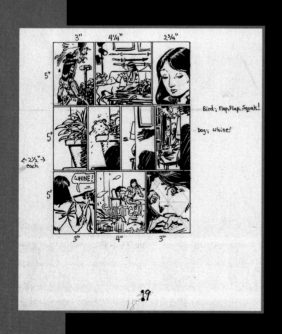

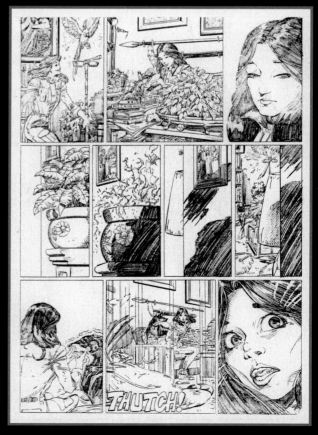

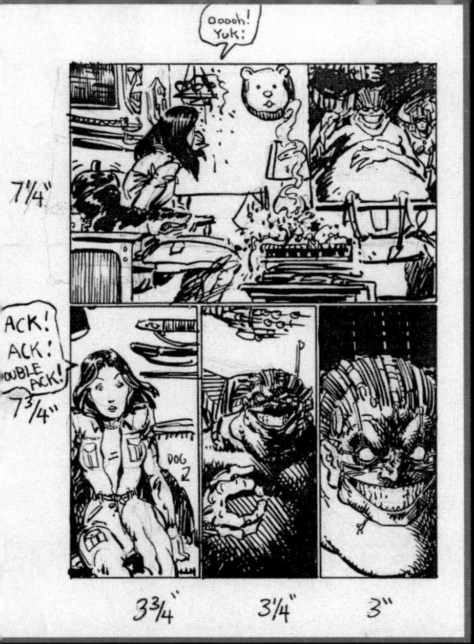
Ooooh! Yuk!
7¼"
ACK! ACK! DOUBLE ACK!
7¾"
DOG
3¾"
3¼"
3"

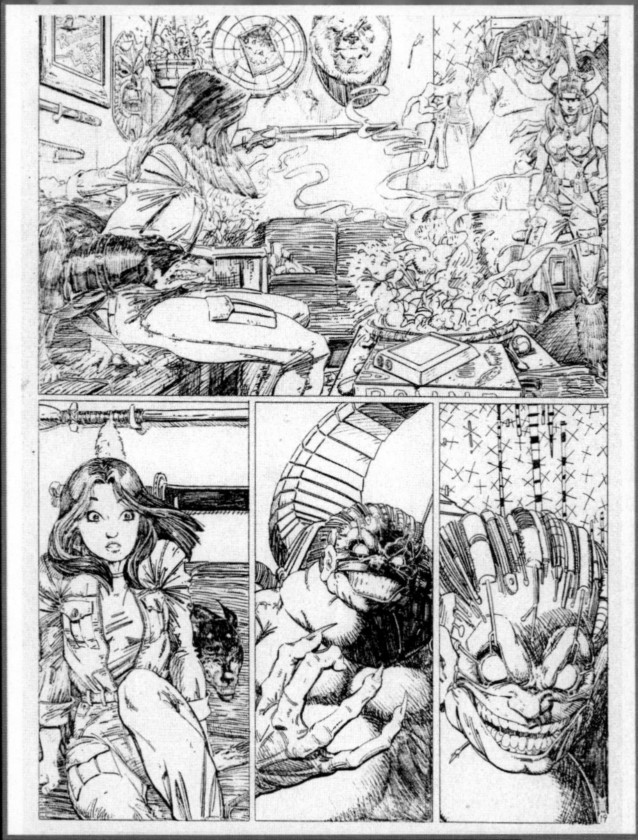

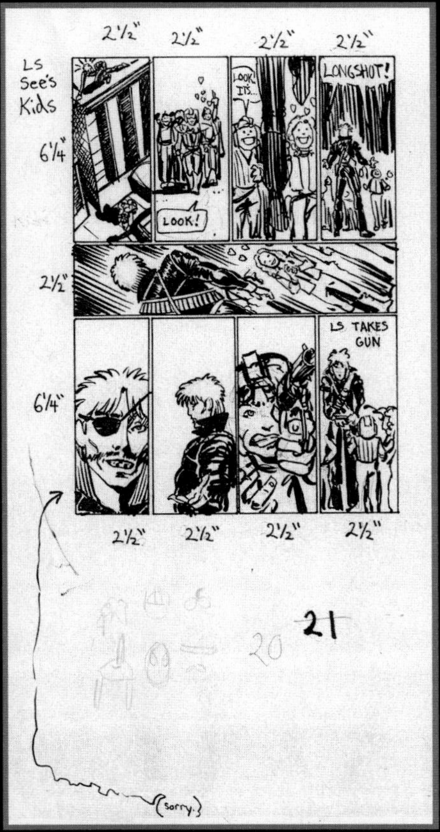
2½"
2½"
2½"
2½"
LS See's Kids
6¼"
LOOK!
LOOK. ITS...
LONGSHOT!
2½"
LS TAKES GUN
6¼"
2½"
2½"
2½"
2½"
(sorry.)
20
21

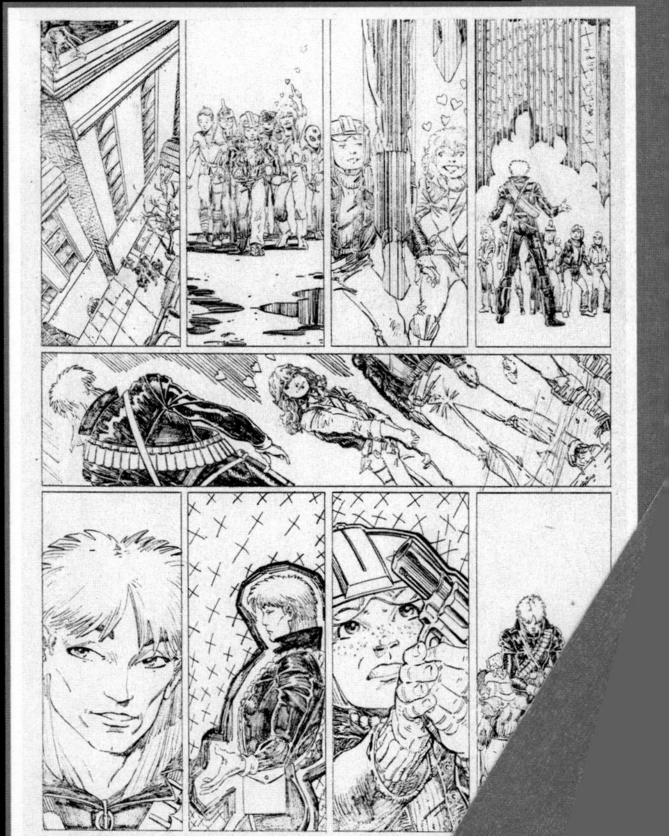

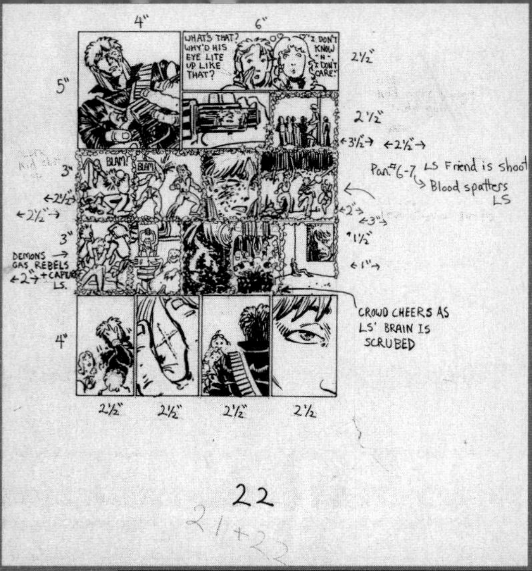
4"
6"
WHAT'S THAT? WHY'D HIS EYE LITE UP LIKE THAT?
I DON'T KNOW -N- I DON'T CARE!
5"
2½"
2½"
BLAM!
BLAM!
Pan# 6-7 LS Friend is shoot
Blood spatters LS
DEMONS GAS REBELS + CAPTURE LS.
CROWD CHEERS AS LS' BRAIN IS SCRUBED
2½"
2½"
2½"
2½
22
21+22

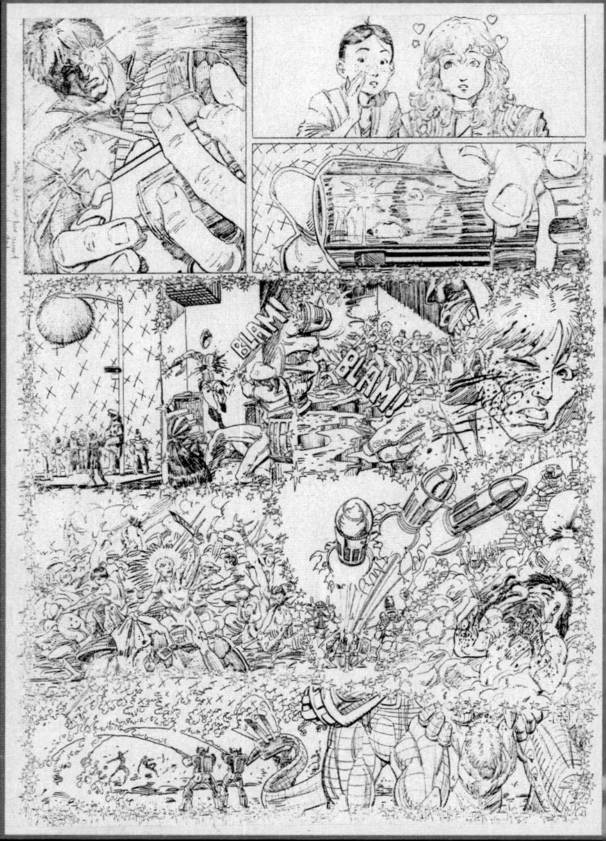
BLAM!
BLAM!

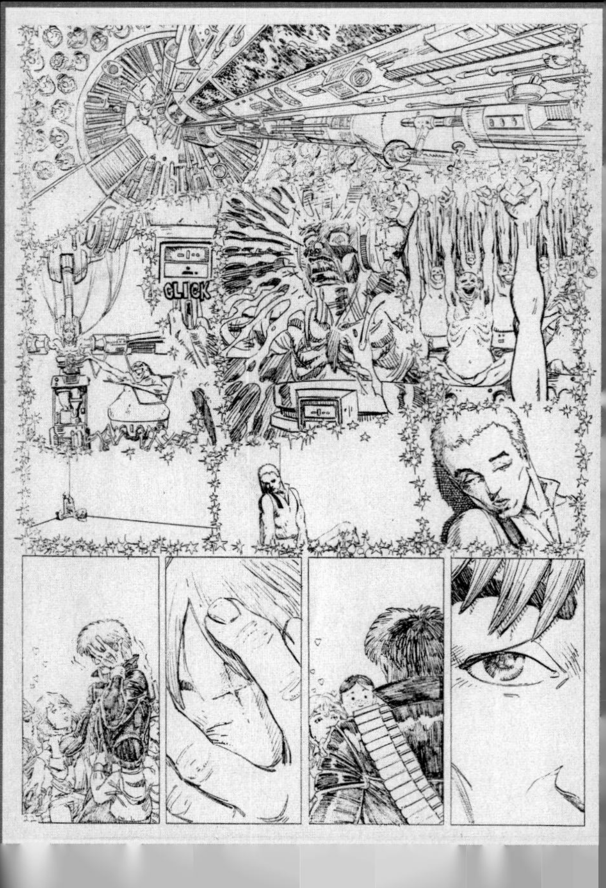
CLICK

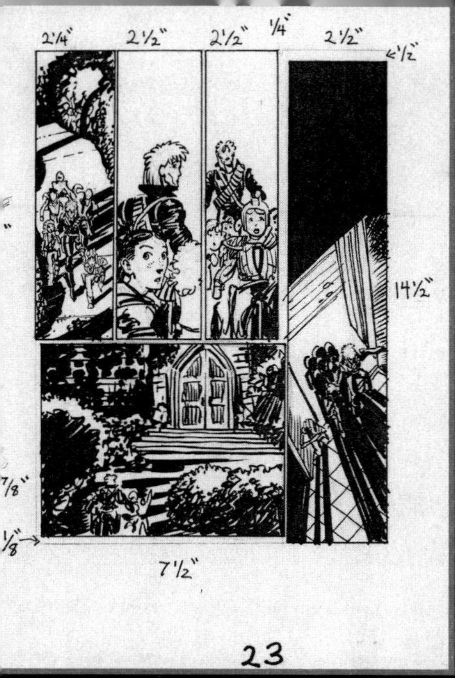
2¼"
2½"
2½"
¼"
2½"
½"
14½"
7/8"
1/8"
7½"
23

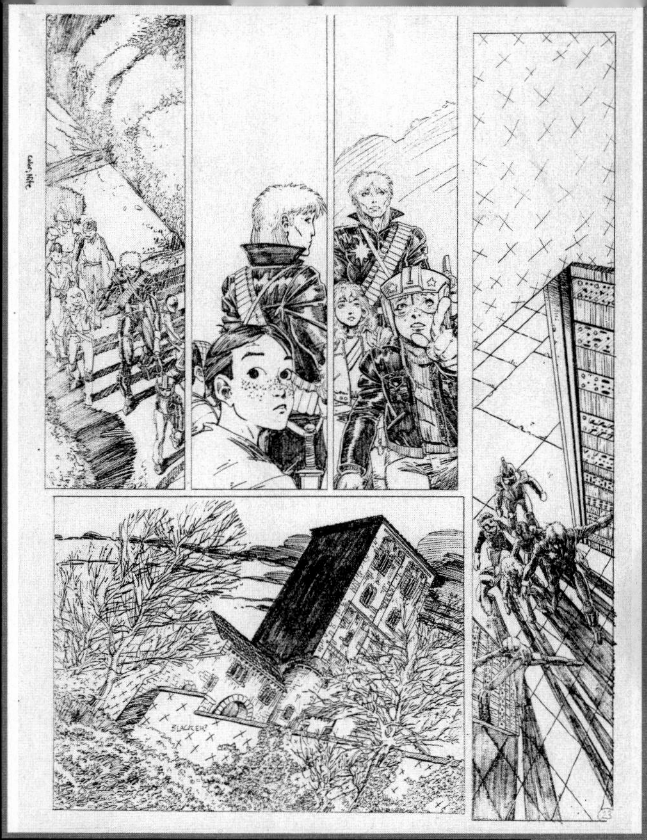
BLACKEN?

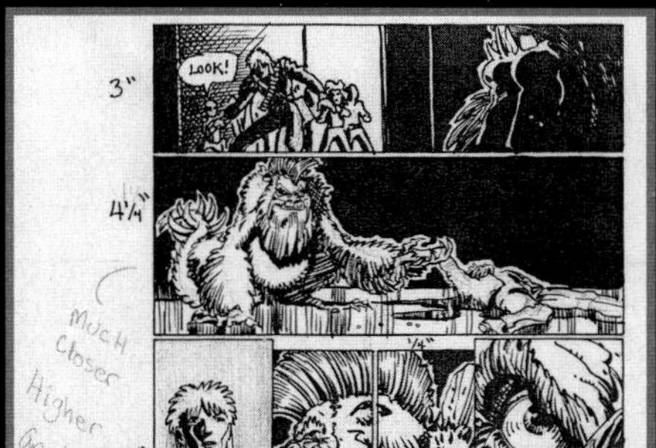
3"
LOOK!
4¼"
MUCH closer
Higher angle
7¾"
RIIIP!
Blink!
TO BE CONTINUED...
2½"
2¼"
2¼"
3"
24

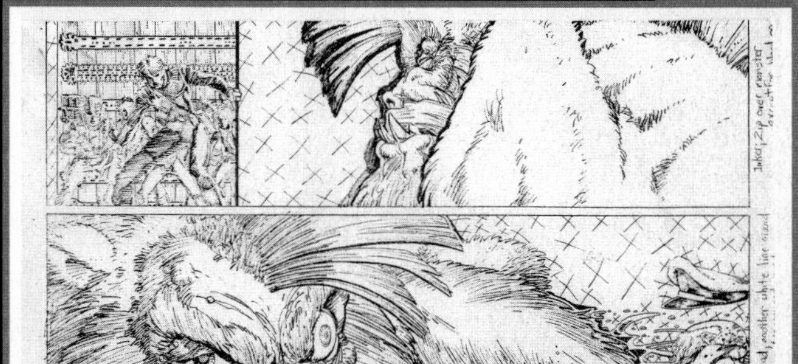

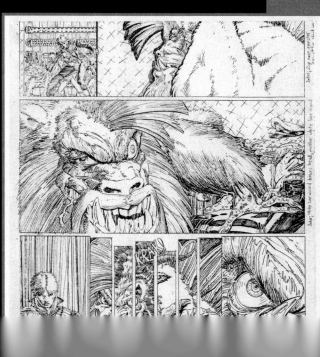

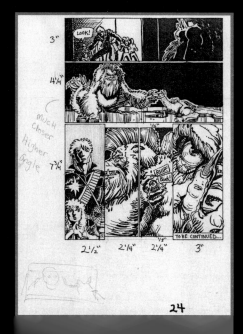

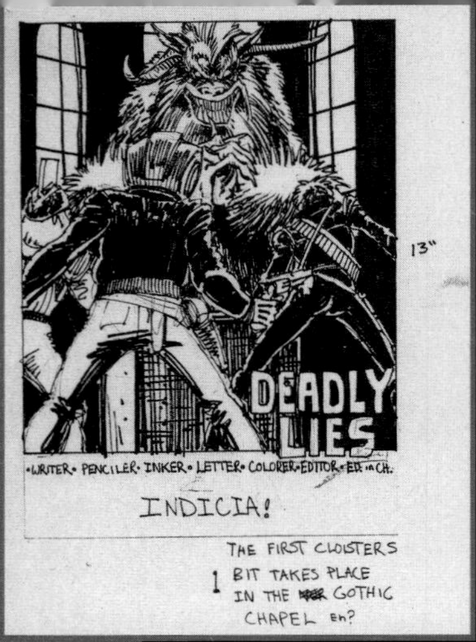
DEADLY LIES
•WRITER• PENCILER• INKER• LETTER• COLORER• EDITOR• ED. in CH.
INDICIA!
13"
1
THE FIRST CLOISTERS BIT TAKES PLACE IN THE GOTHIC CHAPEL eh?
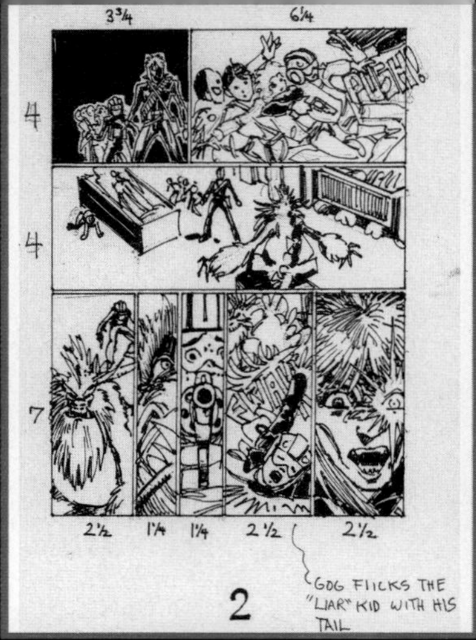
3¾
6¼
SPUSH!
2½
1¼
1¼
2½
2½
2
GOG FLICKS THE "LIAR" KID WITH HIS TAIL
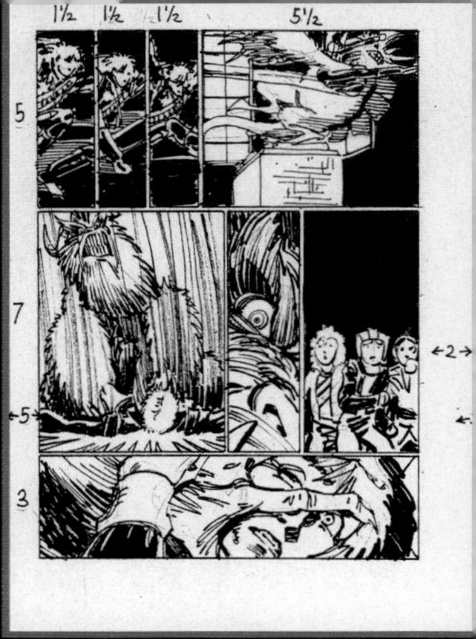
1½
1½
1½
5½
←2→
←5→
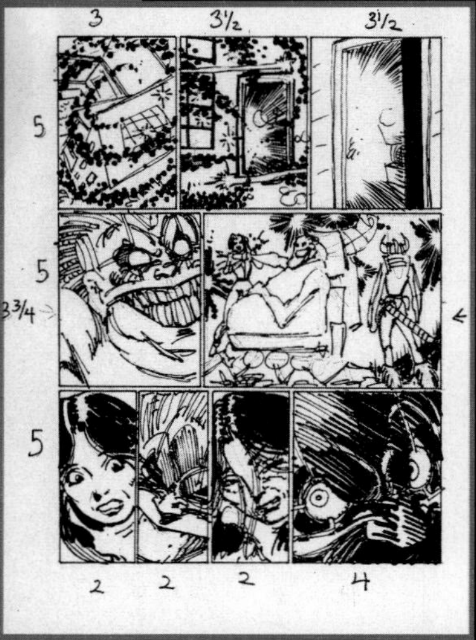
3
3½
3½
3¾
2
2
2
4
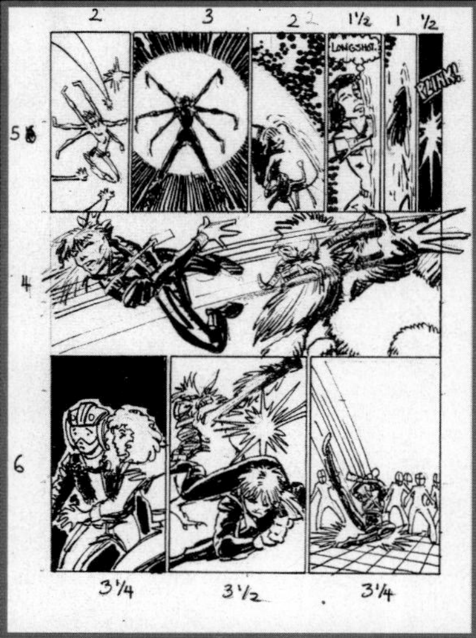
2
3
2
1½
1
½
LONGSHOT
3¼
3½
3¼
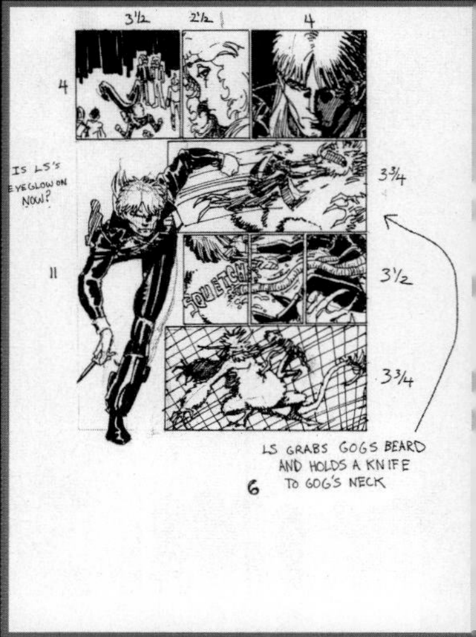
3½
2½
4
IS LS'S EYEGLOW ON NOW?
3¾
3½
3¾
SQUETCH
LS GRABS GOGS BEARD AND HOLDS A KNIFE TO GOG'S NECK
6
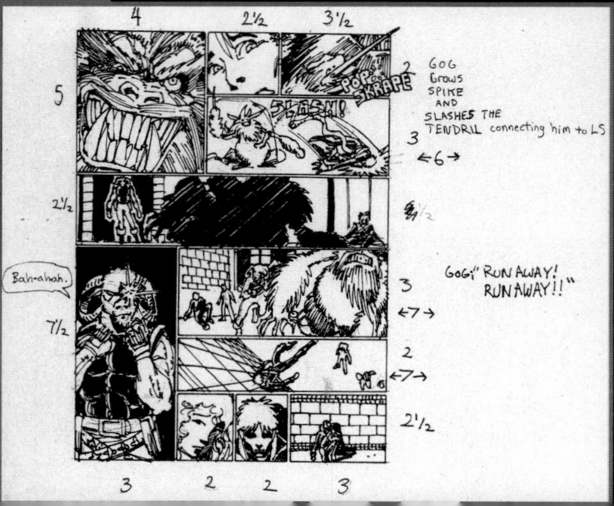
4
2½
3½
POP
SKRAPE
SLASH!
GOG GROWS SPIKE AND SLASHES THE TENDRIL connecting him to LS
←6→
Bah-ahah.
7½
GOG: "RUN AWAY! RUN AWAY!!"
←7→
←7→
2½
3
2
2
3
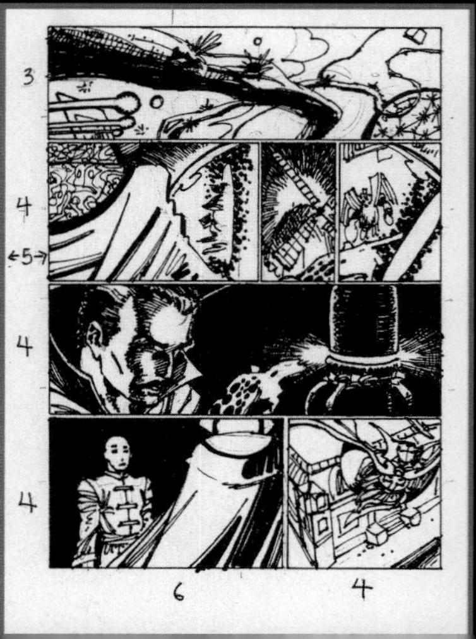
←5→
6
4

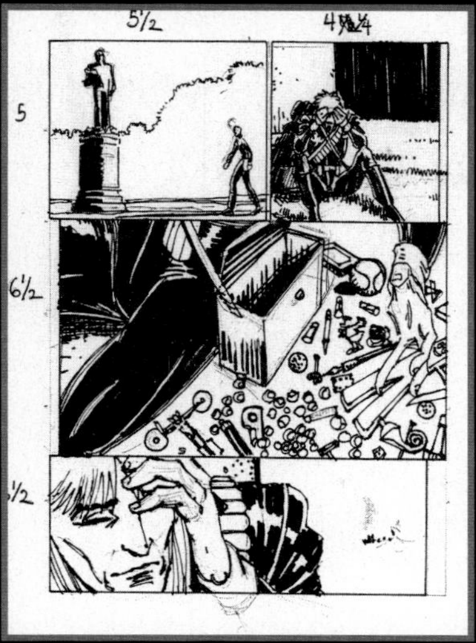

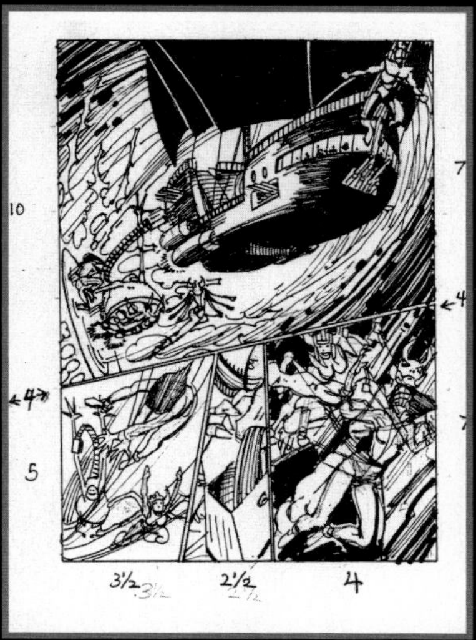

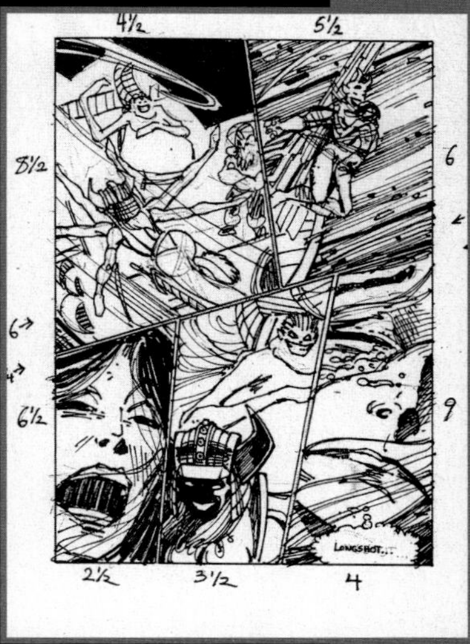
LONGSHOT...

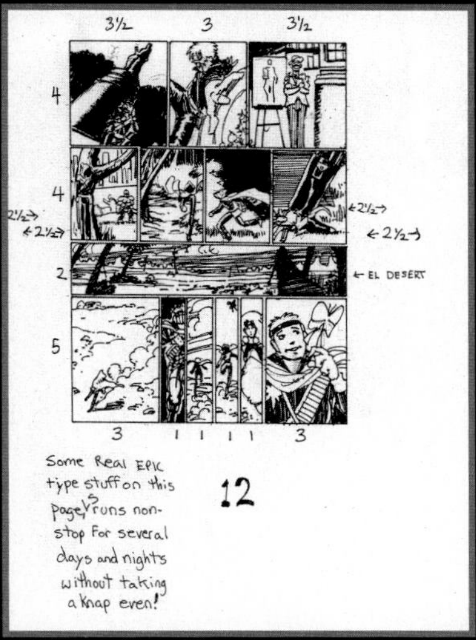
EL DESERT
12
Some Real EPIC type stuff on this page. Its runs non-stop for several days and nights without taking a knap even!

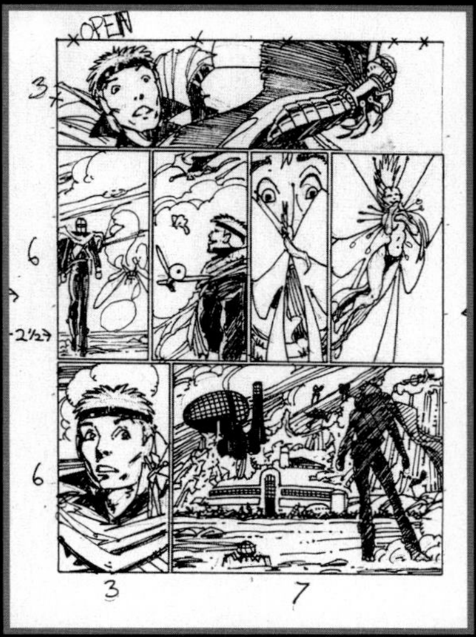
OPEN

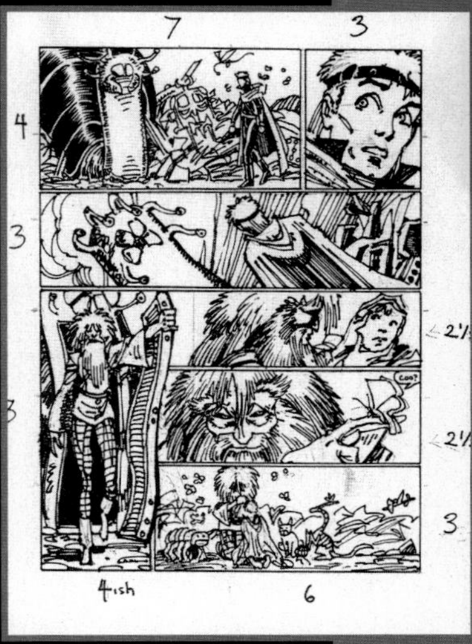

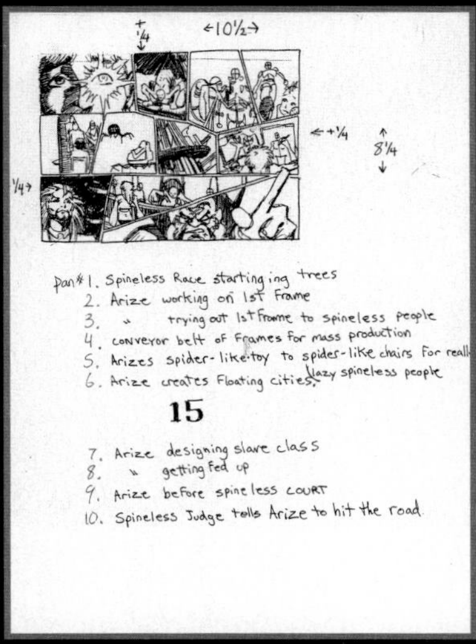
pan#1. Spineless Race starting ing trees
2. Arize working on 1st Frame
3. " trying out 1st Frame to spineless people
4. conveyor belt of Frames for mass production
5. Arizes spider-like toy to spider-like chairs for really lazy spineless people
6. Arize creates Floating cities.
15
7. Arize designing slave class
8. " getting fed up
9. Arize before spineless COURT
10. Spineless Judge tells Arize to hit the road

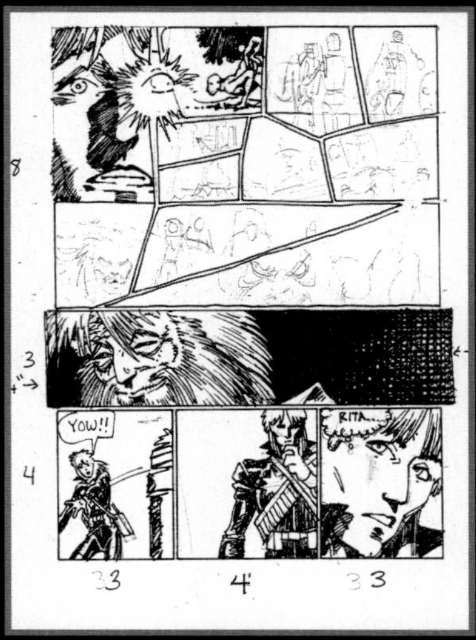
YOW!!
RITA...

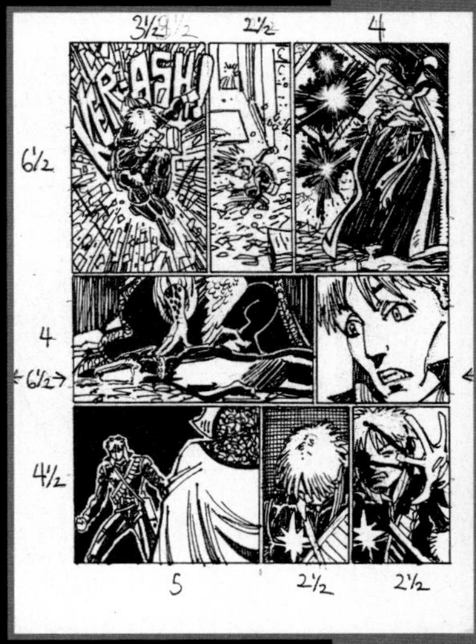

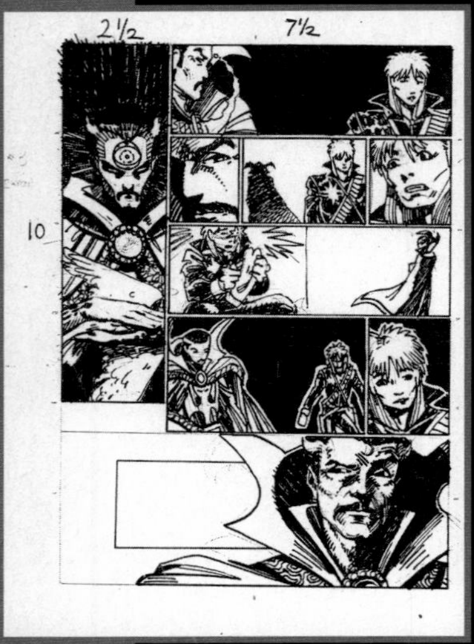
2½
7½
10
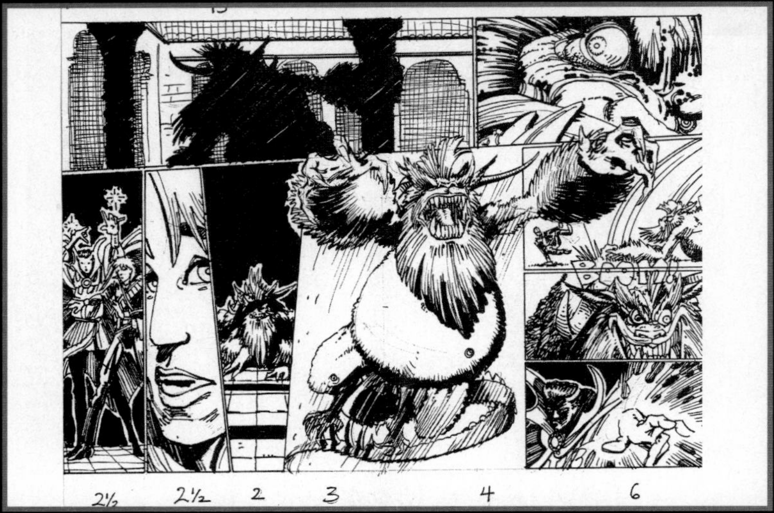
2½
2½
2
3
4
6
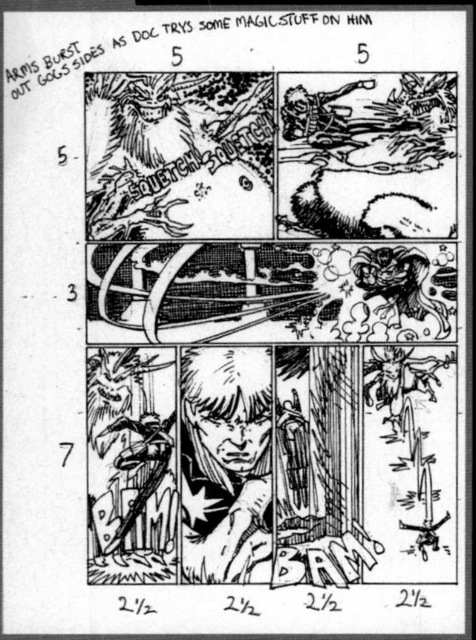
ARMS BURST OUT GOGS SIDES AS DOC TRYS SOME MAGIC STUFF ON HIM
5
5
5
SQUETCH! SQUETCH!
3
7
BAM!
BAM!
2½
2½
2½
2½
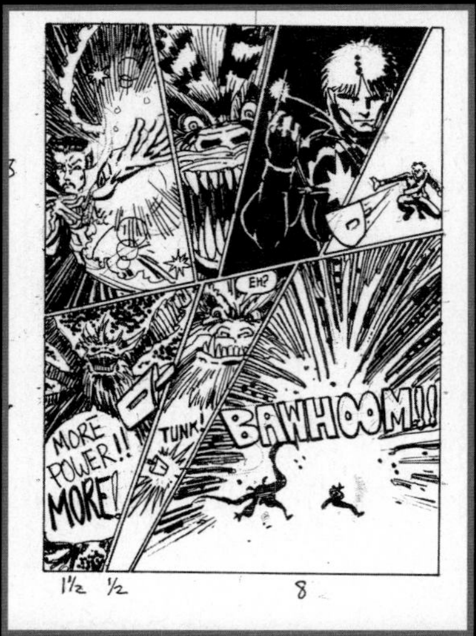
EH?
MORE POWER!! MORE!
TUNK!
BAWHOOOM!!
1½
½
8
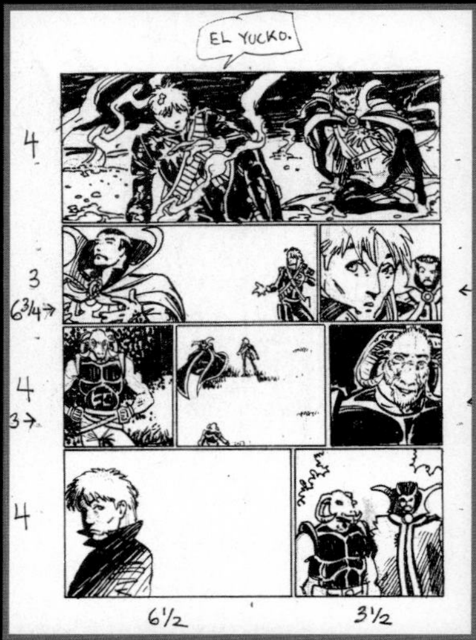
EL YUCKO.
4
3
6¾
4
3
4
6½
3½
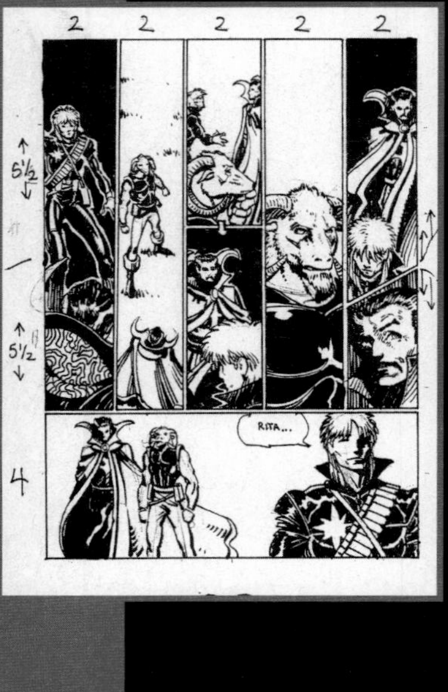
2
2
2
2
2
5½
5½
RITA...
4
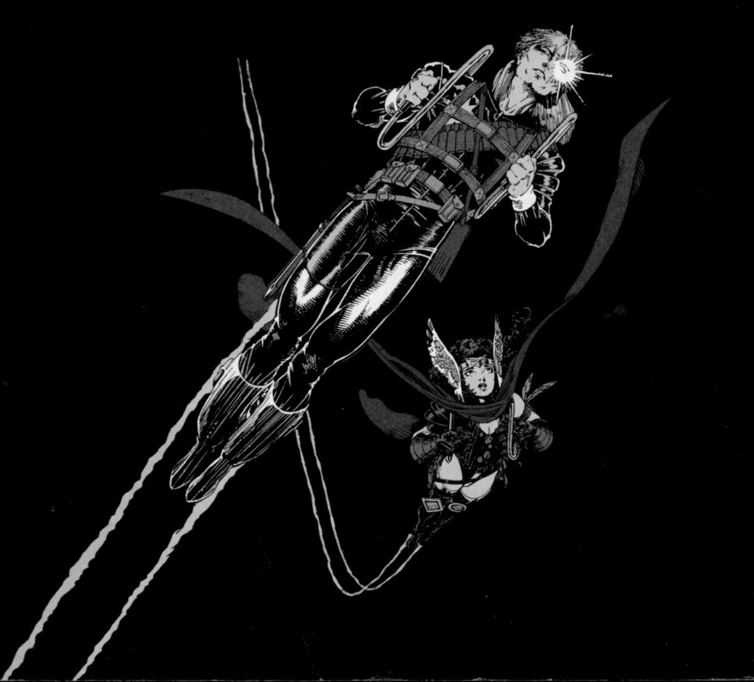

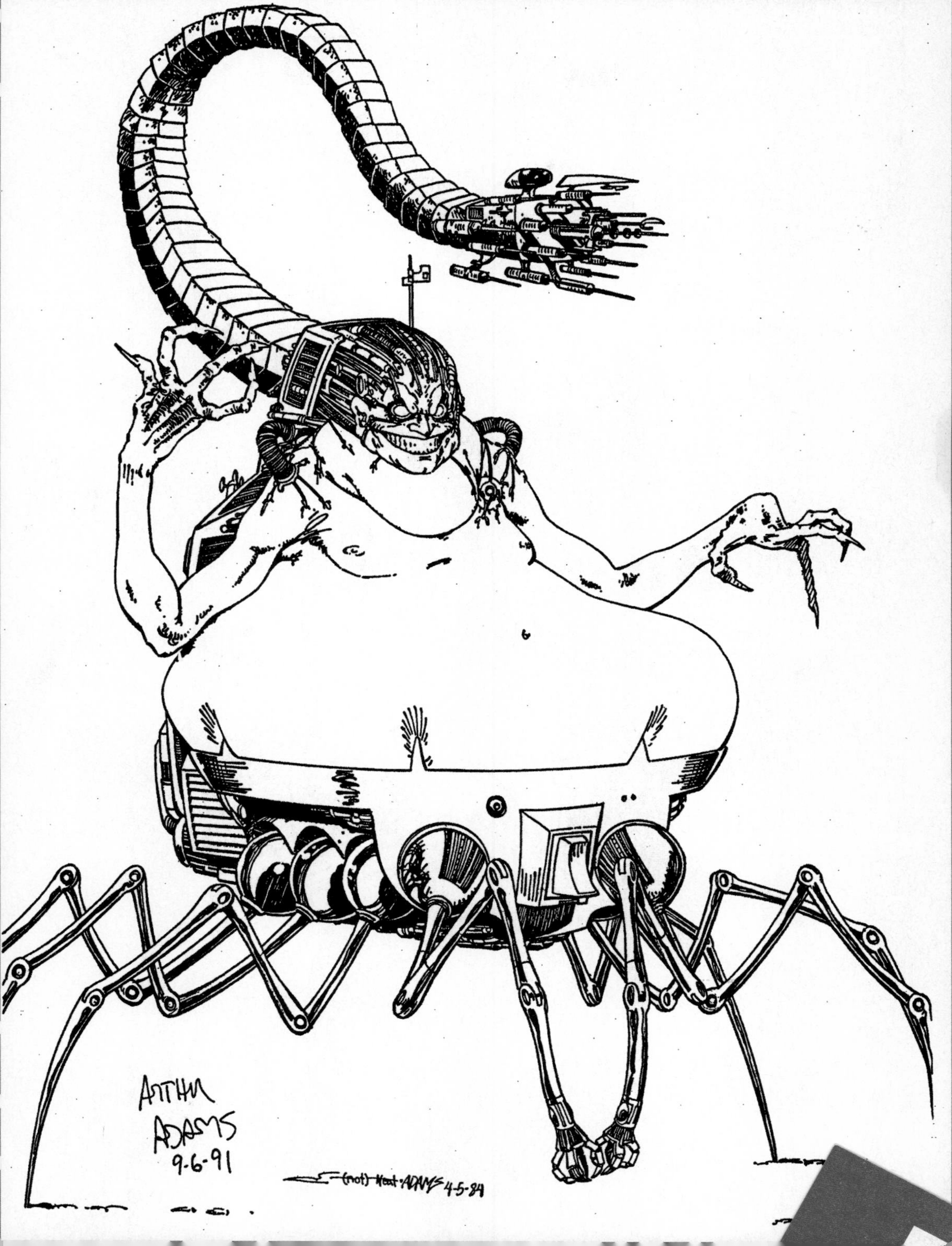
ARTHUR
ADAMS
9-6-91
(not) Neal ADAMS 4-5-84

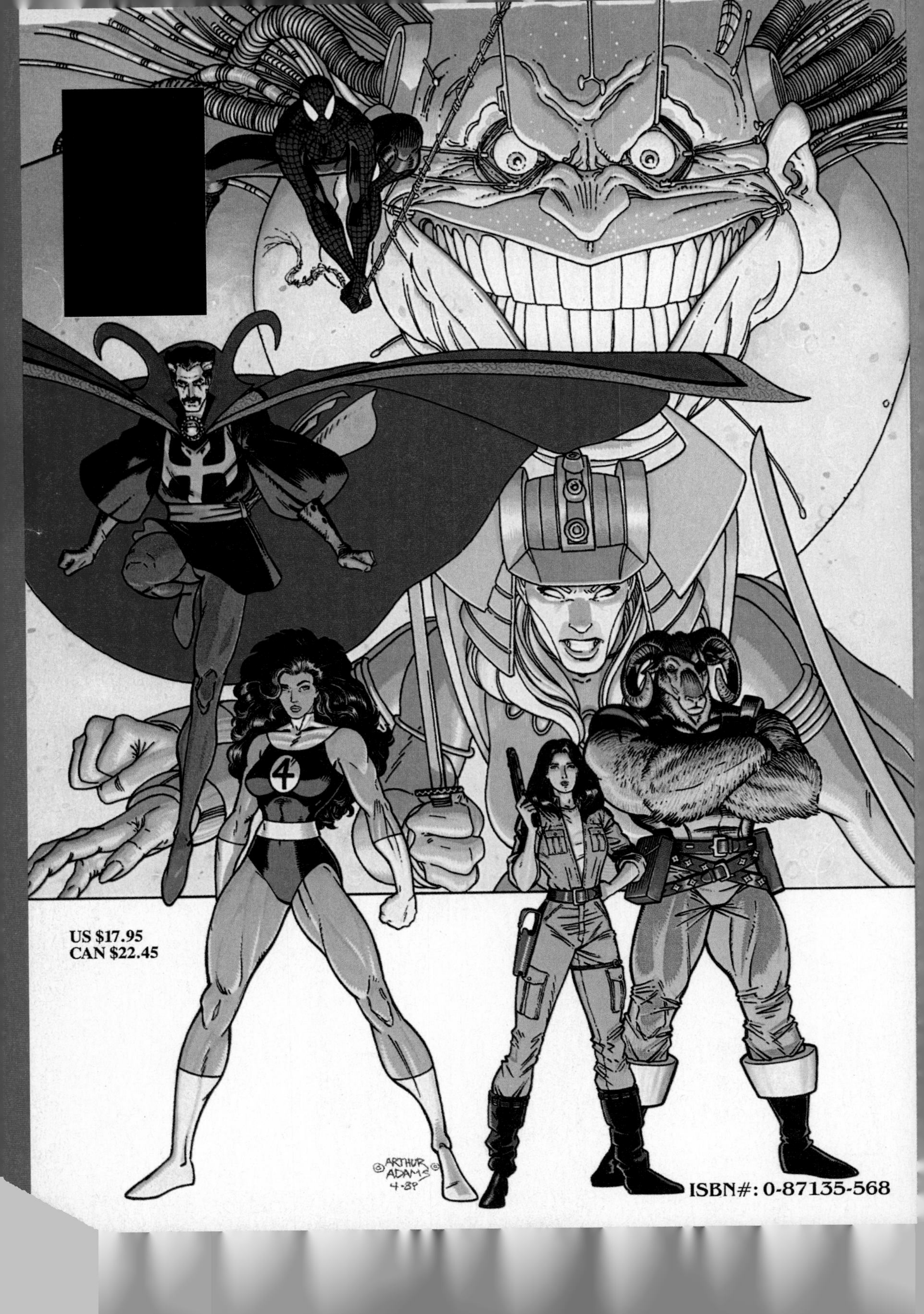
ARTHUR ADAMS
4-89

US $17.95
CAN $22.45

ISBN#: 0-87135-568

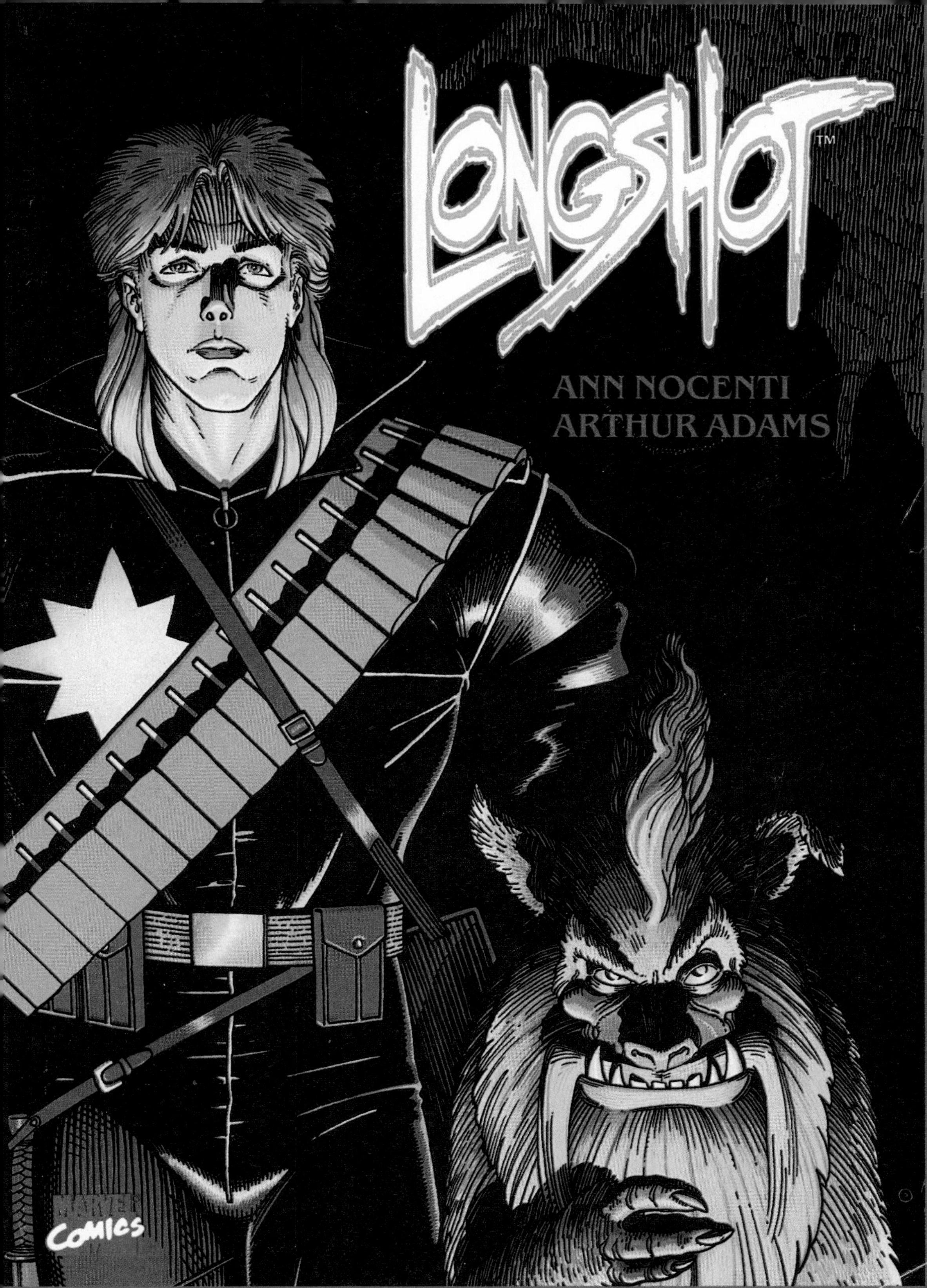
LONGSHOT™
ANN NOCENTI
ARTHUR ADAMS
MARVEL COMICS

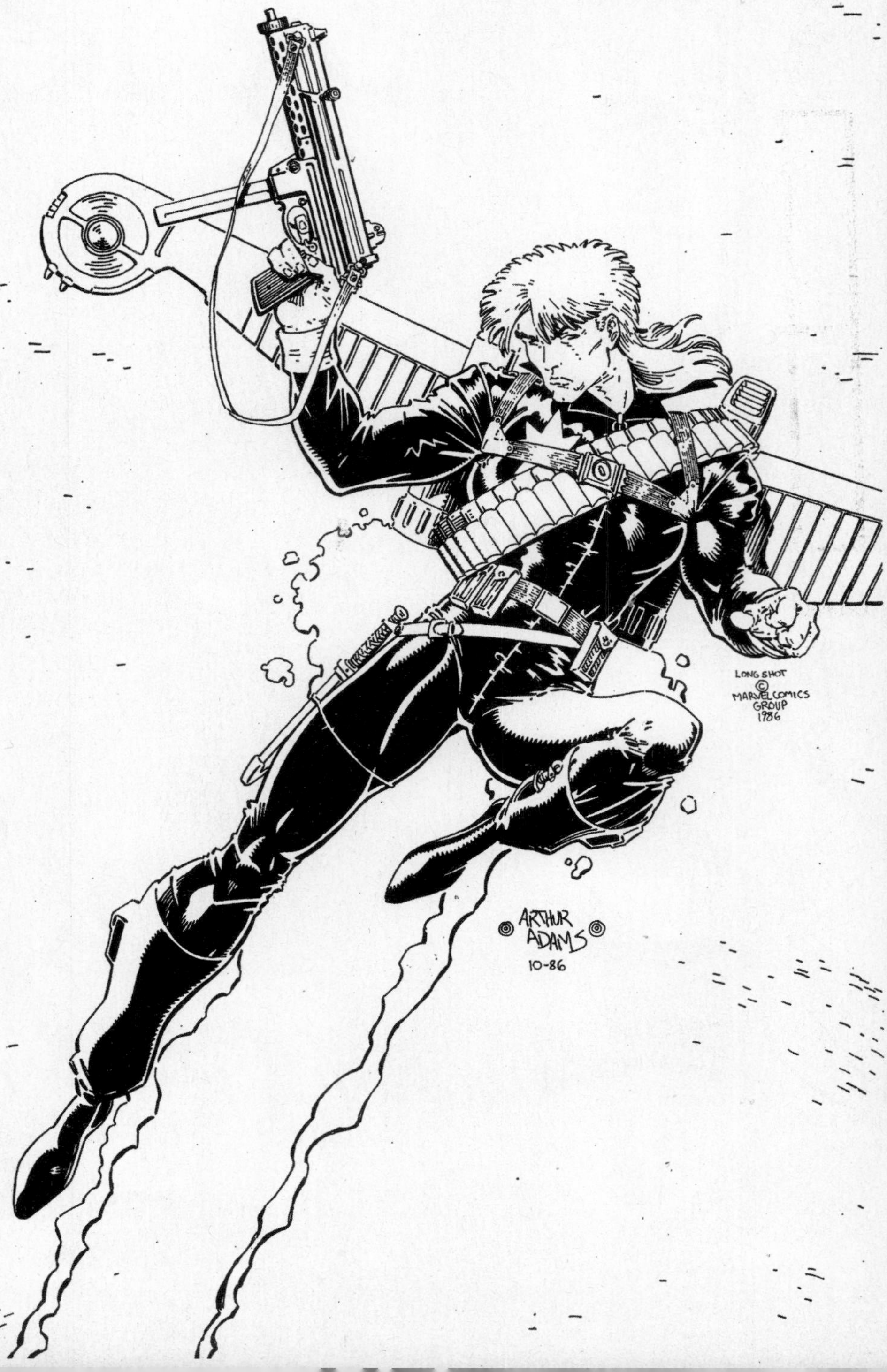
LONG SHOT © MARVEL COMICS GROUP 1986
ARTHUR ADAMS
10-86